Charles Dickens

HIS TRAGEDY AND TRIUMPH

BY EDGAR JOHNSON

FICTION

Unweave a Rainbow:
A Sentimental Fantasy

The Praying Mantis

BIOGRAPHY

One Mighty Torrent:
The Drama of Biography

The Heart of Charles Dickens:
His Letters to Angela Burdett Coutts

ANTHOLOGIES

A Treasury of Satire

A Treasury of Biography

Dickens at Twenty-Five
From the Drawing by Samuel Laurence, 1837

Charles Dickens

HIS TRAGEDY AND TRIUMPH

By Edgar Johnson

VOLUME ONE

1952

Appreciation is expressed to the following for their courtesy in granting permission to reproduce various pictures from their collections in the photographic sections of these volumes:

New York Public Library Picture Collection: pictures 3, 4, 15, 16, 17, 18, 19, 21, 22, 23, 27, 44, 47, 52, 57, 60, 62, 63, 64, 65, 66, 67, 68, 79, 80, 85; Frontispiece, Vol. Two

Dickens House, Doughty Street, London: pictures 11, 20, 25, 43, 53, 59

National Portrait Gallery, London: picture 24

Courtesy of Major Philip Dickens and Dickens House, Doughty Street, London: picture 30

Courtesy of Leigh B. Block: picture 31

Courtesy of Leslie C. Staples: picture 37

Carlyle House, Cheyne Row, Chelsea, London: pictures 40, 41

Reproduced by courtesy of Sir Michael Culme-Seymour: picture 50

Central Office of Information, London: picture 72

William M. Elkins Collection, Philadelphia: picture 84

MANUFACTURED IN THE UNITED STATES OF AMERICA
BY H. WOLFF, NEW YORK

To My Children
Judy and Laurie

Preface

Charles Dickens belongs to all the world. He is a titan of literature, and his own moving life-story, with its radiances of laughter, its conquests of genius, and its dark and fateful drift toward disillusion even in the midst of universal acclaim, epitomizes hardly less powerfully than his works the mingled comedy and tragedy of the human struggle. This book is therefore addressed not only to literary scholars, but to all who find compelling the color and fullness and travail of life itself.

Dickens was himself a Dickens character, bursting with an inordinate and fantastic vitality. The world in which his spirit dwelt was identical with the world of his novels, brilliant in hue, violent in movement, crammed with people all furiously alive and with places as alive as the people. "The Dickens world" was his everyday world. He found his own intimates as funny as Mr. Micawber, Mr. Toots, and Flora Finching, and felt their joys and sorrows as deeply as he did those of the characters in his fictions. His adventures and misadventures were as hilarious or painful as those of Mr. Pickwick or David Copperfield or Pip. And Dickens was not one of those frugal authors who save all their good things for their books. In the profusion of his creativity, in his prodigal exuberance, he poured out through his thousands of letters a wealth of psychological observation and comic episode, a depth of feeling and a vividness of language, that might have enriched a dozen more novels. For these reasons, in narrating the events of his life, I have made copious use of Dickens's own letters. No biographer could convey the flavor of his personality more brilliantly than he has done it himself.

But Dickens is important for more than the sheer intensity with which he reflects experience. He is not merely a great intuitive ob-

server, a mindless sensorium; he is a penetrating commentator on life and modern society. The day is long past when intellectual snobbery contrasted him disparagingly with Thackeray and implied that Dickens was crude in his art and his view of the world an immature one that left him attractive only to children and the semiliterate. The unifying thread of Dickens's entire career was a critical analysis of modern society and its problems hardly surpassed in grasp or scope either by his contemporaries or by any more recent novelists.

In his own day these aspects of Dickens were partly lost in the excessive brilliance of his comedic and dramatic talent, and even today they may be obscured by his reputation as a mere humanitarian sentimentalist. His novels, of course, render his response to experience—and rightly so—primarily in terms of emotion; they do not always completely reflect either his hard-headed practicality as a worker for social reform or his long-headed insight as a social theorist. These found their explicit statement in his other writings—especially in his letters to newspapers and his articles in magazines. Nor can Dickens's social attitudes be fully understood without a careful examination of the pages of Household Words and All the Year Round, the two weeklies over whose pronouncements on all matters he exercised a rigid control for twenty years. Both these publications are crammed with articles on the problems of society—and Dickens printed nothing with which he did not agree. This journalistic activity is significant not only in itself but for the light it throws on his development and on the themes of his novels. But the nineteen volumes of the first and the even more numerous volumes of the second have represented an intimidating bulk of material that few commentators have even attempted to study.

No portrayal of Dickens, finally, can be accurate that ignores the innumerable judgments on public affairs in his personal letters. Only for the last dozen years has there been in print the great three-volume collection running to twenty-five hundred pages and over a million words. And even the published letters are perhaps not half of those

Dickens wrote. In the course of working on this book I have read another thirty-five hundred unpublished documents—including con-
tracts and memoranda and letters written to Dickens, but mostly
letters written by him. Many of these are indispensable for an understanding not only of his emotional life but of his social philosophy and
his career as a reformer. This is especially true of the more than five
hundred letters written to Miss Burdett Coutts, fewer than one-quarter
of which have ever been published, but more than half of which deal
with the charities, slum improvements, and reform movements in
which Dickens served as her guide and almoner.

Interpretation of character, of course, is a matter of judgment, but
in all the narrative parts of this book I have adhered strictly to recorded fact and have invented nothing. Where the facts were unknown and various hypotheses seemed equally plausible I have presented the alternatives. Where different versions of the facts existed,
but one seemed to me more convincing, I have given it in the narrative
and explained in the notes my reasons for rejecting the others. For all
factual statements of any kind I have fully indicated my sources.

Students of Dickens's life will observe that I have accepted as largely
true the information about his relation with Ellen Lawless Ternan
given in Thomas Wright's Life of Charles Dickens and Gladys Storey's
Dickens and Daughter. I have done so because, unsatisfactory though
some of their revelations may be as legal evidence, every additional
fact bearing on the point that I have uncovered totally supports them.
Just as in a saturated liquid solution the salt that it contains may be
invisible to the eye but rapidly crystallizes into visibility with the addition of even a few more grains, so the further evidence that I have
found renders the fact of this association incontestable.

Wright's story, unfortunately, depended upon the testimony of
Canon Benham, who was dead. Miss Storey's depended on the statements of Dickens's daughter, Mrs. Perugini, who was also dead. But
here adduced for the first time is evidence in Dickens's own handwriting, in his diary, in memoranda, and in letters. Some of it was deleted—

with no mark of omission—from the volumes of his letters published
by his sister-in-law Georgina Hogarth and his daughter Mary Dickens;
an effort was made on one of the memoranda to obliterate a very important part of it with overscorings of heavy black ink. These efforts
at suppression or destruction are themselves significant. The written
evidence alone, however, is enough to leave the matter undebatable.

The superheated endeavor to discuss this subject in an atmosphere
of moral indignation has, in my judgment, distorted it through a mis-
placed emphasis on sniggering scandal. It is simply a question of fact,
not of peephole gossip, and our purpose should be to present the facts
and to understand them, not to defend or condemn. There are few,
I imagine, who feel any longer that Wordsworth's youthful liaison
with Annette Vallon destroys all his claims to poetic elevation and
moral insight. Nor do many feel that George Eliot's unconcealed relationship with George Lewes made her a loose woman. If Dickens fell
in love with Ellen Ternan, not in youth, but when he was forty-five
and after years of marriage, and if concern for the welfare of his children and the legal impossibility of divorce forced him to conceal the
fact from the world, we need voice no puritan horror. Dickens's moral
character, like his literary achievement, rests upon a much broader and
grander foundation. At that character who can throw the first stone?

The real importance of this autumnal love lies in the changes it
wrought in the last twelve years of Dickens's life and development as
a writer. It is in this way that I have tried to understand and present
it. The constant endeavor of this book, in fact, has been to integrate
literary interpretation and life interpretation: to make the critical discussion of Dickens's work illumine his personality and the portrayal
of his character clarify his literary achievement. For in the end it is the
same lifeblood that flows in both.

EDGAR JOHNSON

The City College

New York

December 1, 1951

Acknowledgments

One of the joys of such a labor as this book is the generous aid that it receives from many hands. Rare is the bookseller, collector, or scholar who will not put his materials and his knowledge wholeheartedly at the service of a biographer, and the custodians and librarians of every institution are tireless in their assistance. It is with many grateful memories that I voice my thanks to these innumerable helpers.

A primary obligation is to Mr. Henry Charles Dickens, of London, who has not only given me transcripts of letters by his grandfather that are in his possession, but has granted me an all-inclusive permission to quote at will both from Dickens's published correspondence and from the entire bulk of unpublished Dickens letters and other documents and memoranda that I have had the good fortune to trace. Without this kindness the present biography could not exist, and I am deeply appreciative. I am also grateful to the many institutions and collectors who have given me their permission to quote from manuscripts in their possession.

The collections of five great institutions have been the very foundations of my work. The Dickens manuscripts in the Forster Collection of the Victoria and Albert Museum are the core of any investigation into Dickens as a novelist; I here express my gratitude to Mr. J. Wheen, the Librarian of that Collection, and Mr. A. W. Wardrup, the Deputy Librarian, for their help. No less valuable was the aid I received from Mr. Arthur I. Ellis, late Superintendent of the Reading Room and Keeper of Printed Books of the British Museum, and from Dr. Eric George Millar, former Keeper of Manuscripts and Egerton Librarian of the British Museum. As repositories of unpublished letters and other biographical documents three American libraries are unequaled in the world: the Henry E. Huntington Library and Art Gallery, the New York Public Library, and the Pierpont Morgan Library. I am grateful to all three and their officials: especially to Dr. Herbert C. Schulz, Curator of Manuscripts of the Huntington Library; Mr. Robert W. Henderson, Director of the Reading Room of the New York Public Library, Dr. John W. Gordan, the Curator of the Henry W. and Albert A. Berg Collection of that institution, and his able assistant, Miss Adelaide M. Smith; the late Belle Da Costa Greene, former Director of the Pierpont Morgan Library, and Mr. Frederick Adams, Jr., its present Director.

Numerous other institutions and libraries and their custodians have laid me deeply in their debt. Among these I should name the Boston Athenaeum; the Boston Public Library and Mr. Zoltan Haraszti, its Keeper of Rare Books; the Dickens Fellowship and Mr. Leslie C. Staples, Editor of the *Dickensian*, who has never wearied of answering inquiries from me and supplying me with transcripts of materials in the collection of the Dickens House; the Folger Shakespeare Library, Dr. Louis B. Wright, its Director, and Dr. James T. McManaway, Acting Director; the Garrick Club and Major G. W. L. Baddeley, its Secretary; the Houghton Library and the Harry Elkins Widener Collection of Harvard University; the Library of Congress; the Massachusetts Historical Society; the Parrish Collection of Princeton University; the Eastgate House Museum of Rochester and its honorary Curator, the late J. H. Bolton; the Royal Academy of Art and Sir Walter R. M. Lamb, its Secretary; the John Rylands Library of Manchester; and the Yale University Library.

Many private collectors and dealers in autograph letters gave me access to manuscript material. Professor Richard D. Altick sent me microfilm of a collection of Dickens letters he had found in the Pennsylvania Historical Society; Mr. Archibald Barrow of New York, a descendant of the Barrow side of Dickens's family, gave me photostats of Dickens letters in his possession; Major Philip Dickens of Charing, Kent, sent me transcripts of letters and documents in his; Mr. Humphry House, Editor of the new edition of *The Letters of Charles Dickens* now in preparation, and Mr. K. J. Fielding, his Associate Editor, sent me transcripts of many letters they have discovered; Mr. George Macy of New York lent me Dickens's Account Book with Messrs. Coutts and Company for 1865–68; and the late Comte Alain de Suzannet of Lausanne sent me transcripts of letters both to and from Dickens of which he either had the originals or had been given copies. The late Professor Henry Wadsworth Longfellow Dana not only gave me access to all the material in the Longfellow House Papers in Cambridge, Massachusetts, but permitted me to transcribe Dickens letters belonging to him personally. In addition, all of the following generously allowed me to make transcripts of letters and documents in their possession: Mr. Roger W. Barrett of Kenilworth, Ill.; the Carnegie Book Shop of New York; the City Book Auction of New York; the late William M. Elkins of Philadelphia; Mr. Lewis A. Hird of Englewood, New Jersey; Maurice Inman, Inc., of New York; Miss Elena Klasky of New York; Mrs. R. C. Lehmann of London; the late Earl of Lytton; Mr. Ernest Maggs of Maggs Brothers, London; Mr. Carl Pforzheimer of New York; the late Dr. A. S. W. Rosenbach; and the late Ralph Straus.

Mr. Leon Rosenblatt, and Mr. Edward Bachman, both of New York, aided me by generous long-time loans of rare books and pamphlets from their extensive libraries. Mr. Reginald F. R. Barrow of London helped me with information supplied from his erudite genealogical knowledge of the Dickens and Barrow families. My colleague Dr. Leonard Manheim lent me a manuscript copy of his valuable doctoral dissertation *The Dickens Pattern*. Mr. Leigh B. Block of Chicago has allowed me to use among my illustrations a pastel portrait of Dickens never before reproduced.

Still others have responded generously to oral and written appeals for special information: Mr. John L. Bale, Managing Director of Chapman and Hall; Miss Dorothy Barck, Librarian of the New York Historical Society; Mr. George Freedley of the New York Public Library; the late Mrs. Enid Dickens Hawksley; Mr. Jean Hersholt; Mr. H. L. Mencken; the late Professor George C. D. Odell; Mr. Charles Retz; Professor Franklin P. Rolfe; Mr. H. L. Smedley of the Southern Railway Company; Mr. Arthur Swann of the Parke-Bernet Galleries; and Mr. Frank Weitenkampf. Nor should I fail to thank Miss W. Stewart Burt of Gad's Hill Place, Kent, who hospitably received me at Dickens's former home there; the Misses Dingley, of No. 1 Devonshire Terrace, his residence between 1839 and 1851; Alderman C. F. Knight, J. P., Deputy Mayor of Rochester, and Mr. F. C. Biss, Head Verger of Rochester Cathedral, who made pleasant my visits to the city of Rochester and the Cathedral; and Mr. Nicholas Udal, Secretary of the Athenaeum Club, who kindly received me there and lent me Francis Gledstanes Waugh's historical account of that institution. And I should be lacking in gratitude to the City College Library if I failed to acknowledge the protracted loan over successive years of many books that aided my task, and the frequent bibliographical help of the Library staff, especially of Mr. Sidney Ditzion, Mr. Frederick Henry Driscoll, Mr. Joseph R. Dunlap, Mr. Gordon W. Gray, Mr. James Troy Petrie, Mrs. Virginia Naille Cesario, Mrs. Alice R. Scanlan, and Mr. Martin A. Kuhn.

Some parts of this book originally appeared, sometimes in modified form, in various periodicals: the material on the genesis of Dickens's angry pamphlet, "Sunday under Three Heads," in the *American Scholar*, Autumn, 1948, under the title "Dickens and the Bluenose Legislator"; the critical section on *A Christmas Carol* in the *American Scholar*, Winter, 1951–52, under the title "The Christmas Carol and the Economic Man"; the discussion of Dickens's attitude toward Jews in *Commentary*, January, 1950, under the title "Dickens, Fagin, and Mr. Riah"; the account of Dickens's relationship with Richard Bentley in the *Dickensian*, Winter, 1949–50, and Spring, 1950, under the title "Dickens Quarrels with his Publisher"; and the entire critical chapter "The Anatomy of Society," on *Bleak House*, in *Nineteenth-Century Fiction*, September, 1952. It is pleasant to thank these publications and their editors, Mr. Hiram Haydn, Mr. Elliot Cohen, Mr. Leslie C. Staples, and Prof. Bradford A. Booth, for permission to incorporate this material in the present two volumes.

The faith and enthusiasm of my publishers, Mr. Richard Simon and Mr. M. Lincoln Schuster, have been a constant support. I owe a great deal to the appreciative and at the same time keenly critical comments of my friend Henry W. Simon, Senior Editor of Simon and Schuster, who read all of this book in manuscript as its successive parts were produced and made many valuable suggestions.

The deepest debt of gratitude of all I have reserved to the last. This is the gratitude I owe my wife, Eleanor Johnson. Throughout the years of research on which this book is based she worked with me as a fellow student. There is no aspect of the character of Dickens and his associates or of his relationships with them that I have not clarified in my mind by discussion with her, and no judgment of his work that has not profited from her comment. She has not only typed my manuscript in its numerous redrafts, but given the most detailed criticism to its style and structure. Every chapter, every page, almost every paragraph is in some way the better for her painstaking thought. But her influence extends far beyond the purely editorial realm. Her belief in me and in this book have sustained me in my work from its beginnings to this moment of completion.

Contents

VOLUME ONE

[XV]

VOLUME TWO

Part Seven
AT GRIPS WITH HIMSELF: 1846–1851

Part Eight
THE DARKENING SCENE: 1851–1858

Part Nine
THE LAST ASSAY: 1858–1865

Part Ten
THE BOTTOM OF THE CUP: 1865–1870

List of Illustrations

VOLUME ONE

Frontispiece: Dickens at Twenty-Five, 1837

REPRODUCTIONS OF ORIGINAL "PHIZ" DRAWINGS FOR DICKENS'S WORKS

ILLUSTRATION SECTION: DICKENS'S LIFE FROM 1812 TO 1850
(following page 10)

PART ONE

The Anvil and the Iron

1812–1833

A NOTE ON THE NOTES

The bulk of these references, indicated by numbers in roman type, give the sources of the statements and quotations in the text. The numbers in italics, however, mark notes containing supplementary information or discussion.

CHAPTER ONE

Birth and Background

O N the highest strip of ground in the main road from Gravesend to Rochester stands a brick Georgian dwelling with bow windows and a small white bell turret surmounting its gambrel roof. More than a century ago a rather sickly small boy used to cross Rochester Bridge on walks with his father and ascend the two-mile slope to stare with admiration at its rose-and-madder façade and draw a low breath of longing and incredulity when his father told him that if he were to work very hard he might come to live there some day.[1] The house was called Gad's Hill Place and the little boy was named Charles Dickens. The dream came true: he lived there for the last twelve years of his life, and there he died.

His way to Gad's Hill had descended into shabby-genteel suburbs and urban slums; his family's sinking fortunes had jailed the father in the Marshalsea for debt and condemned the despairing child to drudgery and tears in a blacking warehouse. But the child became an office boy, a shorthand writer, a reporter, an author. With *Pickwick Papers*, at the age of twenty-four, he stepped into instant fame, and from then on he marched from triumph to triumph. His readers in England probably numbered more than one out of every ten inhabitants.[2] He was read all over the continent of Europe, from Italy to Russia, and cheerfully pirated by the hundreds of thousands in the United States. From the leading intellectual reviews to the popular press there was no significant disputation of his literary eminence. It would be difficult to name any novelist of our own time who has so commanded the respect of serious criticism and at the same time reached anything like so widespread an audience. In the end, this writer who was the son of a perennially improvident father became the most celebrated literary figure of his time and left an estate equivalent to more than a million dollars today.[3]

Seen thus, the career of Charles Dickens is one of the most glittering of nineteenth-century success stories. But it has darker and profounder depths than can be contained in any such pattern. Beneath the blare of applause there is the heartbreak of his father's imprisonment, the terror of butcher and baker raising angry voices, of insufficient meals choked down with tears, of rooms pawned bare of household goods. Beneath the later fame there is the weeping of a child taken out of school and delivered to toil, all his early ambition of growing up to be a learned and distinguished man crushed within his breast. And, after the first exhilaration of fame, despite a gusto for excitement and a sense of the comic that look like happiness, Dickens was not happy in his good fortune. Sheer vitality and the stimulation of companionship could key him to an electric flow of high spirits. But this only masked an underlying "vague unhappy loss or want of something" which he lamented in the very height of his achievement, and which goaded him to perpetual restlessness and dissatisfaction with himself and the world.[4] There were hidden wounds in his home life, secret burdens and disappointed hopes and loving disillusions, which pride and reserve led him to fight with vigorous activity and with a determined and infectious display of social vivacity. The genial human contact he had always enjoyed became—like his titanic literary labors and the lethal excitement of his public readings—a part of his desperate endeavor to escape a crushing sense of hollowness and futility.

But this personal unhappiness deepened his insight and sharpened his criticism, spurred him to a continued intellectual and artistic growth that turned him from humor and romantic pathos and the lashing of isolated wrongs to the indictment of an entire society. The later Dickens, though he never loses the command of sentiment and hilarity that brought his first fame, becomes a social critic and a social prophet whose amazing imaginative comprehension of his environment illumines the problems of our contemporary world. The early boundless confidence that good will and common sense could conquer all the abuses of society yields to a disillusioned analysis of the endlessly interlinked evils piled up in an economic system dominated by industrialism and material greed. There is a steady line of growth from the glorious humor of *Pickwick* to the penetrating social analysis of

Little Dorrit and *Our Mutual Friend*—an analysis that encompasses the dominant forces of the world we live in today. On one level, then, Dickens was painfully vanquished by the challenges existence posed for him. On another and loftier level he magnificently surmounted them. In this tension between his splendid public success and his deep-rooted dissatisfaction with the world that heaped rewards upon him lies the drama and the pity of his life. Its tragedy grows out of the way in which the powers that enabled him to overcome the obstacles before him contained also the seeds of his unhappiness. Its triumph is that his inward misery stimulated his powers to that culminating achievement of his work.

* * * * *

The baby who was to be named Charles Dickens was born in a little house at 387 Mile End Terrace, Landport, Portsea, on February 7, 1812.[5] On the mantel ticked a small mahogany-cased clock; somewhere in the house there was a little sister called Fanny, only a few months over a year old herself.[6] The building was one of a row of attached brick houses, with two windows to the right of a paneled door between narrow white pilasters, two more windows above, and an attic lit by a low rectangle of window in its sloping roof. A minute square of garden lay between each house and the street, and another square of green behind. John Dickens had exuberantly taken the house when he was married, almost three years before, although its annual rent of £35 was nearly one-third of his entire salary.[7] But now, although it was but a modest house and his income had risen to £140 a year,[8] he was finding it too dear for him. On June 24th, before their baby son was six months old, the Dickens family moved to a cheaper house at 18 Hawke Street.[9]

John Dickens was at this time a lively, talkative, energetic young man of around twenty-six. He worked faithfully at his post, which was that of clerk in the Navy Pay Office; and he talked vividly and entertainingly, even if somewhat magniloquently. He was generous, kindly, warm-hearted; he loved to play host to his friends over a bottle of wine or a hot bowl of punch; his manner was ornately genteel. No one would have guessed that his father, William Dickens, had been steward at Crewe Hall or his mother before her marriage a servant in the house of the Marquess of Blandford, in Grosvenor Square; and that his mother was even now housekeeper at Crewe.

William Dickens had died in 1785, leaving his wife with two children, William and the baby, John.[10] The Crewes took a kindly interest in advancing the education and prospects of their housekeeper's fatherless children. John Crewe (later Lord Crewe), for whom the young child may have been named, had been Member of Parliament for Chester, and was a warm friend of George Canning, then Treasurer of the Navy. When John Dickens was about nineteen years of age he was appointed by Canning, probably through Crewe's influence, to a clerical post in the Navy Pay Office at Somerset House. The date of the appointment was April 15, 1805, and the beginning salary was five shillings a day—not quite £80 a year.[11] The bright young fellow must have given satisfaction to his superiors: a little more than two years later he was made fifteenth assistant clerk at £70 a year plus two shillings extra for every day of actual attendance— [12] a probable total of £100 a year. He had broken away from the menial background of his parents and become a government employee on his way to transforming himself into a member of the gentry. In later years there were family legends of being a branch of the ancient Dickens family of Staffordshire, and Charles Dickens assumed the right to use its crest, which he referred to as "my father's crest: a lion couchant, bearing in his dexter paw a Maltese cross." [13]

At the same time that John Dickens received his appointment another young man was nominated to a clerkship in the same office. This was Thomas Culliford Barrow, whose father, Charles Barrow, had the responsible post of Chief Conductor of Moneys in Town and a suite of rooms in Somerset House. At this time a man of fifty, Charles Barrow was originally a native of Bristol who had made his way to London, where in 1788 he had married Mary Culliford, a daughter of a musical instrument maker. A few years later Barrow became a partner with his father-in-law, Thomas Culliford, and a man named William Rolfe, in a firm that made musical instruments in Cheapside, opposite Bow Church. In 1797 he and his father-in-law retired from the business, and Charles Barrow taught music and ran a circulating library. Then, at the close of 1801, Barrow had been appointed an extra clerk in the Navy Pay Office.

Suddenly, in little more than a year, this man with no previous experience was jumped to the important position he had since occupied, with a salary rising from £330 to £350. It has been suggested and denied that he was related to Sir John Barrow, the arctic explorer, and second secretary of the Admiralty from 1804 to 1845, but such a promotion implies powerful supporting influences, and the Barrows were certainly of markedly higher pretensions than young John Dickens, the steward's and housekeeper's son.[14] But John Dickens and Thomas Culliford Barrow became friends. John was soon asked to Barrow's home, and met his sister Elizabeth. She was a small, pretty girl of about sixteen, with bright hazel eyes, an inordinate sense of the ludicrous, and remarkable powers of comic mimicry, cheerful, sweet-tempered, and well educated.[15]

In the course of the next two years she and her brother's friend fell in love with each other. They were married at St. Mary-le-Strand, opposite Somerset House, on June 13, 1809.[16] The Barrows, it has been asserted, were not too pleased with the match, but there is no evidence that they objected at the time, though they certainly repudiated John Dickens later on. Elizabeth Barrow, in fact, was still a minor and could not be married without her father's consent. He signed the register as a witness, and John Dickens, in nervous excitement, began to sign his name in the wrong place, leaving too little room for his wife's, and then started again higher up.[17] Not long afterward, the married couple proceeded by stagecoach to Landport, where John Dickens was assigned to the paying off of ships at Portsmouth Dockyard.[18] His marriage must have seemed to the young husband another step in his rise into gentility.

Part of Charles Barrow's work was to send money both for salaries and incidental expenses under armed guard to Plymouth, Portsmouth, Sheerness, and Chatham. He also paid tradesmen for repairs, furniture, coal, oil, and other articles needed in the Office. He was entitled to obtain money for these purposes by signing bills of £900 each on his own authority and having them endorsed by the Paymaster to the Navy Board. But about six months after his daughter's marriage, the authorities began to be suspicious of this trusted official and started quietly investigating him. In February, 1810, a Writ of Extent arrived at his office. It transpired that he had been systematically stating false balances since 1803. The deficiency by now was £5,689 3s 3d.[19]

Summoned before the Treasurer, Barrow confessed his guilt, pleading as excuse the burden of a family of ten children and the expenses of constant illness. Expressing bitter regret, he appealed for time to see if a brother in Bristol would not make good the money. A few days later he resigned, still begging not to be sent to jail. But the Treasurer started criminal proceedings, and Barrow absconded to the Continent, from which he never returned to England. (Thirteen years later he turned up in the Isle of Man, outside the jurisdiction of the British law, where he died in 1826.) His household furniture was seized and sold by the Sheriff of Middlesex. It realized £499 9s. The rest of the money that Charles Barrow had embezzled was never recovered.[20]

This shaming business was a severe shock to the family pride of the Barrows. Thomas Barrow, however, did not lose his post in the Navy Pay Office; ultimately, indeed, he rose to be head of its Prize Branch and retired on a pension of £710 a year.[21] For John Dickens the blow may have been more palpable. Any help his father-in-law might have given him toward paying that extravagant £35 a year house rent would have to be found elsewhere now. And already John Dickens was revealing the weakness that dogged him all his life. He was not lazy and he was thoroughly respectable. He was a good father and a good husband. He neither gambled nor drank to excess, though he liked a convivial glass. But he simply could not live within his income. He loved the orotund gesture and the display of hospitality: both of them easier for a bachelor than for a married man with children. Friends about the festal board—as he would have called it—a glowing hearth, songs and toasts, later in the evening deviled mutton grilled over the fire, and a nightcap of punch downed with oratorical sentiments, all these were irresistible to his expansive nature.

Down at Crewe old Mrs. Dickens used to hold the Crewe children fascinated of an afternoon in the housekeeper's room with fairy tales and stories from the pages of history, and sometimes with personal reminiscences.[22] In the years before her retirement in 1820 she grumbled to them about "that lazy fellow John, who used to come hanging around the house," adding "and many a sound cuff on the ear I've given him." [23] But he received cash as well as cuffs on the ear, although she had been too shrewd to give him much. When she died her will bequeathed £500 to William and £450 to John, explaining that he was entitled to no more because he had already received "several sums of money some years ago." [24] Thomas Barrow and his brother John Henry Barrow, a barrister-at-law, were also to receive appeals for aid so often that at last they lost all patience and refused to communicate with John Dickens any further. But they were long-suffering; it took over twenty years to wear them out.[25]

There was no shadow of these future events, though, in the small upstairs bedroom where Charles was born. Although her time was near, his mother, determined to snatch the last possible minute of enjoyment, had put on a dance frock and attended a ball at the Beneficial Society's Hall in Rope Walk. Returning in the small hours, she bore her son before dawn. The child was baptized, as his sister Fanny had been before him, at St. Mary's, Kingston, the parish church for Portsea. In the register for March 4, 1812, his full name is entered as Charles John Huffham Dickens, although "Huffham" is a clerical error for Huffam. Charles was for his maternal grandfather, the absconded Conductor of Moneys; John for his father; and Huffam for his godfather, Christopher Huffam, a prosperous naval rigger whom John Dickens had met while he was at Somerset House.[26]

Shortly after, when Charles was still not five months old, the family's straitened circumstances forced its move to Hawke Street. There was no front garden, the cramped sitting room was up two tiny wooden steps from the street, and a bay window overhung the very paving stones.[27] But baby Charles did not mind, as he and his sister trotted about the little back garden with something to eat, while a maid kept an eye on them through the kitchen area window on a level with the gravel path. He enjoyed, too, being carried in arms to see the soldiers drill at Portsmouth, and a quarter of a century later recognized the exact shape of the military parade as he had seen it when an infant.[28]

Portsea was fun for a small child. It was a fortified town with six gates. Through the Lion Gate on the direct road to London the stagecoach came dashing, to wind up in the yard of the George, the town's principal inn. There were pretty lanes in the surrounding country, and there was a ferry to Gosport, Portsmouth—a penny in fine weather and thruppence in foul. There were plenty of shops and a market three days a week. In these times of the war with the United States and the concluding endeavors of the Napoleonic struggle it was full of sailors and dockyard craftsmen, and of the lively bustle of the military and naval conflict.[29]

Trafalgar, to be sure, had removed all danger of an invasion of Britain. The bombardment of Copenhagen in the autumn of 1807 and the seizure of the Danish fleet had destroyed Napoleon's chances of counterattack by sea. But the Berlin and Milan Decrees had retaliated with the Orders in Council that declared the entire Continent under blockade. These, and England's high-handed seizure and search of American ships for naval deserters, led to angry bickerings with America. The offending measures were repealed in May, 1812, but it was too late— the United States had declared war that very week.[30] These conflicts in the great world meant busy and exciting days even in the routine of the Navy Pay Office.

Suddenly, toward the end of 1814, John Dickens was summoned back to Somerset House in London. He established his family in lodgings at 10 Norfolk Street, near the Middlesex Hospital, between Goodge Street and Tottenham Street. There was now another infant, named Alfred, who had been born in 1813, but who was to die in childhood. Charles had just a faint memory of having come away from Portsea in the winter, but he retained no separate recollections of this first stay in London.[31] Perhaps its impressions were absorbed in the sharper and more painful ones that came to him there later. No one knows exactly how long the family remained in Norfolk Street, or even whether the next three years while Charles was growing from a toddler of two to a child of five were entirely spent in the metropolis, though it is probable that if John Dickens had been assigned to any other post there would be some record of the fact. In the midsummer of 1817, however, he was ordered to the large government dockyard at Chatham, a shipbuilding town that even then melted almost imperceptibly into the cathedral city of Rochester.[32]

[1] John Dickens, a portrait by John W. Gilbert

[2] Elizabeth Dickens, a portrait by John W. Gilbert

DICKENS'S FATHER AND MOTHER

[3] 387 Mile End Terrace, Landport, Portsea, Dickens's birthplace, 1812. Photograph by F. J. Mortimer

[4] 2 ORDNANCE TERRACE, CHATHAM, Dickens's home between the ages of five and nine, 1817-1821

[5] NAVE OF ROCHESTER CATHEDRAL, a childhood haunt. Pen-and-ink sketch by Donald Maxwell

[6] *Above*, 16 BAYHAM
STREET, CAMDEN TOWN, the
Dickens home as financial des-
peration deepened, 1824.
Sketch by F. G. Kitton

[7] *Right*, THE MARSHALSEA,
scene of John Dickens's imprisonment for debt, 1824.
Pen-and-ink drawing by Arthur Moreland

[8] DICKENS AT EIGHTEEN. Miniature by his aunt, Janet Barrow, 1830

[10] DICKENS AT TWENTY-THREE, by Rose Drummond, 1835. He gave this miniature to his fiancée, Catherine Hogarth, as an engagement present

[9] *Below,* MARIA BEADNELL, Dickens's first love, the original of David Copperfield's Dora. From *The Sphere,* February 20, 1909

[11] *Above,* MARY HOGARTH, his wife's sister, dead at seventeen, who inspired the creation of "Little Nell." Portrait by Hablôt Knight Browne

[12] 48 DOUGHTY STREET, LON-
DON. Dickens's home, 1837-1839,
where he wrote *Pickwick, Oliver
Twist,* and *Nicholas Nickleby.*
Photograph by T. W. Tyrrell

[13] *Below,* THE FLEET PRISON,
where Mr. Pickwick was incar-
cerated. After Rowlandson and
Pugin

[14] JOHN FORSTER at twenty-eight,
Dickens's most intimate friend.
Sketch, May 22, 1840, by Daniel
Maclise, R. A.

[15] WILLIAM HARRISON AINS-
WORTH, popular novelist, who introduced Dickens to his first publisher. Sketch by Daniel Maclise

[16] Left, HABLÔT KNIGHT
BROWNE, "Phiz," illustrator of most
of Dickens's books. Drawing by his
son, Walter Browne

[17] THOMAS NOON TALFOURD, Serjeant-at-Law, to whom Dickens dedicated *Pickwick Papers*, the original of Tommy Tráddles in *David Copperfield*

[18] GEORGE CRUIKSHANK, illustrator of *Sketches by Boz* and *Oliver Twist*. Sketch by Daniel Maclise

[19] *Right*, WILLIAM CHARLES MACREADY, famous actor, a lifelong friend

[20] BROADSTAIRS in the 1830's, a favorite Dickens summer resort. Drawing by George Shepherd

[21] SAMUEL ROGERS, sharp-tongued host of the famous "Literary Breakfasts." Sketch by Daniel Maclise, R. A.

[22] LEIGH HUNT, friend of Keats and Shelley, and the original of Harold Skimpole in *Bleak House*. Sketch by Daniel Maclise, R. A.

[23] FRANCIS, LORD JEFFREY, famous Scottish critic, one of those who wept for Little Nell. Portrait by G. Hayter

[24] WALTER SAVAGE LANDOR, the leonine original of Boythorn in *Bleak House*. Portrait by William Fisher

[25] DANIEL MACLISE, "Mac," the painter of the "Nickleby Portrait"

[26] OLD BAILEY AND NEWGATE, scene of the Courvoisier hanging, 1840. (see p. 300) Before such a crowd Fagin would have been hanged

[27] 1 DEVONSHIRE TERRACE, YORK GATE, REGENT'S PARK, LONDON, Dickens's home, 1839-1851, where he wrote *The Old Curiosity Shop, Barnaby Rudge, A Christmas Carol, Martin Chuzzlewit,* and *David Copperfield*

[28] DICKENS in 1839, from the "Nickleby Portrait," painted by Daniel Maclise, R. A.

[29] CATHERINE DICKENS, 1842, Dickens's wife, from the portrait by Daniel Maclise, R. A.

[30] DICKENS'S CHILDREN IN 1841. Charley, Mamey, Katey, and Walter, with the raven, in Devonshire Terrace. Water-color by Daniel Maclise, R. A.

[31] DICKENS, 1840. Pastel portrait
by unknown artist

[32] CATHERINE DICKENS, 1846.
Portrait by Daniel Maclise, R. A.

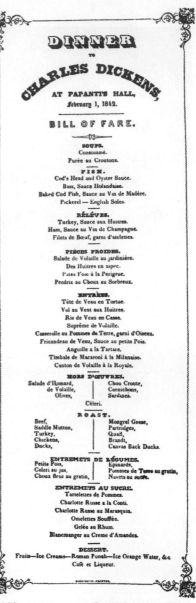

DINNER

TO

CHARLES DICKENS,

AT PAPANTI'S HALL,
February 1, 1842.

BILL OF FARE.

SOUPS.
Consommé.
Purée au Croutons.

FISH.
Cod's Head and Oyster Sauce.
Bass, Sauce Hollandaise.
Baked Cod Fish, Sauce au Vin de Madère.
Pickerel — English Soles.

RÉLÈVES.
Turkey, Sauce aux Huitres.
Ham, Sauce au Vin de Champagne.
Filets de Bœuf, garni d'atelettes.

PIÈCES FROIDES.
Salade de Volaille à la jardinière.
Des Huitres en aspec.
Pâtes Foie à la Perigrue.
Perdrix au Choux au Sorbreux.

ENTRÉES.
Tête de Veau en Tortue.
Vol au Vent aux Huitres.
Ris de Veau en Casse.
Suprême de Volaille.
Casserolle au Pommes de Terre, garni d'Oiseau.
Fricandeau de Veau, Sauce au petits Pois.
Anguille à la Tartare.
Timbale de Macaroni à la Milanaise.
Canton de Volaille à la Royale.

HORS D'ŒUVRES.
Salade d'Homard,   Chou Croute,
de Volaille,   Cornichons,
Olives,   Sardines.
          Céleri.

ROAST.
Beef,   Mongrel Geese,
Saddle Mutton,   Partridges,
Turkey,   Quail,
Chickens,   Brandt,
Ducks,   Canvas Back Ducks.

ENTREMETS DE LÉGUMES.
Petits Pois,   Epinards,
Celeri au jus,   Pommes de Terre au gratin,
Choux fleur au gratin, Navets au sucre.

ENTREMETS AU SUCRE.
Tartelettes de Pommes.
Charlotte Russe a la Conti.
Charlotte Russe au Marasquin.
Omelettes Soufflée.
Gelée au Rhum.
Blancmanger au Creme d'Amandes.

DESSERT.
Fruits—Ice Creams—Roman Punch—Ice Orange Water, &c.
Café et Liqueur.

DICKINSON, PRINTER.

[33] A MODEST COLLATION: The
Hartford dinner menu listed seventy
dishes

[34] DICKENS IN AMERICA, lionized by Boston, 1842. Portrait by Francis Alexander

[35] HENRY WADSWORTH LONGFELLOW, age thirty-three, 1840. Portrait by Cephas G. Thompson

[36] STEAMER "MESSENGER" on which Dickens traveled down the Ohio from Pittsburgh to Cincinnati

[37] SALON, PALAZZO PESCHIERE, the Dickens home in Genoa, 1844

[38] WHERE DICKENS READ *The Chimes* to a circle of friends, December 3, 1844; also the scene of Mr. Tulkinghorn's murder in *Bleak House*. Pen-and-ink drawing by Arthur Moreland

[39] READING *The Chimes*. From left to right the audience includes Forster, Jerrold, Blanchard, Carlyle, Frederick Dickens, Maclise, Fox, Stanfield, Dyce and Harness. Below are Forster, Barham, and Fonblanque. Sketch by Daniel Maclise, R. A.

[40] THOMAS CARLYLE, 1868. From a photograph

[41] JANE WELSH CARLYLE, 1850. Portrait by Karl Hartmann

[42] DICKENS AS CAPTAIN BOBADIL in *Every Man in His Humour*. Painting by Charles R. Leslie, R. A.

[43] GEORGINA HOGARTH, 1850, the sister-in-law who lived in Dickens's home from 1842 until his death. By Augustus Egg, R. A.

[44] ANGELA BURDETT COUTTS, philanthropist, with whom Dickens collaborated in many charitable activities. Portrait by J. R. Swinton

CHAPTER TWO

The Happy Time

THE family was larger now, but it was more prosperous. Five-year-old Charles had a baby sister, Letitia, born in 1816. His mother's eldest sister, Mary, whom the children called Aunt Fanny, had come to live with them when her husband, a naval lieutenant, was drowned at Rio de Janeiro.[1] She probably paid her share of the household expenses (perhaps more, as unattached aunts sharing a home where there are nephews and nieces are apt to do), and John Dickens, who had been given another increase in salary in 1815, was now earning £200 a year, plus extra emoluments.[2]

Consequently he rented a three-story brick house at 2 Ordnance Terrace in Chatham and signalized his standing in the community by subscribing to Wildash's *History of Rochester,* published in 1817. Ordnance Terrace was a row of attached houses having an airy hilltop position looking down toward the lower part of Chatham and the River Medway.[3] There were small front and back gardens, two lovely hawthorn trees, and, across the way, a hay field bright with daisies and buttercups.[4] The neighborhood was genteel. In No. 5 lived Mrs. Newnham, an ancient lady whose glass and picture frames were always covered with yellow muslin and whose tabletops were turpentined and beeswaxed daily. Next door to her was a naval half-pay officer, a bluff old chap who drank his ale, smoked his cigar, raised marigolds, and quarreled bitterly with all the parish authorities.[5]

In Ordnance Terrace the Dickens family had two servants, Jane Bonny and a young girl named Mary Weller who looked after the children.[6] Charles could remember her putting him to bed and humming the evening hymn to him, while he cried on the pillow, "either with the remorseful consciousness of having kicked Somebody else, or

[11]

because still Somebody else had hurt my feelings in the course of the day." [7] She may have been the "very sympathetic nurse" who took the child visiting with her when she went to see friends who had just passed through the ordeal of childbirth. "At one little greengrocer's shop," he wrote, there had been a lady "who had had four children (I am afraid to write five, though I fully believe it was five) at a birth"; and he saw "how the four (five) deceased young people lay, side by side, on a clean cloth on a chest of drawers," reminding the little boy by their complexion "of pigs' feet as they are usually displayed at a neat tripe-shop." [8]

Mary Weller took his imagination on even more horrifying journeys that afflicted him at night, telling him stories of bloody vengeance and supernatural hauntings. One of these gory narratives concerned a certain Captain Murderer who slaughtered his successive wives, baked them in meat pies, ate them, and picked the bones. Ultimately this sinister character met his just fate through a poison injected into the pie crust by a suspicious victim, which caused him to swell up and turn blue and scream until he filled the room from floor to ceiling and finally burst. Still another dismal tale was about a shipwright named Chips who sold himself to the Devil for an iron pot, a bushel of nails, half a ton of copper, and a rat that could speak. Thereafter he found himself haunted by rats, nestling in his pockets, curled up in his hat, dripping from his sleeves, and running up his trouser legs. And worse, he knew what the rats were doing, wherever they were, so that he would sometimes cry aloud, "Oh! Keep the rats out of the convicts' burying-ground! Don't let them do that!" or, "There's two of them smelling the baby in the garret!" In the end, the rats gnawed away the oak of a ship on which he was sailing, and what was left of Chips floated ashore with a great overgrown rat sitting on him, laughing. Little Charles would lie in bed rigid with terror at such horrors projecting themselves before him in the dark.[9]

In the three years before the migration to Chatham, he had not grown so strong and healthy as might have been desired. "He was a very little and a very sickly boy," his friend John Forster wrote, "subject to attacks of violent spasm which disabled him for any active exertion. He was never a good little cricket-player; he was never a first-rate hand at marbles, or peg-top, or prisoners' base; but he had great pleasure in watching the other boys, officers' sons for the most part, at these games, reading while they played . . ." [10]

It was his mother who taught him to read, and, later, the rudiments of English, and even a little Latin.[11] The alphabet Charles learned in thin books "with deliciously smooth covers of bright red or green. What fat black letters to begin with! 'A was an archer, and shot at a frog.' Of course he was. He was an apple-pie also, and there he is! He was a good many things in his time, was A, and so were most of his friends, except X, who had so little versatility that I never knew him to get beyond Xerxes or Xantippe—like Y, who was always confined to a Yacht or a Yew Tree; and Z condemned for ever to be a Zebra or a Zany." [12] At this time, Mary Weller recalled, he had not yet been to school, but Mrs. Dickens, "a dear good mother and a fine woman," had taught him thoroughly well at home. He speedily became, as his nurse put it, "a terrible boy to read," sitting with his book in his left hand, holding his wrist with his right hand, and constantly sliding it up and down while he sucked his tongue.[13]

Later he and Fanny were sent to a dame school upstairs over a dyer's shop in Rome Lane.[14] There was a puppy pug-dog in the long and narrow entry who terrified him by snapping at his undefended legs, and who belonged, as he wrote later, "to some female, chiefly inhabiting a back parlour, whose life appeared to us to have been consumed in sniffing, and in wearing a brown beaver bonnet." In going up the steps—hastily, to escape the dog—he often grazed his knees, and in trying to scrape mud off an unsteady small shoe he usually got his leg over the scraper.[15] The woman who kept the school was a grim old creature upon whom he later partly modeled Mrs. Pipchin and the gloomy establishment at Brighton where little Paul Dombey was one of the inmates. When Charles was puzzled she poked his head with a hard knuckle "by way of adjusting the confusion of ideas in which he was generally involved." [16]

Next door in Ordnance Terrace, at No. 1, were two children, George and Lucy Stroughill, who became playmates of the Dickens children.[17] Charles was invited to Lucy's birthday party. She was "a peach-faced creature in a blue sash," with whom he fell in love, and the two small people sat blissfully "in a shady bower—under a table" consuming sweet foods and liquids, while he imagined this glorified young person to lead a life consisting entirely of birthdays and to be reared exclusively on seedcake, sweet wine, and shining presents.[18]

Although he was still small for his age, outdoor air and sunlight at Chatham were making him stronger and more healthy. Now there were glorious and noisy games in the playing field across the low wall opposite the Terrace. "Here, in the haymaking time," he remembered, "had I been delivered from the dungeons of Seringapatam, an immense pile (of haycock), by my countrymen, the victorious British (boy next door and his two cousins), and had been recognized with ecstasy by my affianced one" (Lucy), "who had come all the way from England (second house in the terrace) to ransom me, and marry me." [19]

On other days, when they played indoors, Charles would rush downstairs and say authoritatively, "Now, Mary, clear the kitchen, we're going to have such a game." Then in would come George Stroughill with his magic lantern, and there would be a spirited acting out of plays. Charles was fond of reciting, too, rendering Dr. Watts's "The Voice of the Sluggard," the admiring Mary recalled, "with *such* action and *such* attitudes!" [20] Fanny was learning to play the piano, and they would sing comic songs together, such as "The Cat's Meat Man," with its recurrent chorus of

> "*Down in the street cries the cat's meat man,*
> *Fango dango, with his barrow and can.*" [21]

This small talent for comic singing gave the sociable John Dickens such delight that he often hoisted Charles up on a table to entertain the guests in his clear, unshy treble, or strolled down into the lower part of the town with the youngster to show him off there.[22] The Dickenses were on visiting terms with the Tribes, who owned the Mitre Inn and Clarence Hotel, a fine old place with beautiful grounds and trees, where Lord Nelson had often stayed. Here, mounted on one of the dining tables, Charles sang sea duets with Fanny. He would begin:

> "*Long time I've courted you, miss,*
> *And now I've come from sea;*
> *We'll make no more ado, miss,*
> *But quickly married be.*"

Then the youngsters would join in a "Sing fol de rol" chorus, she would take the next stanza, and the two would continue alternately:

> *"I ne'er will wed a tar, sir,*
>   *Deceitful as yourself;*
> *'Tis very plain you are, sir,*
>   *A good for nothing elf."* ("Sing fol de rol")

> *"I ne'er deceived you yet, miss,*
>   *Though like a shrew you rave;*
> *But prithee, scold and fret, miss—*
>   *A storm I well can brave."* ("Sing fol de rol")

> *"False man, you courted Sally,*
>   *You filled with vows her head;*
> *And Susan in the valley*
>   *You promised you would wed."* ("Sing fol de rol")[23]

—And so on through long cheerily tuneful sessions, though Dickens in later years told Forster that the memory of his shrill little voice tingled in his ears and made him redden to think what a nuisance he must have been to unoffending grownups called upon to admire him.[24]

It was an innocent and happy time for the young Dickenses. If their family felt any of the economic distresses that followed the end of the wars, the children knew nothing of it. But it is probable that John Dickens, on an undiminished government salary, was benefited by falling prices that were bankrupting businesses, making ruined farmers hang themselves, and pauperizing farm laborers and factory hands by the scores of thousands. The Corn Laws of 1815 helped the landowners and left the poor to starve. The radical press was fought with savage prosecutions, *habeas corpus* was suspended, and starving rioters were tried for treason.

In St. Peter's Fields, Manchester, on August 16, 1819, an orderly and unarmed crowd of sixty thousand men, women, and children were charged into by a regiment of cavalry, who slashed at them with sabers and trampled them under the horses' hoofs. The nervous Government, frightened into ferocity, thanked the magistrates who had ordered the charge, and were surprised by the outbreak of indignation aroused by this "Peterloo Massacre" among respectable citizens.[25]

The fat and corseted Prince Regent, that deplorable and disgraceful old rake who represented the Crown, was more violently despised and execrated even than before. But the only echo of all these events that came to seven-year-old Charles was his being told in confidence about this time by someone "whose father was greatly connected, being under Government, of the existence of a terrible banditti, called 'The Radicals,' whose principles were, that the Prince Regent wore stays, and that nobody had a right to any salary, and that the army and navy ought to be put down—horrors at which I trembled in my bed, after supplicating that the Radicals might be speedily taken and hanged." [26] In later years Dickens recalled a visit that the Prince Regent had paid to Rochester, when his mother ("God forgive her," he interpolated) had perched him on a low wall in front of the Star Theatre to cheer that royal personage.[27]

*   *   *   *   *

It was not until 1821 that John Dickens's incurable financial care-lessness caught up with him again. He had, to be sure, two more children now, Harriet, born in the autumn of 1819, and Frederick, born in the summer of 1820, so that there were five children in the house at Ordnance Terrace, ranging from ten-year-old Fanny down to the baby. But he had received a final salary increase in 1820 to £350 a year, a sizable jump.[28] To the victims of a disastrous fire that destroyed thirty-eight houses on March 3rd of that year, he impulsively contributed two guineas, and was thanked for his efficient and valuable services in a report by the Treasurer of the Relief Committee.[29] On Lady Day (March 25), 1821, however, he found himself forced to give up their pleasant quarters at Ordnance Terrace and move to 18 St. Mary's Place, called "The Brook." [30]

The move was both literally and figuratively downhill. The new home was a small tenement with a front of whitewashed plaster, next door to the Providence Baptist Chapel.[31] From the window of Charles's attic room it was possible to see the spire of St. Mary's Church and the surrounding churchyard with its graves, but there were no such open spaces as the meadow across the way from Ordnance Terrace.[32] The Brook was much nearer the Dockyard, in the crowded lower quarter of Chatham. John Dickens had to put a curb upon his generosity. Mary Weller, who still served them here, recalled no such youthful parties as she had seen at the Terrace.[33]

But Charles, although he was nine by this time, hardly noticed these changes. He found too many other exciting things to become ac-quainted with. Trotting along by his father's side now, when he went to his office in the Dockyard, Charles was wide-eyed for everything—the street posts of cannon and ornaments of shells, and the handsome row of houses for the leading officials.[34] The Navy Pay Office itself, of red brick two stories high, impressed the boy with the gravity of barred arched windows, its strong rooms lined with iron, and "its staid pretense of having nothing worth mentioning to do." [35] He watched the ropemakers and sniffed the smell of tarred rope, heard the anchorsmiths clanging away, saw the blockmakers surrounded by oak chips and wooden shavings, and stood under the huge wooden walls of vessels rising in the slips, amid the exciting clatter and banging.[36] On St. Clement's Day, November 23rd, the artificers had a pageant in which they wore masks and flowing wigs, made doggerel speeches, and paraded "Old Clem" in a chair of state through the town, collecting drink money and singing:

> *"Beat it out, beat it out,*
> *Old Clem!*
> *With a clink for the stout*
> *Old Clem!"* [37]

Sometimes Charles sailed up the Medway as far as Sheerness and the Thames on the *Chatham*, the Navy Pay Yacht, an old tub built two hundred years before, a sluggish sailer in a light wind, but speedy and handy in a stiff breeze. Entranced, he would pass all the ships floating out in the Medway and in the larger stream, bringing with the sight their far visions of the sea.[38] Returning, they would see the Yard from a distance, "snug under hillsides of corn-fields, hop-gardens, and orchards; its great chimneys smoking with a quiet—almost a lazy —air, like giants smoking tobacco." Nearer, they would glide by the gun wharf with its piled-up cannon looking like toys, and the one red-coated sentry on duty like a clockwork figure. Then they would land again at the Stairs, where there was a flotsam of chips and sharp-tanged seaweed.[39]

Lying out in the stream from the mud of the shore they would have passed a black convict hulk "like a wicked Noah's ark," all cribbed and barred and moored by rusty chains, seeming in the eyes of its childish observer "to be ironed like the prisoners" themselves.[40] And back in the Dockyard once more, amid the canvas, and the clanging, and the booming, and the smell of oakum, the boy would stare spell-bound at long files of convict laborers carrying planks of heavy lumber, two tall men sometimes bearing all the weight and a little man in between, with his shoulders three inches below theirs, happily carrying nothing.[41]

Now that he was older, Charles could venture farther afield. On the hill above the town, almost directly behind the Brook, were the Chatham Lines, where the gay bright regiments were always parading and firing; and between Chatham and Rochester, just at the western end of Ordnance Terrace, he could revisit Fort Pitt with its endless succession of sham sieges and sham defenses.[42] Behind Fort Pitt fields, half a mile out of town was a house erected by a recluse named Tom Clarke who lived alone there for twenty-five years, whence it received the name Tom-all-Alone's. Other houses had been built around it, but when the land was needed for a convict prison the soldiers destroyed them with mines, and Charles saw the explosions and the crashing walls.[43]

On the High Street, below the Fort, was Simpson's coach office, which ran a coach to London, mellifluously entitled the Blue-Eyed Maid. The office window displayed an oval transparency that gleamed at night, representing the Maid bowling past a milestone with a full consignment of stylish passengers, all enjoying themselves tremendously.[44] The High Street, meandering along until Chatham merged into Rochester, seemed to boyish eyes "as wide as Regent Street, London, or the Italian Boulevard, Paris." The Guild Hall was "so glorious a structure" that he set it up in his mind "as the model on which the Genie of the Lamp built the palace for Aladdin." Projecting from the Corn Exchange hung a large gilt-framed clock that the boy supposed "to be the finest clock in the world" and found, in later years of manhood, "to be as inexpressive, moon-faced, and weak a clock as ever I saw." [45]

On the southwest side of the High Street loomed College Yard Gate, a cavernous portico with a room above reached by a tiny winding stair in the thickness of the wall. Thence one came into the precinct of the old Cathedral and its shady trees, greensward, and worn gravestones. There was the side entrance giving onto the choir transept and presbytery and then the shady Norman columns of the nave stretching out to the right, the porch, with its ancient carvings, the door opening out of St. Edmund's Chapel on the ruins of the monks' cloisters, and the gray rook-haunted tower soaring over all. Up the slope beyond the cloisters extended the quaint houses of Minor Canon Row and the King's School, and over the brow of the hill to the west the great square pile of Rochester Castle, gaunt and ruinous, with bare holes of windows like the empty eyes of a skull contemplating the river far below.[46]

Across the stream there were rural pilgrimages that Charles took with his father, John Dickens orating all the way in elaborate language and volubly vocalizing. They might go through Strood to Frindsbury, Chalk, or Cobham, although some of these were long walks for a boy of nine or ten. At Cobham were the square Gothic-arched porch and tower of St. Mary Magdalene, and, just across the way, the Leather Bottle, with its long, low-roofed room and fantastic high-backed leather chairs. Past Cobham Hall, then, its octagonal corner towers and innumerable chimneys bristling above a long façade of square-bayed windows and mellow Elizabethan brickwork, they could pass into the shady depths of Cobham Wood and come out by Gad's Hill, where Falstaff robbed the travelers, and the Sir John Falstaff Inn stood to commemorate the fact.[47] Here the boy would always gaze across the road at the ivied front and white portico of Gad's Hill Place. And here, while his father elegantly informed him again that if he were to work very, very hard he might someday come to live there, the boy would heave once more a deep low sigh of incredulity and longing.[48] Then down the Dover Road to Snorridge Bottom, and so back across Rochester Bridge, and home.

The minister of the Zion Baptist Chapel in Chatham during the time the Dickenses lived in St. Mary's Place was the Reverend William Giles. He has been said to have been also the minister of the Providence Baptist Chapel, next door to their house, although it is not likely that he officiated at both churches at the same time.[49] However this may be, Mr. Giles was acquainted with the Dickens family. They were Church of England, though not at all devout, or interested in matters of doctrine. They were not ritualistic nor straitlaced nor iconoclastic, just completely cheerful and worldly. They did not even attend church very regularly. They had no objection, however, to hearing their neighbor preach occasionally, and Charles evidently suffered bitterly from his or some other preacher's long-winded two-hour sermons.

Sitting there uncomfortably on a Sunday, he felt as if his mind were being steamed out of him, hating the minister's "big round face," look-ing "up the inside of his outstretched coat-sleeve as if it were a tele-scope," and loathing "his lumbering jocularity." Haled out of the chapel, the boy would find himself "catechized respecting" the minis-ter's "fifthly, his sixthly, and his seventhly," until he "regarded that reverend person in the light of a most dismal and oppressive Cha-rade." [50] These experiences laid the foundations for his lifelong hatred of Nonconformity and his revulsion from any formal religious affili-ation.

But Mr. Giles had a son, also named William Giles, who had estab-lished a school in Clover Lane around 1817. Subsequently he moved into a larger house at the corner of Rhode Street and Best Street. To his school, about the time they moved to the Brook, Fanny and Charles were sent.[51]

Giles was a young man of twenty-three, an Oxford graduate of more than average ability and cultivation. He speedily recognized in the handsome child with long, light, curly hair a boy of unusual promise. He gave the youngster special attention, and Charles took to his stud-ies with delight and made rapid progress. Outside school, too, he now enjoyed himself with the other boys, who wore white beaver hats and were known as Giles's Cats to distinguish them from pupils in the three other local schools who were called Baker's Bulldogs, Newroad Scrubbers, and Troy Town Rats. With these schoolmates there were romps in Fort Pitt fields, rowing and skating, the color and excitement of Guy Fawkes celebrations around the glowing bonfires, and Twelfth-Night festivities, with Twelfth-cakes and dancing till midnight.[52]

* * * * *

But these everyday boyish enjoyments did not supersede the fanci-ful play of earlier childhood. He had loved reading since his mother had taught him to distinguish "the easy good nature of O and Q and S" from each other.[53] Jack and the Bean Stalk, Red Riding Hood, Valentine and Orson, Robin Hood, the Yellow Dwarf, Mother Bunch: with what brilliant colors they glowed before his mind's eye! Now his imagination received an even more powerful stimulus. His father had become the owner of a cheap series of novels then in course of publi-cation; and he had left them, Dickens wrote in one of the passages of David Copperfield that are literally autobiographical, "in a little room upstairs to which I had access (for it adjoined my own), and which nobody else in our house ever troubled." (It was next to his attic chamber at St. Mary's Place.) "From that blessed little room, *Roderick Random, Peregrine Pickle, Humphrey Clinker, Tom Jones*, the *Vicar of Wakefield, Don Quixote, Gil Blas*, and *Robinson Crusoe* came out, a glorious host, to keep me company. They kept alive my fancy . . . they, and the *Arabian Nights*, and the *Tales of the Genii*,—and did me no harm; for, whatever harm was in some of them, was not there for me; *I* knew nothing of it.

"It is astonishing to me now," the same passage goes on, "how I found time in the midst of my porings and blunderings over heavier themes, to read those books as I did. It is curious to me how I could ever have consoled myself under my small troubles (which were great troubles to me), by impersonating my favourite characters in them— as I did . . . I have been Tom Jones (a child's Tom Jones, a harmless creature) for a week together. I have sustained my own idea of Roderick Random for a month at a stretch, I verily believe. I had a greedy relish for a few volumes of Voyages and Travels—I forget what, now— that were on those shelves; and for days and days I can remember to have gone about my region of our house, armed with the centrepiece out of an old set of boot-trees—the perfect realization of Captain Somebody, of the Royal British Navy, in danger of being beset by savages, and resolved to sell his life at a great price. . . .

"When I think of it, the picture always arises in my mind of a summer evening, the boys at play in the churchyard, and I sitting on my bed, reading as if for life. Every barn in the neighbourhood, every stone in the church, and every foot of the churchyard, had some association of its own, in my mind, connected with these books, and stood for some locality made famous in them. I have seen Tom Pipes go climbing up the church steeple; I have watched Strap, with the knapsack on his back, stopping to rest himself upon the wicket-gate; and I *know* that Commodore Trunnion held that club with Mr. Pickle in the parlour of our little village alehouse." [54]

Besides this noble company, there were the *Tatler* and *Spectator* papers, Johnson's *Idler*, Goldsmith's *Citizen of the World*, and Mrs. Inchbald's *Collection of Farces*.[55] All these had been waiting in that blessed little upstairs room that remained unvisited until a child found his way there. It is impossible to calculate the entire extent of their effect upon him, but the nature and direction of their stimulus is unmistakable. No writer so intimately fuses the familiar and the strange as Dickens does. His physical world is an utterly everyday one of the most prosaic places: Goswell Street, the drab suburbs of Camden Town and Somers Town, Covent Garden Market, the Golden Cross, the poor streets of the Borough—all noted in the sharpest detail. And yet they are transfigured by an inward vision that bathes Bob Cratchit's fireside in glowing warmth and Fagin's thieves' cellar in sordid romance. The clear daylight sanity of *Tom Jones* and the brutal realism of *Roderick Random* are mingled in the works of Dickens with the fantasy of Ali Baba's cave and Sinbad's valley of diamonds.

In later years Dickens remembered how, as a boy "sitting in byplaces near Rochester Castle," with his head "full of Partridge, Strap, Tom Pipes, and Sancho Panza," he had heard of the Yorkshire schools: some boy had come home with a suppurated abscess, "his Yorkshire Guide, Philosopher, and friend having ripped it open with an inky penknife." [56] Dickens's childish imagination had been haunted by a vision of the dirty everyday schoolroom as a hideous dungeon and the schoolmaster as an ogre torturing little boys. The strange ambivalence that endows Wackford Squeers and Dotheboys Hall with a comic nightmare realism is the same as that which bursts out in the image of the M'Choakumchilds of *Hard Times* as utilitarian Morgianas striving to fill their childish vessels brimful of boiling fact and slay the robber Fancy lurking within.[57] Both are implicit in these early years steeped at once in the eighteenth-century realists and in *Don Quixote* and the *Arabian Nights*. The small boy who found the unpretentious Guild Hall of an ordinary provincial town a palace built by the Genie of the Lamp is father to the creator of Quilp and Mr. Jingle, Sairey Gamp, Captain Cuttle, poor mad little Miss Flite, our eminently practical friend Gradgrind, the Circumlocution Office, and Boffin's Dust Heaps: realities in which the commonplace, the comic, the pathetic, and the grotesque are inseparably blended.

In his childhood, too, his imagination received another powerful stimulus, and one which all his life exerted over him the strongest fascination—the theater. At the age of seven he had been taken up to London to behold the splendor of Christmas pantomimes, had delighted in the beautiful complexions of the clowns and their appetite for sausages, exulted in Harlequin and Pantaloon, and "thought that to marry a Columbine would be to attain the highest pitch of all human felicity!" At fair time once, a pantomime had come lumbering to Chatham in Richardson's wagons, and among "a long row of small boys, with frills as white as they could be washed," he had thrilled to the glorious smell of sawdust and orange peel and the confounding of the crafty magician who had been holding the young lady in bondage.[58]

Despite his father's continuing financial struggles, Charles enjoyed exciting tastes of such theatrical fare as Rochester and Chatham could provide. At the foot of Star Hill was the little Theatre Royal, with its two-columned portico and wrought-iron lantern making a tiny square of shelter over the sidewalk just in front of the narrow entrance. Here Edmund Kean and Charles Mathews had sometimes played,[59] and here little Charles, when he was eight and they had still lived at Ordnance Terrace, had precociously clapped his hands for the great Joe Grimaldi, nonpareil of clowns.[60] Later he was occasionally taken to some of the melodramas, farces, and tragedies that held its boards, and was inspired to compose a tragedy entitled *Misnar, the Sultan of India* (founded on one of the *Tales of the Genii*), which won him fame in his childish circle.[61]

His mother's widowed sister, the children's Aunt Fanny, had become acquainted with a Dr. Matthew Lamert, an army surgeon quartered in the Ordnance Hospital at Chatham. The bustling middle-aged man with an abrupt odd way of talking was the figure that later suggested Dr. Slammer, in *Pickwick*. Soon it was understood that he and Aunt Fanny were going to be married. Dr. Lamert had a taste for the drama, and sometimes good-naturedly took his prospective wife's bright young nephew to the Rochester theater. He had a son by a former marriage, who had been to Sandhurst for his education and who often visited Chatham. James Lamert shared his father's theatrical enthusiasm, and got up private performances, in which his father acted, in some of the empty rooms of the almost uninhabited rambling Ordnance Hospital. These the fascinated Charles was allowed to see with eager eyes, drinking in also the wonders of rehearsals and stage business and grease paint and costumes.

On December 11, 1821, Dr. Lamert and Aunt Fanny were married in the parish church at Chatham. They soon left for Ireland, taking Jane Bonny with them as their servant. But James Lamert remained behind as a lodger at the Brook, and became Charles's admired patron and elder friend. He generously continued taking the boy to the Theatre Royal.[62]

It was within these walls that Charles had learned, "as from a page of English history, how the wicked king Richard III slept in war-time on a sofa much too short for him, and how fearfully his conscience troubled his boots." And he recalled how that monarch "made my heart leap with terror by backing up against the stage-box in which I was posted, while struggling for life against the virtuous Richmond." "There, too, had I first seen the funny countryman, but countryman of noble principles, in a flowered waistcoat, crunch up his little hat and throw it on the ground, and pull off his coat, saying, 'Dom thee, squire, coom on with thy fistes then!' At which the lovely young woman who kept company with him . . . was so frightened for his sake, that she fainted away. Many wondrous secrets of Nature had I come to the knowledge of in that sanctuary: of which not the least terrific were, that the witches in Macbeth bore an awful resemblance to the Thanes and other proper inhabitants of Scotland; and that the good King Duncan couldn't rest in his grave, but was constantly coming out of it and calling himself somebody else." [63]

* * * * *

But for Charles the bright sunlight days were fast drawing to a close. Sometime around the autumn or early winter of 1822 John Dickens received an order transferring him back to London. His financial position was now very bad, and before the family's removal there was a sale of the household goods. Their parlor chairs were purchased by the former servant, Mary Weller, who had married a dockyard worker named Thomas Gibson, and been replaced by a little orphan from the Chatham Workhouse whom they took with them to London. The remaining heavy goods were sent to London by water, and John Dickens and his family proceeded there by stagecoach.[64]

It is believed that Charles did not go with the rest of the family to London, but was allowed to stay on in Chatham to finish his school term with Mr. Giles. If so, the other Dickens youngsters, from Fanny, who was now twelve years old, down to the latest baby, Alfred Lamert, who had been born at the Brook the preceding March, were all piled into the coach, and Charles saw them off. The departure of the Micawber family for Plymouth, in *David Copperfield*, hints a memory of this separation: "I think, as Mrs. Micawber sat at the back of the coach with the children, and I stood in the road looking wistfully at them, a mist cleared from her eyes, and she saw what a little creature I really was. I think so, because she beckoned me to climb up, with quite a new and motherly expression in her face, and put her arms around my neck, and gave me just such a kiss as she might have given to her own boy. I had barely time to get down again before the coach started, and I could hardly see the family for the handkerchiefs they waved. They were gone in a minute." [65]

His own stay in Chatham probably ended at Christmas. On the night before he came away, his kind schoolmaster, Mr. Giles, "came flitting among the packing-cases," Dickens remembered, "to give me Goldsmith's *Bee* as a keepsake. Which I kept for his sake, and its own, a long while afterwards." [66] Its philosophic essays on the use of language, on the characteristics of greatness, on the instability of worldly grandeur, its informative articles on the sagacity of insects, the academies of Italy, and the Augustan age of England, its biographical accounts of Maupertuis, Charles XII, and Hypatia, its remarks on the art of the theater and the opera, its short moral tales, might all seem rather precocious reading for a boy in his eleventh year. But William Giles evidently knew his pupil; Goldsmith's graceful humor and gentle charm captivated the boy. The gift was the beginning for Dickens of an enduring affection for Goldsmith and a lifelong fascination with the periodical miscellany.

The happy time was over. It was farewell to the daisied hay field and Mary Weller's tales of poisoned murderers and satanic talking rats, to peach-faced Lucy and the magic lantern, to Fort Pitt and Chatham Lines and the red-coated regiments maneuvering and firing, to the clanging Dockyard, the bright river, and the ships with their far visions of the sea. It was farewell to the arcaded Guild Hall and the marvelous clock, the dim Cathedral and the hoary Castle, the shady verdure of Cobham Woods and the sunlight warming the rosy bricks of Gad's Hill Place. All were about to vanish like the Palace of Aladdin spirited away by the African magician.

In a gloomy drizzle the next morning Charles was stowed away in Simpson's Blue-Eyed Maid, and said good-by to the Chatham of his childhood. He never forgot, he tells us, "the smell of the damp straw in which I was packed—like game—and forwarded carriage-paid, to the

Cross Keys, Wood Street, Cheapside. There was no other inside passenger, and I consumed my sandwiches in solitude and dreariness, and it rained hard all the way, and I thought that life was sloppier than I had expected to find it." [67]

CHAPTER THREE

The Challenge of Despair

T HE new home at 16 Bayham Street, Camden Town, represented a still further decline in the Dickens fortunes. In the early 1820's, to be sure, Camden Town was not the urban slum that it later became. It was separated from London by open fields, with the dome of St. Paul's looming in the distance through the smoke of the City, and there were pleasant walks through the meadows to Copenhagen House. The small jerry-built cottages nestling beneath the quiet shade trees of its streets were inhabited by retired professional men and tradespeople mingled with artisans and laborers.

Bayham Street was a row of about forty houses erected in 1812, with grassy meadows at the back. Next door to the Dickens dwelling lived a washerwoman, and across the way a Bow Street runner. No. 16 itself was a four-room house with a basement and garret, renting for £22 a year. Into this cramped box fitted John and Elizabeth Dickens, the six Dickens children, James Lamert—who was still living with them while awaiting a commission in the Army—and "the Orfling," the small sharp maid-of-all-work from Chatham Workhouse.[1]

Charles had left Mr. Giles expecting that his parents would continue his schooling, but they took no such course. There were no boys near Bayham Street with whom he might become friends, and he sank into a loneliness outdoors and a neglect at home that bewildered and upset him. It stabbed him to the heart that his sister Fanny was in April given a scholarship as a pupil-boarder at the Royal Academy of Music on Tenterden Street, and went away, with the tearful good wishes of everybody in the house, to begin her education, while he remained at home miserable and disregarded.[2] "As I thought in the little back garret in Bayham Street, of all I had lost in losing Chatham," he said bitterly, in later years, to Forster, "what would I have given, if I had had anything to give, to have been sent back to any other school, to have been taught something anywhere!" He could not understand what was happening to him.[3]

"I know my father," he went on, "to be as kindhearted and generous a man as ever lived in the world. Everything that I can remember of his conduct to his wife, or children, or friends, in sickness or affliction, is beyond all praise. By me, as a sick child, he has watched night and day, unweariedly and patiently, many nights and days. He never undertook any business, charge or trust, that he did not zealously, conscientiously, punctually, honourably discharge. His industry has always been untiring. He was proud of me, in his way, and had a great admiration of the comic singing. But, in the ease of his temper, and the straitness of his means, he appeared to have utterly lost at this time the idea of educating me at all, and to have utterly put from him the notion that I had any claim upon him, in that regard, whatever. So I degenerated into cleaning his boots of a morning, and my own; and making myself useful in the work of the little house; and looking after my younger brothers and sisters (we were now six in all); and going on such poor errands as arose out of our poor way of living." [4]

He was eleven now—old enough to feel some awareness of those changes of atmosphere that afflict a worried household. And in their rising desperation his parents found it impossible to guard themselves from any reference to the troubles in which they were engulfed. Charles began to hear of a mysterious and ominous something called "The Deed," which he tremblingly confounded with one of those satanic compacts in the tales with which Mary Weller had terrified him or with the dark deeds of the witches in Macbeth. What dreadful thing had his kind father done? What awful fate was about to descend upon him? The child's imagination shuddered with uncertainty and apprehension.[5]

The Deed was in reality a composition with John Dickens's creditors, who had been pressing him for payment. Tradesmen in Chatham, who were not too resistant to being put off as long as he was employed in the Dockyard there, might reasonably take alarm when he was recalled to London and become more insistent in their demands. There may have been other creditors as well. Did the Barrows come to the aid of their brother-in-law in this emergency? Did John Dickens go to Oxford Street, where his mother was now living on the interest from her savings and a pension from Lord Crewe,[6] and beg money from her? Did he receive any help from Charles's godfather, Christopher Huffam? No one knows; but certainly the meager accommodations of Bayham Street were part of a scheme of retrenchment intended to help meet the payments provided for in the Deed.

Meanwhile Charles solaced his small heart as best he could. James Lamert took pity on his solitude, and made and painted a toy theater for him. Often the boy walked to the top of Bayham Street, where the almshouses were, and stared with vague reflection over the wasteland and the dump heaps rising among the docks and nettles, to the distant cupola of St. Paul's, dim in the haze. Gradually he explored all the surburban areas of Camden Town, Somers Town, and Kentish Town.[7]

Sometimes he was taken in to London to see his uncle, Thomas Barrow, who was laid up at his lodgings in Gerard Street, Soho, with a broken leg which later had to be amputated. Here his uncle's landlady, the widow of a bookseller, still carried on the business, and used to lend the bright-looking lad books, among them Jane Porter's *Scottish Chiefs*, Holbein's *Dance of Death*, and George Colman's *Broad Grins*. The description of Covent Garden in the last of these impressed him so greatly that he stole down to the market and sniffed up "the flavour of the faded cabbage-leaves as if it were the very breath of comic fiction." [8]

His uncle's barber was an eccentric whose hobby was the Napoleonic Wars and the mistakes of Napoleon. The boy wrote a character sketch of this old barber, and another of a deaf old woman who waited on them at Bayham Street, "and who made delicate hashes with walnut-ketchup"; but though he thought them both extremely clever, he never had the courage to show them to anyone.[9]

There were also longer excursions across London to the handsome residence of Christopher Huffam, at 12 Church Row, Limehouse. Here his godfather would show off Charles's comic singing to his friends, one of whom, a boatbuilder, was so tickled that he pronounced the boy to be a "prodigy." [10] The return trip through the night sights of London—the Strand, Covent Garden, the sinister regions of St. Giles—were deliriously exciting to him. Seven Dials exerted a macabre and hideous fascination over his fancy. "Good Heaven!" he would exclaim in later years, "what wild visions of prodigies of wickedness, want, and beggary arose in my mind out of that place!" [11]

But these visits were interrupted by one of the attacks of mysterious spasm and fever that still prostrated him.[12] Throughout this later part of his childhood, indeed, his troubled state was marked by a recurrence of the illnesses that had seemed less frequent in the happy Chatham days. When his fever had subsided, the Deed had redoubled the distresses in Bayham Street. Even the economies there were not meeting its demands. His father's expedients to raise more money were entirely exhausted. At this stage his mother was struck by an inspiration. The time had arrived, she announced, for her to exert herself; she "must do something." She would start a school. Christopher Huffam was believed to have connections in the Indies; he would persuade nabobs and wealthy planters to send their children to her, and they would all grow rich! "Perhaps," thought the sickly lad, "even I might go to school myself." [13]

Energetically Mrs. Dickens rushed about, found a good-sized and satisfactorily located house at 4 Gower Street North, and took it from Michaelmas, 1823, at a rental of £50 a year. A large brass plate was ordered, inscribed "MRS. DICKENS'S ESTABLISHMENT," and fastened to the door. Charles and the workhouse "orfling" were employed to leave laudatory circulars at still other doors. What a brainstorm, born of desperation, was this scheme, that, when they had no money and John Dickens was on the verge of arrest for debt, they should take an expensive house at more than twice what they had been paying; and that Mrs. Dickens, who had no experience in either teaching or administering a school, and who had a family of six small children to take care of, should undertake it! Christopher Huffam, from whom so much had been expected, was apparently able to do nothing for them; indeed, he was immersed in financial difficulties of his own and went bankrupt the following November.[14] The end of the endeavor was characteristic, and is summarized in Dickens's own words: "Nobody ever came to the school, nor do I recollect that anybody ever proposed to come, or that the least preparation was made to receive anybody." [15]

Meanwhile things drifted steadily into a more hopeless state. "I know that we got on very badly with the butcher and the baker," Dickens wrote in the autobiographical fragment, and "that very often we had not too much for dinner." [16] There are further autobiographical scenes in *David Copperfield* from which we can infer that angry tradesmen forced their way into the passage and bawled demands for payment up the staircase, while John Dickens cowered in a room above and tremblingly waited for them to go away so that he could leave the house.[17]

Gradually the distracted parents began selling or pawning their household goods. Charles was often employed in these transactions. First to go were the books they had brought from Chatham, *Peregrine Pickle*, *Roderick Random*, *Tom Jones*, *Humphrey Clinker*, and the rest. Charles sadly took them down from the little chiffonier his father called "the library," and carried them off to a tipsy bookseller in Hampstead Road. More than once the boy found him still in bed, with a cut forehead or a black eye; and the man would try with shaking hand to find the needed shillings from the pockets of his clothes, which lay strewn upon the floor, while his wife, in down-at-heel shoes and with a baby in her arms, berated him shrilly. "Sometimes he had lost his money, and then he would ask me to call again; but his wife had always got some (had taken his, I daresay, while he was drunk), and secretly completed the bargain on the stairs, as we went down together."[18] If the boy was not going to school, he was acquiring an education in the seamier side of human affairs.

* * * * *

But events were soon to stab him with a sharper and more personal anguish. It came, ironically enough, through the kindly intentions of James Lamert. He had ceased to live with the Dickens family before they left Camden Town, but knowing how things were going with them and seeing how Charles was employed from day to day, he made a helpful suggestion. He had grown tired of waiting for his commission and had gone into business as manager for a cousin, George Lamert, who was also his sister's husband. The business was a rival to "Warren's Blacking, 30, Strand," at that time very famous. "One Jonathan Warren (the famous one was Robert), living at 30, Hungerford Stairs, or Market, Strand (for I forget which it was called then), claimed to have been the original inventor or proprietor of the blacking recipe, and to have been deposed and ill-used by his renowned relation. At last he put himself in the way of selling his recipe, and his name, and his 30, Hungerford Stairs, Strand (30, STRAND, very large, and the intermediate direction very small) for an annuity." The purchaser was George Lamert. "In an evil hour for me," Dickens felt, James Lamert now proposed that Charles should make himself useful in the blacking warehouse, at a salary of six shillings a week. During the dinner hour, from twelve to one, he would even give the lad some school lessons every day.[19]

His father and mother accepted the offer very willingly, and on a Monday morning only two days after his twelfth birthday Charles started to work. The event had come upon him with the suddenness of unforeseen catastrophe; and it left him stunned, sick with despair. "It is wonderful to me," he says, "how I could have been so easily cast away at such an age. It is wonderful to me, that, even after my descent into the poor little drudge I had been since we came to London, no one had compassion enough on me—a child of singular abilities, quick, eager, delicate, and soon hurt, bodily or mentally—to suggest that something might have been spared, as certainly it might have been, to place me at any common school. Our friends, I take it, were tired out. No one made any sign. My father and mother were quite satisfied. They could hardly have been more so, if I had been twenty years of age, distinguished at a grammar-school, and going to Cambridge." [20]

It is the shock and bitterness of a hurt child, of course, that speaks in these words—a child so deeply wounded that the hurt is still there, a quarter of a century later, when they were spoken. But if the patience of the family's friends was exhausted, it was hardly to be expected that they should single out one of the Dickens children and offer to be responsible for him. No doubt his harassed parents were thankful enough for James Lamert's well-meant and kindly offer, but they were hardly apt to look upon it or any other aspect of their plight with complacency. Their income was entirely devoured in the endeavor to deal with their debts; and, besides Charles and Fanny, there were four helpless younger children in the family, from Letitia, who was eight, down to two-year-old Alfred Lamert. Nor was there anything unusual, even later at the end of the nineteenth century, in a boy going to work at twelve. The average school life for a child in the 1820's and for a considerable time thereafter was perhaps two years, perhaps eighteen months. Six shillings a week was no bad wage for a boy at the time, and the hours at the warehouse were not more prolonged than usual.

They began at 8 A.M. and ended at 8 P.M., with a lapse of one hour for dinner and half an hour for tea.[21] And despite the comic singing and the admiration of the boatbuilder at Limehouse Hole, neither John Dickens nor his wife suspected that their bright, small-bodied youngster would turn out to be a prodigy.

But in the self-absorbed grief of childhood, Charles hardly realized how frantic his parents were with anxiety, or what a relief even this provision for one of their children must be to them. The boy had an extraordinary desire to learn and distinguish himself, and to him this represented the end of all his hopes. Furthermore, John Dickens's pretensions had led his son to regard himself as a young gentleman, to whom this descent into drudging among common boys with uncouth manners was unspeakably humiliating. One of them, named Bob Fagin, wore a ragged apron and a paper cap, and lived with his brother-in-law, a waterman. Another, whose name was Paul Green, "but who was currently believed to have been christened Poll," was son of a fireman employed at Drury Lane Theatre, "where another relation of Poll's, I think his little sister, did imps in the pantomimes." [22] It was with these that Charles generally worked side by side.

At first, to be sure, James Lamert made some effort to dissociate him from the other boys and give him the noonday hour of daily instruction. The blacking warehouse was a crazy tumble-down old house abutting on the river at Hungerford Stairs. Dirty and decayed, its wainscoted rooms and rotten floors and staircase resounded with the squeaking and shuffling of the old gray rats swarming down in the cellars. Charles sat and worked by himself in a recess of the counting-house, overlooking the coal barges and the river. His task was "to cover the pots of paste-blacking; first with a piece of oil-paper, and then with a bit of blue paper; to tie them round with a string; and then to clip the paper close and neat, all round, until it looked as smart as a pot of ointment from an apothecary's shop." [23] On each of these, finally, he pasted a printed label.

But so inconvenient an arrangement of isolation soon died away, and so did the noon-hour teaching. His small work table, his grosses of pots, papers, string, scissors, paste-pot, and labels, vanished out of the countinghouse and moved downstairs to the common workroom. He was not so young as not to know that he would be slighted and despised if he could not work as well as the others, so despite his suffering he soon made himself as quick and skillful as the other boys. But there was a difference of conduct and manners between him and them that resulted in his being called, perhaps not quite reverentially, "the young gentleman." "Poll Green uprose once, and rebelled against the 'young gentleman' usage; but Bob Fagin settled him speedily." Sometimes the foreman, an ex-soldier named Thomas Gregory, or Harry Tipp, the red-jacketed carman, called him "Charles," but this was mostly when they were very confidential, "and when I had made some effort to entertain them over our work with the results of some of the old readings which were fast perishing out of my mind." [24]

"No words can express the secret agony of my soul," the autobiography goes on, "as I sunk into this companionship; compared these every day associates with those of my happier childhood; and felt my early hopes of growing up to be a learned and distinguished man, crushed in my breast. The deep remembrance of the sense I had of being utterly neglected and hopeless; of the shame I felt in my position; of the misery it was to my young heart to believe that, day by day, what I had learned, and thought, and delighted in, and raised my fancy and my emulation up by, was passing away from me, never to be brought back any more; cannot be written. My whole nature was so penetrated with the grief and humiliation of such considerations, that even now, famous and caressed and happy, I often forget in my dreams that I have a dear wife and children; even that I am a man; and wander desolately back to that time of my life." [25]

But, in his pride, he bottled all his despair within his own breast. "I never said, to man or boy, how it was that I came to be there, or gave the least indication of being sorry that I was there. That I suffered in secret, and that I suffered exquisitely, no one ever knew but I." [26]

* * * * *

Just eleven days later than the Monday on which Charles began his forlorn labors, his father was arrested at the suit of one James Karr for a debt of £40. The first three nights of his detention he was provided with lodgings in the sponging house maintained by the bailiff, while he tried to raise money and avoid being formally committed to prison.[27] Charles, his eyes swollen with tears, spent the week-end running errands and carrying messages for the weeping prisoner. But all efforts were in vain: on Monday John Dickens was taken from the sponging house to the Marshalsea. His last words to the sorrowing lad as he entered the gates were that the sun had set upon him for ever, and they stabbed the boy with anguish. "I really believed at the time," Dickens said many years later, "that they had broken my heart." [28]

The fragment of autobiography continues with reminiscences of later visits to the prison. "My father was waiting for me in the lodge, and we went up to his room (on the top story but one), and cried very much. And he told me, I remember, to take warning by the Marshalsea, and to observe that if a man had twenty pounds a year, and spent nineteen pounds nineteen shillings and sixpence, he would be happy; but that a shilling spent the other way would make him wretched. I see the fire we sat before, now; with two bricks inside the rusted grate, one on each side, to prevent its burning too many coals." [29]

Presently it was dinnertime, and Charles was sent upstairs to "Captain Porter," one of the prisoners there, to beg the loan of a knife and fork. "There was a very dirty lady in his little room; and two wan girls, his daughters, with shock heads of hair. I thought I should not have liked to borrow Captain Porter's comb." Even at such a time of anguish as this the observant boy was always taking things in. He noted the Captain's shabbiness, his untrimmed whiskers, and his bed rolled up in a corner; and, despite the few minutes that he stood timidly wondering on the threshold, he says, "I knew (God knows how) that the two girls with the shock heads were Captain Porter's natural children, and that the dirty lady was not married to Captain P." [30]

John Dickens could not lose his natural ornateness of utterance even in a debtors' prison, but he was dreadfully shaken. The consequences of his easy complacency had at last caught up with him. The failure of the long struggle since they had left Chatham, and the catastrophe of imprisonment, had overwhelmed him with the fear that he was utterly ruined. He became tremulously tragic; it may have been in John Dickens at this time that his son observed that fluttering and frightened motion of the fingers about the lips that he later attributed to William Dorrit in the same misforture.[31]

And there was reason enough to be frightened. There was no way in which he could pay his debts; he must either remain in prison or take advantage of the Insolvent Debtors' Act. He had been in the Navy Pay Office nineteen years, but a man who incurred the disgrace of insolvency could hardly hope to be retained there. In that case, income, pension possibilities, all hope, would vanish.

It might be possible to salvage something from his years of faithful labor by applying for immediate retirement, and getting his pension before he was legally declared insolvent. So, in March, John Dickens obtained from Dr. John Pool, surgeon, of Dover Street, Piccadilly, a certificate stating that he had a chronic affection of the urinary organs that incapacitated him for public duty. In due course, Treasurer of the Navy Huskisson recommended that he be retired on an annual pension of £145 16s 8d (five-twelfths of his salary of £350 a year). But the machinery of government departments moves slowly. Long before the matter progressed any further, John Dickens's efforts to avoid going through the Court had failed.[32]

Meanwhile Charles crept every hopeless day from Gower Street to the drudgery of Hungerford Stairs, and his distracted mother tried to keep things going and the whimpering children fed by pawning brooches and spoons and gradually stripping the rooms bare of furniture. Charles became well known to the pawnbroker's shop, where the broker or his principal clerk, while making out the pawn ticket, would often hear him conjugate a Latin verb or decline *musa* and *dominus*.[33] "My own little bed," Dickens wrote in a passage of *The Haunted House* which is probably autobiographical, "was so superciliously looked upon by a power unknown to me, hazily called 'The Trade,' that a brass coal-scuttle, a toasting-jack, and a bird-cage were obliged to be put with it to make a Lot of it, and then it went for a song—so I heard mentioned, and I wondered what song—and thought what a dismal song it must be to sing." [34] At last there was nothing left in Gower Street but a few chairs, a kitchen table, and some beds; and the family camped out in the two parlors of the emptied house.[35]

It was too far to go from the blacking warehouse to Gower Street within the dinner hour, so Charles usually carried his meal with him or bought it at some neighboring shop. These expenditures he made out of his six-shilling wage. Sometimes, he remembered, he got "a saveloy and a penny loaf; sometimes, a four-penny plate of beef from a cook's shop; sometimes, a plate of bread and cheese, and a glass of beer, from a miserable old public-house over the way: the Swan, if I remember right, or the Swan and something else that I have forgotten. Once, I remember tucking my own bread (which I had brought from home in the morning) under my arm, wrapped up in a piece of paper like a book, and going into the best dining-room in Johnson's alamode beef-house in Clare-court, Drury Lane, and magnificently ordering a small plate of alamode beef to eat with it. What the waiter thought of such a strange little apparition, coming in all alone, I don't know; but I can see him now, staring at me as I ate my dinner, and bringing up the other waiter to look. I gave him a halfpenny, and I wish, now, that he hadn't taken it." [36]

Saturday night was his great weekly triumph. He would walk home feeling the grandeur of having six shillings in his pocket, looking in shop windows, and thinking what it would buy, if only he could afford to spend it. Hunt's roasted corn was then a patriotic substitute for coffee; and sometimes he would part with a little of his small store for some, and roast it on Sunday for a treat. Often he could not resist the extravagance of buying *The Portfolio of Entertaining and Instructive Varieties in History, Science, Literature, and Fine Arts, etc.*, a two-penny magazine that had been started in 1823, and which contained burlesques of plays and outrageous poetic parodies.[37]

The creditors had refused to listen to any proposal of executing a new "Deed," and there was now no recourse but to insolvency proceedings. The law provided that the clothing and personal effects of the debtor and his dependents must not exceed £20 in value. The clothes that Charles wore therefore had to be inspected by the appraiser. He was given a half holiday to call on this official somewhere near the Obelisk, and was terrified lest his grandfather's fat old silver watch, which had been given him by old Mrs. Dickens before the blacking days, and which was now ticking loudly in his pocket, might not bring him over the £20. But the man came out with his mouth full and a strong smell of beer about him, glanced at the boy's poor white hat, little jacket, and corduroy trousers, and said "it was all right." "So I was greatly relieved, and made him a bow of acknowledgment as I went out." [38]

At Lady Day the encampment at Gower Street broke up; the key was sent back to the landlord (who was very glad to get it), and Mrs. Dickens and the younger children went to live in the Marshalsea.[39] Though they were rather crowded, with four small children in the same little room with their parents, it was cheaper than paying for quarters outside. Extra furniture could be hired from the turnkeys, and the prisoners and their families could use a common kitchen or send out during the day to the cookshops for food. Though the debtors could not leave the prison, their families could go in and out freely until the gates were locked at night. And if no one could leave until morning, they were no longer subject to angry siege from their creditors. The Dickens family did not lack for bodily comforts there; John Dickens's income from the Navy Pay Office was still going on. In fact, except for elbowroom they were more easy in prison than they had been for a long time before. They even continued to be waited on by the little general servant from Chatham Workhouse.[40]

The move, however, meant redoubled loneliness for Charles, who did not go with them. Probably there was simply no space for a boy of twelve in his father's prison room, but Charles felt only that he was being abandoned as an outcast. "I (small Cain that I was, except that I had never done harm to any one) was handed over as a lodger to a reduced old lady," Mrs. Elizabeth Roylance, "long known to our family, in Little College Street, Camden Town, who took children in to board, and had once done so at Brighton; and who, with a few alterations and embellishments, unconsciously began to sit for Mrs. Pipchin in *Dombey* when she took me in." [41] Being one of the small waifs in her establishment did not relieve his melancholy loneliness.

His lodging was paid by his father; but now he had to pay, not only for his noonday dinner, but for his breakfast of bread and milk and his supper of bread and cheese out of his own money from the blacking house. "They made a hole in the six or seven shillings, I know well; and I was out at the blacking-warehouse all day, and had to support myself upon that money all the week. . . . I certainly had no other assistance whatever (the making of my clothes, I think, excepted), from Monday morning until Saturday night. No advice, no counsel, no encouragement, no consolation, no support, from any one that I can call to mind, so help me God." [42]

"I was so young and childish, and so little qualified—how could I be otherwise?—to undertake the whole charge of my own existence, that in going to Hungerford Stairs of a morning, I could not resist the stale pastry put out at half-price on trays at the confectioners' doors in Tottenham Court Road; and I often spent in that, the money I should have kept for my dinner. Then I went without my dinner, or bought a roll, or a slice of pudding." Depending on how little money he had, he went to a pudding shop in a court behind St. Martin's Church, where the pudding was dear because it was a special pudding made with currants, or to a cheaper shop in the Strand, which served a stout, hot pudding, heavy and flabby, with great raisins stuck far apart.

"We had half-an-hour, I think, for tea. When I had money enough, I used to go to a coffee-shop, and have half-a-pint of coffee, and a slice of bread and butter. When I had no money, I took a turn in Covent Garden Market, and stared at the pineapples." One coffeeshop in St. Martin's Lane stood near the church and had in the door "an oval glass-plate, with COFFEE-ROOM painted on it, addressed towards the street. If I ever find myself in a very different kind of coffee-room now, but where there is such an inscription on glass, and read it backward on the wrong side MOOR-EEFFOC (as I often used to do then, in a dismal reverie), a shock goes through my blood.

"I know I do not exaggerate, unconsciously and unintentionally, the scantiness of my resources and the difficulties of my life. I know that if a shilling or so were given me by anyone, I spent it in a dinner or a tea. I know that I worked, from morning to night, with common men and boys, a shabby child. I know that I tried, but ineffectually, not to anticipate my money, and to make it last the week through; by putting it away in a drawer I had in the counting-house, wrapped up in six little parcels, each parcel containing the same amount, and labelled with a different day. I know that I lounged about the streets, insufficiently and unsatisfactorily fed. I know that, but for the mercy of God, I might easily have been, for any care that was taken of me, a little robber or a little vagabond." [43]

*   *   *   *   *

Sundays he and Fanny spent at the prison. At nine in the morning he called for her at the Academy of Music on Tenterden Street, Hanover Square, and from there the two walked on, across Westminster Bridge to the Borough.[44] Charles considered his rescue from the blacking warehouse quite hopeless, but felt his solitude so keenly that one Sunday night he broke down and wept before his father. Apparently John Dickens had not thought about it before, but now his kind nature was touched. A back attic was found for the child in Lant Street, not far from the Marshalsea, with a pleasant prospect of a timberyard from its little window. When he took possession of his new abode, he thought it was Paradise.[45]

Now he could breakfast "at home"—in the Marshalsea—going there as early as the gates were open in the morning. He also had supper in the prison, and generally returned to Lant Street at nine o'clock. His landlord there was a fat, lame old gentleman with a quiet old wife and an innocent grown-up son who was also lame—a trio who were to become the Garlands in *The Old Curiosity Shop*. They were very kind to the boy; once all three were about his bed the entire night when he had one of his old attacks of spasm.[46]

Despite the nearness of his new lodgings to the prison, he was separated from his family for most of every day, and he continued to feel very lonely. Sometimes he played on the coal barges with Poll Green and Bob Fagin during the dinner hour, but mostly he was by himself, strolling about the back streets of the Adelphi or exploring the Adelphi arches. Coming home over Blackfriars Bridge and along Blackfriars Road on Saturday nights, he would pass the boot shops and sniff the smell of hatmaking, and sometimes be seduced into going into a show van at a corner to see the fat pig, the wild Indian, and the Little-lady. Even in these small diversions, though, he was alone.[47]

He was still so far from looking the twelve years he had attained that when he went into a bar for a glass of ale or porter to wash down the saveloy and loaf he had eaten in the street, they didn't like to give it to him. One evening he was returning over Westminster Bridge from some errand for his father, and stopped at a public house in Parliament Street, "and said to the landlord behind the bar, 'What is your very best—the VERY *best*—ale, a glass?' For, the occasion was a festive one, for some reason: I forget why. . . . 'Twopence,' says he. 'Then,' says I, 'just draw me a glass of that, if you please, with a good head to it.' The landlord looked at me, in return, over the bar, from head to foot, with a strange smile on his face; and instead of drawing the beer, looked round the screen and said something to his wife, who came out from behind it, with her work in her hand, and joined him in surveying me. . . . They asked me a good many questions, as what my name was, how old I was, where I lived, how I was employed, &c &c. To all of which, that I might commit nobody, I invented appropriate answers. They served me with the ale, though I suspect it was not the strongest on the premises; and the landlord's wife, opening the little half-door and bending down, gave me a kiss that was half-admiring and half-compassionate, but all womanly and good, I am sure." [48]

During the spring Charles was present with some of the family in Tenterden Street to see his sister Fanny receive one of the prizes awarded to pupils at the Royal Academy of Music. He loved Fanny, he was proud of her, and he felt no envy, but the gala occasion reminded him bitterly of the opportunities of which he himself was deprived. "I could not bear to think of myself—beyond the reach of all such honourable emulation and success. The tears ran down my face. I prayed, when I went to bed that night, to be lifted out of the humiliation and neglect in which I was. I had never suffered so much before." [49]

Seizures of his old illness came back to him repeatedly in these days of misery. Agonizing in their constriction of the kidneys, they were doubtless, to a considerable degree, the protests of his poor little body at the unhappiness in his heart. One of them occurred at the warehouse: "Bob Fagin was very good to me on the occasion of a bad attack of my old disorder. I suffered such excruciating pain that time, that they made a temporary bed of straw in my old recess in the counting-house, and I rolled about on the floor, and Bob filled empty blacking-bottles with hot water, and applied relays of them to my side, half the day. I got better, and quite easy towards evening; but Bob (who was much bigger and older than I) did not like the idea of my going home alone, and took me under his protection. I was too proud to let him know about the prison; and after making several efforts to get rid of him, to all of which Bob Fagin in his goodness was deaf, shook hands with him on the steps of a house near Southwark Bridge on the Surrey side, making believe that I lived there. As a finishing piece of reality in case of his looking back, I knocked at the door, I recollect, and asked, when the woman opened it, if that was Mr. Robert Fagin's house." [50]

In the Marshalsea, after his first outburst of despair, John Dickens had recovered his usual bounce. The other debtors, impressed by his combination of swelling port and bonhomie, made him chairman of the committee by which they regulated the internal economy of the prison. It was the business of the committee to ensure cleanliness, provide for coal, hot water, and the means of cooking, and maintain order in the alehouse common room. The new chairman flung himself energetically into his duties. With his consistent talent for managing everything except his own affairs, he did an excellent administrative job and soon was on lordly terms with everyone from the turnkeys to the humblest inmate.[51]

Charles was endlessly curious about all the prisoners and their histories, and untiringly observant of their characters and behavior. Once, when they made a petition for a royal bounty to enable them to drink the King's health on his forthcoming birthday in August, he begged to be allowed to see them affix their signatures to the document. It had been drawn up by John Dickens and was stretched out on a great ironing board. Stationed near by to read the petition to all who were unfamiliar with its contents stood Captain Porter, washed in honor of the solemn occasion. The door was flung open, and a long file of debtors began to come in, each signing it in turn. To anyone who "weakly showed the least disposition to hear it," Captain Porter read every word in a loud sonorous voice, giving a roll to such orotund words as "gracious Majesty," "your gracious Majesty's unfortunate subjects," "your Majesty's well-known munificence": "my poor father meanwhile"—so his son recalled—"listening with a little of an author's vanity, and contemplating (not severely) the spikes on the opposite wall." [52]

Not long after this, the turn of events gave John Dickens his freedom. On the 28th of April his mother died at the age of seventy-nine. Though her pension from Lord Crewe ceased with her death, her savings were considerable. She had transferred £750 to her elder son William in 1813 and now left him another £500; but the £450 willed to John was more than enough to relieve his difficulties. William promptly paid £40 into court for James Karr, on May 5th John Dickens made his petition to be released, the first hearing was held May 27th, and the following day John Dickens was released from the Marshalsea. He had been there just a few days over three months.[53]

* * * * *

The family returned to Camden Town and lodged temporarily with Mrs. Roylance at 37 Little College Street, where Charles had been so miserable in his separation from them. But by June Mrs. Dickens had taken a small house at 29 Johnson Street, an even poorer locality than Bayham Street, adjoining the fields between Somers Town and Camden Town. John Dickens hopefully resumed work at the Navy Pay Office, although his petition to be retired had stated that his health incapacitated him for duty. The debt for which he had been jailed was now paid. Perhaps the authorities would overlook the fact he had gone through the earlier stages toward being declared insolvent, and let him stay on in his post. Not a word was said, though, about taking Charles from the blacking warehouse.[54]

He waited, but nothing happened. The hated and hopeless drudgery continued day after interminable day. Evidently his father's release from prison meant no end of slavery for him. The blacking warehouse had been removed from Hungerford Stairs to Chandos Street, Covent Garden, corner of Bedford Street. Here Charles trudged from Somers Town daily, across Russell Square, with some cold hotchpotch for his dinner, in a small basin tied up in a handkerchief. "I had the same wanderings about the streets as I used to have, and was just as solitary and self-dependent as before; but I had not the same difficulty in merely living. I never however heard a word of being taken away, or of being otherwise than quite provided for." [55]

The new establishment was larger than the old, with several windows on Bedford Street. At one of these, for the sake of light, Charles worked with Bob Fagin. The two boys had become so dexterous in tying up pots that they could turn out a great many in five minutes; they were so brisk at it that sometimes there was a little crowd of people who had stopped to watch them. "I saw my father coming in at the door one day when we were very busy, and I wondered how he could bear it." [56]

Perhaps, when John Dickens saw him in the window, he couldn't bear it. Perhaps, as his son thought, the public exhibition of the boy, engaged in menial toil, struck some chord of pride or of paternal pity in him; for shortly afterward he quarreled with James Lamert: "quarrelled by letter, for I took the letter from my father to him which caused the explosion, but quarrelled very fiercely. It was about me." James Lamert may well have thought it absurdly pretentious, and irritating enough, that an improvident man for whom so many favors had been done should cavil about whether his son worked by a public window or did the same work in private. He told the boy he was very much insulted about him; it would be impossible to keep him any longer. "I cried very much, partly because it was so sudden, and partly because in his anger he was violent about my father, though gentle to me. . . . With a relief so strange that it was like oppression, I went home." [57]

His mother was appalled by the disagreement. Probably John Dickens's tangled affairs were not yet straightened out. There may already have been reason to suspect that he would not be kept on in the Navy Pay Office. In that event, what would they do? How could he make a breach with one of the few well-disposed connections they still retained? How could they afford to throw away even the seven shillings a week Charles had now been earning? She set herself the next day to accommodate the quarrel, and softened James Lamert. "She brought home a request for me to return next morning, and a high character of me, which I am very sure I deserved." [58]

But John Dickens had taken a stand. Something had touched him or hit his pride. His determination was fixed. Charles, he said, should go back to the blacking warehouse no more, but should go to school. On Charles their divergent positions made a deep impression. "I do not write resentfully or angrily," he summarized it, "for I know how all these things have worked together to make me what I am: but I never afterwards forgot, I never shall forget, I never can forget, that my mother was warm for my being sent back.

"From that hour until this at which I write, no word of that part of my childhood which I have now gladly brought to a close, has passed my lips to any human being. I have no idea how long it lasted; whether for a year, or much more, or less. From that hour, until this, my father and mother have been stricken dumb upon it. I have never heard the least allusion to it, however far off and remote, from either of them. I have never, until I now impart it to this paper, in any burst of confidence with any one, my own wife not excepted, raised the curtain I then dropped, thank God." [59]

Indeed, his wife and children never learned either of the blacking warehouse or of his father's confinement in the Marshalsea during his lifetime. They heard of it first in his friend Forster's biography of him after his death. And even Forster learned it, he says, only as it were by the chance of mentioning to Dickens that Charles Wentworth Dilke thought he had once seen him as a child in a warehouse near the Strand. He had gone in there with the elder Dickens (perhaps on that very day when Charles wondered how his father could bear it), given the child a half crown, and received in return a very low bow. Dickens listened to the anecdote in silence, and then spoke on another subject. "I felt," Forster says, "that I had unintentionally touched a painful place in his memory." It was not until some time later that Dickens told him the story, and placed the written narrative of those days in his hands.[60]

The time spent in the blacking warehouse can have been little over four months, five at most.[61] But that had nothing to do with what it seemed to the child, or with the lasting impression it made upon the man. The boy had no way of knowing when his bondage there would ever end, or *if* it would ever end, and he was in a state of absolute despair. "For the adult in desperate straits," as Edmund Wilson points out, "it is almost always possible to imagine, if not to contrive, some way out; for the child, from whom love and freedom have been taken away, no relief or release can be projected." [62] In his secret agony, the hours and weeks prolonged themselves into an eternity. As he remembered them, and projected them, both in the fragment of autobiography he wrote in 1845 or 1846 [63] and in their fictional guise in *David Copperfield*, their hapless victim was a poor little mite of only ten, and their protraction an endless sentence of torment. But that rendering of the facts is profoundly true to their psychological reality.

No emphasis can overstate the depth and intensity with which these experiences ate into his childish soul. For years afterward, he never had the courage to go near Hungerford Stairs; he could not endure it. For years, when he drew near Robert Warren's in the Strand, he crossed to the other side of the way, to avoid smelling the cement of the blacking corks. "It was a very long time before I liked to go up Chandos Street. My old way home by the Borough made me cry, after my eldest child could speak." [64]

But it is more than a mere unavailing ache in the heart, however poignant, and however prolonged into manhood, that gives the Marshalsea and Warren's Blacking their significance in Dickens's life. They were formative. Somewhere deep down inside, perhaps unconsciously, he made the decision that never again was he going to be so victimized. He would fall prey to none of the easy slipshodness of financial imprudence that had been his father's undoing. He would work and subject himself to a steel discipline. No obstacle should stand between him and ambition; no grief or frustration interfere with his strivings. In one sense, the grieving child in the blacking warehouse might be said to have died, to be succeeded by a man of deadly determination, of insuperable resolve, hard and aggressive almost to fierceness. In another, that child never died, but was continually reborn in a host of children suffering or dying young and other innocent victims undergoing injustice and pain; from Oliver and Smike and poor Jo to all the victims of a stony-hearted and archaic social system who throng Dickens's later books. In a final sense, the great and successful effort of his career was to assimilate and understand the blacking warehouse and the Marshalsea, and the kind of world in which such things could be.

CHAPTER FOUR

Ambition's Ladder

IN May, 1827, a brisk new office boy started working for Ellis and Blackmore, attorneys, of 5 Holborn Court, Gray's Inn. He was just a quarter past his fifteenth birthday, and had dropped out of school only that spring.[1] His parents had been finding it hard to meet the fees; that March they had been evicted from their house at 29 Johnson Street for failure to pay their rent,[2] and in the course of the year had acquired another mouth to feed, when their last child, Augustus, was born.[3] They were now living at 17 The Polygon, a very superior part of Somers Town, but they were only "lodgers." [4]

During the previous two and a half years Charles had been at Wellington House Academy, where he had risen to be one of the senior boys, and had probably derived all the benefit he was likely to get from that institution. The child whose eyes had filled with tears of gratitude on hearing his father's intention of sending him back to school [5] had become a romping curly-head given to pranks and wild explosions of laughter.[6] He bore no visible shadow of the blacking warehouse. No more is heard of bouts of fever or attacks of spasm. But no one could have imagined, from the bright unclouded face, how fatefully that past lay within him, or how piercing was his ambition to get ahead.

John Dickens had acted quickly on his decision that Charles should be sent to school again. Within a few days the youngster had been sent to Wellington House Academy near by to ask for a card of terms. When Charles arrived on this errand, the boys were at dinner and the proprietor "was carving for them with a pair of holland sleeves on. . . . He came out, and gave me what I wanted; and hoped I should become a pupil." And at seven o'clock one morning, very soon afterward, before the end of June, 1824, Charles started as a day pupil at Wellington House.[7]

This second schooltime was a buoyant period of recovering from the anguish of the blacking warehouse. Curative instinct sought to blot its memory from his mind, to restore him to the boyhood he had half outgrown. He never spoke of his experiences to his schoolmates, but he well knew what set him off from them and made him different. It was not the things they knew and he had forgotten; he relearned them quickly enough. It was the things he knew and could never forget, which they did not know. "What would they say, who made so light of money," David Copperfield asks, "if they could know how I had scraped my half-pence together for the purchase of my daily saveloy and beer, or my slices of pudding? How could it affect them, who were so innocent of London life and London streets, to discover how knowing I was (and ashamed to be) in the meanest phases of both?" [8]

But all his companions saw was a rather short, plump, fresh-colored youngster, jolly-looking, and given to immoderate laughter for no sufficient reason apparent to them. He dressed with extreme neatness in a pepper-and-salt jacket and trousers, and wore a turn-down collar instead of a frill, so that he looked less youthful than he was. His head he carried with extraordinary erectness.[9] Nobody would have recognized in this well-turned-out lad with the proud head and the uncontrollable laughter the shabby laboring hind he was trying to forget.

Wellington House Academy was located in Hampstead Road, at the corner of Granby Street and Mornington Place. It had a certain local celebrity, and was indeed somewhat better than the average school of its class because its Welsh owner, Mr. William Jones, though no great scholar himself, had the judgment to employ competent masters. "The master was supposed among us," Dickens says in "Our School," "to know nothing, and one of the ushers was supposed to know everything." [10] The teacher believed to know everything was Mr. Taylor, the writing, mathematics, and English master, who shared the younger boys with the Latin master, made out bills, mended pens, and always called at parents' houses to inquire after sick boys, because he had gentlemanly manners. He was lame and played the flute. Mr. Manville, or Mandeville, the Latin master, took pains with the boys who showed ability and a desire to learn, ignored the lazy or stupid, and stuffed onions in his ears in the belief that they helped his deafness.[11] Besides these, there were the junior master, Mr. Shiers, a fat little dancing master who taught the hornpipe, and a brisk little French master.[12]

Mr. Jones, the headmaster, was a sadist, forever smiting the palms of offenders with "a bloated mahogany ruler," "or viciously drawing a pair of pantaloons tight with one of his large hands, and caning the wearer with the other." [13] The pupil-boarders were constantly smarting from his ferocity, especially any of those who, like poor Traddles in *David Copperfield*, appealed to his tastes by a pleasing plumpness. But Charles and the other day boys, who might bear tales home, heard the swish of his cane less often.

The schoolroom was a timber structure parallel to Granby Street in the large playground behind Mr. Jones's residence. Here the boys kept redpolls, linnets, and canaries in all sorts of strange receptacles from desks and drawers to hatboxes, and trained white mice "better than the masters trained the boys." One white mouse, who lived in the cover of a Latin dictionary, "ran up ladders, drew Roman chariots, shouldered muskets, turned wheels, and even made a very creditable appearance on the stage as the Dog of Montargis. He might have achieved great things, but for having the misfortune to mistake his way in a triumphal procession to the Capitol, when he fell into a deep inkstand, and was dyed black and drowned." [14]

The Dog of Montargis was one of the plays that Charles and the other boys amused themselves by staging in toy theaters with gorgeous scenery created by a boy named Beverley, who later became a well-known scene painter. They also did *Cherry and Fair Star*, a dramatic version of Mme d'Aulnoy's fairy tale, *La Princesse Belle-Étoile et le Prince Chéri*, and Pocock's exciting melodrama, *The Miller and His Men*, a lurid story of robbers innocently disguised as millers by day. The mill was so constructed by young Beverley that it could be made at the end to tumble to pieces by means of firecrackers, and did this so realistically that once the police came knocking violently at the schoolhouse door.[15]

All the other things that schoolboys usually do, Charles did. He devoured successive numbers of a penny weekly entitled *The Terrific Register*, "making myself unspeakably miserable, and frightening the very wits out of my head" with tales "in which there was always a pool of blood, and at least one body." [16] He and another boy named John

Bowden wrote stories for a school paper that also contained such items as "*Lost.*—By a boy with a long nose, and green eyes, a very bad temper. Whoever has found the same may keep it, as the owner is better off without it." [17] One of these school friends, who sometimes walked from school with Charles, remembered the Johnson Street home as being in a squalid neighborhood with Rhodes's cow fields at the back of the garden wall, and Charles's mother as a fragile woman who seemed in delicate health.[18]

Of all the boys Charles knew, his closest friend was a youngster named Daniel Tobin, living in George Street, Boston Road, who was an associate and a kind of occasional amanuensis for years afterward.[19] With Tobin and the others Charles chattered about the streets, talking a lingo that they fondly hoped would lead to their being mistaken for foreigners, and playing pranks on old ladies. In Drummond Street once, Charles led his companions in pretending to be beggars, staggering the old ladies by the impudence with which he asked for charity, and then exploding with laughter and taking to his heels.[20]

During Charles's first year at Wellington House Academy, in December, 1825, his father's elder brother William unexpectedly died at the age of forty-three, leaving an estate of some £1,300. Of this, £300 was left to his widow outright, and she was to receive the interest on the remaining £1,000—which was invested in consols—as long as she lived and remained unmarried. But on her death, or in the event that she remarried, these invested funds, after a few other minor bequests, were to be shared in equal parts among his brother's children.[21] The sum that each of the six would eventually obtain was hardly a fortune, but Charles and Fanny at least were old enough by now, and had enough experience of their father's ways, to realize that even so modest a bequest might well prove useful to them.

The next year and a half passed swiftly by. Aside from learning to be something like a cheerful everyday boy again—which may indeed have been enough—it is not certain what Charles learned during this last brief schooling. One thing he did *not* learn, his schoolfellow John Bowden said, was to play the piano; the music master declared it would be robbing his parents.[22] Another fellow pupil, Henry Danson, thought in later years that Charles had not taken Latin, but against this there is testimony that "all the senior boys (and C. D. became one) learned the elements of that language." In fact, he won a Latin Prize, having

been coached by the junior master, Richard Shiers, to whom in gratitude he gave an inscribed copy of the works of Horace.[23]

Aside from an occasional literary allusion, however, of the kind that
constitutes a common stock, Dickens shows few signs of having been
influenced by Roman literature. "There is certainly nothing in Dickens's writings," Hugh Kingsmill remarks with rough justice, "to suggest
that, whether or not he was put into Vergil, any perceptible amount
of Vergil was ever put into him." [24] One can only imagine what the
periods of Cicero and the polished elegances of Horace meant to the
boy who had gone hungry beneath the Adelphi arches and wept in
the spiked shadow of the Marshalsea. Certainly they made no such impression on his boyhood as the eighteenth-century novelists and the
glowing worlds of fairy-tale romance had made upon his childhood.
The classics of the silver age may well have seemed to him very remote
from anything he had known or dreamed. Long before he returned to
declining *musa* and *dominus*, the roots of his inspiration were already
sunk in a far different soil.

*   *   *   *   *

The days when he would leave school had not drawn near without
his mother's having taken thought about his future. She had an aunt,
Mrs. C. W. Charlton, who kept a lodginghouse at 16 Berners Street.
On visits to this aunt she had often met one of the lodgers, Mr. Edward Blackmore, the junior partner in the law firm of Ellis and Blackmore. He considered Charles a clever, good-looking youth, and consented at Mrs. Dickens's earnest request to take him on as an office
boy.[25]

In the seven weeks or so intervening between the time the lad left
school and the time he began with Ellis and Blackmore he spent a short
period with Charles Molloy, a solicitor with offices at 6 Symonds Inn,
Chancery Lane, but it is not known whether this position was merely
temporary or the second one a more attractive later offer. It is possible
that one of his fellow clerks during this brief time was Thomas Mitton,
who had gone to Jonathan Dawson's school in Brunswick Square with
his brother Frederick. Certainly within the next few years Mitton and
Dickens became friends.[26]

The boy who reported for duty to Ellis and Blackmore on that May
morning of 1827 was still rather undersized and looked younger than

his age, but he made up for it by the aggressive bearing with which he wore his blue jacket and the military-looking cap perched jauntily on one side of his head. It promptly earned him a black eye, which George Lear, a fellow clerk, commented on when he returned from delivering papers at a law stationer's. "Yes," Charles replied, "a big blackguard fellow knocked my cap off as I was crossing over Chancery Lane from Lincoln's Inn gateway. He said 'Halloa, sojer!' which I could not stand, so I at once struck him and he then hit me in the eye. A gentleman who was crossing at the same time said to the fellow, 'You blackguard! how dare you hit a little fellow in that way?' His answer was ready,—'Vy, he hit me fust!' " [27]

Shortly after Charles's start with the firm, it moved to 1 Raymond Buildings, where the clerks had a second-floor office overlooking Holborn from which the boy amused himself by dropping cherry stones on the hats of passers-by. When some of these angrily came upstairs to complain, he would answer them with such an air of grave innocence that they often went away convinced that they must have been mistaken.[28] In the intervals of carving his name on the lid of his desk and keeping an account book for his employers in which his own salary rose slowly from ten shillings to thirteen and six and then to fifteen shillings, he also had a keen eye for his surroundings. Mr. Ellis, the senior partner, by his inveterate snuff-taking probably later suggested Mr. Perker in *Pickwick*; and Charles was delighted by queer characters among the clients, one of whom later emerged as Newman Noggs. A classic occasion that he never forgot was when a fellow clerk named Potter, after taking too much wine, insisted "It was the salmon." [29]

But the work itself he found rather dull: getting wills registered, serving processes, carrying documents to and from counsel's offices and courts of law.[30] It was, to be sure, the apprenticeship of a responsible and dignified profession; one might become a prosperous solicitor dwelling in a leafy court of the Temple, or a K.C. in silk terrifying witnesses with his sarcasms, or even a learned judge. Nevertheless, Charles found the law slow and irksome. There was no fascination for him in the scholastic involutions and cumbersome proceedings of a profession that seemed to have no other purpose than entangling its victims for the profit of its adepts. He wanted some more exciting—above all some speedier—way of rising to prosperity.

His mind turned toward journalism, in which during the last two years his father had been engaged.[31] For, as John Dickens had feared, the Navy Pay Office would have none of a man who had become entangled in the Insolvent Debtors' Act. On compassionate grounds, however, and in consideration of his almost twenty years of service and his six children, the Treasurer of the Navy had recommended that he be granted a retirement allowance of £145 a year. The recommendation made its way from Mr. Croker, Secretary to the Admiralty, to the Commissioners and the First Lord, Viscount Melville, and was finally approved. In March, 1825, John Dickens, by then a man of forty-one, had found himself obliged to meet his loss of income by discovering a new means of earning a living.[32]

Save for his careless ways with money, however, and his flowers of speech, John Dickens was no Micawber. In the Chatham days he had published in the London *Times* a two-column account of the great fire that had destroyed thirty-eight homes; [33] perhaps he might become a reporter. With enormous vigor and industry he tackled the difficulties of learning shorthand, to such effect that little over a year later he was one of the Parliamentary corps of the *British Press*.[34] These were among a group of crack reporters who during the time Parliament was in session earned a princely salary of almost fifteen guineas a week, and sometimes, when debate was prolonged into the night, much more.[35] To John Dickens's son the prospect of rising from fifteen shillings to fifteen guineas within a few years looked sufficiently splendid. More enticing still, many men distinguished in other walks of life, Charles learned, had begun their careers by reporting Parliamentary debates.[36] Let him get his foot on the beginning round of that ladder, and he'd climb far enough!

While he was still at Wellington House Academy, he would sometimes take in to the *British Press* what was called "penny-a-line stuff": notices of accidents, fires, or police reports that had escaped the regular reporters, and which was paid for at a penny a printed line.[37] When he left school and started to work, around Easter, 1827, the bustle and excitement of the newspaper office probably had its share in making solicitors' offices seem dull places. A knowledge of shorthand, of course, was almost indispensable for a career in journalism, and he had been told that a perfect command of the mystery of shorthand reading and writing was about equal in difficulty to mastering six languages.[38] But hard work did not disconcert him. With a tenacity of purpose beyond his years, he set himself to the task.

He laid out half a guinea on a copy of Gurney's textbook, *Brachygraphy, or an Easy and Compendious System of Shorthand,* then the most celebrated manual of the subject.[39] Possibly with some help from his father and from one of his uncles, John Henry Barrow,[40] who was a reporter on the *Times,* he gritted his will to master its intricacies. As the months crept on at Ellis and Blackmore, though he often groaned over the toil, and though it necessitated his working far harder than he had ever had to do at Wellington House Academy, he kept at it relentlessly.

"The changes that were wrung upon dots, which in such a position meant such a thing, and in such another position something else entirely different; the wonderful vagaries that were played by circles; the unaccountable consequences that resulted from marks like flies' legs; the tremendous effect of a curve in the wrong place; not only troubled my waking hours, but reappeared before me in my sleep. When I had groped my way, blindly, through these difficulties, and had mastered the alphabet, there then appeared a procession of new horrors, called arbitrary characters; the most despotic characters I had ever known; who insisted, for instance, that a thing like the beginning of a cobweb meant expectation; and that a pen-and-ink sky-rocket stood for disadvantageous. When I had fixed these wretches in my mind, I found that they had driven everything else out of it; then, beginning again, I forgot them; while I was picking them up, I dropped the other fragments of the system; in short, it was almost heart-breaking." [41]

However, life was not all toil. Fanny had been graduated from the Royal Academy of Music in January, 1827, after having studied there under the well-known composer Ignaz Moscheles. She had blossomed into a charming and talented girl with a musical career opening before her. On May 29th she appeared at a benefit for the actor John Pritt Harley, at Drury Lane, where she was announced as "the celebrated pupil of Mr. Moscheles" and played "her master's *Recollections of Ireland*"; the following year, at another benefit for Harley, she gave the same composer's *Anticipations of Scotland*.[42] Through her fellow pupils at the Academy she had friends who joined each other in evenings of piano music and song. Although Charles had been pronounced hopeless at the piano himself, he had not lost his relish for such comic

songs as "The Dandy Dog's Meat Man," [43] or escaped the taste for romantic ballads, and often joined his sister at these melodious gatherings.

He was also busy exploring the life of London. No aspect of its
teeming activity and its gigantic proliferation of streets and squares
escaped his extraordinary observation. He roamed over all the crowded
City, Leadenhall Street, Bishopsgate, Cheapside, and Ludgate Cross,
from Tower Hill and Aldgate Pump to Temple Bar and the Strand. He
knew Palace Yard, Whitehall, the Horse Guards, St. James's Park, the
Golden Cross and the Royal Mews, Piccadilly, Pall Mall, the Quad-
rant, and Regent Street. He was familiar with Vauxhall Gardens,
Knightsbridge, Bond Street, Russell Square, Lincoln's Inn Fields. He
ranged as far as from distant Hampton Court and Richmond to Greenwich, and from New Cross on the Old Kent Road to Hampstead Heath
and Islington. He had seen the drunken revelers staggering home at
early dawn and women bringing in baskets of fruit to Covent Garden
Market, and, long past midnight, watched the baked-potato men and
kidney-pie vendors closing their stalls in the neighborhood around
Marsh Gate and the Royal Coburg Theatre while the lights were still
flaring in the wine vaults and winking out in the cheesemongers' and
tiny chandlers' shops.[44] "I thought I knew something of the town,"
said George Lear, remembering their days together at Ellis and Blackmore's, "but after a little talk with Dickens I found that I knew nothing. He knew it all from Bow to Brentford." [45]

He knew more than the streets; he knew their people. He was fascinated by a dirty old woman, miscalled a laundress, who was paid to
light the fires in their Holborn Court offices and push the dust around
the floor with a broom, and he could brilliantly mimic her ways of
speech and her excuses. "He could imitate, in a manner that I never
heard equalled," Lear testified, "the low population of the streets of
London in all their varieties, whether mere loafers or sellers of fruit,
vegetables, or anything else," and, besides these, all the leading actors
and popular singers of the day, comic or patriotic.[46]

This knowledge of the theater and its performers Charles was gaining with another fellow clerk, Thomas Potter, who shared his passion
for the stage.[47] He had suddenly shot up into a young man and, in a
new brown suit, of which the coat was cut like a dress coat, and a high
hat,[48] felt "a befitting contempt for boys at day-schools." [49] These two

youngsters—Charles was just past sixteen—dined in low-priced res-
taurants on chops and kidneys with a draught of stout, roamed the
town together, and were beginning to experiment in mild Havana
cigars and whiskey and water. They were "thick-and-thin" pals; in one
of the *Sketches by Boz* called "Making a Night of It" he gives a fictional rendering of their relationship in which "the off-hand, dashing,
amateur-pickpocket-sort-of-manner" of Potter is contrasted with "a
spice of romance" in his own disposition, "a ray of poetry, a gleam of
misery, a sort of consciousness of he didn't exactly know what, coming
across him he didn't precisely know why . . ." [50]

After dinner there was the theater. Admission to the galleries was
only one shilling, and around nine o'clock prices were reduced to half.
Since an evening's bill usually included an interlude and a farce in
addition to the main attraction, a good deal of entertainment could
be had at small cost.[51] The only theaters licensed to present the spoken
drama were the so-called "major" theaters at Covent Garden, Drury
Lane, and the Haymarket.[52] Besides these, however, there were a good
many "minor" theaters ostensibly devoted to musical performances,
but mostly these evaded the rules by disguising their offerings with a
few songs and calling them "burlettas." [53] They were forbidden to
compete with the major theaters from October to May, but when
around the beginning of the century the majors began doing plays in
the summer, the others became less scrupulous about observing time
limits. And across Westminster Bridge in Surrey, in the East End, and
to the north and west, there were other theaters controlled by different
regulations, which gave a wide range of performances from melodrama to farce. Astley's, in Westminster Bridge Road, was a circus that
also did plays about savage chiefs and tyrannical Eastern monarchs;
the Surrey, in Blackfriars Road, had nautical melodramas with pirates
and gallant tars; the Pavilion, in Whitechapel Road, dealt in blood-
curdling criminals; the Grecian Saloon, in Britannia Field, Hoxton,
was a sort of cabaret, with a Moorish band and liquid refreshments
served in its gardens.[54]

Finally, in Wilson Street, Gray's Inn Lane, Catharine Street, Strand,
and other places, there were "private" theaters.[55] In these, which were
even cheaper than the other theaters, stage-struck amateurs were allowed for a fee to play Shylock, Captain Absolute, Charles Surface,
or Macbeth. Their patrons, Dickens tells us in *Sketches by Boz*, were

"dirty boys, low copying-clerks in attorneys' offices," and "capacious-headed youths from city counting-houses," who trod the boards under such splendid names as Belville, Melville, Treville, Berkeley, Byron, and St. Clair. For two pounds anyone could be Richard, Duke of Gloucester, and stab King Henry, make love to the Lady Ann, shout "Orf with his ed!" and then, slow and sneeringly, "So much for Bu-u-u-uckingham!" and clash blades in the excitement of the end. "That snuff-shop-looking figure," Dickens goes on, "is *Banquo*; and the young lady with the liberal display of legs, who is kindly painting his face with a hare's foot, is dressed for *Fleance*. . . . The boy of four-teen who is having his eyebrows smeared with soap and whitening is *Duncan*, King of Scotland; and the two dirty men with the corked countenances, in very old green tunics, and dirty drab boots, are the 'army.' " [56] The knowing backstage description of all this makes it clear that Dickens's experience of the private theaters was not limited to the spectators' side of the proscenium.[57]

But these minor dissipations were not making him neglect his office duties, nor had he lost sight of his goal. Ellis and Blackmore had raised his salary to fifteen shillings, though no further. Charles continued to grind away without ceasing at Gurney's shorthand. By November, 1828, he had resolved upon and taken a bold step. He would never become a Parliamentary reporter by grubbing for a firm of attorneys. He was still too young for the reporters' gallery, but it would be better to go his own way and do something that would prepare him for it. His great-aunt's husband, Mr. C. W. Charlton, had a younger relation, Thomas Charlton, Jr., who was a free-lance reporter in the Consistory Court of Doctors' Commons.[58] There he sat in a rented box waiting until one of the proctors engaged him to take down a case. This box Charles could share.[59] He felt confident of his command of shorthand, and was sure that he could earn more than fifteen shillings a week. At the end of November he left Ellis and Blackmore's. He still lacked two months of being seventeen.

* * * * *

Doctors' Commons no longer exists today. Its jurisdiction was taken over by the Probate Court in 1857, and its precincts were torn down. But in 1828 it lay between St. Paul's and the river.[60] An archway from Paul's Chain opened on a stone-paved shady court of old red-brick houses. One of these was the Court; the others were proctors' chambers, with the names of their occupants in white letters on the doors. The inside of the Court was a black-wainscoted and columned room looking like a chapel, Dickens thought, with its farther end fenced off. Inside this area was a raised semicircular platform, and within its curve a pulpit-desk. Doctors in red gowns and gray wigs surrounded the platform; upon it others in black gowns with white fur sat at a green table "like a billiard table without the cushions." Above them, blinking like an owl, sat the presiding judge.[61]

Doctors' Commons was a confusion of different courts, though their members used the same buildings and consisted of the same individuals. It included the Admiralty Court; the Prerogative Office, where wills were registered and filed; the Prerogative Court, which dealt with testamentary matters in the dioceses; the Court of Arches, which was the provincial court of the Archbishop of Canterbury; and the Consistory Court, which was the diocesan court of the Bishop of London. The last of these was the one in which Dickens mainly worked. None of them raised in any way his estimate of the law. They were crabbed, archaic, muddled, expensive of time and money, and obstructive of justice. Watching these "monkish attorneys" manipulating "obsolete old monsters of Acts of Parliament" as they traded on their "ancient monopoly in suits about people's wills and people's marriages and disputes among ships and boats," he felt himself being wrought to a fine mood of scorn and impatience.[62]

Of his first year as a shorthand writer little is known. In the beginning he had plenty of time on his hands as he waited in his box for a proctor to engage his services. As soon as he was eighteen, on February 7, 1830 (the very earliest date possible), he applied for a reader's ticket at the British Museum. C. W. Charlton was one of his guarantors, and Dickens's address was given as 10 Norfolk Street, Fitzroy Square,[63] where his parents were living over a greengrocer's shop.[64] During the next three or four years he read with eager industry, making his way along the little mews from Montague Street, Russell Square, which was then the entrance to the Reading Room. Here he had to pull a rope to summon the "messenger" whose duty it was to admit readers to the building. Up a flight of stairs was a great double room with silent figures bent over tables of books and manuscripts.[65] These days in the Museum, sometimes reading Addison, sometimes the works of Shakespeare or his *Life* by Symonds, sometimes Goldsmith's *History of England*, or Berges's *Short Account of the Roman Senate*, were a valuable supplement to his brief formal education.[66] In later years he would refer to them as the most useful to himself that he had ever passed.[67]

During this time he continued to be a visitor in the homes of his Barrow uncles. The fourth eldest of them, Edward Barrow, had married Janet Ross, a talented miniaturist who did a portrait of Charles when he was eighteen. It is his earliest known portrait, and shows a surprised young face stiffly perched at the top of an enormously high black stock.[68] Janet Barrow had two pretty sisters, Georgina and Thomasina, of whom Charles especially admired Georgina.[69]

In Doctors' Commons he had found it helpful to have a place in which to transcribe his notes, and had taken an office, of which he shared the expense with a proctor named Charles Edward Fenton. Two transcripts have been found of Consistory Court judgments delivered on November 18, 1830, that are in his hand and certified by "C. Dickens, Shorthand Writer, 5 Bell Yard." [70] The cases they deal with arose out of quarrels in the vestry room of the Church of St. Bartholomew-the-Great, Smithfield, and are clearly the origin of "Bumple vs. Sludberry," in the "Doctors' Commons" chapter of *Sketches by Boz*, where both the contestants and the Consistory Court are made absurd enough.[71]

But despite such flickers of comedy, Dickens found law reporting wearisome to him. And, although he was earning his living, it was wearily uncertain; [72] outside of term times, of course, his fees dwindled away almost altogether. Even the addition of practicing in the Metropolitan Police Courts as well as in Doctors' Commons did not swell his income enough.[73] He was unhappy at this monotonous work; and he had other reasons for being desperately anxious to increase his earnings. For he had fallen violently in love with the bright eyes and bewitching curls of a little beauty named Maria Beadnell who had taken him into a delirious captivity that was to fill the coming months with ecstasy and anguish. And even through the luminous mists of love he knew well enough that her father, who was a banker, would not be much impressed by the pretensions of an impecunious youth making a precarious living as a shorthand reporter.[74]

He had to achieve more brilliant prospects, and that speedily. He could not wait forever, hoping for a chance of Parliamentary reporting that never came. Spurred by this necessity, his mind turned to other means of livelihood. He knew he sang a comic song well. He had always been interested in the theater. Perhaps experience in the private theaters had suggested to him that he had more ability as an actor than most aspirants to such a career. He resolved to make an attack upon the stage. Apparently, he did not stop to ask whether Mr. Beadnell would be more impressed by an actor than by a law reporter.[75]

If it were not for the intensity and efficiency with which Dickens went about everything he did, this determination of his might sound not unlike Mrs. Dickens's notion of establishing a school. But with characteristic energy he began a businesslike campaign. He had been going to the theater almost every night for the preceding three years, always seeking the best acting. He had been especially devoted to Charles Mathews, and had sat in the pit whenever that actor played. He now started practicing industriously, even such things as walking in and out, and sitting down in a chair, "often four, five, six hours a day: shut up in my own room, or walking about in the fields. I prescribed to myself, too, a sort of Hamiltonian system for learning parts; and learnt a great number." Besides this self-training, he took a series of lessons from the well-known actor Robert Keeley.[76]

Inspired by renewed hope and by dreams of Maria Beadnell (who had been sent to Paris "to complete her education," and possibly to remove her from the influence of this undesirable young man),[77] he worked away to perfect his acting technique. After weeks of drill, he thought himself sufficiently adept. From his little office in Bell Yard he wrote to Bartley, the stage manager at the Lyceum for Mathews. He stated his age and what he thought he could do, adding that he believed he had "a strong perception of character and oddity, and a natural power of reproducing" what he observed. "There must have been something in my letter that struck the authorities, for Bartley wrote to me almost immediately to say that they were busy getting up the Hunchback (so they were), but that they would communicate with me again, in a fortnight. Punctual to the time another letter came, with an appointment to do anything of Mathews's I pleased, before him and Charles Kemble, on a certain day at the theatre. My sister Fanny was in the secret, and was to go with me to play the songs. I was laid up when the day came, with a terrible bad cold and an inflamma-

tion of the face . . . I wrote to say so, and added that I would resume
my application next season." [78]

* * * * *

But the application was never renewed. At the very moment he was
wavering in his original hopes of doing Parliamentary reporting, the
opportunity came to enter his chosen field. His uncle John Henry
Barrow had in 1828 started a new venture called the *Mirror of Parliament.* It was a sort of Hansard, devoted to a verbally exact and well-
printed transcript of Parliamentary proceedings.[79] John Dickens was
one of its reporters in the Gallery. The Barrows had begun to realize
that their young nephew had ability as well as ambition. Somewhere
early in 1832 he was taken on by his uncle's paper, probably as a super-
numerary of some kind.[80] Not only this, but in the spring of the year
a new sevenpenny evening newspaper, the *True Sun,* was inaugurated
under the editorship of Samuel Laman Blanchard. Dickens became a
member of the reporting staff of this paper from its first day of publication, March 5, 1832.[81]

For the *True Sun* he did general reporting; for the *Mirror of Parliament,* besides whatever assistance he may have given in its offices at
3 Abingdon Street, Westminster, he was specifically a Parliamentary
reporter. It is not clear which engagement preceded the other, but for
a time he certainly worked concurrently on both publications. If he
first entered the Gallery for his uncle's paper, he was, as his friend
Forster claims he was, still only nineteen years of age; [82] if not, less than
a month past his twentieth birthday. Whichever was the fact, to
Charles it undoubtedly seemed that it had taken him a long time to
get there.

But once in the Gallery, he strode rapidly to a position of distinction
—in his own words, "made a great splash." [83] Among the eighty or
ninety reporters there, James Grant of the *Morning Advertiser* declared, he "occupied the very highest rank, not merely for accuracy in
reporting, but for marvellous quickness in transcript." [84] And at Westminster, as it was before the fire of 1834, reporting was not made easy.
Newspapermen were granted no special accommodations; indeed, according to law, there was still a formal prohibition against the publication of debates, and the Duke of Wellington was only one of many

members of Parliament who denied that the English people had any right to know what was said in either House. Reporters had to squeeze through the narrow door of the crowded Strangers' Gallery, and shift as best they could in the back row with five or six rows of seats in front of them.[85] "I have worn my knees," Dickens said, "by writing on them in the old gallery of the old House of Commons; and I have worn my feet by standing to write in a preposterous pen in the old House of Lords, where we used to be huddled together like so many sheep—kept in waiting, say, until the woolsack might want restuffing." [86] Under these circumstances, and against no inconsiderable competition from a body of able and experienced men—many of them veterans in the occupation—this youth in his early twenties achieved pre-eminence. "There never *was* such a shorthand writer!" said one of them.[87]

The young reporter's mind had traveled a long way since he had trembled in childhood at the radicals as terrible banditti who deserved to be hanged. Now he was an ardent reformer. And he reached the Gallery just in time to witness the final stages of the struggle over the Reform Bill of 1832. The death of shapeless, disreputable old George IV in 1830 and the accession of William IV had forced the election of a new Parliament. Bad trade and economic misery had united the nation in a sense of its political wrongs. There was rick-burning in the south, and workmen drilling in preparation for social war in the industrial north. The middle classes feared revolution from below as much as they desired to wrest political power from the aristocracy. Wellington was defeated in Parliament and Lord Grey's ministry formed explicitly on the issue of reform.

The Reform Bill the new Government brought in was a shock to the Tories. Rotten boroughs that had sent one hundred and forty representatives to Parliament were either to be abolished outright or to lose half their members. All £10 householders were to be admitted to the borough franchise, and the seats obtained by disfranchisement redistributed among the large centers of population. The opposition had so little expected anything so drastic that they were stunned and had no plan ready. In the ensuing debate the national will made itself so unmistakable that some of the hostile legislators were intimidated. Within three weeks the Bill passed its second reading by a majority of just one vote.

Further maneuvers forced the election of a new Parliament, in which the Bill had a majority of one hundred and thirty-six. But when it had passed the House of Commons, the Lords threw it out by a majority of forty-one. Popular indignation exploded. There were outrages against bishops and peers. In the south ricks were burning night after night. Unemployment, starvation, and cholera added to the terrors of the winter of 1831–32.

The last stages of these events Dickens witnessed from the Gallery. A new Bill was introduced, modified in some details, but not weakened. When it reached the Lords again, although it passed its second reading, the month of May saw a determined attempt to amend it out of recognition. But the country was equally determined, and Lord Grey knew it. He resigned. During the breathless next ten days it proved impossible for either the Duke of Wellington or Lord Lyndhurst to form an administration. The King was obliged to come to terms with Lord Grey, who consented to return only on securing from his Sovereign a written promise to create any number of peers necessary to carry the Bill. The threat proved enough, and, to a flying of flags and ringing of bells, the Bill became law.[88]

The reformed Parliament was a hard-working group of men far superior in ability to the usual mediocrity of such legislative bodies. It achieved a remarkable legislative record, recasting municipal institutions, passing the first effective Factory Act, and abolishing Negro slavery. It contained such outstanding veterans of debate as Lord Grey, Lord John Russell, and Edward Stanley, later fourteenth Earl of Derby, as well as the Irish leader O'Connell; among the brilliant more recent arrivals were Cobbett, Gladstone, Macaulay, Grote, and the successful novelist Edward Lytton Bulwer.

But although Dickens had a settled antagonism to the Conservatives, who were outnumbered three to one in this Parliament, he was not impressed by the body, or by its members, or by what they accomplished. He saw the House as a place of dull and protracted talk, dominated by a mania for archaic rules and precedents and red tape and sealing wax, and even after its reform hardly less the defender of privileged interests than before. He saw its members, with few exceptions, and those mostly reduced to ineffectiveness by the institution itself, as a mob of brainless windbags, place-warmers, and agents of chicanery and corruption. Even when he knew them to be honest and able, he was apt to dislike them simply for being the kind of men Parliament molded its members into being. He could not bear Lord Grey's "style of speaking, his fishy coldness, his uncongenial and unsympathetic politeness, his insufferable though most gentlemanly artificiality." Years later, in 1862, he told William Charles Kent, "The shape of his head (I see it now) was a misery to me and weighed down my youth." [89]

During the midnight debates of the new Parliament, however, he was working overtime, making as much as twenty to twenty-five guineas a week.[90] And sometimes, for all the ennui generated by dull speakers, there could be moments of intense dramatic excitement and emotion. When O'Connell was speaking against the Bill for the Suppression of Disturbances in Ireland, he drew such an affecting picture of a widow seeking her only son among the peasants killed by soldiers in an anti-tithe riot that the young reporter, abandoning his pencil, was obliged to lay his head on his arms and weep.[91] And after sessions such as this, he and his fellow reporters, who had been spelling each other in three-quarter-hour shifts, would repair to a little tavern in the Palace Yard.[92] Here, in an upstairs room kept sacred to their use, they could write out their copy and compare doubtful passages with colleagues who had sharper ears.[93]

Only one of these associates, however, was really a personal friend.[94] This was Thomas Beard, a reporter for the *Morning Herald,* whom Dickens knew well enough to invite to a party his parents gave on his twentieth birthday.[95] Toward all the rest of his fellow journalists his manner was described as courteous but exceedingly reserved.[96] Leaving them after a late session of the House, he would make his way up Whitehall and the Strand to the lodgings in Cecil Street that he had more recently taken in order to be near his work.[97]

Maria Beadnell was still in Paris, but all week long his professional duties kept him busy until such late hours that he often had to sleep throughout the morning. There were still visits to the theater when he was not on duty in the House, and sometimes on Saturdays convivial evenings with other young men, when they would "knock up a chaunt or two" over punch and cigars.[98] Among these were Beard and perhaps his brother, Francis Carr Beard, who was a young medical student, two other young men named Charles Ross and Henry Bramwell, another named Longhurst, and Henry Kolle, a bank clerk who was also acquainted with the Beadnells.[99] With Kolle he began to ride horseback on Sundays. Writing from North End, Hampstead, that he can procure Kolle an "oss," he jokes about the animal's dismal appearance, and adds, "I am a poor judge of distance, but I should certainly say that your legs would be off the ground when you are on his back." [100]

He had not remained very long in his lodgings in the Strand. "The Cecil Street people," he explained to Kolle, "put too much water in their hash, lost a nutmeg grater, attended on me most miserably, dirted the table cloth, &c., &c.,; and so (detesting petty miseries) I gave them warning and have not yet fixed upon a 'local habitation and a name.'" [101] Soon he was living with his parents again, this time at 13 Fitzroy Street. [102]

Toward the end of July, Dickens had resigned from the *True Sun*, which was not doing well financially. [103] But his position with the *Mirror of Parliament* was now high indeed. Often he was invited to spend the week-end at the home of his uncle John Henry Barrow in Norwood, [104] and his responsibilities on the publication were coming to embrace much more than reporting. By early December he was writing to an applicant for a position, "I shall be happy to avail myself of your assistance when the session commences; and as soon as our arrangements at the *Mirror of Parliament* are completed, I shall write to you." Within the course of the year, it is plain, he had become a sort of sub-editor, entrusted with hiring other members of the staff. And he was being applied to from other directions as well, for to the same correspondent he added: "Had I even received your yesterday's note one day sooner I could have procured you a couple of days employment at the Lambeth Election as a Poll Clerk at a salary of one Guinea per day, having been commissioned by Mr. Tennyson to find no less than *eighteen* young men for that purpose. I regret to say however that the number was completed yesterday morning." [105]

He was still so boyish-looking, however, that it was often hard for mature men to believe how completely he had made himself the master of his profession. During the legislative consideration of the Irish coercion bill (the same one as that upon which O'Connell had reduced Dickens to tears), the Chief Secretary, Edward Stanley, in moving the second reading had spoken at great and eloquent length on the condition of Ireland. His address was so long that the eight *Mirror* reporters, working in three-quarters-of-an-hour shifts, were obliged to put Dickens in to cover the end of the speech as well as the beginning. When it appeared in print, Stanley found all except the first and last parts full of errors. He wished copies of the speech to be circulated in Ireland, and therefore asked the editor of the *Mirror of Parliament* if he would not send the reporter who had taken down those two parts to do the entire speech.[106]

John Dickens, all aglow with pride, was dispatched to fetch his son back from a Sunday in the country and Dickens was sent to Carlton House Terrace. He was shown into a room with newspaper-strewn tables, and told to wait. Mr. Stanley strode in, glanced at the young man suspiciously, and said, "I beg pardon, but I had hoped to see the gentleman who had reported part of my speech." Reddening, Dickens answered, "I am that gentleman." "Oh, indeed," returned Stanley, looking down to hide a faint smile. Dickens was accommodated with a seat in the middle of the room (Stanley tried to induce him to sit at a desk, but the House of Commons had got him in the habit of writing on his knees) and Stanley began striding up and down the room, declaiming his speech, "hour after hour, to the end, often becoming very much excited, and frequently bringing down his hand with great violence upon the desk." [107] When the ordeal was over, Stanley's secretary, Richard Earle, congratulated Dickens in the hall; and after receiving the young man's transcript of his speech, Mr. Stanley wrote a letter of gratitude and compliment to John Henry Barrow for sending so able a reporter.[108]

How far behind now was the ten-years-past misery of the warehouse and the prison! But underneath, no more than half veiled in memory, it had reinforced the strength with which his devotion to Maria Beadnell goaded his ambition. With all the desperate intensity of his nature, he had worked and beaten and hammered away, in a resolution, he said, that "excluded every other idea from my mind for four years, at a time of life when four years are equal to four times four"; and "went at it with a determination to overcome all the difficulties which fairly lifted me up into that newspaper life, and floated me away over a hundred men's heads." [109] Here he was, with a place of distinction among those men, with a hand in running the very paper upon which he had made his debut not many months ago. As he entered his twenty-first year he might well have felt proud of himself. But Maria Beadnell had returned from Paris, his love affair was going with heartbreaking badness, and he was miserable.

CHAPTER FIVE

First Love

THEY had first met in 1829, when he was seventeen. Maria's uncle, John Beadnell, was manager of Smith, Payne, and Smith's banking establishment at 1 Lombard Street; her father, George Beadnell, was also connected with the bank, and later became its manager. He and his family lived next door at 2 Lombard Street. There were three lovely daughters. Margaret, the eldest, was already engaged to a young tea merchant named David Lloyd.[1] Anne, the second, had auburn curls and a tender heart. Maria, the third, was a year older than Charles, and a diminutive siren with dark ringlets, the brightest of eyes, and eyebrows that drew together when she pretended to frown.[2] He thought her "prettily pettish manner" adorable, and her an angel. By the following spring he was abjectly and rapturously enslaved.[3]

Maria was well aware of her own charms and not at all averse to a flirtation with a good-looking boy who could be so entertaining. And there was something about him, too, beneath the shining high spirits and bright flow of words, that made him more interesting than the other boys whom she knew. Mr. and Mrs. Beadnell hardly noticed him at first, although Mr. Beadnell was kind to the boy.[4] To them he was no different from William Moule, absorbed in his elegant ties, or the military-minded Joe Moule, with his enthusiasm for red coats and curling mustachios, or Arthur Beetham, forever buttoned up to his chin as a protection against the cold, or any of the other young men who were always about the house.[5] He was really younger even than the youngest of the girls, and therefore of no possible importance.

During 1830, when he was reading at the British Museum and listening to the drone of voices in Doctors' Commons, Charles passed ecstatic hours in Lombard Street. Anne played the lute and gently sympathized with his infatuation; Maria was ravishing as her fingers wove in and out among the trembling strings of the harp.[6] Surely the sight of that bright face, Dickens thought, would make Satan himself weep and remember the angels singing around Heaven's High Throne![7] Seeing her in a raspberry-colored dress with black-velvet trimming at the top cut in an immense number of Vandykes, he felt his heart pinned like a captured butterfly on every one of them.[8] All his dreams had her for their sun. He would have died for her.[9]

He was not her only worshiper. Among the other young men who clustered around her was one named Henry Austin. He did a pretty painting of her and her little brother George in gouache as Dido and Ascanius for her album, and Charles wrote a feeble but infatuated poem for the opposite page. The two young men were drawn together and became friends. Another tinted sketch that Austin made of Maria, as a milkmaid under a tree, with dangling sunbonnet and a pail by her side, he gave as a present to Dickens.

Everything connected with Maria, Charles found distinctive and admirable. Mr. Beadnell, her father, was an excellent man, so hospitable, friendly, and kind, and of such liberal opinions. Her mother was flawless.[10] (Though, to be sure, she never got his name right, but always called him "Mr. Dickin.")[11] Her sister Margaret sang ballads with a sweet voice, Anne was very well read, and both were witty and sweet-tempered. He even loved Daphne, Maria's little white and liver-colored dog, which "would eat mutton chops if you cut off the fat," and envied that animal's privilege of being clasped to its mistress's breast.[12] Once Maria entrusted him with the commission of matching a pair of blue gloves for her, and how exalted he felt![13]

Meanwhile Mr. and Mrs. Beadnell were beginning to notice him. His family and social position were not striking. His prospects as a mere shorthand reporter in the law courts were nothing to impresss a banker. For a young man who made so little, Maria's parents may have thought, to waste so much of it in the theater showed no very solid character. But, in any case, the thought of anything between him and Maria was absurd; he was not yet even nineteen years of age. Still, they felt mistrustful. "There was something about him that was unfamiliar to them and even a little alarming; a fieriness that was uncomfortable and an outlook not to be approved."[14] But they took no immediate action. Charles continued to call and be invited to dinner, to be enchained by Maria's fascinating little ways, and to indulge in blissful visions of marrying her and loving her forever.

Of course he wanted to marry her. He would work even harder than he had, and accomplish wonderful things. Meanwhile Doctors' Commons (still his only regular source of income at this time) seemed deader and dustier than ever. As the cases dragged their slow length before him, he could take them down almost mechanically now. If he bestowed a thought on them, it was only to wonder, in the matrimonial cases, how married people could be otherwise than happy; and in the prerogative cases, to consider, if the money had been left to him, what steps he would have taken about Maria.[15] It was strange to realize that those dim old judges and doctors "wouldn't have gone out of their senses with rapture at the thought of marriage" to Maria; that she might have sung and played her harp until she led *him* to the verge of madness, "yet not have tempted one of those slow-goers an inch out of his road!" He despised them to a man.[16]

The only discordant element in the enchantment that bathed Lombard Street was Maria's closest friend, Mary Anne Leigh, who called herself Marianne, and who was constantly on the alert to find a meaning for every glance. She was keen to spy out the secrets of every flirtation, and her tongue was spiced with small bits of scandal.[17] With Charles she assumed a teasing, insinuating manner that he found half pleasing, half tormenting. She appeared to seek him out, sometimes alluring, sometimes with a faint tone of malice, sometimes endeavoring to make him confide in her. She provoked a steady series of Beatrice-Benedick verbal sparring matches between them; in one letter to her he speaks of the pleasure "of picking that bone we have to discuss." [18] To him, her behavior seemed extremely puzzling. She was a pretty girl, managing even her attacks with a certain charm, so that Charles hardly knew whether he was attracted to her or detested her. In the main, though, she was a disturbance. He would have preferred to be alone with Maria in a mist of love and beauty.

He was not altogether sure, now, that Mr. and Mrs. Beadnell greeted him as warmly as they had once done, though he had no unmistakable evidence of coldness. The marriage of Margaret Beadnell to David Lloyd, which was to take place on March 2c, 1831, was fast approaching, and all the Beadnell ladies were very busy. When Dickens was not occupied in Doctors' Commons, he walked the streets where the best ladies' shops were in the hope of seeing Maria, and haunted the Bazaar like an unquiet spirit.[19] Once he came upon the three girls, Margaret, Anne, and Maria, with their mother, on Cornhill. The girls were all wearing green merino cloaks; Maria looked bewitching. They were bound for a dressmaker's at St. Mary Axe, to order wedding garments, as Dickens later learned. He gallantly escorted them to the dressmaker's door, where Mrs. Beadnell, evidently seized with an apprehension that he might even come in, said emphatically, "And now, Mr. Dickin, we'll wish *you* good morning." [20]

In May, not long after the wedding, the Beadnells gave a dinner party in Lombard Street.[21] Charles was present, and recited a metrical composition he had written for the occasion, a parody of Goldsmith's "Retaliation," entitled "The Bill of Fare." [22] Primarily, of course, he wanted to amuse the guests, but he may also have hoped that Mr. and Mrs. Beadnell would be struck by its witty thrusts and become more highly impressed by its author. It is always pathetically hard for such a young man to realize how little most businessmen and their wives are apt to care about that kind of cleverness or how small a recommendation they consider it for their daughters' hands.

The verses begin by describing the participants of the feast under the metaphor of items in the banquet, and progress, rather confusedly, to a series of epitaphs upon the same persons, all catastrophically dead after having partaken of it. The Beadnells are given nothing but praise. The host is "a good fine sirloin of beef" and his wife "an excellent *Rib* of the same"; the Misses Beadnell "two nice little Ducks; and very well dressed"; the recently married Lloyds a side dish "Of Honey and sweets in the form of a Moon." Some doubt may be implied whether Mr. Beadnell's enthusiasm for ballot and freedom goes beyond mere words by the statement that "his opinions were always *sound* and sincere," but Mrs. Beadnell is praised without equivocation as "perfection."

Though Dickens allows himself to insinuate Anne's interest in the young bank clerk, Henry Kolle, by a feeble pun that her favorite reading is "*Colley* Cibber," he remains discreet about Maria. He does confess, however, that the departure from this world of one so beautiful and good as Maria would leave him with no desire but for death. There are light hits at some of the other young men: Francis N'Mamara, with his bright yellow gloves and other fripperies, is a dish of "gooseberry-Fool"; William Moule "of a Trifle, a trifling dish"; Joe Moule, with his mania for swords and red uniforms, a victim of *"scarlet fever."* The sharpest epithets are reserved for the Leighs, although they are softened by the tone of jest. Marianne's father, a corn chandler residing at Lea Bridge Road, Clapton, is portrayed as a good-natured drunkard, and Mrs. Leigh implied to be a stupid woman with a tongue dipped in gall; Marianne herself is summed up as a flirt, a pryer into secrets and retailer of scandal, and the greatest tormentor ever known. Himself Dickens describes as

> *". . . a young Summer Cabbage, without any heart;—*
> *Not that he's heartless, but because, as folks say,*
> *He lost his a twelve month ago, from last May"*

and ends the verses by telling how "a sweet pair of eyes sent him home to his grave." [23]

Doubtless he received polite compliments upon this *jeu d'esprit,* which is neither better nor worse than hundreds of such doggerel compositions by clever young men, but there was no sign that Mr. and Mrs. Beadnell were dazzled. Despite their crudeness, the lines reveal an amusing capacity to blow people's eccentricities up into broad caricature that clearly foreshadows the grotesque humors of his later satire. Emotionally the verses are significant for suggesting upon what footing Dickens himself was at that table, and how his feeling for Maria made him regard the others there.

And what were Maria's feelings for him? Was she a teaser and tormentor using her delightful little voice, her gay little laugh only to play with his devotion? [24] Was she a silly, rattle-brained little creature displaying her charms as thoughtlessly as a butterfly dances in the sun, or was she an artful siren entrapping him to feed her vanity? Had she gradually found herself really and troublingly in love with this handsome and sensitive boy, whose high spirits were a wine in the veins, but who had about him, too, a touch of something unintelligibly and frighteningly strange? There is no direct evidence, though years later she seems to have told Charles that she had loved him in these youthful days.[25] The truth of her character and her emotions may well have been, as it so often is, a mingling of all these feelings.

Certainly, however, she and Charles had some kind of secret understanding. They exchanged letters and little gifts,[26] and he believed her words meant that she loved him too, and treasured every keepsake from her with a full heart.[27] It was a time for him of ardor and shining dream and wretched happiness. All delight lay in being with her and all misery, though a delicious misery lit with visions, in being separated from her.[28]

But at last Mr. and Mrs. Beadnell seem to have made up their minds about Charles. (Somehow Mr. Beadnell had also discovered that John Dickens had been in the Marshalsea.) [29] This sparkling but ineligible young man was growing dangerous; Maria had better be got out of his way, where she might forget about him. Suddenly Charles felt his existence "entirely uprooted and my whole being blighted by the Angel of my soul being sent" to Paris "to finish her education." His heart was torn with pain as he thought of the aching emptiness of the days that lay ahead, but he knew he would be sustained by the one perpetual thought of her.[30]

Just when this separation took place is not clearly established. Probably, however, it was toward the latter part of 1831, when Dickens was growing discouraged over his prospects of ever becoming a newspaperman, and formed his extraordinary plan of achieving fame and winning Maria's hand by becoming an actor. There is no reference to her in the surviving correspondence from the early months of 1832, when he was on the *True Sun* and the *Mirror of Parliament*, and just starting to raise himself above the others in the Gallery. Doubtless, though, there were cunning arrangements, as there were later, by which letters could be interchanged without parental interference. Meanwhile Dickens was beginning to form an intimacy with young Henry Kolle, now a calico printer and a declared suitor for Anne Beadnell's hand, but as late as the middle of the year their acquaintance was so slight that Dickens, misled by its pronunciation, spelled his name "Kollie." [31] The letters to him make no mention of Maria Beadnell's name until some time later.

But the Maria who returned from abroad was strangely altered. Now there were coldnesses, quarrels, caprices, reproaches. And, though Charles still visited at Lombard Street, Mr. Beadnell was always about, and there never seemed to be the means of setting things straight. Charles was bewildered and sick and miserable. He tried to appeal to Maria by letters. One of the Beadnell servants named Sarah would come to meet him at Finsbury Place with a basket and a face of good-humored compassion, and carry his letter away and leave him desolate.[32] But presently something cut off this channel of communication too. Maria's father was more vigilant than ever; her unhappy lover was unable to be alone with her long enough to melt the mysterious barrier between them.

In his desperation he appealed to Kolle to place a letter in Maria's hands. He would feel some delicacy in doing so, he said, but that Kolle knew his situation and that he had no objection to Kolle's seeing every syllable of its contents.[33] Kolle took pity on him and delivered the note. Maria replied, asking Charles to send a response by Kolle again, when he came to practice his duet with Anne the next afternoon.[34] From then on Dickens was continually picking up or leaving notes at 14 Addle Street, Aldermansbury, where Kolle resided. But Maria did not grow kinder and Dickens's burden of misery did not grow lighter. Working away in the *Mirror of Parliament* offices, making preparations for reporting the new session of the House, which would begin around the end of January, 1833, he ended the old year and started the new in an agony of uncertainty and foreboding.

His family had moved from Fitzroy Street to 18 Bentinck Street,[35] and his twenty-first birthday was celebrated there, a few days after it actually took place, on February 11th. He would get away from the Gallery by eight o'clock, he announced to Thomas Beard in asking him to come, by changing hours with somebody.[36] Fanny was there, of course, and Letitia, who was now sixteen, and possibly even the younger brothers Frederick and Alfred Lamert, though they were only twelve and ten respectively. Perhaps Augustus, who was still the baby of the family, being only five, and who was his eldest brother's special pet, was allowed to stay up just long enough to see Dickens arrive home from Westminster.

The party was a beautiful one, with music and quadrilles,[37] and, if an account of it in *The Uncommercial Traveller* may be relied on as autobiographical, hired waiters to dispense the refreshments. (This sounds as if John Dickens took a grandiose hand in making the arrangements.) Late in the festivities, Dickens says, "in the crumby part of the night, when wine glasses were to be found in unexpected spots," he managed to get his beloved alone behind a door and speak to her. She called him "a boy," and went away soon afterward. With that "short and dreadful word" scorching his brain, he sought oblivion and found a dreadful headache.[38] The light of the next day's noon found him waking with a heavy head, and all his wretchedness bitterer than ever in his heart. So passed away the happy occasion of his coming of age.

He had no idea of how the early brightness had faded from the air. Painfully, patiently, humbly, he tried to elicit some kind of explanation from Maria. But whatever Maria said or wouldn't say made it no clearer to him. In his low-spirited bewilderment, he appealed to her sister Anne to tell him what was wrong. But all she could find to reply was "My dear Charles, I really cannot understand Maria, or venture to take the responsibility of saying what the state of her affections is," and her tender heart added some quotation about Patience and Time.[39]

His confusion was redoubled by the behavior of Marianne Leigh, who revealed so thorough an acquaintance with facts he thought known only to Maria and himself that he was forced to believe her statement that she had learned them from Maria. But she added many other things, so calculated to excite something even more than ordinary angry feelings, that he hardly knew whether to think that she had invented them or that Maria, for reasons he could not fathom, had given her an account of their relations entirely different from his knowledge of them.[40] Whatever the truth, he distrusted Marianne Leigh's professions of sympathy and doubted her reports of Maria's feelings. He had no desire to tell *her* his side of their discord. He didn't understand why she tried to inject herself into his confidence. He only knew that he liked her less than ever, and wished that she would let him alone.[41] So he stumbled on from day to day in an increasing state of complex misery and fruitless devotion.

Marianne Leigh's conduct, in fact, cannot be explained with any certainty. She may have been only a malicious mischief-maker, delighting in what misunderstandings she could bring about. She may have been secretly in love with Dickens herself, and hopeful of sliding into Maria's place in his heart if she could once bring about their separation. She may have been helping Maria terminate a flirtation of which she was tired, a romantic little drama of which she had had enough— helping get rid of an overserious lover whose importunities were growing troublesome. Possibly what followed was a conspiracy between the two girls, in which he was to be badgered into a state of bewilderment; confused by accusations of faithlessness, or betrayals of confidence, or want of faith and proper loyalty, or saying things about his mistress that were untrue, or any mingling of all these; and finally jilted upon plausible but fictitious grounds that would leave Maria looking as if she had been justified. Whatever Marianne's role—and Dickens knew at last that she had been telling falsehoods, though whether with Maria's knowledge and connivance he did not know—she threw herself at him, was forever in his path, and made herself the main instrument in deepening the breach between her friend and Dickens.

By the middle of March, the strain upon his emotions was more than he could bear. He decided, although only after a painful struggle, that it would be better to separate from Maria altogether than to go on as they had been doing. On the 18th, he wrote to tell her so. "Our meetings of late," he said, "have been little more than so many displays of heartless indifference on the one hand; while on the other they have never failed to prove a fertile source of wretchedness and misery"; he can see that his pursuit has long been worse than hopeless, and to persist in it can only expose him to ridicule. He therefore returns the little present she made him some time since, and the other mementos of their past correspondence. He would not want to hurt her feelings by anything he said, but he would feel it, he wrote, "mean and contemptible of me to keep by me one gift of yours or to preserve one single line or word of remembrance or affection from you. I therefore return them, and I can only wish that I could as easily forget that I ever received them." [42] The bundle of letters he tied up with a ribbon of the same blue as the blue gloves.[43]

His wounded pride could not resist a few words to show that he knew he had been ill treated and knew that he had done nothing to deserve it. He had ever "acted fairly, intelligibly, and honourably, under kindness and encouragement one day and a total change of conduct the next." "I have never held out encouragement which I knew I never meant; I have never indirectly sanctioned hopes which I knew well I did not intend to fulfill. I have never made a mock confidante to whom to entrust a garbled story for my own purposes . . ." (This last sentence implying his suspicions about Marianne Leigh.) In conclusion, he had done nothing and said nothing, he believed, that would be likely to hurt her. He hoped that she, his first and last love, would be happy and have every blessing the world can afford.[44]

He tried to prevent himself from brooding, during the hours he was not busied in the Gallery or in Abingdon Street, by throwing himself vigorously into the preparation of some amateur theatricals that were to be presented in Bentinck Street on April 27th by members of his family and some friends. It was not the last time he was to deal with unhappiness by violent activity. The main piece was *Clari, the Maid of Milan*, remembered today chiefly for containing the song "Home, Sweet Home," by John Howard Payne. On the same bill were "the favourite Interlude of *The Married Bachelor*," and, as a finale, the farce of *Amateurs and Actors*.[45] Dickens made himself producer, director, and stage manager, designed scenery, worried with the stage carpenter about how to produce moonlight, played an accordion in the band, wrote the prologue to the performance, rehearsed the actors—everything.[46] All the Beadnells were to be present; there was no avowed sign that her parents knew how things were with him and Maria; they—and she!—would see what he could do!

Maria had returned his letter to him—not without keeping a copy —and sent with it a reply that raised his hopes into a renewed blaze. He wrote her another note breathing unaltered devotion. She sent it back by hand, wrapped only in a small piece of loose paper.[47] Disillusion was closing in on him, but his longing struggled hard. Deep within, he knew that he should adhere to his resolution of going his way and seeing her no more. By now, for that matter, he hardly ever caught more than the most occasional and infrequent glimpses of her. Many a night, while they were thus falling apart from each other, he came from the House of Commons at two or three o'clock, walked almost three miles to an odd little court back of the Mansion House, and came out by the corner of Lombard Street, only to wander past the place where she slept.[48] In spite of all, though, he could not yet quite nerve himself to face the end.

* * * * *

Henry Kolle, who was now engaged to Anne Beadnell, was playing a Nobleman in two scenes of *Clari*. Early in April, Dickens dropped him a note asking that he and Henry Bramwell be punctual at the next rehearsal, on Monday, and reporting that the scenery was progressing rapidly, the machinery excellent, the decorations good—and expensive —and everything in excellent train.[49] In the middle of the month he was able to say that the scenery was being rapidly completed, the machinery finished, "the curtain hemmed, the orchestra complete, and the manager grimy." [50]

Kolle had announced that he would be married to Anne on May 22nd. Dickens offered his "heartfelt congratulations . . . because you are, or at all events will be, what I never can, happy and contented." "Now turning from feeling and making oneself miserable," he added, could Kolle spare one evening to rehearse his part: Thursday was to be a rehearsal of *Clari* with the band, Friday week the dress rehearsal, and the performance on Saturday, April 27th.[51] But Kolle, immersed in the excitement of his approaching wedding, missed his rehearsal, and the nervous manager took it as a slight. He and his family knew, he wrote, "that a little flow of prosperity is an excellent cooler of former friendships, and that when other and more pleasant engagements can be formed, visits, if not visits of convenience, become irksome." As Saturday was fast approaching, however, he would like to know if Kolle intended to retain the part; if not he must entrust it to other hands.[52]

Kolle must have understood the sore heart that prompted Dickens's spleen and the little rift was mended. The evening came. Among the other players were Henry Austin and Thomas Mitton, John Dickens, Fanny and Letitia, and their uncle Edward Barrow. Dickens played Rolamo, and three other roles, and the accordion as well. Maria was in the audience, but there was none of the sweetness of having her peep backstage, eager and anxious for his success. She remained in the audience, cold and remote. And when the performance was over, and they went upstairs, Marianne Leigh threw herself in his way all the rest of the evening.[53]

Sixteen days later Maria saw Dickens, and evidently explained her coldness by reproaching him with having discussed their relations with Marianne Leigh and betrayed intimate and personal details to her. Dickens vehemently denied it at once; rushing home, he learned from his sister Fanny that Marianne had for days and even weeks been claiming that he had made her his confidante. He was bitterly indignant that Fanny had not told him before.[54] If Fanny owed a duty to Maria, she owed a greater one to him; all the more, he wrote Maria, "*because she knew* what Marianne Leigh had said of *you*; she heard from you what she had said of *me* . . . If I were to live a hundred years I would never forgive it." [55]

But he was even more distressed that Maria could believe him so indelicate and dishonorable. As if, remembering how they once had been, and "the happy hopes the loss of which have made me the miserable reckless wretch I am," he could ever "breathe the slightest hint to any creature living of one single circumstance that ever passed between us"—and least of all to Marianne Leigh! He believed he now understood quite clearly the deceitful part she had played: telling him falsehoods about Maria's feelings, and telling Maria falsehoods about him. Quite unasked, Marianne had volunteered the information, he now wrote Maria, "that *you* had made her a confidante *of all that had ever passed between us without reserve.*" Though she had detailed facts that made him believe this, he had never, by word or deed, made a confidante of her.[56]

His first impulse had been to go at once to Clapton and tax her with her "duplicity and disgusting falsehood"; his next, to prevent any further misrepresentation by her, to do it in writing. But then it struck him that Miss Leigh's malice might, since he had learned of her conduct through Maria, be directed against her. Consequently he sought out Kolle and asked him to take a letter to Maria, telling what he planned to do and asking her consent to his sending a note he had already written.[57] He would not detain Maria or intrude upon her attention by any more observations. "I fear I could say little calculated to interest or please you. I have no hopes to express, no wishes to communicate." "I have been so long used to inward wretchedness and real, real misery that it matters little, very little to me what others may think of or what becomes of me."[58]

Maria's reply interpreted his indignation at the thought that *he* could have confided in Marianne Leigh as a criticism of *her* having done so. It also pettishly implied that he had been seen so often immersed in such intimate conversation with Marianne that he could hardly have the aversion for her that he stated. Dickens admitted that he had been hurt by the fact that, knowing his aversion to Marianne, Maria should have confided in *her*, of all people. He granted that Marianne had thrown herself in his way of late, but denied that he had had, then or ever, any pleasure in speaking to her. "Kind words and winning looks" from her—he quoted Maria's phrases—he had never sought or been moved by. "*Unkind* words and cold looks" from Maria he had suffered again and again, as her will altered and her pleasure changed. "I have borne more from you than I do believe any living creature breathing ever bore from a woman before." The very last time he had seen Maria, he had heard, even among her own friends, "remarks on your own conduct and pity—pity, Good God! for my situation."

Maria had indicated that she would like to see any note he proposed sending to Marianne. He replied that he would send her by Kolle a copy of the note that he would send if he sent any. On this point he was not asking if Maria approved, only if she had any reason to object.[59] The following day, May 17th, he enclosed the proposed letter to Marianne Leigh in a stiff, hurt little note to Maria, saying that he would make any alterations she proposed and begging her to return the enclosure to him. He had begun without salutation; at the close he wrote: "I find I have proceeded to the end of my note without even inserting your name. May I ask you to excuse the omission and to believe that I would gladly have addressed you in a very, very different way?" [60]

The letter to Marianne Leigh, bearing the same date, began by returning her album, "which I regret to say want of a moment's time has quite prevented my writing in." It went on to her claim that he had made a confidante of her, which, if it had had "the slightest foundation in truth," would have stamped him "as a dishonourable babbler." "Passing over any remark which may have been artfully elicited" from him "in an unguarded moment," he knew he had made a confidante of no one. Her interposition, however well intentioned, had been "productive of as much mischief as it had been uncalled for . . . I would much rather mismanage my own affairs than have them ably conducted by the officious intereference of anyone." In conclusion, he said, it was "because I am really and sincerely desirous of sparing you the meanness and humiliation of acting in the petty character of an unauthorized go-between that I have been induced to write this note." [61]

The evening of the very day these two letters were written, Kolle's brother gave a farewell bachelor dinner for him. Innumerable bottles of hock were opened. It was a Friday night; Dickens would have no Parliamentary duties again till the following week. There had been no further sign from Maria. As Dickens looked across the board at Kolle and reflected that he was so soon to marry Maria's sister, it is easy to imagine what thoughts and emotions filled him at the memory of those months of wasted tenderness and undeserved humiliation. The end of the evening for him was such that he was still recovering two days later and wrote to Kolle, "Yesterday I felt like a maniac, today my interior resembles a lime basket." [62]

But he had made a final resolution. He was no longer even received in Lombard Street. With Kolle's marriage and Anne's departure from her parents' home, he would lose his only means of communication with Maria. He would make one last effort to restore the old tenderness and trust. He begged Kolle to deliver an appeal which he now penned: "Sans Pride, Sans Reserve, Sans everything but an evident wish to be reconciled." [63]

In his letter to Maria he soberly and earnestly pleaded his hope that they might try again. "I will allow no feeling of pride, no haughty dislike to making a reconciliation to prevent my expressing it without reserve. I will advert to nothing that has passed, I will not again seek to excuse any part I have acted or to justify it by any course you have ever pursued; I will revert to nothing that has ever passed between us —I will only openly and at once say that there is nothing I have more at heart, nothing I more sincerely and earnestly desire, than to be reconciled to you. . . . I have no guide by which to ascertain your present feelings and I have, God knows, no means of influencing them in my favour. I have never loved and I can never love any human creature breathing but yourself. We have had many differences, and we have lately been entirely separated. Absence, however, has not altered my feelings in the slightest degree, and the Love I now tender you is as pure and as lasting as at any period of our former correspondence. I have now done all I can to remove our most unfortunate and to me most unhappy misunderstanding. The matter now of course rests solely with you . . . I could entreat a favourable consideration on my own behalf but I purposely abstain from doing so because it would be only a repetition of an oft told tale and because I am sure nothing I could say would have the effect of influencing your decision in any degree whatever. . . . Let me entreat you to consider your determination well whatever it be and let me implore you to communicate it to me as early as possible." [64]

When Maria's answer came, it was cold and reproachful. His clear statement of a refusal to engage in any more accusations or excusings or justifyings, and his fair suggestion of wiping the slate clean, she had utterly ignored. Dickens realized that all his serious endeavor to place their relationship upon a stable foundation of understanding and responsiblity had brought him back to exactly where he was before. To go on would mean no more than a renewal of the old round of neglect and fleeting favor, of self-abasement for him and caprice from her. Maria would never be any different. Appeals were entirely useless. He understood it at last, and went his way.[65]

*   *   *   *   *

Years later they were to meet again, when she would no longer be the exacting and tyrannous little beauty who had tormented a loving boy. Dickens, too, would be altered out of all recognition from the hurt and puzzled and still adoring youngster who finally mustered courage to forego a hopeless pursuit instead of waiting for her to dismiss him when she had wearied of playing with his heart. But the imprint of his youthful sufferings would be neither forgotten nor eradicated, and their second encounter was to have for him consequences no less fateful than their earlier relationship.

What these four years of loving Maria Beadnell had done for Dickens and done to him, he himself in the course of time came partly to understand. All the imagination, romance, passion, and aspiration of his nature she had brought into flower and she would never be separated from. Not, of course, that he would never have had these qualities save for her, but she vitally influenced the form they assumed. His intense capacity for suffering, and for feeling with suffering— which the suppressed but unforgotten misery of the Marshalsea and the blacking warehouse had ground into his being—his misery over her made still more sharply a part of him. It revived and re-emphasized those shapes of suffering that he remembered so well: the suffering of helplessness and of undeserved humiliation.

The wounds his defeat left him to heal as best he could deepened two ways of sublimating his self-pity until they formed a characteristic psychological pattern. A grief or an annoyance, he had found, could be exorcised by being magnified to such grotesque proportions that it exploded into the comic and was lost in laughter. And, alternatively, the private emotion could be transcended by being used as a means of understanding and sympathizing with other living creatures, with whose joys and griefs one merged one's own. Both these forms of sublimation Dickens displays again and again, both in his personal life and in his artistic career.

His love and his unhappiness hardened Dickens's determination to cut through all material obstacles. He well knew how much his shabby background and his mediocre prospects had to do with his ineligibility as a suitor—for though he fought against admitting the cogency of all these objections to him, he saw and recognized their existence as clearly as the Beadnells did. Neither they nor his hard-hearted little mistress, perhaps, would have been so obdurate if his financial position had been different. In desperate earnest and animated by the one absorbing hope, the vision of desire, he had set himself to fight his way out of poverty and obscurity.[66] The loss of that hope came just as his efforts were beginning to be rewarded with recognition. The experience focused into burning clarity his realization of the importance of financial status and his impassioned resolve never again to be a victim of indigence. He always remained warm-heartedly generous to others, and with prosperity he became lavish in expenditure, but in business he was to grow relentlessly set on obtaining the last fraction of what he regarded as his due. And no less in certain other directions, when his will was pitted against the will of others, he was to become adamantine in the determination that not he but they must always give way.

Linked with this overbearing and domineering tendency, and rooted in the same hidden causes, was an excessive vulnerability to psychological pain. In society it rendered him, on occasion, uneasy, shrinking, and oversensitive; and, on others, truculently assertive of his independence.[67] In his writing it accounts for the difficulty he exhibits until almost the close of his career in delineating love between men and women as anything other than an idealized unreality, a sentimental tenderness, or a sort of comic pathos. He can think of David Copperfield adoring an etherealized child-bride or poor Mr. Toots painfully and hilariously infatuated with Florence Dombey: it took him a lifetime to be able to deal with a Bradley Headstone so desperate in his thwarted passion for Lizzie Hexam that he must beat his hand bloody against a cemetery wall while beads of agony stand out on his brow. But it would be a shallow reading of human character that failed to see Bradley Headstone latent in the youthful Charles Dickens so caught and ground between his hurt pride and his anguished passion.

All the rest of his emotional life he lay under the shadow of this lost love, which in its darkest places merges with the shadow cast by the spiked wall of the Marshalsea and the imprisoning shades of the blacking warehouse. He tried to write it down when he attempted his autobiography, but that part of his story he could not bear to show even to his closest friend, could not bear even to have anyone read after he was dead; he lost courage and burned it.[68] The most eager craving for affection and sympathy he therefore almost habitually armored in a stern isolation and reserve that were no less real for all the bright mask of exuberance he presented to the world. Able to fling himself buoyantly into friendly intercourse with all kinds of men, and sympathize with their gaiety and grief, he locked his own most intimate griefs in his heart, revealing them only to a few, and to those few only in part. The wasted tenderness of his youthful love for Maria Beadnell, he said years afterward, "made so deep an impression on me that I refer to it a habit of suppression which now belongs to me, which I know is no part of my original nature, but which makes me chary of showing my affections, even to my children, except when they are very young." [69]

If there were a Fate that had deliberately aimed at forming the young man who now stood upon the threshold of his career, it could hardly have gone about its task more effectively than circumstances had done. Follow the sensitive, imaginative child living in a bright-colored world of happiness; the drop into an abyss of an absolute despair; the rescue just in time to spare his nature from being coarsened or his courage from being broken, and the healing reprieve after that agonizing experience of cosmic injustice. But had there been only one such experience, it might have come in the course of time to seem an accident, and the lines drawn by the Marshalsea and Warren's Blacking might have been gradually obliterated. The exaltation, the wretched happiness, the ultimate and inexorable misery of his love for Maria Beadnell bit in those lines with so bitter an acid that they could never again be blurred, not even by the lifetime of triumph now beginning to dawn.

PART TWO

Climb to Fame

1833–1837

CHAPTER ONE

The Career Takes Shape

DICKENS did not allow his heartache to impair the efficiency with which he did his work for the *Mirror of Parliament*. As a child he had known with precocious intuition that he should be slighted unless he were as quick and dexterous as the others, and pride had made him hide his tears and labor at the hated wrapping of the blacking bottles. The intervening years had only deepened that pride to indomitable fierceness. From the inconvenient back row of the Stranger's Gallery, with the glare of chandeliers in the misty atmosphere blurring the view of the benches, and the members of the House sprawling about, coughing, oh-ing, groaning, Parliament was a spectacle of noise and confusion worse, Dickens said, than Smithfield on market day or a cockpit in all its glory.[1] But there he sat at his task day after day and night after night, his pencil indefatigably jotting down its curves and dots and skyrockets and flies' legs. No grief or hopelessness could shake the performance of his duties.

No sooner had the Irish coercion bill become law than Edward Stanley had at once resigned his post as Irish Secretary and entered the Colonial Office to frame the Bill for the Abolition of Slavery in the Colonies. Dickens recorded the debates on this measure, saw young Mr. Gladstone leap up to deny in an indignant maiden speech that the administrator of his family estates in Demerara was a "murderer of slaves," heard Bulwer's address about keeping faith with the Negro and O'Connell's valedictory "There is nothing to add; the House must divide!" as he tore up the notes for his own speech. Dickens was in the Gallery during Macaulay's notable contributions to the passing of the Act that abolished the commercial monopoly of the East India Company and remade that body into a corporation charged solely with the ruling of Hindustan. It is probable that in the previous year he witnessed the defeat of Sadler's Ten Hours Bill and the rejection of Lord Ashley's Bill to limit the working hours of adults; during 1833 he certainly heard the legislators debating the recommendations of the Royal Commissions on laboring conditions in the factories and on the operations of the Poor Law.[2] Out of these debates emerged Lord Althorp's Factory Act of 1834, the first effective act of factory regulation, and the new Poor Law, which Dickens was to attack so violently in *Oliver Twist*.[3]

It would be misleading to say that Dickens was indifferent to the results of these legislative proceedings, but he grew steadily more skeptical of their being attended by any real benefits to the nation as a whole. Though he certainly did not desire to see the Conservatives returned to power, he could not help noting that in the Whig House where they were a negligible minority there was a determined effort to defeat or emasculate the very measures for which he felt most sympathy: those designed to ameliorate the lives of the poor and their children. Whatever hopes he might have entertained that the Reform Bill would change the nature of Parliament evaporated before this demonstration that the privileges of landowners and industrialists still took precedence over the welfare of the people. The accomplishments of the reformed legislature, not inconsiderable in fact, to his imperious demands seemed paltry.

The truth was that he was impatient of the very way in which legislative bodies act. Nothing in his past experiences had given him any very high respect for the wisdom of his elders or any reverence for flagrant respectability. The dry fictions of the law as he had known them in solicitors' offices and its interminable tergiversations in Doctors' Commons had left him intolerant of meaningless verbal forms. The kinds of solid members of the community he had observed in both filled him with impatience for conventional viewpoints. He could be affectionately amused at his father's elaborate turns of phrase, but he had no filial affection for Parliament. There the endless, empty verbosity and the snail's pace it enforced, the contrast between lofty professions on the floor and jobbery behind closed doors, the mutilation inflicted on the most desirable measures before they could be enacted, all served only to antagonize and disgust him. Some few members excepted, such as Lord John Russell, whom he warmly esteemed, Parliament seemed to him merely a device for obstructing the passage of proper legislation. Dickens's sentiments on the subject are accurately echoed by David Copperfield:

"Night after night I record predictions that never come to pass, professions that are never fulfilled, explanations that are only meant to mystify. I wallow in words. Britannia, that unfortunate female, is always before me, like a trussed fowl; skewered through and through with office-pens, and bound hand and foot with red tape. I am sufficiently behind the scenes to know the worth of political life. I am quite an Infidel about it, and shall never be converted." [4]

But as he sat in the dark rear row of the Strangers' Gallery or pushed his way through its narrow two-foot door at the end of a session, he kept these thoughts to himself. He continued to perform his duties with assiduity and dispatch. After the unsatisfactory Cecil Street lodgings where they had put water in the hashes, he had for a time taken a room on the top floor at 15 Buckingham Street, in order not to be too far from Abingdon Street and the Palace Yard on late nights, but during most of his time on the *Mirror of Parliament* he was still living with his family on Bentinck Street.[5]

Young Henry Austin and Thomas Beard, from the Gallery, were often there, as well as Thomas Mitton, who had by now given up his clerkship and was starting out as a solicitor himself. Fanny Dickens had re-entered the Academy of Music in 1832 for further study,[6] and the next year there entered a young composer named John Hullah who became a friend to both Fanny and Charles.[7] There were more amateur theatricals in the Dickens home, for which Dickens wrote a burlesque extravaganza entitled *O'Thello*, with lyrics fitted to well-known airs and with John Dickens in a role suggestively named "The Great Unpaid." [8] Dickens continued to be intimate with Henry Kolle and his wife, the gentle-hearted Anne, at whose wedding he had served as best man, and to go out to see them in their home at Newington.[9]

The *Mirror of Parliament* could pay its staff well during Parliamentary sessions, but at other times Dickens still had to fall back upon his old work at Doctors' Commons or other occasional employment as a stenographer for Public Boards or Commissions.[10] John Henry Barrow, by this time strongly impressed with his nephew's abilities, made efforts to get him a post on one of the dailies. There were no vacancies on the staff of the *Times*, with which Barrow was connected. Dickens himself wanted to get on the *Morning Chronicle,* a strongly liberal paper with whose views he sympathized. A former *Times* man, John Payne Collier, whom Barrow had known for five or six years, had become subeditor in charge of Parliamentary reporting for that paper. Barrow praised Dickens to Collier, and asked him to give the young man a letter of recommendation.[11]

Collier, however, was cautious. The *Chronicle* was on the verge of being taken over by new proprietors, of whom the moving force was John Easthope, a stockholder who had been in Parliament for St. Albans and for Banbury.[12] Easthope was an irascible man, who became known to his subordinates as "Blasthope"; Collier had no desire to risk his neck for an unknown youth. Where was the young man educated? What were his qualifications? The first inquiry Barrow rather evaded, saying only that Dickens was the son of a former clerk in the naval department at Portsmouth; to the second he replied enthusiastically that his nephew was extremely clever, wrote shorthand well, and had worked for the *True Sun.* How old was he, Collier demanded, and where had he been employed before being on the *True Sun?* Once again Barrow was somewhat vague: his father's financial difficulties had driven him to earn a living in any way he could; "at one time he had assisted Warren, the blacking-man, in the conduct of his extensive business," and had written advertising jingles for him. He jocosely implied that his nephew was responsible for the rhyme used in Warren's advertisement of a dove mistaking its own reflection in a polished boot for its mate:

> "*I pitied the dove, for my bosom was tender;*
> *I pitied the sigh that she gave to the wind;*
> *But I ne'er shall forget the superlative splendour*
> *Of Warren's Jet Blacking, the pride of mankind.*" [13]

Collier was amused by the verse, but felt he should meet its author before committing himself to a recommendation. Barrow suggested that he come out to Norwood for dinner that Saturday and make the acquaintance of the young man. Accordingly, on July 27, 1833, Collier dined with Barrow, the latter's uncle Culliford, Dickens, and a few others. He was surprised by a youthfulness so extreme as to show no trace of beard or whisker. But it was not long before he had decided that Barrow had by no means exaggerated his smooth-cheeked neph-

ew's cleverness. The younster was good company, too, and the evening
was convivial. After considerable urging, Dickens sang a couple of
comic songs, one of them of his own invention, about a milkmaid with
enticing eyes named "Sweet Betsey Ogle," and her amorous adventures
with a barber. "We were all very merry," Collier wrote in his Diary,
"if not very wise." At the end he hesitated no longer about writing
the recommendation.[14] But it proved ineffective; Dickens received
no offer of a post on the *Morning Chronicle.*

He had begun to write small fictional sketches based on types of
London life he had observed and people with whom he had come in
contact. In one of these he used Marianne Leigh's loud and red-faced
father, the corn chandler of Clapton.[15] Disguised under the name of
Octavius Budden of Poplar Walk, he is shown crudely trying to curry
favor with a cousin in Somerset House who has £10,000 in the funds.
The cousin, Mr. Augustus Minns, is a prim and middle-aged bachelor
with a horror of dogs and children, upon whom Mr. Budden's coarse
insensibility, large white dog, and revolting small son produce the
reverse of the impression aimed at. It is not a superlatively brilliant
story, but there are some amusing scenes of Mr. Minns agonizing
while the dog devours a bit of toast butter-side-down on his carpet and
undergoing an embarrassing meal at Budden's dinner table.[16]

"With fear and trembling" one twilight evening toward winter
Dickens stealthily dropped this sketch "into a dark letter-box in a dark
office up a dark court in Fleet Street." [17] This was the office of the
Monthly Magazine, subtitled "The British Register of Literature, Sci-
ences, and Belles Lettres." It was an old established periodical with
a circulation of about six hundred, published from Johnson's Court
by a bookseller named Andrew Robertson who had his shop at 84
Fetter Lane.[18] Just that October it had been sold by Charles Tilt, its
former owner, to a Captain Holland who had fought with Bolivar in
South America and who was now editing the magazine to voice his
own ardent liberalism.[19] Holland had no money to pay contributors,
but he gave fledgling authors a chance to appear in print. Dickens
waited in trepidation to see what would happen to the first literary
effort with which he had courted publication.

On a December evening, just before closing time, he stepped into
a bookshop on the Strand and asked for the new number of the
Monthly Magazine. Would his piece be there? A little birdlike shop-

man gave him a copy from the counter; Dickens paid his two and six, and turned aside to glance hastily and nervously through the pages.[20] There it was!—"A Dinner at Poplar Walk"—"in all the glory of print." It had been accepted; he was an author! So agitated that he wished only to be alone to take in what had happened, he turned out of the crowded Strand and strode down the pavement of Whitehall to take refuge in Westminster Hall from the eyes of pedestrians. There for half an hour he paced the stone floor under the dark rafters and time-stained carvings, "my eyes so dimmed with pride and joy," he said, "that they could not bear the street, and were not fit to be seen." [21]

More exciting news was to follow. Captain Holland liked the story so well that he sent "a polite and flattering communication" to its author "requesting more papers." [22] Dickens made the proud announcement to Kolle and his wife that the little paper "you saw lying on my table," with its name "transmogrified from A Sunday out of Town to A Dinner at Poplar Walk," was to be "the first of a series" in the *Monthly Magazine*. "I am so dreadfully nervous," he added, "that my hand shakes to such an extent as to prevent my writing a word legibly." [23]

A week after its appearance, Dickens's story was pirated in the *London Weekly Magazine*, a publication which until the preceding March had been named *The Thief*, but which in changing its name had not changed its nature. Not without a certain pleased vanity, Dickens passed this news also on to the Kolles, and wrote them he was "in treaty" with the *Monthly* and planning his next paper, "Private Theatricals." He suggested, with his love to Anne, that when their expected child was born he would like to be god-father if it "could afford to have one poor god-father." Between these two parts of his letter he apologized for having been so busy at his uncle's for a week past that he had been unable to get out to see them at Newington. Nor could he respond to their invitation even now, for "pleasure in the shape of a very nice pair of black eyes call me to Norwood." [24] Possibly the black eyes belonged to Georgina Ross, the young sister-in-law of his uncle Edward Barrow; but there can be no doubt whose eyes Dickens hoped would see these records of his doings.[25]

Meanwhile the contributions to the *Monthly* continued apace. In January, 1833, appeared "Mrs. Joseph Porter Over the Way," a sketch based on Mrs. Leigh's malicious tongue and the amateur performance of *Clari*.²⁶ Three more followed in rapid succession: "Horatio Sparkins" in February; "The Bloomsbury Christening" in April; the two parts of a longer story called "The Boarding House" in May and August. The earlier sketches had borne no author's name; with the August contribution came the first use of the signature "Boz." ²⁷ This had arisen out of Dickens's jesting nickname for his seven-year-old brother, Augustus, "whom in honour of the *Vicar of Wakefield* he had dubbed Moses." The child's nasal mispronunciation of Moses as "Boses" was facetiously adopted and shortened to "Bose," and had finally become "Boz" by the time Dickens borrowed it for his own pseudonym. "Boz was a very familiar household word to me, long before I was an author." ²⁸

* * * * *

In the same month that Boz was thus born, Dickens achieved his ambition of becoming a regular Parliamentary reporter on a daily newspaper. Though the *Morning Chronicle* had had no opening the year before, now, under new ownership, it was strengthening its staff to give more bellicose competition to the *Times* and to provide the Whigs with a vigorous daily organ. John Black, the editor, had recently taken on Eyre Evans Crowe, author of *A History of France*, as Paris correspondent, and George Hogarth as music and theatrical critic.²⁹ Joseph Parkes, the Parliamentary agent of the Whigs and a powerful figure behind the political scenes, was helping in the reorganization. Parkes engaged Thomas Beard as a reporter, and asked him to recommend a colleague. Beard had no hesitation in naming Dickens as "the fastest and most accurate man in the Gallery." ³⁰ He was engaged at the "Fleet Street minimum" (paid by all papers except the *Times*) of five guineas a week.³¹ This was less than he had been earning on the *Mirror of Parliament*, but it continued all year round instead of ceasing when Parliament was not in session.

Never since the shabbiness of his blacking-warehouse days had Dickens allowed himself to be other than neat and well turned out. But now he celebrated the prosperity of an assured annual income by blossoming out into something of a dandy. Payne Collier mentions meeting him in "a new hat and a very handsome blue cloak with velvet facings, the corner of which he threw over his shoulder *à l'Espagnol*." He was overflowing with vivacity and high spirits. "I overtook him," Collier says, "in the Adelphi, and we walked together through Hungerford

Market, where we followed a coal-heaver, who carried his little rosy but grimy child looking over his shoulder; and C. D. bought a half-penny worth of cherries, and . . . gave them one by one to the little fellow without the knowledge of the father." Popping the cherries into the little one's eager mouth, Dickens was quite as delighted as the child.[32]

Under John Black, the *Morning Chronicle* had had a long and honorable record of liberal journalism. A blunt, thickset farmerlike Scotsman, never seen on the street without a huge mastiff and a thick cudgel, a truculent fighter who had sent out a dozen challenges to duels, Black was also a scholar and booklover whose fifty thousand volumes in Greek, Latin, English, French, and Italian crammed even the halls and pantries of the apartment he occupied over the *Chronicle* offices at 322 Strand.[33] He was a philosophical radical, a close friend of James Mill, and a disciple of Bentham, but no slavish follower of any man. He could not be stampeded by popular excitement; he poured indignation on the Peterloo Massacre but was unable to regard the divorce proceedings against Queen Caroline in 1820 as the persecution of a saint and martyr. He could see faults on his own side and merits in his opponents. Doctrinaires fumed when Black demolished Cobbett's rhetoric and doubted his honesty, recognized virtue in Canning, and found even Wellington sometimes in the right.[34]

Black's influence during the decade preceding the Reform Bill had been no slight one. John Stuart Mill, who began writing for him around 1823, pays tribute to Black's importance for the advance of progressive opinion. Black, he said, was "the first journalist who carried criticism and the Spirit of Reform into the details of English institutions. Those who are not old enough to remember those times can hardly believe what the state of public discussion then was. People now and then attacked the constitution and the borough-mongers, but no one thought of censuring the law or the courts of justice; and to say a word against the unpaid magistrate was a sort of blasphemy. Black was the writer who carried the warfare into those subjects, and by doing so he broke the spell. Very early in his editorship he fought a great battle for the freedom of reporting preliminary investigations in the Police Courts. He carried his point out and the victory was permanent." [35] "He kept up an incessant fire . . . ," Mill summarized in his *Autobiography,* "exposing the absurdities and vices of the law and the courts of justice, paid and unpaid, until he forced some sense of them into people's minds." [36]

This was the editor under whom Dickens was to work. But the *Morning Chronicle* had been losing ground of late years because the owner, William Clement, had lacked capital to maintain an adequate staff and Black had been unable to do everything by himself. When it changed hands in 1834 it brought only £16,000, one-third of its price in 1821. The new owners were John Easthope; Simon McGillivray, a merchant influential in the Canada and the Hudson's Bay Companies; and James Duncan, the Paternoster Row publisher of the Old Testament in Hebrew.[37] Easthope, their leading spirit, was an irritable superior, but he was not afraid to spend money to get results. With his vigorous though often quarrelsome support, Black was able within a few years to bring the circulation up from one thousand to six thousand.[38] This placed it well ahead of every other London newspaper except the *Times*, although that paper still retained its commanding lead. (It should be remembered that the price of sevenpence that the high stamp duty forced upon newspapers placed them out of reach for nearly all except prosperous people; there were no papers with mass circulations until much later in the century.)

Dickens speedily found himself leading a life of varied and exciting movement. When the House was not in session he was sent all over the country to report political meetings. What was probably his maiden assignment was that of covering the reception for Earl Grey at Edinburgh in September, 1834, when that nobleman was given the freedom of the city. Dickens and Beard made the trip to Leith by sea. Dickens was in intense high spirits, and unspeakably delighted to notice a sandy-haired commercial traveler on board reading "The Bloomsbury Christening" in the April number of the *Monthly* with roars of laughter.[39] One can sympathize with Dickens's excited interest. What had tickled the traveler *that* time? Was it the proud father's discovery that the infant's restlessness all night was not fever but a pin stuck in the leg? Was it the omnibus full of wringing-wet passengers? Was it the description of Mrs. Kitterbell's light hair and white face as reminding one of a cold fillet of veal? [40]

In Yarmouth Roads they ran into boisterous weather, and Dickens's exhilaration was considerably damped by seasickness. In Edinburgh he quickly recovered his gusto and sent in to the *Chronicle* for September

17th an account of the preparations being made to dine one thousand five hundred guests in a special banquet pavilion on Calton Hill above the city.[41] The following day the paper had eleven closely printed columns covering the reception and cold collation at Dalkeith, the noble earl's acceptance of the freedom of the city at the Waterloo Hotel, with Princes Street one mass of brilliant banners and military bands, and the ceremonial dinner that took place that evening.[42] This story, describing the glittering chandeliers, the stone-gray walls ornamented with armorial bearings, the painted ceiling, and the crimson pillars, and giving the speeches in full, was probably the joint work of Dickens and Beard.

One passage, however, is indubitably pure Dickens. The guest of honor and the principal visitors, as usual, were late, and one gentleman, the account says, overcome by the "cold fowls, roast beef, lobster, and other tempting delicacies . . . appeared to think that the best thing he could possibly do, would be to eat his dinner, while there was anything to eat. He accordingly laid about him with right good-will, the example was contagious, and the clatter of knives and forks became general. Hereupon, several gentlemen, who were not hungry, cried out 'Shame!' and looked very indignant; and several gentlemen who were hungry cried 'Shame!' too, eating, nevertheless, all the while, as fast as they possibly could. In this dilemma, one of the stewards mounted a bench and feelingly represented to the delinquents the enormity of their conduct, imploring them for decency's sake, to defer the process of mastication until the arrival of Earl Grey. This address was loudly cheered, but totally unheeded; and this is, perhaps, one of the few instances on record of a dinner having been virtually concluded before it began." [43]

Irreverently frisky, this, in dealing with a solemn feast! How unbelievable it would have seemed to the flippant young reporter as he looked at Lord Grey and felt his familiar exasperation at the very shape of that noble lord's head, that seven years later fame would raise him to that same eminence as Edinburgh's guest of honor receiving the freedom of the city! Not that even so grandiose a vision would have changed his sentiments. About politics and politicians Dickens was simply unable to feel worshipful. At another public dinner, when the Earl of Lincoln floundered through a few halting words and resumed his seat in confusion, Dickens wrote: "Lord Lincoln broke down, and sat down." "There was a good deal of enquiry at the Clubs," Payne Collier recorded, "and at the Athenaeum in particular, who had ventured to write such a droll laconic account of Lord Lincoln's failure?" but Collier told no one that his youthful associate was the author.[44]

When the Houses of Parliament burned to the ground in October, Dickens sympathized with the popular feeling on their destruction. Thomas Carlyle gives an eyewitness account of the fire: "The crowd was quiet," he says, "rather pleased than otherwise; whewed and whistled when the breeze came, as if to encourage it. 'There's a flare-up for the House of Lords!' 'A judgment for the Poor Law Bill!' 'There go their *Hacts*!' [the unpopular Six Acts of 1819] Such exclamations seemed to be the prevailing ones: a man sorry I did not see anywhere." [45] To Dickens the origin of the fire symbolized the results of a social system cumbered by useless tradition. Accounts had formerly been kept on splints of notched elm called "tallies." Even when this primitive system was superseded in 1826, the worm-eaten sticks were still preserved for another eight years. When the revolutionary suggestion was made that they be disposed of, instead of letting the poor have them for firewood, they were stuffed into a stove in the House of Lords, where they set fire to the paneling and started a conflagration that destroyed the entire building. It demonstrated, Dickens liked to say later, how "all obstinate adherence to rubbish which the time has long outlived is certain to have in the soul of it more or less what is pernicious and destructive, and will one day set fire to something or other." [46]

*   *   *   *   *

Back in London after the Grey dinner, Dickens continued working busily. He had the first of four London *Street Sketches* in the *Morning Chronicle* on September 26th, and another contribution, "The Steam Excursion," in the October *Monthly*.[47] By this time George Hogarth and John Black were both in on the secret of the identity of Boz, and Black was repeatedly predicting that Dickens would go far.[48] The half dozen or so pieces he had already produced were attracting some attention. It was not usual for periodicals to comment on the articles published by other periodicals, but the *Weekly Dispatch*, which made a feature of reviewing the more popular magazines, singled out for praise no fewer than three of his pieces as they appeared in the *Monthly*.[49] The popular dramatists, too, began to pay him the compliment of stealing from him. In mid-October the *Chronicle* sent him to review a new farce by J. B. Buckstone at the Adelphi, which turned out to be derived from his own "Bloomsbury Christening," with numbers of his jokes stolen outright. Dickens noted the plagiarism good-naturedly enough in his review, but he wrote a letter to the editor of the *Monthly* protesting against "the kidnapping" of his offspring,[50] which that periodical published with the comment, "Our pages seem to be pigeons which every dramatist thinks he is at liberty to pluck." [51]

In the course of 1834, the fact that Dickens was Boz became an open secret in the Gallery and on the *Chronicle*. Visiting the paper's offices in the Strand, William Harrison Ainsworth noticed the young reporter's flashing face and was told his identity. Ainsworth immediately made his acquaintance and began giving the younger man a good deal of friendly attention. He was seven years Dickens's senior, his historical novel *Rookwood* had recently scored a sensational success, he was a spectacular figure in the literary world. Small, handsome, dressed to the height of dandyism and ornately jeweled, he glittered in the best-known intellectual salons, and whatever he wrote was sure of eager readers. Dickens was soon imitating his style of waistcoat, and Ainsworth was to introduce Dickens to his publisher, a young Manxman named John Macrone.[52]

Meanwhile, though Dickens now had an income of £275 a year, he was still shadowed by financial difficulties. John Dickens was either falling into old ways again or had never amended them. He was no longer on the *Mirror of Parliament*; John Henry Barrow and Thomas Culliford Barrow had lost all patience and disowned him. Though he had managed to find employment as a reporter on the *Morning Herald*,[53] whatever his earnings there may have been, he was unable to live within them. He was forever in debt to tradesmen, and was constantly borrowing and struggling through a sea of troubles. In a letter to Kolle at this time, Dickens refers to his father's ways as "the damnable shadow" cast over his life.[54] By November, 1834, his father's affairs had reached a state of crisis. A creditor named Burr refused to wait any longer. This time the son took charge. He stripped himself of all the cash he had on hand to stave off disaster, and appealed to Mitton for a loan of "what you can possibly spare till Saturday"; in another note he begged an additional four shillings.[55]

But of course John Dickens was found to have still other creditors.

He went out with his son Alfred in the endeavor to obtain some money, and when his efforts were unsuccessful simply failed to return home. In Bentinck Street the family were in great tribulation. Mrs. Dickens became ill. Dickens was not as much worried as the others; his father, he explained to Mitton, had developed the habit of disappearing when there were troubles of this kind.[56] Waking next morning, Dickens learned that his father "had just been arrested by Shaw and Maxwell, the quondam wine people," and was in Sloman's sponging house in Cursitor Street.[57]

Undaunted, Dickens set himself to straighten out the tangle. His loyalty would not allow him to stand by and see them all suffer from his father's imprudence. He was fond of his prodigal father, too, despite all his improvident ways with money; he couldn't let him go to prison again even if he richly deserved it. And so he took the first step in a course that was to saddle him throughout his life with helpless or idle dependents, and render him a prisoner of his own efficiency. As soon as his day's work was finished, he visited John Dickens in Cursitor Street, and found out the extent of his embarrassments. He provided for his father's temporary needs by asking Mitton to cash an order for £5 which had arrived too late to take it to the agent in the City to whom he usually went.[58] He arranged for his mother, the girls, and the younger children to take cheaper lodgings near Bentinck Street, and took his brother Frederick into chambers with him at Furnival's Inn.[59] He persuaded a bill broker to renew a note for two months for "the usual *moderate* bonus," got Edward Barrow (evidently more amenable than his brothers) to lend his signature to some document, and mortgaged his salary for two weeks to pay the removal expenses.[60]

By the middle of December Dickens had worked out a solution of the family problems. "We have much more cause for cheerfulness than despondency after all," he resiliently told his friend Beard.[61] The £35 he had had to pay in advance for his three empty back rooms at 13 Furnival's Inn, together with the other sums he had had to lay out, had evidently exhausted his resources, for he was obliged to borrow £5 for current expenses from Beard.[62] He had "no *dishes*, no curtains, and no french polish" in his rooms as yet, and therefore deferred a "projected flare" till a few days later, but he faced the end of the year in good spirits.[63]

During these first few days in his new residence Dickens received an unexpected visit from Ainsworth's publisher Macrone, who brought with him an American journalist, Nathaniel Parker Willis. They drove from St. James's Square to Holborn and alighted before the pale brick court of Furnival's Inn, with its cornice and Ionic stucco pilasters. Willis followed Macrone up the three flights of stairs "into an uncarpeted and bleak-looking room, with a deal table, two or three chairs and a few books, a small boy" who was Dickens's brother Frederick, "and Mr. Dickens for the contents." Misled by the narrow stairs and the bare room, Willis thought the place a shabby tenement and Dickens an impecunious journalist.[64] In reality Furnival's Inn was inhabited largely by solicitors with comfortable incomes. The rent of £35 a year that Dickens paid was not small, and he himself would have been in no difficulties but for his father's debts.

Dickens, while receiving his guests, changed a ragged officecoat "for a shabby blue." Possibly embarrassed himself, or possibly trying to relieve their embarrassment at finding him so ill prepared to entertain callers, he treated them with an eagerness of courtesy that Willis again misinterpreted as being "overwhelmed by the honor" of a visit from Macrone. As he sat on a rickety chair, Willis thought, "My good fellow, if you were in America with that fine face and your ready quill, you would have no need to be condescended to by a publisher." [65] He little realized how far Dickens was from having the slightest tendency to let himself be patronized by anybody.

* * * * *

Early in January Dickens reported the elections at Ipswich and Sudbury, in Suffolk.[66] No sooner had he returned to London than he was ordered to Essex to cover further elections there.[67] At Chelmsford the elections had not begun, so he went on to Colchester, returned to Chelmsford the following morning, and then, being unable to get a saddle horse, drove a gig the twenty-four miles to Braintree. "I wish to God you could have seen me," he reported to Beard, "tooling in and out of the banners, drums, conservative emblems, horsemen, and go-carts with which every little green was filled . . . Every time the horse heard a drum he bounced into the hedge on the left side of the road; and every time I got him out of that, he bounded into the hedge on the right side. When he *did* go, however, he went along admirably." [68]

On January 31, 1835, the proprietors of the *Morning Chronicle* inaugurated an evening paper under the name of the *Evening Chronicle*. George Hogarth, their music critic, was made editor of this new venture, and he asked Dickens to write for its first number a sketch similar to the four *Street Sketches* that had appeared between September and November. Dickens at once agreed. Then it occurred to him to suggest that he might do a series of such articles. If he did, would they think he "had any claim to *some* additional remuneration (of course, of no great amount) for doing so?" [69] The proposal was approved, and his salary was increased from five to seven guineas a week. Not yet quite twenty-three, he was already earning more than his father had ever received in the Navy Pay Office.[70]

George Hogarth, the editor of the new paper, had been a Writer to the Signet in Edinburgh, one of a privileged class of legal practitioners before the Court of Session. He had been a friend of Sir Walter Scott and one of the trusted advisers whom he consulted after his ruin in the financial crash of 1826. Hogarth's sister had married James Ballantyne, the elder of the two brothers running the printing business in which Scott was a silent partner. Hogarth himself married one of the daughters of George Thomson, "the friend of Burns." The connection had probably come about through Hogarth's interest in music, for his father-in-law was the editor of six volumes of folk airs with lyrics drawn from Burns, Scott, and Byron, and with accompaniments he persuaded Beethoven and Haydn to compose for some of them, as well as many by Scottish composers. In 1832 Hogarth left Edinburgh to become editor of the *Halifax Guardian*, and gave up that post to join the staff of the *Morning Chronicle* less than three months before Dickens was taken on.[71]

The older man—Hogarth was already fifty—rapidly developed a friendly interest in his young colleague and invited him to his home off the Fulham Road, where Dickens became a friend of the family. The eldest daughter, Catherine, who was nineteen at this time, was a pretty girl with a rosy complexion, heavy-lidded blue eyes, and a slightly retroussé nose; among her sisters the next in age was a sweet, grave-looking child named Mary, who was only fourteen, just a little older than Dickens's brother Frederick. In the course of a few months Dickens was passing many hours in Chelsea, and began giving lessons in shorthand to Robert, Hogarth's eldest son.[72]

During the next seven months Hogarth printed twenty of Dickens's sketches in the *Evening Chronicle* at irregular intervals.[73] They ranged from word pictures of street scenes, pawnshops, glaring gin palaces, Astley's Circus, and the poor amusing themselves at Greenwich Fair, to little vignettes of character or miniature narratives based on people or events he remembered from the Ordnance Terrace days in Chatham. Now that he had a remunerative outlet for his work he notified the *Monthly Magazine* that he would write no more unpaid stories, but Captain Holland was as short of cash as ever, and therefore Dickens's contributions to that periodical ended with the publication in January and February of "A Passage in the Life of Mr. Watkins Tottle." [74]

The new vitality of the *Morning Chronicle* was sharpening the professional antagonism between that paper and the *Times*. Through a new system of "extraordinary expenses" the *Times* had managed at a cost of £290 to print the speeches at the Edinburgh banquet for Lord Grey the very next morning, and jeered at the *Chronicle*, whose report appeared a day later, for labeling it "By Express." [75] When Lord John Russell offered himself for re-election in South Devon, after accepting the office of Home Secretary in Lord Melbourne's ministry, Dickens and Beard therefore made careful preparations to beat the *Times*. They set out for Exeter in a pelting rain that never stopped, and on May 1st in the midst of a downpour in the castle yard Dickens recorded Lord John's speech while two good-natured colleagues "held a pocket-handkerchief over my note-book," he said, "after the manner of a state canopy in an ecclesiastical procession." [76] On the first stage of the return journey, Dickens had poor horses; on the second, he "bribed the post-boys tremendously and we came in literally neck and neck"; the roads were extremely muddy and the *Times* men ordered four horses; Dickens did the same; in the end Dickens got to London before they did, with a longer and more accurate account than any other paper.[77]

Lord John was defeated and Dickens was deaf and rheumatic from exposure to the rain; but the *Spectator* noticed his accomplishment as "a feat" and John Black clapped him on the shoulder delightedly.[78] The *Times* had no better resource than to vent its spleen on its rival by calling it "that squirt of filthy water" and describing it as a "licentious" feeder "on falsehood and lies," to which the *Chronicle* retorted that "the poor old *Times*, in its imbecilic ravings, resembles those unfortunate wretches whose degraded prostitution is fast approaching neglect and disgust." These are not, to be sure, unusual examples of the journalistic amenities of the age; the *Standard* called the *Globe* "our blubber-headed contemporary" and the *Chronicle* dismissed the *Morning Post* as "that slop-pail of corruption." [79] But the *Times* thundering from Printing-House Square and Black bellowing in return from the Strand make it easy to see where Dickens found Pott and Slurk, the rival editors in *Pickwick*.

After the exciting dash to Exeter and back, Dickens was in London most of the time until November. He and Catherine Hogarth were in love with each other, and Dickens had taken a room in Selwood Place, just around the corner from the Hogarth home at 18 York Place, to be near her as often as his duties allowed.[80] But he had not yet cleared off the debts he had contracted at the time of his father's arrest, so they were deferring their marriage until his financial position was brighter. As a loverlike service, during July he read the printers' proof slips for *Journies through Italy and Switzerland*, a volume written by Catherine's great-uncle William Thomson and published in 1836 by Macrone.[81]

No sooner had the series of sketches Dickens was contributing to the *Evening Chronicle* drawn to a close than he was undertaking a new series proposed to him by Vincent Dowling, a former colleague in the Gallery who was now the editor of *Bell's Life in London*. These were signed "Tibbs," a pseudonym probably derived from the character of Beau Tibbs, in Goldsmith's essays. There were a dozen of them, running from September 27, 1835, to January 17th of the following year, under the general title of *Scenes and Characters*.[82] Like the pieces in the *Evening Chronicle*, these sketches varied from clear-cut pictures of streets and places to lightly satirical portrayals of character with touches of pathos.

Dickens's acquaintance with Harrison Ainsworth, which had begun in the previous year, had warmed into friendship. Ainsworth, who was separated from his wife, had taken a pleasant dwelling named Kensal Lodge, on the Harrow Road near the village of Willesden. Here the widow of a cousin, Mrs. Eliza Touchet, a clever, sarcastic, fascinating talker, who was twelve years Ainsworth's senior, acted as his hostess, and Ainsworth did a good deal of entertaining. At his dinner table could be found Father Prout keeping the company in a roar with classical witticisms, the brilliant young artist Daniel Maclise, the famous

George Cruikshank taking more wine than anyone else and presently roaring a street ballad or dancing the hornpipe, Disraeli in his gold-flowered waistcoat and Edward Bulwer extravagantly loaded with jewels, the ingenious minor canon Richard Barham making sly but good-natured personal allusions, Samuel Laman Blanchard, the editor of the *True Sun*, William Jerdan, the editor of the *Literary Gazette*, the scholarly Dyce, and many others Dickens presently came to know.[83]

Leaving Kensal Lodge with Ainsworth's publisher, Macrone, one evening to walk back to Holborn, Dickens was delighted to learn that his companion was also going to Furnival's Inn. The publisher told him that his *Sketches* were "capital value" and should be collected into a volume for publication. Macrone added the suggestion that they might be illustrated by Cruikshank. This was an exhilarating thought, for Cruikshank had long been a famous cartoonist. He had established his reputation among the radical caricaturists fifteen years before, at the time of the trial of Queen Caroline, with a series of brilliant savage portrayals of George IV, in which the shapeless bulk of the King had appeared now as an Oriental voluptuary lolling on a couch, now as a disgraceful reprobate cowering before the bar of public opinion. Cruikshank's pre-eminence in his work was so unchallenged that his name alone ensured a large sale.

Macrone and the young author soon reached an agreement. Dickens would write a sufficient number of additional sketches to make the contents fill two volumes; Macrone would pay him £150 for the copyright of the first edition and publish it early in 1836.[84] Dickens was filled with excitement. Albany Fonblanque, the editor of the *Examiner*, liked his sketches; so did Samuel Carter Hall, of the *New Monthly Magazine*; William Jerdan of the *Literary Gazette*, whose approval was enough to make the reputation of any author, had praised them. Dickens saw a new realm of achievement opening before him.

He already stood, he knew, in the topmost rank among the reporters of the Gallery. But what was it to be a mere journalist, even a journalist with some reputation as a clever writer, in comparison with being a man of letters whose work was published in book form! His brain was seething with ideas for dozens of additional sketches: "The Cook's Shop—Bedlam—The Prisoner's Van—The Streets—Noon and Night —Banking-Houses—Fancy Lounges—Covent Garden—Hospitals and Lodging Houses." [85] Once he began, the future was illimitable!

CHAPTER TWO

Boz Is Born

Dickens had enthusiastically committed himself to a task that involved prodigal expenditures of energy. It was a tendency that was to recur at every crucial stage of his later career. All at the same time, now, he was continuing to give full attention to his newspaper duties, turning out his series for *Bell's Life in London*, writing additional sketches for his book, and preparing the volume for the press. John Black, to be sure, thought so highly of Dickens's talents that he spared him a great deal of the mere drudgery of a reporter's life. "Any fool," he told Charles Mackay, "can pass judgment, more or less just or unjust, on a book or a play, but 'Boz' can do better things; he can create works for other people to criticize. . . . Keep 'Boz' in reserve for great occasions. He will *aye* be ready for them." [1]

Nevertheless, Dickens knew he would be obliged to go to Bristol early in November to cover the Stroud by-election in which Lord John Russell was the Government candidate, so he wished before he left to settle as many details concerning his book as possible. He rushed about collecting proof slips of the articles that had appeared in the *Evening Chronicle*, planned additional sketches, and discussed possible titles for the book with Macrone. Captain Holland had sold the *Monthly Magazine* to the firm of Cochrane and Macrone, from which Macrone had withdrawn when he set up as a book publisher. From his former partner, however, he could easily obtain copies of the sketches that had appeared there. Macrone suggested calling them something like *Bubbles from the Brain of Boz* in parody of Head's *Bubbles from the Brunnens of Nassau*.[2] Dickens felt this to be rather pointless. "What do you think," he asked Macrone, "of

*"Sketches by Boz
and
Cuts by Cruikshank*

---

*Etchings by Boz
and
Woodcuts by Cruikshank."* [3]

"I have begged Black," Dickens went on, "to get old Alderman Wood to take me to Newgate—as an amateur of course. I have long projected sketching its Interior, and I think it would tell extremely well. It would not keep you waiting, because the printer has plenty to go on with; and a day's time is a handsome allowance for me—much less [obviously a slip for "more"] than I had when I was writing for the Chronicle." [4] Two nights later he added, "I am by the mercy of Black and The Chronicle proprietors, at home this evening—It would be an insult to suppose it worth your while to walk or cab so far East, for Scotch Whiskey and Cigars, would it not?" [5]

The order to Bristol came on November 7, 1835, forcing Dickens to break off an engagement for that very evening to meet Cruikshank for the first time and discuss the illustrating of the *Sketches*.[6] Dickens and Beard were again a team. They arranged that as soon as Lord John Russell had finished speaking, one of them would dash to Marlborough in a chaise, transcribing his notes as he rode. At Marlborough a horse express would be waiting to rush the report to London.[7] Since the *Times*, Dickens wrote his subeditor, had thought only of having a chaise and four all the way, a rider on horseback should beat them hollow. The speeches following Lord John's would be sent by Cooper's Company's coaches leaving Bristol at six-thirty the next morning.[8]

Making preparations at the George and Pelican in Newbury, Dickens was surrounded by a chaotic confusion of road maps, roadbooks, ostlers, and postboys.[9] After a cold journey, he and Beard arrived at the Bush Inn, Bristol, and were kept up all night writing out their reports.[10] The next night they reported a dinner at Bath, twelve miles away; after sharp work, and staying up all night again, they snatched a little sleep and returned to London. The Russell dinner had made the next morning's edition with three and a quarter columns on page three, and was concluded in another three columns the day after: a great triumph.[11]

In town Dickens had a hundred things to attend to. After several further delays, he finally conferred with Cruikshank on the sixteen illustrations that were to go with the two volumes.[12] Filled with the excitement of their project, Dickens could not forbear adding to a letter condoling with Macrone for the death of an infant son, the glorious news that Cruikshank thought they would be able to publish by Christmas. Soon, however, he was indignant at Cruikshank's taking his desire for speed rather coolly, and saying that he would "have 'a' plate next week, and 'two' the week afterwards"—until he remembered that Cruikshank had also said each plate would contain four subjects.[13] But at the end of a fortnight, he was hot again at Cruikshank for being slow.[14] With startling speed this neophyte was adopting a peremptory tone about the veteran artist and telling Macrone "I think he requires the spur." [15] In between these activities he was completing the additional sketches he was doing to fill the two volumes. He was gratified by Macrone's praise of "The Black Veil," and even more by his confirmation of the opinion already expressed by Hogarth and Black that "A Visit to Newgate" would "make" any book.[16]

The middle of December took Dickens to Kettering to watch the by-election there, and he entrusted a stint of proofreading to Hogarth.[17] Party feeling in Northamptonshire was running so high that Dickens expected violence. "Such a ruthless set of bloody-minded villains" as the Tories, he said, "I never set eyes on, in my life." [18] Before the hustings a gang of horsemen rode their way into the audience with bludgeons and loaded riding crops; one of them cut about him with an iron part of his stirrup-leather and another brandished a pistol, had his nose bloodied by a thrown stick, and would have fired into the crowd had not his arms been pinioned by two companions.[19] "No one speaker on the Conservative side," Dickens wrote for the *Chronicle*, "made the slightest allusion to, or expressed any regret for, this disgraceful proceeding." [20]

The polling two days later was riotous with "bells ringing, candidates speaking, drums sounding, a band of *eight* trombones," and "the blue swine" of conservative voters fighting, "drinking and guzzling and howling and roaring." [21] Dickens and four of his fellow reporters, in no very good odor in a Tory town, retired with a bagatelle board to his room over the stable yard, locked the door, and ordered a dinner of "cod and oyster sauce, roast beef, and a pair of ducks, plum pudding,

and mince pies." "Damn the Tories," he concluded, "—They'll win
here I am afraid." [22]

In the midst of this hum of activity, Dickens had still other irons in
the fire. The young composer John Hullah, who had been at the Academy of Music with Fanny, was planning an operetta with a Venetian
background, to be called *The Gondoliers*, and asked Dickens to supply
the libretto. With the assurance that was becoming characteristic of
him, Dickens took charge of Hullah's idea, had him drop the Venetian
setting, and transformed it into a bucolic drama of would-be seducers,
rustic maidens, and upstanding farmers. "While I am at home in England," he told Hullah, "I am in Venice abroad indeed." He could work,
he argued, with effect on a play where the characters behaved like
people he saw and heard every day; it could be done in the style of the
old English operas whose beauty he admired; and it would not require
the costly and elaborate *décor* of an Italian scene.[23] Hullah yielded, in
part no doubt to the impact of Dickens's arguments, but in part, too,
one feels, to the force of Dickens's personality. It was not the last time
Dickens was to seize another man's notion and transform it beyond
recognition. Hogarth introduced Dickens to John Braham, the famous
tenor, who was opening the new and splendid St. James's Theatre in
the middle of December, and it was arranged that the operetta should
be submitted to him as soon as possible.[24]

By Christmas Dickens had almost finished the dramatic portion of
the operetta, though the lyrics were still to do.[25] He spent the first part
of January sending out announcements of his *Sketches* to magazine
and newspaper editors, and working out with Macrone the wording of
the advertisement for the press. He expected at any moment, he wrote
Macrone, to hear from Cruikshank that his work was finished, and
they would then go together to spend an evening with the artist and
see the plates. He would arrange with the printer at the *Chronicle* that
the advertisement should be placed at the head of a column. He would
write to Dilke that he was the author of the volumes Macrone was
sending. There were uncertainties about *exactly* when the book would
be ready; could Macrone throw any further light on the subject? [26]

His other activities, of course, could not slacken in the midst of these
personal excitements. He reported the procession and ceremony on the
occasion of Lord Melbourne's opening the Licensed Victuallers' School
at Kennington.[27] He also led a successful strike of reporters on the

Morning Chronicle against being required to sign an agreement that the management desired to impose upon them.

What was objectionable in the agreement is not known. The importance of the dispute, however, lies in the way Dickens put himself at the head of the group and outlined the strategy they should follow. He would ask Easthope, he told Beard, if a refusal to sign would result in dismissal. If it would, they would sign under protest, announcing that they would then all seek the first annual engagement they could get elsewhere. If not, they would refuse to sign, but express their willingness to concur in any other reasonable arrangement. Easthope had no wish to lose the services of his two star reporters and the best part of his reporting staff, and gave way. Dickens gained considerable fame on Fleet Street at having conducted the case so triumphantly.[28]

*   *   *   *   *

Sketches by Boz was published on February 7, 1836, its author's twenty-fourth birthday.[29] Volumes were dispatched to Catherine's Edinburgh relatives, and complimentary copies inscribed to Easthope and John Black.[30] Dickens also presented an inscribed copy to Edward Stanley, by then become Lord Stanley, who had so highly praised his accuracy at the time of the Irish Disturbances Bill.[31] Still another went to the generous and amiable Thomas Noon Talfourd, formerly a law reporter for the *Times*, a Serjeant-at-Law, and since 1835 a member of Parliament for the town of Reading.[32] Copies were also sent to the *Sun*, the *Spectator*, the *Athenaeum*, the *Literary Gazette*, the *Court Journal*, and other periodicals.[33]

A paragraph in the *Morning Chronicle* heralded the book's appearance at the end of the week, and two days before its publication there was a review by Hogarth which praised its style as like Washington Irving's "in his happiest hours," and likened "A Visit to Newgate" to Victor Hugo's "Dernier Jour d'un Condamné." Its author, Hogarth said, was "a close observer of character and manners, with a strong sense of the ridiculous and a graphic faculty of placing in the most whimsical and amusing lights the follies and absurdities of human nature. He has the power, too, of producing tears as well as laughter. His pictures of the vices and wretchedness which abound in this vast city are sufficient to strike the heart of the most careless and insensitive reader." [34]

Provokingly, copies did not reach the Sunday papers in time to receive immediate notice, and three of the dailies whose reviews had been in type for days were prevented by the pressure of other matters from printing them at once,[35] but Dickens was deeply moved by "Hogarth's beautiful notice." [36] He was confident that there was every reason to anticipate the book's being a success. Other favorable reviews, in fact, continued to appear. The *Literary Gazette* for February 15th spoke of his "talent" and "fidelity" and was struck by the "genuine acquaintance with his subjects" revealed in these scenes of common life "cleverly and amazingly described." The *Satirist*, the same week, found the two volumes "in their way inimitable" and their author "a man of unquestionable talent and of great and correct observation." John Forster reviewed it favorably in the *Examiner*, the *Athenaeum* praised it, and so did the *Sun*, the *Sunday Times*, and the *Sunday Herald*.[37] The *Morning Post*'s review in March, Dickens joyfully reported, was "as good as Hogarth's." [38] By the end of that month he was writing to his uncle Thomas Culliford Barrow of "the great success of my book, and the name it has established for me among the publishers." [39] In August there was a second edition, and in 1837 there were two more.[40]

It was no coincidence that the reviews all emphasized Dickens's knowledge of his subjects and his closeness of observation. The subtitle of the *Sketches* proclaimed them "Illustrative of Everyday Life and Everyday People," and more than half the contents strictly deserved that description. They are facts—of street and shop and tavern and jail—reported with extraordinary precision and vivacity. The rest are mainly a kind of low-comedy fairy tale wherein a farcical poetic justice overtakes drapers' clerks passing themselves off as men of fashion, needy or greedy men courting unattractive females with money, and snobbish merchants anxious to be acquainted among the great.[41] But even these conventional subjects are keyed to so exact an observation of middle-class behavior and surroundings as to transcend their stock-comedy patterns and rise into an eccentric documentary realism.

Both the sketches and the stories underline that brilliant reporting talent with which Dickens began, and which he never lost throughout his life. This aspect of his writing has misled some admirers into a mania for ferreting out the living model of Mr. Merdle and discovering in what drowsy village the real Blue Dragon dispensed good cheer. To treat the fictions as a hidden hunting ground of mere fact is of course a distortion of Dickens's true genius, and yet it is rooted in a significant feature of his way of working. No writer takes more pains to seize upon the most striking characteristics of actual places and people and incorporate them into the creations of his imagination. Dickens would roam for an entire morning through Bevis Marks to find an appropriate house for Sampson Brass,[42] and bid his illustrator look upon a specific London merchant to realize the physical type of Mr. Dombey.[43] The novels are crammed with vivid portrayals of localities that thousands of his readers will recognize, from the narrow lanes darkened by the walls of Lincoln's Inn to the tall genteel houses between Portland Place and Bryanston Square.

In the *Sketches*, the outstanding triumph of this descriptive faculty is the sharp accuracy with which it captures exactly what the everyday observer would note as most characteristic and colorful, if only he *were* observant enough to do so. There is no distortion, no oddity of choice, but the very essence caught and transfixed, so that whether the scene is a shabby secondhand shop, a gin palace glittering with gilt and mirrors, an excursion steamer jammed with people, the flaring lights of a pantomime at Greenwich Fair, or a crowded slum with broken windows and slimy gutters,[44] the details are still as true and the picture as convincing as when it flowed from Dickens's pen. The two companion sketches of "The Streets"—"Morning" and "Night" [45]—take us through successive hours of the twenty-four in a series of vignettes in words that are a startling urban parallel to Monet's experiments in painting the same scene under the different atmospheric conditions of the various hours.

But the *Sketches by Boz* are no mere exercise in smooth journalistic objectivity, however vivid. The personality of their author lights a hundred perspectives and sharpens a thousand epithets. Dickens had suffered enough from the mistakes and inadequacies of his elders to have no reverence for age and experience. He had understood enough of the selfishness and blundering stupidity of constituted authority to have no respect for respectable opinion. In his rebellion against both there is a youthful violence that is sometimes mere smart self-assertion but that is not infrequently an angry scorn for the unimaginative cruelty that calls itself common sense. He can sympathize with the underpaid milliners' and staymakers' apprentices,[46] and pity the scantily clad ballad singer with the wailing child whose only reward from the passing crowd is "a brutal laugh at her weak voice." [47] Such sights, he says, "will make your heart ache—always supposing," he adds bitterly, "that you are neither a philosopher nor a political economist." [48] Man's indifference to the welfare of his fellow man, he had already seen, harvests its dreadful toll of poverty, prostitution, drunkenness, and crime. Well-bred ladies and gentlemen might do something more generous and useful than recoil from the sixteen-year-old streetwalker whose features are already branded with depravity "as legibly as if a red-hot iron had seared them" and whose later career "in crime will be as rapid as the flight of a pestilence . . . in its baneful influence and wide-spreading infection." [49] Instead of turning with cold disgust from the sodden drinking of the poor, they might try to "suggest an antidote against hunger, filth, and foul air," which drive the inhabitants of the slums to seek oblivion from their misery.[50] In such comments we already hear the clarion-tongued crusader who will make the world ring with the evils of political and industrial exploitation.

If the interests suggested by Dickens's first published volume thus anticipate the social themes of his novels, its style and characters no less clearly foreshadow his astonishing literary achievement. At this stage, to be sure, he is often crude and clumsy, falling sometimes into a polysyllabic turgidness that shows little of the startling verbal felicity he came to command. He indulges in a showy and cocksure jibing full of the fierce vanity and hardness of youth. He abounds in flip puns and knowing word-plays: about young men who are "fond of mails, but more of females," [51] and shopkeepers behind in their rent who "lock the door and bolt" themselves,[52] and crowded roads where "horses won't go on, and wheels will come off." [53]

Mingled with such conceits, however, we may enjoy much that is more gloriously comic. Here, for example, is a splenetic red-faced speaker, in "The Parlour Orator," whose forensic style is a rich foretaste of the ludicrous rhetoric of Chadband in *Bleak House*:

" 'What's freedom? Not a standing army. What's a standing army? Not freedom. What's general happiness? Not universal misery. Liberty ain't the window-tax, is it? The Lords ain't the Commons, are they?' " [54]

And here is a chorus of cabmen swarming over the Tuggses at Ramsgate Pier who arouse the same order of chuckle we give the cabman in *Pickwick*:

" 'Nice light fly and a fast trotter, sir,' " said one: " 'fourteen mile a hour, and surroundin' objects rendered inwisible by ex-treme welocity!'

" 'Large fly for your luggage, sir,' " cried a second. " 'Wery large fly here, sir—reg'lar bluebottle!'

" 'Here's *your* fly, sir!' shouted another aspiring charioteer, mounting the box, and inducing an old grey horse to indulge in some imperfect reminiscences of a canter. 'Look at him, sir! Temper of a lamb and haction of a steam-ingeine!' " [55]

But those knowing comments Dickens is constantly tempted into making, though they often sound like mere cockney smartness, are by no means limited to the showy wisecrack. He has innumerable witty thrusts and comic images. He will describe a small child as having "a damp piece of gingerbread in his hand, with which he had slightly embossed his countenance," [56] or speculate on why it is that there is a class of men in London who "appear to have no enjoyment beyond leaning against posts." [57] Or he describes how stage fathers suddenly discover "that somebody whom they have been in constant communication with, during three long acts," is their own child. " 'Ah! what do I see? This bracelet! That smile! These documents! Those eyes! Can I believe my senses?—It must be!—Yes—it is, it is my child'—'My father!' exclaims the child; and they fall into each other's arms, and look over each other's shoulders." [58]

Observation so acute merges imperceptibly into creation. What the mind notes with such vividness it will presently be calling up and soon surpassing in imagination. Indeed, time and again in *Sketches by Boz* we see Dickens's imagination in the very act of taking fire and rising into a realm far above that of mere factual reporting or even shrewd satire, though it be the most commonplace experience that provides the spark. In one of the most remarkable of the sketches, "Meditations in Monmouth Street," he stands before the window of a secondhand clothing emporium, merely looking at a collection of old boots and shoes. Before he knows it, he finds himself fitting "visionary feet and legs" into them:

"There was one pair of boots in particular—a jolly, good-tempered, hearty-looking pair of tops, and we had got a fine, red-faced, jovial fellow of a market-gardener into them, before we had made their acquaintance half a minute. . . . There were his fat legs bulging over the tops, and fitting them too tight to admit of his tucking in the loops he

had pulled them on by; and his knee-cords with an interval of stocking;
and his blue apron tucked up round his waist; and his red neckerchief
and blue coat, and a white hat stuck on one side of his head; and there
he stood with a broad grin on his great red face, whistling away, as if
any other idea but that of being happy and comfortable had never
entered his brain.

"This was the very man after our own heart; we knew all about him;
we had seen him coming up to Covent Garden in his green chaise-cart,
with the fat tubby little horse, half a thousand times; and even while
we cast an affectionate look upon his boots, at that instant, the form
of a coquettish servant-maid suddenly sprung into a pair of Denmark
satin pumps that stood beside them, and we at once recognized the
very girl who accepted his offer of a ride, just on this side the Hammer-
smith suspension-bridge, the very last Tuesday morning we rode into
town from Richmond."

Fast on the heels of these two Dickens conjured up a smart female
in a showy bonnet who stepped into "a pair of grey cloth boots, with
black fringe and binding," and began trying to flirt with the gardener,
who paid no attention "beyond giving a knowing wink." "His indifference, however, was amply recompensed by the excessive gallantry of a
very old gentleman with a silver-headed stick, who tottered into a pair
of large list shoes . . . and indulged in a variety of gestures expressive
of his admiration of the lady in the cloth boots, to the immeasurable
amusement of a young fellow we put into a pair of long-quartered
pumps, who we thought would have split the coat that slid down to
meet him, with laughing." [59]

With what vivacity Dickens here creates, in one flash of the imagination—from a heap of old shoes—an entire cast of brightly differenti-
ated figures, with what speed establishes a set of relations among them!
Here, and in other passages like this, the volume reaches its climactic
achievement, and foreshadows the incredible fecundity that was to
be. Though *Sketches by Boz* is full of the flaws and shortcomings that
disclose it to be the work of an apprentice, it is also full of something
more than promise: of a kind of not entirely ripe fulfillment. Apprentice work indicating an apprentice so enormously gifted and even here
so precociously skilled might well banish all surprise if its author, in
his very next effort, leaped into the circle of the masters.

*   *   *   *   *

Dickens's own confidence in his prospects had been raised to a state of effervescence. For hot upon the publication of the *Sketches* he had received a proposal to write a serial work in twenty installments. Although it would mean turning out twelve thousand words a month in addition to all his regular newspaper duties, it would pay nine guineas a sheet and add a clear £14 monthly to his income. With this he felt he and Catherine might venture to marry. "The work," he wrote her, "will be no joke, but the emolument is too tempting to resist." [60] Only a short time before he had offered to write again for the *Monthly Magazine* at eight guineas a sheet, but the new editor, James Grant, had found that his employers were no more able to pay the contributors than Captain Holland had been.[61] The contrast between his present state and that of two short years ago must have been strong in Dickens's mind when he met Captain Holland himself on the street, and allowed that impecunious worthy to invite himself to Furnival's Inn for a glass of grog and some oysters the next night.[62]

Out of this new undertaking Dickens had agreed to, *Pickwick Papers* came into being. It is curious to reflect how easily Mr. Pickwick, Sam Weller, Jingle, and all the rest of that extraordinary company might have remained in the realms of the unborn; for the proposition came to Dickens almost by chance and only at the end of an involved chain of coincidences. A young publishing firm named Chapman and Hall was just starting a monthly *Library of Fiction*, edited by Charles Whitehead. Before the sale of the *Monthly Magazine* Whitehead had been employed on that periodical, where he had noticed Dickens's stories. He therefore wrote Dickens asking him to contribute to the *Library of Fiction*.[65] Dickens responded by agreeing to write "The Tuggses at Ramsgate," which was to appear at the end of March with an illustration by the popular comic artist Robert Seymour.[64] The latter, who had gained the public fancy with his burlesque sporting pictures, had conceived the idea of a series of plates depicting the mishaps of a "Nimrod Club" of cockney sportsmen.[65] Seymour tried to get several people, including Theodore Hook and Henry Mayhew, to do the accompanying humorous text, but all these efforts fell through. Eventually he broached his notion to Chapman and Hall, for whom he was illustrating the *Squib Annual of Poetry, Politics, and Personalities*.[66]

Edward Chapman liked it and wrote William Clarke, who had

tickled the humor of the town with a comic work called *Three Courses and a Dessert*, inquiring if he would collaborate with Seymour. This letter received no reply. Seymour, impatient to have his plans for the new year settled, kept pestering Chapman for action. Chapman had been impressed by Dickens's sketches in the *Monthly Magazine*, although he had not known the name of the author and was unaware of the fact that he was writing for the *Chronicle*. Through Whitehead he had learned Dickens's identity.[67] Although his story for the *Library of Fiction* was not yet delivered, it occurred to Chapman that Dickens might tackle this new enterprise. Boz's *Sketches*, just off the press, were obtained and looked through; it was decided that he would do. To Furnival's Inn, therefore, on the morning of February 10th, repaired little Mr. William Hall, the junior partner of Chapman and Hall, to lay the proposal before Mr. Charles Dickens.[68]

At Christmas Dickens had taken larger and sunnier rooms, facing south, at 15 Furnival's Inn, but he did not actually move into them until the middle of February.[69] So the steep stairs with the brass-bound railing that Hall ascended were the same as those Nat Willis and Macrone had climbed the previous year. The young man who threw open the door was just three days past his twenty-fourth birthday, but, with his smooth face and his luxuriant brown hair waving down over his shoulders, he looked much younger. Only the keen eyes and the eager, restless air of energy marked the strength within. Nothing even hinted the determination that could steel the sensitive mouth.

As Dickens took in the brisk, birdlike little figure of his visitor, he broke into a shout of recognition. This was the very man who had sold him the copy of the *Monthly Magazine* containing his first story to appear in print! The transaction had been charged with no such inner excitement for Hall, of course, as it had been for his youthful customer, and he did not remember it. But the two agreed to hail the incident "as a good omen, and so fell to business." [70] Hall had the proposition all cut and dried. The members of Seymour's Nimrod Club were to go out shooting, fishing, and so on, and involve themselves in difficulties through their lack of dexterity. The writing was only a hack job to go with the plates, and the payment offered was no more than might have been commanded by half a hundred journeyman authors. But to Dickens, earning seven guineas a week on the *Morning Chronicle* and picking up small sums by irregular contribu-

tions to other periodicals, a dependable addition of fourteen guineas
a month to his income was tempting. He knew at once that he would
accept the offer—but only on his own terms.

With swift conclusiveness he marshaled his conditions before the
publisher. Though born and partly bred in the country, he himself
was not much of a sportsman except for walking. The idea of sporting
misadventures was not novel. (The comic annuals and sporting magazines, in fact, were full of calf-brained lieutenants and thick-skulled
squires jovially immersed in brandy and buffooneries, stumbling
through booby mishaps in field and stream.) Having disposed of
Seymour's idea, Dickens added that it would be infinitely better for
the plates to arise out of the text, and that he should like to take his
own way through a free range of English scenes and people; he was
afraid, in fact, he would ultimately do so in any case, whatever course
he might prescribe to himself at starting.[71] All this amounted to the
cavalier suggestion that instead of *his* illustrating Seymour, as had
been proposed, Seymour should illustrate *him*. The cheeky young
fellow who had not hesitated to say that the veteran Cruikshank required a touch of the spur did not intend to be subordinate to Seymour.

What William Hall thought of his host's audacity can only be con-
jectured. One thing is clear: he was impressed. If it crossed his mind
that it might be hard to manage a young man who so coolly announced
that, whatever he agreed to, he would probably wind up by doing as
he pleased, the cautionary reflection was blown away in the gale of
Dickens's magnificent self-assertion and confidence. This was a writer
they must certainly obtain! Hall assured Dickens that there ought to
be no trouble in meeting his views, and went into details about the
manner of publication.[72]

He suggested that the book be brought out in monthly parts of about
twelve thousand words each, totaling twenty issues selling at a shilling
apiece.[73] There was an element of novelty in this scheme, although
it had previously been used for Pierce Egan's *Tom and Jerry*. For the
most part, however, serial publication had been a means of bringing
out cheap reprints of works like the Bible, the *Pilgrim's Progress*, and
the *Book of Martyrs*. Generally, it had been standard practice, since
Scott's publication of *Kenilworth* in 1821, to issue original works of
fiction in the form of the three-volume novel selling at one and a half
guineas.[74] But there was no reason why the serial form of publication

should not be applied to new works of all kinds. Many people would find it easier to pay a shilling once a month than twenty times that amount all at once, and even the sum total was one-third cheaper than the standard price. Furthermore, the publisher had a chance of making his money twice over, for readers who wouldn't bother with a serial or who had lost some of the installments might still pay the entire price when the book was published in boards. The interview ended with Dickens and Hall in thorough accord.[75]

The junior partner hurried back to the Strand and urged that Dickens be given his way. Edward Chapman concurred. But to Seymour the new turn in the plan came with a painful jolt. He was an excitable and touchy person, given to fits of gloom, and it was almost more than he could bear to see *his* pet scheme being wrested away from him and twisted completely out of shape. Worse still, it was all too clear that he would be playing second fiddle to the hack originally called in merely to concoct a story around his plates. But here it was already running into February, time pressed, he had no other plans, and Chapman and Hall now seemed determined to do things in the mangled way suggested by this young upstart or not to do them at all. Seymour swallowed his spleen and grudgingly consented.[76]

The discussion between the partners and the expression of their decision to Seymour had taken only two days. They at once dispatched a letter to Dickens summarizing the terms of the understanding as they had been orally agreed upon. Dickens took exception to only one detail: he thought the time in advance of publication specified for copy being in their hands unnecessarily long and suggested that for each installment to reach them five weeks ahead of publication ought to be ample. This point, like all his others, having been conceded, Dickens turned his mind to the work he had agreed to write.[77]

It was understood that the story was to be entertaining and humorous, but not a single character, scene, or situation had been so much as mentioned in their discussions, or even conceived in Dickens's mind. But with that fertility of invention which could fill a window of secondhand shoes with living people, he at once imagined his central character. He tells of this event in one of those bare little sentences that history makes famous when time has invested their flatness with pregnancy. "I thought," he said simply, "of Mr. Pickwick." [78]

Within two days more he was writing the first number. "Pickwick," he announced to Chapman and Hall, "is begun in all his might and glory." [79] Another three days, and he had "Pickwick and his friends on the Rochester coach," "going on swimmingly" with Alfred Jingle, who, Dickens felt sure, would "make a decided hit." [80] The name of Pickwick he borrowed from that of the well-known coach proprietor of Bath, Moses Pickwick.[81] The shorter title, *The Pickwick Papers*, which from the beginning he used alternatively with the full one, *The Posthumous Papers of the Pickwick Club*, may have been suggested by the fact that Whitehead, one of whose books was entitled *The Autobiography of Jack Ketch*, had jestingly spoken of writing a sequel to this book under the title of *The Ketch Papers*.[82] Dickens had retained the apparatus of the Pickwick Club as a relic of Seymour's original scheme, and good-humoredly thrown in Mr. Winkle, with his terror of horses and his ignorance of guns, as a special concession to the artists's love of boastful but incompetent sportsmen.[83]

But Seymour did not feel mollified, and had trouble producing illustrations to the publishers' liking. His first sketch of Pickwick was a tall, thin man. Edward Chapman at once protested. Pickwick must be fat; "good humor and flesh had always gone together since the days of Falstaff." [84] For Seymour's benefit he described a friend of his own at Richmond, "a fat old beau who would wear, in spite of the ladies' protests, drab tights and black gaiters." [85] It was a type Seymour knew. In Robert Penn's *Maxims and Hints for Anglers*, three years before, he had drawn just such a figure, plump, bald-headed, and bespectacled, tenderly holding an umbrella over a brood of ducks in a thunderstorm.[86] This figure he accordingly used again; the publishers and author were delighted, and it became the world's image of the immortal Pickwick. Still filled with reminiscences of his own plan, he drew for the cover page of the monthly parts a cockney blazing away at an unconcerned little dickybird on a near-by branch and Mr. Pickwick dozing over a fishing line in a punt, although in the story Mr. Winkle never manages to aim so straight and Mr. Pickwick never goes fishing at all.

Meanwhile preparations were being made for Dickens's marriage to Catherine Hogarth. He had agreed on a three-year tenancy of his chambers at Furnival's Inn before there had been any such prospect as Chapman and Hall's offer,[87] and he could not afford to lose the £50 a year he paid in rent, so the young couple decided to start housekeeping there. Kitchen equipment and additional furniture now had to be obtained, and Catherine frequently came in from Chelsea with her younger sister Mary, who was to live with them after they were married, and stayed overnight in the Dickens home at 34 Edwards Street, Portman Square. Mrs. Dickens was buying linen for them, attending to covering the sofa, and helping to transform the bachelor quarters so as to fit them for their new feminine inmates.[88] Dickens, in high fettle, went about acquiring all sorts of objects: "a pair of quart decanters, and a pair of pints, a chrystal jug, and three brown dittoes with plated tops, for beer and hot water, a pair of lustres, and two *magnificent* china jars"—all great bargains.[89]

Writing the second number of *Pickwick* went more slowly than he had imagined it would. "The sheets," he confessed to Catherine, "are a weary length—I had no idea there was so much in them." [90] He was obliged to write in intervals between his other work; on Sunday, March 20th, he told her he would have to be at his desk till one or two that night.[91] The impatience and excitement with which he was looking forward to their wedding day two weeks hence may have made application difficult. "Here's another day off the fortnight," he exclaimed the next afternoon. "Hurrah!" [92]

Everything was in readiness for the two great events. Macrone had already paid him £50 of the price agreed on for *Sketches by Boz*, and gave him the remaining £100 on Thursday, March 24th.[93] Chapman and Hall had sent him a draft for £29 to pay for the first two numbers of *Pickwick*.[94] Two days later, with a large advertisement in the *Times* and an entire page in the *Athenaeum*, of which the upper half was devoted to *The Pickwick Papers*, they announced the forthcoming publication of its first number for March 31, 1836. Next day there were shorter advertisements in *Bell's Life in London*, the *Observer*, *John Bull*, the *Weekly Dispatch*, the *Satirist*, the *News and Sunday Herald*, and the *Times*.[95] On the day of publication, the *Library of Fiction* made a simultaneous appearance, with Boz's story, "The Tuggses at Ramsgate," and an advertisement of *Pickwick*.[96] Dickens looked forward to the success of the enterprise and his approaching marital happiness in as high spirits as ever Mr. Pickwick and his friends bowled along on top of the Commodore while it rolled to Rochester.

CHAPTER THREE

Catherine

THERE seemed to be little resemblance between Catherine and the love whom Dickens had ceased to see three years before. Maria Beadnell was a tiny and teasing charmer with enchanting ringlets; Catherine, though not large in build, was a full-bosomed lass with long, dark hair waving down over her shoulders and a sleepy voluptuousness more suggestive of the south than of the Scottish north.[1] Her blue eyes were large and heavy-lidded, her mouth small and red-lipped, her behavior slow-moving and unassuming.[2] She had little of Maria's impulse to vivacious and light-headed chatter, though when in spirits she would burst into bright laughter and often had a delayed sweet smile.[3] But she was not seldom in low spirits, during which she indulged in a feeling of vague crossness or causeless melancholy.[4] These moods sometimes impelled her to display toward her lover a mingling of petulance and capriciousness that sounds like an echo of her predecessor's "prettily pettish" ways. Despite their striking differences, indeed, Catherine reveals on closer examination certain haunting similarities to Maria Beadnell reminiscent of Marcel Proust's belief in a fatality drawing one always to fall in love with the same underlying qualities and always to repeat in love the same mistakes.

Dickens's entire determination, though—perhaps conscious, perhaps unconscious—was that he would not repeat the same mistakes. He did not intend again to be slavishly subservient under ill-treatment; he would be neither the plaything of high spirits nor the whipping boy of low spirits. His letters to Catherine during the period of their engagement are tender and devoted, and there is no doubt that he was in love with her. But even in the lovers' quarrels that are sometimes mirrored there, he reveals none of the wild misery of worship that

trembled through his letters to Maria and none of the miserable and
hurt endeavor to regain his own dignity in the midst of humiliation.
He was gentle but firm, and he speedily reduced Catherine to the position of pleading to be forgiven for her exhibitions of ill-humor.

The realization that Catherine was subject to these fits of moodiness
and spleen did not come to him, to be sure, until after they became
engaged, when the lover was allowed to feel what would have been
spared a stranger. In his earliest visits to the Hogarths the attraction
had not even been Catherine but her father, who was Dickens's superior on the papers for which they both worked and for whom Dickens
felt both liking and respect. George Hogarth was an unassumingly
friendly man of gentlemanlike manners,[5] and although he was self-
educated he had in the hard-working Scots way made himself a person
of considerable cultural attainments. He had mingled with literary
society in Edinburgh, been on friendly terms with Scott's son-in-law,
John Gibson Lockhart, as well as with the great novelist himself, and
was even mentioned in Christopher North's *Noctes Ambrosianae.*[6]
He was the editor of an anthology of poetry and prose, mainly by Yorkshire authors, called *The White Rose of York*, and his *Musical History,
Biography, and Criticism* was published early in 1835.[7] The ambitious
young writer not merely liked him for himself and for his encouraging
attitude, but fundamentally had far more esteem for the kind of attainment Hogarth represented than he had for a mere successful businessman like George Beadnell.

Little by little the rural Chelsea home, with its large household of
young people, became a pleasant refuge from his bachelor chambers
at Furnival's Inn and the cramped family quarters and financial stringency of Edwards Street. Catherine, with her buxom figure and rose-
petal complexion, and her younger sister Mary, whose admiration for
Dickens was unbounded, listened eagerly to his adventures as a reporter, and doubtless giggled at his account of the Grey banquet being
gobbled down before it officially began, and at his horse bounding in
and out of hedges all the way to Braintree. Catherine was not stupid,
although she did not shine in conversation; she possessed no verbal
wit, but when she was feeling happy her gaiety could overflow in joyfully far-fetched puns.[8] Dickens felt sure that her culture might be
assumed in the daughter of so gifted a father, and gradually fell under
the spell of her somnolent charm.

With the Hogarths he was on a very different footing than he had been with the Beadnells, who even now might not have been much impressed by his magazine stories and newspaper articles or by his rise in what had not yet become a recognized profession. But Hogarth himself was a journalist and saw in Dickens a writer of extraordinary promise. There was no question of his hearty approval when Dickens and Catherine became engaged in the spring of 1835. Everyone was pleased, and Dickens had his portrait in miniature painted on ivory by Rose Drummond and gave it to Catherine as a betrothal present.[9]

It was not long, though, before he had a taste of Catherine's sulkier moods. In the earliest known letter of those he sent her, written in May, some three weeks after their engagement, he reproached her for the "sudden and uncalled for coldness with which you treated me just before I left last night." It pained him, he began, to say one word that could bear the appearance of unkindness, but this was the second time she had indulged recently in such a display, and he owed a duty to himself as well as to her. He "could not have believed that such sullen and inflexible obstinacy could exist in the breast of any girl in whose heart love had found a place." And he proceeded to read her a stiff little lecture on her conduct:

"If a *hasty* temper produces this strange behaviour, acknowledge it when I give you the opportunity—not once or twice, but again and again. If a feeling of you know not what—a capricious restlessness of you can't tell what, and a desire to teaze, you don't know why, give rise to it—overcome it; it will never make you more amiable, I more fond, or either of us more happy." If she is already tired of him, let her say so—"I shall not forget you lightly, but you will need no second warning." She may depend upon it, though, that what she does not take the trouble to control for a lover, she will not for a husband.

He knew as well as if he were by her side, he concluded, that her impulse on reading this note would be "one of anger—pride perhaps, or to use a word more current with your sex—'spirit.'" But she must realize that he has written thus neither to hurt her nor to make her resentful, only because he "cannot turn coolly away and forget a slight" from her as he might "from any other girl" to whom he was not deeply attached. "If you knew the intensity of the feeling which has led me to forget all my friends and pursuits to spend my days at your side . . . you could more readily understand the extent of the pain so easily inflicted, but so difficult to be forgotten." [10]

A remarkable, even an alarming, letter for a young woman to receive from a fiancé of three weeks' standing! One more experienced or more cynical than Catherine, or even more endowed with cunning, might have felt that whether the upbraiding were justified or unjustified in the particular instance, this was a tone too lofty to promise well for her comfort, however genuine the affection that accompanied it. Though Dickens disavowed any claim to be her superior, he was unmistakably monitorial.

But Catherine had no guile and was no fighter. She knew she had in fact behaved peevishly. That knowledge weakened whatever impulses of pride might have held her back. She sent Dickens a frightened and remorseful note asking his forgiveness and begging him to love her "once more." Dickens was magnanimous. Her note revealed, he said, all the amiable and excellent feeling in which he believed her unrivaled; if she would only "*shew* the same affection and kindness" when she felt "disposed to be ill-tempered," he would "have no one solitary fault to find" with her. It was unnecessary for her to ask him to love her again: "*I have never ceased to love you for one moment, since I knew you; nor shall I.*" [11]

Catherine tried to control her moods, and during the summer Dickens took lodgings in Selwood Place, just around the corner from her father's house, to be near her whenever his work for the *Chronicle* or his sketches would allow.[12] He was hoping to be able to let his chambers at Furnival's Inn,[13] but when this expectation was disappointed he proposed that they begin their married life there. "You have often told me," he wrote, "that you could be happy anywhere with me," and "I have neither fear nor despondency about the matter." [14] Writing away industriously, even when the same sketch needed to be revised for the fifteenth time he was still in the most joyous of spirits.[15] Once, when the Hogarths were all quietly sitting in the family drawing room, "a young man dressed as a sailor jumped in at the window, danced a hornpipe, whistling the tune, jumped out again, and a few minutes later Charles Dickens walked gravely in at the door, as if nothing had happened, shook hands all round, and then, at the sight of their puzzled faces, burst into a roar of laughter." [16]

Often his "dearest Kate," as he now called her, came tapping at his door with her sister Mary to share his breakfast with him. Once he asked her to indulge his "childish wish" of having her make his breakfast for him: "It will give me pleasure," and it will be excellent practice for her "against Christmas next." [17] Sometimes, worn out with work, and with an aching head, he facetiously complained of "furteeg," [18] or at three o'clock in the morning lamented that he had not seen her since seven o'clock of the previous evening, a deprivation that "seems an age." [19]

That October Catherine and her mother both came down with scarlet fever after Dickens had spent an evening with them. He was in great anxiety for them, and somewhat worried, too, lest he get it himself. He sent his brother Fred with black-currant jam to ease Catherine's throat, recommended chloride of lime to purify the air of her room, went again and again to see how she was, and wrote, "Should you not be well, I *must* see you, and *will not be prevented*." [20]

His letters abounded in little endearments. She was his "ever dearest Katie" and his "dearest love" and "Dearest darling Pig" and "My Dearest Life." "God bless you my dearest Girl," he would write, and add "99ooooooooooooooooooooooooooooooooooooooooooooooo kisses." [21] By October he had to be back in Furnival's Inn again, working furiously to gather together his *Sketches* for publication by Macrone, writing the supplementary ones despite a cold so severe that he tottered on his legs and could hardly see for dizziness, and trying to meet Cruikshank for a conference about the illustrations.[22] Going to see him at his home in Pentonville, Dickens looked at the new houses there; they were pretty and well situated, but the cheapest was £55 a year, which was too much.[23] Four days later his cold was so much worse that he felt obliged to stay at home, and sent Kate a copy of Ainsworth's *Rookwood* that he had borrowed from Macrone to aid her "in getting through the day." [24]

Kate, however, finding that all these demands upon Dickens's time kept him away from her, began to feel neglected and aggrieved. She complained of being in "low" spirits[25] and tried to make him sorry for her by saying in baby-talk with a childish pout that she was "coss," [26] reiterating that he could come to her if he would and that he took pleasure in being away,[27] and accusing him of stiffness and formality in his letters.[28] Dickens patiently reasoned with her and tried to reassure her. However strongly disposed to be "coss" she was, surely she must see that he had no alternative but to set to work as best he could? [29] "You may be disappointed:—I would rather you would—at not seeing me; but you cannot feel vexed at my doing my best with the stake I have to play for—you and a home for both of us." [30] He was sorry to perceive that she had not subdued her "distrustful feelings and want of confidence," though he loved her "far too well to feel hurt by what in any one else would have annoyed me greatly." [31]

But all that Kate seemed to have been able to learn from their conflicts was to substitute a feeble plaintiveness for sullen coldness or angry reproach. With these disturbances, and the pitch at which he was working, and possibly his father being in financial straits again— "Father was worrying me here this morning," he wrote in one letter, "until nearly two o'clock"[32]—Dickens had a recurrence of his old attacks of spasm more severe than any he had suffered since he was a child. "It still continues exceedingly painful," he told Kate, "and my head is aching so from pain and want of rest that I can hardly hold it up." [33]

It is not surprising, therefore, if he sometimes lost patience and spoke with a certain asperity. Shortly after his return from reporting the dinner to Lord John Russell at Bristol, when he had been going through Newgate to gather material for his sketch of that prison, he wrote that he hoped she had "no new complaints either *bodily* or *mental*: indeed I feel full confidence after last night that you will not have a renewal of the latter." [34] Finally he attained a kind of philosophic resignation on the subject. Working on the first installment of *Pickwick*, he told her that though he liked the *matter* of what he had written that day, "the quantity is not sufficient to justify my coming out tonight. If the representations I have so often made to you, about my working as a duty, and not as a pleasure, be not sufficient to keep you in the good humour, which you, of all people in the world should preserve—why then, my dear, you must be out of temper, and there is no help for it." [35]

*　　*　　*　　*　　*

Despite these cloud-shadows, however, the year of their engagement was a time of happiness and hope. Dickens was constantly in and out of the house in York Place, and Kate and Mary occasionally came in to London escorted by Dickens's younger brother Fred, who was sent to Brompton for the purpose.[36] Sometimes, on a sunny day, Dickens would walk out along Piccadilly, crossing the road at Hyde Park Corner and continuing on the same side as Slater the upholsterer's until he met the two girls coming along Brompton Road to meet him.[37] About his visit to Newgate and the House of Correction,[38] he would have lots of amusing anecdotes to tell her, he wrote Kate; and surely she would like to hear the latest bulletin about his chastising the butcher's boy, being threatened with a warrant for assault, and reply- ing that he would be intimidated by "no more insolent attempts to extort money." [39]

There was theater-going, too, at Covent Garden, Drury Lane, the Adelphi and probably the Olympic,[40] where the beautiful, brilliant, and naughty Mme. Vestris staged extravaganzas with remarkable imaginative delicacy and grace. Sometimes Dickens had to write a notice of a new play, sometimes he had the use of the *Chronicle* news- paper pass. On at least one occasion the management of the Adelphi sent a pass to a private box, and Dickens grandly invited Beard and the Hogarths to fill it.[41] The introduction Mr. Hogarth had given him to Braham, and the great tenor's receptivity to the operetta Dickens was doing with Hullah, also brought tickets to the red-and-gold mag- nificence of the St. James Theatre, just opened on King Street on the 14th of December. "I would very much like you to see a place and a set of people," Dickens wrote Kate, "in which we are likely to be so much interested."[42]

Meanwhile John Pritt Harley, who had become Braham's stage manager, had asked Dickens to write a one-act farce with an amusing part in which Harley himself could appear, and Dickens began to turn his story "The Great Winglebury Duel" into a play under the title of *The Strange Gentleman*.[43] These two theatrical enterprises he carried on simultaneously with his sketches for *Bell's Life in London* and the *Chronicle*. The first scene of the operetta, which he and Hullah had agreed to call *The Village Coquettes*, was finished by the middle of November.[44] Early in December Dickens was submitting the book of the songs to Hogarth's criticism and announcing that he had only two more scenes to write, but in January he was beginning the second act, he told Kate, "with a scene founded on your suggestion." [45] Near the end of December he wrote, "I am finishing my Duel"; in February he asked Chapman and Hall if they would care to publish *The Strange*

Gentleman.[46] But then there is no further mention of the operetta until late spring or of the farce until the autumn.

As the day of their wedding drew near, Dickens worked more furiously than ever in order to clear his desk for the few days' leisure of the honeymoon. Two political dinners were taking place in Liverpool and Birmingham which he might have to report,[47] colds confined him to his rooms,[48] there were "more irons in the fire: more grist to the mill." [49] His letters to Kate were full of rueful little explanations for delays in seeing her, and tender rallyings to keep in spirit: "Is it my fault that I cannot get out tonight? I must work at the opera." [50] "Not low this morning I hope?—You ought not to be, dear Mouse, and are very ungrateful if you are." [51] "A note, and not me. I am very—very—sorry.... If you are unjust enough to be cross, I will not deprecate your anger, or ill humour. I have at least equal reason to be so; forced as I am to deny myself the least recreation, and to sit chained to my table, when a regard for my own health, or my own wishes, would move me away." [52] And he adds other cajoleries and pet names: "Dearest Titmouse," "Darling Tatie," "My dearest Wig," "an unlimited number of kisses," "I should like to have you by me—*so* much." [53]

On the last day of March Dickens wrote his uncle, Thomas Culliford Barrow, announcing his approaching marriage. Though he was marrying on the £50 from Macrone and the modest financial prospects of his agreement with Chapman and Hall, he felt proud of the favorable reception given *Sketches by Boz*, and confident about his future. He was not a little pleased, too, with the merits of the match he had made, describing Kate to his uncle as "the daughter of a gentleman who has recently distinguished himself by a celebrated work on music, who was the most intimate friend and companion of Sir Walter Scott, and one of the most eminent of the literati of Edinburgh."

"There is no member of my family," he went on, "to whom I should be prouder to introduce my wife than yourself," but his uncle's attitude toward his father made that impossible. "If I could not as a single man, I cannot as a married one, visit a relation's house from which my father is excluded; nor can I see any relatives here who would not treat him as they would myself." This was a painful decision, Dickens wrote, for he could not forget when he was Thomas Barrow's "little companion and nurse, through a weary illness," nor the many proofs he had received in later days of his uncle's interest and affection. Nor would he ask his uncle to alter his determination, even though he felt it an injustice to his father's real character. But though Barrow thus made it impossible for them to know each other again on the terms of intimacy and friendship Dickens would desire, at heart he would ever be an affectionate nephew.[54]

Since Kate was still some six weeks short of being of age, it was necessary that they have a special license officially stating that she married with her father's consent.[55] Dickens, of course, knew all the ins and outs of Doctors' Commons, and on March 29th obtained from the Vicar General's Office[56] the proper authorization in the name of the Archbishop of Canterbury. Four days later, on April 2, 1836, he and Catherine were married very quietly at St. Luke's Church, Chelsea, and there was an unpretentious wedding breakfast at Mr. Hogarth's home in York Place.[57] The rector of the church was the Reverend Charles Kingsley, father of the author of *Westward Ho!* It was the curate, however, not the rector, who made them man and wife.[58]

The ceremony and the wedding breakfast were so simple that Thomas Beard, who served as best man, was able in later years to remember nothing about it save that he and Macrone were the only guests outside the members of the Dickens and Hogarth families.[59] Dickens had originally asked Macrone to fill that office, but the ladies had unanimously exclaimed, he wrote, "that I *must* be attended to the place of execution by a single man." [60] Henry Burnett, who was now engaged to marry Dickens's sister Fanny,[61] described the event long afterward: "I can see him now, helping his young wife out of the carriage after the wedding and taking her up the steps" of her father's house "in the Fulham Road, then standing opposite orchards and gardens as far as the eye could reach." [62] At the wedding breakfast, "A few common, pleasant things were said, healths were drunk with a very few words . . . and all seemed happy, not the least so Dickens and his young girlish wife." [63]

That evening the young couple arrived at Mrs. Nash's little slatted cottage on the north side of the Gravesend Road in the tiny village of Chalk, not far from Chatham and the scenes of Dickens's childhood. Here they spent the one-week honeymoon that was all the time Dickens had before his work compelled him to return to town.[64] At the end of the week, he and Kate went back to London and his chambers at

Furnival's Inn, where a newly purchased sideboard, the freshly covered sofa, and all Dickens's bargains, from the brown beer jugs to the pair of lusters, were arranged within the three rooms.

With them in these modest quarters would be staying Kate's sixteen-year-old sister Mary, who was developing into a beautiful and interesting girl.[65] She was dazzled by the genius and fascination of her brother-in-law, and he found it impossible to speak too highly in her praise. Her intelligence, her virtues, and her beauty were constantly on his lips.[66] In her portrait painted during the following year by Hablôt Knight Browne, she has dark, smooth hair, a high, pale forehead, and a pensive face rather more suggestive of melancholy than Kate's, but Dickens found her merry, sweet, and gay as well as good.[67] The two sisters were tenderly devoted to each other; even in childhood they had never had a single quarrel or moment of anger.[68] Soon Mary was their constant companion. She made her way more deeply and intimately into Dickens's heart even than either of his own sisters. She became, he said of her, "the grace and life of our home"; "so perfect a creature," he believed, "never breathed." [69]

*   *   *   *   *

So Dickens began his married life. He had an ideal picture in his imagination of what marriage should be like, a sweet and brightly colored domesticity in which at the end of his day's work he would turn for happiness to the fond looks and gentle ways of his wife.[70] There would be no more of "the moping solitude of chambers," but always the warm companionship of their own fireside, where he would tell her "rationally what I have been doing" throughout a day whose pursuits and labors would all have for their mainspring her "advancement and happiness." [71]

It was a dream no more unreal or egotistic than most people form of their future marital relations, and no more ignorant of the adjustments each would have to make if their life together was to run smooth. Not the least of the ways in which Dickens is extraordinary is that he actually did learn from experience, and refused to be with Kate the servant of whim or caprice that he knew he had been with Maria Beadnell. The reward of his entire surrender then had been to have his heart torn and his pride shattered; this time the surrenders should not be made by him. Naturally, he overcompensated. It would not be true to say he did not love Kate, but it must be said that there were reservations in his love and that he regarded her from a certain judicial if affectionate elevation.

These aspects of their relationship are implicit in the entire tone of his correspondence with her. He denied feeling himself her superior, but one does not deny what there is no danger of anyone thinking. Her displays of coldness and temper drew from him neither the grief nor the anger of the desperate lover, only the assurance that he had been "hurt" by her conduct and the calm "advice" to overcome her defects of temper. So a father might speak to a refractory child, so long as he remembered that it *was* a child, and even parents are not free from explosions of anger. Undoubtedly Kate had moods of sulky ill-humor and was unreasonable in her inability to see that he could not neglect his work to go and hold her hand when she was in low spirits, and Dickens refused to yield on these matters. He was patient, kind, and reasonable—but he definitely spoke as one in authority, not as an equal. If she could not refrain from being sullen and obstinate with him, let her say so, and he would take himself off. It was an ultimatum that fixed their relative positions once and for all.

But though Dickens could force Kate to surrender, he did not see her character more clearly than most lovers are apt to do. He thought her tendency to pout and feel "coss" and complain of the long stretches of work in which he left her alone would melt away in the sweetness of intimacy. He did not observe that she understood no better than she had at the beginning the claims of the imaginative labors that chained him to his desk. He knew that she was gentle and compliant; he did not realize that the incapacity to resist which made her go down before his will also made her an easy prey to the mistrust and passive self-pity he told her to overcome. If Kate could not fight him, neither could she overcome a weakness that rendered her more immovable to change than if she had met him with the strength of hot defiance. She was amiable, devoted, unenterprising, lachrymose. She would no doubt have made an admirable wife to a placid gentleman of comfortable means. But Dickens had his way to make by his energies and his gifts; and his nature, flashing from elation to misery and back in an instant, was all wire-drawn intensity.

Dickens understood his own nature and its springs little better than he did Kate's. He knew what he wanted and what he did not want; he did not know what those facts might portend. With his boundless confidence in the power of the will—which had already made him so different from the sickly and heartbroken little boy of only twelve years ago —it was impossible for him to believe that the will has limits. He could not imagine that there were elements in his own character as well as in his wife's beyond the ability of the will to alter. He saw the changes he had made; he did not reflect that he might not have been so able to mold himself to a different pattern. He was fiercely sure that all achievement is possible. And therefore he could not conceive that Kate might not change at all or that he might grow less patiently and gently critical than he had been during the period of their courtship.

Already deeply grained in Dickens was a quality whose existence he himself did not come to realize clearly until long after, when he referred it to the wound Maria Beadnell had given his heart. But even before that, so far as all his deeper emotions were concerned, he had become intensely reserved, and his unhappiness over her had only sharpened a tendency already there. His companions in the blacking warehouse had never received from him any explanation of how he came to be there or any sign of his secret grief, and his schoolfellows had never known that hidden shame of his life which no one, in fact, except John Forster, was ever to hear until Dickens was in his grave. Mere acquaintances of later years were apt to believe that Dickens was all spontaneity and warm-hearted intimacy; and his friendliness was entirely sincere, of course, in its way. But it did not involve his taking people really into his confidence. He did that with very few and the appearance of intimacy with all the others was imaginative and dramatic exuberance. He had told Maria Beadnell all his heart; it would be only with the greatest difficulty that he could so let himself become defenseless again.

He did not do so with Kate. He could be playfully tender with her, and even tell her with a gravely affectionate restraint that he loved her greatly; but some last surrender, some inner heart of his heart he did not yield, and could not yield to anyone. He probably could not and did not conceal from her his father's continuing misadventures, but the fact that he never told her of the blacking warehouse is curiously symbolic. Surely she would have pitied him for his sufferings? Yes, but though he pitied himself he could not bear to be pitied. He yearned for tenderness and yet trembled away from it as a net in which he might be entangled. It was the same fear that later made him repress the manifestations of his love even for their children except when they were very young. There were depths in his being that he shrank from exposing to the gentlest touch.

With these obstacles to complete intimacy between them, it was probably unfortunate that Dickens and Kate began their married life with a third person in their household. Kate loved her sister deeply, and Dickens enveloped her in an imaginative idealization, but for a young married couple to have anyone else in their home is an inevitable restraint, and even more of one if they are living together in only three rooms. Neither husband nor wife can be so singly impelled to explore each other's resources as a companion. Neither can behave in a way so spontaneously and solely generated by considerations of his relationship to the other. Whatever problems there may be between them are more apt to be suppressed in the interests of seeming harmony than solved by the attainment of real harmony.

The existence of a permanent guest in the household is fraught with other dangers. If Mary Hogarth had been troublesome and tactless, Dickens would certainly have resented her presence as an imposition. In fact she was sweet, considerate, and happy-spirited, and bathed Dickens in an admiration that probably had its share in generating his praise of her. When the third member of the family is a beautiful and adoring young girl who admires her sister's husband beyond measure, it is easy for him to believe that any flaws in the serenity of his home are no fault of his, and easy for him, too, without quite realizing that he is doing so, to exalt the younger sister at the expense of the other. In the occasional small frictions of any home, a husband so situated may not always reflect that it is easier to be a perfect guest than to be a perfect wife. Elements such as these one senses in the beginnings of Dickens's married life. His eulogies of Mary Hogarth were indubitably innocent in all conscious feeling, and there is no evidence for assuming that Kate ever imagined them to be otherwise, or resented them or felt any twinge of jealousy or diminished love for her sister.[72] But there is still the possibility that the entire lives of Charles Dickens and his wife might have been different if when they had set up housekeeping in Furnival's Inn they had been alone.

Could a sufficiently prescient observer, connecting all the facts about them, have forecast the course they were to travel? With their future a part of the past to us, it is impossible to say, although it is always tempting to concentrate on all the little hints that might lead one to conclude that what did happen happened inevitably. But certainly no one, not Dickens himself, in whose breast some of the most significant of the facts were locked as secrets, knew what they all were or was prepared to understand their meaning. No one did anticipate what was going to happen, probably no one could have done so. The unbelievable success of *The Pickwick Papers*—the amazing trajectory of Dickens's career from that point on—and its impact on his character and outlook, were all beyond the powers of the wildest imagination to foresee. Catherine might well have lived happily enough if Dickens had been a busy journalist and minor literary man with a home in some leafy London suburb. It was more uncertain how she would do as the wife of an enormously ambitious, volatile, and determined genius who would soon be moving as a conqueror among the great of his time.

CHAPTER FOUR

"Pickwick Triumphant"

T HE first number of *Pickwick* had consisted of a modest four hundred copies, set up and run off in one evening by Mr. Aked, the
foreman of the printing establishment, after the other workmen had
left.[1] Nevertheless, Chapman and Hall evidently had strong hopes for
the new publication, and made unusually vigorous efforts to obtain
as much newspaper publicity as possible. Their first full-page spread
in the *Athenaeum* with the *Pickwick Papers* featured in the upper
half, and a corresponding announcement in the *Times*, had been followed up by a whole cluster of smaller advertisements in all the more
important weeklies. During the first week after publication, besides
the large advertisement in their own *Library of Fiction*, they ran advertisements in the *Times*, the *Morning Post*, the *Court Journal*, and
the *Age*.[2]

But at first the critical reception was chilly in comparison with the
praise that had greeted *Sketches by Boz*. The opening chapter of *Pickwick*, with its crude satire on learned societies and Parliamentary manners, struck the *Atlas* as representing a vein of "exhausted comicality":
it dismissed the new work as a "strange publication" that professed
"to be funny," but was in fact "excessively dull." Neither the *Times*
nor the *Observer* reviewed it at all, though the *Times* printed Mr. Pickwick's bewildered dialogue with the cab driver about the horse that was
forty-two years old and kept in the shafts to prevent his falling down.
The Bath *Herald* found Dickens's humor "enigmatic" but "harmless." [3]

Nor were sales other than discouraging. After the first number,
acting on the advice of Charles Tilt, the wholesale bookseller, Chapman and Hall sent out fifteen hundred copies of each number to the

provinces "on sale or return," but for the first five numbers an average of fourteen hundred and fifty of these came back.[4] The London sales gave no reason to increase the quantity of their printings.[5]

Relations with Seymour were uneasy. The touchy artist had not been mollified by the retention of his club idea or by the invention of Mr. Winkle as the boastful and blundering sportsman. Even though Mr. Tupman and Mr. Snodgrass were also good material for him he was still chafing at being relegated to second place. Despite the fact that the prospectus of the story had mentioned Kent and the Medway among the scenes of the book, he convinced himself that the visit to Rochester was a deviation from the agreed plan. The whole second number seemed to exasperate him. His indignation boiled over at the tragic melodrama of "The Stroller's Tale" and its dying clown. This interpolated story, which Dickens had probably inserted by way of working off "copy" and lessening the demands upon his time in the days prior to his honeymoon, Seymour angrily took as a deliberate violation of the tone of broad comedy he felt he excelled in. He couldn't even ignore it; the story was so prominent a part of the number that it would clearly have to supply the subject for one of his four engravings.[6]

Inwardly seething, Seymour forced himself to the distasteful task. When the drawing was done, Chapman and Hall didn't like it; neither did Dickens.[7] The publishers adroitly passed on to Dickens the problem of dealing with the fretful artist by suggesting that the young author and the older man had better meet face to face and discuss future plans. So far the two had not so much as seen each other; Dickens was delighted to do so. There is no indication of whether or not Chapman and Hall gave him any hint of Seymour's resentment.[8] On April 14th, less than a week after returning from Chalk, Dickens wrote Seymour that he was asking Chapman and Hall in for "a glass of grog" the following Sunday evening and hoped the artist would be able to come too.[9]

In his opening paragraph he tactfully praised Seymour's rendering of "our mutual friend Mr. Pickwick," and added that he was happy to be able to congratulate the artist, the publishers, and himself on the success of their enterprise. Although more favorable reviews had by this time appeared—in William Jerdan's *Literary Gazette*, Fraser's *Literary Chronicle*, the *News and Sunday Herald*, *Bell's Life in Lon-*

don, and the *Spectator*—the feeble sales might have excused Seymour if his irritation went up another few degrees at this remark and if he thought the "success" might have been more pronounced had they kept to *his* scheme. But worse was to follow.

He had seen Seymour's sketch for "The Stroller's Tale," Dickens continued, and thought it "extremely good; but still, it is not quite my idea"; he would feel personally obliged if Seymour would make another drawing. "The alterations I want," he went on with calm unconscious arrogance, "I will endeavor to explain." The woman should be younger, the "dismal man" less miserable and looking more sympathetic and solicitous, the sick man emaciated but not repulsive. "The furniture of the room," he concluded, on a note of praise again, "you have depicted *admirably*." [10] Seymour must have been gratified to have it conceded that he could draw a bed and a three-cornered table, and that it was merely the people he had got all wrong.

On the appointed evening, Sunday, the 17th, Seymour arrived at Furnival's Inn. Edward Chapman was not there; William Hall, it appears, must have been; Kate and Dickens's brother Frederick were.[11] Their interview, Dickens said, was "short," and Seymour "certainly offered no suggestion whatsoever" about the contents of *Pickwick*.[12] Seymour in fact had no ideas except his sense of grievance at having been supplanted and his vague notion about cockney sportsmen that had been superseded. No other account than Dickens's of what took place at that meeting is known to exist. One imagines Seymour, though, uneasily trying to assert his own age and established reputation against Dickens's extreme youth and comparative obscurity, and nettled at his host's failure to be abashed, simmering with the injustice of seeing his original idea discarded and his own powers of comic invention ignored, threatening—or indecisively half threatening—to withdraw and let some younger and less distinguished man take over the menial job.

But if Seymour adopted any such course, he had no chance against Dickens. The younger man already felt the stirring of his own powers. Very courteous, very handsome, very happy, seemingly calm but seething with excitement within, he takes his stand. The future course of *Pickwick* will be determined entirely by himself, and he must reserve the right from time to time to issue such instructions about the illustrations as he deems necessary. His publishers are completely in accord with him on this point—here a confirmatory glance at little Mr. Hall.[13] Whatever the exact course of the brief meeting, Seymour went away committed to illustrating whatever Dickens wrote. They parted with an appearance of cordiality, but inwardly Seymour was sick with the humiliation of defeat.[14]

Next day he set to work on "The Dying Clown" again, but in his perturbed emotion he spoiled the plate. He had done only two illustrations out of the four, and time was getting on. All the next day, Tuesday, he worked hard at the re-engraving. Wednesday morning young Frederick Dickens came knocking on his brother's door at Furnival's Inn with startling news. Seymour had gone into the summerhouse in his garden at Islington, placed the muzzle of a fowling piece in his mouth, and blown out his brains. There was a letter close beside the body:

"Best and dearest of wives—for best of wives you have been to me —blame, I charge you, not any one, it is my own weakness and infirmity. I don't think any one has been a malicious enemy to me; I have never done a crime my country's laws punish with death. Yet I die, my life it ends. I hope my Creator will grant me peace, which I have prayed for in vain whilst living." [15]

In his studio was found the completed plate of "The Dying Clown." The overwrought man had finished the hateful assignment and then gone out and killed himself.

Dickens received the news with consternation and anxiety.[16] Just how much he knew of Seymour's kickings and rebellions with Chapman and Hall cannot be determined, or how much he may have sensed beneath the surface in their one polite, brief meeting. But he could not have failed to guess that the unhappy artist's suicide had been precipitated by his failure to control the project he had initiated. And yet it could hardly be said that Dickens was to blame. He was not obliged to accept an offer in a form uncongenial to him, and there was no reason why he should not propose any changes in it that he pleased. It would have been absurd to suspect that a man he did not even meet until later would blow his brains out because Dickens's ideas were adopted rather than his own. Even the pathetic phrases of the poor artist's farewell note plainly absolved anyone else from having driven him to his deed, and their unbalanced thought-processes reveal a mind in no normal state. But with all these facts conceded, it would still be a shock for anyone to know that the course he had followed was instrumental, however innocently, in leading a fellow creature to take his own life. Dickens had not been cruel or ruthless; there was no way in which he could have anticipated and prevented Seymour's act. His genius had merely annihilated the weaker man.

The distress he felt was legitimately mingled with a certain anxiety. Seymour's engravings had been the reason for bringing *Pickwick* into existence; with the artist dead before the second number had even appeared in print, might not the publishers decide to drop the whole enterprise? And what, then, would Dickens do to replace the additional fourteen guineas a month on the strength of which he had married? It was true that the more recent reviews were all favorable, including Jerdan's powerful *Literary Gazette*,[17] but there was no universal clamor of applause and no rush of orders to set the presses roaring.

* * * * *

That Chapman and Hall, in fact, decided to go on—influenced, no doubt, by Dickens's own determination—appears little less than a magic of personal magnetism. But in the same way that this extremely confident young man had persuaded them to follow his suggestions rather than Seymour's original plan, and had emerged as the dominant force in the work, so he had managed to infect them with something of his own enthusiasm. He did more. Chapman and Hall not only went on with *Pickwick*; they agreed that a new artist should be chosen to take Seymour's place, and that Dickens should have the final voice in choosing him and superintending his work.[18]

Rapid action had to be taken. Chapman and Hall published an announcement dated April 25th, one week after Seymour's death, reassuring the four hundred people more or less who might have seen the first number: "Arrangements are in progress which will enable us to present the ensuing number of the *Pickwick Papers* on an improved plan which, we trust, will give entire satisfaction to our numerous readers." [19] The second number appeared with the three engravings that were all Seymour had finished; nothing else could be done without what might prove a disastrous delay in publication. Meanwhile they conferred with Dickens on the "improved plan," and cast about for a man to illustrate the third number.

George Cruikshank might have seemed the natural choice, but he was booked up with as much work as he could handle; and after having chafed at Cruikshank's slowness while *Sketches by Boz* was going through the press, Dickens may not have felt that Cruikshank sufficiently appreciated the importance of promptitude. Some three months after Seymour's death, Cruikshank sent them a very youthful artist named John Leech, whom he thought promising. By that time, of course, a choice had been made.[20] Dickens saw several other applicants in Furnival's Inn. Among them came a young Anglo-Indian giant with a broken nose, one William Makepeace Thackeray, who showed him two or three sketchy line drawings completely different in style from Seymour's elaborate etchings.[21] Thackeray imagined he had been chosen; he exultantly dined a young fellow artist named Hablôt Knight Browne on sausage and mashed potatoes to celebrate.[22] But actually Dickens found his drawings quite unsuitable. Time pressed, and still no one had been chosen.

John Jackson, an engraver who worked for Chapman and Hall, then suggested that they approach Robert William Buss, who had supplied an illustration for Dickens's "A Little Talk about Spring and the Sweeps" in the third number of their *Library of Fiction*.[23] Buss was a well-known artist who had done portraits of numerous actors, including Mathews, Harley, Buckstone, and Vanderhoff; he had also exhibited subject pictures at the Royal Academy: *Watt's First Experiment with Steam, The Introduction of Tobacco by Sir Walter Raleigh, The Biter Bit, the Musical Bore*.[24] Several of these were humorous and many of them had been engraved. Furthermore, Buss already had a reputation as an illustrator of books. He had begun work on another painting for the Academy, but he agreed as a favor to Chapman and Hall to make a sample sketch for them.[25] This sketch may have been "The Review at Chatham," illustrating an episode from the second number. It was not used—that number had already appeared in print —but was evidently regarded as promising enough to justify selecting Buss for the task.[26] Obligingly, he set aside his painting and concentrated on the illustrations for the third number.

Fortunately, there were now only two to be made. For the "improved plan" that Dickens and his publishers had been discussing turned out to be that Dickens should supply eight more pages of story each month and that the number of engravings should be reduced from four to two! Dickens seized the occasion to suggest that, since he was to increase his contribution, they increase his *rate* of remuneration from nine to ten guineas a sheet "until the appearance—say of the fourth or fifth number"; and then increase it again "in the event of the sale of the Work increasing as we expect"! Meanwhile, he argued, it would cost them only an additional two pounds a number.[27] (A sheet consisted of sixteen pages, and the enlarged number would amount to two sheets, or twenty guineas.)

Buss did not have the standing of Seymour and doubted Hall's solemn assurance that they were offering him the same rate; [28] even with the two guineas more that Dickens was asking it is likely that Chapman and Hall were cutting down costs or at the very least breaking even. The new plan of more text and fewer illustrations was accordingly announced to the public as one that "entails upon the publishers a considerable expense, which nothing but a large circulation would justify them in incurring." [29]

Buss had experience in wood engraving, but unfortunately he knew nothing about etching. He dropped everything else and worked night and day in the two or three weeks he had before the plates must be turned in, but he could not make himself even passably competent in so brief a time. Because of his inexperience in laying it, he found that the wax invariably broke under the etching point. When the time grew short he had no choice but to take his two designs to a professional engraver, to be etched and bitten in. "The work," Buss said, "he did very well, but . . . the free touch of the original work was entirely wanting." There was no more time, however. These two unsatisfactory plates had to be placed in the printer's hands, "abominably bad" though Buss confessed them to be.[30]

Chapman and Hall felt almost desperate. They had laid out considerable sums in advertising; the artist whose name would have been a powerful selling point was dead with only seven etchings done; the man who had followed him was a failure; sales were still lagging, and they might have to foot a heavy loss. Dickens had convinced them that the book ought to go well, but illustrations were then regarded as essential to a book's success. Fortunately, John Jackson had another suggestion. A pamphlet entitled *Sunday Under Three Heads* which Dickens had just written under the pseudonym of "Timothy Sparks" had four illustrations that admirably caught its flashing combination

of high-spirited common sense and caricature. Why not try the artist
who had supplied them? [31]

This was young Hablôt Knight Browne, who had dined with Thackeray on the night he fancied *he* had been chosen to be the illustrator
of *Pickwick*. Browne was still a few months short of twenty-one, but
had already scored notable successes in his work. He had been apprenticed to Finden, the line engraver, studied water-color drawing, and
worked in the "Life" School in St. Martin's Lane. At the age of seventeen he had earned the medal of the Society of Arts for the best representation of a historical subject, and had just won a prize offered by
the Society with a laughable etching of *John Gilpin*.[32] Browne was shy
and extremely nervous, but Dickens took to him at once. Better still,
the young artist immediately hit the mark with his etching of Mr.
Pickwick and Sam Weller in the yard of the White Hart. His first few
plates were signed "Nemo," but then came the famous pseudonym of
"Phiz," which marked the long years of his artistic collaboration with
"Boz." [33] Publishers and author felt that Browne was decidedly their
man. So Chapman and Hall sent a curt note to R. W. Buss dispensing
with his services.[34]

Buss was thunderstruck. He had dropped work on his Academy painting at a time that rendered it impossible for him to make that year's
date of entry any longer, and he had believed himself definitely engaged for the entire course of the work. He knew his first two plates had
been disappointing, but he thought he had done as well as could reasonably be expected on such short notice and was sure his subsequent
efforts would be better. (In fact, less than a year later he was doing the
etching of his own plates for Henry Colburn, then a much more important publisher than Chapman and Hall, and illustrating books by
some of the best-known authors of the time, such as Mrs. Trollope's
The Widow Married and Captain Marryat's *Peter Simple*.[35]) But
Chapman and Hall claimed that he had only been on trial and felt
they could afford no further risks. People who heard Buss's side of the
story advised him to go to law, "but Hall," he said, had been "cunning
enough to know that his promises in the name of the firm were but
verbal, made with me alone in my painting room, and so took a mean
advantage." [36] Whether or not Hall had misled him, the firm certainly
repaid the favor Buss did them by dismissing him with brusque ingratitude.[37]

Though the illustrating problem had been overcome, sales still lingered in the doldrums.[38] The second number was reviewed in the *Sun*, the *Morning Post*, Captain Marryat's *Metropolitan Magazine*, and even as far afield as the Bath *Chronicle*; the third was praised in *John Bull*, which predicted for the publication "a high place in the ranks of comic literature." [39] But it is doubtful if more than four or five hundred copies of each number had been sold.[40] In February Dickens had effervescently announced that Pickwick was "begun in all his might and glory"; but three months later that worthy's circulation was so poor that Dickens agreed to let his own remuneration be reduced to ten guineas a number.[41] When Macrone offered him £200, early in May, for a three-volume novel to be entitled *Gabriel Vardon, the Locksmith of London,* he was glad to accept it. This new work of fiction he rashly calculated he might be able to complete by the end of November or soon thereafter.[42]

Meanwhile he did not allow himself to be discouraged. *The Village Coquettes,* which had been hanging fire, needed to be completed and put in Braham's hands. The proprietor of the St. James's Theatre would soon be leaving town; a day's delay at this time might mean a month's after the season had begun. Some of the lyrics had to be altered to accord with Hullah's music, there was a dramatic duet to be worked out, and the "Finale" to be composed; Hullah's part of the work dragged. "When, oh *when,*" Dickens pleaded desperately, "will this music be ready?" [43]

Finally, though, book and music were finished and submitted to Braham. Hogarth had already spoken in Hullah's behalf to Cramer and Company, the music publishers, who were eager to buy the score.[44] Braham's answer, when it came, was enthusiastic. Talking with Hogarth, he was full of Dickens's "works and 'fame,' " expressed an earnest desire to introduce Boz to the public as a dramatic writer, and added that he intended to produce the opera within a month after he opened at Michaelmas. He wished, however, to have a low comedy part for Harley introduced into the play, and this involved rewriting some of the rest of it.[45]

* * * * *

During these same weeks, despite all these preoccupations and his work on *Pickwick,* Dickens made the time to indite an angry pamphlet which is significant of his entire viewpoint at this period. Toward the end of April he had listened indignantly to the reintroduction in Parliament of a bill offered by Sir Andrew Agnew that would have prohibited not merely all work but all recreation on Sunday.[46] Agnew had been repeatedly bringing up or supporting measures of this stamp since 1832, only to have them defeated or deferred to the next session. In April, 1834, Edward Bulwer had argued powerfully against the bill of that year that it not merely had no warrant in Scripture but was antisocial and un-Christian.

Dickens felt infuriated by the persistence with which this repressive and puritanical measure was introduced. But he was even more infuriated by its discriminatory character, as a bill that would bear down on the pleasures of the poor, forbidding them the few harmless enjoyments available to them at the same time that it left the well-off complacently untouched. It was another illustration of the harsh tendency to consider working people mere beasts of burden with no right to any indulgence save the briefest possible surcease from toil. Writing in a hot rage, Dickens tore off a molten political pamphlet called *Sunday Under Three Heads: As it is; As Sabbath Bills would make it; As it might be made.* By working at top speed, he got it in print by June, signed with the pseudonym "Timothy Sparks." [47]

Dickens dedicated it caustically to Dr. Blomfield, the Bishop of London, who had raised pious hands of horror over the viciousness of Sunday excursions among the lower classes. It irritated him to hear the upper-class cant about the poor not knowing their stations in life because the workman bought his wife a ribbon for her dress and his child a feather for her bonnet, and the entire family sallied forth for one day's outing after six devoted to work. What was so criminal, he asked, about these good-humored crowds with their picnic baskets and bundles of bulging apples on the decks of the river steamers? What was the enormity of climbing Windmill Hill, strolling among the trees of Greenwich Park, gliding past the meadows of Twickenham, or glimpsing the cornfields and orchards of Kent? Only a gloomy fanaticism would insist on closing the shops for people who work so late that they have no other time to buy their Sunday's supplies with their Saturday night's wages. Only an intolerant zeal would demand that coffee-stalls be barred on Sunday mornings to dwellers in single rooms who had nowhere else to obtain their breakfasts.[48]

The enthusiasts for whom Sir Andrew spoke, professing to be horrified about the desecrating of the Sabbath, wanted to shut the bakeshops and deprive poor folk of their weekly hot dinnner of mutton and browned potatoes. Look at it being borne home, Dickens bids us, "amidst a shouting of small voices, and jumping of fat legs," while the baby in his mother's arms on the doorstep, "not precisely understanding the importance of the business in hand, but clearly perceiving that it is something unusually lively, kicks and crows most lustily, to the unspeakable delight of all the children and both the parents." [49] Such a scene of innocent delight "would fill Sir Andrew Agnew with astonishment; as well it might, seeing that Baronets, generally speaking, eat pretty comfortable dinners all the week through, and cannot be expected to understand what people feel, who only have a meat dinner on one day out of every seven." [50]

The iron-hearted man who would deprive such people of their only pleasures, Dickens points out, would be doing his best to drive the respectable poor into the filth, disease, fornication, and drunken squalor that characterized the wretched slum-dwellers of St. Giles and Drury Lane. Dire poverty deprived these of even the humble relaxation, the breath of country air, the game of cricket, available to the more fortunate. They had no amusement for the mind, no means of exercising the body.[51] Consequently they flew to the gin shop as their only resource, and then, when they lay wallowing in the gutter, "your saintly law-givers lift up their hands to heaven, and exclaim for a law which shall convert the day intended for rest and cheerfulness, into one of universal gloom, bigotry, and persecution." [52]

But hardly less objectionable than its oppressiveness to the poor was the "deliberate cruelty and crafty injustice" with which Sir Andrew's bill exempted the rich from its provisions. They might continue to have their servants cook their Sunday dinners and to travel in their escutcheoned carriages; "the whole of saintly venom" was directed against the licensed victualer and the rumbling hackney coach that served the artisan and his family. Nothing forbade the fashionable promenade, the Sunday feast, the private oratorio; it was only the public newsroom and the public debate which might enlighten the people that must be guarded against. All of his usual indulgences were preserved to the man of wealth; he never lacked them, and therefore they were "necessary" to him. But the poor man who saved his money to enjoy some little luxury on a Sunday must not have it; for he usually did not, and therefore it was *not* "necessary" to *him*.[53]

"It is customary," Dickens wrote, "to affect a deference for the motives of those who advocate these measures, and a respect for the feeling by which they are actuated. They do not deserve it. If they legislate in ignorance, they are criminal and dishonest; if they do so with their eyes open, they commit wilful injustice; in either case, they bring religion into contempt. But they do NOT legislate in ignorance. Public prints, and public men, have pointed out to them again and again, the consequences of their proceedings." [54] Neither genuine piety nor honest ignorance, Dickens insists, explains the way in which this bill has been repeatedly brought forward, but "an envious, heartless, ill-conditioned dislike" of seeing humble people cheerful and happy, and a selfish, un-Christian pride filled with a sense of its own high worthiness and of the shortcomings of others.[55]

It was ludicrous for these holy hypocrites to quote criminals on the scaffold who blamed their fate on falling into dissipated ways on the Sabbath. The same argument would abolish all holidays whatever, and frown on teaching people to write because some fell into forgery.[56] Instead of making Sunday into a day of lassitude and dejection, it should be made into one of rational enjoyment. Let people play outdoor games, go on walks, take excursions by boat or coach. Let the British Museum, the National Gallery, and the Gallery of Practical Science be open to working men on the one day they could go to these places instead of closed at that very time. Let the fields neighboring London resound to the stroke of the bat, the ring of the quoit, and the sound of laughing voices—and vice would be weakened, true religion strengthened.[57] Surely God can never intend, Dickens concludes, "that the more a man strives to discharge [his] duties, the more he shall be debarred from happiness and enjoyment." Sunday legislators should remember the words of the Master "whose precepts they misconstrue, and whose lessons they pervert—'The Sabbath was made for man, and not man to serve the Sabbath.' " [58]

Sir Andrew's bill was thrown out on its second reading on May 18th by a majority of thirty-two votes.[59] Dickens's blast had nothing to do with this defeat, however, since it was not printed until June. When the bill was reintroduced yet once more in 1837, in fact, it was approved by the House of Commons, but lingered in committee until

Parliament was dissolved by the death of William IV. Sir Andrew was not elected to the new Parliament and no other legislator took any step to push his bill again. Possibly Dickens's pamphlet had by this time added its mite to a weight of public sentiment that discouraged further endeavors to force the measure.

The greatest significance, however, of *Sunday Under Three Heads* lies in its indication that Dickens had already attained a defined social attitude. It clearly displays the stand he was taking toward rich and poor, and reveals the broad sympathy with which he surveys the duties and enjoyments of existence. It contains the core of that warm-hearted humanism and humanitarianism that glowed within him throughout his entire life. Its satire upon the intolerance and narrowness of the dissenting clergy, too, strikes a characteristic and prophetic note. The Nonconformist preacher of the pamphlet, with his intemperate denunciations and frantic thumping of the pulpit, and the groaning enthusiasm of his congregation, did not precede by many months the red-nosed and hypocritical Stiggins in *Pickwick*, who is followed in turn by the drunken Melchisedech Howler of *Dombey and Son* and the oily Chadband of *Bleak House*. Flagrant rectitude was always to make Dickens see red.

*   *   *   *   *

Meanwhile, on the *Chronicle* he continued to be assigned to all the most important news events. Toward the end of May he went down to Suffolk and reported O'Connell's speech at Ipswich, amid intense excitement and fears of mob violence.[60] And on June 22nd he covered the Melbourne-Norton trial. The defendant in this notorious case was no less a personage than the Prime Minister, Lord Melbourne, and there was supposed to be scandalous evidence that the beautiful and charming Caroline Norton had been his mistress.

The Court of Common Pleas at Westminster was jammed that morning, Dickens reported, with members of the *beau monde* who had bribed attendants as much as ten guineas a seat to hear the sensational details.[61] The case turned out to rest on nothing but the spiteful tattle of discharged servants. The witnesses were proved to be of the lowest moral character, and the supposedly incriminating letters between the lady and her alleged lover were so empty of any such implications as to suggest Dickens's parody of them in Bardell vs. Pickwick:

"Dear Mrs. B.—Chops and Tomato sauce. Yours, Pickwick." "I shall not be at home tomorrow. Slow coach. Don't trouble yourself about the warming-pan." At half-past eleven that night, the jury acquitted Lord Melbourne without leaving the court,[62] and a few minutes later the House of Commons cheered the verdict. Dickens, exhausted with his prolonged labors, fell into bed and stayed there all the following day.[63]

Since the publication of *Sketches by Boz* he had agreed with Macrone on a second series, also to be illustrated by Cruikshank, and was hard at work visiting Bedlam and gathering material in other places for additional sketches.[64] He and Kate were now on terms of friendly intimacy with Macrone and his wife, the ladies exchanging visits and notes, and the two families inviting each other to dinners of roast goose and sending messages of sympathy whenever any of them was unwell. Macrone suggested that he take fifteen-year-old Fred into his accounting house, an offer Dickens pondered over accepting. "I have deliberated a long time," he told Macrone, "about the propriety of keeping him at his present study, but I am convinced that at his present period of life, it is really only so much waste time." [65] So, if Macrone would agree to Frederick's taking his tea at home, in order that Dickens might still "set his studies for the night, and see what he is at," [66] Fred would sit himself upon a stool to be initiated into business habits forthwith; and if Macrone really wanted "any sharp young fellow, you can not have one better suited to your purpose." [67]

By the latter part of July, the revisions in *The Village Coquettes* were completed. On Saturday evening, the 23rd, a small party of friends assembled in Furnival's Inn to hear Dickens read the play and try the music.[68] They were all enthusiastic in their praise. At the end of the first act, Macrone offered to buy the copyright of the first edition.[69] Braham also, when the new version was placed in his hands, spoke of it in the highest terms. His musical director Stansbury, he reported, was charmed by it; " 'I sang it to him,' " Dickens quoted Braham, " '—all through'!!!" To Hogarth, Braham said, "Depend upon it, Sir, that there has been no such music since the days of Sheil, and no such piece since the Duenna." Harley said it was a sure card, adding: "Bet you ten pounds it runs fifty nights." [70]

And, to top all these glittering prospects, *Pickwick* at last turned the corner. The sales were still going but languidly as Dickens finished the fourth number, in which Mr. Pickwick comes upon Sam Weller cleaning shoes in the White Hart Yard and determines to take Sam into his own employ. That June there were only two notices in London papers, one in *Bell's Life in London,* the other in the influential *Literary Gazette.*[71] But the editor of the *Gazette,* William Jerdan, reading this fourth number, found Sam Weller irresistible and wrote Dickens a letter counseling him to develop so striking a character to the utmost.[72] Mr. Pickwick's discovery of Sam in fact marked the crucial point in *Pickwick's* fortunes. During July, sales began to swell, orders for back numbers started coming in; all at once it was a flood.[73] By the end of the month Dickens was writing in excited capitals at the close of a letter to Macrone: "PICKWICK TRIUMPHANT." [74] In August, Chapman and Hall suggested that from November they pay him £25 a month.[75] Before the end of its course Pickwick was selling forty thousand copies of every number.

Some of the highly charged activity and glory of these weeks radiates from a letter Dickens wrote to Catherine's grandfather, George Thomson, at the end of July. His exultation fairly crackles through the phrases: "I am at present engaged in revising the proof sheets of the second Edition of the Sketches which will shortly appear; I am preparing another series which must be published before Christmas, I have just finished an opera which will be produced at Braham's Theatre in October, I have to get Mr. Pickwick's lucubrations ready, every month . . ." Why can't the Thomsons, he demands, all come down from Edinburgh for a visit?—"imagine what delightful evenings we might spend at this season of the year—what a family party we should be, on the first night of this never-sufficiently-to-be-talked-of opera . . . Catherine is extremely well, and has got up a most admirable stock of good looks. She has not yet quite recovered from the high and mighty satisfaction she derived from a supper of her own invention and arrangement which we gave to our first little party a week ago, but with this exception she is quite herself, and desires a thousand loves to a thousand relations and friends whose names I have no room to write, and couldn't spell if I had." [76]

The skyrocketing sales of *Pickwick* brought Dickens offers of further work, which he gaily accepted.[77] The editor of the *Carlton Chronicle,* just started that June, wanted a series of fortnightly sketches at liberal rates. "The circulation, I believe," Dickens told Macrone, "is a small one. So much the better—Fewer people will see the Sketches before they are corrected. It is all among the nobs too—Better still. They'll buy the book." [78] Thomas Tegg, the publisher of cheap reprints, offered £100 for a children's book to be called *Solomon Bell the Raree Showman*, which Dickens agreed to finish by Christmas.[79] All this was in addition to the regular installments of *Pickwick*, the three-volume novel promised to Macrone, and his newspaper work on the *Morning Chronicle*, not to mention that both his farce and the operetta would soon be going into rehearsal.

Now that the popularity of *Pickwick* was established, however, almost every week brought more golden opportunities. The preceding March, through Hogarth,[80] Dickens had met Richard Bentley, the New Burlington Street publisher, a short, pink-faced man with bristling hair and huge whiskers, a fluent talker who exuded a warm bonhomie. Bentley had recently dissolved his partnership with Henry Colburn. The two men were furious rivals, Colburn had managed to retain their best authors, and Bentley was consequently on the alert for new talent. He was a clever and daring businessman who did things in a grandiose way; within two months of their meeting he decided that Dickens was a rising figure.[81] He therefore proposed that Dickens write a novel for him, but was disappointed to discover that Macrone had forestalled him, apparently by a matter of weeks, and that Dickens was contracted to Macrone.[82]

Dickens must also have been sorry, for in the course of the next three months he secured or believed he secured from Macrone a release from the engagement to write *Gabriel Vardon*, evidently by connecting it up in some way with the agreement about the second series of his *Sketches*.[83] He also succeeded in canceling his arrangement about a child's book with Thomas Tegg.[84] Around the middle of August, Dickens told Bentley he was now free to consider a contract. Bentley promptly offered to buy the entire copyright of *two* novels of undetermined titles and subject matter and with no time limit specified for their delivery, for the sum of £400 each.

Dickens was shrewdly aware not merely of his soaring market value but of his swelling literary prestige. Confidential friends advised him, he wrote Bentley on August 17th, that he should demand £500. He should be sorry "to appear anxious to drive a hard bargain," but he did not feel the additional sum unreasonable in view of "the rapid sale of *everything* I have yet touched" and "the anxiety I should feel to make it a work on which I might build my fame . . ." The assured emphasis on future fame is especially striking in a young man who is just scoring his first triumph. "Recollect," he concluded, "that you are dealing with an author not quite unknown but who, so far as he has gone, has been most successful." [85] Bentley accepted the amendment, and Dickens signed a contract for both books on August 22nd. This leap to £500 and the extremely flexible conditions show how Dickens's prestige had risen skyward in the fifteen amazing weeks since he had agreed with Macrone to do *Gabriel Vardon* for £200.

*　　*　　*　　*　　*

After these breathless developments, Dickens and Kate relaxed for five or six weeks in a little cottage they took at Petersham for the latter part of August and most of September.[86] But even so Dickens was constantly shuttling back and forth, between its rural sports of strolling in the meadows, riding horseback, and rowing on the stream, and the business activities of London [87]—now demanding why he hadn't seen Browne's designs for the next number of *Pickwick*, now getting proofs of his own manuscript,[88] now dropping in to see how things were going at the St. James Theatre.[89] Braham had decided to put on *The Strange Gentleman* before *The Village Coquettes*, but some of the same players were in both; one of these, Miss Julia Smith, was "a very knowing little person," Dickens reported to Hullah, "*rather* fat, but not a bit too much so, with a very nice smiling pretty face." [90]

Near the end of September Dickens and Kate returned to town, and invited Beard to be one of the party that would see the opening of *The Strange Gentleman* on the 29th.[91] It is a conventional farce of cross-purposes and confused identities, but its elaborate misunderstandings, though mechanically arranged, are ingenious, and it is easy to see that they would be ludicrous enough in the hands of skilled actors. Except for a few lines suggestive of Sam Weller, however, which are given to a comic "boots," its superficial staginess only faintly echoes the rich humor Dickens was already achieving in *Pickwick*. Mme. Sala, one of the leading actresses of the day, scored a resounding success as the portly Julia Dobbs, relentlessly bent on marrying anyone she could capture, whether it was a weak-witted young nobleman or a complete stranger. Dickens's friend Harley was a riot as the "strange gentleman" fleeing from a duel and terrified to believe himself surrounded by an innful of lunatics. The piece ran for almost sixty nights and was put on again after the new year—no inconsiderable success.[92] It gave still wider currency to the name and fame of Boz.

Dickens's contributions to the *Carlton Chronicle* lapsed after the publication of two sketches, that aristocratic publication—together with *Bell's Life in London*—apparently finding it simpler and cheaper to pirate some of his articles as they appeared concurrently in the *Morning Chronicle* and the *Evening Chronicle*.[93] Dickens wrote a letter to Easthope suggesting that the proprietors of the papers remonstrate with the offending periodicals and at least get them to acknowledge the source from which they derived the articles.[94]

In October the printers were to set to work on the second series of *Sketches by Boz*. Dickens agreed with Cruikshank on eight illustrations for the first volume, and left the manuscript with the artist so that he could be quite exact in following the descriptions.[95] He was entertained and a little irritated to hear that Cruikshank proposed to make editorial changes in the text. "I have long believed Cruikshank to be mad," Dickens wrote Macrone; the publisher would oblige him by telling the artist that Dickens was amused by his presumption and that if he had done any such thing "I should have preserved his emendations as 'curiosities of Literature.' " Perhaps it would be a good idea to drop Cruikshank altogether and let the illustrations be done by "his" Pickwick man, who was already favorably known "by his connection with that immortal gentleman." [96]

This small friction was smoothed over, however, and artist and author continued on friendly terms. But he was quite certain, Dickens told Macrone, that he could not get out the second volume before Christmas; the time was too short.[97] In fact, he found entire days being consumed by the preparations for *The Village Coquettes*, and on top of this came a severe attack of facial rheumatism that confined him to his bed and made it impossible for him to write at all for a fortnight.[98] "I cannot do more than one pair of hands and a solitary head can execute," he desperately wrote Cruikshank, "and am really so hard pressed just now that I must have breathing time." [99] In the end, he found it impossible to supply the material for a second volume at all, and at last, in December, 1836, the book appeared in one volume.[100]

During the course of the fall there had been a slight and ludicrous run-in between Dickens and Cramer's, the music publishers who were bringing out the published version of *The Village Coquettes*. They feared that "the young ladies" in boarding schools might feel their modesty shocked by such lines in the lyrics as Squire Norton's

> "A *winter's night has its delight,*
> Well *warm'd to bed we go.*"

"If the young ladies are especially horrified at the bare notion of anybody's going to bed," Dickens told Hullah, "I have no objection to substitute for the objectionable line

> " '*Around, old stories go.*'

"But you may respectfully signify to Cramers that I will see them d- - - -d before I make any further alterations." [101]

The Village Coquettes opened at the St. James's Theatre, with *The Strange Gentleman* on the same bill, on Tuesday evening, December 6th. With his newspaperman's feeling for publicity, Dickens sent not only complimentary tickets but books of the songs to the Editor of the *Examiner* and to various other editors and dramatic critics.[102] Braham himself played the wicked Squire Norton in a hunting coat of scarlet velvet, and John Parry was Young Benson in rustic garb and a preposterous wig with long ringlets that wobbled over his brow. At the end of the performance the audience screamed for Boz, who "appeared, and bowed, and smiled, and disappeared," the critic of the *Examiner* wrote, "and left the audience in perfect consternation that he neither resembled the portraits of Pickwick, Snodgrass, Winkle, or Tupman. Some critics in the gallery were said to have expected Sam Weller. The disappointment was general and deeply felt." [103]

Backstage, Mme. Sala's son, a small boy of ten, was a witness to all the excitement of the occasion. He was patted on the head by Braham, chucked under the chin by Parry, and saw a "very young gentleman with long brown hair falling in silky masses over his temples," "dressed up to the very height of the existing fashion," but with eyes "full of power and strong will, and with a touching expression of sweetness and kindliness on his lips." [104] Throughout the engagement, in fact, Dickens was constantly in the wings and the greenroom, drinking in the intoxication of the experience. When *The Strange Gentleman* was put on again, a little later, Dickens is even supposed once or twice to have stepped on the stage in the minor role of one of the waiters.[105]

Hullah's music was well received, but most of the reviewers did not think much of the play. "Have you seen the Examiner?" Dickens wrote Hullah. "It is *rather* depreciatory of the opera, but like all their critiques against Braham, so well done that I cannot help laughing at it, for the life and soul of me. I have seen the Sunday Times, the Dispatch, and the Satirist, all of which blow their little trumpets against unhappy me, most lustily." [106] The play pretty well deserved what the reviewers said of it, but Hullah's music was charming, the eighteenth-century costumes were pretty, and audiences found it enjoyable. Later still it had a successful run at an Edinburgh theater.

Many of the reviews were affronted by the endeavor to exploit the literary prestige of Boz, which was already extraordinary, as a means of packing the house. It was not then customary for dramatic authors to appear in theaters and take curtain calls, and many of the papers clearly thought that the cries for Boz came from a claque. The *Morning Herald* was "utterly amazed" when the green curtains parted and he actually appeared. The *News* thought Dickens "extremely ill-advised to come forward to receive the congratulations of a *packed* house." Even Jerdan's well-disposed *Literary Gazette* commented unfavorably on the innovation: "When will this ridiculous nonsense end? Will they have Bulwer on the Covent Garden stage next Wednesday at the close of 'La Vallière'? Why had they not Serjeant Talfourd after 'Ion'?" The dramatic critic of the *Examiner*, a clever young man named John Forster, was gentler to the author, but more wittily devastating to the play: "We have a great respect and liking for 'Boz,' " he wrote. "*The Pickwick Papers* have made him, as our readers are very well aware, an especial favourite with us; and we have no idea of his being exhibited gratis. Bad as the opera is, we feel assured that if Mr. Braham will make arrangements to parade the real living 'Boz' every night after that opera, he will insure for it a certain attraction." [107]

For that matter, Dickens had friends who disapproved of his letting Chapman and Hall bring out *Pickwick* in monthly parts, and spoke of it slightingly as "a low, cheap form of publication" that would ruin his rising hopes.[108] The only style suitable to the dignity of a man of letters, they felt, was the three-volume novel selling for a guinea and a half, not this scrabbling for the shillings of the impecunious. But

Dickens had no such delicate notions of dignity, and no desire to limit his audience to an élite. He valued the laughter and the tears of the poor as much as he did the acclaim of the rich. From the beginning he had a keen awareness of the value of publicity and considerable adroitness in seizing and using it. In the full surge of his career he advertised brilliantly; all London would be flooded with his bright orange posters when he was bringing out a new book. And there could be no doubt now of the victorious course the *Pickwick Papers* was running.

* * * * *

The reviews and newspapers were almost a unanimous chorus of praise. Appreciation in the press ranged from *John Bull's* declaration that the September number of *Pickwick* was irresistibly good and that "Smollet never did anything better," to the *Metropolitan Magazine* of the following January comparing Mr. Pickwick and Sam Weller to Don Quixote and Sancho Panza.[109] But more than this, readers in every class of society from high to low became Mr. Pickwick's devoted admirers and followed his adventures from month to month with roars of loving laughter.[110] "Judges on the bench and boys in the street," wrote Forster, "gravity and folly, the young and the old, those who were entering life and those who were quitting it, alike found it to be irresistible." [111] At a locksmith's shop Dr. Shelton Mackenzie came upon a group of twenty men and women who were too poor to afford the shilling that would buy a monthly part and who were renting a copy at twopence a day from a circulating library, which one of them read aloud to the others.[112] "An archdeacon," wrote Thomas Carlyle, "with his own venerable lips, repeated to me, the other night, a strange profane story: of a solemn clergyman who had been administering ghostly consolation to a sick person; having finished, satisfactorily as he thought, and got out of the room, he heard the sick person ejaculate: 'Well, thank God, *Pickwick* will be out in ten days any way!' " [113]

Out in the country Mary Russell Mitford, the author of *Our Village*, was amazed that her friend Miss Jephson hadn't heard of *Pickwick*, and bore testimony to Dickens's triumph: "I did not think there had been a place where English was spoken to which 'Boz' had not penetrated. All the boys and girls talk his fun—the boys in the streets; and yet they who are of the highest taste like it the most. Sir Benjamin Brodie takes it to read in his carriage between patient and patient; and

Lord Denman studies *Pickwick* on the bench whilst the jury are deliberating. Do take some means to borrow the *Pickwick Papers*. It seems like not having heard of Hogarth, whom he resembles greatly, except that he takes a far more cheerful view, a Shakespearean view. of humanity." [114] And to Elizabeth Barrett she writes that she holds Dickens "to be the next great benefactor of the age to Sir Walter Scott." [115]

Before the last number of *Pickwick* had appeared in its green-paper covers, the plump and amiable little figure with its gaiters and its benevolently glittering spectacles, together with Sam Weller and his other friends, had become more than national figures—they had become a mania. Nothing like it had ever happened before. There were Pickwick chintzes, Pickwick cigars, Pickwick hats, Pickwick canes with tassels, Pickwick coats of a peculiar cut and color; and there were Weller corduroys and Boz cabs.[116] There was a *Pickwick Comic Almanac*, a *Pickwick Treasury of Wit*, a *Sam Weller's Pickwick Jest Book*, and a *Pickwickian Songster*. There were innumerable plagiarisms, parodies, and sequels—a *Pickwick Abroad*, by G. W. M. Reynolds; a *Posthumous Papers of the Cadger Club*; a *Posthumous Notes of the Pickwickian Club*, by a hack who impudently called himself Bos; and a *Penny Pickwick*—not to mention all the stage piracies and adaptations.[117] People named their cats and dogs "Sam," "Jingle," "Mrs. Bardell," and "Job Trotter." [118] It is doubtful if any other single work of letters before or since has ever aroused such wild and widespread enthusiasm in the entire history of literature. Barely past the age of twenty-five, Charles Dickens had already become a world-famous figure beaten upon by a fierce limelight which never left him for the remainder of his life.

While this process was no more than beginning, Dickens himself felt an intimation that he was achieving something greater than he had ever aimed at. "If I were to live a hundred years," he wrote Chapman and Hall on November 1, 1836, "and write three novels in each, I should never be so proud of any of them as I am of Pickwick, feeling as I do, that it has made its own way, and hoping, as I must own I do hope, that long after my hand is withered as the pens it held, Pickwick will be found on many a dusty shelf with many a better work." [119] Wonder still lingers in the words. Dickens could hardly have dreamed how fully the years would realize his proudly humble wish.

CHAPTER FIVE

Knight of the Joyful Countenance

CRITICISM: *Pickwick Papers*

Nor is wonder inappropriate. For the greatness of *Pickwick* seems almost inadvertent, as if powers within its author more vital than any of his conscious purposes had seized upon him and declared themselves. It is easy for the prophet after the event to perceive the enormous talent in *Sketches by Boz* and the promise it holds of future achievement. But even great brilliance often gutters out into failure; though we might not be surprised to learn that the author of the *Sketches* had become a major writer, who would have foretold it? And, above all, who would have predicted that a book undertaken as a hack piece of journalism, issued in installments as it was turned out month by month, and begun only a few weeks after the appearance of his first book, when its author was still a youthful twenty-four, should be not merely one of his own great fictions, but one of the world's masterpieces of sane and inexhaustible laughter?

In the beginning the story didn't even have much of a plan. What little there was came from cheerfully tacking together notions suggested by three or four people.[1] All Dickens had in his own mind hardly amounted to more than a clownish parody of the great eighteenth-century novels that had filled his boyhood with glory: a farcical echo of the lusty adventures of Tom Jones and Partridge or Roderick Random and Strap. He knew only in the faintest way what he intended to make of Mr. Pickwick, and what he finally did make of him turned out altogether different.[2] A further stumbling block was that at first Dickens imagined the publication in monthly numbers compelled each installment to be more or less a complete story in itself.[3] Such a string of disconnected episodes might have limited Mr. Pickwick and

[157]

Sam Weller to the comedy effects of Jeeves and Bertie Wooster. Only by slow degrees did the discrete opening scenes merge into one large and airy landscape as Dickens's imagination broadened to the vision of a world—the comic, heroic, illimitable Pickwick world stretching away, as Chesterton finely says, in "a maze of white roads, a map full of fantastic towns, thundering coaches, clamorous market-places, uproarious inns, strange and swaggering figures." [4]

Even less promising than the shapeless plan were the hackneyed characters and situations. Both were lifted from the shelves of stock comedy. Pickwick is the gullible old fool who can be duped by any sharper, Tupman the plump, middle-aged dandy, Winkle the inept and timid pretender to sporting valor, Snodgrass the philistine's patronizing image of the feebly poetical, half fraud and all fool. The figures surrounding them are stamped from the same materials: the greasy adventurer, the man-hungry old maid, the pompous and ignorant magistrate, the fraudulent solicitors, the raffish medical student and drunken apothecary, the shrewish landlady who terrifies her husband and her lodgers with fainting fits and fury. Even the embarrassments through which the Pickwickians stumble are largely the familiar ones of slapstick misadventure: Mr. Pickwick having his breath knocked out by the indignant cabman, the borrowed coat that involves the frightened Mr. Winkle in an incomprehensible duel, Mr. Tupman's courtship and the plot by which the irrepressible Jingle supplants him, Mrs. Bardell's hysterical jubilation when she mistakes for a proposal of marriage Mr. Pickwick's announcement that he is hiring a manservant.

The opening chapter is dull enough to justify the *Atlas* reviewer's strictures on its "exhausted comicality." Its wooden imitation of Parliamentary proceedings has none of the gleaming silliness that shines in the later accounts of the Eatanswill election and the ludicrous editorial rivalries of the *Gazette* and *Independent*. Perhaps the impatience Dickens felt with his constant attendance in the Gallery blunted his sense of fun in dealing with the long-winded eloquence he heard there. The only good joke in the chapter travesties a famous occasion when Brougham provoked a brawl in the House of Commons by accusing Canning of "monstrous truckling for the purpose of obtaining office." [5] The two avoided being committed to the Serjeant-at-Arms by accepting a pacific suggestion that Brougham's words applied to

Canning's "official not his personal character." Mr. Blotton's explanation that in calling Mr. Pickwick a humbug he was using the epithet
only "in its Pickwickian sense" [6] faithfully echoes the formal lunacy of
its model. There is surely an excessive piety, though, in finding it, as
some worshipers do, a transcendant stroke of hilarity.

Not until the next chapter, in fact, does Dickens enter into his own
enlivening realm. Then, all at once, with the horse kept in harness
"two or three weeks" "because of his veakness," and the cabman's
jumping-jack pugnacity, Mr. Jingle's jerky monologue, and the Pickwickians' devout absorption in his adventures, we find ourselves breathing the first tang of its unusual air.[7] And these waggish goings-on provide a clue to the secret of Dickens's peculiar magic. Staid scholars have
spent far too much time debating from what ephemeral fiction of the
time Dickens may have borrowed Jingle's fantastic utterance, or in
what forgotten play he found the hint of Sam's famous "Wellerisms."[8]
Anyone could invent the *idea* of Jingle's disjointed jargon. Anyone
could construct Wellerisms by mere mechanical ingenuity: " 'No
noose is good noose,' as the criminal said ven they sprung the trap
from under him." But nobody except Dickens could fill these bare
outlines with such rich and glorious nonsense, endow their speakers
with such fantastic life, and transform the stalest comedy entanglements into situations gravely and irresistibly ludicrous.

What Dickens does is to *irradiate* these stock characters and stock
situations with high-spirited fantasy. It is nothing that Mr. Jingle
speaks in hiccuping fragments. It is everything that when he speaks
to prescribe a raw beefsteak for Mr. Tupman's black eye he immediately conjures up so preposterous an image of the injured gentleman
resorting to a more unusual remedy: "cold lamp-post very good, but
lamp-post inconvenient—damned odd standing in the open street
half an hour with your eye against a lamp-post—eh,—very good—ha!" [9]
The picture fills Jingle's telegraphic syntax with a wild vitality seeming to pour out of its speaker; Mr. Jingle *is* the man who says precisely
that. And in the same way he *is* the man who drapes himself romantic-
ally against the mantelpiece in the Rochester ballroom, and—merely
for the mischievous fun of it—gazes with a devout and melancholy
simper on the fat little widow.[10] These endowments in behavior, which
on the surface are irrelevant embellishments to the stock character of
the strolling trickster, are in fact the qualities that make Jingle a living

Mr. Wardle and his friends under the influence of "the salmon"

creation. Without the extravagant additions he would be nothing but a puppet; with them he is at the least a puppet galvanized into cheeky animation.

Into an amazing number of the three hundred or so characters who throng the Pickwick world Dickens breathes this profusion of unexpected detail with prodigal creativeness. The fat boy, who at first seems all slumberous belly, waking only to engulf a pigeon pie and closing greedy eyes the instant the last morsel goes down, surprises us by a sudden amorousness intruding on his gluttony,[11] or by telling the old lady, "I wants to make your flesh creep." [12] The poetical Snodgrass, usually a rather tenuous figure, emerges queasily from the shades after too much indulgence in the bottle. " 'It wasn't the wine,' " he murmurs "in a broken voice. 'It was the salmon.' " His revered leader, Mr. Pickwick, is only more brilliantly illuminated by the draughts that have so nearly extinguished Mr. Snodgrass: " 'Hurrah!' " he echoes a gasping cheer from Mr. Winkle, "taking off his hat and dashing it on the floor, and insanely casting his spectacles into the middle of the kitchen.—At this humorous feat," Dickens adds, "he laughed outright." [13]

The people of *Pickwick* not only reveal themselves in such fantastically unpredictable deeds; *their* behavior releases the most ridiculous self-revelation in others. During Mr. Pickwick's trial, Mrs. Cluppins baffles Mr. Justice Stareleigh by saying a door was "on the jar"; "Partly open," Serjeant Snubbin explains; "She *said* on the jar," demurs the little Judge with a cunning look, and continues to feel distrustful even when the Serjeant assures him the meaning is the same. Or take another interchange from a later moment when Sam Weller is in the witness box:

" 'Oh, quite enough to get, Sir, as the soldier said ven they ordered him three hundred and fifty lashes,' replied Sam.

" 'You must not tell us what the soldier, or any other man, said, Sir,' interposed the Judge; 'it's not evidence.' " [14] How abysmally the speaker gives himself away with this irrelevant and imbecile snippet of judicial wisdom!

Even animals and lifeless objects in *Pickwick* display a risible and troublesome individuality. Mr. Winkle's gun goes off by itself [15] and won't go off when he pulls the trigger,[16] hits nothing when he aims at a pigeon and Mr. Tupman when he aims at nothing; [17] Mr. Tupman's gun brings down a plump partridge when he merely shoots in the air with his eyes shut; [18] the street door playfully closes itself on Mr. Winkle, ejecting him shivering in his dressing gown into the night air of the Royal Crescent.[19] Still more bothersome to Mr. Pickwick's entire circle are their adventures with horses, a species they all regard with deep misgivings. Mr. Winkle scrambles up into the saddle of his mount—an animal towering to enormous height—like a man getting up the side of a battleship; perching there with all the sensations of a landlubber in a crow's-nest, he is bewildered to have the creature drift mysteriously up the street "with his head towards one side of the way and his tail to the other"; once dismounted, he tries in vain to get back on again while the animal coyly backs away in skittish circles. Meanwhile, Mr. Pickwick's carriage horse punctuates a constant jerking of the head with a series of sudden darts and abrupt stops—a procedure that leaves Mr. Snodgrass and Mr. Tupman equally baffled to imagine what the beast can "mean." The day's doings become sheer nightmare when Mr. Winkle's horse escapes and Mr. Pickwick's bolts and smashes their chaise against a bridge: the rustics they meet believe the remaining animal stolen and refuse to stable him, so that the Pickwickians are obliged to trudge miles of dusty road leading the useless and embarrassing nag by the reins. " 'It's like a dream,' ejaculated Mr. Pickwick, 'a hideous dream. The idea of a man's walking about, all day, with a dreadful horse that he can't get rid of!' " [20]

Almost all the events in *Pickwick* are related in a sedate and even solemn manner that intensifies their humor. Dickens has left utterly behind the clumsiness which in *Sketches by Boz* often began by assuring the reader that something inordinately amusing was going to happen. Now he never tells us that anything comical is about to occur, but his infectious drollery of vision takes us captive by itself. It is easy to sympathize with Sir Edmund Gosse's boyhood "rapture of unresisting humorous appreciation" over *Pickwick*, and almost impossible not to share it. "My shouts of laughing at the richer passages," he writes, "were almost scandalous . . . I felt myself to be in the company of a gentleman so extremely funny that I began to laugh before he began to speak; no sooner did he remark 'the sky was dark and gloomy, the air was damp and raw,' than I was in fits of laughter." [21]

The glory to which Gosse responded is indeed a light of triumphant laughter that shines even through the later and more shadowed part of *Pickwick*. It radiates from Dickens's delight in his own impish insight into the grotesque—that insight which at the Grey banquet had enabled him to seize on the spectacle of gentlemen eating and crying "Shame!" and still gobbling as fast as they could—and which now, with a rising sense of harmonious achievement, becomes a kind of cosmic vision. At last he had vanquished the obstacles that had beset him and exorcised—almost—all his ancient sorrows, so that they seemed but comic hobgoblins, mock wraiths of woe. He had made a place for himself in the world, and a comfortable income. He was a man of letters, with a successful volume in print. Before *Pickwick* had struck the public fancy, even before the first number had been published, Dickens was completely confident of its success. "Pickwick is begun," he had written his publishers, "in all his might and glory." [22] He was newly married to a wife he loved, still breathing the dewy and intoxicating fragrance of that strange tenderness. There were gay evenings at the theater with Kate and her sister, and even more glowing evenings of love and laughter around his own hearth. For perhaps the first time since the Chatham days Dickens was utterly happy. He had risen above the miserable past of the blacking warehouse and the Marshalsea, transcending with laughter the evil forces in the world that create along with other bitter things those dark places of suffering. No wonder that a glorious surge of creative affirmation lifts the *Pickwick Papers* high into the radiant light of the sun and makes it a joyful masterpiece.

*   *   *   *   *

What dark and perilous things Dickens had to transcend is hinted by a number of brief and isolated stories set within the framework of the book. Edmund Wilson has called attention, in *The Wound and the Bow*, to their cardinal importance for the biographer and psychologist.[23] They claim only a very small number, to be sure, of *Pickwick's* 325,000 words, and they are negligible enough in literary merit. But the striking thing is that Dickens should have intruded into the bright texture of a comic novel these gloomy tales of poverty and persecution, revenge, insanity, and despair. Their presence betrays a vein of morbid horror in Dickens deeply significant of his submerged griefs and fears.

The revelation is all the more impressive because in his later work these lurid preoccupations with criminal resentment, terror, and rebellion were to rise, like the bloody ghost of Banquo, again and again. Save for the healing sunlight of laughter, the bitter vapors hidden within this region of his soul might well have spread and made him a fellow wanderer with Edgar Allan Poe through regions of haunted and phantasmal dread. But though the dark vision never conquered the daylight vision, in all the novels there are scenes as if imaged through the fumes of the witches' cauldron that portend how slight a change in the balance of Dickens's emotional forces would have turned the Dickens world into a Dostoevskian world of guilt and anguish: Fagin's last night in the condemned cell, all crouched into a shape of huddled nightmare, the hangman Dennis dragged pleading and screaming to the gibbet, Jonas Chuzzlewit skulking through the crimson wood, Bradley Headstone remembering ever the struggle by the weir and the crash of the heavy club, John Jasper muttering through his opium daze of the dangerous journey he has taken over unknown deeps.

The *Pickwick* tales no more than crudely anticipate such themes, and have hardly a scintilla of the intensity Dickens was to achieve in melodrama.[24] But in their very clumsiness they divulge compulsive emotional drives that would be masked in more skillfully contrived fictions. In one, a pantomine clown dying in the direst poverty believes in his delirium that his wife intends to kill him.[25] In a second, a worthless father's neglect and bad example have helped lead his son astray. Returning home after seventeen years from a sentence of transportation, the son finds his father a disgraceful, diseased workhouse pauper. In his guilty fear the terrified old wretch strikes the son across the face with a heavy stick, the embittered son seizes the old man by the throat, and the latter, bursting a blood vessel, falls dead.[26] In a third, a madman whose insanity has long gone undetected, and who has exulted in the ease with which he deludes men who grovel before his gold, ultimately turns violent, runs amuck, and is confined in a barred cell.[27]

But the tale of the "Queer Client" is the most revealing of them all. A prisoner named Heyling, confined for debt in the Marshalsea by the vindictiveness of his own father-in-law, has undergone the heartbreak of having his wife and son die of sorrow and slow starvation. Meanwhile the old man has refused to do a single thing for the relief of his own child and grandchild. When Heyling inherits money, he dedicates his life and fortune to revenge. He buys up at enormously inflated rates certain promissory notes that the old man had signed on the understanding that he would be allowed to renew them. Then, taking advantage of the fact that this agreement had never been put in writing, Heyling has his agent demand payment at a time when it means his enemy's ruin. The old man loses all his property and disappears to escape debtors' prison himself; but his relentless pursuer traces him to the scene of Dickens's own childhood suffering: "the meanest-looking house" in "a desolate place" "called Little College Street," in Camden Town. Here Heyling appears and states his determination to send his miserable victim to jail. The old man dies in a fit, and Heyling is never heard of again.[28]

These synopses are hardly worse than the stories they outline. Though as interludes the stories are only a kind of small mud-clogged backwater in the clear and sparkling flood of *Pickwick*—they average fewer than four thousand words each—and though the artistic damage they do is slight enough, it is significant that they found their way into the book at all. The interpolated tale, of course, is an old fictional device, running from Cervantes and Lesage through Fielding and Scott. But in these writers there is no such disharmony between the shorter story and its larger frame and no such inferiority to the whole as here in *Pickwick*. Dickens's four brief tales are not merely exercises in a conventional form; they spring from emotional experience he has been unable either to dismiss or to get into perspective. Everything about them—their bathos, their tone of hysteria, their irrelevance to the fabric they are patched into, their magnified distortions of auto-biographical matter—suggests the meaningful forces behind Dickens's failure to realize their artistic badness. "The Dying Clown" he even believed would "create considerable sensation." [29] Such blindness to flaws, however trivial, in one of his own masterpieces—and in a writer seldom so gravely deceived later in his career—shows with glaring clarity how far from healed were his childhood wounds.

It is evident that for Dickens the emotional reality of those horrors in his own past is all overcast with images of cruelty and persecution. How could such things be if there were not some vindictiveness, of man or fate, hounding their victims? How could the dreadful descent into the poverty of Camden Town, the hopeless and hideous despair of prison cells, be rendered in all their desolation except in analogy to delirium and insanity? When the awful threat rose as an inescapable fact before a man's eyes, was it unbelievable that his heartstrings should literally crack and the man fall dead? The very memory seared upon Dickens's brain was as of the madness of hell or a bestial nightmare. Even the most hysterical fancies were not out of key with that feverish reality. He knew very well that his anxious mother had had no desire to hurt him, but his heart cried out that if she had made him go back to the prison of the blacking warehouse she would indeed have killed him. He knew very well that his warm-hearted wastrel of a father was no brutal ruffian, and he loved his father. Nevertheless, his judgment also said that if the courage and abilities of Charles Dickens had been crushed in the vulgar surroundings of the blacking warehouse, the fault would have been his father's. "Who does not wish to murder the father?" Ivan Karamazov was to demand. Dickens never asks Dostoevski's fierce and searching question outright, but his imagination hovers round it half fascinated. And there was no need to disguise his hatred for all that wore men down even to the sacrificing of their children. *That* he hated in all its disguises, in every institution of society— the workhouse, factory, slum, and prison, the bodies made to darken and distort law. How gladly, in grim exultant symbolism, he could fancy his fingers tighten around their throats!

Remembering always what that small boy had been, and how he had felt his sufferings, it is less remarkable that they should have left a heritage of raw pain and horror than that he ever soared beyond the shadow of their night. Indeed, only the happy seed-time that had gone before in Chatham and Rochester makes intelligible the Dickens we know, and even so, if the dark days had lasted too long the earlier flowering might have withered like a plant kept in a cellar. Childhood had nourished his imagination with the gold of fairy tales, and the dip of Kentish orchards and cloud-dappled hilltops, and comic ballads trolled on tables, and the breezy world of the eighteenth-century novel; it had stored happiness in his memory and love in his heart. Is it surprising that when this great happy novel of glorious challenge to the powers of darkness gets under way, it should start rolling along the Dover Road and straight for Rochester and the sunlight?

For indeed, though Dickens had told William Hall he would like to take his way among a free range of English scenes and people,[30] for him it is Kent that is the heart of England, and the Kentish junketings have the most genial glow in all *Pickwick*. The few ventures beyond the home counties are much more dominantly satiric in tone. At Ipswich Mr. Pickwick has his embarrassing adventure in the Great White Horse with the lady in curlpapers, and tangles with that titan of legal erudition, Mr. Nupkins.[31] At Bath, while Lord Mutanhed stares through Mr. Pickwick, and the Dowager Lady Snuphanuph bullies him at whist, Sam Weller is edified by the gorgeous liveries and lofty tone of life belowstairs.[32] At Eatanswill—a borough not otherwise identified than by its being on the way to Norwich—Mr. Pickwick moves blandly through an atmosphere violent with the political recriminations of Fizkin and Slumkey [33] and mingles with Count Smorltork and a crowd of equally glittering celebrities at Mrs. Leo Hunter's masquerade breakfast.[34]

But in all these scenes there is nothing that resembles the affectionate lingering over Rochester Bridge and the old Castle, the Bull Inn, Chatham Lines and Fort Pitt, and the green meadows, the tingling winter sports, the roaring fires and good cheer of Dingley Dell. Mr. Wardle's Christmas party is bathed in those warm tones of good-fellowship and hearty enjoyment which Dickens made so deeply his gift to that festive season and which only Washington Irving's *Bracebridge Hall* had painted in anything like such colorful hues before. The plump host himself, his old mother in her lavender-silk gown, the teasing Isabella and Emily Wardle, and Arabella Allen, with her neat ankles in their fur-trimmed boots, diffuse a pleasant cheer that brightens the entire story with its normal and healthy charm.[35]

*   *   *   *   *

Meanwhile a more serious theme—one that is to dominate all the latter half of this comic novel—has been thrusting itself into the main stream of the action. It is that theme of injustice which had proved only a bathetic failure in the interpolated stories; but this time Dickens was to handle it with brilliant success. Mrs. Bardell, Mr. Pickwick's landlady, has made the muddle-headed error of imagining that he has asked her to marry him. A firm of shyster solicitors, Dodson and Fogg, have persuaded her to sue him for breach of promise. Not long after —"another wronged man," as Edmund Wilson points out—"he will land in the debtors' prison, where a good many of the other characters will join him and where the whole book will deepen with a new dimension of seriousness." [36] For what Wordsworth called "the burden of the mystery"—the existence of suffering and evil—never ceases to lie with a heavy weight upon all life. Great comedy is no evasion of this knowledge, no closing of the eyes upon it, but as true a victory over it as the exalted acceptance of tragedy. Without ever denying or falsifying the dark realities, comedy rises triumphantly above them in a glorious flood of laughter. Evil is neither subdued nor destroyed, and yet it is somehow by the sheer ringing affirmation of the human spirit transcended, and thereby conquered.

This catharsis which is the essence of comedy is nowhere more utterly victorious, not even in Aristophanes, than in the irresistible hilarity of Mr. Pickwick's trial for breach of promise.[37] Boldly adapting a scene from Surtees's *Jorrocks's Jaunts and Jollities*, fusing with it hints from the Melbourne-Norton trial, impudently caricaturing in Serjeant Buzfuz and Mr. Justice Stareleigh two living figures (Serjeant Bompas and Sir Stephen Gazelee), Dickens marvelously raises the whole sordid shakedown he is revealing to heights of ecstatic travesty. Mrs. Bardell's drooping entrance, the frenzied recollection with which she kisses her child, her relapse "into a state of frantic imbecility" in which she requests to be informed where she is, the sympathetic side-turned weeping of Mrs. Cluppins and Mrs. Sanders, Dodson and Fogg's entreaties "to compose herself," [38] all set a tone of high farce from which the foolery constantly soars to still loftier heights.

Serjeant Buzfuz is superbly outrageous throughout. He solemnly explains that since Mrs. Bardell's dead husband had been a single gentleman before he married her, it never occurred to Mrs. Bardell's trusting heart to be suspicious of single gentlemen.[39] He rhetorically describes Mr. Pickwick's supposed machinations: "The serpent was on the watch, the train was laid, the mine was preparing, the sapper and miner was at work." He thunderously defies the helpless Pickwick to "bully" or "intimidate" him by indulging in gestures of indignation and dissent.[40] He fantastically reads the most deeply compromising significance into Mr. Pickwick's notes about chops and warming-pans.[41] All these scandalous distortions enhance our delight when Sam Weller administers a setback:

" 'Now, attend, Mr. Weller,' said Serjeant Buzfuz, dipping a large pen into the inkstand before him, for the purpose of frightening Sam with a show of taking down his answer. 'You were in the passage and yet saw nothing of what was going forward. Have you a pair of eyes, Mr. Weller?'

" 'Yes, I have a pair of eyes,' replied Sam, 'and that's just it. If they wos a pair o' patent double million magnifyin' gas microscopes of hextra power, p'raps I might be able to see through a flight o' stairs and a deal door; but bein' only eyes, you see, my wision's limited.' " [42]

Spectators titter, Serjeant Buzfuz looks vexed and foolish; and we

whet our appetite for Sam's next stroke. It comes quickly. Will Sam
tell the court, the Serjeant asks, what was said about the trial when he
visited Mrs. Bardell's?

" 'Vith all the pleasure in life, Sir,' replied Sam. 'Arter a few unim-
portant obserwations from the two wirtuous females as has been examined here today, the ladies gets into a very great state o' admiration
at the honourable conduct of Mr. Dodson and Fogg—them two gen'l'-
men as is settin' near you now.' This, of course, drew general attention
to Dodson and Fogg, who looked as virtuous as possible.

" 'The attornies for the plaintiff,' said Mr. Serjeant Buzfuz, 'well,
they spoke in high praise of the honourable conduct of Messrs. Dodson
and Fogg, the attornies for the plaintiff, did they?'

" 'Yes,' said Sam, 'they said what a very gen'rous thing it was o'
them to have taken up the case on spec, and to charge nothin' at all for
costs, unless they got 'em out of Mr. Pickwick.' " [43]

But this passage at arms is no more than a momentary check to the
course of Mr. Pickwick's discomfiture. Mrs. Cluppins and Mrs. Sanders are encouraged in an orgy of irresponsible surmise.[44] Mr. Winkle
is badgered beyond the verge of desperation.[45] Mr. Pickwick's quoted
words are ingeniously and damagingly amended past all recognition.[46]
Soothed by the Serjeant's voice, the little judge sleeps on and off, waking in an occasional silence to write something down with an inkless
pen, and looking "unusually profound, to impress the jury with the
belief that he always thought most deeply with his eyes shut." [47] His
summing-up from what he can decipher of his notes is classic: "If Mrs.
Bardell was right, it was perfectly clear Mr. Pickwick was wrong, and if
they thought the evidence of Mrs. Cluppins worthy of credence they
would believe it, and, if they didn't, they wouldn't." [48]

In the end, Mrs. Bardell is awarded damages of £750.[49] Chicanery
has won the battle; innocence is completely and ludicrously routed.
And yet never has the comedy slackened. Mr. Pickwick retains our
sympathy, and, indeed, rises in our respect, but his mishaps arouse our
inextinguishable merriment. The sniggering scoundrelism of his foes
has been exposed in a gleaming rain of ridicule. Trickery and stupidity
combine to defeat the right, and nevertheless above their victory a
triumphant derision soars to an annihilating vision of their moral
meanness. Here, in truth, Dickens is one of the great humorists, freeing

our imaginations from the bondage of respect for the sordid manipulations of the law with a laughter of ringing delight.

And with this scene there is a change of atmosphere, as of a cloud gathering above a sunlit summer landscape. During the months of Mr. Pickwick's imprisonment in the Fleet, the shadow of the Marshalsea and its chevaux-de-frise that had entered Dickens's heart when he was a child begins to lengthen over the story. There is no oppressive gloom in the delineation even of this place of horrors, but there is more than enough of suffering seen with deep sympathy to make an undaunted heart an act of courage. The panorama passes before our eyes: the haggard victim of chancery who still expects to be out in an hour or so, the damp and greasy vaults Mr. Pickwick at first supposes to be coal cellars, the raffish ne'er-do-wells shuffling greasy cards in a cloud of tobacco smoke, the emaciated and sobbing young woman with a child in her arms, the fortunate legatee ruined by quarrels among his fellow heirs, the dying prisoner who gasps in the hot, polluted air.[50] "Twenty years," he exclaims, "twenty years in this hideous grave! My heart broke when my child died, and I could not even kiss him in his little coffin. My loneliness since then, in all this noise and riot, has been very dreadful. May God forgive me! He has seen my solitary, lingering death." [51]

At the heartlessness with which the absolutely destitute among the prisoners are treated, Dickens cannot contain his indignation. He knows well enough, and gives examples to show, that there are vicious wastrels there who have amply deserved their incarceration. But that even these should be allowed to dwell in filth unless they have means to bribe their jailors, and that impoverished victims of legal injustice should be condemned to sink in slow misery, while the burglar and the pickpocket must be cared for, fills him with wrath. "We no longer suffer them to appeal at the prison gates to the charity and compassion of the passers by," he bursts out; "but we still leave unblotted in the leaves of our statute book . . . the just and wholesome law which declares that the sturdy felon shall be fed and clothed, and that the penniless debtor shall be left to die of starvation and nakedness." [52] Mr. Pickwick remarks that the idlers and rascals hardly seem to mind their imprisonment at all, and Sam Weller confirms the observation: "It's the t'other vuns as gets done over, vith this sort o' thing: them downhearted fellers as can't svig away at the beer, nor play at skittles neither;

them as vould pay if they could, and gets low by being boxed up. I'll tell you wot it is, sir; them as is always a idlin' in public-houses it don't damage at all, and them as is alvays a workin' wen they can, it damages too much." [53] No wonder that at last, in the squalor and noise and turmoil, Mr. Pickwick can bear no more. "I have seen enough," he says. "My head aches with these scenes, and my heart too. Henceforth I will be a prisoner in my own room." [54]

The reader may be surprised around this time by the realization that Mr. Pickwick has long since been behaving like a man of heart and sense. The silly old fool, solemnly busied in the investigation of tittlebats and tricked by any impostor, started to disappear with the unmasking of Mr. Jingle, and has since imperceptibly faded away. Nearly all the major characters in the book, indeed, are transmuted into humanity and dignity. We almost forget Mr. Winkle's grotesqueness as horseman and hunter when he is ensnared by the demure and black-eyed Arabella Allen and begins acting no more foolishly than any other honest gentleman in love. We lose sight of the absurd figure plump Mr. Tupman made as an Italian brigand in his loyalty to his imprisoned leader. Old Mr. Wardle and Mr. Perker cease to be caricatures and become personalities.

Mr. Pickwick himself and Sam Weller are the supreme examples of this transformation. Sam's sharp knowingness and his loyalty early make him a good deal more than a comic cockney with a pat verbal formula. And even Mr. Pickwick's gullibility gradually becomes merely an excess of goodness that renders it difficult for him to suspect guile in others. He is visibly more sensible at Ipswich and Bath than he was at Rochester and Eatanswill. He acts with dignity and judgment when he is dragged before Mr. Nupkins. If he betrays an incautious anger under the leering provocations of Dodson and Fogg, he does not thereby make himself ridiculous. His decision to go to jail rather than submit to their frame-up is quixotic but not silly, and his ultimate surrender dictated by a generous unwillingness to involve other victims along with him. He emerges as a noble figure of benevolence and magnanimity, bathed in the light of Sam's intense devotion and guarded by Sam's shrewder judgment of the unscrupulousness in men.

Mr. Pickwick's chance meeting with those two precious scoundrels, Jingle and Trotter, now reduced to the deepest misery in the Fleet, reveals more powerfully than any previous scenes the deepening humanity with which he is conceived. By these destitute outcasts he has been tricked and wronged. He has indignantly pursued them from town to town, but now he cannot restrain his pity. Jingle, no longer the smirking rascal he was, breaks down under this unexpected sympathy. "Good fellow," he says. "Ungrateful dog—boyish to cry—can't help it —bad fever—weak—ill—hungry. Deserved it all—but suffered much— very." Mr. Pickwick glances from the distressed stroller to the hollow-cheeked Job Trotter, "trying to look stern, with four large tears running down his waistcoat." And the scene ends not with the hearty cuff they have deserved, but with Mr. Pickwick bestowing help for their needs.[55] It is impossible not to feel the justice of Sam's famous tribute: "I never heard, mind you, nor read of in story-books, nor seen in picters, any angel in tights and gaiters . . . but mark my words, Job Trotter, he's a reg'lar thorough-bred angel for all that; and let me see the man as wenturs to tell me he knows a better vun." [56]

The changes in Mr. Pickwick's companions are slighter: the fantastic outlines in which they were drawn have simply been allowed to melt into a humanity retaining its original oddity but no longer merely ludicrous. Mr. Pickwick's transfiguration, however, from gull to angel, is radically different, and even among Dickens's early reviewers there were some who pointed out its inconsistency. Against their accusation, Dickens defended himself with a characteristic mingling of touchiness and ingenuity. "I do not think this change will appear forced or unnatural to my readers," he remarks, "if they will reflect that in real life the peculiarities and oddities of a man who has anything whimsical about him, generally impress us first, and that it is not until we are better acquainted with him that we usually begin to look below these superficial traits, and know the better part of him." [57]

This is brilliant special pleading, but it is not we who have become better acquainted with Mr. Pickwick. It is Dickens whose conception has broadened. He started, as Cervantes did in *Don Quixote*, with a comic butt, and, like Cervantes, found that his slapstick puppet began to breathe and grow into something more wisely and tenderly humorous than he had foreseen. The plump and gullible buffoon who talks so foolishly and behaves so fatuously turns into a sensible gentleman who speaks with dignity and acts nobly. Thereby his misadventures gain new depths of meaning and richness; they move into a world where the laughter transcends superficial clowning and is steeped in the humor of reality. In the light of this achievement, who would want Dickens to have maintained a trivial consistency to his crude beginning?

* * * * *

What Dickens has done, in fact, has been to devise a new literary form, a kind of fairy tale that is at once humorous, heroic, and realistic. Unlike the flat world of farce or the misty dream world of romance, it is as solid and ponderable as England itself, and full of the actual sights and sounds and places of England. Mr. Pickwick loses himself in the labyrinthine corridors of the Great White Horse, smells the shrimps and tar of Chatham, hears the drums and trumpets and the drunken shouts of the electors at Eatanswill, slides the frozen ponds and walks the flowery meadows of the Kentish countryside, breathes the crisp air of an outside journey by stagecoach, and in one of those novel vehicles that Mr. Raddle calls a "cabriouy" rattles through the streets of a London only recently equipped with gas lamps.[58] It is a world bursting with hundreds of people as grotesque as those to be found in any street: Mr. Stiggins soaking up pineapple brandy and extolling the virtues of tea and temperance with the other members of the United Grand Junction Ebenezer Temperance Association; [59] Mr. Nupkins browbeating court officers and prisoners alike with an impartial ignorance of the law; [60] the loyal freemen of Muggleton with their Christian hatred of Negro slavery abroad and devotion to the factory system at home; [61] the learned members of the legal profession and their "ingenious machines put in motion for the torture and torment of His Majesty's liege subjects, and the comfort and emolument of the practitioners of the law." [62] It is a world seen with no endeavor to deny the reality of ignorance, foolishness, malice, stupidity, prejudice, scoundrelism, suffering, vice, and evil.

But it is also a world in which, as in the world of the fairy tale, its innocently guileless hero can experience no irretrievable loss and meet no inextinguishable sorrow. He can be overwhelmed in ridiculous embarrassments and temporarily victimized by the plots of designing men, but he bears a charmed life. Ultimately he and all those over whom he extends the aegis of his protection are destined to regain a cheerful serenity, from which they will go on to new adventures no less assured of a happy ending. Mr. Pickwick is a Knight of the Joyful

Countenance, as rotund as Cervantes' Knight of the Rueful Countenance is lean, followed by a more faithfully protective squire, and as fated for triumph as his predecessor was for failure. He is a beaming fairy godfather to almost all the world, forever rescuing maidens and bestowing them on their true loves, succoring the oppressed, shaming even the cheats and petty tricksters with his kindness. His very existence and personality represent a kind of magic; if not that of the ugly duckling turned into a swan, a very foolish goose transformed into an angel in gaiters!

In *Pickwick Papers* we see again the seminal influence of Dickens's childhood reading new-minted into fresh creation. Mr. Pickwick begins by being as silly a fellow as Jack who sold the cow for a handful of beans and ends no less heroically. He is a middle-class and middle-aged version of the miller's son protected by a cockney puss-in-boots, an Aladdin checking no fewer than two African magicians in the persons of Dodson and Fogg, a gay but undeniable Christian escaping the Fleet dungeons where so many are imprisoned by the Giant Despair. All the ogres are there, revealed as the ogres of everyday, and all the forty thieves, with most of them lawyers; and the symbolic evils of the fairy tale and allegory have become the real evils of the real world for whose discovery Dickens had been prepared by the fierce insight of Smollett and by Fielding's wide, clear gaze. The very scenes of *Pickwick*, though free from Smollett's astringency and coarseness, are steeped in his knowledge of the shadier sides of existence; and the invigorating air that streams through them has blown over the same highroads and coppices and downs that Fielding knew. The great achievement of his predecessors in picaresque realism and comic epic Dickens blends with the magic of romance into a unique and novel triumph of his own. With *Pickwick* he invented the realist fairy tale. It was to recur in much of his future work.

"Bless his old gaiters," exclaims Sam Weller, when Mr. Pickwick is involved in Mr. Winkle's nocturnal interview with Arabella Allen, "He's a keepin' guard in the lane vith that 'ere dark lantern, like a amiable Guy Fawkes! I never see such a fine creetur in my days. Blessed if I don't think his heart must ha' been born twenty-five year arter his body, at least!" [63] But though the hero of the realist fairy tale has the heart of youth and can escape the powers of darkness, he cannot slay them. There they remain athwart all the sunlight and lyricism of the world. Mr. Pickwick can touch the hearts of Jingle and Trotter; Dodson and Fogg he cannot touch. He can escape the Fleet himself; he cannot destroy it or the evils for which it stands. In *Barnaby Rudge* Dickens's imagination would flame to the destruction and burning of the Fleet, but shudder back from the chaotic forces thereby released. Only by slow degrees did he come to see clearly the shadowy powers behind the Fleet and to realize that they were what needed to be destroyed.

PART THREE

Troubles and Triumphs

1837–1839

CHAPTER ONE

Metamorphosis of a Journalist

Even before *Pickwick* began its spectacular rise, Dickens had been eager to give up his post on the *Morning Chronicle*. He was tired of having his bones bruised in wild nocturnal gallops over the byroads of England, tired of trying to fit his writing into the uncertain hours left over from reporting, above all he was tired of the House of Commons. "I devoutly hope ere next session," he had written in June, "I may make some arrangements which will render its sittings a matter of indifference to me—as the story-books say—for ever after." [1] But these plans evidently fell through; at the end of October he was resigning himself to spending another session in the Gallery. [2]

Within a few days, however, the situation changed. Richard Bentley was planning to establish a new magazine and asked Dickens to assume its editorship. At first calling it the *Wits' Miscellany*, when his friends laughed him out of this [3] Bentley changed the name to *Bentley's Miscellany*. He offered Dickens liberal terms—£20 a month for his editorial duties, and another twenty guineas for contributing sixteen pages of his own writing to each month's issue, the copyright of which was to belong to Bentley. This was at a rate more than 75 per cent higher than Chapman and Hall were paying him for *Pickwick*. The new agreement was unconnected with the novel contract between Bentley and Dickens except for the provision that at the conclusion of *Pickwick* Dickens might write another novel for Chapman and Hall, instead of being pledged to give his very next two to Bentley. Signed November 4, 1836, the agreement was for one year, renewable at Bentley's option for another three. [4] In total, Bentley's terms handsomely surpassed the seven guineas a week Dickens had been getting on the

Chronicle, and, with the £300 a year he was beginning to receive from *Pickwick,* gave him a dependable income of almost £800.

As soon as these arrangements were concluded, Dickens wrote a letter of resignation to the proprietors of the *Morning Chronicle.* To Easthope personally, he expressed his "warmest and most sincere thanks for all the courtesies and kindnesses" received at his hands, and promised before his departure to write the additional sketches for which he had been paid.[5] But Easthope, irritated at losing a valuable employee, dispatched a furious blast accusing Dickens of having discourteously left the office without waiting to see him, and of having been paid for three sketches that had never been delivered.

Dickens began a temperate response, excusing himself of any intentional discourtesy by explaining that he had left Mrs. Dickens waiting in a neighboring shop and had been obliged to return for her. As for the sketches, he had followed the same course as in the former series, writing at his convenience, and the paper, in the same way, publishing at its convenience rather than on a regular schedule. But in the course of the letter his own temper took fire and his tone sharpened. He would return the six guineas with the utmost pleasure, he wrote indignantly, and he only wished he could return at the same time every sixpence he had received beyond his regular salary, although he had rendered the money's worth.

Easthope's intemperate letter, he went on, might have been expected when a servant gave warning and took himself elsewhere. But *he* had expected some written acknowledgment of his work in their behalf. "I may say now, that on many occasions at a sacrifice of health, rest, and personal comfort, I have again and again, on important expresses in my zeal for the interests of the paper, done what was always before considered impossible, and what in all probability will never be accomplished again. During the whole period of my engagement wherever there was difficult and harassing duty to be performed—travelling at a few hours' notice hundreds of miles in the depth of winter—leaving hot and crowded rooms to write, the whole night through, in a close damp chaise . . . under every possible circumstance of disadvantage and difficulty—for that duty I have been selected. And I did not think when I made great efforts to perform it, and to eclipse (as I have done, again and again) other papers with double the means, that my reward at last would be . . . a fear lest at the close of two years, I should have received six pounds six, too much!

"Depend upon it, Sir," Dickens concluded scathingly, "that if you would stimulate those about you to any exertions beyond their ordinary routine of duty, and gather round you competent successors of the young men whom you will constantly find quitting a most arduous and thankless profession, as other prospects dawn upon them, this is not the way to do it." [6]

With these words Dickens turned his back on his reporting days. Easthope no doubt felt his own outburst had gone too far, for he ran a favorable notice of the forthcoming appearance of *Bentley's Miscellany* in the *Chronicle*. Through John Payne Collier he let Dickens know that he thought he should be thanked and felt much hurt by Dickens's angry letter. But Dickens was obdurate. Easthope's notice was no more than would have been given "the first number of a new periodical of Bentley's" under any other editor. As for their parting, "I cannot retract one syllable," he insisted; Easthope's only quarrel with him was "that I should ever have contemplated having anything better to do than reporting for the Chronicle." [7]

In later years, however, when he looked back on his newspaper experiences, Dickens remembered them with more affection. "I went into the gallery of the House of Commons," he said at a Newspaper Press Fund dinner in 1865, "when I was a boy not eighteen, and I left it—I can hardly believe the inexorable truth—nigh thirty years ago. I have pursued the calling of a reporter under circumstances of which many . . . of my modern successors, can form no adequate conception. I have often transcribed for the printer, from my shorthand notes, important public speeches in which the strictest accuracy was required . . . writing on the palm of my hand, by the light of a dark lantern, in a post-chaise and four, galloping through a wild country, and through the dead of night, at the then surprising rate of fifteen miles an hour. . . . Returning home from excited political meetings in the country to the waiting press in London, I do verily believe I have been upset in almost every description of vehicle known in this country. I have been, in my time, belated on miry bye-roads, towards the small hours, forty or fifty miles from London, in a wheelless carriage, with exhausted horses and drunken postboys, and have got back in time for publication, to be received with never-forgotten compliments by the late Mr.

Black, coming in the broadest of Scotch from the broadest of hearts I ever knew." [8]

For John Black, indeed, Dickens retained the warmest affection. "It was John Black that flung the slipper after me," he would often say; and "Dear old Black! my first hearty out-and-out appreciator," he exclaims in a letter to Forster the year he died.[9] And in time, even toward the proprietors of the *Chronicle* he came to feel more amicable. "There never was," he wrote Forster in 1845, "anybody connected with newspapers, who, in the same space of time, had so much express and post-chaise experience as I. And what gentlemen they were to serve, in such things, at the old Morning Chronicle! I have had to charge for half-a-dozen breakdowns in half-a-dozen times as many miles. I have had to charge for the damage of a greatcoat from the drippings of a blazing wax-candle, in writing through the smallest hours of the night in a swift-flying carriage and pair. . . . I have charged for broken hats, broken luggage, broken chaises, broken harness—everything but a broken head, which is the only thing they would have grumbled to pay for." [10]

But now, his ties with the *Morning Chronicle* severed, Dickens flung himself into the task of lining up potential contributors for *Bentley's Miscellany*. He wrote Douglas Jerrold, author of the popular comedy *Black-eyed Susan*, whom he had not yet met, proposing to call on him and obtain the promise of a paper for the first number.[11] He recommended to Bentley the literary talents of Charles Whitehead, who had first recommended him to Chapman and Hall.[12] He asked Macrone for the address of the Reverend Francis Mahony, who wrote witty mystifications in verse under the pseudonym of Father Prout.[13] For the opening number, he himself wrote "The Public Life of Mr. Tulrumble" and sent it to Cruikshank, who was doing most of the magazine's illustrations.[14]

*   *   *   *   *

With Macrone, Dickens continued to be on the best of terms. All through the autumn he dropped in at Macrone's place of business in St. James's Square about the publication of the second series of *Sketches by Boz*. Kate was expecting their first child during the winter and seldom came with him, but he was often accompanied by Mary Hogarth, whose pretty face and charm aroused admiring comment there.[15] In Macrone's office, which was adorned with busts of distinguished men, they met the sculptor responsible for some of them, the

sweet-tempered Angus Fletcher, whom Dickens affectionately nicknamed "Kindheart." Macrone's wife was also expecting a child earlier
in the fall; friendly messages passed between the families and the two
husbands often dined at each other's residences.[16]

But suddenly these amicable relations were shattered. As Dickens
described it two years later, "A dispute arose between myself and Mr.
Macrone, whether an agreement for a novel, which we had together,
was not understood to be cancelled between us." [17] Ainsworth had told
Macrone in August that Dickens was contracting to write a novel for
Bentley,[18] but Macrone had taken no action—which would seem to
support Dickens's belief that Macrone had in fact released him from
his agreement to write *Gabriel Vardon*. With the news of the projected
magazine, however, Macrone flew into a rage. He wrote Dickens an
intemperate letter of complaint and of angry accusation against Bentley.[19] Dickens's reply was unsatisfactory. Macrone, in his agitation,
asked Ainsworth for his advice.

It is impossible, on the known evidence, to determine the rights of
the case. Perhaps Macrone, early in July, had casually said he would be
willing to cancel their agreement and then later, when *Pickwick* soared
into success, regretted it, while Dickens, upon this oral assurance, had
gone ahead in his arrangement with Bentley. Dickens's behaviour during
the entire dispute is that of a man indignantly resentful of a piece of
chicanery. On the other hand, Ainsworth apparently believed Macrone
entirely sincere, and indicated no doubt of his statements. Certainly
Macrone had neither returned the letter of agreement nor destroyed
it, but still had the document.

His appeal to Ainsworth put him in an equivocal position. Ainsworth and Dickens were on the friendliest terms, and the younger novelist was a frequent guest at Ainsworth's home. But Ainsworth had also
introduced Dickens to Macrone, and felt that the publisher was entitled to fulfillment of his contract. He himself had refused offers from
Bentley and other publishers, considering himself bound to Macrone.[20]
He told Macrone that he had blundered in losing his temper and vilify-
ing Bentley. Publishers generally, Macrone included, were constantly
wresting authors from each other. Nevertheless he condoled with Macrone on the loss of Dickens as a serious misfortune; he was "unquestionably a writer of the first order." Even Bentley's offer, Ainsworth
considered, was inadequate to his worth; he ought to have received

£800 for a novel, and the £200 Macrone had offered was preposterously small. "I am exceedingly sorry for your loss. You will not easily repair it." [21]

Macrone protested the assumption that Dickens was lost. Did he not have Dickens's letter of agreement? Doubtless the friendliest course for Ainsworth to have followed would have been, not to advise Macrone secretly, but to ask permission to discuss the subject with Dickens. This, however, he did not do. He felt uncomfortable, he insisted that he must not be quoted, but agreed that Dickens was bound. The fact that the agreement specified no date of delivery for the novel was unfortunate, but it did not entitle Dickens to violate it. Macrone should put himself into legal hands at once. [22]

Whether or not Macrone consulted solicitors is unclear. What he did do, much to Dickens's irritation, was to continue to advertise *Gabriel Vardon* as a forthcoming publication. Their relations became so strained that they ceased to communicate with each other directly. When Macrone offered on December 1st to buy the entire copyrights of the first and second series of *Sketches by Boz*—he had previously bought only the copyrights of their first editions—the negotiations were carried on by Thomas Hansard, the printer. Dickens asked £50 more than the £200 Macrone offered for both copyrights, and demanded that Macrone cease advertising a novel by him and return his letter. [23]

Hansard objected to making these negotiations dependent on settling the dispute over *Gabriel Vardon*. Dickens replied, with some asperity, "You will allow me to observe, that knowing nothing of my misunderstanding with Macrone, you are not competent to judge of the propriety of my connecting it with the offer for the two copyrights. I decline entering into any negotiation with Mr. Macrone having reference to any other engagements than those I have mentioned above, so long as that misunderstanding remains in its present state." [24] His irritation was sharpened by the fact that on that very day Macrone had sent an advertisement of *Gabriel Vardon* for inclusion in the next number of *Pickwick*, which Chapman and Hall rejected at Dickens's request. Still chafing, Dickens sent around to Bentley's the next morning asking them to refuse any similar advertisement for the *Miscellany*. [25]

But, as Ainsworth had seen, Macrone had Dickens at a disadvantage. As the agreement "was not actually cancelled, he had the legal power of enforcing it, or claiming damages against me." [26] Whether Macrone could have collected damages for Dickens's failure to produce a literary work of unpredictable earning power, whether he could even have enjoined his writing for any other publisher, is very doubtful.[27] But Dickens feared these possibilities and worried lest publicity on his technical breach of contract gravely injure his reputation.

Consequently, whatever the good faith in which Dickens had believed himself released, Macrone's unyielding position forced him to a compromise. On January 5, 1837, after six weeks of acrimony, he accepted only £100, instead of the £250 he had at first insisted upon, for the entire copyright of both series of *Sketches*, but with this sum he received the agreement he had believed canceled.[28] "First and last by these books," he told Mitton bitterly, "I had some £400, Macrone had some £4,000 . . ." [29]

But meanwhile he seemed to be free of Macrone, and he had already thrown himself full force into his new pursuits. His association with his brisk and genial publisher speedily ripened into the warmest friendship. Bentley inaugurated a series of literary dinners in the "red room" of his offices in New Burlington Street. Here Dickens met for the first time many of their contributors who were friends of Bentley's, and deepened his acquaintance with others. After one of the first of these evenings, on December 1st, he wrote Bentley, "I kept very quiet, purposely. Since I have been a successful author, I have seen how much ill-will and jealousy there is afloat, and have acquired an excellent character as a quiet, modest fellow. I like to assume a virtue, though I have it not; it has served me with a subject more than once." [30] Bentley was delighted with his new editor, and insisted on his being proposed for membership in the Garrick Club, to which he was elected early in January.[31]

Success also smiled on his playwriting. Despite its poor reception by the dramatic critics. *The Village Coquettes* was doing well enough on the stage, and was published by Bentley in December with a dedication to John Pritt Harley.[32] At the same time Chapman and Hall brought out *The Strange Gentleman*, and Dickens took Hablôt Browne around to Harley's dressing room at the St. James's to sketch him in one of its scenes.[33] Harley was so pleased with his success in the title role that he begged Dickens to write another farce for production in the spring.

Dickens ended the year, despite the necessity of completing the next installment of *Pickwick*, in a round of social activities. From one party he arrived home at one in the morning "dead drunk, and was put to bed by my loving missis. We are just going," he added, "to Chapman's sister's quadrille party, for which you may imagine I feel remarkably disposed." [34] There was a holiday turkey sent by Mitton's partner, Charles Smithson, of which Beard and Mitton were invited to partake.[35] And on Christmas Day, at Kensal Lodge, Harrison Ainsworth initiated the longest and most deeply intimate friendship in Dickens's life by introducing him to the literary and dramatic critic of the *Examiner*, John Forster.[36]

* * * * *

It was strange that they had not met before. Forster had been in London since 1828. The son of a cattle dealer at Newcastle-on-Tyne, he had come up to University College and then entered the Inner Temple. He had speedily made his way into journalistic and literary circles, become a friend of Charles Lamb and Leigh Hunt, joined the staff of the *Examiner* when he was no more than twenty years of age in 1832, and been dramatic critic on the *True Sun* throughout a period overlapping Dickens's brief employment on that paper.[37] On a visit to the offices of the *Chronicle* he had even seen Dickens on the staircase during the strike of its reporters, been struck by his "keen animation of look," and learned that "young Dickens" was the spokesman who had "conducted their case triumphantly." [38] Albany Fonblanque, the editor of the *Examiner*, had the saltiest appreciation of the *Sketches by Boz* and was always praising them to his young coadjutor. And Forster had written a laudatory review of *Pickwick* in the *Examiner* on September 4th and a depreciatory but not unfriendly comment on *The Village Coquettes* when it was produced.

Voluble, opinionated, overbearing, and quarrelsome, Forster was also sincere, deeply interested in literature, and selflessly faithful to his friends. Untiring in his endeavors to serve authors whose work he admired, and a man of perceptive taste, he was even now trying to prod Ainsworth into finding a publisher for Browning's *Sordello* and pressing Macready to stage his *Strafford*. Although he was to attach himself with special devotion to Dickens, many other writers, Landor, Tennyson, and Carlyle among them, came to know and be grateful for his generous helpfulness. Thackeray declared of him, "Whenever anybody is in a scrape we all fly to him for refuge—he is omniscient and works miracles." [39] If during the lengthening years his voice grew stentorian, his convictions dogmatic, his behavior dictatorial, and his manner pompous, in that portly, grim-jawed figure there was a deep loyalty that never swerved in its affections.

But the person whom Dickens beheld when they met at Kensal Lodge in 1836 was a serious young man with a mane of dark hair, a firm chin, sensuous lips, and dark intense eyes shadowed beneath level brows.[40] Two months the novelist's junior, he wore a self-assured sobriety contrasting oddly with Dickens's boyish effervescence that made him seem considerably older. He carried himself in a way that satirical observers said was modeled upon Macready's stage presence, stalking into a room hand on heart, intoning in his loud voice some such formula as "It is with infinite regret" or "Believe me I feel it sensibly." [41] Detractors called him "Fuz-Buz, a man of brummagem sentiment," [42] but this was a malicious distortion, for though Forster was blunt and sometimes even rude, he was honest to the point of belligerence. "A most noisy man," Carlyle said he was, "but really rather a good fellow . . . and with some substance in his tumultuary brains." [43] He and Dickens—opposites in many ways—warmed to each other at once. Dickens was all fire and charm; Forster thorny but solidly dependable. Although they often quarreled—Forster fought with everybody—the friendship then begun survived all shocks and lasted until Dickens's death thirty-four years later.

The young man Forster saw at that first meeting looked amazingly youthful, with a marked expression of openness and candor. His face revealed no more beard than a girl's, and his head was covered with rich brown hair in luxurious abundance and was carried in a manner extremely spirited. "He had a capital forehead, a firm nose with full wide nostril, eyes wonderfully beaming with intellect and running over with humour and cheerfulness, and a rather prominent mouth strongly marked with sensibility." But above all his face had that in it, Forster summarized, "which no time could change, and which remained implanted on it unalterably to the last. This was the quickness, keenness, and practical power, the eager, restless, energetic outlook on each several feature, that seemed to tell so little of the student or writer of books, and so much of the man of action and business in the world. Light and motion flashed from every part of it." [44]

Though the two young men were strongly attracted, they were prevented from meeting again for almost two months [45] by Kate's approaching confinement and Dickens's search for larger living quarters than the three rooms at Furnival's Inn.[46] Meanwhile he sent Forster copies of both series of his *Sketches* "as a very small testimony of the donor's regard" and "of his desire to cultivate" a friendship between them, adding to these formal phrases a more direct hope that Forster would "receive them for my sake, and not for their own." [47]

On the morning of January 6th Kate's labor began. Dickens's mother and Mrs. Hogarth both arrived to hover anxiously and give help. Dickens and Mary went out to buy a little table for Kate's bedroom, dispatched on the errand, perhaps, by the two mothers to get them out of the way. They wandered up and down Holborn and the neighboring streets for hours, going from one dealer to another. At last they came back to the very first shop they had looked into, and had passed half a dozen times since because Dickens was too diffident to ask the price.[48]

The baby, a boy, was born at quarter past six that evening, and was consequently a Twelfth-Night child. He was named Charles after his father.[49] The two grandmothers remained at Furnival's Inn for the night, so that there was no place for Mary. Dickens took her out to her father's house at Brompton, but she was back again next morning taking care of the entire small household for the remainder of the month. "I shall never be so happy again," Dickens said in his diary a year later, "as in those chambers three storeys high—never if I roll in wealth and fame." [50]

The first issue of *Bentley's Miscellany* made its appearance in the world only a few days before the birth of Dickens's child. It made an immediate success—thereby falsifying Theodore Hook's malicious prophecy that its title was "ominous—'Miss-sell-any.' " [51] The second number sold six thousand copies; at the end of six months they were "fairly inundated with *orders*." [52] It was a cheerful magazine of humorous tales and articles, lively and sometimes melodramatic biographical sketches, ghost and adventure stories, light verse, facetiae, and even an

occasional brief dramatic farce. Its contributors came to include
Dickens's friend Whitehead and his father-in-law Hogarth, William
Jerdan, Father Prout, Captain Medwin, Dr. Maginn, Samuel Lover,
James Morier, author of *Hajji Baba of Ispahan*, James Fenimore
Cooper, Thomas Love Peacock, Bentley's close friend Barham—anon-
mously—and of course Dickens himself.

He tackled his editorial duties with determination and energy. Even
the "Answers to Correspondents" showed his tremendous industry
and attention to detail. They overflowed with a bold high-spiritedness,
and revealed the young editor's almost boisterous determination to
do and say exactly what he pleased.[53] Rejected articles were accompanied by individual letters of tactful explanation, and promising
contributors received detailed criticisms brightened by friendly praise.[54]
He recommended Phiz, "my Pickwick artist," to Bentley as a pictorial
contributor, and passed upon all illustrations with an eagle eye.[55] Into
his own new story, *Oliver Twist*, beginning in the February number,
"I have thrown my whole heart and soul," he wrote, ". . . and most
confidently believe he will make a feature in the work . . ." [56]

Oliver Twist was a bold departure from the genial tone of *Pickwick
Papers*. Instead of safely echoing the humor and hilarity that had set
all England roaring with affectionate laughter, Dickens embarked on
a scathing denunciation of the new Poor Law and moved on to a lurid
and somber portrayal of London's criminal slums. The comedy had a
bite he had seldom previously attempted even in painting the Fleet
or describing Dodson and Fogg. Bumble, the workhouse beadle, is
comic, and the stupefied pallor of the workhouse master when Oliver
"asks for more" [57] is ludicrous, but the laughter has an acid quality
and Bumble is slowly subjected to a kind of vindictive ferocity.

The very language of the opening pages is characterized by a scalding sarcasm. At the end of the first chapter, describing Oliver's birth,
"Oliver cried lustily," Dickens wrote. "If he could have known that
he was an orphan, left to the tender mercies of church-wardens and
overseers, perhaps he would have cried the louder." [58] And in the following chapter Dickens spoke of the orphans in the baby farm as
"juvenile offenders against the poor-laws" who "perversely" "sickened
from want and cold, or fell into the fire from neglect, or got half
smothered by accident," or were sometimes "overlooked in turning

up a bedstead or inadvertently scalded to death when there happened to be a washing—though the latter accident was very scarce, anything approaching to a washing being of rare occurrence." [59] When Oliver burst into tears at being gently spoken to by the magistrate, "He might be excused for doing so," Dickens commented grimly, "for the words were kindly said, and strange sounds frighten one." [60]

It took courage to risk alienating his readers by providing them in this second novel with emotions so different from what they were expecting. But Dickens was building a career, not merely consolidating a sudden popularity. He would consider anxiously how to make his readers receptive to what he wanted to say; he would not consider saying only what they wanted to hear. The impatience that had often seethed within him when gentlemen in Parliament indulged in high-flown oratory untinged by even a touch of real human sympathy, or droned out statistics with no consciousness that their figures represented enjoying and suffering human beings—all this warm feeling of the life that politicians and economists forgot was simmering in his heart and demanding that he make himself its spokesman.

It was from a closely related sentiment that *people* must not be sacrificed to any abstract principle, however righteous in appearance, that he had flamed into the indignation of *Sunday Under Three Heads*. Nothing could have made Dickens limit himself to the prudent exploitation of a popular vein. But his themes themselves are no product of abstract principle. Playful or fiery or pathetic, they burst into existence out of all the most powerful impulses of his nature. And so, even while Bob Sawyer trembles at the tongue of Mrs. Raddle and Stiggins sways with drunken belligerence at the temperance meeting, there is welling into Dickens's imagination the picture of a helpless child surrounded in a dreadful place by hideous companions.

His fusion of bravery and instinct justified itself. Masses of readers hated Bumble and laughed at him with an angry laughter; they loathed Fagin and shuddered at Sikes. The pathos and the horror of Dickens were as triumphant as his humor had been. It proved that *Pickwick* was no flash-in-the-pan achievement. Rendered gloriously self-confident by its reception, Dickens definitely determined to give up his rooms in Furnival's Inn. His lease there still had until Christmas, 1838, to run, but he could afford the loss now. In good earnest he

began looking for a house suitable to a growing family and in a neighborhood befitting an established author.

*   *   *   *   *

While house agents were searching in their behalf, Dickens, Kate,
and Mary went down for a few weeks to the cottage at Chalk where
he and Kate had spent their honeymoon.[61] Kate was not yet fully recovered from her confinement. Through the latter half of January she
had been, he wrote Bentley, "in a very low and alarming state," and
he had to stay with her constantly, "being the only person who can
prevail upon her to take ordinary nourishment." [62] And under the
stress of his own work Dickens had been having violent headaches
and been "ordered as much medicine as would confine an ordinary-
sized horse to his stall for a week." [63] Meanwhile, he was irritated and
inconvenienced by the fact that Cramer's were being very dilatory in
paying Hullah and himself the money due them on *The Village Coquettes,* and its revival at the St. James's was doing such poor business
that Braham was inviting them to write as many free orders as they
wished in order to fill up the house.[64]

At Chalk, Dickens finished revising the farce he was writing for
Harley, "a comic burletta in one Act," called *Is She His Wife?* and
sent it to young George Hogarth, his brother-in-law, to copy for him.[65]
It is an ineffective piece with an elaborate comic intrigue based on a
series of misunderstandings among all the characters and including a
somewhat strained scene between a bored husband and a nagging wife
only recently married.[66] Although Braham paid £100 for this piece,
and produced it at the St. James's on March 6, 1837,[67] Harley did not
score anything like the success with it that he had with *The Strange
Gentleman,* and it enjoyed only a short run. It has been inferred from
this farce that Dickens was bored on revisiting the scene of his honeymoon, but his only letter from there was serenely cheerful and its
references to Kate were quietly affectionate.[68]

On several occasions during this brief visit Dickens had to go up
to London again on business. Once house agents kept him so busy
that he nearly missed his coach back to Chalk, but they had found him
a house. It was a pleasant twelve-room dwelling of pink brick, with
three stories and an attic, a white-arched entrance door on the street
level, and a small private garden in the rear. It was located just north

of Gray's Inn at 48 Doughty Street, a genteel private street with a lodge at each end and gates that were closed at night by a porter in a gold-laced hat and a mulberry-colored coat with the Doughty arms on its buttons.[69] Dickens leased it for three years beginning Lady Day (March 25th) at £80 a year,[70] obtaining from Bentley an advance of £100 on their novel contract to pay the expenses of getting it ready and moving in.[71]

The Doughty Street home was soon full of lively doings. In addition to Mary, young Frederick Dickens—by this time sixteen—was now a member of the household, and added to its high spirits. A full-lipped, snub-nosed youth, with raised eyebrows and an amusingly oily laugh, he had a ludicrous gift for comic imitations in which Dickens abetted him.[72] The bright first-floor sitting room often resounded with Kate's and Mary's happy laughter.

During his mornings Dickens did editorial work for the *Miscellany*, and wrote *Oliver Twist* and *Pickwick* in his upstairs study overlooking the garden. In the afternoons he took long walks or went horseback riding with Ainsworth.[73] As fast as he turned out *Oliver* he sent the manuscript to Cruikshank for illustration, suggesting among other subjects the attempt to bind Oliver to Mr. Gamfield the chimney sweep, and his reception by Fagin and the boys.[74]

The little family circle was often joined in the evenings by his younger sister Letitia, who had become engaged in January to Henry Austin. Dickens felt a warm esteem and affection for this old friend, with whom he had so many times listened to Maria Beadnell's harp in Lombard Street. He had once even suggested that Austin share his bachelor chambers at Furnival's Inn, "an offer that I would make to no other creature living," [75] and he was now delighted at the idea of the closer relationship. "Had I a marriageable daughter," he told him, "(which thank God I have not) of all the young men I know or ever did know, I should delight in seeing her set her cap at you . . ." [76]

Henry Burnett, the young man to whom Fanny was engaged, was a singer like herself and had already had a little experience on the operatic stage. When he took Braham's role as Squire Norton in *The Village Coquettes* in April he was billed as from the Theatre Royal, Edinburgh. On the eve of his debut John Dickens wrote Harley a characteristic note, identifying himself at the top of the page as "John Dickens, father to Charles": "I beg your sympathy on behalf of the young hero Burnett who is to come out under your auspices on Monday night. He has been for some time engaged to my eldest daughter, wholly a love affair, and it has occurred to me that your knowing the relationship in which he is about to start to my family, may not lessen the interest as regards the success of a first appearance in this case." [77]

Burnett in later years described one of the visits he and Fanny made to Doughty Street when Dickens was working, as he sometimes did, in the evening:

"One night in Doughty Street, Mrs. Charles Dickens, my wife and myself were sitting round the fire cosily enjoying a chat, when Dickens, for some purpose, came suddenly into the room. 'What, you here!' he exclaimed; 'I'll bring down my work.' It was his monthly portion of 'Oliver Twist' for Bentley's. In a few minutes he returned, manuscript in hand, and while he was pleasantly discoursing he employed himself in carrying to a corner of the room a little table, at which he seated himself and recommenced his writing. We, at his bidding, went on talking our 'little nothings,'—he, every now and then (the feather of his pen still moving rapidly from side to side), put in a cheerful interlude. It was interesting to watch, upon the sly, the mind and the muscles working (or, if you please, *playing*) in company, as new thoughts were being dropped upon the paper. And to note the working brow, the set of mouth, with the tongue tightly pressed against the closed lips, as was his habit." [78]

On March 31st came the first anniversary of the publication of *Pickwick*. In celebration of a good fortune far transcending anything that any of them had anticipated, the publishers sent Dickens as an honorarium, in addition to the sums that had been agreed on, a check for £500 and gave a dinner in honor of the anniversary. "Accept my very best thanks for your handsome communication," Dickens told them, "and for the time and manner you chose for making it which renders it doubly gratifying." [79] The dinner took place on Saturday, April 8th, and caused yet another delay in Dickens and Forster meeting each other again. Regretting that he must decline an invitation for that night, Dickens explained, "I have long been engaged to the Pickwick publishers to a dinner in honour of that hero which comes off tomorrow." [80]

On the last day of April Dickens celebrated his editorial dignity by inviting his new publisher Bentley to dinner. Portly John Dickens was there, and George Hogarth, Mary, and one of the younger Hogarth sisters. It was a merry evening. Dickens sang comic songs and gave imitations of well-known actors. The fun was unceasing and so were the successive glasses of the brandy punch. Not until almost midnight did Bentley think of leaving, and then Dickens pressed him to a final glass, which, by that time, he would gladly have avoided. Dickens begged his lovely young sister-in-law Mary to add her persuasions, and Bentley yielded. "At the hands of this Hebe," he wrote, "I did not decline it." [81]

Never had a writer's position more splendidly and amazingly changed than Dickens's during these twelve months. At its beginning he was merely a successful journalist with the foreshadowings of a literary reputation, the author of a first volume of sketches reprinted from newspapers and magazines, glad to take on a job of hack writing in order to afford to get married. Now he was a family man living on an income more than doubled in a comfortable house with a pretty wife, an infant son, and an adoring and deeply loved sister-in-law. He was the editor of a magazine impressively prosperous from its inception. He was already more than halfway through one incredibly popular novel and had started another that bade fair to be hardly less so. Above all, he was on the road to being famous. Mr. Pickwick, bursting out of his green covers, had beamingly played the fairy godfather in actual fact, and magically transfigured the life of his own creator.

CHAPTER TWO

Lost Love

B UT soon there were shadows on the brightness. Early in May, a
few weeks after they had so happily settled themselves at Doughty
Street, Dickens experienced his first and possibly his greatest loss. The
death of Mary Hogarth shook the family, and in Dickens left scars
as deep as those of his youthful love for Maria. But where Maria had
brought him bitter disillusion, Mary set in motion in the springs of
his imagination a vision of ideal womanhood that was never realized
for him again. How far Mary was all he thought her, we cannot know.
Her light shone briefly on his life. But her memory never faded from
his mind, nor his love for her from his heart.

Almost from the beginning, when, as a girl of sixteen, Mary had
come to stay with them shortly after their honeymoon, her complete
and immediate responsiveness had won her a unique place in his affections. On New Year's Day, six months after her death, despite all
the successes the year had brought him, he confided his grief to his
diary: ". . . if she were with us now, the same winning, happy, amiable
companion, sympathising with all my thoughts and feelings more than
anyone I knew ever did or will, I think I should have nothing to wish
for, but a continuance of such happiness." But with an "awful suddenness," [1] just when she was about to share with him and Kate the
triumphs of his rising position in the world, she was gone.

The week after the dinner for Bentley, Mary had gone to Brompton
to spend two days with her mother. She returned in time to accompany
Dickens and Kate to the St. James's Theatre on Saturday night. They
reached home in the highest spirits, and after good nights were said
and lights put out downstairs, Mary "went upstairs to bed at about one
o'clock in perfect health and her usual delightful spirits." [2] She had

hardly closed her door, had not even had time to undress, when Dickens heard her utter a strange choking cry. Rushing into her room, he saw that she was severely ill. Kate joined him; Frederick ran for a doctor. During the night and the next morning she grew worse. Every remedy that skill or anxiety could suggest was tried. But although no danger was "apprehended until nearly the very last," Dickens wrote, "she sank under the attack and died—died in such a calm and gentle sleep, that although I had held her in my arms for some time before, when she was certainly living (for she swallowed a little brandy from my hand) I continued to support her lifeless form, long after her soul had fled to Heaven.

"This was about 3 o'clock on the Sunday afternoon. They think her heart was diseased. It matters little to relate these details now, for the light and life of our happy circle is gone—and such a blank created as we can never supply." [3] In an agony of grief Dickens slipped a ring from her pale hand and slid it on his own finger.[4] It remained there until his death.

The entire family was stunned by the catastrophe. Mrs. Hogarth, who had been brought to her daughter's bedside, lost consciousness and remained insensible for a week thereafter.[5] Kate herself, overwhelmed with the unexpected sorrow, "made such strong efforts to console her, that she unconsciously summoned up all her fortitude at the same time, and brought it to her own assistance." [6] As Dickens reflected on Mary's sweet and gentle spirit and recalled her joyful vitality, his heart ached with wretchedness. "You cannot conceive," he wrote the day after her death, "the misery in which this dreadful event has plunged us. Since our marriage she has been the peace and life of our home—the admired of all for her beauty and excellence—I could have better spared a much nearer relation or an older friend, for she has been to us what we can never replace, and has left a blank which no one who ever knew her can have the faintest hope of seeing supplied." [7]

The burial was in Kensal Green Cemetery on the Harrow Road. "I feel that as tomorrow draws nigh, the bitterest part of this calamity is at hand. I hope that, for that one day at all events, I may be able to bear my part in it with fortitude, and to encourage and console those about me. It will be no harder trial to anyone than myself." [8] And sometime afterward he asked Ainsworth, whose home was near by, to have the cemetery gardener "plant a rose tree or a few little flowers on that early grave" [9] for which he himself had composed the inscription on the tombstone:

MARY SCOTT HOGARTH
DIED 7TH MAY 1837
YOUNG, BEAUTIFUL, AND GOOD,
GOD IN HIS MERCY
NUMBERED HER WITH HIS ANGELS
AT THE EARLY AGE OF
SEVENTEEN

For years it was Dickens's hope to be buried in that same grave.[10]

When all was over, he was so prostrated that, although he had been obliged to borrow money from Edward Chapman for the funeral expenses, he felt unable to go on with his writing. Never before or again were his habits of industry or his sense of responsibility to his readers so shaken that he was totally unable to work. He took Kate off with him to a small farm in rural Hampstead. "I have been so much unnerved and hurt," he wrote Ainsworth, "but the loss of the dear girl whom I loved, after my wife, more deeply and fervently than anyone on earth, that I have been compelled for once to give up all idea of my monthly work and to try a fortnight's rest and quiet." [11]

There was no number of *Pickwick Papers* for the end of May,[12] and in the June issue of *Bentley's Miscellany*, instead of an installment of *Oliver Twist*, there was a notice of explanation: "Since the appearance of the last number of this work the editor has to mourn the sudden death of a very dear young relative to whom he was most affectionately attached and whose society has been for a long time the chief solace of his labours." [13]

This notice, however, did not prevent the most fantastic rumors from breaking out. All literary London knew by this time who Boz really was, but there were persons who nonetheless gravely maintained that *Pickwick* was the work of an association that had disbanded, that Boz was a prisoner who had been many years in King's Bench, that he was a Catholic, that he was bred to the Bar, that he was a youth of eighteen so shattered in health by his literary labors "that there was not the slightest chance of his ever publishing another number." [14]

The brief two weeks' rest after the funeral passed quietly in the little, secluded cottage. Surrounded by a large garden, it had a veranda, and a cherry tree blooming in an angle of the house. There they were alone, except for visits from a few close friends. Beard was asked to join them "in the old way." [15] From Kensal Lodge, by a crossroad skirting north of London, Ainsworth made his way over on horseback,[16] and he and Dickens went riding together. And in the latter part of the month John Forster finally broke through the obstacles that had limited their meetings to a few business encounters, by paying his first call on Dickens while he was at Hampstead.[17]

Kate, too, had been dreadfully shaken by their ordeal and a short time after suffered a miscarriage,[18] but in the country solitude she slowly attained some peace. The bond between herself and Mary had been so close, Dickens recorded, that "she has nothing to remember but a long course of affection and attachment, perhaps never exceeded. Not one cross word or angry look on either side even as children rests in judgment against her, and she is now so calm and cheerful that I wonder to see her." [19]

The anguish, for Dickens, was not easily softened. Writing to Beard while at Collins's Farm, he poured out his heart: "Thank God she died in my arms, and the very last words she whispered were of me. . . . The first burst of grief has passed, and I can think and speak of her calmly and dispassionately. I solemnly believe that so perfect a creature never breathed. I knew her inmost heart, and her real worth and values. She had not a fault." [20]

When he revisited the cemetery a month after her death he felt her loss as painfully as ever. "I saw her grave but a few days ago and the grass around it was as green and the flowers as bright, as if nothing of the earth in which they grew could ever wither or fade. Beneath my feet there lay a silent but solemn witness that all health and beauty are but things of the hour. . . .

"Those who are left behind to recollect what she was here; to miss her sweet face and winning smile, and all the countless endearments that a guileless heart and affectionate nature gave birth to, are indeed objects for sympathy and compassion. Among these mourners as none loved her better living, so . . . none laments her more constantly and deeply in death . . ." [21]

For every correspondent to whom he had to make the sad announcement, he reiterated her praises and repeated his own misery. "From the day of our marriage the dear girl had been the grace and life of our home, our constant companion, and the sharer of all our little pleasures. . . . We might have known that we were too happy together to be long without a change.

"The change has come, and it has fallen heavily upon us. I have lost the dearest friend I ever had. Words cannot describe the pride I felt in her, and the devoted attachment I bore her. She well deserved it, for with abilities far beyond her years, with every attraction of youth and beauty, and conscious as she must have been of everybody's admiration, she had not a single fault . . ." 22

* * * * *

As the months went by he thought of Mary with ever-increasing love. In the fall, thanking Mrs. Hogarth for a lock of Mary's hair, he wrote, "I have never had her ring off my finger by day or night, except for an instant at a time, to wash my hands, since she died. I have never had her sweetness and excellence absent from my mind so long. I can solemnly say that, waking or sleeping, I have never lost the recollection of our hard trial and sorrow, and I feel that I never shall. . . . I wish you could know how I weary now for the three rooms in Furnival's Inn, and how I miss that pleasant smile and those sweet words which, bestowed upon our evening's work, in our merry banterings round the fire, were more precious to me than the applause of a whole world could be. I can recall everything we said and did in those days, and could show you every passage and line we read together." And, remembering Mary's companionship on the day Charley was born, he thought of the approaching birth of his second child next March. "You and I will probably be oftener together in Kate's coming confinement, which will be a truly heavy time to me, reminding me how we spent the last." 23

In his diary, on January 6th, the first anniversary of Charley's birth, his marking of this event was wholly taken up with recalling Mary's presence on that day and mourning the lost happiness of the Furnival's Inn days. A few days later he copied out a passage from Sir Walter Scott's diary: " 'She is sentient and conscious of my emotions *somewhere*—where, we cannot tell, how, we cannot tell; yet would I not this moment renounce the mysterious, yet certain hope that I shall see her in a better world, for all that this world can give me.' " And he observed that these thoughts "have been mine by day and by night, in good spirits and bad, since Mary died." [24]

During her lifetime there had been natural boundaries to the development as well as the expression of his feelings for his adoring sister-in-law. And if he had idealized her then into the unattainable of perfection, it was no doubt partly because she was in fact unattainable. But the accident of her early death not only eased the barriers; it made that perfection permanent and unassailable, forever safe from the hazards of time. If he had, before her death, idealized her partly because he loved her, from then on he loved her even more because he could idealize her forever.

Her image came to him nightly in visions which he anticipated with longing and told to no one. But on a visit to Yorkshire nine months after her death he was moved to reveal them to Kate: "Is it not extraordinary that the same dreams which have constantly visited me since poor Mary died follow me everywhere? After all the changes of scene and fatigue, I have dreamt of her ever since I left home, and no doubt shall till I return. I should be sorry to lose such visions, for they are very happy ones, if it be only the seeing her in one's sleep." [25] With this injudicious violation, however, of his instinct toward secrecy about them, the dreams ceased, and Mary came to visit his slumbers only once again in later years. These dreams and the fact of their cessation on being divulged made a deep impression on him, though he perceived no special significance in their coming to an end with his mentioning them to Kate. Nevertheless, the episode stamped itself so unforgettably and strangely on his memory that five years after, in a letter to Mrs. Hogarth, he wrote, "After she died, I dreamed of her every night for many months—I think for the better part of a year—sometimes as a spirit, sometimes as a living creature, never with any of the bitterness of my real sorrow, but always with a kind of quiet happiness, which became so pleasant to me that I never lay down at night without a hope of the vision coming back in one shape or other. And so it did. I went down into Yorkshire, and finding it still present to me, in a strange scene and a strange bed, I could not help mentioning the circumstance in a note I wrote home to Kate. From that moment I have never dreamed of her once, though she is so much in my thoughts at all times (especially when I am successful, and have prospered in anything) that the recollection of her is an essential part of my being, and is as inseparable from my existence as the beating of my heart is." [26]

In the course of time, he was able to think and speak of her in quiet terms of peace and hope. When William Bradbury, the printer, lost his own child some two years after Mary's death, Dickens wrote to him: ". . . I lost in one short night a young and lovely creature whom— I can say even to *you* now—I loved with the warmest affection that our nature is capable of, and in whom I had the fondest father's pride. The first burst of anguish over, I have never thought of her with pain —never. I have never connected her idea with the grave in which she lies. I look upon it as I sometimes do upon the clothes she used to wear. They will moulder away in their secret places, as her earthly form will in the ground, but I have long since learnt to separate her from all this litter of dust and ashes and to picture her to myself with every well-remembered grace and beauty heightened by the light of Heaven . . ." [27]

But the image of her death he could not fully conquer. At about this time he was drawing near the end of *Oliver Twist*, and he found himself unable to carry out his original intention of having Rose Maylie die. He could not bear to describe the fair young creature breathing her last amid the blossoms of May.

Two years later, Mary dominated his imagination again, throughout the whole story of Little Nell, in *The Old Curiosity Shop*. He felt such anguish at the approaching death he had planned for his child heroine that he spun out the narrative to delay the moment when he must face the ending. When it could no longer be put off, ". . . I am the wretchedest of the wretched," he wrote Forster. "It casts the most horrible shadow upon me, and it is as much as I can do to keep moving at all." Nobody, he said, would miss Nell as he would. "It is such a very painful thing to me, that I really cannot express my sorrow. Old wounds bleed afresh when I only think of the way of doing it: what the actual doing it will be, God knows. . . . Dear Mary died yesterday, when I think of this sad story." [28]

Toward the end of October, 1841, Mary's grandmother died, and suddenly, a few days later, her brother George, at the age of twenty. "For God's sake be comforted," he wrote Mrs. Hogarth, "and bear this well, for the love of your remaining children.

"I had always intended to keep poor Mary's grave for us and our dear children, and for you. But if it will be any comfort to you to have poor George buried there, I will cheerfully arrange to place the ground at your entire disposal. Do not consider me in any way. Consult only your own heart. Mine seems to tell me that as they both died so young and so suddenly, they ought both to be buried together." [29]

But although to Mrs. Hogarth he generously minimized the cost to him of this sacrifice, and even made himself useful by attending to the burial arrangements, he could not suppress a desperate outcry to Forster: "It is a great trial to me to give up Mary's grave; greater than I can possibly express. I thought of moving her to the catacombs and saying nothing about it; but then I remembered that the poor old lady is buried next her at her own desire, and could not find it in my heart, directly she is laid in the earth, to take her grandchild away. The desire to be buried next her is as strong upon me now, as it was five years ago; and I *know* (for I don't think there ever was love like that I bear her) that it will never diminish. I fear I can do nothing. Do you think I can? They would move her on Wednesday, if I resolved to have it done. I cannot bear the thought of being excluded from her dust; and yet I feel that her brothers and sisters, and her mother, have a better right than I to be placed beside her. It is but an idea. I neither think nor hope (God forbid) that our spirits would ever mingle *there*. I ought to get the better of it, but it is very hard. I never contemplated this—and coming so suddenly, and after being ill, it disturbs me more than it ought. It seems like losing her a second time." [30] And in response to a suggestion of Forster's the next day, he replied in despair, "No, I tried that. No, there is no ground on either side to be had. I must give it up. I shall drive over there, please God, on Thursday morning before they get there; and look at her coffin." [31]

With this last look he laid the aching pain of her to rest. The following year he was on his triumphant tour of America with Kate, and, overwhelmed by the "tremendous spectacle" of Niagara, he wished longingly that "the dear girl whose ashes lie in Kensal-green, had lived to come so far along with us." [32] In Genoa in 1844, when the seed of other troubles was already stirring within him, Mary's spirit came to him for the last time in a dream. "I was not at all afraid, but in a great delight, so that I wept very much, and stretching out my arms to it called it 'Dear,'" and awoke "with the tears running down my face." [33]

And in a letter to Forster in 1848 he was still marking the anniversary of her loss: "This day 11 years poor dear Mary died." [34]

But out of his imagination she never died. The imprint of all the virtues he attributed to her was marked upon his innermost being. Throughout almost his entire literary career his novels continue in their portraits of young girls to reveal glimpses of now one and now another aspect of her shining image. Possibly for him the memory of her playful charm threw over even coquettish little Dolly Varden in *Barnaby Rudge* a hue of rose not always there for his readers, and Mary's gaiety and tenderness certainly animate loving, laughing Ruth Pinch in *Martin Chuzzlewit*. His vision of her nobler qualities recurs again and again, in Florence Dombey's devotion to her brother and father, in David Copperfield's serene and perhaps too perfect Agnes, in the tender Ada Clare of *Bleak House*, in the sacrificial spirit of Little Dorrit. The very sentimentality that we sometimes find in their delineation is only a further index to the transcendent goodness with which he endowed Mary in his heart.

The memory of her death, too, deepened the pathos with which Dickens was always to contemplate youth or innocence condemned to die. It was agonizingly present to him in the last hours of Little Nell, and six years later it suffused with tenderness the death of Paul Dombey. It lends a dignity to the fading away even of David Copperfield's foolish, frivolous child wife Dora. There are organ tones of the same solemn emotion in the death of the poor crossing sweeper Jo in *Bleak House*. Eighteen years after Mary's death Dickens adapted to fictional purposes in "The Holly Tree" the literal story of the dreams of her that ceased when they were once confided to Kate. Even in the last book that he completed, *Our Mutual Friend*, echoes of her loss are still lingering in the poignant death of Betty Higden's grandchild, little Johnny.

It is impossible to exaggerate the significance of this early love and early sorrow for Dickens. His devotion to Mary was an emotion unique in his entire life, not only more enduring and unchanging than any other, but one that touched his being in a way no other did. Unlike Maria Beadnell, who tortured his heart and his pride and taught him to be forever on his guard, unlike Kate, whose slow-minded and pedestrian goodness he ultimately found impossible to mold into the shining pearl of perfection, unlike one or two others of later years, who stimulated his imagination or fired his passions but proved unable to sustain his invariable desire to idealize them, Mary alone remained elevated by her death to her high altar. Not only did she become the recipient of an idealizing emotion of which his wife, even during the days of their courtship, had never been the object, but Mary's gradual enshrinement in Dickens's memory subjected Kate to comparisons that she could not possibly equal—that perhaps no living person could have done—and had its share in the slow growth of the catastrophe that years later overtook the married life of Dickens and Kate.

Ascent of the Rocket

O N the 18th of November, 1837, at the Prince of Wales Tavern in Leicester Square, a banquet was held to celebrate the completion of England's most popular and important contemporary work of fiction. Just before "*the* toast of the evening," "the head waiter . . . entered, and placed a glittering temple of confectionery on the table, beneath the canopy of which stood a little figure of the illustrious Mr. Pickwick." [1] For, after nineteen months of steadily mounting success, *Pickwick* had at last come to its triumphant close. It was a merry company and a merry occasion.

The principals had good reason to feel delighted. In welcoming Dickens as their guest of honor, Chapman and Hall put in his hands a check for £750. Above the sums they had contracted to pay him, they had presented him with what Forster later estimated as another £2,000 and Edward Chapman remembered as £2,500. They could well afford this generosity, for they had made about £14,000 from their investment in the unknown young man whom Hall had sought out to do a piece of literary hack work. [2] Promptly on the Monday following, Dickens opened an account in Coutts's bank with an initial deposit of £500.

In contrast to the frictions that were already developing between him and Richard Bentley, Dickens had for Chapman and Hall the warmest of feelings. Early in their connection he had declared that he would be "the most jolter-headed scribe alive" [3] if he ever entertained any notion of dissolving their pleasant association. With generous bonuses and gifts, they had created a human bond between themselves and an author sensitively responsive to friendly ties. "I cannot tell you," Dickens had written them in the previous summer, "how very much I am gratified and delighted by the receipt of your most unique and beautiful present, which I shall lay up in lavender for my boy to show his boys—and girls likewise—as a Pickwickian relic of his respected father. . . ." [4]

Now, he was much moved by the affection of his friends and the excitement of the occasion. He occupied the chair, and the genial Thomas Noon Talfourd made an excellent vice-chairman at the other end of the table. Besides the two publishers, those present included Hogarth and the beaming John Dickens, the dignified and stately actor William Charles Macready, Ainsworth with his gusty laugh, the witty and epigrammatic Jerdan, editor of the *Literary Gazette*, the Irish novelist Samuel Lover, and Forster, of course, who had come striding in with his impatient tread. Possibly present also, though there is no record of it, was Thomas Hill, a cheerful and aged little cupid "with a face like a peony," a collector of rare books who gave literary dinners, and whom Dickens is known to have invited.[5]

The dinner and the wines, Ainsworth said, were both capital.[6] And Jerdan recalled that at the table "the pleasant and uncommon fact was stated . . . that there never had been a line of written agreement, but that the author, printer, artist, and publisher had all proceeded on simple verbal assurances, and that there never had arisen a word to interrupt the complete satisfaction of everyone." [7] It was true that there had been no formal contract, although there had, of course, been exchanges of letters agreeing on terms. In the course of the evening Dickens received from his publishers a set of silver "Apostle" spoons with characters from *Pickwick* instead of the Twelve Apostles on the handles.[8] And at the height of the festivities Talfourd, following the magnificent appearance of Mr. Pickwick in confectionery, proposed Dickens's health "in a very good speech," Macready noted in his diary, "and Dickens replied—under strong emotion—most admirably." [9]

By this time, after the first shock and suffering over Mary's death, Dickens's life was settling into a pattern prophetic of the future. His days hummed with the electric energy of a dynamo. Before *Oliver Twist* was more than half finished he began his third novel. His circle of friends grew constantly larger. And, only eight months after the modest *Pickwick* dinner, he received what almost amounted to official recognition as one of England's celebrities.

*   *   *   *   *

Following his brief retreat to Collins's Farm in June, the summer had found him back at Doughty Street going ahead with the last installments of *Pickwick*, superintending the *Miscellany*, and resuming *Oliver Twist*. On the latter he worked carefully and with close attention to factual accuracy. He thanked Charles Ross for a "statistical Magazine" with "tables contemning juvenile delinquency that I was particularly anxious to see in a well digested form." [10] To a gentleman who had charge of the press reporters for the City Courts he wrote: "In my next number of Oliver Twist, I must have a magistrate; and casting about for a magistrate whose harshness and insolence would render him a fit subject to be 'shewn up' I have, as a necessary consequence, stumbled upon Mr. Laing of Hatton Garden celebrity." Might he, under these circumstances, "be smuggled into the Hatton Garden Office for a few moments some morning?" [11] This personage duly appeared as Mr. Fang in *Oliver Twist*.

Once the initial obstacles to their seeing each other had been passed, the intimacy with Forster grew at a rapid pace. Dickens sent him the parts of *Oliver* already published, and was delighted with his enthusiasm.[12] Forster in turn sent Dickens one of the biographies of the *Statesmen of the Commonwealth* that he was contributing to Dionysius Lardner's *Cabinet Cyclopaedia*. "I don't know what to say," Dickens told him, "about your beautiful present . . . Conclude that I am like the parrot who was doubly valuable for not speaking, because he thought a great deal more." [13] And a few days later he wrote, "Believe me that I require no present to render more lively my assurance of your friendship or my deep conviction of its worth. . . . It shall go hard, I hope, ere anything but Death impairs the toughness of a bond now so firmly riveted." [14]

Richard Bentley, however, did not take as enthusiastically to Forster as Dickens did. They met on a river excursion to Blackwall, where Bentley was having a party for dinner. He had invited Forster at Dickens's request and was introduced to him on the steamer going down the Thames. "This ill-mannered man broke up the pleasure of the party," Bentley declared, "by some rude remarks at several of my guests; so markedly rude as almost to precipitate personal violence." [15] His unfavorable opinion, however, did not prevent his subsequently contracting to publish one of Forster's books.

Although Dickens had already been having differences with Bentley over the *Miscellany*, their dispute still simmered below the boiling point. But with Macrone there was a renewal of trouble, which now brought Forster actively into Dickens's affairs and started him on his long role of unofficial business manager. Dickens learned that Macrone planned to reissue the *Sketches* in monthly parts got up in green covers exactly imitative of *Pickwick*. Already irritated at hearing that Macrone was "making thousands" from the copyright he had hastily sold, he felt that three simultaneous publications "must prove seriously prejudicial to my reputation," and might even damage the sale of *Pickwick*. He asked Forster to try to dissuade Macrone by reminding him how cheaply he had purchased the *Sketches*, how much money he had already made, and further, that when he obtained their copyright he had not even hinted at publishing them in this form. If he still persevered in his scheme he was to be warned that Dickens would advertise everywhere that the reprint was against his wishes and brought him no profit.[16]

But Macrone was unfrightened. The *Sketches*, he insisted to Forster, were now his absolute property. If Dickens had chosen to surrender the copyrights to get out of writing the novel he had promised, that did not alter Macrone's right to make as much from them as he could. If he had been the loser, Dickens would not have given back any of the purchase money. He should not be expected to indemnify Dickens for acting in panic or bad judgment.[17] Macrone's position, in fact, was sound. The only part of it that smacked of sharp practice was the proposal to reap an advantage from the *Pickwick* harvest by a misleading duplication of its green covers.

Forster saw that he must alter his attack. He knew from Dickens that Chapman and Hall would advance the money to repurchase the copyrights, and asked what Macrone would take for them.[18] The £2,000 Macrone demanded "opened so wide a mouth," Forster considered, that he "would have no part in the costly process of filling it," and advised Dickens to "keep quiet for a time." [19] But that was just what Dickens could not do. He was too vexed and impatient. Some further negotiations took place and Macrone presented an estimate of his probable profits. He "peremptorily refused," Dickens wrote Forster, "to take one farthing less than the two thousand pounds . . . Hall, whose judgment may be relied on in such matters, could not dispute the justice of the calculation." [20]

The fact was that Chapman and Hall had reflected that if the *Sketches* were *going* to appear in monthly numbers, they and the author might as well profit. With the *Pickwick* system of distribution, they might attain a far larger sale than Macrone could and own the book at the same time. They therefore suggested putting up the money to buy the copyrights jointly, deducting Dickens's share from the profits.[21]

Perplexed about what to do, Dickens sought further advice from Forster. But he was not at home, and Macrone refused to wait.[22] In desperation Dickens consented. Macrone received £2,250, a sum that may have allowed for expenses already incurred in the projected reprint.[23] "Was I right?" Dickens asked Forster. "I think you will say yes." "I could not say no," Forster comments, "though I was glad to have been no party to a price so exorbitant. . . ." [24]

From this time forward there was hardly any of Dickens's work that Forster did not see and comment upon in manuscript. Regularly he took off Dickens's hands the burden of correcting proofs, beginning with the fifteenth number of *Pickwick*, which Dickens sent him "by Fred, who is on his way with it to the printers." [25] With the sixteenth, Dickens wrote Forster that he could not go for an intended ride that day: "Here I am slippered and jacketted . . . and can't get out.

"I am getting on, thank Heaven, 'like a house o' fire,' and the next Pickwick will bang all the others. I shall expect you at 1.

"If you know anybody at St. Paul's, I wish you'd send round and ask them not to ring the bell so, I can hardly hear my own ideas . . ." [26]

Forster became also his constant companion in the long walks and rides by which Dickens believed he rested from his mental labors. Always just one jump ahead of the printer, he nevertheless managed on many a day to clear his writing table by eleven, ride out to Richmond or Twickenham, lunching on the road and returning to Doughty Street for six o'clock dinner.[27] He ought to dine in Bloomsbury Square today, Dickens would tell Forster, but he would rather ride. "So engage the osses." [28] Or, "Where shall it be—oh where—Hampstead, Greenwich, Windsor? WHERE????? While the day is bright, not when it has dwindled away to nothing! For who can be of any use whatsomdever such a day as this, excepting out of doors?" [29]

Walking, he put in seven or eight miles at a fast pace. "Is it possible that you can't, oughtn't, shouldn't, mustn't, *won't* be tempted, this gorgeous day!" "Come, come, *come*, and walk in the green lanes. You will work the better for it all the week. COME!" [30] "You don't feel disposed, do you, to muffle yourself up and start off with me for a good brisk walk over Hampstead Heath? I knows a good 'ous there where we can have a red-hot chop for dinner, and a glass of good wine"—an invitation that led to their first experience of Jack Straw's Castle.[31] At Hampstead, too, they often came to dine at the Spaniards, with its worn flagstones, low-ceiled bar, and narrow-paned lattice windows.[32]

Occasionally Ainsworth and Talfourd joined them on their rides, which in these days of glowing energy were an even more favorite exercise for Dickens than walking. They would go out by Twyford Abbey and the winding Brent to Perivale and Greenford, through the vale of Middlesex, and home by Stanmore and Harrow. Or they would cross Old Oak Common to Acton, stopping at Berrymead Priory to greet Edward Lytton Bulwer, clatter on through Acton's narrow High Street with its raised pavement and old red-tiled houses, past "Fordhook," Henry Fielding's beloved home, and the long village green of Ealing, through orchard-bordered lanes to Chiswick, and circle home again by Shepherd's Bush and the Scrubs.[33] Ainsworth's sharp-tongued cousin Mrs. Touchet, a famous horsewoman in her youth, called them "Cockney horsemen" in scorn of their riding style, although of course not one of the group was a native Londoner.[34]

Dickens and Bulwer did not become intimate for a number of years, but they were already on a friendly footing and occasionally dined at each other's tables. Bulwer's rapid literary success, with *Paul Clifford, Eugene Aram, The Last Days of Pompeii,* and *Rienzi,* his luxurious scale of living, and perhaps his consciousness of his distinguished social position, evoked among many of his fellow writers a good deal of spiteful resentment. "A thoroughly *satin* character," one of them remarked, "but then it is the *richest* satin." [35] Bulwer, however, was magnanimously quick to recognize the merits of others. Although the rising star of Dickens threatened to eclipse his own, he gave to *Pickwick,* from its earliest numbers, the warmest praise, even "before the depth beneath its humor was acknowledged," as he wrote to Forster, "yea, tho' I foresaw that he of all men was the one that my jealousy might best be aroused by." [36] And Dickens paid public tribute in later years to the generosity with which Bulwer stood far above all the "little grudging jealousies" that sometimes disparage the brightness of literature.[37]

In the middle of June Forster took Dickens round to Covent Garden to present him to Macready. With the great actor Forster was on terms of warm friendship, despite the trials he inflicted on Macready's furious temper by tactless contradiction. Macready was forty-four and famous in Shakespearean roles; Forster was only twenty-five, but he would arrogantly attempt "to dictate how a Shakespearean sentence should be emphasized," a dogmatism doubly irritating in a youth whose very bearing seemed an imitation of Macready's own.[38] For all Forster's bumptiousness, though, and the violence of their clashes, Macready valued Forster's good qualities, and received his visitors cordially in his dressing room. "I was glad to see him," he wrote of Dickens,[39] and their meeting started a lifelong friendship unmarred by a single quarrel or trace of bad feeling.

In the course of these warming companionships, Dickens and Kate, with Hablôt Browne, took a week's holiday across the Channel in July, dashing merrily from Calais to Ghent, Brussels, and Antwerp. "We went this afternoon," Dickens wrote Forster, "in a barouche to some gardens where the people dance, and where they were footing it most heartily—especially the women, who in their short petticoats and light caps look uncommonly agreeable.

"A gentleman in a blue surtout and silken berlins accompanied us from the hotel and acted as curator. He even waltzed with a very smart lady (just to show us, condescendingly, how it ought to be done), and waltzed elegantly too. We rang for slippers after we came back, and it turned out that this gentleman was the Boots. Isn't this French?" [40]

On their return the young Dickenses entertained frequently at dinner parties in Doughty Street. Harley was a constant visitor, with Cruikshank and his wife, "with Burnett and his'n," with Talfourd and Macready.[41]

> *"Two aunts and two uncles, a sister and brother*
> *Dine with us next Thursday; will you make another?"*

Dickens expansively words one invitation.

Nor did he forget other friends of long standing. He introduced Hullah to Macready, who produced Hullah's new opera, *The Barbers of Bassova*, the next November at Covent Garden.[42] To poor old Captain Holland, who had started him off in the *Monthly Magazine*, and was now in Paris, twelve guineas must be sent for old times' sake.[43]

Beard needed money; in lending it Dickens entreated his old friend "not to turn your thoughts to this small enclosure until you have devoted every ten pounds you have to every demand that presses upon it." [44]

Part of August and September Dickens spent with Kate and eight-months-old Charley at Broadstairs, a picturesque Kentish seaside resort where the Macreadys often went for summer bathing.[45] Hardly more than a fishing village at the time, it zigzagged in three crooked old streets to the edge of the white chalk cliffs.[46] From its perch there, surrounded by fields of rippling corn, it looked down on the blue water of a toy semicircular bay with an old wooden pier and, farther out, the ocean "winking in the sunlight like a drowsy lion." At low tide the fishing boats lay on their sides like exhausted fish and the "brown litter of tangled sea-weed and fallen cliff" looked "as if a family of giants had been making tea" and untidily thrown "their tea-leaves on the shore." [47]

"I have walked upon the sands at low-water, from this place to Ramsgate," Dickens reported to Forster, "and sat upon the same at high-ditto till I have been flayed with cold. I have seen ladies and gentlemen walking upon the earth in slippers of buff, and pickling themselves in the sea in complete suits of the same. I have seen stout gentlemen looking at nothing through powerful telescopes for hours, and when at last they saw a cloud of smoke, fancying a steamer behind it, and going home comfortable and happy. I have found out that our next neighbour, has a wife and something else under the same roof with the rest of his furniture—the wife deaf and blind, and the something else given to drinking." [48] To these scenes Forster came down for a visit, and they had a "merry night" at the Albion Hotel.[49]

*   *   *   *   *

Back in London in the fall, Dickens superintended the appearance of the final double number of *Pickwick*, and dedicated its first edition in book form to Talfourd in friendship and recognition of his efforts to get through Parliament a copyright bill extending an author's rights for sixty years.[50] At that time, not merely did they expire with the writer's death, but even during his life he had no protection against piracy in the form of abridgment or alteration. There was, of course, no international copyright, and publishers of all countries appropriated the works of foreign authors. Dickens had made detailed suggestions on the provisions of Talfourd's bill, and was disappointed when its defeat left no recourse except to begin over again.

About the innumerable dramatic piracies of his own work, however, he was still able to feel reasonably calm. "Well; if the Pickwick," he wrote, "has been the means of putting a few shillings in the vermin-eaten pockets of so miserable a creature, and has saved him from a workhouse or a jail, let him empty out his little pot of filth and welcome." [51] Later on, he was to be less philosophic about piracy and plagiarism. Even at this time, indeed, he was careful not to countenance these liberties with his work. To a firm of American publishers who offered him £50 in acknowledgment of the profits from their own edition of *Pickwick*, he replied with a courteous ambiguity of phrase that "under the circumstances" he should not feel "quite at ease" in drawing upon them for the proffered sum. He would, however, be happy to enter into arrangements with them for transmitting early proofs of *Oliver Twist*.[52] Though polite and willing to do business, he would not in any way imply his acquiescence in his work having been used without his permission.

The prodigal and even reckless energy with which Dickens kept both these novels running concurrently, sometimes barely a week ahead of the printer, was already arousing amazement and doubts of his ability to keep it up. Abraham Hayward in an otherwise highly laudatory critique in the October *Quarterly Review* remarked that "Mr. Dickens writes too often and too fast," and warned that if he persisted in this course his fate was certain: "he has risen like a rocket, and he will come down like the stick." Dickens granted much truth to this notice but, already oversensitive to all but the most lavish praise, chose to give it a personal motive. "I think Hayward has *rather* visited upon me, his recollection of my declining his intimate acquaintance . . ." [53]

But, though swift in resentment, Dickens melted readily to forgiveness. Bitter as he had been against Macrone, when he learned that the publisher had suddenly died in September, leaving his affairs in confusion and his widow and children destitute, he joined with Ainsworth in a plan to help them—a benefit volume by writers who had been connected in business "with poor Mr. Macrone." [54] Cruikshank donated illustrations, and Dickens, in addition to his other work, contributed a story and attended to all the details of getting the volume into print.

Even in the following spring, while he was getting his next novel, *Nicholas Nickleby*, under way, he was busied in correspondence and negotiations for this volume.

Meanwhile, during the first week in November, Dickens and Kate spent a few days at Brighton. It was their first visit there, and the weather was stormy. "It blew a perfect hurricane," Dickens wrote Forster, "breaking windows, knocking down shutters, carrying people off their legs, blowing the fires out, and causing universal consternation. The air was for some hours darkened with a shower of black hats (second hand) which are supposed to have been blown off the heads of unwary passengers in remote parts of the town, and have been industriously picked up by the fishermen." His notions of the place, he added, were "consequently somewhat confined: being limited to the Pavilion, the chain-pier and the sea." 55

But even for this time it was hard to forget the excitement of *Oliver*. "I have had great difficulty in keeping my hands off Fagin and the rest of them in the evenings; but as I came down for rest, I have resisted the temptation, and steadily applied myself to the labour of being idle. Did you ever read (of course you have though) Defoe's History of the Devil? What a capital thing it is! I bought it for a couple of shillings yesterday morning, and have been quite absorbed in it ever since." 56

Returning from this holiday, Dickens sat to Samuel Laurence for a portrait which the artist insisted on presenting to him.57 It shows a young man whose assured face and firm jaw reveal the will that vitalized his imaginative powers. Dickens evidently liked it, for he had Laurence do a portrait of Kate too. No record tells, however, what Dickens thought of a somewhat different view of him, a slightly earlier pencil sketch of Cruikshank's, portraying him as a dandified D'Orsay figure in frock coat, tight trousers, and enormous silken cravat, with a delicate face and curling hair.

It was in the midst of these sittings that the banquet for *Pickwick* occurred. At the same time Chapman and Hall revised their arrangements with Dickens. For, although they were on the best of terms, Dickens had no share in the copyright, and Forster had been pressing emphatically for the justice of his having a legal part of the profits. Forster had established himself by now as a sort of literary adviser and arbiter to Chapman and Hall, swinging into their offices at 186 Strand as though the whole place belonged to him and telling everyone ex-

actly what must be done.[58] Under his influence, they agreed to give
Dickens a one-third share in the copyright of *Pickwick* after five years,
in consideration of a contract signed on that very day, November 18,
1837, for a new periodical work of undecided title to succeed it. There
must previously have been an oral understanding about this novel, for
it had already been referred to in Dickens's dealings with Bentley.
Dickens was to receive £150 for each of its twenty numbers, and the
publishers were to have the copyright for five years, after which it re-
verted to Dickens in its entirety.[59]

Shortly after, the publishers sent Dickens three copies of *Pickwick*,
luxuriously bound by Hayday, which he gave to Kate, Ainsworth, and
Forster.[60] "Accept your copy," he wrote Forster, "with . . . a hearty renewal (if there need be any renewal when there has been no interruption) of all those assurances of affectionate regard which our close
friendship . . . has every day implied. Our boy took the measles last
Saturday to celebrate his birthday, and has been ill ever since. 'He's got
'em very mild' in nursery phrase, so I am not sorry for it will now be
quickly over." [61]

The preceding Saturday, December 9, 1837, had not in fact been the
baby's birthday, but his christening, delayed from June by Kate's illness
and miscarriage after Mary's death, and then postponed until now she
was two-thirds of the way through another pregnancy. "We christen
the living wonder," he wrote Beard, "on Saturday, at 12, at New Pan-
cridge"—an anticipation of the way in which Mrs. Gamp might have
described New St. Pancras Church.[62] The boy was to be named Charles
Culliford, but when the clergyman asked what the child's names were
to be, John Dickens excitedly cried out "Boz!" in consequence of
which the full name that appeared on the register was Charles Culliford Boz Dickens.

Their good friend Miss Burdett Coutts was the godmother. One of
the partners in Coutts and Company, Edward Marjoribanks, had introduced Dickens late in 1835 to Angela Burdett, shortly to dazzle the
imagination of society as Miss Burdett Coutts, heiress to two enormous
fortunes.[63] The fifth daughter of Sir Francis Burdett, himself a radical
reformer, she was resolved to use her wealth to help those less fortunate. Between the twenty-three-year-old author and the earnest twenty-
one-year-old heiress, from their very first meeting, there was a deep
sympathy and understanding that made them lifelong friends. To Kate

Dickens and the Dickens children Angela Burdett Coutts became a kind and generous friend. But more meaningful than these personal ties was the fact that Charles Dickens became the guiding conscience of her philanthropic career, and she the power through which Dickens was to bring about many a practical achievement in which the world did not even suspect his hidden hand.

The new year brought an endless round of demands on Dickens's time. Cruikshank had to be set straight about the illustrations for *Oliver*: "I have described a small kettle," Dickens pointed out, "for one on the fire—a *small* black teapot on the table with a little tray and so forth—and a two ounce tin tea cannister. Also a shawl hanging up —and the cat and kittens before the fire." [64] He paid a melancholy visit to Kensal Green.[65] He succeeded in getting Lord Stanley to appoint his brother Frederick to the Secretary's Office in the Custom House.[66] In the midst of other engagements he had to refuse an invitation from Mme. Sala, the original Julia Dobbs in *The Strange Gentleman*, to meet the Honorable Caroline Norton, whose trial he had reported in his newspaper days.[67]

Dining at Talfourd's, he heard him read his new play, *The Athenian Captive*. Dickens had been much impressed by Talfourd's previous play, *Ion*, which had been a great success under Macready's management, and was astonished to hear that the actor had curtly dismissed the new play with the words "This is not *Ion*." [68] "What has come to Macready?" Dickens asked Forster. "Has management driven him mad?" [69] But ultimately Macready gave way, and Dickens passed on to Ainsworth the inside story: "A word in your ear. Macready *objected* to Talfourd's play—declined it, in fact; whereupon Talfourd grew fierce and Macready more manageable and less manageriable . . ." [70]

Despite all his other commitments, Dickens was at the same time planning to collaborate with Ainsworth on a book to be entitled *The Lions of London*, which Ainsworth had originally contracted to write for Macrone. But the pressure on his energies became crushing; "my month's work," he complained, "has been dreadful,—Grimaldi [an editing job for Bentley], the anonymous book for Chapman and Hall [the *Sketches of Young Gentlemen*], Oliver, and the Miscellany. They are all done, thank God, and I start on my pilgrimage to the cheap schools of Yorkshire (a mighty secret of course) next Monday Morning." [71] In fact, with his next novel, *Nicholas Nickleby*, already bursting its bonds to get started, he was far too busy to take on this enterprise with Ainsworth and it was later abandoned.

The theme of *Nicholas Nickleby* had been vaguely shaping itself in his mind around the abuses in the Yorkshire schools that had made such a deep impression on him in his Chatham days. With his "head full of Partridge, Strap, Tom Pipes, and Sancho Panza," he had heard tales of these schools that even then invested them with such a nebulous horror in his imagination that he had never forgotten them.[72]

Purporting to give an education and board their pupils for the cheapest of fees, the Yorkshire schools were notorious for negligence, cruelty, and pedagogical incompetence. William Shaw, who kept an academy at Bowes, near Greta Bridge, was sued by the parents of two children who became totally blind there through infection and gross neglect. During the trial it was testified that the boys were given maggoty food, that as many as five usually slept in a single flea-infested bed, that they were often beaten, that ten boys had lost their sight there and been given no medical treatment. Shaw was convicted and paid damages of £500 but continued to conduct his school.[73] The small churchyard at Bowes has the graves of twenty-five boys from seven to eighteen who died there between 1810 and 1834.[74]

There were similar schools in other parts of Yorkshire, largely used, of course, as a means of getting rid of illegitimate and other unwanted children. They advertised "no extra charges" and "no vacations," and took their pupils entirely off the hands of those responsible for them for as little as twenty guineas a year. But they also victimized a considerable number of impecunious but well-intentioned parents. Dickens aimed to inform the ignorant and expose the vicious.

With his strong journalist's feeling for documentation, he decided on a trip to Yorkshire for direct observation of his material. Not that he intended to make a photographic copy of any one school or pillory any one offender. He was well aware of the endless arguments that could be generated about whether an individual was representative of a system. "Fictitious narratives," he said, "place the enormities of the system in a much stronger point of view"; [75] they had the force of powerful generalization. But the propaganda novel, as he might have further explained, gained tremendously in vividness through being embodied in concrete details. The eye of the reporter could sharply note the facts, the novelist's imagination transform them from statistics into a symbol dyed in emotion.

On January 30th, then, a blustery cold morning, he set off in the Mail from the Saracen's Head. "Phiz" went along to note the pictorial background. After traveling through howling snowstorms they reached, about midnight of the second day, "a bare place with a house standing alone in the midst of a dreary moor." This was the George and New Inn, at Greta Bridge. They warmed themselves before a "rousing fire halfway up the chimney," and in the morning, after a breakfast of "toast, cakes, a Yorkshire pie, a piece of beef about the size and much the shape of my portmanteau, tea, coffee, ham and eggs," they went for a look at Bowes Academy.[76]

To avoid suspicion, Dickens traveled under an assumed name, pretending to be in search of a school for the son of a widowed friend. But William Shaw, the one-eyed master of the Academy, was mistrustful and let them see very little. From Greta Bridge the investigators took a post chaise for Barnard Castle, a town about four miles away. Charles Smithson, Mitton's friend and partner and a native of Yorkshire, had given Dickens a letter in support of his assumed character to Richard Barnes, an attorney there. [77] Barnes was most cordial and Dickens and Browne had dinner with the "jovial, ruddy, broad-faced" old fellow.[78] He gave them two introductions to local schoolmasters, but himself avoided all talk on the subject of schools. That night, however, he turned up at their inn, and after some embarrassed hesitation explained that their errand had been weighing on his mind all day.[79] Then, with a sudden rush, his feelings burst through his legal caution: "Ar wouldn't mak' ill words amang ma neeburs, and ar speak tiv 'ee quiet loike. But I'm dom'd if ar can gang to bed and not tell 'ee, for weedur's sak', to keep the lattle boy from a' sike scoondrels while there's a harse to hoold in a' Lunnon, or a goother to lie asleep in!" [80]

Dickens made a survey of the schools at Barnard Castle, and also looked at those in near-by Startforth. On the return trip, he and Browne stopped off and attended services in York Minster, where they saw the gorgeously hued window called the "Five Sisters" and heard from Dr. John Camidge, the organist, the fifteenth-century legend of its origin that Dickens soon inserted in the second number of *Nicholas Nickleby*.[81]

He was back in Doughty Street after a week's absence, and attacked the new book at once. "I *have* begun!" he announced to Forster on February 7th—his twenty-sixth birthday. "I wrote four slips last night, so you see the beginning is made. And what is more I can go on: so I hope the book is in training at last." And with his ebullient spirits, he looked forward, although it was still winter, to another out-of-doors jaunt: "The snow will take away the cold weather, and then for Twickenham." [82] Two days later he told Forster triumphantly, "The first chapter of Nicholas is done." [83]

* * * * *

When Mary, their second child, was born early on March 6, 1838, Dickens asked Forster to help him ride off his excitement, declaring, "I can do nothing this morning." [84] On the way home they dined at the Red Lion in Barnet, after going fifteen miles out on the Great North Road, and brought in their horses dead lame.[85] Three days later he wrote Forster, "I was thinking about Oliver till dinner-time yesterday, and just as I had fallen upon him tooth and nail, was called away to sit with Kate. I did eight slips however, and hope to make them fifteen this morning." [86]

By the end of the month Kate was well enough to go with Dickens to Richmond. Having been out of London when *Pickwick* first appeared, he was mildly superstitious about being away when *Nickleby*'s first number came out on April 1st. But he couldn't resist riding into town to learn how it had gone. He sent Forster an imperious summons: "Meet me at the Shakespeare on Saturday night at eight; order your horse at midnight, and ride back with me." One o'clock was sounding from St. Paul's before they were on the road, after startling news had prolonged their dinner into an exultant festivity. The next evening, at the Star and Garter, Dickens, Kate, and Forster marked a triple celebration. It was their second wedding anniversary, and Forster's twenty-sixth birthday, and *Nickleby* on its first day had sold almost fifty thousand copies! [87]

During June and July Dickens rented a cottage at Twickenham [88] and had a stream of summer visitors and week-end guests—his mother and father, his younger brothers, Henry Burnett and Fanny, Henry Austin and Letitia, Talfourd, Ainsworth, and Mitton, who was drafting Dickens's will.[89] Beard, who had been ill and was on leave from his newspaper work, was invited for an extended visit.[90] Bentley and Hul-

lah came to stay overnight.[91] Forster, of course, was always on the
scene, and had been "elected president of a balloon club . . . on condition of supplying all the balloons," for the children, whom Dickens
had nicknamed "the Snodgering Blee" and "Popem Jee." [92]

New faces, too, turned up in this Twickenham summer, and later
at Broadstairs, where they spent August and September. Among these
was the playwright Douglas Jerrold, soon to be editor of *Punch*—a
little man, almost deformed, but "bright-eyed, quick, and eager in
spirit." [93] And since Thackeray had applied to do the *Pickwick* illustrations, Dickens had grown better acquainted with him at the Garrick Club and published a story of his, "The Professor," in the September, 1837, *Miscellany*.[94] The towering, squash-nosed young man
was now a frequent dinner guest, as was also the Scotch-Irish painter
Daniel Maclise, whom Dickens had met through Ainsworth.[95] A way-
ward, delightful fellow, as Dickens described him, Maclise's glorious
enjoyment of idleness, the amusing serenity with which he faced the
most provoking mishaps, and his quaint mingling of sharpness and
simplicity made him a sparkling holiday companion.

Another new friend in the living flesh, though an old one on the
printed page, was Leigh Hunt. A youthful friend of Shelley and Keats,
he had written a brave editorial attacking the Prince Regent as "a fat
Adonis of fifty," a companion of gamblers and demireps, deep in debt
and disgrace. The attack sent Hunt to jail, where he papered his cell
with rose-patterned wallpaper, was visited by Byron, Moore, Lamb,
and Bentham, and admired by every liberal in England. He was a poet
of considerable grace and charm, and, as a critic and essayist who interpolated descriptions of familiar scenes and people, was one of the formative influences of Dickens's own youth; indeed, there had been reviewers who imagined Hunt the author of *Sketches by Boz*. After a
life of trials he was now, at fifty-four, still as slim and brisk as a boy,
animated, sweet-tempered, full of whimsical and gay-hearted fancy.
He had touched Dickens by a delicately worded tribute to the epitaph
on Mary Hogarth's grave, and in July Dickens sent him an American
edition of *Pickwick* and the numbers of *Oliver* and *Nickleby* so far
published, hoping that Hunt would find some "vibration of the old
chord you have touched so often and sounded so well . . ." [96]

Another old friend who turned up in correspondence was Dickens's
kind Chatham schoolmaster, William Giles, who sent him a silver

snuffbox inscribed to "the Inimitable Boz," a signature Dickens had been using with gay exuberance in the *Miscellany*'s "Answers to Correspondents." [97] Warmly acknowledging the gift, Dickens sent Giles copies of his published books, and promised to send a set of *Oliver Twist* when it appeared in book form.[98]

Around this time, also, Dickens met Dr. John Elliotson and first became interested in mesmerism. Professor of the Practice of Medicine at London University, Elliotson was the first physician to use the stethoscope and was one of the founders of University College Hospital. He was also a daring innovator in unorthodox realms of knowledge and, as the first president of the Phrenological Society, one of the pioneers in experimenting with the use of mesmerism to relieve pain. Conservative opposition to these activities forced him to resign his chair. Dickens saw Elliotson magnetize sufferers totally unable to sleep into mesmeric slumber and witnessed some remarkable feats performed by a Belgian boy. Under mesmerism and blindfolded, the boy read the name of the maker of Kate's Geneva watch when it was held behind his head and also gave correctly the number inside its case.[99]

Throughout the summer and fall Dickens's popularity continued mounting to ever greater heights. A letter of these months bears witness to his prestige even in America and strikes a prophetic note of a journey already in his mind. Lewis Gaylord Clark, a New York magazine editor, asked him for a contribution. "I should be very happy to write for the *Knickerbocker*," Dickens replied, "but I do assure you, that I have scarcely time to complete my existing engagements. So I think I must defer this pleasure, until I visit America, which I hope to do before very long . . ." [100]

Oliver Twist was now almost finished and poured itself out of Dickens in a fever of creation. He often wrote till late at night, something he never did in later years. "Hard at work still. Nancy is no more," Forster learned one October night. Dickens had shown the pages describing Nancy's death to Kate, "who was in an unspeakable '*state*'" at those sickening thuds that beat out the girl's life, "from which and my own impression, I augur well. When I have sent Sikes to the devil, I must have yours." [101] Soon he had done that too, painting with hideous power, as Chesterton says, "the besieged house, the boy screaming within, the crowd screaming without, the murderer turned almost maniac . . . the escape over the roof, the rope swiftly running taut, and death, sudden, startling, and symbolic." [102]

There remained only to sum up the rest and put an end to the merry and black-hearted old Fagin, "who is such an out and outer that I don't know what to make of him." "No, no, don't, don't let us ride till to-morrow," he appealed to Forster; he could do nothing else till the last word was written. [103] "My missis is going out to dinner, and I ought to go, but I have a bad cold. So do you come, and sit here, and read, or work, or do something, while I write the LAST chapter of Oliver, which will be arter a lamb chop" and "a bit o' som'at else." [104] Talfourd had been pleading in behalf of Charley Bates, and even of the Artful Dodger, as earnestly "as ever at the bar for any client." Dickens discussed with Forster what should be their fate. "How well I remember that evening!" exclaimed Forster, who was present when Dickens at last threw down his pen. [105]

During the intervening weeks Dickens had been in frequent communication with Cruikshank about the illustrations. "I have written a long chapter since I saw you, but it has no subject. . . . In the meantime may I venture to call your attention to the last published No. (which I enclose) and to suggest that possibly there may be one more subject there?" [106] In August, "I find on writing it," he told Cruikshank, "that the scene of Sikes's escape will not do for illustration. It is so very complicated, with such a multitude of figures, such violent action, and torch-light to boot, that a small plate could not take in the slightest idea of it." [107]

Nevertheless Cruikshank achieved a striking plate of Sikes poised beside the chimney on the steep roof of the besieged house. Dickens, to be sure, returning with Forster from a visit to Liverpool and Manchester on November 18th, when the books were already on the stalls, regarded all the illustrations for the third volume as very bad. [108] Two of them, above all, he considered "a vile and disgusting interpolation" on the true feeling of the tale and, through Forster, asked Bentley to delete them from the next printing. In "Sikes attempting to destroy his dog," Forster said, the animal looked like a tailless baboon, and "Rose Maylie and Oliver" resembled a Rowland Macassar frontispiece to a sixpenny book of forfeits. No time should be lost in getting rid of both. [109]

Dickens was somewhat more tactful. About "Rose Maylie and

Oliver," he wrote Cruikshank, "I am quite sure there can be little difference of opinion between us . . . May I ask you whether you will object to designing this plate afresh, and doing so *at once*, in order that as few impressions as possible of the present one may go forth? I feel confident you know me too well to feel hurt by this enquiry. . . ." [110] Cruikshank did design a substitute for this plate, but nothing seems to have been done about the "tailless baboon."

Oliver Twist was the first of Dickens's books to be published under his own name. Forster gave Bentley directions that the title-page should read:

> Oliver Twist
> in 3 Vols.
> By Charles Dickens author
> Of the 'Pickwick Papers.' [111]

From then on, in public comment, his name and Boz were used interchangeably.

* * * * *

No sooner was *Oliver Twist* out of the way than Dickens, in spite of the fact that he was finding *Nicholas* hard going, promised Macready a new farce for Covent Garden. He wrote a feeble and laborious concoction entitled *The Lamplighter*, of which Macready, after giving it a second reading, wrote in his diary, "Manifest disappointment. It went flatly, a few ready laughs . . . broken in upon by the horse-laugh of Forster, the most indiscreet friend that ever allied himself to any person." Macready believed that Forster had "goaded Dickens to write this farce, and now . . . would *drive* it upon the stage. God defend me from my friends! . . . I cannot sufficiently condemn the officious folly of this marplot, Forster, who embroils his friends in difficulties and distress in this most determined manner." [112]

But Macready's growls often had other causes than their seeming provocations, and an incident of the previous year was perhaps still rankling within him. Incensed at some offense, he had "retired in high dudgeon from the Garrick Club," and Dickens had loyally resigned with him. Forster agreed that Macready was right, but then infuriated him by announcing that he thought he would stay in the club after all. The actor's testy imagination saw Forster's tactful sympathy as a dark plot to make him resign. He had no doubt, Macready added bleakly, that Forster had "instigated" Dickens to leave the Garrick too! [113]

Forster, however, changed his mind about *The Lamplighter*, and agreed that it should be vetoed. Macready, somewhat nervous about Dickens's reaction, tried to soften its rejection and warmly thanked him for his effort. Dickens replied that his only disappointment was in not having been able to be of some use to Macready. "An answer which is an honour to him," Macready commented. "Dickens and Bulwer have been certainly to me noble specimens of human nature . . ." [114]

Although Macready told Dickens that *Oliver Twist* was utterly impractical for the stage,[115] the usual crew of piratical adapters had seized upon it long before it had run its course in the *Miscellany*. One version at the Surrey Theatre was so excruciatingly bad that in the middle of the first scene the agonized novelist lay down on the floor of his box and never rose until the curtain fell.[116] Nevertheless, Dickens hankered to make a dramatic version himself, and suggested it to Frederick Yates, who was currently scoring an enormous success at the Adelphi with *Nicholas Nickleby*.[117] Despite his general resentment of the liberties taken with his work, Dickens was delighted with Yates's performance: "*that glorious Mantalini*," he wrote, "*is beyond all praise.*" [118] Nothing came of Dickens's plan to dramatize *Oliver Twist* himself, but he saw and applauded later productions at the Adelphi, both of that book and of *The Old Curiosity Shop*, in which Yates played Fagin and Quilp.[119]

Meanwhile, Dickens had gone up at the end of October, again accompanied by Browne, to the Midlands and North Wales to see the cotton mills. On the way Dickens was enraptured by the ruins of Kenilworth but cold to Warwick Castle and had little to say about Stratford.[120] The following day they proceeded by way of Birmingham and Wolverhampton to Shrewsbury. On Dickens's imagination the industrial north made an impression of lurid and melodramatic horror, "miles of cinder-paths and blazing furnaces and roaring steam-engines" looming through fog and smoke like some enormous Alberich's cave of clamorous glares, "such a mass of dirt gloom and misery," he wrote Kate, "as I never before witnessed." [121]

From Shrewsbury they made a rapid tour of North Wales—Llangolen, Bangor, Capel Currig, and Conway—and thence to Liverpool.[122]

Here Forster joined them and the three went on to Manchester. Ainsworth had given Dickens letters of introduction to some friends in his native city, the bulky James Crossley and Gilbert Winter and Hugh Beaver.[123] Over the dinner table at Stocks, Winter's home on Cheetham Hill, Forster provoked a verbal duel with a local canon, but was judged by native opinion "completely extinguished" by the sharper wit of his northern antagonist. At this same table Dickens dined with the brothers William and Daniel Grant, merchants and manufacturers, of Cheeryble House, upon whom he was shortly to model the Cheeryble brothers in *Nicholas Nickleby*. And at a breakfast party at Stocks a cousin of Ainsworth's, James Bower Harrison, saw Dickens smiling over some proof sheets of that story, and noted his polished boots, drawing-room-like attire, and almost effeminate good looks.[124]

On his return to London, Dickens wrote Edward Fitzgerald, the poet and translator of *Omar Khayyam*, "I went, some weeks ago, to Manchester, and saw the *worst* cotton mill. And then I saw the *best*. *Ex uno disce omnes*. There was no great difference between them. . . . But on the 11th of next month I am going down again, only for three days, and then into the enemy's camp and the very headquarters of the factory system advocates." Lord Ashley—later the seventh Earl of Shaftesbury—who had been fighting the horrors of factory conditions since 1833, had offered, through Fitzgerald, to have Dickens shown what the mills were like, and in asking Fitzgerald to convey his gratitude Dickens wrote feelingly, "With that nobleman's most benevolent and excellent exertions, and with the evidence which he was the means of bringing forward, I am well acquainted. So far as seeing goes, I have seen enough for my purpose, and what I have seen has disgusted me and astonished me beyond all measure. I mean to strike the heaviest blow in my power for these unfortunate creatures, but whether I shall do so in the 'Nickleby,' or wait some other opportunity, I have not yet determined." [125]

But although horror and indignation sank deep in his heart, Dickens could not deal with things still so strange to his imagination as those dust-laden mills and their thunderous machines. He could take lethal notes on a brutal police-court magistrate or a tyrannical schoolmaster and work them into the background of what he already knew of criminal slums and childhood suffering; the sodden misery of nineteenth-century industrialism spreading like a slow sore through the factory towns and the potteries and the iron foundries was to elude his pen for years to come. Not until a decade and a half later, in *Hard Times*, the fiercest and bitterest of his books, would he strike that "heaviest blow" against those dark satanic mills and the greed that imprisoned helpless human beings in their dismal shades.

Dickens made the second trip to Manchester in the middle of January, combining further investigation with a public dinner for Ainsworth and himself. Originally planned for Ainsworth, the dinner turned out ambiguously to include Dickens also as guest of honor, after Ainsworth had generously lauded him to his Manchester friends as now "installed in the throne of letters vacated by Scott." [126] But Ainsworth was magnanimously free from jealousy. He and Forster and Dickens were now on terms of such warm fellowship that they had formed a club consisting only of themselves, called the Cerberus Club. They rode and dined with each other constantly, and drank toasts to each other out of special glasses appropriately etched with a three-headed emblem.[127] Although Ainsworth had been "devilish nervous about the speechifying," the dinner went off brilliantly.[128] It was a high point, as well as one of the happiest incidents, of Ainsworth's career. For, despite the huge success of *Jack Sheppard*, he was now being steadily eclipsed by the young man whose first book he had recommended to its publisher.

The day after the banquet James Crossley had them to dinner at his house, and astonished them mightily by the sight of his triangular table with his portly form wedged between its apex and the wall. Dickens, proposing his health, said, "During the whole evening, seeing the peculiar position our host occupied, I could not help being reminded of Dr. Primrose's famous family picture in *The Vicar of Wakefield*, and I have been wondering all night how ever he should be got out, but still more amazed how he ever got in." [128a] It was probably on this visit also that Beaver found Dickens reading an adverse review of his work that said, "What is good is not original, and what is original is not good," and in later years remembered Dickens stamping up and down the room, greatly upset, and swearing, "They shall eat their words!" [129]

*   *   *   *   *

But he need hardly have exercised himself. Only a few weeks earlier, he had heard the pleasant news from Edinburgh that the powerful critic Lord Jeffrey was giving *Oliver Twist* the highest praise. "It has done wonders here in the way of sale," Dickens wrote, "and as to Nickleby, I don't know when he is going to stop." [130] With these triumphs, not only the doors of London's literary and artistic circles but those of the great world were opening ever wider before him.

The young man who had put on a shabby coat to receive Nat Willis in a three-pair rear in Holborn now issued brilliantly waistcoated and magnificent of neckcloth from his own doorway to visit mansions in Curzon Street and St. James's Place. The patchily educated shorthand writer, who had doggedly bent over books at the long tables in the British Museum to repair the gaps in his reading, now met men who came from public schools and universities and country houses with libraries and galleries, who had traveled in France and Italy and spoke the languages of those countries. How would Dickens adapt himself to the leonine Walter Savage Landor, with his classical learning and alarming temper, the glittering cosmopolitan dandy Count D'Orsay, the icily sardonic Samuel Rogers, the steep-nosed social gorgon Lady Holland, the witty Lady Blessington?

Anyone less superbly self-assured than Dickens might have been intimidated, and perhaps beneath his alert poise even he knew some tremors. But mingled with a resolution to make his way everywhere, there was a proud though veiled resentment at the insolence of privilege, and a consciousness of his own gifts, which made him determined to hold his own and not allow himself to be patronized. Against the mere arrogance of caste, indeed, he came to maintain a prickly truculence. He had quickly experienced, of course, some of that odd upperclass snobbery that regarded a writer as a strange animal to be exhibited, made to go through its tricks, and patted on the head if it were docile. His feelings may be divined from a sentence in *Nicholas Nickleby* that peeps out incongruously from a description of the modest demeanor of Mr. Lillyvick at the Kenwigses' party: "If he had been an author, who knew his place, he couldn't have been more humble." [131] But Dickens felt the glamour of power and prestige, too, and though no one could more sharply repel any attempted condescension, he was pleased by his new importance. With his vivid perception of the color of any group, and the mimetic talent that had made him at one time think of becoming an actor, he rapidly acquired the tone and manner of his surroundings.

In 1836 Talfourd had introduced Dickens to Count D'Orsay, a dilettante man-about-town whose ornate and startling dress inspired some of Dickens's later extravagances. In his white greatcoat, blue-satin cravat, skin-tight primrose-colored gloves scented with jasmine, and hair precisely curled, D'Orsay might have seemed effeminate were it not for his polished ease and six-feet-four of height.[132] He lived at Gore House with his wife's stepmother, the widowed Countess of Blessington, in relations of which the world felt deeply suspicious.

In consequence, although Lady Blessington was beautiful, witty, and charming, few women frequented her famous literary salon. But hardly a well-known man in London failed to appear in her mirrored drawing room and long, magnificently arched and columned library with its white-and-gold furniture.[133] Everyone talked freely on these celebrated evenings, without stiffness or formality. Wellington would be grimly amused by the talking crow she had saucily taught to repeat his own "Up, Guards, and at 'em!" That brilliant clergyman, Sydney Smith, scattered sparkling showers of harmless wit. Disraeli might tell of Beckford's fantastic spire at Fonthill Abbey and the subterranean vault in which he proposed to be entombed with a Spanish dwarf. Landor could be heard talking in his vehement and impassioned manner or giving a roar of laughter, throwing back his magnificent head with its mane of hair. Other guests often there were Captain Marryat, author of the well-known sea stories; Sir Martin Shee, the painter; Albany Fonblanque, the editor of the *Examiner*; Bryan Waller Proctor, better known as "Barry Cornwall"; Lord Lyndhurst, the Lord Chancellor; and Lord Durham, famous for the remark "A man could jog along on forty thousand pounds a year." And sometimes, leaden-eyed and silent in a corner, sat Prince Louis Napoleon, while in the shining center of the room D'Orsay and the others whipped up a lively froth of humor in key with the flowing of the champagne.

Dickens first went to Gore House with Talfourd.[134] Lady Blessington had asked the dramatist to bring a young writer to help entertain the aging Landor, whom Dickens later described as "like forty lions concentrated into one Poet." And Gore House remained one of the places he thoroughly enjoyed. "Lady Blessington," he wrote, "wears brilliantly, and has the gloss upon her, yet."[135] Before his return from Genoa in 1845, he assured her, ". . . I mean to come to Gore House with such a swoop as shall astonish the poodle . . ."[136]

If Gore House was luxuriously Bohemian and cosmopolitan, Samuel Rogers's classic little mansion at 22 St. James's Place represented the severely literary. A banker and poet whose *Italy* and *Pleasures of Memory* had a bloodless elegance, Rogers made a triumphant career of the cautious but smoothly firm determination to enjoy a place in the sun. Born in 1763, he could remember the heads of rebels on Temple Bar, had seen Garrick act, knocked on Samuel Johnson's door in Bolt Court, and talked there with Boswell. He had known Fox, Burke, Sheridan, Mme. de Staël. For all his wealth, he spent only £2,000 a year. Stumping out on foot to parties in stately salons, he walked home even on the rainiest nights, and entertained everyone of note at small economical breakfasts where the guests were expected to be brilliantly entertaining on topics chosen by their host.[137] Now in his seventies, he looked on the world with a pale head, white, bare, and cold as snow, through large blue eyes, cruel and disillusioned as the frigid epigrams that fell from lips tight above a sardonic shelf of chin. With him, said Thomas Moore, one walked on roses, but with a constant apprehension of the thorns among them.

But he could be gracious too. Whereas most of the great world hardly troubled to conceal its feeling that Dickens's wife was rather negligible, Samuel Rogers was always gentle to her and affable when he visited at the Dickens home. Kate developed a trustful affection for the grizzled old man [138] that she did not extend to many of her husband's other friends. Although ladies were not excluded from the famous literary breakfasts, Kate, however, was never one of those present. She had no conversation, and Rogers, for all his kindness, would not endanger the sparkle of his table by a dead weight.

Though the setting of these morning feasts was small, it dripped opulence. For a young man so recently timorous about asking the price of a table in Tottenham Court Road, its richness of *décor* was as impressive as the tone of its talk. The Titians, the Raphael Madonna, the little St. George that Rogers believed to be a Giorgione, hung gold-framed against walls of crimson damask. Among other treasures were Milton's receipt for *Paradise Lost*, framed upon a door, and Roubillac's death mask of Pope. The mantelpieces were by Flaxman; luxuriously bound volumes and rare editions were shelved in bookcases painted by Stothard with scenes from Boccaccio, Chaucer, and

Shakespeare. "Sam hives very comfortably," Sydney Smith liked to say.[139]

Holland House, one of the great Whig strongholds, gave huge crushes that Rogers's miniature drawing rooms could never have accommodated. The old Elizabethan mansion had a noble entrance hall, liveried footmen who led one up the grand staircase to a lofty dining room with gilded wainscoting and a long library containing, Macaulay said, all the books in the world that one ever wished to read.[139a] The guests were less literary, more political and diplomatic than those at Gore House, and their arrogant hostess disciplined them like a drill sergeant. Those who could provide her table with game, venison, cheeses, or foreign delicacies were ruthlessly forced to pay up for the privilege of being bullied, interrupted, or silenced at the will of their hostess.

"Lay down that screen, Lord Russell," Lady Holland would say brusquely. "You will spoil it." Or to Rogers, whom she liked, "Your poetry is bad enough, so pray be sparing of your prose." She once interrupted Macaulay, who was being long-winded about the Christian Fathers, by bursting in with "Pray, Macaulay, what was the origin of the doll?" Whereupon he cheerfully turned to a dissertation upon Roman dolls. She ordered her guests to draw the curtains, close the window, ring the bell; only Sydney Smith ventured impertinently to ask if he should also dust the room. A fierce old autocrat in the habit of being obeyed and entertained, she was described by Carlyle as looking in profile as a falcon might if its bill were straight.

Not until 1838 did Dickens meet this fearsome apparition. Lady Holland rather grandiosely asked Bulwer "if Boz were presentable, and became the condescending with a man of genius, a thing not to be forgiven," wrote Bulwer in his journal; "so I growled and snapped." [140] Taking these noises as sufficient testimonial, Lady Holland commanded Talfourd early in July to present his little friend. Unfortunately, the wedding anniversary of Letitia and Henry Austin prevented Dickens's acceptance. Talfourd then had to be out of London for a while, and Dickens privately hoped that "another opportunity" would not materialize until his return, clearly feeling the need of some friendly support on the first visit.[141]

Sometime later in the summer he successfully passed through the ordeal of presentation. When he dined at Holland House, Lady Holland's sister found him intolerably dandified, but thought his face "beautiful, because blended with his intelligence there is such an expression of goodness." [142] Lady Holland was also impressed by him, and Dickens, with the instinct he often had about people, felt the kindness that she concealed behind that harsh façade. When some witticism of Sydney Smith's supposed to have been made at her table appeared in the *Miscellany* without his knowledge, he hastened to assure her that he had had nothing to do with the babbler from whom it was obtained, and that he detested the impertinence and vulgarity of printing private conversations.[143]

Another event of the year 1838 indicates how absolute now was Dickens's conquest of the cultivated world: his introduction to a pair of little old ladies, the Misses Mary and Agnes Berry. Both now around seventy-five, for several decades they had made their town house at Curzon Street a center of the most exclusive circles of the literary and fashionable world. Their associations went back not merely to the days of Chesterfield and Garrick, but to those of Swift and Pope, and well-nigh to those of Addison and Congreve. They had been young girls when Horace Walpole was in his seventies, and the witty old worldling had fallen in love with Mary. They had been intimate with Georgiana, the renowned Duchess of Devonshire, and known the Duchess of Queensbury, who had been a youthful beauty at the Court of Queen Anne. For Thackeray they symbolized all the glamour of the English past.

But Dickens had no such reverence for tradition. Perhaps, too, he failed to recognize the patent of distinction thus conferred on him. For when the two mittened and gentle old creatures called on the Dickenses during the summer at Twickenham to ask them to dinner, Dickens excused himself on the ground that he was working frantically on the next installment of his new book. But the world had decided that this remarkable young man had really arrived; eager and desperate, they invoked the aid of Sydney Smith.

"The Miss Berrys," he wrote Dickens, "live only to become acquainted with you," and he conveyed a second invitation, for "Friday 29th or Monday July 1st." "The Miss Berrys and Lady Charlotte Lindsay," he wheedled enticingly, "have not the smallest objection to be put into a Number, but on the contrary would be proud of the distinction: and Lady Charlotte, in particular, you may marry to

Newman Noggs. Pray come, it is as much as my place is worth to send them a refusal." [144] Dinner with the Misses Berry Dickens consequently had, and evidently found the experience agreeable, for he dined with them again on a number of later occasions.[145]

But the high point of the year, the seal of an almost official sanction, was Dickens's election to the Athenaeum Club. Founded in 1824, it was primarily a cultural rather than a political or social institution, designed as a gathering place for England's men of achievement. Its original committee, which included Sir Walter Scott, Samuel Rogers, Sir Thomas Lawrence, Sir Francis Chantrey, and Lord Spencer, had chosen its first members from the benches of bishops and judges, the Royal College of Surgeons, and the Society of Antiquaries, and its membership now included the leading scholars, men of letters, artists, scientists, and statesmen.

The Athenaeum is still housed in the nobly proportioned building on Waterloo Place that was designed for it by Decimus Burton. Its Roman-Doric portico of six columns has a frieze with triglyphs carved in Bath stone by John Henning. The lofty hall is modeled on the Temple of the Winds at Athens. Pillars of primrose marble with gilded capitals support a wagon-vaulted ceiling, and the great staircase rises, under a central lantern fifty-four feet above the floor, to the statue of Pallas presiding over the landing. On the left of the entrance a Pompeian dining room with five great windows overlooks the garden; on the right, behind a morning room with a blue-and-gold Venetian ceiling, there is a more intimate writing room only twenty-three feet by twenty, with Opie's portrait of Dr. Johnson on the wall. Running the entire width of the building on the floor above, the great drawing room rears its twelve columns and sixteen pilasters between red-damask walls with three carved marble fireplaces.[146]

Such was the grandiose institution of which Dickens became a member in June of 1838. He had been proposed by Talfourd and seconded by Serjeant Storks. Among the forty persons eminent in art, literature, and science who were brought in at the same time were Macready, who had failed of election three years before, Grote, the classical scholar and historian, and Charles Darwin. Thackeray had to wait until he was forty before he was granted the freedom of those august portals, and Browning until he was fifty-six. Both had then been known to the world for years and could point to a long series of literary productions. Dickens, at the time he achieved the same honor, had written only two published books, and had two others appearing in serial form. Within a brief career of two years and by the age of twenty-six, he had attained not merely the widest popular success and admission to the most famous salons, but one of England's most coveted distinctions.

CHAPTER FOUR

The Break with Bentley

DURING the two years of Dickens's rocketing fame, his relations with the pleasant, pink-faced owner of the *Miscellany* had ceased to be as amicable as they had been at first. When Dickens had been obliged to buy off Macrone from bringing out *Sketches by Boz* in green-covered installments imitative of *Pickwick*, Bentley had made negotiations more involved by suggesting to Macrone that he might purchase them himself. Dickens granted to Bentley that he "had a a perfect right to step in and bid for these apples of discord . . . but the interference was not the less injurious to my interest": it had stiffened Macrone's demands by giving him magnificent notions of the price he might get.[1]

In addition, editor and publisher disagreed about the conduct of the *Miscellany*. Bentley had the right to veto any article, but aside from this Dickens was supposed to be in complete charge. His inexperience and his limited literary acquaintance at that time, however, had led Bentley to solicit contributions from his own friends, and the two men had developed the practice of settling the contents of the magazine in an informal editorial discussion.[2] Nevertheless, Dickens did not regard this procedure as in any way surrendering his own editorial powers.

Differences first arose over their financial arrangements. The *Miscellany's* popularity had led to a revision of the original agreement as early as March, 1837. Bentley desired the right to retain Dickens as editor for another five years instead of three, and, if he so nominated, for five beyond that. He also wanted the exclusive use of Dickens's periodical writings, aside from the successor to *Pickwick* (which he had already agreed might be written for Chapman and

Hall), and he offered Dickens an additional £10 monthly for every thousand by which the magazine's circulation exceeded six thousand.

To Dickens these terms did not compensate for his abstention for so long a period from any other periodical writing. He proposed that the renewal clause for a second five years be omitted, that he be given £250 or twelve months' notice if Bentley decided to discontinue the magazine, and that his salary be regularly increased on the publication of the sixth, twelfth, twenty-fourth, and thirty-sixth numbers.[3] After consultations with Forster, he accepted a compromise. Bentley was to have the options on his services. Dickens was to have the notice or £250, but half of this was to be a set-off against the novels. And his increases would be £10 for the first additional thousand of monthly circulation and £5 for each further five hundred.[4] "I have the most unfeigned pleasure in saying that the arrangement . . . is alike highly satisfactory to me and highly creditable to yourself," Dickens wrote Bentley, adding his regret that in his irritation he might have used "expressions of feeling" that gave Bentley pain.[5]

However, the terms on which Bentley was to have the two novels were not affected. And soon Forster came to suspect that they had been disposed of too hastily. Dickens reluctantly confirmed him. "It is a very extraordinary fact (I forgot it on Sunday) that I have NEVER HAD from him a copy of the agreement . . . I fear he has my second novel on the same terms as the first. This is a bad look-out but n'importe we will try and mend it. You will tell me you are very much surprised at my doing business in this way. So am I, for in most matters of labour and application I am punctuality itself." [6]

There was, however, a bright side to the situation. Bentley had often expressed his earnest desire to be liberal. Surely when Dickens's growing popularity was taken into account, Bentley would concede the justice of changes. "Will you have the goodness," Dickens wrote him, "to turn the matter over in your mind, and let me know . . . what the footing is, on which you propose to place me, and what the terms you intend to offer?" [7]

They met with complete friendliness in New Burlington Street, and Bentley urged Dickens to state his own views. Dickens had no definite proposition to offer. Bentley suggested that Dickens visit him at Brighton when he had further considered the matter.[8] But Dickens was so behind in his work that he could not leave London for a day.

Therefore he wrote to Bentley proposing that he increase to £600 the sum to be paid for permission to publish three thousand copies (instead of the entire copyright) of *Barnaby Rudge*, the first of the novels. He further proposed that Bentley pay £700 for permission to publish the same number of *Oliver Twist*, which he now referred to as the second novel, deducting from that sum whatever had been paid for its appearance in the *Miscellany*. He declared that this was his "fixed conclusion," and that if Bentley invoked his "power to hold me to the old agreement," "I shall abide by the strict letter of my agreement respecting the Miscellany, and arrange my future plans with reference to it, accordingly." [9]

Behind this implied threat may have lurked a realization that Bentley would hardly consider his proposal "a fair and very reasonable one." For *Oliver Twist* was not the second novel he had agreed to write; it was part of the monthly sixteen pages he was to contribute to the *Miscellany*. In essence, Dickens was trying to make one literary work fulfill two separate agreements, and only conceding the deduction of the remuneration for its magazine publication.

Feeling swamped by his threefold labors of editing, finishing *Pickwick*, and writing *Oliver Twist*, he also pleaded for a respite, asking if it "would hurt the Miscellany if (the announcement that I was about to begin a new tale therein, being meanwhile very conspicuously displayed) I wrote nothing in it for a number. I really see no other way of making a start with Oliver, for I no sooner get myself up, high and dry, to attack him manfully then up come the waves of each month's work, and drive me back again into a sea of manuscript." [10]

Whether or not Bentley replied to this, he evidently said nothing about the modification of the novel agreements, for Dickens pressed for an answer. Bentley suggested that they meet again at New Burlington Street. At this meeting, he said, his own behavior was friendly but Dickens was cold and restrained. Bentley pointed out that their agreement was mutually binding and that *he* could have obtained no reduction had Dickens's popularity declined, but expressed his willingness to *present* Dickens with the additional sums. For this, however, he insisted on the entire copyrights, as already agreed. Moreover, he refused to consider *Oliver Twist* as the second novel; it had now been running through five numbers of the *Miscellany* and the copyright of those published parts already belonged to him.[11]

Dickens was much irritated. With *Oliver* only half done, he threatened to stop writing it altogether. His object, Bentley thought, was to provoke an angry retort, but Bentley controlled himself, although holding firmly to his position. Dickens then suggested that Serjeant Talfourd arbitrate the dispute. Bentley objected that Talfourd was a friend of Dickens, and proposed that he should nominate a co-referee, to which Dickens agreed.[12]

Instead of approaching Talfourd, Dickens appealed to his old friend Thomas Beard. Only to gain time, he said, Bentley wished "a friend of mine to meet a friend of his" for discussion. "I merely want to concede this to him for the sake of appearances without in the slightest degree departing from my point." [13] But the "friend" Beard met in New Burlington Street was Bentley's solicitor, John Gregory. Beard feared he might injure Dickens without knowing it if he tried to deal with a man trained in legal minutiae. He therefore indicated that he had power only to discuss, not to settle.

At his report Dickens blew up. As "the disinterested, unprejudiced, private friend whom you were to select with so much care—was no other than your own Solicitor," he wrote Bentley, any further communication between them would be unpleasant. He requested that his monthly remuneration and all correspondence about the *Miscellany* be sent him through some third party.[14]

This outburst Gregory interpreted as an effort to strengthen a feeble case by picking a quarrel. But "Mr. Boz" was a valuable editor. He must have no pretext for anger. He consequently advised Bentley to send a conciliatory letter offering to submit to arbitration by a mutually reliable friend.[15]

When Bentley called at Dickens's home in Doughty Street to give him his salary, he learned that Dickens was on holiday at Broadstairs. He wrote saying that it was at the office and requesting an early meeting to confer about the next issue. Dickens made no reply, but sent his brother for the money. Bentley again called fruitlessly at Doughty Street; a few days later he received a note declining to have any further communication with him except by letter.[16]

Bentley became concerned lest Dickens was neglecting the *Miscellany* altogether. Stopping in at the printer's, he learned that without consulting him Dickens had sent in numerous papers to be set up in type. Bentley confirmed the selection of almost all, but vetoed two or three, as he had the right to do, and directed that the usual place on the first sheet be kept open for Dickens's installment. But, to be certain of something for the leading position, Bentley set in reserve a story that he and Dickens had agreed to use.[17]

Meanwhile, to avoid recourse to law, Bentley accepted an offer from Cruikshank to mediate the dispute. "Cruikshank has been here," Dickens wrote Forster after the first of several visits, "—deputed by Bentley to say nothing." [18] Cruikshank reported that Dickens rigidly refused to entertain any proposition that did not recognize *Oliver Twist* as the second novel of their agreement. This course Cruikshank advised. Somehow he had picked up the odd impression that the public were "heartily tired of 'Oliver Twist'" and that it was "more likely to injure the Miscellany than otherwise." If Bentley accepted it as the second novel, Cruikshank seemed to think, he might drop it out of the magazine entirely! [19]

Bentley speedily disabused him of this notion. But the struggle with Dickens was proving more difficult than he had anticipated; Dickens might very possibly refuse to perform any of his obligations. Suppose Bentley won a court case, what good would that do? A sullen editor and a reluctant novelist were worse than none. Meanwhile, *Pickwick Papers* grew more deliriously popular every day, and whatever the eccentric Cruikshank thought, *Oliver* certainly was a drawing card the *Miscellany* could ill afford to lose. If he wished to retain the services of this spectacularly successful young man, Bentley at last decided, he must yield. He empowered Cruikshank to offer Dickens a larger sum for the two novels and to consent that *Oliver Twist* be regarded as the second novel.[20]

But hard upon this concession came an angry letter from Dickens. He was bitterly indignant at the changes Bentley had made in the October issue. His whole arrangement had been altered, articles inserted that he had never even seen in manuscript, and this course persisted in despite his notice that he would revise no such papers. "By these proceedings I have been actually superseded in my office as Editor . . . They are in direct violation of my agreement with you, and a gross insult . . ." He therefore declined any further connection with the *Miscellany* beyond "this month—no longer." [21]

Almost on top of this Bentley received a bewildered note from Cruikshank. Only the day before he had thought everything smoothed out. Now Dickens was making "a stand upon his editorial right." Cruikshank urged Bentley to resolve the contention in a friendly way. There might still "be time to get out the 'Oliver Twist,' in the next Number." (It will be noted that Cruikshank's judgment of the story seems to have altered.)[22]

Bentley, however, was not uncholeric. He had exercised great control over himself. Only the day before, learning that Dickens objected to the piece he had ordered set up in type, he had withdrawn it, although *he* felt he had the right to insist on its insertion. Now his own temper was aroused. He had "no alternative but that of consulting my legal advisers," he wrote Dickens, and announced his intention of holding him to all his agreements.[23]

Dickens replied curtly: "Mr. Molloy . . . is my solicitor. . . . Of course it *is* my intention to abide by the determination I have given you notice of, or I should not have announced it." [24] And to Cruikshank Dickens wrote that there would be no *Oliver Twist* that month.[25] To fill the gap he sent in a labored satire on learned societies, called "Full Report of the First Meeting of the Mudfog Association for the Advancement of Everything."

An ineffectual interview now took place between Bentley, Gregory, and Molloy. Gregory advised Bentley he was convinced Dickens's real grievance was that other editors of similar magazines were more highly paid. Bentley could decide either to insist on the agreement and proceed against Dickens, or accept a pecuniary loss as the cost of retaining him as editor. If the latter, Gregory should learn from Molloy what price Dickens exacted, in order to discover "whether it is worth your while to be cheated to that extent or to try the result of an action." [26]

Gregory certainly did not understand Dickens. So far, none of his complaints had even mentioned an inadequacy of salary. He did say the remuneration originally agreed upon for the novels was inadequate; he would not have hesitated to say the same about his editorial salary. And although he *had* made the agreements, he had undoubtably been victimized by his inexperience. (Harrison Ainsworth had thought, at the time, that Dickens should have been offered £800, not £500, for each of the two novels; since then Dickens's value had grown steadily.)

Furthermore, it was an error to imagine that Dickens was using Bentley's editorial interferences only as a trick to drive a better bargain. From the beginning he had complained, with some asperity, on these points. "I must beg you once again," he wrote in one letter, "not to allow anybody but myself to interfere with the Miscellany." [27] He had rigid ideas of his own dignity and authority as editor, which he resisted seeing infringed even at the hands—in a man of Dickens's character one might say especially at the hands—of his employer. Nothing would put Dickens's back up more fiercely than the notion that he might be intimidated by a superior.

This does not mean that there was no acquisitiveness in his motives, nor that his financial dissatisfaction had no connection with his resentment of editorial interferences. Nor does his desire for a more equitable return for his work justify his actions. For he had made the agreements. He was not entitled to repudiate them because he now saw that publisher would gain more than author, or because he could now get more elsewhere. But it was understandable that he chafed at "the consciousness that my books are enriching everybody connected with them but myself," [28] and that he should struggle to amend the discrepancy. Less defensible are the weapons he used.

But they won the first round of the duel. Bentley decided that Dickens was too valuable to lose. In September he surrendered, conceding practically all he had refused in August. He would consider *Oliver Twist* the second of the novels and pay £600 and £700 respectively for the first three thousand copies of each; after that they should be published on joint account with author and publisher sharing equally in the profits. Although he retained the copyright on all Dickens's other contributions, he agreed that should any of these be separately reprinted, they would also be on joint account. Finally, as additional bait, he offered to raise Dickens's salary as editor to a straight forty guineas a month independent of circulation and retroactive from the beginning of Dickens's editorship.[29]

These proposals, however, did not salve Dickens's wounded editorial dignity. There must be no more unregulated interferences; his powers and Bentley's must be clearly defined. Otherwise he would not resume his duties. In a stiff little note Molloy indicated that

Dickens had performed his final services.[30] But Bentley also had his dignity to maintain. He would not be a nonentity on his own magazine. He must have more than the negative right of veto. Dickens had promised some contributors exaggeratedly high sums; he must not be thus committed without his approval.[31]

In an attempt to reach a compromise there was a conference at which Forster represented Dickens and Gregory's partner Follett represented Bentley. Almost all day long the men struggled over a draft agreement, settling point after point in Dickens's favor.[32] Finally the agreement, dated September 28, 1837, provided that he would edit the *Miscellany* for three years from December, 1837, dropping both the previous five-year options. His salary would be £30 a month, plus £10 additional when sales exceeded six thousand copies and £5 for each additional five hundred. Bentley retained his right of veto, could originate three articles in every number, and made all arrangements about contributors' payments. *Oliver Twist* would continue in the *Miscellany* till midsummer, 1838, and be published in book form on Dickens's supplying the remainder of the copy and receiving £500 for it on the 1st of May. On this book Bentley would have a three-year copyright, after which half the copyright would revert to Dickens. *Barnaby Rudge*, in three volumes, was to be delivered on similar terms before or during October, 1838, for £700.[33]

Dickens had scored an almost complete victory—in some respects, indeed, considerably more than he had originally contended for. Their respective editorial powers were clarified, he was to receive more than he had demanded for both novels, and he not only won his main point about regarding *Oliver Twist* as the second novel but no deductions were to be made for its periodical appearance.

* * * * *

But the peace that now ensued was only an uneasy lull. Bentley felt he had been subjected to extortion. Dickens burned at his struggle to obtain a reasonable sum for the novels and at what he considered the infringement of his editorial powers. Beneath the surface cordiality, there smoldered bitter resentments. Bentley, however, endeavored to be conciliatory. He and Dickens dined together again. "Bentley was here yesterday," Dickens wrote Forster in October, 1837. "He at once gave in about Barnaby Rudge"—Dickens wanted it deferred to the end of October, 1838—"and said I could direct Molloy to alter the agreement as I liked to meet the object in view." [34]

Bentley had acquired a life of the famous clown Grimaldi, long-windedly and clumsily arranged by Thomas Egerton Wilks from auto-biographical notes. He proposed that Dickens revise it. Dickens stipulated that his name should appear only as editor, not as author, and demanded a minimum of £300 and a half share of the profits after deduction of expenses, to which Bentley agreed.[35] Dickens did no original writing, except for an introductory and possibly a concluding chapter. His revisions, mostly drastic abridgment, he dictated to his father, who vastly enjoyed his exalted office as amanuensis. The book's reception surprised Dickens, who thought little of it. "Seventeen hundred Grimaldis have been already sold," he wrote Forster during the first week of publication, "and the demand increases daily!!!!!!!!!!! !!!!!!!!!!!!!!!!!!!!" [36]

The restored cordiality did not long endure. Even while Dickens was pushing forward on the revision of the Grimaldi manuscript, editor and publisher resumed their clashes. Although their new agreement gave Bentley the right to initiate three articles in each issue, the two men differed repeatedly about editorial direction. Some of Bentley's friends were apparently being published by his desire only, and wished to extort Dickens's approval as well, which he tenaciously refused to give. "I will not bind myself," he wrote Bentley, "to any man, either to commend Mr. Wilks, or Mr. Hughes, or Mr. Richard Hughes or Mr. Alfred Brown or anybody else." [37] "I have exercised an impartial judgment on Mr. Wilks's previous productions," and "do not choose to recognize him as a regular contributor to the Miscellany, although *you* have the power of inserting his compositions if you like." And in some indignation, Dickens adds, "Let the matter drop here. We shall never agree about it I see plainly. Mr. Wilks's conditions are exceedingly presumptuous and arrogant . . ." [38] And again, "I do not choose Captain Marryat to suppose that *I* pillage his articles from American papers, and advertize his name as a contributor to the Miscellany. . . . I cannot and will not bear the perpetual ill will and heart-burnings and callings and writings consequent upon my accepting papers which are never inserted." [39] By this time, it is clear, Dickens's powers over the magazine were almost entirely annulled.

"Order the Miscellany just as you please," he told Bentley wearily. "I have no wish or care about the matter." [40]

Presently Dickens discovered Bentley to be making petty deductions when his contributions were short, by a page or half page, of the sixteen pages he was supposed to supply each month. As he had often cut them to make them fit into the space left after he and Bentley had worked out the rest of the magazine, it is difficult to acquit Bentley of tactlessness at the best, or avoid suspecting that, still rankling over their previous differences, he was relieving his feelings by seizing upon a technicality. But it was not a safe, even though legal, liberty to take with Dickens. If Bentley really desired friendly relations, he might better have forgotten these cheese-paring economies—they totaled some sixteen guineas for the entire year—instead of risking a good will that might have brought him profits in thousands. For Dickens reacted to these annoyances as if stung. Did Bentley think it liberal, he asked "to your editor and principal contributor to deduct his half pages and count him down by the line"? Did he not think "the pains and care bestowed upon the tale of which you count the words" deserved a better return? Did he "consider that such treatment (so different from any I have received elsewhere) is likely to make me wish for a very long continuance of our business connection?" [41]

However, their relations staggered on through 1838. But as Dickens tried to finish *Oliver Twist* sufficiently in advance of its completion in the *Miscellany* to have it at the book printer's that winter, he realized that it would be impossible to have *Barnaby Rudge* ready by November, as he had agreed. Nothing of literary merit or popular appeal could be turned out so hastily. Consequently he now wanted Bentley to make the same change for this novel that had been wrested from him for *Oliver*. Would it not be more to Bentley's interest, he suggested in February, as well as within the scope of Dickens's ability, if *Barnaby Rudge* succeeded *Oliver* in the *Miscellany* and were published afterward in three volumes? Would this not be better than his undertaking, at the conclusion of *Oliver* in the magazine, a new series for it while at the same time writing *Barnaby* for separate book publication? The production every month of a large installment of three separate works (for Dickens was already starting *Nicholas Nickleby* for Chapman and Hall) would have been, he felt, beyond Scott himself. This way, he "could do the best for you as well as for myself" and the

Miscellany would suffer, he assured Bentley, no gap in his contributions. "Just think of this at your leisure. I am really anxious to do the
best I can for you as well as for myself, and in this case the pecuniary
advantage must be all on your side . . ." [42]

But Bentley did not at all agree. He insisted on keeping *Barnaby
Rudge* and Dickens's contributions to the *Miscellany* two distinct
matters, which Dickens repeated it was impossible for him to accomplish. And if it was unrealistic for Dickens to have undertaken them
in the first place, it must be remembered he was still a newcomer to
his profession. To have allowed him to undertake them was certainly
no less unrealistic of Bentley, who was a publisher of long standing.
Dickens can hardly be cleared, however, of recklessness and, even, of
disingenuousness when he undertook still another work for Chapman
and Hall less than a fortnight after he assured Bentley that it was impossible for him to perform what he was already committed to. [43] Although he never turned out the comic book, *Don's Annual Register
and Obituary of Blue Devils*, which he then agreed to have ready for
Christmas, Bentley would hardly have felt more faith in Dickens's
arguments if he had known about the matter.

The wrangle over *Barnaby Rudge* spread itself out over the next
six months, while the writing of *Oliver Twist* was drawing within
sight of its close and the shining sun of *Nicholas Nickleby* was rising
upon the world. That June saw Dickens's election to the Athenaeum.
In July Bentley visited him at Twickenham overnight to try to iron
out their difficulties. [44] At last, after conferences with Bentley's advisers, it was agreed that the sum for *Barnaby* be increased to £600,
and Dickens's main demand that it be published in the *Miscellany*,
instead of a separate series, was conceded. [45]

But in January their uneasy peace broke down again. Dickens was
still exasperated by editorial interferences: articles he accepted never
appeared in the *Miscellany*, others were delayed for months. To one
plaintive contributor he explained that there were at least thirty such
papers lying about for a full twelve months, adding, "These delays
are not more annoying to anyone than to me." [46] In addition he found
Bentley's premature notices of the appearance of *Barnaby* irritating.
As far back as November, Forster had asked Bentley, "Is it exactly
prudent to use the expression 'forthwith' respecting the appearance
of *Barnaby* in the Miscellany?" [47]

All these sources of friction, and *Barnaby Rudge* still to be begun and threatening to crush him with the weight of work, so chafed Dickens that Forster had much trouble to restrain him from throwing over the agreement altogether. "The immense profits which Oliver has realized for its publisher and is still realizing," Dickens complained; "the paltry, wretched, miserable sum it brought me . . . and the consciousness that I have still the slavery and drudgery of another work on the same journeyman-terms; the consciousness that my books are enriching everybody connected with them but myself, and that I, with such a popularity as I have acquired, am struggling in old toils, and wasting my energies in the very height and freshness of my fame, and the best part of my life, to fill the pockets of others . . . all this puts me out of heart and spirits: and I cannot—cannot and will not— under such circumstances that keep me down with an iron hand, distress myself by beginning this tale until I have had some time to breathe; and until the intervention of summer, and some cheerful days in the country, shall have restored me to a more genial and composed state of feeling."

With this outburst Dickens enclosed a letter he was determined to send Bentley, demanding a six-month postponement in the starting date of *Barnaby Rudge.* "Go it MUST," he told Forster. "It is no fiction to say that at present I *cannot* write this tale." But for Forster, he said, he would repudiate the agreement altogether. "For I do most solemnly declare that morally, before God and man, I hold myself released from such hard bargains . . . This net that has been wound about me, so chafes me, so exasperates and irritates my mind, that to break it at whatever cost—*that* I should care nothing for—is my constant impulse. But I have not yielded to it. I merely declare that I must have a postponement very common in all literary agreements . . ." [48]

An eloquent and heartfelt utterance, certainly. But the facts are colored in personal emotion. For Bentley had neither entangled Dickens in a net nor forced him into slavery. It was Dickens's terms that had been agreed on from the beginning, and Bentley had repeatedly modified them in Dickens's favor. In addition to the pieces for the *Miscellany,* two novels had been contracted for; they were now become simply the contributions to the magazine and were being paid for, besides, at a considerably higher price. For Dickens's name as editor, if not his services, Bentley was also giving a salary rising with the circulation to probably double the sum originally agreed upon.

Bentley, however, was indubitably profiting to an enormously greater degree than Dickens. And he resisted every concession until it was wrung from him by the realization that these golden fruits might vanish. Chapman and Hall had also gained more from *Pickwick* than Dickens had, but it is significant that he did not resent them as he did Bentley. Later, it is true, Dickens left them, but with no such acrimonious and protracted quarrel. Nor was Dickens the only person with whom Bentley had troubles. There were difficulties over the publication of a novel by Mary Russell Mitford.[49] From Forster Bentley demanded repayment of a £150 advance on a canceled book agreement, at the very time he himself was asking Forster to restore it.[50] He quarreled with Ainsworth and with Cruikshank.[51] Some years later he tried to pare down the sums he paid his old college friend Richard Barham, who promptly obtained twice as much from Bentley's rival, Colburn.[52]

It is certainly clear that if Dickens was a man of growing determination, Bentley bristled with difficult traits. And, although it is true that Dickens was unscrupulous in pressing his artist's advantage of declaring a kind of literary strike if Bentley insisted on what was nominated in the bond, the revisions Dickens demanded represented a common-sense view of fairness even if they were not embodied in contractual law. Much of the trouble between these two determined men lay in the absolute sale of a copyright for a lump sum, a practice common between all publishers and authors during the period. This procedure might work fairly for an established writer of stable position, but it would naturally be unsatisfactory to an author like Dickens whose popularity constantly outstripped every attempted readjustment. Had there been anything like the contemporary sliding scale of royalties, the conflict between them might partly have been avoided.

Not entirely, however. For a certain residue of their hostility was ultimately temperamental. Despite all his surface bonhomie and cordiality, Bentley had strong authoritarian impulses. The enterprise that he owned, he intended to manage. He must have a finger in every part of the direction: the acceptance, rejection, and commissioning of manuscripts, their rate of remuneration, the contents of each issue. As a successful publisher he considered his literary judgment better than that of the editor he had put in what he evidently regarded as nominal, but Dickens insisted must be real, charge of the *Miscellany*. Dickens, too, was proud and determined to have his own will. In the end, Bentley's every way of doing things rasped him: the small deductions for half-page shortages, the delays in running pieces long accepted, the petty assertions of his rights that Bentley could not resist making even in the very act of yielding a point.

The last of these tendencies appeared in his reply to Dickens's demand for a delay in *Barnaby Rudge*. Bentley ostentatiously underlined his own flexibility by professing himself "desirous . . . at all times to meet your wishes even at the expense of my own convenience." Although he could find no clause in their agreement that entitled Dickens—and he now quoted Dickens's own words—" 'to require a postponement of six months,' " he would raise no objection to Dickens's wish. Only *he* required that Dickens undertake to suspend all work except *Nicholas Nickleby*, and refrain from writing "any work or portion of a work of any description during that period." [53]

But this Dickens could not promise. He had already agreed to edit the benefit volume for Macrone's widow, which was to be published by Colburn. He had not yet given up, although he had done no work on, the comic book he was to have had for Chapman and Hall for Christmas. Bentley's response assuredly was very embarrassing to an author demanding a six months' vacation during which he washed his hands "of any fresh accumulation of labour." If Dickens had "heart and spirits" to tackle a comic annual and an editorial job for Bentley's former partner Colburn, Bentley might ask, why had he none to do his long-contracted work for the *Miscellany*?

Far from being embarrassed, however, Dickens greeted the demand Bentley attached to his concession by an explosion of anger. Within two days he repudiated any further connection with the *Miscellany*. In vain Bentley tried to shake this determination. He even offered to acquiesce in Dickens's writing the comic annual, of which he had learned by now, if Dickens remained nominal editor of the *Miscellany* and agreed not to conduct any other periodical. For this mere use of his name Bentley offered £40 a month.[54] But Dickens was adamant, and advanced the counter suggestion that his friend Harrison Ainsworth become the editor. Then, and then only, although still withdrawing, Dickens would express himself as friendly toward the magazine.

Bentley was furious but desperate. He spoke bitterly of what he stigmatized as Dickens's dishonorable conduct, and resisted having Ainsworth forced upon him.[55] Dickens refused to budge. Bentley asked Barham to confer with Dickens and Ainsworth, and Barham told him frankly that Ainsworth would make a very eligible choice for the editorship. He submitted to Bentley a memorandum of Dickens's proposals, which he felt "fair and reasonable." Dickens would write a paper for the next number of the *Miscellany* pleasantly announcing his resignation and expressing his friendship for the new editor. He would write gratuitously two further papers within the next six months. He would give Ainsworth *personally* any information that might help him in conducting the magazine, and would regard it as a point of honor not to edit, conduct, originate, or write for any other magazine whatever until the end of 1839.[56]

Reluctantly Bentley agreed. He realized how little possibility there was of getting what he wanted by a chancery suit; at enormous expense he might ruin Dickens but still be as far as ever from furthering his own ends. Nor would a rancorous court battle aid the *Miscellany* or enhance its standing with other authors. There remained only to settle the disposition of *Barnaby Rudge*, on which Bentley still had claims not surrendered with Dickens's departure from the magazine.

After several tentative draft agreements, the final one provided that *Barnaby Rudge* was to be delivered to Bentley on January 1, 1840, for publication in three volumes, an extension three months longer than Dickens had been demanding. He was to undertake, until then, no other work except *Nicholas Nickleby*, the comic annual for Chapman and Hall, and the benefit book for Mrs. Macrone. For *Barnaby Rudge*, Bentley agreed to pay £2,000 outright, another £1,000 if the sale exceeded 10,000, and still another £1,000 if the sale came to 15,000: a possible total of £4,000 for the entire copyright of the book which, two years before, Dickens had agreed to write for only £500.[57]

It was a bitter pill for Bentley to swallow. Dickens was triumphant at having "burst the Bentleian bonds." [58] In the February, 1839, *Miscellany* he withdrew in a "Familiar Epistle from a Parent to a Child, Aged Two Years and Two Months." The infant for whom he had cared since birth, he said, he handed over to his good friend Mr. Ainsworth with his best wishes and without gain or profit to himself, for it had "always been literally 'Bentley's' Miscellany, and never mine."

* * * * *

But nine months later, when the delivery date for *Barnaby Rudge* was drawing near, Dickens had no more than two chapters written.[59] He was finding it hard going, for all his disciplined powers of concentration, and his long delay in starting reinforces the suspicion that, by now, he didn't *feel* like writing *Barnaby* and was laboring against the grain. For, although he complained of the strain of writing *Nicholas Nickleby*, it had not taken all his time. He had dropped the comic annual but had written instead an anonymous potboiler that Chapman and Hall published in January under the title of *Sketches of Young Couples*. For this he received only £200,[60] and there can be no doubt that *Barnaby Rudge* would have brought in the full £4,000 agreed to by Bentley. (*Nicholas Nickleby* was at that time selling around fifty thousand copies a month.) Mercenary reasons were not the cause of his delay, nor does it seem possible that Dickens, for all his prodigious energy, could have expected to finish a three-volume novel in three months.

The book's stormy history may well have built up within him an insuperable internal resistance to it. He had had trouble about it with Macrone, before its title was changed from *Gabriel Vardon, the Locksmith of London*. It had been a bone of contention through all the bitter hostilities marking his two years on the *Miscellany*. Deep within him, he wished to be free of Bentley altogether. Whether or not he consciously put it off in the Micawberlike hope of something turning up that would justify his refusing to finish it, he certainly now pounced upon two excuses he conceived Bentley's conduct to give him.

First, he resented Bentley's improper use of his name. "Mr. Bentley in his advertisements and hired puffs of other books with which I never had . . . any possible connection," Dickens wrote his attorneys, "has repeatedly used my name and the names of some of my writings in an unwarrantable manner . . . calculated to do me serious prejudice." Second, he disapproved of what he termed Bentley's practice of bringing out a three-volume novel for twenty-five shillings and then, while the booksellers' shelves still groaned with unsold copies, republishing it in fifteen weekly parts for a shilling each.[61]

These accusations Bentley's son and successor characterized after Dickens's death as false.[62] Their truth and importance, however, are matters of interpretation. As the publisher of *Oliver Twist* Bentley was justified in "puffing" that book. Dickens neither claims Bentley represented him as the author of books he did not write, nor states how the use of his name or his books damaged him. As for the cheaper editions, if true save as an unusual accident, Bentley would be a curiously incompetent man of business willfully destroying his own sales or, even if the immediate losses were not his, endangering future sales. On the other hand, Dickens was too clever a controversialist to risk a statement demonstrably untrue. But he may here have seized upon a few exceptional occurrences to support his contentions. There was no use, he insisted, in Bentley's advertising that the book was "preparing for publication." He was working on something else, and the manuscript would not be ready on January 1st. This, he concluded, the agreement distinctly provided for by giving Bentley the right under those circumstances to cancel it.

But Bentley, of course, had no such desire. Gregory reminded Dickens's attorneys that Bentley had already granted several postponements, that this one would be "provably of pecuniary loss"; what compensation did Dickens propose? [63] Meanwhile, Bentley went on advertising *Barnaby Rudge*, and Dickens announced a new publication by Chapman and Hall. Gregory noted that, whereas Dickens's solicitors had merely said the manuscript would not be ready on time, Dickens had now declared a positive determination to violate the agreement.[64]

Mitton called on Gregory to say that if Bentley's advertisements continued, Dickens would advertise denials. Did he or did he not, Gregory demanded, intend to write the book he had agreed to write? Mitton was unprepared to answer, and Gregory wished him good morning.[65] It was, Dickens exclaimed in fierce exultation, "War to the knife . . . with the Burlington Street Brigand." [66]

For another week all was quiet. "The Brigand is sleeping," Dickens wrote Edward Chapman, "but I suspect with one eye open." [67] Macready offered his own services for mediation. "So much disgust and suffering," he wrote, "must interfere with you seriously in every way." [68] But in the privacy of his diary, Macready considered Dickens quite wrong. "He makes a contract which he considers advantageous at the time, but subsequently finding his talents more lucrative than he had supposed, he refuses to fulfil the contract." [69]

Dickens, however, was no less convinced that he was entirely right, and refused Macready's offer with grateful thanks. "I am exceedingly anxious that you should understand that I do not reject your good offices from any obstinate or wrong-headed feeling, but simply because I *know* the hopelessness of any mediation just now, and know this man as well as anybody living. The law, bad as it is, is more true and more to be trusted than such a hound as he, and *unless* he gives me the opening for a negociation, I must . . . submit to its vexations with what philosophy I can. If I were a builder or a stone-mason I might fulfill my contract with him, but write for him I really cannot unless I am forced and have no outlet for escape." [70]

The hysterical sincerity of this letter reveals that what Dickens felt now was an almost obsessional hatred of Bentley. "The advertisement was repeated today in the Times and Herald and the dog's solicitors (God forgive me for libelling his good animals) doggedly inform us that they mean to repeat it. The contradiction, therefore . . . appears in the evening papers tomorrow . . . This done, he means, as he tells us, to advertise the agreements—and that done, I don't know what happens." [71]

Bentley prepared to carry the battle into the pages of the *Miscellany*, with an account of the dispute that would outline the "one-sided agreement" Dickens complained about. The result, his friend Barham was sure, would be slaughterous: "Only *be still* for a moment," he wrote Bentley persuasively, "& your reply may be a *smasher* . . ." [72] Meanwhile, Dickens was threatened with a chancery suit and belligerently retorted that no court in England should compel him to write the novel. [73]

Slowly, from this high moment of defiance, the dispute simmered down to its final settlement. Bentley was advised by expert legal counsel that he could not obtain an injunction restraining Dickens from the publication of any new work until the delivery of *Barnaby*. His only recourse would be to a court of law for damages. [74]

A protracted series of negotiations took place, Forster representing Dickens's interests, and the editor of the *Literary Gazette*, William

Jerdan, who felt friendly to both parties, representing Bentley. At last, in June, 1840, they arranged a settlement that both antagonists accepted.[75] Dickens was to pay Bentley £1,500 for the assignment to him by Bentley of his interest in *Oliver Twist* and the relinquishment of all further claims upon Dickens's writings, either produced or promised. In addition, Dickens also purchased the Cruikshank plates for *Oliver Twist* and the copies of that novel remaining in stock for £750. Chapman and Hall agreed to finance Dickens and to deduct the sum from £3,000 they would pay him for a six-month copyright of *Barnaby Rudge*.[76] Thus Dickens concentrated the publication of all his books in one firm, his "trusty friends" Chapman and Hall, whom he proclaimed "the best of booksellers, past, present, and to come." It was a daring prediction, but at last Dickens was happy and satisfied.[77]

With Bentley, who thereby lost the most remunerative author of his time, it is impossible not to sympathize. For he had had the law on his side at every stage of their contention. Against his clear claims was only Dickens's burning sense of injustice and ruthless determination not to yield, even to the law. It was Bentley's misfortune that his legal remedies were so expensive and uncertain that they were feeble weapons, although from every legal point of view he was in the right and Dickens entirely in the wrong.

The imponderables, however, are more difficult to assess. For if Dickens had no case, he did have a grievance. It was genuinely unjust that the talent which had achieved so tremendous a popularity should have profited so much less than the hands which distributed its work. The heart of their breach, however, was a clash of radically opposed temperaments—even from the very first disputes over Dickens's attempt to have *Oliver Twist* fulfill two commitments, to the same struggles over *Barnaby Rudge*, and his postponement and final wrenching of it free from Bentley's grasp. Although Bentley spoke of his desire to be generous, he disputed every guinea. And every concession—he did make six of them!—was extorted from a reluctance that resisted long enough to destroy any grace in its final yielding. Nor were matters helped by his subsequent petty economies on the enormously successful *Miscellany* and his wrangles about editorial authority. Dickens expressed gratification at some of their earlier readjustments, but he found, in the end, that he had to fight for whatever he got.

From their three-year duel Dickens emerged not only completely victorious but with a will forged into a weapon of steel, his sense of power immeasurably sharpened, his tenacity immovably strengthened. Strong from the days of his delicate and unhappy boyhood his will had always been, but it had operated with a certain diffidence and almost as an invisible force in his struggles to surmount obstacles. His imperiousness and his indignation had flared on only a few previous occasions when he had become convinced that he was being ill-treated. Never before had it tempered itself to the rigors of a prolonged conflict with an individual foe. Always clever in shaping the facts of a dispute to his advantage, he became a brilliant controversialist, highlighting every weakness in the position of his adversary with biting sarcasm. Never, from the time of his struggle with Bentley, did Dickens surrender in the smallest point to any antagonist. Even in repose the set of his features and the high carriage of his head often conveyed an impression of spirited defiance. And once opposed, whether by adverse literary critics, his publishers, his friends, members of his family, or the entire American press, he hardened into a relentless determination that was to sweep fatefully through all the sorrows and successes of his life.

CHAPTER FIVE

The Will in Command

Around the wine-red mahogany table in Doughty Street friends raised their glasses to toast Dickens on his twenty-seventh birthday. Ainsworth and Forster, the other two members of the Cerberus Club, were there of course, and Tom Mitton, Browne, Dickens's mother and father, the latter bursting with pride and conviviality, Fanny and her personable husband Henry Burnett, Laman Blanchard, who had been editor of the *True Sun* in Dickens's days there, and Leigh Hunt, with his gentle grace and luminous eyes.[1] Hunt found Dickens "as pleasant as some of the best things in his books," [2] and exclaimed, "What a face is his to meet in a drawing-room! It has the life and soul in it of fifty human beings." [3] To the flashing animation of Dickens were added, after dinner, the jollity of Harley and the sculptor Angus Fletcher.[4]

It had been, Dickens felt, "a most prosperous and happy year." [5] For its feverish contentions with Bentley had never really dampened his spirits or poisoned the enormous excitement with which he dashed at experience; indeed, even in disputation he laid about him with the fierce enjoyment of one glorying in giant combat. His freedom from editorial subjection to a man he found unendurable was a triumph that cast its light backward over all the excitement of the struggle. And what radiant prospects lay ahead!

The immediate future, to be sure, brought Dickens a problem. For his father had again become a source of embarrassment. His financial irresponsibility had not diminished with middle age. He was the same grandiloquently improvident personage he had always been, forever running up bills with tradesmen, forever behindhand in his payments, forever signing "deeds" and making compositions with his creditors.

But Dickens was to deal with his father's infirmities far more sternly this time than he had five years ago, when he mortgaged his own salary to get John Dickens out of Sloman's sponging house. The status he had achieved in the world gave him a sense of his own importance and power and made him resentful of such shabby doings. Further, in the past two years he had learned to enforce his own will by taking a stand and insisting that everyone else must yield.

For some time now, unknown to Dickens, his father had been up to his old ways. No sooner was *Pickwick* a success than he was on Chapman and Hall's doorstep for a £4 loan to tide him over some trifling trouble. Little Mr. Hall, pacing up and down the room, murmured "something that sounded like, 'Well, it's not business, you know'; while Mr. Chapman, with a mild, meditative smile, rejoined: 'Oh, but we *must*; we can't refuse him so small a sum as that!' " [6]

Then, in February, 1837, before this sum was repaid, John Dickens had another "moment of some difficulty," and advanced an ingenious proposition for extending Chapman and Hall's obliging assistance. Would they deduct the amount already due, plus interest, from the enclosed promissory note for £20 and send him the balance? Their failure would "be productive of fatal consequences." To be sure, he added, the publishers might consider this request an intrusion: "I feel it to be so; but, recollecting how much your interests are bound up with those of my son . . ." [7]

By July he needed another £15 to pay the rent. "Mind," he wrote, "the subject is one of settlement by 2 o'clock, and unless I so arrange it, I am lost." [8] A little later a document marked "Confidential" bore witness to another loan. He now owed Chapman and Hall £55 5s., but had to have £50 at once to save him "from perdition." [9] By this time even John Dickens was embarrassed by the possible appearance of obtaining money "as it were . . . under false pretenses," so he proposed insuring his life in their favor for £100 for three years. When "a man is placed in the situation in which I have placed myself, all but subjected himself to the laws of his country, he will snatch at a straw to save himself not from drowning, but a scarcely milder sentence." [10] The money must be had "by one o'clock tomorrow" to avert "the most awful consequences." "I am sure it will reflect no disgrace on you that you have to this extent assisted the father of one with whom it has been your lot to do business . . ." [11]

At the end of 1837 he apologized for not paying them until "more pressing demands, such as threatened my liberty, are satisfied," and thanked them for not telling Charles about these matters: "I am sure it could have led to a breach of a most distressing nature." [12] But early in the next year he begged a further renewal. "All sorts of annoyances," he wrote, had driven him almost to madness.[13] Then, at last, he was arrested once more for debt, and coolly invited his son's publishers to "do the needful."

His affairs grew constantly more tangled. And his other victims were less discreetly complaisant than Chapman and Hall. Although he had even been selling sheets of manuscript and autographs to scrape together cash, his involvements were too great. He received a notice of eviction from his house; he was liable to arrest on behalf of innumerable tradesmen.[14] At last, toward the end of February, 1839, shortly after the buoyant birthday dinner, his piled-up debts could no longer be concealed from his son.

Dickens acted with authoritative, with dictatorial, speed. It was intolerable that his father's shady dodges should be allowed to soil his good name and subject him to a kind of blackmail if he wished to avoid the disgrace of seeing John Dickens again in jail. He would come to the rescue, of course, but it must be in the way he thought best. Above all, no such disgraceful situation must ever be allowed to arise again.

He would settle his father and mother and Augustus in a house in the country—in Exeter, remote from London. He would pay the rent they owed and contrive some temporary living arrangement for Frederick. Alfred, who had shown a tendency to follow in his father's footsteps by dunning Chapman and Hall for small loans, had already been put to studying engineering in Yorkshire. To the tradesmen "let them say nothing," Dickens ordered. "The only hope I have of making any composition short of paying in full is founded on their being previously non est inventus." Undoubtedly John Dickens's bills had been allowed to mount on the certainty of their being honored by his son, and Dickens therefore saw no point in being more out of pocket than he could help. To his mother he gave the choice of taking the coach with him or joining him a few days later. His father would have to get out of town and could reach Exeter in a week. "This promptitude is *necessary,*" Dickens wrote Forster, "and worth a thousand prospective resolutions." [15]

Flurried, perhaps, by this ruthless dispatch, his mother did not accompany him. Dickens took his place alone in the Telegraph—the coach for Exeter—and the next morning, strolling along the Plymouth high road, exactly a mile out of Exeter at Alphington he came upon a little white cottage with a for-rent sign. It had a vegetable and flower garden, an orchard, and a splendid view of Exeter with a glimpse of the cathedral towers rising to the sky. Within, it was "bright as a new pin," freshly painted and papered, with an excellent parlor, a beautiful drawing room and two or three bedrooms, all for £20 a year. [16]

Dickens quickly signed an agreement with the landlady, a fat and fresh-faced old widow in the cottage next door. Toasts were drunk in beer, and then he dashed off to the upholsterer, "coming over the upholsterer's daughter," he wrote Forster, "with many virtuous endearments, to propitiate the establishment and reduce the bill." [17] He bought some tables and imitation rosewood chairs, a couch, secondhand red curtains for the sitting rooms, two secondhand carpets, a tent bedstead and white-dimity furniture for the best bedroom, glass, crockery, garden tools, and coal. The whole cost of fitting up the cottage he estimated as less than £70. [18]

Dickens was in high spirits. He wrote Forster that he was sure his mother and father would be happy there, and sent Kate directions for his mother to take the coach from its starting place at the Black Bear, Piccadilly. [19] To Mile End Cottage consequently came Mrs. Dickens, and, on Saturday, John Dickens, Augustus, and the dog Dash. There was no resisting the relentless whirlwind of Dickens's will. But before going off into exile, John Dickens rather plaintively asked Chapman and Hall what he would do in a little place like Alphington. [20] He was only fifty-three, and despite his unreliability with money he had always been industrious.

But Dickens, in a letter inviting Beard to see his "new turn-out," a handsome carriage he had purchased for Kate and was redecorating at a cost of £15, was confident that he had "the governor" settled for life. [21] And, indeed, at first John and Elizabeth Dickens seemed pleased with the pretty rural retreat that was so different from the faded London lodgings they had known for years. But at the end of a month there was an "unsatisfactory epistle from Mother"; by June both parents were writing "hateful, sneering letters." "I do swear," Dickens groaned, "I am sick at heart with both her and father too." [22]

Gradually, however, his "prodigal parent" and his mother grew reconciled. By July of the following year Dickens found them apparently "perfectly contented and happy" and the "little doll's house" beautifully kept.[23] Chastened by the drastic fate that had overtaken him, perhaps a little afraid of his son, and, above all, with fewer opportunities in Devonshire, John Dickens made some improvement in his ways. But he never reformed entirely; in 1841 and 1844 Dickens again had to pay some of his debts.[24] Little by little, though, his banishment became less absolute. In August of 1841 he and his wife stayed at Broadstairs with Dickens,[25] and his spirits were bounding with an exuberantly wild scheme to "proceed to Paris to consolidate Augustus's French." [26] By the end of 1842 he had been allowed to return to London again. In later years he turns up at Greenwich, the Isle of Man, and finally in London once more.

No sooner had his father's troubles been straightened out than Dickens was obliged to "buckle-to again and endeavour to get the steam up" on *Nicholas Nickleby*. "If this were to go on long," he told Forster, "I should 'bust' the boiler. I think Mrs. Nickleby's love-scene will come out rather unique." [27] He also had ready for the printer the benefit volume for Mrs. Macrone, now entitled *The Pic-Nic Papers*.[28] Meanwhile, an after-flurry of his tempestuous breach with Bentley had broken out.

"That noblest work of God, in New Burlington Street," was, Dickens wrote Ainsworth, spreading the allegation around town that Forster had incited Dickens to break his contract, and further had villainously "entangled and entrapped the innocent and unsuspecting bookseller" into precipitating the rupture. Dickens appealed to Ainsworth to deny these accusations. He could testify that Forster had in fact refused to intervene in Dickens's behalf. Ainsworth knew that Bentley had ignored Forster in the final negotiations because he had himself told Dickens the proposed terms, and knew that Forster had been astonished to hear them. Forster must be set right *"without the delay of an instant."* "Believe me, Ainsworth," Dickens wrote earnestly, "that for your sake no less than on Forster's account this should be done." Otherwise it would look very much as if, to stand well with Bentley, Ainsworth were suppressing the testimony that would clear

Forster. "I do not mean to hurt or offend you by anything I have said, and . . . I should be truly grieved to find I have done so. But I must speak strongly because I feel strongly. . . ." [29]

The vehemence of this letter and its expressed uncertainty as to exactly how, aside from Bentley's statements, these rumors had started, suggest that Dickens suspected Ainsworth of not being altogether guiltless of conniving at them. And Ainsworth might well have felt no very cordial sentiments at the moment toward Forster, who had recently written a violently adverse review of *Jack Sheppard*.[30] For a while Ainsworth was ruffled, and the services of Barham were called on to smooth his feelings and obtain from him what the good-natured canon called "a plain manly good-tempered statement." [31] The friendship was resumed, but with a certain coolness; some time passed before Dickens wrote to Ainsworth with full cordiality again.

Another annoyance of the spring was an echo of Dickens's troubles with Macrone. During these two years that the dead publisher's affairs had been in Chancery, Thomas Hansard, the printer, had never been paid for setting up the second series of *Sketches by Boz*. It occurred to him that Dickens could be made to foot the bill. He claimed that Dickens had been a half partner in the book, and was consequently liable for the whole. Dickens was hotly indignant. Hansard knew he was no partner; he had acted for Macrone in the sale of the copyright of the *Sketches*, and "not a word said he then of his bill being unpaid or my having been a partner." The whole claim was a lie, and Dickens refused to pay a sixpence. Mitton forwarded this answer to Hansard's attorneys, who evidently advised him to drop the matter.[32]

By this time, in early May, Dickens had removed for the summer to Elm Cottage, Petersham. Here there were the same generous hospitalities and lively pastimes as in the preceding summer at Twickenham. Though in childhood Dickens had been sickly and unskilled in games, he was now ardent at quoits and bowls, pursued battledore and bagatelle with relentless activity, and even leaped the bar against such vigorous athletes as Beard and Maclise, keeping it up long beyond the stage where his competitors had retired panting. He also attended the Petersham races almost daily, and worked himself far harder than the horses.[33]

Maclise was at Petersham a good deal this June, for Chapman and

Hall had commissioned him to paint a portrait of Dickens that was to be engraved by Finden and used as the frontispiece to *Nicholas Nickleby* in its three-volume form that autumn. He was a laborious craftsman and throughout the bright summer days studied Dickens in countless sketches which he destroyed in dissatisfaction. "Maclise has made another face of me," Dickens reported at the end of the month, "which all people say is astonishing." [34] Out of this grew the brilliant "Nickleby" portrait, alive and gleaming as if reflected in a mirror, of which Thackeray said that it was the real "inward Boz" no less than his outward presentment.[35]

George Cruikshank also came down to Elm Cottage, bursting with enthusiasm over a cockney variant he had recently heard of the ancient ballads of Lord Bateman or Beichan. With this discovery he had regaled a dinner of the Antiquarian Society, and was now drawing illustrations for it.[36] Hearing Cruikshank mournfully intone the words of the Turk's daughter to the imprisoned Lord,

> "O in sevin long years, I'll make a wow,
> For sevin long years, and keep it strong,
> That if you'll ved no other voman,
> O I will v-e-ed no other man," [37]

Dickens offered to polish it into an even more solemn absurdity. He told Cruikshank to ask his sister Fanny to take down the music and *"to be sure to mark the shakes and the expression."*[38] And although he kept secret his part in "The Loving Ballad of Lord Bateman," he not only wrote a burlesque introduction and notes, but altered lines and substituted a new last verse. Cruikshank published the ballad with plates that Dickens considered a triumph of comic draftsmanship: "You never," he assured him, "did anything like those etchings— never." [39]

*   *   *   *   *

During the course of the summer, as he got into the home stretch of *Nicholas Nickleby*, he began to think a good deal about his future relations with Chapman and Hall. If Forster could only learn *their* intentions it might prove very helpful. Dickens had received offers, he wrote Forster, to publish anything he wrote at a percentage of the profits and no risks to himself, but he felt well disposed toward his present connection and if they behaved with liberality he would not leave them on any consideration. But they must be primed to "do something handsome, even handsomer perhaps than they dreamt of doing." If they did so, they would find him tractable. Knowing all this, and knowing that when *Barnaby Rudge* was written he would be clear of all engagements, Forster should put before them "the glories of our new project" and make them realize "that if they wish to secure me and perpetuate our connection, now is the time for them to step gallantly forward . . ." [40]

Edward Chapman and William Hall were majestically summoned to Forster's chambers in Lincoln's Inn Fields to hear this ultimatum. They presented themselves there in amenable mood. No doubt anything that Mr. Dickens desired would be entirely satisfactory. Might they not, however, be given a few details about what "the glories of our new project" were? They would also like to have some intimation of what Mr. Dickens would consider a proper financial arrangement to be. [41] The answer to both these humble inquiries came promptly, in a letter bursting with creative vitality, that outlined a scheme with enough ideas for three enterprises.

The new project was a weekly periodical to be sold for threepence a copy, modeled somewhat upon Addison and Steele's *Tatler* and *Spectator*, or Goldsmith's *Bee* (again the influence of the Chatham reading), only far more popular. Mr. Pickwick and Sam would reappear in a little club of interesting characters; there would be "amusing essays on the various foibles of the day"; there would be a set of Arabian Nights tales by Gog and Magog, the Giants in the Guildhall; there would be a series of Savage Chronicles, "something between Gulliver's Travels and the Citizen of the World," satirizing British magistrates by portraying "the administration of justice in some country that never existed." Dickens might even pledge himself to go to Ireland or America, and write a series of descriptive sketches and traditional legends after the plan of Washington Irving's *Alhambra*.

The financial terms he demanded showed that he had not forgotten a single detail of his protracted struggle with Bentley. He must be a proprietor of the paper with a share in its profits. He must be guaranteed a weekly minimum sum for his own contributions. He must choose any other collaborators that *he* saw fit, who were to be paid by the publishers on his order according to a fixed and agreed scale. Or they might pay him for the whole of each number, and he would make whatever arrangement *he* chose for other contributions. None of these payments, however, were deductible from his share of the profits. Finally, if he went abroad, there must be additional provision about his traveling expenses.[42]

If he and his publishers agreed on terms, Dickens was ready to start publication on March 31, 1840. In the course of July calculations were made, proposals offered and rejected, modifications accepted.[43] For the opening numbers at least of the new publication (which was to turn into *Master Humphrey's Clock*) it was agreed that Dickens was to be the sole contributor and that, whatever might be the success of the shorter papers he wrote, he would provide some continued story at the intervals. Phiz would be joined by George Cattermole in providing the illustrations, which were to be woodcuts dropped in the text instead of separate full-page plates.[44]

The financial part of the agreement Dickens and Forster subjected to exacting scrutiny. Chapman and Hall's profit from the sale of the monthly numbers alone, not counting the book sales, of *Pickwick* and *Nickleby* had amounted to £14,000 each. But the new publication, being more expensive, would be less profitable. Unknown to Chapman and Hall, Dickens rigidly checked all their estimates with printers and papermakers, who pronounced them perfectly accurate. The arrangement that was hammered out by July 25th, although not signed until almost the eve of publication in March, represented not merely another startling increase in Dickens's remuneration but a significant alteration in the very nature of his relationship to his publishers.[45]

First, Chapman and Hall gave him an additional £1,500 on *Nicholas Nickleby*. Second, they paid him £50 a week for the new work, which even with a liberal allowance for assistance would net him £38. They paid all expenses of advertising, printing, and illustrating. Third, they paid Dickens half the realized profits on each number, but bore all the loss on an individual number if there were any. Thus, Dickens explained to Mitton, Chapman and Hall would begin getting half profits only after the first 20,000. "If the work went on for two years and were to sell 50,000 (which Bradbury and Evans think certain, but which I confess I do not, though there is a good chance of it) my profits would be between ten and eleven thousand pounds, and theirs five thousand," over and above the £50 per week guaranteed. "I think this very good—as good as could be," he concluded as his vision grew even more enthusiastic, ". . . and as to time, if it continues to be popular it may go on for five years as well as for two." [46]

Clearly Dickens had proved no inept pupil in the school of business experience. Only four years before he had diffidently asked if his employers on the *Chronicle* would not perhaps think him entitled to *some* additional remuneration for the additional contribution of his sketches—and had been more than happy to receive an increase of two guineas a week. Now, with Forster's aid and advice, he made a bargain not merely shrewd but stringent and, as Forster put it, one in which he would rightfully not only always be the gainer but always the greatest gainer. The "hard bargains" that had perpetually lagged behind his furiously mounting sales, the "slavery" "on journey-man terms" "to fill the pockets of others" were a thing of the past. Henceforth he would see to it, and his would be the "iron hand," that he had full control of his work. His earnings would be proportional to his sales, his would be the major share of the profits, and he would have no losses at all.

While these matters were being settled, Dickens went in to London on July 20th to attend a farewell banquet for Macready.[47] Despite Dickens's usual touchiness to adverse criticism, his friendship for the great actor had not been impaired by his discouragement of Dickens's ambitions as a dramatist. The previous year he had written for the *Examiner* a breathless eulogy of Macready's heart-rending performance in *King Lear*,[48] and had been most enthusiastic about the whole course of Macready's management of Covent Garden. The actor's magnificent Shakespearean revivals had won ovations. He had encouraged current drama by producing the works of such living dramatists as Bulwer, Miss Mitford, Browning, and Talfourd. But his period at Covent Garden had been financially disastrous and he had announced his approaching abdication that March at a dinner of the Shakespeare Society that turned into an informal and affectionate testimonial.[49] Dickens, in the chair, had enchanted Mrs. Cowden Clarke, the compiler of a Shakespeare concordance, by his "superlatively handsome face" with its "magnificent eyes," and by the feeling and understanding with which he spoke of the theater.[50] Macready, too, was deeply moved by his eloquent review of the Covent Garden enterprise.

After the last performance under his management on July 16th, there was a formal farewell dinner on the 20th at which Dickens proposed the toast to the late Covent Garden Company. During the summer Macready was Dickens's guest at Petersham; [51] in August Dickens visited the Macreadys at Elstree and served as godfather to their little son Henry.[52] In return he asked Macready to be godfather to the child he was innocently expecting to be "the last and final branch of a genteel small family of three which I am told may be looked for in that auspicious month when Lord Mayors are born and guys prevail." [53]

At the end of August, Dickens took his family down to Broadstairs again, where he rented for a month a little house with a beautiful view of the sea.[54] Here he worked hard at winding up *Nicholas Nickleby*.[55] Seeing Rogers through the window at the Albion, he left a card on him, and later drove with him to Dover when the old poet left for Paris. Harley and his sisters were at Broadstairs, and he walked one night on the terrace with them.[56] But otherwise, there was little to distract him from his task. Fred came down for a visit, and Chapman and Hall brought some sketches of Browne's for *Nickleby* and imparted "intentions as to a Nicklebeian fete," he wrote Forster, "which will make you laugh heartily. . . . It has been blowing great guns for the last three days, and last night (I wish you could have seen it!) there was such a sea! . . . I staggered down to the pier, and, creeping under the lea of a large boat which was high and dry, watched it breaking for nearly an hour. Of course I came back wet through but it was most superb." [57]

At two o'clock in the afternoon of September 20th he wrote the last lines of *Nickleby*, and rushed off immediately with Kate and Fred to Ramsgate to dispatch the copy to the printers, so that proofs would be at Forster's when Dickens got to town. "Thank God," he noted in his diary, "that I have lived to get through it happily." [58] "I have had pretty stiff work," he had told Forster, ". . . and I have taken great pains. The discovery is made, Ralph is dead, the loves have come all right, Tim Linkinwater has proposed, and I have now only to break up Dotheboys and the book together. I am very anxious that you should see this conclusion before it leaves my hands, and I plainly see therefore that I must come to town myself on Saturday if I would not endanger the appearance of the number." [59] They worked till past midnight correcting proofs in Lincoln's Inn Fields, and he took Forster back with him to Broadstairs for a few days before they all returned to London.[60]

The "Nicklebeian fete" came off on Saturday, October 5th, at the Albion in Aldersgate Street.[61] Macready was chairman, Jerdan vice-chairman, and besides Chapman and Hall, and the printers Bradbury and Evans, the guests included Forster, Talfourd, Beard, Maclise, the artist George Cattermole, Harley, red-cheeked little old Tom Hill, the marine and landscape painter Clarkson Stanfield, who also painted scenery at Drury Lane, the well-known artist Sir David Wilkie, and Hablôt Browne, nervously timid, lurking in a corner or trying to hide behind a curtain.[62]

The banquet provided by the hosts on this occasion, Macready thought, was even "*too* splendid."[63] Chapman and Hall, following the tradition of Constable's presentation to Scott of his portrait, made a personal and at the same time magnificent occasion out of formally presenting to Dickens the portrait by Maclise which hung impressively over the table. Wilkie said there had been nothing like Dickens "issuing his novels part by part since Richardson issued his novels volume by volume," adding that as many letters were written Dickens "to implore him not to kill poor Smike as had been sent by young ladies to the author of *Clarissa* to 'save Lovelace's soul alive.' " [64]

In the casual conversation that followed the speeches, Macready asked Dickens about his handsome young brother-in-law, Burnett, from whom Browne had drawn the physical type of Nicholas Nickleby. Was it really so that he intended to quit the stage? Dickens, surprised, said he had heard nothing of it. After making inquiries, he wrote Macready a few days later that on the contrary Burnett was painfully anxious for an engagement. In the same letter he promised that there was a "mighty" copy of *Nickleby* binding for Macready, but not yet ready; "the binder when questioned on the subject, shakes his head mysteriously and says, 'never mind,' which his intimate friends take to be a kind of dark hint that it is to be something uncommon." [65] Macready bestirred himself in Burnett's behalf, and Dickens thanked him when he forwarded the anticipated volumes shortly after. "The red represented my blushes at its gorgeous dress; the gilding all those bright professions which I do *not* make to you; and the book itself, my whole heart for twenty months, which should be yours for so short a term, as you have it always." [66]

The last week in October Dickens spent awaiting the birth of the new baby. "I go to bed every night," he wrote, "to horrid nightmares, concerning a nurse who is not to be found, a doctor with a night-bell that can't wake him, and a cab with a motionless horse and wheels that go round without moving onward." [67] But on the 29th of the month Dickens's third child, Kate Macready, arrived without mishap.[68] Two weeks later Dickens was advising Macready, "Kate progresses splendidly and, with me, sends her best remembrances to Mrs. Macready and all your house." [69]

Beneath the surface, however, Dickens's home life had not been perfectly serene during the last year and a half. From the time of Mary's birth rifts had appeared that were known only to his closest friend. "What is now befalling me," Dickens sadly reminded Forster almost twenty years later, "I have seen steadily coming, ever since the days you remember when Mary was born . . ." [70] In *Oliver Twist* and *Nicholas Nickleby* Mrs. Corney and Miss Petowker hint the possibility of wives turning out very different from what they had seemed before marriage. In *Pickwick* there had been scenes of husbands lashed by the sharper sides of their wives' tongues and subjected to faintings and hysterical outcries. And although these are drawn entirely from lower-class life and handled as farce, the comedy has an acid edge and the theme is a recurrent one in the later novels.

Even toward Kate herself, Dickens's letters now begin to reveal a trace of something that only half disguises itself in jest. In anticipation of his sarcastic impatience later with her physical awkwardness and mishaps, he makes game of her blunders. Remarking to Forster on her garbling someone's name, "By a happy touch of Kate's accustomed cleverness," he writes, "I find now that the name is Mullrainy." [71] And toward her family, too, his attitude is shifting. "The Loving Ballad of Lord Bateman" has a note on critical mothers-in-law: "During the whole of her daughter's courtship, the good old lady had scarcely spoken, save by expressive smiles and looks of approval. But now that her object is gained, and her daughter fast married (as she thinks), she suddenly assumes quite a new tone . . ." "This is an exquisite touch of nature," Dickens comments, "which most married men, whether of noble or plebeian blood, will quickly recognize." [72] Great weight cannot, of course, fairly be given to such stock situations of farce. But, in the light of his later feelings about Mrs. Hogarth, his exploitation of them even at this time is not without significance. And for Kate's uncle and aunt, the Thomsons, "All I can say regarding the visit of Mr. and Mrs. T.," he now writes Forster, "is, damn the impudence of Mr. T." [73] The distinguished Edinburgh family, friends of Burns and of Sir Walter Scott, are no longer so impressive in Dickens's eyes as when he boasted of them to his uncle Thomas Barrow.

These changes in his attitude, of course, reflect the rising distinction of Dickens's own social contacts. And as they widened there were more and more of them in which Kate did not share. It was not merely that many of them, like the Shakespeare Society, the Antiquarian Society, and the dinners of the Literary Fund and the Theatrical Fund, were almost exclusively masculine gatherings, or that Kate was often obliged by pregnancy to remain at home, although doubtless these facts played their part. It was not even that the social position of Lady Blessington and Lady Holland was such that conventional ladies did not go to Gore House and Holland House. Kate was not invited to Mr. Rogers's breakfasts or to great fashionable gatherings of the distinguished because she could not sustain a role in society. She could look wholesome, even pretty, and behave with good breeding, but she hardly sparkled. Even acidulous Jane Carlyle, for all her cleverness, often sat at home while her husband stalked off like a gawky and black-coated Isaiah to some elegant feast at Lady Ashburton's. The wives of famous authors had no social position as such in London's upper circles, nor had they the privilege sometimes granted ladies of great name, of being received despite an insignificance of personal distinction.

Toward other women in society, especially if they were young and pretty, Dickens could not resist an attitude of gallant roguish-raillery. Of a nineteen-year-old niece of Mrs. Touchet, he wrote Ainsworth, "If I were a single man I should hate her husband mortally." [74] And of another unknown lady, in a note to Forster, "Yes—I wrote to that effect to the beautiful Mrs. F, whose eyelashes are in my memory. Would you know this hand? Oh Evins, how misty I am." [75] It was all harmless enough, a kind of high-spirited play-acting, but of dubious reassurance to the wife of a husband whose "magnificent eyes" lingered in other women's memories. Nevertheless, for the time being, the rifts were neither deep nor destructive of true affection and devotion.

* * * * *

Dickens went back to London in the fall determined, at last, to get a start on the much-put-off *Barnaby Rudge*, which at this stage he was still supposed to write for Bentley. Now he would dash it off, and clear the way for his new project. To Cruikshank he proclaimed his intention of going at it "tooth and nail" and having some "MS by the middle of the month for your exclusive eye." [76] A little later, "Thank God, all goes famously," he announced. "I have worked at Barnaby all day, and moreover, seen a beautiful (and reasonable) house in Kent Terrace, where Macready once lived, but larger than his." [77] For with his three children, his redoubled prosperity, and the luxurious scale of living that he had seen in Rogers's little mansion on the Green Park, Dickens had decided that he needed a larger and more magnificent residence than the house in Doughty Street. "Barnaby has suffered so much from the house-hunting," he had presently to tell Forster, "that I mustn't chop today." [78] Then, with a renewal of industry he reported, "All well. Barnaby has reached his tenth page," although promptly thereupon he dawdled again, reading *Christabel* and *Wallenstein* instead of working.[79]

Macready praised his own location in Clarence Terrace, looking directly east into the Regent's Park, as the most healthful in London, and for a while Dickens favored that neighborhood. But in November, just south of the York Gate into the park, he found so exactly what he desired that he was on tenterhooks lest he fail to get it. "A house of great promise (and great premium), 'undeniable' situation and excessive splendour, is in view," he wrote Forster. "Mitton is in treaty, and I am in ecstatic restlessness." [80] This was No. 1 Devonshire Terrace, a handsome structure with a spacious brick-walled garden between it and the New Road.

The entrance, set back a little from the street, had an impressive portico of brick and stone, and curving into the garden were two semicircular bow windows rising the height of the house. Within, a large vestibule opened on a spacious square hall and a stairway curving up to the left, a library on the right with steps descending into the garden, and behind these, splendid with ornamental columns, a dining room that also overlooked the garden and the coach house in the rear. On the floors above were a drawing room and bedrooms and nursery.[81]

By the middle of November Dickens was "in agonies of house-letting, house-taking, title proving and disproving, premium paying, fixture valuing, and other ills too numerous to mention. If you have the heart," he added, "of anything milder than a monster, you will pity me." [82] But he obtained the house on a twelve-year lease, and promptly entered upon a series of magnificent improvements. John Chapman, "a genius in houses," was called in to suggest elaborate installations of water closets.[83] With the image of Rogers's luxury in his mind, and with Forster's sumptuous tastes to encourage him, Dickens replaced deal doors with paneled mahogany, and wooden mantels with carved marble. Doughty Street had been rather meagerly furnished with holdovers from Furnival's Inn and stray pieces Dickens and Mary had picked up one by one from secondhand dealers. At Devonshire Terrace these would do for no more than the attic and upper bedrooms. For the reception rooms and chief bedrooms entire new suites were ordered. There were conferences with drapers and upholsterers, white spring roller blinds were made to measure for the dining-room windows, curtains festooned, deep-piled carpets laid, shining mirrors set in the walls to reflect the lights when Mr. and Mrs. Charles Dickens entertained.[84]

The library, which was also the author's study, was very different from the little back room in which Dickens had written at Doughty Street. When George Lewes, the friend of George Eliot, had visited Dickens there in 1838, that scholarly booklover had seen "nothing but three-volume novels and books of travel, all obviously presentation copies from authors or publishers." Though he had not expected to find Dickens "a bookworm, not even a student," the random collection had been a shock.[85] But the fitted shelves at Devonshire Terrace displayed fine bindings, books of plates, pamphlets, and a representation of the great writers that had been conspicuously absent before. And a few years later, when Tom Hill died, Dickens attended the auction of his old friend's effects, and added rare books from that bibliophile's collection to his own library.[86]

A library was among the visible signs of the place one had achieved in the world, an appurtenance of success like a carriage, and works of art for one's walls. Only in his childhood and in the days of his ambitious striving for self-improvement had Dickens been a voracious reader; and his childhood reading had all been dreaming romance, his later efforts an unsystematic plunging in random directions. Not that they had failed to be of the greatest value; if Dickens was no assiduous scholar, he tore through those books that were valuable to him, almost fiercely soaking up their riches. As Samuel Johnson remarked, there are men who see more in the coach to Hampstead than others do on the grand tour of Europe.[87] The comments Dickens made on those books he found time to read in his busy later career—more numerous and more varied than he is ordinarily given credit for—are always vividly alive, and often sharply penetrating. But it is doubtful that the well-stocked shelves of Devonshire Terrace ever meant to him what that little upstairs room in Chatham had, whence came forth to keep him company Tom Jones, Dr. Primrose, Don Quixote, and Robinson Crusoe in a glorious host.

One part of that Devonshire Terrace library, however, is more richly significant—the table by the garden windows where Quilp and Dick Swiveller, Barnaby and his raven, Pecksniff, Sairey Gamp, Scrooge, Micawber, Peggotty, Betsey Trotwood, and Mr. Dick were magically to rise into life from his pen. There, in a deep, mysterious inner world Dickens lived with his imagination. The rest of the library, and all the house, its dignified entrance, its curving stair, the ornately capitaled columns in its dining room, its walled garden, its coach house with horse and carriage and groom, are a splendid embodiment of ambition. They are the work of a practical will that had made itself as sharp and steely as a knife, the proofs of his success in the outer world Dickens had determined to conquer. Seeing the carriages of the great and famous sweep up to that portico, hearing Dickens devising noisy fun in the garden and nursery for his happy children, who would have suspected that the cheerful house was haunted by a sickly small boy dreaming in a corner of Rochester Castle, by an unhappy child-waif creeping from Bayham Street to the blacking warehouse?

PART FOUR

Deeper Cast

1839–1841

CHAPTER ONE

The Thieves' Den and the World

CRITICISM: *Oliver Twist* and *Nicholas Nickleby*

THE three novels with which Dickens had now established his literary eminence all glow with his characteristic endowments. They are bursting with vitality. *Pickwick Papers* had swiftly ripened to an affectionate hilarity that made Dickens a master of luminous humor unexampled by any writer since Shakespeare. *Oliver Twist* blazes with a sulphurous melodrama in which horror is fused with angry pathos. *Nicholas Nickleby* mingles the indignation of *Oliver* with the loose, sprawling comedy of *Pickwick*. But their differences are only the flashing facets of a many-sided brilliance. For deep in all three there already runs the vein of social criticism that was to become dominant in Dickens's entire career. They share a unity of viewpoint and of underlying purpose that makes them logically related in the great unfolding of Dickens's powers.

From the sunny landscape of *Pickwick*, no more than dappled with shadow, *Oliver Twist* plunges into a confined world of darkness, an oppressive, lurid intensity from the workhouse to the criminal slum and the jail. In its heart lurks the smoky and fetid thieves' kitchen where the Artful Dodger leers and Fagin grins in mirth through the greasy air. Almost all its interiors are bleak and gloomy: the workhouse where half-starved boys whimper with hunger in the bare stone hall and scrawny hags hang over the beds of the dying, the peep-holed back room of the Three Cripples, the ruined warehouse where Monks terrifies Bumble by night. Even when Oliver rests asleep at Mrs. Maylie's, just beyond the window loom Fagin and Monks, darkening the sunlight like two monstrous demons. The very outdoors huddles under a heavy sky of evil. Nancy lurks in black shadow on the slimy steps of

London Bridge, Sikes wanders in horror-haunted flight away from and back to the city, the waving torches glimmer on the mud of Folly Ditch while the murderer clambers over the tiles of the barricaded house. And the end narrows in relentlessly with Fagin cowered in the condemned cell, gnawing his nails and glaring at the close wall.

This progression from the suffering of gaunt and beaten children to the jeering Dodger and the ferocious Sikes and Fagin, foul with evil, is not, of course, merely a piece of melodramatic contrivance. For it was Dickens's bitter conviction that the cold-hearted cruelty that treated pauperism as a crime brought forth its dreadful harvest of criminality and vice. He did not deny the evils of the old system of the dole, nor by any means advocate a return to it. But the intended reform of the new Poor Law, far from accomplishing its purpose, either broke or brutalized the spirit of its victims. If the sturdy pauper gave a wide berth to the workhouse bastille, how often did he drift to the stews of Whitechapel and Saffron Hill? For one Oliver Twist how many Noah Claypoles were there, who gravitated inevitably from the charity school, that taught only idleness and cringing, to the pickpocket school and the training ground for spies and burglars that taught all too well?

During the forty years preceding the enactment of the new Poor Law of 1834 the percentage of paupers had doubled. By the "Speenhamland Act" of 1795 the farm laborer's wages had been fixed at an immovable figure that ignored the rising cost of living and denied him the benefit of bargaining for his services. Instead, he received from the parish for himself and each mouth he had to feed a weekly pittance that varied with the price of a loaf of bread. Meanwhile the landlords were trebling their rents, and agricultural labor, supported by home relief, had been reduced to a state of ragged and hollow-cheeked indigence on the verge of starvation.[1]

Pauperism became, as G. M. Trevelyan says, "the shameless rule instead of the shameful exception." [2] There was no incentive to industry or saving. No matter what they did, a large proportion of laborers were condemned to pauperism for life. And huge families of children were no longer a liability; they even added a trifle to their parents' miserable scale of subsistence. A resulting tide of population eddied into the towns to add its competition to the pool of unemployed factory workers; industrial labor became hardly better off than farm labor. The entire system thus successfully kept wages down, but it also pauperized the laboring class and shattered its self-respect. Under such a dole, shiftlessness was easier and even more profitable for many than industry and personal pride.

The new Poor Law of 1834 was designed to remedy these evils. Its drastic surgery destroyed all encouragement to live in the lap of idleness and pauperism. There was no dole to supplement low wages. The unemployed laborer was no longer allowed to subsist with his family on an allowance from the parish; his home was ruthlessly broken up, father, mother, children, separated and consigned to the workhouse. And the workhouse life and its rations were deliberately made grimmer than the very poorest subsistence he could earn by outside work.[3] For, in addition to discouraging pauperism, economy also was a motive in the new regulations; within three years the cost of poor relief diminished by 36 per cent.[4]

In theory the new Poor Law distinguished between the helpless and the man or woman who could work but wouldn't. In practice, however, it mingled the idler, tramp, drunkard, and prostitute in the same workhouse with the aged, ill, and infirm, and with the foundling children. The children suffered worst of all. Badly educated or left entirely illiterate, branded with the workhouse stigma, associating with men and women of doubtful character, apprenticed at an early age to get them off the rates as quickly as possible—perhaps as chimney sweeps under some master like the Gamfield of *Oliver Twist*—the parish boys were almost predictably doomed to a later career indistinguishable from that which Oliver so narrowly escaped.[5]

Oliver was born under the old Poor Law. But his infancy in the pauper baby farm, "where twenty or thirty other juvenile offenders against the poor-laws rolled about on the floor all day, without the inconvenience of too much food or too much clothing," [6] could equally well have been under the new dispensation. And when, at the age of nine, Oliver returned to the workhouse to be educated by picking oakum from six in the morning on,[7] the Poor Board had the reformed system in full swing. "The members of this Board," Dickens writes, "were very sage, deep, philosophical men; and when they came to turn their attention to the workhouse, they found out at once, what ordinary folks would never have discovered—the poor people liked it! It was a regular place of public entertainment for the poorer classes; a tavern where there was nothing to pay; a public breakfast, dinner, tea, and supper all the year round, a brick and mortar elysium, where it was all play and no work. 'Oho!' said the Board, looking very knowing; 'we are the fellows to set this to rights; we'll stop it all, in no time.' So they established the rule, that all the poor people should have the alternative (for they would compel nobody, not they), of being starved by a gradual process in the house, or by a quick one out of it." [8]

Dickens's "three meals of thin gruel a day, with an onion twice a week, and half a roll on Sunday," [9] was, of course, an exaggeration, as Humphry House points out. But not a gross one, as he goes on to show by quoting the approved daily ration for an able-bodied man: 12 ounces of bread, 1½ pints of gruel, 5 ounces of cooked meat, ½ pound of potatoes, and 1½ pints of broth. Women and children over nine received slightly less; children under nine were fed "at discretion." "It is fairly plain," House adds, "which way discretion would veer." [10]

These facts explain why the newly apprenticed Oliver's eyes "glistened at the mention of meat" when some scraps that had been put by for the dog were placed before him. "I wish," Dickens bursts out bitterly, "some well-fed philosopher, whose meat and drink turn to gall within him" ("philosopher" is always Dickens's name for the political economist), "whose blood is ice, whose heart is iron; could have seen Oliver Twist clutching at the dainty viands that the dog had neglected. I wish he could have witnessed the horrible avidity with which Oliver tore the bits asunder with all the ferocity of famine. There is only one thing I should like better, and that would be to see the philosopher making the same sort of meal himself, with the same relish." [11]

In the long run, no doubt, the changed order enabled wages to find a natural level and helped to end that artificial depression of earnings that had degraded the working classes. And in a painfully longer run it took the administration of the workhouses out of the hands of people like Bumble, who were holdovers of the days of outdoor relief. But the early reports of the Poor Law Commissioners are severe in their strictures upon unsuitable officers retained from the old system. The typical fault of the old, however, was wasteful and dirty feeding, not underfeeding, whereas it was the calculated intention of the reform to make the diet sparse.[12] And it is specifically the harshness and the starvation regimen of the new that Dickens lashes with all his fury. Bumble illustrates, no doubt, the stupidity of employing the old officers for its administration; but Mrs. Corney symbolizes the frigid brutality of an economic system that condemned the ill, the aged, and helpless children to misery in the name of destroying temptations to idleness.

It is noteworthy that Bumble has some human sympathy in him, and that Mrs. Corney has none. When Oliver weeps in heartbroken loneliness, Bumble is obliged to clear his throat huskily and pretend to a "troublesome cough." [13] On another occasion he says, not unkindly, "don't cry into your gruel; that's a very foolish action, Oliver." "It certainly was," Dickens comments, "for there was quite enough water in it already." [14] But there is never a faltering in the fierce cruelty of Mrs. Corney bullying her starved and cringing victims while the workhouse crones titter in sycophantic delight; "in them, as in many future instances," George Gissing remarks, "Dickens draws strictly from his observation." [15]

He was no less accurate in delineating the foul areas of St. Giles and Saffron Hill and the slums of Whitechapel, Rotherhithe, and Bethnal Green. With hideous realism he painted the squalid shops of Field Lane flaunting the silk handkerchiefs bought from pickpockets, the piles of old iron and bones and stolen, fusty clothes rusting and rotting in grimy heaps. He plunged into tortuous alleys deep in churned-up mud, into dark hallways reeking with odors of decay, rooms blackened with dirt and soot, cellars splotched with green damp. Vividly he revealed the streets of blighted houses, the screaming children, the villainous faces, the drunken men and women wallowing in filth, although even he could not bring himself to say plainly that the filth consisted of offal and the emptyings of chamberpots and privies.

What these places were like was known to those familiar with government reports and the Reports of the Society for the Suppression of Mendicity. For most people, however, they were merely vague unrealities or "mysteriously wicked regions" haunted by thieves, vagrants, and prostitutes, where cholera festered in dirt and vice.[16] But to his readers Dickens gave them a dreadful and concrete reality. Even so, many denied that they could possibly be true; as late as 1850 there were public men who claimed that Jacob's Island was—what it emphatically was not—simply a figment of Dickens's imagination.[17]

His primary objective, in fact, was fidelity to the criminal slum world he was depicting. He would have nothing to do with romanticizing poverty into the picturesque, he would have none of the gallant bandits of romance, gay in crimson coat and lace ruffles, cantering bravely over moonlit heaths or trolling a song with sparkling glass held high, surrounded by a glamorous circle of elegant harlots. Instead, he would show the fatal ease with which a workhouse orphan like Oliver, running away from the harsh master to whom he was apprenticed, might fall into the clutches of a gang of lawbreakers and be subjected to their corrupting influence. That miserable reality Dickens painted in all its deformity—the villainous receiver of stolen goods, the brutal robber and his rum-drinking trull, the ruffian band of boys being trained in crime, with the "great, black, ghastly gallows" always stretching up behind them. He was not writing, Dickens said, for those delicate-minded readers who could not bear to hear the truth about crime when it appeared in fustian jacket and dirty stockings, and for them he would not abate one hole in the Dodger's coat or one scrap of curlpaper in Nancy's disheveled hair.[18]

But, despite this note of spirited defiance, Dickens's method was not that of an absolutely uncompromising naturalism. Although Oliver has been brought up in a workhouse, nothing in his vocabulary and accent seems to mark his vulgar background. Dickens deliberately refused to "offend the ear"[19] by reporting all the oaths and indecencies that fell from the lips of Sikes and Fagin. He would make it clear that Nancy was a burglar's drab, but he would not insist on the physical details of their relationship, nor would he suggest the sex-drenched atmosphere in which a gang of young criminals like the Dodger and Charley Bates would live.

With the fundamental truth of the facts he was portraying, of course, Dickens never tampered, and Fagin's school for young pickpockets was drawn from observed reality. An autobiographical narrative published later in the century, *Sixty Years of Waifdom*, describes a woman in Whitechapel training boys to sneak a purse from her pocket without tinkling a bell attached to it, and tells of a thieves' tutor who claimed to have taught no fewer than five hundred in twenty years.[20] Even the Dodger's farcical scene in the police court is not fan-

George Cruikshank

Oliver's reception by Fagin and the boys

tastically exaggerated. A dozen years after the appearance of *Oliver Twist*, Dickens and Mark Lemon were walking in the Edgware Road when the latter caught a pickpocket feeling in his coat; their captive accused them in court of being "swell mob-men" and Dickens of being a "fence" who had been sentenced to jail.[21] And as accurately based on observation as the cruelty of Mrs. Corney are the sodden ferocity of Sikes and Fagin's readiness to betray his human tools to the gallows after they have outlived their usefulness. But the generalizing epithets in which Dickens described these figures skulking through "cold, wet shelterless midnight streets" and sprawling in "foul and drowsy dens" [22] where vice lay closely packed, softened and blurred the loathsomest details of dirt and stench.

For it was Dickens's aim not to turn the stomach but to move the heart. So motivated, he always had his eye on how much his readers could stand. If they would turn away in revulsion from the picture of maggoty corpses of dead cats rotting in piles of ordure in the streets, and flies clustered on the festering eyelids of babies, Dickens would not forfeit their attention by thrusting these physical horrors before them. The evil that was being done to the spirits of human beings was more important even than the hideousness and disease in which their bodies were steeped, dreadfully though the two were linked. He had rather, he said, "lead to the unavoidable inference" that a world existed "of the most debased and vicious kind, than to prove it elaborately by words and deeds." [23]

It enhanced rather than detracted from his purpose that he was able to introduce a bitter and pitiful comedy into the workhouse scenes and endow Fagin with a sinister hilarity. His strategy was always to fuse drama, pathos, and laughter with a realism pleading for humane feeling, not to evoke mere nauseated recoil. Of the essential facts he was determined to reveal he would sacrifice not one iota; and these would be more than sufficient to arouse the emotions and stir indignation.

All these details, however, are woven into a luridly melodramatic plot that poses—in the very process of overcoming them—undeniable problems of belief for the reader. The mystery of Oliver's birth is a complex rigmarole involving the rightful inheritance of an estate and destroyed proofs of identity. Since the illegitimate Oliver will obtain his father's bequest only if his name throughout his minority remains unstained by any act "of dishonour, meanness, cowardice, or wrong," [23a] his evil half-brother Monks bribes Fagin to seduce him into crime. (It is significant of Dickens's sympathies with the downtrodden, however, that he reverses the conventional melodramatic formula by making the *legitimate* Monks the vicious one and the bastard Oliver a child whose goodness even the most degraded surroundings have not destroyed.) The cloak-and-lantern villainy of Monks, skulking up dark stairs and slinking to conspiratorial meetings in deserted mills by night, reeks of the stage. No less theatrical are the two chances that bring Oliver, even before his identity is discovered, first under the protection of his father's old friend Mr. Brownlow, and second into the home of his mother's sister, Rose Maylie. Harry Maylie is cut out of the most heroic pasteboard, and Rose Maylie drips a syrupy sweetness transcending patience. That even so unreal a scoundrel as Monks should be foiled by the unworldly Brownlow staggers critical faith no less than the coincidences that prove Oliver to be Rose's nephew and the child of Brownlow's dead friend.

Such flaws in the very reality Dickens has invoked are not to be defended. And yet two things may be said about them. First, that Dickens's own undeviating faith in what he has imagined exerts a magical spell in which we hardly observe the implausibility of these melodramatic embroideries. Second, that the sheer power and speed of the story compel us to intense emotional participation. We believe partly because we want to believe and partly because its rapid intensity gives us no time to stop. Whatever skeptical reservations we may feel about the contrived plot arise only after the story is ended and the light of everyday has melted its fierce, dark hypnosis.

No doubt this is an art inferior to that of *Pickwick*, which is frankly a comic fairy tale with a hero who cannot be destroyed by the dragons of reality. But in *Oliver Twist*, evil men and hideous institutions have a genuine power to harm, and Oliver may really be injured. Its canons of verisimilitude are therefore somewhat different from those that were appropriate to the Pickwick world. Despite the artificiality of its complicated intrigue, however, *Oliver* violates those standards in no significant way. It is guilty of no underlying unreality in the conception of its main characters and no falsification of its criminal world.

So understood, the plot and the stage language are simply the conventions through which Dickens conveys reality. Throughout he knows and insistently emphasizes the fact that even the vilest environment cannot utterly obliterate or corrupt the principle of good in its victims. And if Oliver talks rather more like a little gentleman than is altogether plausible, he has been so drawn that it is not unbelievable to see in him that principle "surviving every adverse circumstance and triumphant at last." [24] And if Nancy's language seems somewhat unnaturally to change from that of the bedraggled whore she is when her sympathies have been aroused by the frail child who has been thrown in her way, the conflict between her devotion to Sikes and her pity for Oliver is wholly convincing. "It is emphatically," Dickens wrote, "God's truth, for it is the truth He leaves in such depraved and miserable breasts; the hope yet lingering behind; the last fair drop of water at the bottom of the dried-up weed-choked well." [25] No less true is Oliver's struggling resistance to the pollutions by which the Dodger is already indelibly stained. It is the wonder but the truth of humanity that it *does* so struggle.

No more are Sikes and merry old Fagin and the cynically high-spirited Dodger fictional distortions. Their corruption sharply portrays the influence of evil surroundings on callous and insensible natures. A masterly vividness bathes the burly thief and the sinister fence. Sikes's bullying speech and sodden silences, his slouching gait, his ferocious hand and murderous rages, give him a physical reality as fiercely menacing as his brutal character. Still more loathsomely memorable is Fagin, now crouching before the fire and glancing over his shoulder with swift and craven suspicion, now dropping soft hints or wheedling hypocritical endearments, again laughing or rushing from the room with a howl of terror. Fagin is one of those nightmare images, often recurrent in his creator's mind, that Dickens regarded with a loathing so fascinated as to be half horrible enjoyment: an image of hilarious evil delighted in cunning self-applause. Daniel Quilp, the deformed dwarf of *The Old Curiosity Shop*, in whom malice boils up into an atrocious playfulness, is a grotesque mutation of the image. Still another this time a fantastic caricature of false gentility—is Mr. Chester, in *Barnaby Rudge*, consistently appreciating his own duplicity.

These figures of brute ferocity and insidious evil embody all the dreadful and lurid power of the book. The grinning knavery of Fagin and the violence of Sikes continually threaten collision. In the end Fagin incites Sikes to the fury that sends him rushing off to murder Nancy and precipitates the book into the wild race of its culminating horrors. "You won't be—too—violent, Bill?" the old villain whispers.[26] Then follow the pistol beaten into the bloody face, the reflection of the pool of gore quivering on the ceiling, the ghastly flight, the peddler's chant that he can remove "pitch-stains, mud-stains, blood-stains," Sikes's desperate escape and delirious wandering.[27]

All this feverish melodrama Dickens conveys with a sharp and sensitive psychological penetration, sometimes startling in its revelation. Sikes tries in vain either to escape or to face the haunting figure always close behind him. "If he shut out the sight, there came the room with every well-known object—some, indeed, that he would have forgotten, if he had gone over its contents from memory—each in its accustomed place." [28] Such a passage shows that Proust was not the first novelist to be aware of the machinery of unwilled memory.

From this wild fury, the closing scenes of Fagin's trial and last night alive plunge us with intensified force into that atmosphere of dark repressive confinement that has dominated the book. All the eyes of the courtroom glaring down hotly upon the villainous old man, his tense listening, his mind wandering over trivia like a snapped pencil point and the broken iron spike before him even while he burns with the terror of death, his beating his hands raw against the door of his cell, his unwashed flesh crackling with fever, the hollow boom of the iron bell reverberating within those narrow walls—all strike the same note. With the arrival of the jailor, speaking his name, comes a detail of extraordinary power: "'That's me!' cried Fagin, falling instantly into the attitude of listening he had assumed upon his trial. 'An old man, my Lord; a very old, old man!'" [29] And then the scene speeds on to its end, Fagin's face retaining no human expression but rage and terror while he struggles with the attendants and sends up cry after cry.

*   *   *   *   *

From this world of crowded evil *Nicholas Nickleby* escapes into the bright outer air again. But not entirely; it mingles the sunlight of *Pickwick* with the darkness of *Oliver*. Cheats and rascality and thievery are forever forcing themselves into its jubilant high spirits: Mr. Gregsbury, the slippery M.P., the United Metropolitan Improved Hot Muffin and Crumpet Baking and Punctual Delivery Company, the mean and penny-pinching Gride, the dissolute Sir Mulberry Hawk and his toadies Pluck and Pyke. Under the bleak winter skies of Yorkshire there is the dungeon squalor of Dotheboys Hall, and in Lambeth the mean inn where Squeers crouches burning papers with Peg Sliderskew. In the glittering opulence of the Park Lane hotel Sir Mulberry drinks feverishly with his cronies; in the dark street without he furiously slashes at Nicholas with his whip. And overhead in Ralph Nickleby's house in Golden Square the gloomy garret with the iron hook in the ceiling awaits him while the black cloud that Ralph sees in the stormy heavens pursues him to his doom.

But in contrast to these scenes of melodrama and satire, *Nicholas Nickleby* opens also into a wide realm of genial warmth and high-hearted laughter hardly less glorious than that of *Pickwick*. Mr. Mantalini cajoles his wife with the most improbable endearments ever invented by the mind of man: "my essential juice of pine-apple"; "She who coils her fascinations round me like a pure and angelic rattle-snake." [30] Mr. Lillyvick remembers the romantic details of Mrs. Kenwigs's courtship: "'Mother,' she says, 'I love him!' 'What do I hear?' cries her mother; and instantly falls into strong conwulsions." [31] A little later, Mr. Lillyvick is gloomily dissatisfied to learn that *"l'eau"* is the French for "water." "Lo, eh? I don't think anything of that language—nothing at all." [32] At Portsmouth we meet the diminutive but somewhat withered child actress, the Infant Phenomenon, and the impudent Mr. Folair, and Miss Snevellicci, with her delightful skipping gait and charming flirtatious confusions, and the jealous Mr. Lenville, so disastrously surprised by the outcome of his proposal to pull Nicholas's nose before the company. With Mrs. Nickleby and Kate we see cucumbers and vegetable marrows showered over the wall by the enamored old gentleman in the gray-woolen stockings. And at the Saracen's Head we hear honest John Browdie roaring and choking and getting black in the face with laughter. Riotous farce and broad comedy tumble after each other with breathless hilarity.

Nicholas Nickleby thus fuses the inexhaustible laughter of *Pickwick* with the somber themes of *Oliver Twist*. The tattered clothing and meager diet of Dotheboys Hall, its cold and brutality and beatings, its basin of brimstone and treacle, reveal in colors almost as dark as *Oliver Twist* all that neglect and mistreatment and persecution of children against which Dickens had ranged his powers. Smike, with his brains literally battered into feebleness by ill-usage, is the lachrymose symbol of victimized childhood. Ralph Nickleby, Gregsbury, the Wittiterleys, and Sir Mulberry Hawk caricature the forces of business greed, political chicanery, and social snobbery that Dickens had seen and struggled against in his career as solicitor's clerk, shorthand writer, Parliamentary reporter, and rising young author. It is bursting through the indignation of these serious themes that there surges the Pickwickian spirit, effervescent, swirling and pirouetting in sheer irresponsible humor and good humor. On its tide come thronging Mrs. Nickleby, Miss La Creevy, Newman Noggs, the Kenwigses, John Browdie, the Mantalinis, Vincent Crummles and his theatrical troupe, Fanny Squeers, and all the rest of that grotesque and glorious company.

Nickleby, however, lacks the essential unity and coherence that blankets all of *Oliver* with its heavy evil—evil that is no melodramatic embroidery on the workhouse and slum themes, but part of the very canvas. In *Nickleby*, on the other hand, the diverse threads are loosely woven together, its varied scenes and crowds of characters related to each other in a sprawling picaresque improvisation in the eighteenth-century tradition of *Tom Jones* and *Roderick Random*. And yet, no more than *Tom Jones*, is the story really lacking in structure. It opens when the indigent widow, Mrs. Nickleby, arrives in London with her children, the youthful Nicholas and Kate, to seek the aid of her husband's brother Ralph. He has no intention of parting with a penny more than he can help, but he sees a chance to use Kate as a decoy with the wastrels to whom he lends money. His cynical exploitation of the charms of his pretty niece while her brother Nicholas is got out of the way, his later machinations against the heiress Madeline Bray, and Nicholas's return to foil these schemes, provide a plot almost as involved as that of *Oliver Twist*. For plot purposes, however, it hardly matters *where* Nicholas is; his experiences as a teacher in Yorkshire with Squeers and as an actor in Portsmouth with Vincent Crummles are purely arbitrary. Dotheboys Hall gives Dickens the chance to expose the schools, but Nicholas's life would have been little different had he never seen the place. And Kate might as well have been a seamstress or a governess as a milliner at Mme. Mantalini's and a companion to Mrs. Wittiterley.

But the triumphant achievement of the book is that these gratuitous interludes start into a life so far exceeding their structural importance as to represent, in fact, *Nicholas Nickleby*'s most vivid claim upon our memories. The reason that people recall its complications of intrigue as wandering and more formless than they are, is that long after they have forgotten the reason why Ralph Nickleby hangs himself and forgotten the very existence of that pale and tedious martyr Madeline Bray, they cannot forget Ralph fleeing before the avenging cloud and a host of other scenes and characters whose relationship to the plot has been extinguished by their vividness.

For it is the details that take possession of the story, dominate the story, are the story. What would be mere rococo embellishment in

Theatrical emotion of Mr. Vincent Crummles

another novel becomes the very *raison d'être* of this. No one except a
child reads *Nicholas Nickleby* to find out if the wicked uncle is defeated: Nicholas is the hero and Kate the heroine—both endowed with
pretty much the qualities such figures should have, and no more than
real enough to sustain their roles; we know that all will come well in
the end. We are worried by no desperate need for Nicholas to rush
back to London and rescue Kate. But we do feel a desperate need for
Crummles to say farewell with a stage embrace, laying his chin on
Nicholas's shoulder and looking over it. There is no pressing need to

hasten the cluster of betrothals in the last chapter; there is a pressing need for Mrs. Nickleby to gabble wanderingly about the Prince Regent's legs and Miss Biffin's toes and then accuse her bewildered listeners of woolly-mindedness. Everywhere the individual scenes are vibrant with this anarchistic vitality.

And what a wealth they spread before us! Nicholas reflecting on the apelike appearance of Squeers: "He is an odd-looking man. What of that? Porson was an odd-looking man, and so was Doctor Johnson; all these bookworms are." [33] Squeers smacking his lips over the watered-down milk and saying, "Ah! Here's richness!" [34] Fanny Squeers writing of Nicholas's assault on her father that "the two forms are steeped in his Goar," and that her mother's comb was driven "several inches into her head. A very little more and it must have entered her brain." [35] Mr. Mantalini praising his wife's "graceful outline" and depreciating the society ladies he had fascinated: "The two countesses had no outlines at all, and the dowager's was a demd outline." [36] All the actresses helping Mrs. Lillyvick put down her husband while Mr. Snevellicci kisses them one by one. Mr. Lenville inserting a dance into a drama of mother and child thrust out into the streets: " 'Do you remember,' " the distressed lady will say, " 'that dance, my honest friend, which in happier days you practised with this sweet angel? It never failed to raise my spirits then. Oh, let me see it once again before I die!' There it is—cue for the band, *before I die*—and off they go." [37] The fertility of invention and the unflagging pace with which these episodes stream from Dickens's pen are a triumph of frolicsome creation.

He displays, too, a striking ingenuity in distinguishing between the theatricality of his actors and actresses and that of his serious characters. Although they all move in an atmosphere of the stage, the players are fundamentally histrionic in a way that the others are not. Mr. Crummles's and Miss Snevellicci's very feelings are steeped in the conventions of the boards; they see reality in terms of stylized sentimental melodrama. But though Kate and Nicholas and Ralph often speak an artificial stage idiom, the springs of their conduct are not false to reality. If Kate and Nicholas are insufficient as characters (Ralph is more subtly conceived), it is not because they violate belief, but because they seldom enlarge it beyond the area of the expected. They embody no subtle revelations in human behavior, no psychological surprises.

Like all good melodrama, however, they are not unreal; they are an enhanced version of an elementary reality.

Even the well-born blackguard Sir Mulberry Hawk, in his brutal, sullen debauchery, has this kind of truth, limited and flamboyant but not basically false. Sneering at Ralph Nickleby and yet deep in his financial toils, accepting his hospitality and striving furiously to seduce his niece, Sir Mulberry is nevertheless something more than pure grotesque. Part Mephistopheles, part cad, he flatters his own vanity by enacting a role picturesquely satanic. He glories in his own image as one of brilliant evil; he never sees himself as mean and vulgar. And with a chivalry of hatred, Dickens gives him a grandiose viciousness that Thackeray would never use in painting the Honorable Frederic Deuceace or Rawdon Crawley. Undeniably, there is a cutting truth to Thackeray's portrayals. But though his sordid and stupid gamblers, fleecing petty tradesmen and then fleeing to the Continent, are true, they are no truer than Dickens's swaggering scoundrels. Thackeray reveals the man by his outward actions; Dickens distorts the actions into a surrealist projection of their emotional reality.

The rendering of Ralph Nickleby mirrors more complex depths with a penetration to which commentators have not done full justice. Fundamentally Ralph is neither businessman nor miser; he is a man goaded by a suppressed feeling of self-betrayal into still bitterer assertions of power. For a little more money he could have a clerk twice as useful as Newman Noggs, but Ralph wants someone he can bully and despise. He is grasping, not scrimping; his drawing room dazzles the eyes with mirrors and splendid furniture. If it were only money he desired, he might be primarily a speculator or an entrepreneur, not a usurer. But what Ralph wants is to sneer at his victims even as he entices them into his clutches, to be hard, cutting, and sarcastic, to grind them down, to have them beg and be refused.

These are the marks of a man bolstering up his ego with brutality and deeply gnawed by unadmitted hatred for himself. And they explain why Ralph hates Nicholas with a galling sense of humiliation that he furiously strives to deny. In Nicholas's face he sees the face of the dead brother whom he once loved, in Nicholas's generous heart and proud integrity virtues that he only pretends to himself to despise. Within him struggle vague intimations that he has strangled all the better potentialities he once possessed, but he grinds the awareness down beneath his will. For Kate, a helpless girl who presents no challenge to his pride, he occasionally feels a faint pity, but Nicholas's haughty contempt fills him with vindictive and guilty fury. Exposing his niece to seduction and outrage, though with recurrent qualms, fiercely shaken off, deep in his twisted heart he hates himself and his libertine clients.

Under these circumstances, his need to humble Nicholas becomes a maniacal obsession, and his inability to do so, the downfall of all his schemes at Nicholas's hand, a frustration that drives him beyond the edge of sanity. To see him as only a sharp moneygrubber in whom it would be ridiculous to be motivated by revengeful feelings out of which he could not make a farthing is to overlook the consistent strokes that define his real character. In his final torment of intolerable defeat, crude as is the machinery of dupes, wastrels, forced marriages, and stolen wills in which he appears, Ralph himself is no unreality but a powerful sketch touching depths of profound and almost Dostoevskian drama.

There is little, however, to be said for the Cheeryble brothers, those philanthropic merchants modeled upon the Grant brothers of Manchester. They are merely a crude device for giving Nicholas a position in London and providing him with a prosperous future. In his preface Dickens noted that they were real people and "that their liberal charity, their singleness of heart, their noble nature, and their unbounded benevolence, are no creations of the Author's brain." [38] But it is not only impossible to believe that the overgrown elderly babies whom Dickens presented as the Cheerybles could ever have been successful in business; to most modern readers they are thoroughly tiresome in their hand-rubbing, their unctuous smiles, their childlike benevolent glee. Indeed, to some they are even nauseating: two "gruesome old Peter Pans," Aldous Huxley calls them.[39] And even in Victorian England there were dissenters to their charitable bullying. It was "quite as probable," said *Fraser's Magazine*, that Ralph Nickleby "would have been foiled by Lord Verisopht or Smike, as by a couple of such unredeemed and irredeemable old idiots" as "these pot-bellied Sir Charles Grandisons of the ledger and daybook." [40]

Of the success of the Dotheboys Hall scenes, however, out of which the book had its inception, there can be no possible doubt. Though they fill less than one-tenth of the entire narrative, they are painted in colors that unforgettably mingle the most painful sufferings with a caustic and searing comedy. But the absurdity of the Squeers family is more than a mere comic antidote to the revelations of cruelty. Both aspects of the handling fuse into a singleness of effect essential for Dickens's purpose: the satiric display of Squeers's ignorance deflates his educational pretensions as sharply as the portrayal of his brutality destroys all his claims of fitness for the care of children.

There can be no doubt, though, that the comedy also serves to make the emotional atmosphere more bearable, and that here, as in *Oliver*, Dickens displays an extraordinary skill in rendering dreadful material without either falsifying it or alienating the reader. "One paragraph, admirably written," notes George Gissing, "puts before us the picture in all its hideousness; in the next we read, 'And yet this scene, painful as it was, had its grotesque features, which, in a less interested observer than Nicholas, might have provoked a smile.' " [41] And thereafter Dickens brilliantly alternates between horror and laughter. The paragraph to which Gissing refers portrays the victims of that harsh schoolroom:

"Pale and haggard faces, lank and bony figures, children with the countenances of old men, deformities with irons upon their bony limbs, boys of stunted growth, and others whose long meagre legs would hardly bear their stooping bodies, crowded on the view together; there were the bleared eye, the hare lip, the crooked foot, and every ugliness or distortion that told of unnatural aversion conceived by parents for their offspring, or of young lives which, from the earliest dawn of infancy had been one horrible endurance of cruelty and neglect. There were little faces which should have been handsome, darkened with the scowl of sullen, dogged suffering; there was childhood with the light of its eye quenched, its beauty gone, and its helplessness alone remaining; there were vicious-faced boys, brooding with leaden eyes, like malefactors in a jail; and there were young creatures on whom the sins of their frail parents had descended, weeping even for the mercenary nurses they had known, and lonesome even in their loneliness." [42]

But hard upon this follows "the first class in English spelling and philosophy." "C-l-e-a-n, clean," Squeers explains his system, "verb active, to make bright, to scour. W-i-n, win, d-e-r, der, winder, a casement. When the boy knows this out of book, he goes and does it."

After spelling "b-o-t, bot, t-i-n, tin, bottin, n-e-y, ney, bottiney," the boy goes out and weeds the garden. "A horse is a quadruped, and quadruped's Latin for beast, as everybody that's gone through the grammar knows"; and "As you're perfect in that," Squeers adds to an other boy, "go and look after *my* horse, and rub him down well, or I'll rub you down." [43]

Nor is Squeers's ignorance only a comic exaggeration. As late as 1851, 2½ per cent of the schoolmasters and mistresses in private schools signed their census returns with a mark.[44] As for Squeers's cruelty, the preface to *Nicholas Nickleby* points out "that there are upon record trials at law in which damages have been sought as a poor recompense for lasting agonies and disfigurements inflicted upon children by the treatment of the master in these places, involving such offensive and foul details of neglect, cruelty, and disease, as no writer of fiction would have the boldness to imagine." [45]

Dickens never claimed, in fact, to be a pioneer who ferreted out hidden evils. The abuses he exposed had been heard of by thousands. It was part of his strength that what he told his readers they already knew to be true.[46] His originality did not lie in the fact that his moral and social themes were unfamiliar, but that he made paupers, chimney sweeps, maltreated school children, seamstresses and milliners' assistants, thieves, and pickpockets, not pallid abstractions in a statistical report or empty names in news items, but living human beings. His power streamed from the intensity with which he demanded the sympathies of his readers for the emotions and sufferings of actual people. He attacked evils not because they were wrong economics or wrong politics, but simply because they were wrong.[47] And *Oliver Twist* and *Nicholas Nickleby* were clarion peals announcing to the world that in Charles Dickens the rejected and forgotten and misused of the world had a champion.[48]

CHAPTER TWO

Master Humphrey's Clock Strikes One

"I AM utterly lost in misery, and can do nothing," Dickens wrote Forster. "I saw the Responsibilities this morning, and burst into tears. The presence of my wife aggravates me. I loathe my parents. I detest my house. I begin to have thoughts of the Serpentine, of the Regent's Canal, of the razors upstairs, of the chemist's down the street, of poisoning myself . . . of hanging myself upon the pear-tree in the garden, of abstaining from food and starving myself to death . . . of murdering Chapman and Hall and becoming great in story (SHE must hear something of me then—perhaps sign the warrant: or is that a fable?), of turning Chartist, of heading some bloody assault upon the palace and saving Her by my single hand . . ." [1]

It was just two days after Queen Victoria's marriage to Prince Albert. And Dickens was infectiously carrying Forster and Maclise along with him in a wild fantasy of all three being madly in love with their young Sovereign. Maclise, a great favorite with the Queen, excited the jealous envy of the other two through being asked to paint secret pictures for the bride to give the Prince on his birthday. All Dickens could do was join a throng of privileged spectators in the great stand at the Athenaeum. Here also sat Kate with eleven hundred and thirty ladies and children, to watch the procession go by for the Coronation and Royal Wedding, and admire Miss Burdett Coutts in her carriage, wearing the tiara of Marie Antoinette. The Queen, Dickens had been told, was fond of his books.[2] But what was that to a lover wearing a marriage medal near his heart and weeping over her portrait!

Although the jest had deeper undertones for Dickens, it was symbolic of the high spirits of these rushing days when he was getting settled in his splendid new home and making preparations for the "great

[292]

new project"—the weekly periodical he was to start in the spring for
Chapman and Hall. For had Dickens not played with the same prodigious vitality that he brought to his work, he could hardly have produced the staggering total of over a million words since the beginning
of *Pickwick*. From a positive fury of industry at his writing table—and
from the feverish alarms of his last fracas with Bentley—he turned to
a no less furious renewal of energy in diversion—extravagant pranks
like this one about the Queen, rides through country lanes, prowls
through London slums, playgoing, rural sports, dining at the tables of
the great, gatherings at home, bathing at Broadstairs, dashing from
Exeter to Stratford and Manchester.

Since December, when the move to Devonshire Terrace was made,
Dickens had done a good deal more entertaining than working. Cards
were left on new acquaintances, and old friends like Beard were invited to dinner.[3] Especially throughout the Christmas holidays elaborate parties kept the servants up late night after night,[4] and finally exhausted even the tremendous turkey that Bradbury and Evans sent
Dickens as an annual remembrance. In order that they "might have a
becoming idea of its astonishing capabilities," Dickens wrote them
the day after the New Year, "the last remnants of that blessed bird
made its appearance at breakfast yesterday—I repeat it, yesterday—
the other portions having furnished forth seven grills, one boil, and a
cold lunch or two." [5]

In the course of February half a dozen friends received delirious
letters announcing his desolate infatuation with his young Queen. To
the bewildered Landor, in Bath, Dickens wrote that he was wandering
"up and down with vague and dismal thoughts of running away to
some uninhabited island with a maid of honour . . . I have my eye upon
Lady ——, principally because she is beautiful and has no strong
brothers." [6] He told his friend T. J. Thompson that he and Maclise,
"raving with love," had prowled about Windsor, so heartbroken at the
glowing windows of the royal bedchamber "that I, your humble servant, lay down in the mud of the Long Walk, and refused all comfort . . ." The letter ended with a bequest of his body to his royal mistress: "I should wish to be embalmed and to be kept (if practicable)
on top of the triumphal arch at Buckingham Palace when she is in
town, and on the northeast turret of the Round Tower when she is
at Windsor." [7]

Farcically indulged though it was, more than one biographer has felt that, behind the comic mask of being in love with a young queen who never could be his, there is "the image of another girl—also a queen in her way—who was lost: the Mary who was so constantly in his dreams." [8] Living or dead, a ghost or a queen, either way lost and unattainable, she still haunted him poignantly. And unconsciously he combined this opportunity to symbolize his sense of loss with an irresistible indulgence in playful fantasy. It was a fantasy in which he struck divergent chords, as it reflected divergent depths within him. With abandoned shift from the *Orlando Furioso* vein, he wrote Monckton Milnes an account of a street ballad popular in Seven Dials and supposed to be sung by the Queen herself:

> *"So let 'em say whate'er they may,*
> *Or do whate'er they can;*
> *Prince Halbert he vill allvays be*
> *My own dear Fancy Man."*

In the same letter he quoted a burlesque catechism in which John Bull voices his opposition to the "wast and enormous expenditer" involved "vith respectin' to" this importation of "German sassages from Saxe Humbug and Go-to-her." [9]

Mingled with Dickens's pretense of love-insanity were jests about a pet raven now a member of the family, a talkative and rambunctious bird named Grip, who alarmed the children and lady visitors by pecking at their ankles. Edwin Landseer facetiously remarked that Dickens was "raven mad." [10] This pleasantry distorted itself from mouth to mouth until by autumn rumors were circulating that he was out of his mind. "What do the papers mean," his cousin James Lamert wrote from Cork, "by saying that Charles is demented . . . ?" [11] Chapman and Hall passed on the same report, and Dickens ground his teeth about it in half-serious, half-comic indignation.

Grip, the raven, survived by little more than a year the pun he had inspired, though that was long enough for him to serve as the model for his namesake in *Barnaby Rudge*. Dickens wrote his friends characteristic descriptions of the bird's demise. When it first fell ill, a bird fancier had been called in to administer a powerful dose of castor oil. The next morning, much better, Grip had "so far recovered his spirits as to be enabled to bite the groom severely." [12] But he had a relapse, in which he talked to himself incoherently. "On the clock striking twelve he appeared slightly agitated, but he soon recovered, walked twice or thrice along the coach-house, stopped to bark, staggered, exclaimed Halloa old girl (his favourite expression), and died.' [13]

The bird fancier assured Dickens that "he never see sich a thoroughgoing, long-headed, deep 'owdacious file,' " and scouted the groom's resentment of being bitten: " 'Why, what has he agin that bird? That little man could no more stand agin him in pint of sense and reason than I could agin the ghost of Cobbett.' " [14] "The raven's body . . . was taken off to be stuffed, but has not come home yet. He has left a considerable property (in cheese and half pence) buried in different parts of the garden; and the new raven——for I have a successor— administers to the effects. He had buried in one place a brush . . . a very large hammer, and several raw potatoes, which were discovered yesterday." [15]

*   *   *   *   *

Meanwhile, during January, Bentley had made his last desperate effort to enforce the delivery of *Barnaby Rudge*, and reduced Dickens to distraction by those newspaper advertisements that heralded its forthcoming publication. Although the manuscript was supposed to have been completed by the first of the year, Dickens had in fact written no more than a couple of chapters,[16] and was hysterically determined on finding reasons for not giving the book to Bentley at all. His old enemy's newspaper announcements threw him into a fever of resentment. "For today," he noted desperately, "the vagabond has stopped my clock—and he knows that as well as I." [17]

The "clock" Bentley had momentarily stopped was, of course, *Master Humphrey's Clock*, the title Dickens had finally decided on for his new weekly periodical, now fast taking definite shape. "I have a notion of this old file in the queer house," he told Forster, "opening the book by an account of himself, and, among his other peculiarities, of his affection for an old quaint queer-cased clock . . . Then I mean to tell how that he has kept odd manuscripts in the old, deep, dark, silent closet where the weights are; and taken them from thence to read . . . And thus I shall call the book either Old Humphrey's Clock, or Master Humphrey's Clock," [18] he decided, ". . . if so be that there is no danger of the pensive confounding 'Master' with a boy." [19] Resiliently he threw off the fury of his vexations with Bentley. By the middle of

January he had finished the first number and brought the Guildhall Giants on the scene.

Confident as Dickens was of his own popularity, he still did not fully realize the position he had attained, or the intensity of the appetite for his works that he had created. He imagined that he must find some novelty to give his public if he was not to wear out his success. Consequently he conceived his Arabian Nights-Gulliver-Mr. Spectator salmagundi of Master Humphrey and Mr. Pickwick sitting beside the old clock and Gog and Magog telling various unconnected tales of old times in the shadowy Guildhall. Since his childhood reading of the *Spectator* and the *Tatler* and Goldsmith's *Bee*, he had been fascinated by the periodical miscellany. He was completely unprepared for the discovery he would soon unhappily make that his readers did not want sketches, tales, essays, squibs on current absurdities; that, like Oliver Twist, they were asking for more, and they refused to be satisfied with anything less than another full-scale novel from his pen.

But meanwhile, with his head full of visions of the contents of that "dark, silent closet," he went off to Bath with Forster at the end of February on an overnight visit to Landor. The noble, warm-hearted, hot-tempered old poet had grown deeply interested in Dickens and his work since their first meeting at Lady Blessington's, and had followed both *Oliver Twist* and *Nicholas Nickleby* with responsive emotion. "Tell him," he wrote Forster, "he has drawn from me more tears and more smiles than are remaining to me for all the rest of the world, real or ideal." [20]

In Landor's lodgings in St. James's Square, Bath, with Italian paintings crowded over all the walls and even the doors, there was a glorious evening of luminous conversation over the wine. Dickens treated the older man with just the right measure of respect, but "allowed his wit to play about him, bright and harmless as Summer lightning," and the Olympian Landor was in turns grave, violent, tender, and thunderous with tremendous and extravagant laughter.[21] During this evening Dickens sketched out to his two companions an imaginative fancy that had seized his mind.[22] With further reflection it grew into a tale of gentle pathos. Two days later he had succumbed to its hold over him and decided to substitute for a "witch-story" that was originally to have filled the third number of *Master Humphrey* this "little child-story."[23] And by the time of his return to London he had invented various titles, on which he asked Forster's opinion. Should it be *The Old Curiosity Dealer and the Child* or simply *The Old Curiosity Shop?* [24]

The child heroine of the story conceived that night in Bath had no greater admirer among the many who loved her than Landor. Upon Nell, he thought, "Juliet might for a moment have turned her eyes from Romeo." When, in later years, he was reminded that she had been born on that visit, he would confirm the fact with one of his whimsical outbursts of comic violence: never had he regretted anything so much, he exclaimed, as his having failed to buy "that house . . . and then and there to have burnt it to the ground . . . that no meaner association should ever desecrate the birthplace of Little Nell." And then, conscious of his listeners' sense of his absurdity, he would break into a thundering peal of laughter.[25]

The expansion of *The Old Curiosity Shop* from a short story to a full-length narrative was in part a result of the increasing hold it took upon Dickens's feelings. But even more it was a consequence of Dickens's ability to adapt himself to adverse circumstances, and there can be no doubt that it saved him from what might have proved a grave setback. The first number of *Master Humphrey* was to go on sale on Saturday, April 4th, and Dickens again observed his custom of leaving town on the eve of publication. He had spent a pleasant evening at Richmond with Forster and Maclise the night before, and on Friday Dickens and Kate went to Birmingham. Here Forster hastened to them with the exciting news that almost seventy thousand copies of the *Clock* had been sold. Jubilant at another triumph, they prolonged their holiday somewhat longer than they had expected to, and, joined by Dickens's brother Alfred (who was studying engineering near Birmingham), made excursions to Shakespeare's house at Stratford and Johnson's at Lichfield. These jaunts ended in a comic misadventure. They had underestimated their expenses and made no provisions for credit. To pay their railway fares back to London they had to send Alfred out to pawn their gold watches.[26]

"The clock goes gloriously indeed," Dickens wrote when he had returned to town. "What will the wiseacres say to weekly issues *now?* and what will they say to any of those ten thousand things we shall do together to make 'em writhe and stagger in their shoes. Thank God for this great hit. I always had a quiet confidence in it, but I never expected *this*, at first." [27] His exultation, however, proved short-lived. The public had flocked to *Master Humphrey* under the impression that it was another Dickens novel. With the second number the sales fell off alarmingly; by the third their decline was disastrous.[28] There was a hasty editorial conference at Chapman and Hall's offices in the Strand. Dickens flung himself at once into the breach. He would expand *The Old Curiosity Shop* into a long serial, postponing the appearance of its first chapter from the third number to the fourth, where it would be announced as a continued story. Meanwhile Mr. Pickwick and Sam Weller would reappear in several intervening numbers and stem the tide while he was enlarging the plan of the story and getting it under way.[29]

Once started, Dickens progressed with dispatch and enthusiasm, though he felt rushed by the short intervals between numbers—all the more so because his sudden change of plan had given him no time to get ahead of his story. He also felt harassed by the necessary brevity of weekly installments. "I was obliged to cramp most dreadfully what I thought a pretty idea in the last chapter," he complained. "I hadn't room to turn." [30]

Nevertheless his enjoyment of the tale grew steadily. Dick Swiveller's "behaviour in the matter of Miss Wackles," he wrote Forster, "will, I hope, give you satisfaction. I cannot yet discover that his aunt has any belief in him, or is in the least degree likely to send him a remittance . . ." [31] At the end of May, resolved on getting on with his pressing task, Dickens decided to spend June at Broadstairs, dashed down there, and rented 37 Albion Street for the month. "I don't know of a word of news in all London, but there will be plenty next week, for I am going away," he wrote Forster jokingly on the eve of departure. ". . . I am doubtful whether it will be a murder, a fire, a vast robbery, or the escape of Gould, but it will be something remarkable no doubt. I almost blame myself for the death of that poor girl who leaped off the monument upon my leaving town last year. She would not have done it if I had remained, neither would the two men have found the skeleton in the sewers." [32]

Within two hours of his arrival at Broadstairs he had, as he invariably did, rearranged the furniture in all the rooms, set out his writing table with the neatness peculiar to him, and installed a good array of bottles labeled "Gin," "Brandy," and "Hollands," together with wine, in the dining-room closet. "The sea is rolling away, like nothing but the sea, in front of the house," he wrote Beard, "and there are two pretty little spare bedrooms waiting to be occupied." [33] And to Maclise:

> "My foot is in the house,
>   My bath is on the sea,
> And before I take a souse,
>   Here's a single note to thee,"

adding, "come to the bower which is shaded for you in the one-pair front, where no chair or table has four legs of the same length, and where no drawers will open till you have pulled the pegs off, and then they keep open and won't shut again. COME." [34]

Two weeks later the entire family were "as brown as berries," and Dickens was beginning No. 15.[35] "There is a description of getting gradually out of town, and passing through neighbourhoods of distinct and various characters, with which, if I had read it as anybody else's writing, I think I should have been very much struck. The child and the old man are on their journey, of course, and the subject is a very pretty one." [36]

*   *   *   *   *

Back in London in July, a sudden impulse took Dickens to see the hanging of the murderer Courvoisier. At dinner the day before the event he had been disgusted to learn that his brother Fred morbidly planned to join a circle of reporters who were witnessing the event. But by the close of the evening his own curiosity got the better of him, and he carried Maclise and Burnett off with him to see the preparations.

Before the prison the barriers were already crowded three deep, at eleven o'clock, with men and women who would wait until eight the next morning for the spectacle. Streams of people pressed through all the streets on their way to the scene; by one o'clock, the pavements were a surging sea, and nearly all the windows in the houses opposite the jail were rented to spectators. "Just once," Dickens exclaimed, "I should like to watch a scene like this, and see the end of the Drama;" and he suddenly plunged into a house facing "the drop." Maclise marched Burnett up the stairs after him to a room from which they looked down on the throng below.

At four o'clock began the banging of hammers on the scaffold. By this time the mob stretched beyond St. Sepulchre's Church, jammed so tight that the pickpockets who were everywhere had no room to operate, and women who fainted from the pressure remained wedged upright though unconscious. From this packed mass came a constant tumult of men and women bawling slang obscenities. "Why, there stands Thackeray!" cried Dickens suddenly, pointing out where he towered head and shoulders above the crowd. At eight the church bells struck and the multitude gave a yell. At last the wretched murderer appeared, "feeble and agonized . . . with wringing hands—uplifted though fettered—and moving lips as if in prayer." The bloodthirsty mob remained to the very end, and only then, after what Burnett called "a ghastly night in Hades with demons," could Dickens and his friends get away.[37]

The experience sharpened Dickens's horror of making a public spectacle out of executions and deepened his loathing for the hideous gloating of the mob. Granting that the public safety required murderers to be exterminated—and even this he considered debatable— there was no excuse for disposing of them in such barbarous fashion and with such evil effects upon the witnesses. It was a subject about which he felt deeply and later wrote with striking understanding of criminal and mob psychology.

The remainder of July and August passed in less lurid diversions. The week after the hanging, Miss Coutts gave a grand ball; the announcement that there would be a Royal Duke and Duchess among the guests prompted Dickens to ask whether gentlemen were expected to wear court dress: "I have already appeared in that very extraordinary costume and am prepared for the worst." [38] Kate had a feminine visitor at Devonshire Terrace for whom, Dickens wrote Maclise, he had "conceived a horrible aversion, and whom I *must* fly. . . . She is the ancient mariner of young ladies. She 'holds me with her glittering eye' and I cannot turn away. The basilisk is now in the dining room and I am in the study, but I *feel* her through the wall. She is of a prim and icy aspect, her breast tight and smooth like a sugar loaf, she converseth with fluency, and hath deep mental lore. . . . I went out last night and in my desolation, had my hair cut—merely to avoid her." [39]

Dining with Dr. Elliotson, he made the acquaintance of the Reverend Chauncey Hare Townshend, a gentleman who shared their host's enthusiastic interest in mesmerism and who had written a little book called *Facts in Mesmerism*. [40] Meanwhile, the first semiannual volume of *Master Humphrey's Clock* was drawing to a close, and Dickens asked Samuel Rogers for permission to dedicate it to him.[41] And toward the end of August, Dickens invited Harley and a number of other friends to be present at the christening of baby Kate Macready on the 25th, when a fatted calf would be served in celebration. "It (the calf, not the baby) is to be taken off the spit at 6." [42]

Although Dickens was managing these social distractions, and enjoying himself, he found the perpetual effort to keep at least one jump ahead of the printer fatiguing. "Mr. Shandy's clock," he wrote Landor, "was nothing to mine, wind, wind, wind, always winding am I; and day and night the alarum is ringing in my ears, warning me that it must not run down. When I received that Swing-like letter of yours, such visions of Bath sprung up and floated about me that I rung the bell for my portmanteau and putting it on a chair looked hard at it for three quarters of an hour—Suddenly a solemn sound from the clock jarred upon my ears; and sending it upstairs again, I sat down with a sigh to write." [43]

Made tense possibly by weariness and work, Dickens gave way to exasperation one August night in Devonshire Terrace when Forster was more tactlessly domineering than usual. The only other guests were Maclise and Macready, whose diary tells the story without saying what the dispute was about. "Forster got on to one of his headlong streams of talk (which he thinks argument)," Macready wrote, "and waxed warm . . ." Sharp observations followed, then personal retorts. Dickens broke in; Forster endeavored to carry things off with a high hand. Losing his temper, Dickens burst out that this was his house and he should be glad if Forster would leave it. Kate ran from the room in tears. Forster started to stamp out, but Macready stopped him, pleading that they should not let one angry instant destroy a friendship valuable to both. Dickens, regaining self-control first, admitted "that he had spoken in passion, and would not have said what he said, could he have reflected." But he could not help adding that he "could not answer for his temper under Forster's provocations"; given the same offense, he would do just the same again.

It was a painful scene. Forster, distressed at the thought of wrecking their friendship, no longer wished to walk out and end it forever, but neither could he be satisfied with the expressions of regret that Dickens now repeated. His pride demanded some more humbling apology that Dickens's pride in turn would not give. And so Forster remained feebly vacillating in the middle of the room, neither going nor letting the subject drop, but, as Macready put it, "skimbling-skambling a parcel of unmeaning words." Only after protracting the uncomfortable situation, and finding he could obtain no more, did he at last make "a sort of speech, accepting what he had before declined. He was silent and not recovered—no wonder!—during the whole evening." [44]

Dickens was very much grieved about the episode, he wrote Macready the next day. And yet, reason with himself as he would, he could not be penitent. With all the regard he had for Forster, and their close friendship, he could not close his eyes to the fact that he did not quarrel thus with other men. There was "no man, alive or dead, who tries his friends as he does. . . . I declare to you solemnly, that when I think of his manner (far worse than his matter) I turn burning hot and am ashamed and in a manner degraded to have been the subject of it." [45] Nevertheless, Dickens regretted his passion and intemperance, and they resumed their friendship, as they were always to do through many other similar trials.

*　　*　　*　　*　　*

In September Dickens was once more at Broadstairs, this time in Lawn House, a small villa with a cornfield between it and the sea.[46] "Come down for a week, come down for a fortnight, come down for three weeks, come down for a month," he begged Maclise. "It's charming, and the house a most brilliant success—far more comfortable than any one we've had." Fletcher was there, he added, committing all manner of absurdities, as usual, sketching beggars and idiots whom he dressed in fragments of his own attire, asking the sailors to find "half a dozen old apostles" to pose for him, reading Wordsworth and Mrs. Hemans to stray groups he came upon on the terrace. The first time he went bathing, he fell heavily into the water, letting out a howl like a wolf as its coldness struck him. "You never heard anything so horrible! And then he splashed about like a fleet of porpoises, roaring most horribly all the time, and dancing a maniac dance which defied description." [47]

Nothing, however, was allowed to distract Dickens from his writing table and *The Old Curiosity Shop*. "I have effected a reform," he wrote Forster, "by virtue of which we breakfast at a quarter before eight, so that I get to work at half-past, and am commonly free by one o'clock or so, which is a great happiness. Dick is now Sampson's clerk, and I have touched Miss Brass in Number 25, lightly, but effectively I hope." [48] He pressed steadily onward all through September and into the first week of October, despite an attack of facial rheumatism that tortured him desperately. "I am as bad as Miss Squeers," he told Chapman and Hall, "—screaming out loud all the time I write." [49] Two days later, of Nell's journey with her grandfather through the Midlands, he wrote Forster, "You will recognize a description of the road we travelled between Birmingham and Wolverhampton; but I had conceived it so well in my mind that the execution doesn't please me quite as well as I expected." [50]

Although the end of the story was not yet written, when Dickens returned to London he helped Frederick Yates with a dramatization of it at the Adelphi and "made a great many improvements . . . with divers pieces of bye-play" at the rehearsals. But he had no faith in its merits and didn't have the heart to be at the first night; Kate and Fred went without him.[51] Only in Yates as Quilp did he have any confidence.

His misgivings over the stage version were sharpened by the emotional tension of nerving himself for Nell's death. "All night," he wrote, "I have been pursued by the child; and this morning I am unrefreshed and miserable." [52] Forster had pressed upon him the artistic necessity of this death, and Dickens agreed that it was the only possible ending,[53] but as it began to be foreshadowed in the narrative he was "inundated with imploring letters recommending poor little Nell to mercy." [54] He suffered from it so intensely as to feel "the anguish unspeakable." [55] Writing George Cattermole a description of Nell lying dead upon her couch to aid him in illustrating the scene, he burst out, "I am breaking my heart over this story . . ." [56] As he remembered the bitterness of death that he had known, Nell's features seemed to reveal transparently the image of the dead face he had loved and his old wounds bled again.[57]

Dickens's readers were drowned in a wave of grief no less overwhelming than his own. When Macready, returning home from the theater, saw the print of the child lying dead by the window with strips of holly on her breast, a dead chill ran through his blood. "I have never read printed words that gave me so much pain," he noted in his diary. "I could not weep for some time. Sensations, sufferings have returned to me, that are terrible to awaken . . ." [58] Daniel O'Connell, the Irish M.P., reading the book in a railway carriage, burst into tears, groaned, "He should not have killed her," and despairingly threw the volume out of the train window.[59] Thomas Carlyle, previously inclined to be a bit patronizing about Dickens, was utterly overcome.[60] Waiting crowds at a New York pier shouted to an incoming vessel, "Is Little Nell dead?" Landor felt that her story might have beguiled Desdemona of her tears. Lord Jeffrey was found by a friend, Mrs. Henry Siddons, in his library with his head bowed upon the table; he raised it and she saw that his eyes were bathed in tears. "I had no idea that you had any bad news or cause of grief," she said, "or I would not have come. Is anyone dead?" "Yes, indeed," he replied, "I'm a great goose to have given way so, but I couldn't help it. You'll be sorry to hear that little Nelly, Boz's little Nelly, is dead." [61]

But the misfortunes of Nell and her unhappy grandfather, with the interwoven lives of the Nubbles family, Quilp, Sampson and Sally Brass, Dick Swiveller, and the Marchioness, were the turning point in the fortunes of *Master Humphrey's Clock*. Dickens's most sanguine hopes for the story proved justified; before its end as many as one hundred thousand copies of each number were being purchased.[62] Dickens had saved himself from what might have been a most disastrous reversal in the ever-swelling tide of his hold upon his readers. And, as Forster observes, no story that he had thus far written had so strengthened the bond between him and his readers into one of personal attachment, or so deepened the feeling that he was no less a master of pathos than of humor.

Unlike *Pickwick Papers*, this had been achieved by no stroke of lucky appeal, but by deliberate design. Dickens knew that his position depended on his readers, who could not be argued or battered into liking what they did not like. Though he was not afraid to assert views to which they might be opposed, he worked assiduously to provide a kind of writing that they would enjoy. Good fortune had given him the command of their laughter and tears, and he never despised the gift. The verdict that he might resent from a reviewer, he accepted from the beating of his readers' hearts. And so, when the public response to the first few numbers of *Master Humphrey's Clock* warned him that it might break down at any minute, he had quickly altered its scheme. He had divined what was needed, and supplied the want. The public desired from him long continued stories of mingled drama, comedy, and pathos; henceforth that was what he should give them.

Not for another ten years, and then only with a much more adroit and calculated appeal to popular taste, would he attempt, in *Household Words*, another weekly periodical built upon his cherished miscellany plan. And even then, keeping an eagle eye on its circulation figures, he would carefully buttress the appeal of shorter articles with longer narratives. In 1841, however, he was not yet the master journalist who could devise and conduct a successful weekly magazine at the same time that he pursued his career as a novelist. He had saved *Master Humphrey's Clock* from failure simply by reverting to his primary role as a writer of fiction. Consequently the close of the one story in its pages was followed immediately by the beginning of another. Of the original *Clock* machinery he revived Master Humphrey and his friends for only the few pages necessary to bridge the gap between *The Old Curiosity Shop* and *Barnaby Rudge*, that often postponed task for which he had at last found a potent motivating force.

CHAPTER THREE

Emergence of a Radical

THE writing of *Barnaby Rudge* was a time of enormous development for Dickens, although it continued to give him almost as much trouble as when he was struggling to write it for Bentley. "I didn't stir out yesterday," he wrote Forster, "but sat and *thought* all day; not writing a line; not so much as the cross of a t or the dot of an i." "Last night I was unutterably and impossible-to-form-an-idea-of-ably miserable," but the next morning he managed to go to work "in good twig" by concentrating his mind steadily upon it.[1] He worked on, despite disinclination and bilious disorders, and in the intervals between forcing himself to keep going, saw Ainsworth, with whom he was on cordial terms again, and accepted invitations from Lord Jeffrey and Lord Denman.[2] Old Tom Hill had died, and at the sale of his effects Dickens bought some of his books and "a cup, made from the Bard's Mulberry tree," which he presented to Macready.[3] "I have done nothing today but cut the Swift, looking into it with a delicious laziness in all manner of delightful places, and put poor Tom's books away."[4]

Preparations for the appearance of *Barnaby Rudge* considerably antedated its first installment on February 13, 1841. Cattermole had drawn an inordinately ornate and many-gabled inn, with which Dickens was greatly pleased, to represent the Maypole, and was soon doing Gabriel Varden's house and The Warren.[5] From the artist's studio at Clapham Rise, with its dark nooks and tapestried walls, its quaintly carved escritoire, its frowning Giorgione knight glaring down from above the bookcases, and the light of a brass pedestal lamp glinting on ancient suits of armor and antique weapons, emanated almost three dozen of the illustrations used in *Master Humphrey's Clock,* and the artist's home saw many dinners with Dickens and his friends as the guests.

In this studio, after sitting over their port at dinner, or in the cavernous drawing room with the heavy carved furniture that had once belonged to Lord Byron in the Albany, would assemble a group calling themselves "the Portwiners"—Dickens, Forster, Thackeray, Bulwer, Charles and Edwin Landseer, Macready, Mark Lemon, Maclise. While a great log of ship timber blazed on the hearth and fumes of incense rose from the cigars, conversation glowed with anecdote and wit. Dickens joked about an "omnibus tout" nicknamed Sloppy who haunted the Ship Tavern at Charing Cross, from which they took their departure for Clapham. Thackeray buttonholed Forster over one of Cattermole's drawings of a waterfall to express his wonder that anyone could get such an effect "with only a bit of charcoal." "*And brains*," added Forster with Johnsonian decision through a cloud from his cigar. Edwin Landseer slowly shook his head, "like a physician over a patient he despairs of," to convey that he was "entranced, beyond verbal expression," by a water color representing Macbeth. Meanwhile the kettle boiled, and Dickens, frantically squirting lemon juice into his eyes and over his floreate waistcoat, brewed the punch for the company.[6]

During the latter part of January, Kate was expecting the birth of their fourth child, an event that delayed itself from the 23rd, when Dickens was aroused at four in the morning by what seemed the beginning of her birth pangs, until more than two weeks later.[7] Throughout the entire time, Kate was extremely unwell. Finally, on February 8th, the child was born, "a jolly boy" who was to be named Walter Landor Dickens.[8] Despite the prolonged strain of the delay Kate made such an amazingly rapid recovery that toward the end of the month she was able to go with Dickens to spend a few days at the Old Ship at Brighton.[9]

On his return Dickens found himself in early March again obliged to deal with his father's debts.[10] This time they had assumed so embarrassing a form that he had Mitton insert in the newspapers a notice the deliberate vagueness of which does not disguise what John Dickens had been doing: "Certain persons having or purporting to have the surname of our said client have put into circulation, with a view of more readily obtaining credit thereon, certain acceptances made pay-

able at his private residence or at the offices of his business agents";
and it went on to give warning that for the future Dickens would pay
no debts except those contracted by himself or his wife.[11]

*   *   *   *   *

Old associates continued to reappear in his life together with the
new circle brought him by his fame. Writing to one of these—either
a schoolfellow or a companion of his newspaper days—Dickens said,
"Happily, though I have made many friends, I have never since my
schooltime lost *one*." Only the other day "a little pale schoolmaster
who taught me my letters"—obviously William Giles—had "turned
up miraculously" "in a high state of preservation." Indeed, the "pleasantest and proudest part" of his correspondence, Dickens concluded,
was that in which he had stored the congratulations of those whom
he had known in less successful times. "I really cannot tell you how
much pleasure I have derived from the receipt of your warm-hearted
and welcome letter . . ." [12]

Despite the unrelenting pressure of his work, Dickens wrote generously long letters of kind but vigorously honest comment to the
would-be authors who were constantly sending him their work.
Though he praised what he could, he was severe on fancy writing.
How, he asked, did one "spell a tiger from all thoughts of harm,"
"clasp blood springs with tendril fingers," or "fold love's banner o'er
a lady's brow"? [13] It was foolish and wrong, Dickens told the same
young writer in a second letter, to plead the absence of needful revision. The question was not what he thought but his power of expressing his thought. "How can I judge of that, upon your mere
assurance that you have the power of writing regular verse, but have
not taken the trouble to exert it?" "I do not remember to have ever
had . . . any composition sent me by a young man (and I have had a
great number) who did not give me to understand that it was the
worst he had ever written, and he had much better ones at home."
Despite these shrewd thrusts, however, Dickens remained gently sympathetic. "If I seem cruel it is only to be kind. You do not know, and
can form no conception of the misery," he said, of men who had mistakenly chosen a literary career or of the dreadful beggary of their lives.
With "these dismal scarecrows" before his eyes, Dickens concluded,

"I must know well what your qualification is, before I encourage you in your perilous desire." [14]

Another of these literary neophytes came to Dickens's attention just as he was leaving the *Miscellany*. A man named John Overs had sent in some songs for the different months of the year, stating that he was a carpenter and had written them in his spare time.[15] Dickens would gladly have published them but would ask no favors of Bentley. He learned that Overs was self-educated, had a wife and family of small children, and earned thirty shillings a week as foreman to a manufacturer of medicine chests.[16] Dickens felt uneasy about the risks and anxieties of a literary career for such a man, but Overs explained that his aspirations were humble, that he thought these pursuits as harmless as the alehouse or the skittle ground, and that he did not neglect his daily work but felt sufficiently rewarded simply in enjoyment and self-respect. Touched by "arguments so unpretentious and so true," Dickens made no further efforts at dissuasion and tried to advance the poor carpenter's literary career.[17]

He gave one of Overs's compositions to Ainsworth when he took over the editorship of the *Miscellany*. He had Overs send the songs, with Dickens's comment on them, to *Tait's Magazine*, at Edinburgh, where they were published.[18] But of a poetic drama by Overs he could not speak favorably. "The father is such a dolt, and the villain *such* a villain, the girl so exceptionally credulous, and the means used to deceive them so very slight and transparent, that the reader cannot sympathize with their distresses." [19]

During the following year, Dickens made time in his busy schedule to help Overs with revisions. Sitting down to revise one of his protégé's stories, and finding that he could not do so without having Overs at his elbow, he appointed a time for them to work on it together: "If you can be with me at 12 *exactly* next Sunday, I can spare you an hour and a half"; and he begs Overs not to "mention any slight pains I may be at in your behalf (which are in truth so many pleasures to me)." [20] And on a story about Wat Tyler's rebellion, Dickens made a comment that significantly foreshadows his approach to the climactic riots of *Barnaby Rudge*: "I object on principle to making Wat such a thorough-paced villain, because a rebel on such grounds has a certain claim to one's sympathy, and I feel that if I had lived at his time I should have been very likely to have knocked out the collector's brains myself . . ." 21

Not many writers would take time from so busy a career to comment in detail on the compositions of unknown young men or to spend hours revising their work. In addition, he was also struggling to shorten the delays in publishing *The Pic-Nic Papers* for the benefit of Mrs. Macrone. "Poor thing," he commented, "she needs it sadly." Just when all the contributions that had been donated for it were ready, Colburn, the publisher, aroused Dickens's indignation by rudely deleting Landor's offering. Resenting the insult offered by "this sneaking vagabond" to a distinguished writer, Dickens at first refused to send in his own piece, a fictional adaptation of *The Lamplighter*, the farce originally written for Macready. But in pity for the unhappy widow Dickens gave way, and when the book was published later that summer of 1841 he was able to put £300 into her hands.²²

In April, Angus Fletcher sent down from Scotland a portrait bust of Dickens upon which he had been engaged and which, Dickens told him, was "considered by everyone (by Maclise at the head of them) *much more like* in the marble than in the cast. Kate wrote to thank you for it, but was guilty of the small omission (a very slight one) of forgetting to put it in the post." In the same letter, announcing an intended visit to Edinburgh that June, Dickens begged Fletcher not to intercede against any testimonial that might be planned. "*Stop nothing*," he urged, for he was "coming northward really as an acknowledgment of the kind opinion of the Northern people." That very morning, he added, he had called on Jeffrey, who was visiting London. "His enthusiasm relating to the Old Curiosity Shop, exceeded even what you had prepared me for . . . I came out of the house more delighted than if I had been ten thousand pounds the richer than when I went in . . ." ²³

From Washington Irving in America came no less gratifying praise. "I wish I could find in your welcome letter," Dickens replied, "some hint of an intention to visit England. I can't. I have held it at arm's length, and taken a bird's-eye view of it, after reading it a great many times, but there is no greater encouragement in it this way than on a microscopic inspection. I should love to go with you,—as I have gone, God knows how often—into Little Britain, and Eastcheap, and Green Arbour Court, and Westminster Abbey. I should like to travel

with you outside the last of the coaches down to Bracebridge Hall.
It would make my heart glad to compare notes with you . . . about all
those delightful places and people that I used to walk about and
dream of in the daytime, when a very small and not over-particularly-
taken-care-of boy . . ." [24]

All this time *Barnaby Rudge* was continuing to exact its demands
upon Dicken's time. Shortly before leaving for Edinburgh, he apologized to Lady Blessington for not having sent a promised article to
The Keepsake, which she was editing, reminding her that he had "a
clock which always wants winding," and promising to supply it upon
his return. And, alluding to the mesmeric experiments of Townshend
and Dr. Elliotson, "Have you seen Townshend's magnetic boy?" he
added. "You heard of him, no doubt, from Count D'Orsay. If you get
him to Gore House, don't, I entreat you, have more than eight people
—four is a better number—to see him. He fails in a crowd, and is
marvellous before a few. . . . I am a believer in earnest . . ." [25]

*   *   *   *   *

Barnaby Rudge was now driving on to the fury of the Gordon
Riots. The writing was going better than it had, though Forster took
exception to what he regarded as Dickens's too favorable view of Lord
George Gordon. "Say what you please of Gordon," Dickens rejoined;
"he must have been at heart a kind man, and a lover of the despised
and rejected, after his own fashion. He lived upon a small income,
and always within it; was known to relieve the necessities of many
people; exposed in his place the corrupt attempt of a minister to buy
him out of Parliament; and did great charities in Newgate. He always
spoke on the people's side, and tried against his muddled brains to
expose the profligacy of both parties." [26] Forster was more successful
in advising Dickens against a fancy he at first had of having the riots
led by three splendid fellows who should ultimately be revealed to
have broken out of Bedlam.[27]

As his imagination plunged into the surging tumult of the riots
themselves, Dickens's emotions boiled up in strange turmoil. Fear
and horror of the ferocities of mob violence mingled with fierce sympathy for the wrongs of the oppressed rising like fiends to avenge
themselves in destruction. Dickens obviously shared with the rioters
an orgiastic joy in the flaming demolition of Newgate amid clamor

and smoke. He shuddered and at the same time he exulted in this overthrow of authority. In spirit he was more than half at one with the mob in its assault upon the sinister old prison. "I have just burnt into Newgate," he wrote Forster excitedly, "and am going in the next number to tear the prisoners out by the hair of their heads." [28]

These pages—the most powerfully written in the book—are deeply colored both by his own past experience and by the public strife taking place almost as these very scenes were being written. The jail was the dark symbol of suffering and imprisonment that had indelibly branded his memories of childhood, the cruel bond that united him with all the suffering and exploited. As a solid citizen he might set his face against social disorder, but deep within how could he not rejoice at those flaming beams and crashing walls? The actual riots of 1780, to be sure, around which his story centered, had supposedly sprung from anti-Catholic fury, and though Dickens himself strongly disliked the Catholic Church, as a good liberal he deplored persecutions of any faith. The events of that uprising, however—churches and homes burnt wholesale, the prisons of London broken upon, the Bank of England attacked—suggest deeper discontents than feeling only against the Roman Catholics, and strongly resemble the storming of the Bastille and the lootings in Paris that were the first signs of revolutionary violence in 1789.

Dickens certainly read mutterings of this deeper rebellion in the disturbances that were his theme. But more, in the world around him, he saw ominously vivid signs of the same dangers swelling to greater desperation. The years immediately preceding 1840 had been years of industrial depression. The Chartist agitation for universal suffrage and laboring-class representation in Parliament had collapsed in 1839 into rioting among the South Welsh miners. In Manchester during the following year the cotton mills stood empty while threatening jobless men filled the streets; the whole North of England went out on one gigantic general strike that the authorities were able to put down only by firing into the crowds. In 1841 there was a brickmakers' strike ending in bloody riots.[29] These were the events that Dickens and the readers of *Barnaby Rudge* in its weekly numbers had before their eyes as they responded to the excitement of its smoking pages.

Dickens had never thought of himself as one of "the people"—

even in the blacking warehouse he had always been "the young gentleman," and painfully humiliated by the common associations to which he had been reduced. His emotions and his ambitions were deeply those of the respectable middle class, and he shared its fear of seeing the foundations of society disrupted by violence. And yet he felt at the same time an obscure inward identification not only with the poor but even with the bloody rebellion that he described in such fascinated horror. As a prosperous householder he feared the mob, but the child who had wrapped bottles from dawn to dark shared its feelings about a brutal society in which government protected privilege.

These attitudes were reflected not solely in the ambiguous overtones of *Barnaby Rudge,* but were increasingly coming to the surface in his feelings and actions. When he was acknowledging the receipt of Lord Ashley's speech "moving the Children's Employment Commission," Dickens had not been able to forbear "cursing the present system and its fatal effect in keeping down thousands upon thousands of God's images." [30] And when Dr. Southwood Smith, the Chief Commissioner, put the report of the Commission in his hands, Dickens read with anger and horror of the dreadful ways in which even small children were worked in the mines. He found no less cause for fury in a later report on conditions in the factories and iron foundries.[31] The two reports painted hideous pictures of dark tunnels no larger than a good-sized drain through which seven-year-old children dragged loaded carts to which they were chained; of girls clad only in ragged trousers working in the dark, often up to their knees in water, alongside men who wore nothing; of girls carrying heavy loads of coal up steep ladders a distance exceeding the height of St. Paul's Cathedral; of horrible accidents constantly occurring, and not even the most ordinary precautions taken to prevent them; of deformed and stunted boys toiling fourteen hours a day, fed on offal, struck with bars, burned by showers of sparks from red-hot irons, pulled by the ears till the blood ran down.[32]

About these revelations Dickens arranged with Macvey Napier, the editor of the *Edinburgh Review,* to write an article of burning comment as soon as the report was officially laid before Parliament and could legally be referred to.[33] And he warmly applauded Lord Ashley for refusing to take government office because Sir Robert

Peel "hadn't made up his mind" and would not pledge himself to factory improvement. He also contributed to Albany Fonblanque's *Examiner* during the summer of 1841 a series of angry rhymed squibs on the Tories and other opponents of factory regulation. For though he hated those utilitarians who were ready to show that neither wages nor laboring conditions could be improved without economic disaster, he sympathized with the more humanitarian wing of utilitarianism that the *Examiner* represented.

The bitterest of these lampoons was a new version of "The Fine Old English Gentlemen," "to be said or sung at all Conservative Dinners":

> *"I'll sing you a new ballad, and I'll warrant it first-rate,*
> *Of the days of that old gentleman who had that old estate;*
> *When they spent the public money at a bountiful old rate*
> *On ev'ry mistress, pimp, and scamp, at ev'ry noble gate,*
> > *In the fine old English Tory times;*
> > *Soon may they come again!*

> *"The good old laws were garnished well with gibbets, whips, and chains,*
> *With fine old English penalties, and fine old English pains,*
> *With rebel heads, and seas of blood once hot in rebel veins;*
> *For all these things were requisite to guard the rich old gains*
> > *Of the fine old English Tory times;*
> > *Soon may they come again!*

.   .   .   .   .   .

> *"The bright old day now dawns again; the cry runs through the land,*
> *In England there shall be—dear bread! in Ireland—sword and brand!*
> *And poverty, and ignorance, shall swell the rich and grand,*
> *So, rally round the rulers with the gentle iron hand,*
> > *Of the fine old English Tory days;*
> > *Hail to the coming time!"* [34]

Everywhere Dickens looked, and in every direction his mind ran, he noted conditions to arouse indignation. Walking at his vigorous pace, sometimes by day, sometimes by night, through the crowded areas of Houndsditch, Whitechapel, or Seven Dials, observing the filth, the congestion, the inadequate water supply, and knowing, as he well did, what consequences in disease and crime they engendered, he swore to himself that he would strike blow after blow against these evils. Hearing the shrill voices of children, with no place to play but the refuse heaps of the streets and without proper schooling (there were fourteen thousand children in Bethnal Green, Lord John Russell was to point out, and only two thousand attending any school at all),[35] Dickens saw how hoodlumism and corruption inevitably sprouted from the very cobblestones. How could it fail that a hideously high proportion of these victims of dirt and ignorance should make their way to Coldbath Fields and Bridewell and Newgate, and how could even a few humane prison governors like Chesterton and Tracey help them then? [36] Only fundamental changes in society's treatment of these problems could strike to the root of the evil. "How radical I am getting!" Dickens wrote Forster in August, 1841. "I wax stronger and stronger in the true principles every day." [37]

Dickens had been sympathetic to the Chartist program of manhood suffrage, vote by ballot, annual Parliaments, abolition of property qualifications for election to Parliament, payment of members, and division of the country into equal electoral districts.[38] He agreed with Carlyle's declaration in a thick pamphlet entitled *Chartism* that the movement voiced a just protest against a social organization dominated by privilege and wealth. Parliamentary reform had not accomplished much that Dickens regarded as valuable, nor would it, he was convinced, so long as Parliament was controlled by the aristocracy, the industrialists, and the rich merchants. The middle class, of which he was himself a member, would never help the masses, as some people hoped. It was only "the fringe on the mantel of the upper class," [39] its interests identical with the governing hierarchy into which it steadily merged.

Consequently, although Dickens reveals no trace of Carlyle's doctrine of leaders divinely born to command and a populace endowed only with the right to obey, he shared Carlyle's scorn for a Parliament that represented only a sham aristocracy. Carlyle's philosophy did not plainly display to nineteenth-century readers the ominous Fascist overtones it reveals today; its real drift was disguised by a mysticism in which his dictators merged vaguely with the poets and prophets and heroic light-bringers of legend. Dickens saw in Carlyle the denunciation of an incompetent cruelty that condemned the poor to starve in cellars and garrets; he did not see the iron fist that would have crushed all freedom.

All Dickens's writings, indeed, from *Oliver Twist* to *Our Mutual Friend*, make it clear that he was not advocating tyrannic authority, however kindly in intention. He objected not merely to the stupid cruelty but to the arbitrary power of Bumble. He objected not merely to the poorhouse being a place of terror but to old Betty Higden being forced into any poorhouse at all against her will. What Dickens really desired was not subservience to a benevolent despot; it was emancipation from the "accursed gentility" and enthronement of privilege that blighted England. Carlyle's searing contempt for Parliament therefore seemed to Dickens to voice his own unbelief in a government that did not represent the people.

*   *   *   *   *

The two men had met in February, 1840, at a dinner given by Charles Buller, where Lord Morpeth, M. Guizot, and Lord and Lady Holland were among the other guests. Carlyle was tickled to see "the little bob" Dickens gave in greeting Lady Holland, "a brown-skinned, silent, sad, concentrated, proud old dame," Carlyle said. "Notable word she spake none—sate like one wont to be obeyed and entertained." Dickens he observed with close attention, and described later, a bit superciliously, though with more good will than he usually gave his fellow guests:

"Know, Pickwick was of the same dinner party, though they did not seem to heed him much. He is fine little fellow—Boz, I think: clear blue intelligent eyes that he arches amazingly, large protrusive, rather loose mouth, a face of the most extreme *mobility*, which he shuttles about—eyebrows, eyes, mouth and all—in a very singular manner while speaking. Surmount them with a loose coil of common coloured hair, and set it on a small compact figure very small and dressed á la D'Orsay rather than well—this is Pickwick. For the rest, a quiet, shrewd-looking little fellow, who seems to guess pretty well what he is and what others are." [40]

There is no record of what Dickens thought of Carlyle's dour figure, with its blazing eyes and shaggy hair, its set jaw and protruding underlip giving the whole face an expression of dogged determination and of gloom. Nor, although Carlyle obtained Dickens's support, with that of Talfourd and Bulwer, in founding the London Library in 1840, did any close acquaintance develop between them until several years later.[41]

Carlyle's disdain of the lawmakers at Westminster, however, strongly confirmed Dickens's disillusioning experience of sitting in the Reporter's Gallery, the repeated spectacle of good men like Grote, Lord Ashley, and Lord John Russell being defeated in the most necessary reforms by callous political obstruction. Nevertheless, when Dickens was offered the opportunity in 1841 to forward social reform from a seat in the House of Commons, he hesitated for a few days. In May Lord Melbourne's Government fell, and a group of citizens from Reading asked Dickens to stand as their second candidate with his friend Talfourd. Dickens courteously refused on the ground that he could not afford the expense of a contested election. "I beg you to understand," he replied, "that I am restrained solely (and much against my will) by the consideration I have mentioned . . ." [42] Partly, no doubt, he was merely being polite to Talfourd's supporters in order not to injure his friend with them. When a few days later they suggested that the Government might support his candidacy even to the extent of paying the entire cost of the contest, he again refused. He could not compromise his independence by putting himself under any such obligations.[43] And in later years his position hardened into the firm conviction that Parliament was no sphere for him, and hardly for any public-spirited man who did not want to be worn down by repeated frustration. Therefore, although he received many offers even of uncontested seats, he always declined.

This concern with public welfare that paradoxically kept him from accepting a seat in Parliament was, from the very beginning, an animating force in Dickens's work. He was a writer who strove to do more than excite or entertain; he was critical of the world he portrayed. *Sketches by Boz* had its flickering flame-tongues of wrath for the miseries of milliners' apprentices and the hopelessness that drove the slum-dweller to the gin palace; and *Pickwick* clearly makes its points against hypocritical temperance reformers, corrupt borough elections, the inequities of Chancery, and the abuses of prison administration. But, as he swept into the full stride of his career, his most striking growth was in the scope and penetration of his criticism.

As he saw the murky skies and glaring furnaces of Wolverhampton

and the factories of Manchester, as he felt the impact of Dr. Southwood Smith's report on the conditions in the coal mines, as he revisited the jails and devoured the statistics on juvenile delinquency,
as he struggled with his own ambiguous reactions to the riots of
Barnaby Rudge, he realized that dirt and poverty and crime were not
caused only by the depravity and evil of individuals. He began to move
toward an understanding of the intricate network that bound all these
things he hated into a linked system dominating every major institution of society.

The time would come when he no longer struck merely at the
cruelty of the workhouse and the foundling asylum, the ignorance
and brutality of the cheap schools, the enslavement of human beings
in mines and factories, the hideous evils of slums where crime simmered and proliferated, the injustices of the law, and the cynical corruption of the lawmakers betraying the welfare of the country to the
entrenched privilege they represented. He would not cease to assail
any of these distortions of decency, but his comprehensive vision
would perceive them all as no more than vicious symptoms of the
great evil permeating every field of human endeavor: the entire structure of exploitation on which the social order was founded. And the
fiercest of his attacks he would direct against that golden-faced idol
with a heart of iron and bowels of brass.

CHAPTER FOUR

The Neglected and Misused

CRITICISM: *The Old Curiosity Shop*
and *Barnaby Rudge*

NEITHER *The Old Curiosity Shop* nor *Barnaby Rudge* attacks
social injustice directly. They make no such onslaught against
specific institutions as *Oliver Twist* made against the workhouse and
Nicholas Nickleby against the Yorkshire schools. They voice little of
that slashing antagonism to a cold-hearted economic philosophy that
merely rationalized society's evils, and which Dickens had already
scored as one of the great evils itself. But as the awareness grew within
him that amputation of the individual evil would not cure the diseased
social organism, these two books brought from him not further
diagnosis of the symptoms but lyrical outcries against the very fact
of that disease and its deadly destructiveness.

These narratives are as different from each other as the shadows of
Oliver are from the outdoor brightness of *Nickleby*. *The Old Curiosity
Shop* paints glowing pictures of the hard-working Nubbles family, and
renders with humorous pathos that starved little household drudge,
the Marchioness, in the damp underground kitchen where she spends
her days. During the wayfarings of Nell and her grandfather it gives
a brief, horrifying glimpse of the Black Country and the dark industrial conflicts that are being engendered there. And Nell herself is a
pathetic symbol of all the forgotten and ignored, left to wander
through the difficulties of their existence as best they may.

Barnaby Rudge, however, sweeps over these themes in a more tempestuous key. Its tones reverberate fiercely in the resentments against
the world of Hugh, the brutal and embittered hostler at the Maypole,
and they swell into the dreadful clamor and hideous fury of the rioters

[319]

who storm burning and destroying through the streets of London. Their violence Dickens sees as the inevitable consequence of grievances ignored by governors who feel no sense of responsibility for the welfare of the governed. It is with a stinging irony that in the end he shows the strong arm of the law—so slow to prevent and so heavy to repress—wreaking vengeance on the most helpless and oppressed of those who had been literally maddened to rebellion.

During the time in which *Barnaby Rudge* and *The Old Curiosity Shop* were published, coquettish little Dolly Varden captivated readers and Nell broke everyone's heart. But since then there have been strong reservations about the merits of both books. Not, to be sure, that parts of them have ever failed to be admired: the tumultuous narrative of the *Barnaby Rudge* riots seething with mounting turmoil through two hundred furious pages, and in *The Old Curiosity Shop* all the comic scenes and most of the melodramatic ones. Many readers, however, have found the earlier half of *Barnaby* slow-going and its humor mechanical, and many more have felt the death of Little Nell to be overdone in its sentimental pathos.

But no reader of *The Old Curiosity Shop* resists the ludicrous appeal of Dick Swiveller, with his glorious love of the highfalutin gesture, his "unerring instinct," as G. K. Chesterton says, "for the perfect folly of a phrase." [1] Where others drink and sleep, he quaffs "the rosy" and snatches "a wink or two of the balmy." [2] Hear him gloomily murmuring to his inamorata, "Miss Wackles, I believed you true, and I was blessed in so believing, but now I mourn that e'er I knew a girl so fair yet so deceiving." [3] When she falters her regrets for trying to arouse his jealousy by flirting with the market gardener Cheggs, out of what Byronic depths of bitterness he replies: "Sorry, Ma'am! Sorry in the possession of a Cheggs!" [4] Hear him exclaim, "Some wine there. Ho!" and then behold him "handing the tankard to himself with great humility" and "receiving it haughtily." [5] He is at the same time overwhelmingly absurd and entirely real, for he knows that he is absurd, and goes on being so because it pleases him. The solitary poetic delight that the *mot juste* was to Flaubert, that is the joy Dick Swiveller feels in great gulps of ludicrously grandiose words.

Dick is only one, however, among the rich attractions of *The Old Curiosity Shop*. Kit Nubbles takes his mother and the younger children to Astley's Circus, and later to an oyster shop, where little Jacob miraculously eats oysters for the first time "as if he had been born and bred to the business," and the baby sits "good as gold, trying to force a large orange into his mouth" and "making indentations in his soft visage with an oyster-shell." [6] Nell and her grandfather have supper at the Jolly Sandboys with the Punch and Judy men, while the performing dog who is in disgrace mournfully grinds "Old Hundredth" on the organ and the traveling showmen talk about what becomes of worn-out old giants. The morose Thomas Codlin makes disinterested endeavors to ingratiate himself with Nell at the expense of his good-natured partner Short: "Recollect the friend. Codlin's the friend, not Short. Short's very well as far as he goes, but the real friend is Codlin—not Short." [7] To Nell's innocent inquiry about wax-works, "Is it funnier than Punch?" Mrs. Jarley indignantly shrieks, "Funnier! It is not funny at all," and grandly explains, "It's calm and—what's that word again—critical?—no—classical—that's it—it's calm and classical." [8] There is an endless wealth of such scenes, ranging with effortless brilliance from the poor Nubbles household and the kindly middle-class Garlands in London to the varied people Nell and her grandfather encounter on their journeyings, the bargees, the gamblers and low life of the race tracks, the starved and desperate laborers of the Midlands.

Despite its profusion of people and places, they are all woven into a simple narrative structure. Old Mr. Trent, Nell's senile grandfather, anxious to provide for her future, has gradually fallen prey to a gambling mania, frenziedly borrowing at exorbitant rates from Quilp, until the old curiosity shop and all its contents are seized in repayment by the dwarfish usurer. Nell and her grandfather flee from London into the country, the old man in a kind of childish terror, Nell to take him from the temptations of the gaming table. Kit Nubbles, formerly their boy-of-all-work, takes service with the Garland family, but Quilp, who hates him for his devotion to Nell, conspires with his knavish legal advisers, Sampson and Sally Brass, to make it appear that Kit has stolen money from their office. Dick Swiveller, who is employed as a clerk there, foils this plot with the aid of their little kitchen servant, whom Dick calls the Marchioness. Meanwhile both Quilp and the old man's brother have been trying to trace the fugitives, Quilp for further persecutions, the brother to restore them to comfort and prosperity. They have moved through the hideous regions of the industrial north, the child slowly sinking into illness. When they gain refuge,

Little Nell and the Old Man looking back at London

after long wanderings, with the schoolmaster of the ancient parish church of Tong, the struggle and exposure have been too severe for Nell. Only a few hours before the brother at last finds them, the child has died, under circumstances of prolonged and intensified pathos.

The reservations felt about *The Old Curiosity Shop* have, of course, been concerned with none of its comic successes, but with the character and fate of Nell. To almost the degree that Dickens's contemporaries luxuriated in grief over her death, modern readers have often been coldly indifferent and even derisive. Aldous Huxley voices the typical indictment in accusing Dickens of bad writing, of sentimentality and gush, and of a lachrymose emotional vulgarity. The "sticky overflowings" of Dickens's heart, writes Huxley witheringly, billow from him "in an atrocious blank verse" while he drowns his intelligence and wallows in his own tears.[9]

It is true that Dickens indulges his own emotion by prolonging over too many pages the narrative of Nell's slow decline. Some of the sad details—the old man weeping in dark corners of the church, the mortuary conversations with the schoolmaster and the sexton, the little boy begging her not to become an angel—are contrived and unconvincing. There is a lugubrious excess in the sobbing iambic rhythms of the close. But though the execution is faulty, the emotion is neither excessive nor inappropriate; it is as if a heart-rending requiem were rendered on a barrel organ. The medium is inferior, but the feeling is noble. That was what moved Dickens's contemporaries.

And it must be emphasized that readers like Landor and Carlyle, Washington Irving and Lord Jeffrey were not uncritical, they were not men of vulgar and sentimental taste. Their discriminations were rigorous, often severe. But for them the defects that we see were either trivial or nonexistent; the pathos that makes us uncomfortable moved them deeply. Rather than our being entirely right and Dickens's contemporaries entirely wrong, the fact is that we live in a different emotional climate from theirs.

Though much has been said about Victorian restraint, emotionally it is we who are restrained, not they. Large bodies of modern readers, especially those called "sophisticated," distrust any uncurbed yielding to emotion. Above all when the emotion is noble, heroic, or tender, they wince in skeptical suspicion and distaste. A heartfelt expression of sentiment seems to them exaggerated, hypocritical, or embarrassing. They can bear the pathos of Ilusha's death in *The Brothers Karamazov*; Dostoevski dignifies it by involving it in a preoccupation with the problem of evil. They can bear the Marchioness in *The Old Curiosity Shop*; Dickens disinfects her pathos by infusing it in humor. But pure pathos they can bear only in very attenuated quantities.

This fear of sentiment, however, is far less deeply rooted in human feelings than the sentiment of the Victorians. Our response is the deviation and theirs approaches closer to the norm. Homer's heroes easily dissolve in tears and Dante swoons under the pain of Beatrice's displeasure. The troubadours and the Elizabethan dramatists and sonneteers were not afraid of emotional extravagance. Shakespeare's Imogen in *Cymbeline* and Hermione in *The Winter's Tale* are exquisite exercises in pathos; and Fletcher's *Faithful Shepherdess* and Ford's *The Broken Heart* reveal how far the Caroline dramatists were ready to go in indulging a tearful mood. And in the eighteenth century many a coarse, hard-riding, hard-drinking country landowner like Fielding's Squire Western would sit weeping while his daughter played some tender ballad on the harpsichord. It is in fact not we, but Dickens and the Victorians, who are in the central stream of natural emotion.

There are explanations, of course, for our peculiar fear of sentiment as sentimental. With the enormous growth of popular fiction, vulgar imitators have cheapened the methods they learned from great writers and coarsened their delineation of emotion. Dickens's very powers marked him out as a model for such emulation. In consequence, we read the death of Nell, or of Paul Dombey, not as Dickens's contemporaries did, but distracted by memories of all the facile tears that have dripped through fiction since. But when *The Old Curiosity Shop* appeared in 1840, it touched chords of feeling of which people were not ashamed with a novel and tender hand. As Gissing truly says—and Gissing was no ready emotionalist—"Little Nell struck readers not only as pathetic, but as fresh and original, which indeed she was; overfamiliarity robs us of the delight which was inspired by a new vein of fiction, discovered and worked by a master spirit." [10]

*   *   *   *   *

Some of the newness of *The Old Curiosity Shop* assuredly lies in its daring fusion of the picaresque novel and the novel of sentiment. No writer has absorbed his forerunners more thoroughly than Dickens, but not many youthful writers have varied them more freely. *Pickwick Papers* and *Nicholas Nickleby* sum up and develop the picaresque tradition of Defoe, Fielding, and Smollett; but Dickens writes with a warmth and color and tenderness entirely his own. *The Old Curiosity Shop* sums up and develops the sentiment of Goldsmith and Sterne, but allows the pathos to unfold against a sharp background of urban scoundrels and countryside mountebanks. Recognition has never been given to how much Nell's touching little odyssey gains, not merely in picturesque color, but in essential feeling, from these lights and darks: by alternating with the bold and grotesque villainy of Quilp and the sneaking villainy of Sampson Brass, and by moving through the world of Punch and Judy men, strollers, jugglers, gypsies, dancing dogs, and traveling wax-works. The story in fact is composed simply of these contrasting pictures, the rough men and bad

places, and the child passing among them all, untouched and unstained, until the last scenes in the quiet village and the ancient
church are dissolved by death.

They make of *The Old Curiosity Shop* a sad Hans Christian Ander-
sen fairy tale, a summer transformation of some story of a snow prin-
cess slowly melting away. Indeed, for all the vivid solidity with which
it renders sordid realities like Quilp's wharf and Sampson Brass's
house in Bevis Marks and the rapacious figures around Nell and her
grandfather, the entire tale has about it something fabulous. The distorted objects crouching in dim corners of the curiosity shop, the fantastic carvings and threatening forms, harmlessly prefigure the uglier
shapes of evil that will beset their journey in a world dark with lurking
dangers.

Everywhere fairy tale merges into reality. The monstrous Quilp in-
vades the house with his fawning legal henchman Brass, and lolls goggling in the child's bed like some demon breathing fire and smoke.
The old man and the child creep out at dawn in desperate flight; across
the whole country Quilp pursues, looming suddenly and horribly into
the moonlight through the black archway of a town gate. But he fails
to see the child cowering in the shadows, and again the fugitives escape. They are never safe, though; legions of dangers and betrayers
encompass them about. Plucking hands of restraint or injury reach
out, as in an enchanted forest, wherever they pass, but always they
move on. And still, although the young heroine is never harmed, the
doomed journey has but one inevitable goal.

For the good powers and personalities fail to help, just as the wicked
dwarf and his black legal magic failed to entangle. Though they too
set out in pursuit, to bring happiness to one frail child, though they
have all the resources of intelligence and wealth, and though they
trace her over England from town to town, they arrive too late. "All
the good fairies," writes G. K. Chesterton, "and all the kind magicians,
all the just kings and all the gallant princes, with chariots and flying
dragons . . . go after one little child who had strayed into a wood, and
find her dead." [11]

The story is more than a fairy tale, however; it is a kind of fable, and
as always in fable deeper implications run below than appear on the
surface. The grandfather's crazed pursuit of fortune at the gaming
table, his belief that there he will gain the gold that will make his

grandchild a lady, the delusions that victimize the very object of his tenderness and bring her to her death, have profounder meanings and wider ramifications than the derangement of one feeble old man. Whenever money is at stake the two wanderers meet with treachery and greed. Only the unconventional, the lowly, and the unworldly really treat them kindly—eccentric, warm-hearted Mrs. Jarley, the rough bargemen and the lonely furnaceman crouching beside his ashes, the poor schoolmaster. Respectable society speaks in the hectoring voice of Miss Monflathers, reproving poverty and misfortune as moral stigmas. The whole bizarre company, as Rex Warner notes, suggests that "Dickens is describing forces which are bigger than the characters themselves, and is embodying in his people and scenes the cruelties and delusions which he observes in wider society." [12]

In no far-fetched sense, indeed, *The Old Curiosity Shop* may be read as a fantasy upon a no less fantastic nineteenth-century dream. What oriental silks and spices, Spanish gold, the exploitation of the New World, the wealth of the slave and rum trades had been to the imagination of earlier periods, stock-market speculation became to the early industrial age. Gas-lighting syndicates, muffin-baking companies, railway shares, Eden land corporations, and Peruvian mines were to shower lucky investors with sudden affluence that would enable them to live in idle luxury, magically transformed into ladies and gentlemen. The stock market was at once Golconda and gaming table, pouring forth the "shining yellow boys" [13] that dazzled the vision of Nell's grandfather.

Since the close of the Napoleonic Wars the stock-gambling mania had spread in waves of rapacity and ruin. Speculative losses had been the death of Sir Walter Scott. In 1836–37, Dickens had seen the beginnings of the railway-speculation madness that was to reach delirious heights in the forties. And these were only symptoms of an acquisitive greed callous to the suffering it caused. Everywhere in mine and mill and factory profits took their toll of maimed bodies and gaunt frames and embittered hearts, and exacted dreadful sacrifices of children's happiness and children's lives. Herod's massacre of the innocents was kind in comparison with the massacre of the innocent and helpless that went on every day for gain. These considerations, if not all consciously present to Dickens's mind as he sorrowed over the death of Little Nell, were part of his background of thought and feeling, dark with his knowledge of childhood in London's slums, burned deep in his memory by the horrors of Southwood Smith's mine-and-factory reports. Through them Nell is transfigured from a single suffering child into a symbol for all the victims of a society that might discover too late, as Midas did, that it had killed its children, but not even gained his gold.

Of the meanest evils produced by that society the misshapen Quilp and his degraded helpers Sampson and Sally Brass are grotesque embodiments. Quilp portrays its heartless cupidity; Brass and his sister the dirty and crawling dishonesty that will twist itself and every instrument of law to the service of chicanery, swallowing sneers and snarls together with its spoils. Quilp deliberately spurs the grandfather forward upon his disastrous course, ensuring himself with usurious agreements, and takes possession of the curiosity shop when he sees that his victim has lost everything else. Brass devises the legal and illegal tricks that his horrible little employer exacts. Degraded as both of them are, it is dubious that Dickens draws any deep moral distinction between them and many an exalted financier and his counsel.

The characterizations of the two Brasses are masterpieces at the same time of the loathsome and the ludicrous. That gaunt and bony amazon, Sally Brass, inhaling snuff and wiping her pen upon her dress, at once laconic and tormentingly malicious, shares her brother's avarice to its last depth, and would be beyond measure indignant if he abated a particle of it. But she nevertheless delights to thwart him and to taunt him with his groveling cowardice, and grimly enjoys his sufferings under Quilp's persecutions. Sampson Brass, sniggering with subservient admiration at every insult the dwarf bestows upon him, soaked with rain and shivering with cold in Quilp's leaky little summerhouse, drinking boiling liquor at his host's behest, never ceases to exclaim in cringing and pretended rapture, "He has the richest humour!" "Such spirits!" "Quite eccentric!" "Amazingly whimsical!" [14] Every stroke in the delineation of this precious pair is filled with a laughter like the stinging of a whip until it dies away in the horror of their last hideous appearance, crawling along the streets on cold nights looking into kennels for offal and refuse food.

But the supreme grotesque creation of the book, melodramatic, comic, hateful, crackling with vitality, is Daniel Quilp. He lives in an atmosphere of satanic hilarity, plaguing his very coadjutors like a demon bubbling with malignant glee. He grotesquely lolls his tongue out at his mother-in-law when she happens to catch his eye in a mirror, meanwhile saying in a tone of bland affection, "How are you now, my dear old darling?" [15] When there is a knock at the door he bounces through it flailing his arms in furious attack upon the visitor. He eats hard-boiled eggs shell and all, devours gigantic prawns with their heads and tails on, chews tobacco and water-cress at the same time, drinks hot grog direct from the saucepan in which it has just been boiling on the fire. He maltreats the boy at his wharf and snarls extraordinary threats at him: "You dog, I'll beat you with an iron rod, I'll scratch you with a rusty nail, I'll pinch your eyes, if you talk to me." [16] He varies these ferocities by wheedling his wife or her mother with a solicitude even more terrifying, or making jokes of a fantastic and elaborate facetiousness. He reduces all his dependents to a half-fascinated terror and dominates every scene in which he appears with such electric intensity that even when he is dead the reader almost hopes he will poke his head into a room to make one more atrocious remark.

If Quilp is a gargoyle perversion of cruelty, Dickens makes it clear that the mere callousness of upper-class indifference to the poor may be hardly less brutal. Miss Monflathers, the proprietor of the young ladies' seminary, feels that the lower classes were made only to toil unremittingly in factories and on farms. When Nell comes to leave handbills advertising Mrs. Jarley's Wax-Work, "Don't you feel how naughty it is of you," Miss Monflathers says severely, "to be a wax-work child, when you might have the proud consciousness of assisting, to the extent of your infant powers, the manufactures of your country; of improving your mind by the constant contemplation of the steam-engine; and of earning a comfortable and independent subsistence of from two-and-ninepence to three shillings per week?" [17] Dr. Watts's poem about the little busy bee, with its emphasis on a due proportion between work and play, is only for genteel children, for whom the work means painting on velvet and fancy needlework, Miss Monflathers remarks: for poor people's children there should be nothing but toil.

The satiric indignation of this scene is underlined by the later episodes in the dark inferno of the industrial regions, hideous with stagnant pools and blighted vegetation, where strange engines writhe like tortured creatures and shriek like souls in anguish, while wan and half-naked men, women, and children scowl from the doorless entries of tottering houses and a black vomit of smoke blasts all life. Where is the justice, cries one woman, of forgiving the attempted theft by a neighbor's son because he is deaf and dumb, and transporting *her* son, who was deaf, dumb, and blind to right? "You gentlemen have as good a right to punish her boy, that God kept in ignorance of sound and speech, as you have to punish mine, that you kept in ignorance yourselves. How many of the girls and boys—ah, men and women too— that are brought before you, and you don't pity, are deaf and dumb in their minds, and go wrong in that state, and are punished in that state, body and soul, while you gentlemen are quarrelling among yourselves whether they ought to learn this or that?" [18]

That is Dickens's own outcry, sounding again and again through the pages of this book, and through all his work. It is reinforced, too, by terrible pictures of industrial unrest painted in lurid colors of grim warning. Dark figures move among the blazing furnaces, calling to one another with hoarse cries. One worker tells Nell that he and five hundred others have been thrown out of work for three months; his third and last child has just died of starvation. No wonder, then, Dickens comments, that "bands of unemployed labourers paraded the roads, or clustered by torchlight round their leaders, who told them, in stern language, of their wrongs, and urged them on to frightful cries and threats," and that "maddened men, armed with sword and firebrand, spurning the tears and prayers of women who would restrain them, rushed forth on errands of terror and destruction . . ." [19] Their superiors and rulers were negligently sowing seeds of cruelty and hatred. Let them beware lest they themselves were cut down in a harvest of vengeance.

* * * * *

In *The Old Curiosity Shop* the notes of sympathy for the oppressed and of dark warning are subordinated to the grotesque comedy and lyric pathos. Only here and there does it give a glimpse of the fiery depths beneath the peaceful surface of society. These disorders, latent in it, approach dominance in *Barnaby Rudge*, boiling up in those two hundred tumultuous pages of mob fury that are its most impressive and exciting achievement, like a volcanic eruption bursting out of the black subterranean cauldron within which its flames and molten lava have been seething. No narrative of physical action that Dickens ever produced, not even the French Revolution scenes in *A Tale of Two Cities*, surpasses these parts of *Barnaby Rudge* in continuous power, speed, and violence.

Despite their surging passion, however, *Barnaby Rudge* is the least satisfactory of all Dickens's full-length books. Among its defects are a clumsy and broken-backed plot, with which the feeble-witted Barnaby, its central character, has no organic connection. His father is supposed to have been murdered, with his employer, years before the story opens, but actually he had killed and robbed his master and then disappeared. Mrs. Rudge and her son live in a cottage on the estate of Mr. Haredale, the brother and heir of the elder Rudge's victim. Haredale's niece Emma is in love with Edward Chester, whose polished and cynical father is her uncle's mortal enemy. Jo Willet, whose father owns the village inn, the Maypole, loves Dolly, the daughter of the London locksmith, Gabriel Varden. Dolly laughs at Jo's love-making, he enlists in the army, Mr. Chester disowns his son, and Mrs. Rudge disappears with Barnaby in order to escape the secret blackmailing visits of her husband.

There is then a five-year gap in the story, after which everyone is brought together again in the tumults of the anti-Catholic riots precipitated in 1780 by Lord George Gordon. Barnaby is enticed into joining the rioters who burn the Maypole and Mr. Haredale's house and kidnap Dolly and Emma. But the two girls are rescued by Jo, who has returned from the war in America; Dolly has repented her coquettishness; Haredale kills the elder Chester in a duel, discovers the secret of his brother's death, and hands the elder Rudge over to justice; Emma and Edward marry; and Barnaby's mental deficiencies are invoked to obtain a pardon for his share in the riots.

The earlier half of the story, before the five-year break, is slow, even sluggish and impeded in movement, in a way that seems to reflect the difficulty Dickens had in getting started on it. Much of its comedy is mechanical and tiresome. The dull conceit of old John Willet, the slow-witted landlord of the Maypole, is all too often merely dull rather than funny. Barnaby, for all his crazed imagination, attains to no more than flashes of fantastic life, and his mother creeps through the book in a tediously lugubrious resignation. The elder Rudge is an incredible silhouette of sneaking villainy, skulking in obscure corners and forever turning up at midnight. The sentimental heroine of the story, Dolly

Varden, with her cherry-colored ribbons and her coquetry, is coyly kittenish beyond almost all bearing. Young Edward Chester and Emma Haredale, the romantic leads, have the usual conventional virtues and no personality whatever. Few of the major figures, in fact, are very striking, and only in some of the minor ones does Dickens reveal his characteristic power.

Sim Tappertit, the locksmith's apprentice, is not among the successes. His conceit of his own importance, his illusion that he can subdue the proudest beauty by "eyeing her over," and his infatuation with the shapeliness of his legs are little better than stock comedy. And the mockery with which Dickens portrays the secret meetings of the 'Prentice Knights is ludicrous, of course, as a picture of conspiratorial labor organizations. Better is Mrs. Varden's servant Miggs. The volubly illiterate commiseration with which she stirs up discord between her mistress and the long-suffering Varden is good, and so is her spiteful and surreptitious jealousy of the locksmith's pretty daughter. "My situations is lowly, and my capacities is limited, and my duties is to humble myself . . . Ho yes! My only becoming occupations is to help young flaunting pagins to brush and comb and titivate theirselves into whitening and suppulchres . . ." [20]

That plaintive and self-pitying martyr Mrs. Varden is a brilliant addition to Dickens's gallery of trying women. Complaining dolefully that Varden is "glum and silent" when he is most cheerful, expressing submission "with a kind of solemn titter," she dampens the poor man's spirits daily in a series of relentless stages: "Therefore, if you please, Varden, we'll drop the subject"; "No, you did not begin it, oh dear no, not you, my dear!"; "I know my duty. I need know it, I am sure. I am often obliged to bear it in mind, when my inclination, perhaps, would be for the moment to forget it. Thank you, Varden." [21]

They are a remarkable series, these women, from the termagant Mrs. Raddle and the shrewish Mrs. Sowerberry, through the fascinating Miss Petowker, whose alteration after marriage proves such a surprise to the unfortunate Mr. Lillyvick. Mrs. Varden is more elaborately drawn than any of her predecessors, and with a richness of domestic detail that suggests more prolonged and closer observation. Although Dickens hardly ever copied without variation from a living model, he did adapt the recognizable traits even of those very near to him. Mrs. Nickleby's scatterbrained gabble, for example, renders his mother without her sense of humor. The wife of one of Dickens's Barrow cousins described Catherine Dickens as a complaining woman, and suspected that the novelist was nagged in his home.[22] As early as the birth of their eldest daughter Mary, there was friction between husband and wife, though it is not at all likely that Dickens exhibited the meek good nature of Gabriel Varden. Thomas Wright notes that Kate's mother, Mrs. Hogarth, appears as Mrs. Jiniwin, Quilp's mother-in-law in *The Old Curiosity Shop*, and that her word-conflicts with the dwarf, "or something like them, certainly took place in real life." "Quilp," he adds, "was, in a sense—in his love for monkey tricks, for instance—Dickens himself as seen by the eyes of Mrs. Hogarth." [23]

Dolly Varden, exasperating though she is, in one way represents Dickens's most successful portrayal of a pretty young woman so far: she is alive. Unlike Rose Maylie, she is no mere image of all the virtues drowned in sugar syrup, and unlike Madeline Bray no colorless symbol of the hero's affections. We can easily believe that when Mrs. Varden was her daughter's age she was the same kind of pouting coquette that Dolly is, and see Dolly's pretty petulance gradually turning into her mother's whimpering, self-righteous discontent. In relationship to Jo Willet she is a callous little tormentor; in relationship to her own desires, a silly little fool defeating the very ends she has at heart. As characterization this would all be admirable if we were not invited to look on these very qualities with indulgent affection as parts of her bewitching cuteness, and to find her delightful even when our patience is being tried by her half-witted refusal to tell her lover that she loves him.

*　　*　　*　　*　　*

But the major claim of *Barnaby Rudge* to consideration is not in its characterizations; it is in the roaring flames and furious movement of the anti-Catholic tumults around which the book is built. Though Dickens himself was no friend to the Catholic faith, he is painstakingly fair to its adherents. No word of theological judgment appears in the narrative. Lord George Gordon, the half-unbalanced agitator who precipitated the riots, is portrayed as a deluded bigot, and his secretary Gashford as an unscrupulous schemer. In the mob whatever small number of sincere fanatics there may be are lost among the hordes of the desperate and miserable who are swept on to wild destruction by ruffians, criminals, and malcontents. Mr. Haredale, the only Catholic painted in any detail, is blunt-spoken and gloomy, but a man of conscience; and none of the Catholics in the book are revealed in the mean lights that illumine their enemies, as silly, like Mrs. Varden, or hypocritical, like Miggs, or cynical and vindictive, like Sir John Chester.

Even Mr. Haredale's morose rudenesses, in fact, are partly designed as a foil to the polished insincerities of Chester, whom Dickens detests with the same intensity that he did Sir Mulberry Hawk and depicts with the same chivalrous hatred. In consequence, Chester does have a glittering if artificial reality, and there is even a picturesque integrity in his composing his face to a well-bred smile as he dies stabbed through the heart by his old enemy Haredale. As a picture of Lord Chesterfield, of course, upon whom he was modeled, he is pure caricature. Chesterfield was a great master of worldly wisdom, but he does not deserve Chester's eulogy of him: "In every page of this enlightened writer, I find some captivating hypocrisy which has never occurred to me before, or some superlative piece of selfishness to which I was utterly a stranger." [24] Nor would Chester be likely to make any such remark, nor be doing himself justice if he did. But to Dickens he stands for all the freezing self-centeredness of the aristocracy at its worst, and all its merely specious standards of good manners.

This symbolic aspect of Chester is profoundly related to Dickens's conviction that the riots were deeply rooted in mass bitterness, and that hatred of Catholics was only their proximate, not their fundamental, cause. For Chester has seduced and deserted a gypsy woman subsequently hanged at Tyburn, and his bastard son Hugh, the hostler at the Maypole, feels a savage rancor at his position in the world and a bloodthirsty determination to avenge himself. When father and son, without knowing their relationship, are brought together, the privileged gentleman uses the brutalized product of his own neglect only as a tool, tempting and leading him into further depravity. Even when their blood tie becomes known and the son is condemned to the gallows in whose shadow he was born, Sir John indifferently denies the relationship and shrugs off all responsibility.

No more cogent symbol could be found for a society that denied its own children—denied even the relationship of brotherhood between the prosperous and the impoverished, that ignored and neglected the masses, exploited and maltreated and corrupted them, left them to

filth and ignorance, refused to accept any responsibility for them unless they were in the last stages of destitution, and then, if they fell
into vice and crime, let the law take its brutal course to the last measure of severity. What wonder that Hugh asks how he could have
learned, "born as I was born, and reared as I have been reared . . . in
this hardened, cruel, unrelenting place," and stretches his fist to
heaven: "Upon these human shambles, I, who never raised his hand
in prayer till now, call down the wrath of God! On that black tree, of
which I am the ripened fruit, I do invoke the curse of all its victims,
past, present, and to come." [25]

That the riots were really an outbreak of social protest Dickens implies repeatedly throughout the story. He implies it in a significant
interchange between Hugh and Dennis the hangman at Lord George's
headquarters in Welbeck Street: "No Popery, brother!" cries the
hangman. "No Property, brother!" responds Hugh. "Popery, Popery,"
interposes the secretary. "It's all the same!" cries Dennis. "It's all right.
Down with him, Muster Gashford. Down with everybody, down with
everything!" [26] It is implied too, in the defense of the blind man
Stagg: "It's the cant of you folks to be horrified if a blind man robs,
or lies, or steals; oh yes, it's far worse in him . . . than in you, who can
see, and work, and are not dependent on the mercies of the world. A
curse on you! You who have five senses may be wicked at your pleasure; we who have four, and want the most important, are to live and be
moral on our affliction. The true charity and justice of rich to poor, all
the world over!" [27]

The social forces represented by Sir John Chester, and the social
consequences represented by Hugh and Dennis and Stagg, not religious hatred of the Catholics, are the true causes of the riots. Dickens
makes this clear by emphasizing that except for a sprinkling of "honest
zealots," the mob is "composed for the most part of the very scum and
refuse of London, whose growth was fostered by bad criminal laws,
bad prison regulations, and the worst conceivable police," [28] and by
showing how scores of destitute wretches and other poor creatures (including innocently suggestible people like Barnaby) are swept into
the torrent of destruction. And as the turmoil rages ever more fiercely
it swells into outrages totally unconnected with its supposed causes.
Churches as well as Catholic chapels are gutted, mansions like the
Bloomsbury Square residence of Lord Mansfield—who was not a

The Hangman

Catholic—sacked and put to the torch, all the jails of London forced
and their prisoners released.

In following the course of the riots, except for the fictitious wrecking of the Maypole and the burning of Mr. Haredale's house, Dickens
adheres with great fidelity to historical sources. He had a numerous
collection of contemporary pamphlets and accounts from current
periodicals like the *Political Magazine,* and there is a copy of Robert
Watson's *Life of Lord George Gordon* annotated in his hand.[29] But
all the fire and intensity of his narrative, of course, is Dickens's own,
although he may have been partly influenced by Sir Walter Scott's
description of the storming of the Tolbooth in *The Heart of Mid-
lothian.* And when Dickens's vision grows molten, what awful scenes
he paints with awful power:

"There were men there, who danced and trampled on the beds of
flowers as though they trod down human enemies, and wrenched

them from the stalks, like savages who twisted human necks. There were men who cast their lighted torches in the air, and suffered them to fall upon their heads and faces, blistering the skin with deep unseemly burns. . . . On the skull of one drunken lad—not twenty, by his looks—who lay upon the ground with a bottle to his mouth, the lead from the roof came streaming down in a shower of liquid fire, white hot; melting his head like wax." [30] "The gutters of the street, and every crack and fissure in the stones, ran with scorching spirit" from broken casks, around which people lay in heaps, "and drank until they died. While some stooped with their lips to the brink and never raised their heads again, others sprang up from their fiery draught, and danced, half in a mad triumph, and half in the agony of suffocation, until they fell, and steeped their corpses in the liquor that had killed them. From the burning cellars, where they drank out of hats, pails, buckets, tubs, and shoes, some men were drawn alive, but all alight from head to foot; who, in their unendurable anguish and suffering, making for anything that had the look of water, rolled, hissing, in this hideous lake, and splashed up liquid fire which lapped in all it met as it ran along the surface, and neither spared the living nor the dead." [31]

The aftermath to all this maddened violence underlines Dickens's view of its significance. Administrative authorities that had felt no call to redress the grievances of the misused and outcast, that had taken no steps to prevent the uprising and been dilatory enough in getting it under control, were swift and harsh to chastise. Organized society, which denied being its brother's keeper, was ready enough to be his judge. But by no means all of the worst offenders were even apprehended, and many who were condemned were mere victims only slightly involved in the crimes for which they were punished. "It was a most exquisite satire," Dickens writes, upon the degree to which religious hatreds had caused the outbreak, "that some of these people owned themselves to be Catholics, and begged to be attended by their own priests." Two cripples, one with a wooden leg, the other dragging his twisted limbs along with a crutch, were hanged in Bloomsbury Square; another boy in Bow Street; other lads in various quarters of the town. "Four wretched women, too, were put to death. In a word, those who suffered as rioters were, for the most part, the weakest, meanest, and most miserable among them." [32]

The mob scenes of *Barnaby Rudge*, as we have seen, are a strange fusion of exultation and fascinated horror that gives them a curious emotional ambiguity. But there is no ambiguity in the social attitudes the book implies. The only possibility of misreading it would be to assume that the evils of 1780 had been completely eradicated by a more humane and enlightened world. Dickens gave no encouragement to that misapprehension. He looked upon the assumptions underlying the social order with a profoundly critical eye. He was, as he claimed to be, a radical, though he adhered to no doctrinaire faith and had no dogmatic panacea. He did not want to abolish private property. He did not wish everything to be controlled by the state. But neither did he fear state interference to correct social and economic injustices.

What Dickens did desire was that government should represent the people and that its concern should be the welfare of the people, not that of a privileged group of classes. He desired the laws of society to be better, not worse, than the law of the jungle; to cease being weighted against those who had too little and in favor of those who already had more than enough. He desired to see the poor lifted out of the circumstances, not of their making, that hampered their struggles: slum surroundings, illiteracy, incredibly protracted labor under hideously unsanitary conditions for starvation wages. He desired to see an active hand of brotherhood extended to the poor and ignorant and ignored and misused. And he made the very central theme of *Barnaby Rudge* the grim implicit warning barely suggested in *The Old Curiosity Shop*. Uprisings were not always quelled. Unless their selfish indifference yielded to a change of heart, gentlemen might someday rue the hell-fury they had blown to burning in poor men's hearts.

CHAPTER FIVE

Triumph in Scotland and the
Eve of a New Departure

EVEN before Lord Jeffrey arrived in London in April, 1841, he had been earnestly pressing Dickens to visit Scotland. Jeffrey himself drove about Edinburgh declaring there had been "nothing so good as Nell since Cordelia," [1] and the whole city, he wrote Dickens, was eager to welcome him. During the preceding year Dickens had been thinking of going to Ireland, but now his mind began to run instead on Rob Roy's country, Arthur's Seat, and the lochs and glens of the Highlands. The meeting with Jeffrey instantly crystallized his intention.

Though Dickens had dined with Jeffrey on the critic's previous visit to London in 1839,[2] there had been no intimacy; but as the two men came to know each other better, their mutual esteem deepened into friendship. The older man thought the dinners in Devonshire Terrace too sumptuous for a man with a family—even though *Master Humphrey's Clock* was selling forty-four thousand copies a week—and found the novelist reserved in company, but delightful in personal conversations and in long walks through the Regent's Park.[3] Dickens warmed to Jeffrey's charm and wit, and to a kindness in Jeffrey's manner to him which was half that of a father, half of an elder brother.

The very day following their second meeting Dickens determined that on June 21st he would take the road to Scotland. He asked his friend Angus Fletcher to bespeak the needful accommodations at an Edinburgh hotel and perhaps keep them company later: "You shall be our 'Dougal' to the Highlands, and I your bailie." As for the dinner Dickens had heard they were planning to offer him in Edinburgh, he told Fletcher that despite his "quiet ways" he "would not for the

[338]

world" reject their cordiality. "Therefore I say, stop *nothing*; and be assured that I should accept any testimonial of that or any other kind, in the full height of the spirit in which it would be bestowed—and very gladly and proudly." [4]

Dickens and Kate left London two days earlier than originally planned, and on the evening of the 22nd took up quarters at Edinburgh's Royal Hotel. "I have been this morning to the Parliament House," he wrote Forster the next day, "and am now introduced (I hope) to everybody in Edinburgh. The hotel is perfectly besieged, and I have been forced to take refuge in a sequestered apartment at the end of a long passage, wherein I write this letter. They talk of 300 at the dinner. We are very well off in point of rooms, having a handsome sitting-room, another next it for Clock purposes, a spacious bed-room, and large dressing-room adjoining. The castle is in front of the windows, and the view noble. There was a supper ready last night which would have been a dinner anywhere." [5]

The ceremonies of lionization began immediately. Judges, the Solicitor-General, the Lord-Advocate, and other dignitaries all came to call. Sir William Allan squired Dickens around Edinburgh, and his daughter took Kate to visit the house where she was born.[6] In the Hall of the Courts of Law, Dickens was introduced to "the renowned Peter Robertson," "a large, portly, full-faced man, with a merry eye, and a queer way of looking under his spectacles." Here, too, striding up and down at a slashing pace, and dogged by a wiry, sharp-eyed terrier, was John Wilson, Professor of Moral Philosophy at the University, the "Christopher North" of *Blackwood's Magazine*, who was to preside as chairman of the dinner in place of Jeffrey, who was ill.[7] A burly giant nearing his sixtieth year, with "the bluest eye you can imagine," wild hair streaming from under a broad-brimmed hat, unconventionally dressed in a blue-checked shirt without a waistcoat, he looked less like a man of letters than some hale old mountaineer from the Highlands.[8]

The two days before the great event were packed with bustle.[9] Dickens effervesced everywhere and charmed everyone. "He was a very fountain of mirth, bonhomie, and surprising anecdote," said Lewis Spence, an aged relative of Kate's. "Every word sparkled," and left people with the feeling that he was an angel and a genius.[10]

The public dinner took place on Friday, June 25th. More than seventy people had been turned away for lack of room, and besides some two hundred and seventy diners cramming the room to the throat there were almost two hundred feminine spectators.[11] As the guest of honor made his appearance the band struck deliriously into "Charlie Is My Darling," and cheers rang through the room.[12] "It was a most magnificent show," Dickens said, "and the shouting perfectly awful." For once he had come upon a scene that he professed himself staggered to describe. "It beat all natur'." [13]

How different was Dickens's position now from that of seven years ago, when he had been an obscure reporter gazing across the sea of tables in the pavilion to the high table where Lord Grey had then been the guest of honor. Now the music and the clamor and the speeches were for him. Robertson convulsed the company with laughter by an imaginary interview between Squeers and Scott's Dominie Sampson, culminating in the latter worthy schoolmaster's "Pro-di-gi-ous!" [14] Wilson, although ill, "plucked up like a lion" and spoke eloquently on the genius, the sympathy with his fellow men, and the spirit of truth, honor, and integrity that pervaded all Dickens's creations, and concluded by assuring him that all Scotland regarded him with admiration and love.[15]

As Dickens rose to reply he was interested to note his own calm and realize that, "notwithstanding the enthoosemoosy, which was startling," he was "as cool as a cucumber." How remarkable it was, though, "to see such a number of grey-headed men gathered about my brown flowing locks!" [16] He began speaking with absolute poise. If he felt their warm and generous welcome less, he said, he would be better able to thank them. But as it was, it left him "all heart and no lips, yearning to respond. . . . I thank you again and again, with the energy of a thousand thanks in each one, and I drink to you with a heart as full as my glass . . ." [17]

The parallel between his own reception and that tendered Earl Grey was rendered complete four days later. The Lord Provost, Council, and Magistrates voted him by acclamation the freedom of the city of Edinburgh.[18] What a triumph for a young writer of twenty-nine, to be accorded a recognition not bestowed upon the veteran statesman until his seventieth year! The parchment scroll recording the honor Dickens framed and hung upon his study walls, where it remained to the end of his life.[19]

During the week-end he had visited Jeffrey at Craigcrook. The following week was a rush of breakfasting, lunching, and dining. A Scotch county asked Dickens to represent it in Parliament, but he refused although this time the offer was "free, gratis, and for nothing." He made a public appearance at the theater, attended an evening party given by the Treasurer of the Town Council, had supper with the artists of Edinburgh.[20] The expenses of his visit were proving more than he had calculated, and he had failed to bring a checkbook, so that he was obliged to ask Edward Chapman to send him a £50 note.[21] At last, at seven-thirty in the morning on Sunday, July 4th, he took the stage for Stirling and a brief tour of the Highlands, somewhat wearied by his tumultuous honors.[22] "I sigh for Devonshire Terrace and Broadstairs, for battledore and shuttlecock," he wrote Forster; "I want to dine in a blouse with you and Mac . . ." [23]

With Fletcher as their guide, Dickens and Kate made their way through the Trossachs to Loch Katrine, trudged in a pouring rain through a rocky pass to see the island of the Lady of the Lake, and drove on, wet to their skins, another twenty-four miles to Loch-Earn-Head. When they arrived at their inn, they found the fires in their rooms not yet lighted, and Fletcher ran back and forth between the sitting room and the two bedrooms wielding "a great pair of bellows, with which he distractedly blew each of the fires out in turn." But his "habit of going into kitchens and bars, disconcerting at Broadstairs," was welcome here; it brought them a meal of oatcake, mutton, hotchpotch, trout from the loch, small beer bottled, marmalade, and whiskey. This they enjoyed while the sky made itself "a vast water-spout" that never left off emptying, and the mists were stalking about, "and the clouds lying down upon the hills."

The inn, Dickens said, looked "like a white wall with windows in it by mistake." The sitting room was a good size, but the bedrooms were so small that it was "impossible for you to move, after you have taken your boots off, without chipping pieces out of your legs. There isn't a basin in the Highlands which will hold my face; not a drawer which will open after you have put your clothes in it; not a water-bottle capacious enough to wet your tooth-brush." Nevertheless, at this inn they remained three days, and Dickens was able to dispatch the next installment of *Barnaby Rudge*,[24] before they proceeded on through the pass of Glencoe to "some place which no man ever spelt but which sounds like Ballyhoolish." [25] (Ballechelish.)

The approach to the pass lay through "the most desolate part of Scotland, where the hill-tops are still covered with great patches of snow" and the moors and mountains were sprinkled with huge masses of rock making it look like "the burial place of a race of giants." "Glencoe itself is perfectly *terrible*. The pass is an awful place. It is shut in on each side by enormous rocks from which great torrents come rushing down in all directions." Among the rocks were "scores of glens, high up, which form such haunts as you might imagine yourself wandering in, in the very height and madness of a fever." [26]

Bad weather made it impossible for them to ferry across an arm of the sea to Oban, and forced their return in a drenching rain through Glencoe in order to reach Inveraray. "If you should happen to have your hat on," Dickens wrote Forster, "take it off, that your hair may stand on end without any interruption." For if Glencoe "had been tremendous the day before, yesterday it was perfectly horrific. . . . Through the whole glen, which is ten miles long, torrents were boiling and foaming, and sending up in every direction spray like the smoke of great fires. They were rushing down every hill and mountain side, and tearing like devils across the path, and down into the depths of the rocks. Some of the hills looked as if they had cracked in a hundred places. Others as if they were frightened, and had broken out in a deadly sweat. In others there was no compromise or division of streams but one great torrent came roaring down with a deafening noise, and a rushing of water that was quite appalling."

At one place they had to cross a foaming stream on a tiny foot-bridge of slippery planks with only a trembling rail on one side between them and the broken rocks below. The carriage, plunging into the swollen ford farther downstream, sank so deep that only the horses' heads and the postboy's body were visible amid the turmoil of the rushing water. "It made me quite sick to think how I should have felt if Kate had been inside. The carriage went round and round like a great stone, the boy was as pale as death, the horses were struggling and plashing and snorting like sea-animals, and we were all roaring to the driver to throw himself off and let them and the coach go to the devil, when suddenly it all came right (having got into shallow water) and, all tumbling and dripping and jogging from side to side, climbed up on the dry land." [27]

*   *   *   *   *

Returning to London in the middle of July quite exhausted by all these adventures, Dickens cleared up a few matters of business before going on to Broadstairs for August and September. The chief of these grew out of a small flurry of hard feeling between him and his publishers the preceding fall. The purchase of *Oliver Twist* and *Barnaby Rudge* was covered only by a letter from Dickens to Chapman and Hall. Their solicitor, a Mr. Chapman of Richmond, quite unrelated and "with no very strong family likeness to Mr. Chapman of the Strand," had insisted with an injurious discourtesy of language that to make Dickens's debt binding in law as well as in equity he must sign a deed covering the amount of the advance, and had drawn up a document positively insulting in the stringency of its terms. Smithson (no intimate friend to Dickens) declared it a commitment that any solicitor should have dissuaded a client from demanding, and Dickens flatly refused to sign it.

Finally he did sign a bond securing the advance. But if Chapman and Hall, forgetting their old friendly relationship, were going to treat him as a stranger of doubtful honesty, he would not have on record the letter in which he had expressed warm appreciation of their kindness in advancing the money. He therefore demanded its return. Chapman and Hall responded at once that this action had given them much pain and offered to return the bond. Immediately mollified, Dickens warmly assured them that their letter had restored the feelings of trust and esteem "which have so long subsisted and should always subsist between us." As for the bond, since they thought they could trust him without it, "I would rather you threw it into the fire with your own hands—for I can trust you to do it." [28]

This debt, plus various advances bringing the total to £3,019 9s. 5d., was secured to Chapman and Hall by a lien on Dickens's share in the stock and copyrights of the books he had so far written, and was being further liquidated by turning over to them one-half of his profits from *Master Humphrey's Clock* above his weekly £50. Whatever part of it still remained unpaid by July 2, 1845, they could then call in. But

Dickens was uncertain that the future earnings of these works alone would be enough to repay Chapman and Hall in full. What if he died before the debt was discharged? He had resisted an endeavor to bind him with degrading conditions, but he did not wish them to risk a loss of the debt. He therefore now insured his life for £2,000 and placed the policy in their hands as a further security.[29] Always anxious to be fair and even magnanimous, though sensitive to the smallest pinprick of a grievance, Dickens would bestow in friendship the equivalent of what he would not yield to distrust.

At Broadstairs, Dickens addressed himself to concluding *Barnaby Rudge* and directing the production of the illustrations for it. Cattermole had drawn the mob at the Maypole smashing bottles and drinking out of the best punch bowls while John Willet, fallen back in his chair, regarded them with stupid horror.[30] "The rioters went, sir, from John Willet's bar," Dickens now wrote him, "(where you saw them to such good purpose) straight to the Warren, which house they plundered, sacked, pulled down as much of as they could, and greatly damaged and destroyed. They are supposed to have left it about half an hour. It is night, and the ruins are here and there flaming and smoking."[31] Throughout the next month Dickens dispatched Cattermole a series of vignette descriptions for the scenes he desired to have depicted.

Meanwhile there was a steady miscellany of other correpondence between the "dips and airings" of the seaside.[32] Beard must come down by the Ramsgate boat as soon and as often and for as long as he could, and Mitton must also be a visitor.[33] To the carpenter-writer, John Overs, Dickens wrote "good news from Mr. Cruikshank"; the artist had accepted for publication in his new magazine, *George Cruikshank's Omnibus*, the little sketch of "The Postilion" that Dickens had liked.[34] "The sun is sparkling on the water so that I can hardly bear to look at it," Dickens wrote Forster. "The tide is in, and the fishing-boats are dancing like mad. Upon the green-topped cliffs the corn is cut and piled in shocks; and thousands of butterflies are fluttering about, taking the bright little red flags at the mast-heads for flowers, and panting with delight accordingly. (Here the Inimitable, unable to resist the brilliancy out of doors, breaketh off, rusheth to the machines, and plungeth into the sea . . .)"[35]

With the end of *Barnaby Rudge* it had been decided that Dickens would discontinue *Master Humphrey's Clock* and revert to publication in monthly parts.[36] Despite its enormous sales while it was running *The Old Curiosity Shop*, the *Clock's* circulation had trembled and fallen since, and was now around thirty thousand. In addition, the strain of meeting a weekly deadline was becoming too exhausting for Dickens to carry on alone. Nor did either he or Chapman and Hall feel confident that his readers would respond to a periodical written mainly by other hands than his.[37] It had therefore been tentatively agreed that they should go back to the tried green format of *Pickwick* with a new serial to begin in March.[38] Dickens went up to town on August 20th to discuss this matter. Walking about Lincoln's Inn the next day, preparatory to carrying Forster off to dinner with the publishers, Dickens revolved the subject in his mind.

Was it really judicious for him to follow one story by another without any interval in this way? "I remembered that Scott failed in the sale of his very best works, and never recovered his old circulation (though he wrote fifty times better than at first) *because he never left off.*" Had Dickens perhaps not spoiled his own great success by running it to death and giving his imitators the models that enabled them to deluge the town with every kind of trash and rot? Would he not do better, with a view to his future fame, to stop now, to publish not another word for a year, and then come out with a complete novel in three volumes and "put the town in a blaze again"?

These ideas sorted out in his head, Dickens put them before Forster. Would Forster, who could state them more forcibly for Dickens than he could himself, lay the case before Chapman and Hall after dinner that day? Let them stop the *Clock* on November 27th, as planned, but advertise, instead of the new serial in March, a novel in three volumes to come out a year from then. That agreed, the question to be put to Chapman and Hall was, what would they give him for one-half the copyright of that book, over and above the sum of £2,000 in quarterly installments that he would require for his living expenses during this year of retirement?

At dinner the two publishers were sanguine and cheerful. William Hall, "his pocket full of figures and estimates," toasted "Success to our new undertaking." Then Forster announced that he was going to startle them by something Dickens had mentioned to him just half an hour before. He was sure, however, that it was right, and certain they would say so too. He then stated with great force Dickens's argument, adding to it a number of other considerations, including the effect that the year's cessation might have upon the sales of what Dickens had already written.

Little Hall and big Chapman were as if knocked down by a thunderbolt. Chapman recovered first. Looking forward, he said, for twenty years, not for two, he believed that Dickens was right. Then little Hall chimed in that "He thought so too," but doubted whether the year's silence should be broken with three volumes or new monthly parts. Oh, the volumes, certainly, Dickens and Forster rejoined. The general principle of temporary retirement, however, was agreed on, and Chapman and Hall had only to consider what terms they could offer. Assured of more than half a year's rest from novel-writing, Dickens returned triumphantly to Broadstairs.[39]

* * * * *

During this London visit he had seen John Overs, who had depressing news of himself. He had recently been having pains in his chest; the doctors now told him that his lungs were infected. He could not possibly live very long, they said, if he continued to work as a cabinetmaker, a task that necessitated his being on his feet for at least twelve hours a day.[40] Dickens promptly sent him for a more expert diagnosis to Dr. Elliotson, who confirmed the opinion.[41]

Dickens gently passed this information on to Overs. Dr. Elliotson, he assured Overs, "says emphatically, that he has cured several such cases. I *know* that, under God, there does not live a man in whose hands you would have as much reason to hope for a perfect restoration to health. . . . If my own life, or my wife's . . . were in peril tomorrow, I would trust it to him, implicitly." To these encouragements Dickens added that Elliotson had sent a £5 note to help Overs meet his immediate needs. "Tell me whether I shall send you the whole sum at once, or a part—and consider that I have put another five to it, and am your banker to the amount of Ten Pounds." [42]

After reflecting on what might be done for Overs, Dickens wrote and described his case to Macready. "It has occurred to me as just possible that you might at some time or other find you wanted such a person in some capacity about the Theatre—as a kind of upper messenger, or doorkeeper, or in any capacity where a diligent, respectable, sober fellow, of very creditable appearance and manners would be a desideratum. I can vouch for him most thoroughly in every respect. He has been in the habit of coming backwards and forwards to me for three years, and I know him to be a man of that kind that only this country and this time give birth to." [43] Macready at once replied that a place should be found for Overs at Drury Lane that fall. "His word is his oath," Dickens told Overs, "and you may be assured he will not forget you." [44]

Mid-October saw Overs installed in a minor post at the theater. But with what may have been a sick man's peevishness, soon he was not at all satisfied. He felt himself underpaid by comparison with the stage carpenters and scene painters. He disliked some of Macready's regulations. He felt offended at the fact that he had made several unsuccessful efforts to see Mr. Bryden, Macready's manager, and voice these grievances directly.[45] Dickens was ill at this time, but he allowed Overs to call at Devonshire Terrace and heard him through a mood of complaining unhappiness.[46] He saw at once that Overs would not remain at the theater a month. He was startled to indignant disapproval, however, when Overs followed up this visit by sending him a long letter of criticism that he proposed dispatching to Macready.

If Overs was dissatisfied, Dickens replied, let him resign at once. But it was presumptuous of him to lecture Macready on the management of his own enterprise. Overs in turn felt aggrievedly that Dickens was biased in Macready's favor by friendship. In another letter to Dickens he lamented pathetically the change he felt in the latter's feelings toward him.

Dickens administered a stinging reproof. His feelings about Overs *had* changed, he admitted. The carpenter's last note, accusing him of irascibility and injustice, showed why. How ridiculous for Overs to expect that as a disabled man doing odd jobs he should be paid on a scale commensurate with craftsmen doing skilled work! How fantastic for him to measure himself against Macready, a man who had raised himself to the summit of his art! How preposterous for him to lecture this gentleman and assume the tone of a martyr oppressed by an ogre of cruelty! "I am disappointed in you," he concluded. "Disappointment, of course, slackens my zeal to serve you; but I still entertain the desire; and I would do so, if I had the opportunity." [47]

Frightened, Overs made a humble "submission." Evidently, he wrote, he was unfit to associate with gentlemen. But Dickens wanted no submission. "I hate it; have no right to exact it. . . . All I want is that for your own welfare and happiness, you should submit yourself, if I may use the expression, *to* yourself." Overs should not mistake a loud-tongued belligerence for a worthy independence. "Let this matter rest where it is," Dickens concluded. If Overs wished to see him, he would be at home any Sunday except the next one.[48]

*　　*　　*　　*　　*

Meanwhile, the August and September days at Broadstairs had been bright and vigorous. With *Barnaby Rudge* rapidly progressing to its last page and the prospect of a respite, after some six years of steady writing, Dickens's spirits soared like a balloon. He would emerge from his morning's work eager to whip everyone else up to a pitch of exhilaration matching his own. Broadstairs was now full of friends and members of his family: Maclise, Angus Fletcher, Mitton, the Macreadys, John Dickens and his wife on a visit from Alphington, Fanny and Henry Burnett, Fred Dickens taking off a few days from his post in the Treasury, a little later Henry Austin and Letitia. The Smithsons also had taken a house at Broadstairs, where Mrs. Smithson's brother, T. J. Thompson, was among their guests.[49]

Dickens's contagious gaiety spread among them as if champagne were flowing. Fred, with his weary expression and raised eyebrows, made ludicrous remarks and outrageous puns that Dickens capped with even more absurd ones, though he pretended to be disgusted when Kate too joined the game, and vowed he was deteriorating under this bad example. Kate would perpetrate her small, harmless attempts, "turning up her eyes in affected terror of his wrath and terminating in a pretty little *moue*," while Dickens went through a pantomime of tearing his hair and writhing in attitudes of anguish. Then Fred's oily laugh would sound through the air, followed by an abrupt bray from Mitton which ended in such an extraordinary sound that everyone was convulsed.[50]

On other occasions, when they went sailing, Fred and Dickens would keep the sailors in a broad grin by roaring out a series of nautical commands with the greatest gravity and earnestness: "Now then, a reef in your taffrail," "Sheepshank your mizzen," "Abaft there!

brail up your capstan-bar," "Haul up your main-top-gallant-sprits-sail-boom!" [51]

In the evenings there were cards, guessing games, dancing, and strolls down to the pier or the Tivoli Gardens. Under Dickens's influence "Vingt-et-un" and "Loo" became totally unrecognizable and usually ended in a round of unblushing cheating and uproar, after which the stakes were thrown in a pile and distributed. Dickens was brilliant in routing everybody at "Animal, Vegetable, or Mineral," although he himself failed to guess a vegetable object mentioned in "mythological history" and belonging to a queen, and was chagrined to have it identified as the tarts made by the Queen of Hearts. [52]

Dickens was sometimes persecuted in their strolls out of doors by his own celebrity. At the Tivoli Gardens one evening, while the others were dancing a quadrille inside, he found himself being followed persistently by a wide-eyed and wide-eared admirer, upon whom he turned at last with the question: "Pray, sir, may I ask, are you a native of this place?" "No—no—sir, I am not!" stammered his pursuer. "Oh! I beg your pardon," Dickens reponded. "I fancied I could detect *Broad-stares* on your very face!" And the next day, walking along the sands, with Fletcher in his eccentric way cutting extraordinary capers on ahead, Dickens observed some strangers mistaking his friend for himself. They had evidently heard the rumor of Dickens's insanity, and stared at Fletcher's antics open-eyed. "Ah! How sad!" one of them sighed, wagging his head mournfully. "You see it's quite true. Poor Boz!" [53]

Among the guests at the Smithsons' were two ladies whose surnames have not survived, one of them, no longer in her first youth, named Millie, and her considerably younger friend Eleanor P——. [54] The latter had met the Dickenses at the home of a relative in London the year before, and was thrilled at the renewal of the acquaintance. Mrs. Dickens she had found "a pretty little woman, plump and fresh-coloured," with a retroussé nose, a small, red-lipped mouth, and "large, heavy-lidded, blue eyes" that wore a sleepy look and moved slowly. [55] After her first terror of Dickens had subsided, she was riveted by the marvelous power of his eyes, lighting into such a luminous depth of hue that for the moment she could see nothing else. His features, too, expressed a rare harmony of strength and delicacy of perception, but his style of dress disappointed her, with its loud expanse of waistcoat and the finicking patent-leather-toed shoes. In the course of the dinner she was fascinated by his alternations of mood. At intervals he would drift seemingly far off with a rapt, veiled look, then, with a sudden twinkle and comic lift of an eye-brow, returning to the conversation, he would break forth into a wittily twisted version of all their casual remarks that they thought he had not even noted.[56]

With this young lady and her more mature friend Dickens pretended at Broadstairs to be in love. Rhapsodically he called them, in turns, "My charmer," "Beloved of my soul," "Fair enslaver," and "Queen of my heart." He entreated them to dance: "Wilt tread a measure with me, sweet ladye? Fain would I thread the mazes of this saraband with thee"; and then went through a stately burlesque of the dance with a deportment mingling the airs of Turveydrop with those of Malvolio.[57] "'Tis my lady! 'Tis my love!" he exclaimed dramatically, hand on heart. "Oh, that I were a glove upon that hand, that I might touch that cheek!" "Which of us do you intend to be Juliet to your Romeo?" Millie inquired. Whereupon, with a swift upset, "Whichever you choose, my little dears," Dickens replied, and strolled off.[58] Eleanor P—— was horribly frightened of him and at the same time half bewitched. At last she gathered courage to confess her terror and tell him he looked like a forest lion. Dickens, laughing, promised that he would henceforth be less intimidating: "I will roar you as gently as any sucking dove!" [59]

But Eleanor P—— came to feel that she was not the only one who was afraid of Dickens. His whole family, she noted, held him in awe and were appreciably subdued in his presence, as if they feared to arouse his wrath. Of them all Frederick, with his burlesque impersonations, showed it least. But his mother, in the face of his displeasure, hardly dared indulge her love of dancing except with her son-in-law or some other relation; and that old buck, her husband, for all his corklike optimism and orotund phraseology, also kept a sharp eye on Dickens's moods.[60] Their young observer probably did not know, of course, that only the preceding June the father had again bobbed up out of debt only by the help of his son. John Dickens's financial tricks with Dickens's name might explain the prodigal parent's feeling like a bad boy at the time—and the son like an exacting father.

In general, though, Dickens was in tearing high spirits that September. Discussing Byron's *Childe Harold*, he criticized the words

"Dazzled and drunk with beauty" and "The heart *reels* with its fulness" as less suggestive of Venus than of gin-and-water, then without warning slapped his brow, tossed his waving hair, and exclaimed, "Stand back! I am suddenly seized with the divine afflatus!" Taking up a pencil, he looked wildly around for paper, and finding none, stalked to the window and wrote on the white-painted shutter:

> "*LINES TO E. P———. AFTER BYRON*
> *"O maiden of the amber-dropping hair*
> *May I, Byronically, thy praises utter?*
> *Drunk with thy beauty, tell me, may I dare*
> *To sing thy paeans borne upon a shutter?"* [61]

One evening on the pier, as the tide rippled in under the darkening sky, impelled by some demon of mischief, Dickens flung his arms around Eleanor P——and whirled her down the incline of the jetty to the water's edge, where he clung with her to an upright pole, proclaiming his intention to hold her there till the wild waves overwhelmed them both in watery death. While she struggled, the water splashed over their feet. "O! my dress," she cried; "my *best* dress, my *only* silk dress will be ruined!" and then, with a wild shriek as the water surged up to her knees, "Mrs. Dickens! help me!—make Mr. Dickens let me go."

"Charles!" Kate called. "How can you be so silly? You will both be carried off by the waves, and you'll spoil the poor girl's silk dress." "*Dress!*" Dickens shouted scornfully. "Talk not to me of *dress!* . . . Am I not immolating a brand-new pair of patent-leathers still unpaid for? . . . In this hour of abandonment to the voice of destiny, shall we be held back by the puerilities of silken raiment? Shall leather or prunella (whatever that may be) stop the bolt of Fate?"

Here Eleanor managed to struggle free, and fled with her *only* silk dress clinging round her saturated limbs, leaving a watery track behind her, feeling, in Mr. Mantalini's words, like "a demned moist unpleasant body." To make her distress worse, Mrs. Smithson, blaming Dickens not at all, told her in dignified displeasure to run home and take off her wet things, adding severely that she was "*surprised*" at her young guest.[62]

From the scene of these unrestrained diversions, Dickens sent Edward Chapman a burlesque warning against his approaching marriage. He should reflect, before it was too late, about the precipice on which he stood. "To see a fellow creature—and one who has so long withstood—still if—will *nothing* warn you." Following these broken phrases came a succession of postscripts:

"P.S.—Pause.
  Put it off.
P.P.S.—Emigrate.
P.P.P.S.—and leave me the business—I mean the Strand one." [63]

* * * * *

During the preceding two weeks Dickens had occasionally been running up to London to discuss the details of his new understanding with Chapman and Hall, and Mitton had been drafting its provisions.[64] On September 7th an agreement was signed. Dickens was to have his rest from writing, but Hall's counsel had prevailed against publication in three volumes, and the new work was to appear in monthly numbers beginning November, 1842. During its publication Dickens was to receive £200 a month, calculated as one of the expenses, and, in addition, three-quarters of all the profits. Six months after the novel's completion, upon paying Dickens one-fourth of the value of all existing stock, Chapman and Hall were to have half the future earnings. During the fourteen months before publication started, Dickens was to draw £150 a month (instead of the £2,000 in quarterly installments he had originally suggested) as an advance against his three-quarters of the profits.[65] "M[acready] was quite aghast last night," Dickens wrote exultantly on September 9th, "at the brilliancy of the C. and H. arrangement . . ." [66]

Hardly had these matters been settled before Dickens impulsively dashed in a new direction. In the early plans for *Master Humphrey's Clock* vague thoughts of a visit to Ireland and even to America had been in his mind. That weekly was about to cease, but the desire to see the New World now took violent possession of him. "Washington Irving writes me that if I went, it would be a triumph for me from one end of the States to the other, as was never known in any nation."[67] His reception in Edinburgh would pale beside it. Would it not be a sad mistake to miss this opportunity his leisure gave him? America had long exercised a fascination over his mind. The United States symbolized for him the goal of liberty and democracy toward which he hoped that England might be tending. It was the glowing promise of a future in which the worn-out snobberies, aristocratic privileges, and corruptions of the Old World gave way to a better scheme of things and men were valued according to their character and accomplishment. "I am still haunted," he wrote Forster, "by visions of America, night and day. . . . Kate cries dismally if I mention the subject. But, God willing, I think it *must* be managed somehow!" [68]

PART FIVE

The New World

1842

CHAPTER ONE

The American Dream

With Dickens, to form a desire was to be overwhelmed with hot haste for its realization. At once he began to devise reasons why he should set out for the United States without delay. Mrs. Trollope's *Domestic Manners of the Americans* had given a caustic picture of the new country, and Harriet Martineau's *Society in America* had also found much to criticize. It was to their books, and others like them, that Tony Weller referred when he suggested that Mr. Pickwick take passage "for Merriker" and then "come back and write a book about the 'Merrikins as'll pay all his expenses and more, if he blows 'em up enough." [1] Dickens was convinced that he could understand, as neither of these ladies possibly could, a democratic kingless country freed from the shackles of class rule.

What, then, if he "ran over to America" [2] for four or five months, and returned with a one-volume book that would redress the balance of their disdainful praises and prevailing tone of depreciation? "In going to a New World," he prescribed, "one must utterly forget, and put out of sight the Old one and bring none of its customs or observations into comparison"; or, at the very least, remember how much brutality there was in England. "I think you are *rather* hard on the Americans," he told Andrew Bell, the author of another of these works, "and that your dedication like Mrs. Trollope's seems to denote a foregone conclusion." [3]

These judicious reflections Dickens was to find easier to preach than to practice. He did not realize how deeply he was permeated by European ways of looking on things, or how much that was alien he would find in the United States. But Chapman and Hall leaped at his proposal of an American notebook and speedily regarded the idea of the American visit as quite settled.[4]

Dickens had another motive for his impulse besides the loadstone of America alone. He had read Lockhart's *Life of Scott* and Scott's *Diary*. The touching story of the grand and worn-out old man's journey to Italy had brought home to him the desirability of traveling in youth and "plenitude of power," instead of dragging through a pilgrimage shadowed by illness and decay.[5] What might not the sight of Naples and Rome have meant to Scott in the fullness of his vigor! What might not the great scenes of the world mean to Dickens while he still was young!

"Now to astonish you," he announced his decision to Forster. "After balancing, considering, and weighing the matter in every point of view, I HAVE MADE UP MY MIND (WITH GOD'S LEAVE) TO GO TO AMERICA—AND TO START AS SOON AFTER CHRISTMAS AS IT WILL BE SAFE TO GO." [6] Chapman and Hall were instructed "to make every enquiry about the fares, cabins, berths, and times of sailing; and I shall make a great effort to take Kate *and* the children." [7] Kate was in tears whenever the project was even mentioned. How could they travel with four small children, she wept, little Charley not yet five, Mamey and Katey younger still, and the baby less than a year old? Her lamentations were so grievous that Dickens asked Macready's advice and help. Ought he to take the children or leave them at home? [8] Somehow Kate must be constrained to "a reluctant consent." All her dismay made Dickens deviate not one jot from his determination; but until all arrangements were made he found rest, sleep, appetite, and work destroyed.[9]

Macready decidedly recommended that the children remain behind and generously offered to care for them in his own home.[10] At the thought of leaving her darlings Kate rained more tears than ever. Dickens begged Macready to add his persuasions. He would not use so selfish an argument, Macready told her, as the delight of seeing "that grand country." But it was her *duty* to go with her husband and *"must be a source of happiness to her."* She could be sure that he and Mrs. Macready should be anxious "to fulfil in the strictest sense every duty of friendship" in their care of the children. She should view the matter in its proper light, and make it happier by putting a smiling face upon it.[11]

Poor Kate was incapable of the smiling face, but she did give way. Instead of accepting the Macreadys' offer for the entire six months Dickens and Kate were to be away, it was decided that Fred should take charge of the children during the earlier part of it. Kate felt comforted by this arrangement, for all the children were fond of Fred.[12] Maclise further cheered her by painting a small group portrait of them, a pretty water color in which Charley and Mamey held glasses of wine while Katey looked at pictures in Strutt's *Antiquities of England* and baby Walter stretched out his arms behind her.[13] Consoled by these things, and by the fact that her highly capable maid Anne would be with her to lighten the rigors of the journey, Kate grew reconciled and could even talk gaily about it, Dickens reported,[14] though she probably still dropped many tears in secret.

Accommodations were immediately taken on the British and North American packet *Britannia*, sailing from Liverpool on January 4th for Boston. By September 26th Dickens was writing to Washington Irving and Lewis Gaylord Clark, the editor of the *Knickerbocker Magazine*, announcing his arrival in the third week of the new year "upon the soil I have trodden in my day-dreams many times and whose sons (and daughters) I yearn to know and be among." [15]

Coming back to London from Broadstairs at the end of September, Dickens was suddenly stricken ill.[16] A few trivial symptoms previously ignored became graver, and he learned that he had a fistula, the result of laboring overlong at his desk. It would have to be removed by an operation rendered unspeakably painful by the fact that surgery had not yet developed the use of anesthetics. The ordeal took place on October 8th, and left Dickens so weak that he was obliged to lie on the sofa every day while Kate wrote his letters to his dictation.[17] Within ten days, however, he was able to go out on short visits and take a daily airing in his carriage, and had regained his usual spirits.[18] By the beginning of November he had taken himself first to Richmond and then to the White Hart at Windsor to restore himself to health.[19]

*   *   *   *   *

On their return from Windsor in the middle of November, Dickens was plunged into innumerable preparations for departure. Warned that both the *Argus* and the *Britannia*, in which he was insured, were "very doubtful offices," he decided to "get rid of those policies for any little money they may fetch." [20] He had no trouble in taking out a policy for £5,000 with the *Eagle*, although its officers emphatically demanded a contradiction of the rumors about his insanity.[21]

His friends were assiduous in obtaining for him letters of introduction to outstanding people in the major cities of the United States. To be sure, Dickens already felt as if he were well acquainted in New York. He had corresponded with Lewis Gaylord Clark; and in the four or five letters he had exchanged with Washington Irving he and the distinguished American writer were already warm friends. At Macready's on several occasions he had met one of the actor's great friends, David Cadwallader Colden, of New York, whose wife was a sister-in-law of Lord Jeffrey's.[22] In addition, Dickens took from his friend the Reverend William Harness an introduction to Bishop Wainwright.[23] Through Landor's friend John Kenyon he secured letters to George Ticknor, the historian of Spanish literature, Charles Sumner, and other leading citizens of Boston.[24] For presentation in Philadelphia he had a letter to Lucretia Mott, the well-known Quaker antislavery advocate, and another from Charles Leslie, the painter, to his brother-in-law Henry C. Carey, the publisher.[25] These preparations concluded with a ceremonial call on Edward Everett, the American Minister in London, whom Dickens found shy and cold in manner.[26]

Entire new wardrobes also must be ordered. Kate, still weeping softly on occasion, rustled in and out of a rainbow profusion of pretty new frocks, traveling dresses, gowns suitable for whatever glamour of Embassy balls and White House dinners. Dickens must have the most elegant of coats and trousers, a blaze of velvet and satin waistcoats, golden chains and tie-pins and rings. As one of the most distinguished authors of the day, he would allow no sartorial deficiencies to dim the magnificence of his triumphal progress.

Where he should go, and all the details of the journey, Dickens worked out with Forster, aided by advice from Macready based on his own travel experience in America. Edward Marjoribanks, of Coutts and Company, helped with information about the state of American roads, and arranged for a letter of credit for £800.[27] An American journalist who called at Devonshire Terrace on the eve of the departure found Dickens's study piled high "with Marryat's, Trollope's, Fidler's, Hall's, and other travels and descriptions of America," and blazing "with highly-colored maps of the United States." Dickens chatted in happy excitement, volatile with anticipation.[28]

December was feverish with eleventh-hour activities. Landor came up from Bath to attend the christening of his ten-months-old godson.[29] Letters of welcome from America were arriving and demanding to be answered, and letters of farewell needed to be written. A Boston portrait painter, Francis Alexander, asked Dickens to sit for him.[30] Mrs. Samuel Carter Hall sent a copy of Catlin's *North American Indians*.[31] An invitation from Miss Coutts had to be declined because every day of that third week in December was engaged, but Dickens promised to come some morning to say good-by and take her order for a bottle of Niagara water or a neat tomahawk.[32] Talfourd's little daughter asked him to her birthday party, but Dickens explained that he had to spend the last days before his departure with his own children.[33]

Not all his friends approved the approaching visit. "Aren't there disagreeable enough people to describe in Blackburn and Leeds?" Albany Fonblanque asked.[34] Lady Holland tried to dissuade him from going at all, saying plaintively, "Why cannot you go down to Bristol and see some of the third and fourth class people there and they'll do just as well?" [35] And Kate, of course, still despaired whenever she thought of the entire width of the Atlantic between herself and her children.

On New Year's Eve the Dickenses dined with Forster, and on New Year's Day he had dinner at Devonshire Terrace with them. After dinner some sparkling Moselle was opened to drink their happy return, then the wine cellar was sealed up, and the house was in readiness to turn over to General Sir John Wilson, who had rented it for the six months of Dickens's absence.[36] There was a farewell call on Macready, whose heart was quite full at the departure of his friend.[37] The next day, a Sunday, good-bys were said to Fred and the children, and Forster accompanied Dickens and Kate to Liverpool, whence they were to sail on Tuesday the 4th.[38]

The *Britannia*, a packet of 1,154 tons, the first Cunard steamer to commence the mail service across the Atlantic, had made her maiden voyage in 1840.[39] Going on board in the cold bright sunlight, with a thin crust of morning ice crackling under their heels on the deck, they made their way below. In the preposterous box that was their stateroom they were hilarious about its minute area, into which they could no more force their two portmanteaus than a giraffe could be got into a flowerpot,[40] and Dickens sat roaring aloud upon something that the stewards called his bed, but which he said he believed to be a muffin beaten flat.[41] He demonstrated that, by nearly closing the door, twining in like serpents, and counting the washing slab as standing room, very nearly four people could be insinuated into it at one time.[42]

Back at the Adelphi Hotel that evening, the proprietor, Mr. Radley, provided a magnificent dinner that included turtle, cold punch, hock, champagne, and claret.[43] Before going to bed Dickens wrote a letter to Lord Brougham, with whom he had developed a friendly acquaintance. Always eager to do his father-in-law a service, Dickens called attention to Hogarth's works on music and history, and recommended a new book by him for publication by the Society for the Diffusion of Useful Knowledge.[44]

The next afternoon Dickens, Kate, and Forster crowded up the gangway, under the huge red funnel pouring out smoke and the tangle of masts and spars for the auxiliary sails, amid a confusion of wild stewards and swarming luggage.[45] Forster presented Dickens with a pocket Shakespeare as a farewell gift.[46] Presently Dickens and Kate saw their last of Forster as the small paddle-wheeler that had set them on board drew away from the side of their vessel in the gathering fog.[47]

*   *   *   *   *

The passage across the Atlantic was one of the stormiest in years. Dickens was sick for the first five days, Kate for six and in the utmost terror throughout the entire voyage.[48] Beard had presented Dickens with a medicine chest for the voyage: "If you could only have seen me, Beard, endeavoring (with that impossible pair of scales, and those weights, invisible to the naked eye) to make up pills in the heavy weather, on the rolling Atlantic! If you could only have seen me,—when Kate and Anne were deadly fearful of shipwreck, bent on raising their spirits with calomel, and ringing the changes on all the bottles in that mahogany box, to restore their peace of mind!" [49]

The ship continued to roll so heavily that when the travelers played whist they stuffed the tricks into their pockets to keep them from disappearing: "five or six times in the course of every rubber we are all flung from our seats, roll out at different doors, and keep on rolling until we are picked up by stewards." [50] "Four dozen plates were broken at dinner. One steward fell down the cabin-stairs with a round of beef, and injured his foot severely. Another steward fell down after him, and cut his eye open. The baker's taken ill; so is the pastry-cook. . . . Twelve dozen of bottled porter has got loose upon deck, and the bottles are rolling about distractedly, overhead." [51]

Ten days out so violent a gale struck that the smokestack had to be lashed with chains and ropes to prevent its being blown over and setting fire to the decks and cabins with red-hot sparks. Next noon, while the sea ran mountainously high, smashed lifeboats hung from their davits in a faggot of crazy boards, the planking of the paddle-boxes had been torn away so that the wheels dashed spray over the decks, storm sails were set, and the chimney sagged in its knotted rigging, white with crusted salt to its belching top. Kate moaned in her berth, and in the ship's cabin Dickens found only four out of the eighty-six passengers rubbing their hands with the cold.[52] Throughout these wild experiences Dickens tried to spread cheer by borrowing an accordion from the steward and regaling the ladies' cabin with his performances.[53]

On the fourteenth day the sea grew comparatively smooth, and the decks tolerably dry. Two days later they were piloted into Halifax Harbor with a light wind and a bright moon. Suddenly the ship struck. Passengers rushed on deck in a panic, sailors kicked off their shoes and threw off their jackets to swim ashore (for the lifeboats were broken fragments littering the deck), breakers roared ahead as the vessel drove upon the surf and frantically worked her paddle-wheels backward. Rockets were thrown up, blue lights burned, soundings taken every two minutes. Only Captain Hewett remained calm. The pilot's folly had driven them upon a mudbank, but they had scraped over it, and anchored now in a sort of little pond, surrounded by rocks and shoals, but perfectly safe. The tide was already past ebb. With the morning they would be able to float free.[54]

By nine-thirty they were gliding along a broad stream, the sun shining brightly on the white wooden houses, flags flying, and crowds shouting on the quays. The wharf to which they were heading was paved with upturned faces, the gangway thrust out almost before they were made fast.[55] Arm in arm with the ship's doctor, Dickens immediately went ashore for some oysters.[56] "Then, sir, comes a breathless man . . . shouting my name as he tears along. . . . The breathless man introduces himself as the Speaker of the House of Assembly; *will* drag me away to his house; and *will* have a carriage and his wife sent down for Kate, who is laid up with a hideously swoln face.

"Then he drags me up to the Governor's house (Lord Falkland is Governor), and then Heaven knows where; concluding with both houses of parliament, which happen to meet for the session that very day, and are opened by a mock speech from the throne delivered by the governor . . . I wish you could have seen the crowds cheering the Inimitable in the streets. I wish you could have seen judges, law-officers, bishops, and law-makers welcoming the Inimitable. I wish you could have seen the Inimitable shown to a great elbow-chair by the Speaker's throne . . . listening with exemplary gravity to the queerest speaking possible, and breaking in spite of himself into a smile as he thought of this commencement to the Thousand and One stories in reserve for home and Lincoln's Inn Fields and Jack Straw's Castle.— Ah, Forster! when I *do* come back again!" [57]

The *Britannia* lay over for seven hours at Halifax and then stood off for Boston. There was squally weather in the Bay of Fundy, but two days later, on the afternoon of Saturday, January 22nd, Dickens stood on deck in the dry frosty air watching New England rise from the green sea.[58] Soon they were in Boston Harbor, but long before the boat was moored "a dozen men came leaping on board at the peril of their lives, with great bundles of newspapers under their arms . . . 'Aha!' says I, 'this is like our London Bridge': believing of course that these visitors were news-boys. But what do you think of their being EDITORS? And what do you think of their tearing violently up to me and beginning to shake hands like madmen?" (Dickens was mistaken in his identification the second time as well as the first; they were reporters.) "If you could have seen how I wrung their wrists! And if you could but know how I hated one man in very dirty gaiters, and with very protruding teeth, who said to all comers after him, 'So you've been introduced to our friend Dickens—eh?' " [59] Another of these reporters, however, Dr. Palmer, an acting editor of the Boston *Transcript*, after learning that Dickens had made no advance arrangements for hotel accommodation, raced ahead to the Tremont House and ordered rooms and dinner for him." [60]

*   *   *   *   *

The Charles Dickens whom the reporters saw was a young man of middle size, wearing a shaggy greatcoat of bear or buffalo skin that might have been envied by a Kentucky woodsman. Open over his chest, it revealed a brown frock coat, a red-figured waistcoat crossed by a gold watch-guard, and a voluptuously folded cravat with a double pin and chain. His brown hair hung in ringlets on each side of a face animated, glowing, and cordial.[61]

Soon Dickens was shaking hands with T. Colley Grattan, the British Consul, who had come on board to meet him, and with Francis Alexander, the artist.[62] Accompanied by the young Earl of Mulgrave, a lively fellow passenger with whom Dickens had struck up a friendship, the entire party went ashore.[63] Alexander conveyed them in his carriage from the waterfront through the business district up State Street to Court, and so to Tremont Row and the Tremont House, a four-story hotel with a Grecian portico [64] "a trifle smaller," Dickens wrote, "than Finsbury Square." [65] "It has more galleries, colonnades, piazzas, and passages than I can remember, or the reader would believe."[66]

Dickens bounded into the lobby, his face aglow, shouting "Here we are!" as the lights burst upon his party.[67] By this time it was already dark, and after presenting Kate with a bouquet of flowers, Alexander left them to sit down with Lord Mulgrave to a handsome dinner in a spacious sitting room. Invitations began to pour in from the moment it was known where they were staying.[68] Hardly was dinner over before a delegation arrived from the "Young Men of Boston" to invite him to a dinner in his honor. Their number included James Russell Lowell, then a youthful twenty-two. Dickens willingly accepted, and the first day of February was named for the occasion.[69]

Despite the fatigues and excitement of their arrival, Dickens's vitality was not exhausted, and about midnight he and Lord Mulgrave sallied out for a look at the city.[70] Boston was then a town of 125,000, with shade trees lining the well-paved streets and porticoed houses whose grass plots were enclosed by iron railings. Back Bay was open water and swamp, and the main residential area included Boylston Street, Temple Place, Sumner, Winter, and Franklin Streets. The shopping district stretched from Washington Street and Scollay Square to the waterfront.

Dickens was in the most elated of spirits. It was a stinging night, but in the light of the full moon everything stood out sharp and glittering. Muffled in his fur coat, he ran over the shining snow in the middle of the streets, keeping up a continual shout of uproarious laughter as he read the signs on the shops and observed the architecture of the new country. Emerging into Washington from Tremont Street, he and Lord Mulgrave lost their way, but kept gaily on until they arrived opposite the Old South Church, where Dickens—probably in sheer high spirits—gave something between a shout and a scream. One of a crowd of boys who had followed them was mightily bewildered by this riotous response, and puzzled in his mind as to whether it could be because of some mysterious resemblance to St. Paul's or Westminster Abbey.[71]

Sunday morning, walking down to the Custom House with Lord Mulgrave, Dickens was impressed by the brightness of the signs with their gilded letters, the redness of the brick, the whiteness of the stone, the greenness of shutters, the polish of the doorknobs and plates, all shining with a prim neatness like a child's toy.[72] In the afternoon he and Kate unpacked, and placed Maclise's sketch of the children on a table; later he was sketched by Pierre Morand in the hotel parlor, and interviewed by Dr. Palmer for the *Transcript*. At tea with Lord Mulgrave and Grattan, it was decided that Dickens would have to hold a daily reception to accommodate the throngs eager to see him, with Grattan introducing the guests.[73] Dickens was still blissfully unaware of the flood that was about to descend upon him.

When George Ticknor called next morning he found Dickens sitting to Henry Dexter, the sculptor, who was doing a bust of him while Dickens tossed off autographs in response to the hundreds of requests that had come in the mail. In the afternoon he was led through cheering crowds that lined the streets to the State House, looking down upon the Common from the top of Beacon Hill. Here he was shown the chambers in which the House of Representatives and the State Senate met, and introduced to John P. Bigelow, the Secretary of the Commonwealth, and Josiah Quincy, the President of the Senate. Rushing back to his hotel for supper, he then pushed his way across the street through a surging mob to the Tremont Theatre, where he was escorted by the managers into a gaily decorated box, and had to bow and smile while the orchestra played the Boz Waltzes especially composed for the occasion and the audience cheered him nine times.[74]

The bill consisted of *Charles O'Malley,* a dramatization of *Nicholas Nickleby* written and acted by the comedian Joe Field, and an entertainment devised by the same versatile gentleman, entitled *Boz: A Masque Phrenologic.*[75] The skit included a sly hint at the way in which native no less than foreign writers were injured by the lack of an international copyright agreement. "Boz" is made to say of his projected visit to "Columbia":

> *"Besides, I'm told they'd rather* read me *there,*
> *For* nothing, too! *yet not for that I* care:
> *Although, no doubt, their authors would delight*
> *To see me paid, So get themselves thus 'Right':*
> *But pshaw! I must not quarrel with the 'Trade,'*
> *In golden smiles more richly am I paid;*
> *Happy, when gone, if they my wish recall—*
> *God bless their Literature and bless them all!"* [76]

It was the earliest mention of a theme that was to sound a discordant note in the triumph of this American visit.

With Dickens's first sitting to Alexander his lionization began to swell to embarrassing proportions. Ladies pressed into the studio to stare at him until Dickens bolted for the door, only to be mobbed there and forced to retreat and lock himself within. When hunger obliged him to emerge for lunch they were still besieging the doorway, and surged about him instantly again, seizing his hand to "claim the privilege," [77] clinging to him while they furtively snipped bits of fur from his coat to treasure as souvenirs,[78] and filling the passage with a soprano clamor of adulation. At last the distracted author was forced into flight for the Tremont House with his coattails flying behind him. "Really, it is too bad," commented an onlooker, "that he should get such an idea of the ill-breeding of our people." [79]

Social engagements continued in ever-mounting proportions. Cornelius Felton, "heartiest of Greek professors," the younger Richard Henry Dana, Charles Sumner, and Henry Wadsworth Longfellow were among the callers.[80] There were dinners with William Hickling Prescott, the historian, with Francis Gray, the leader of the Wednesday Evening Club and a dominating figure among the intellectuals and men of letters, dinners with other prominent citizens.[81] There was a great ball at Papanti's Dancing Academy, in Tremont Row, with its twelve high windows, its great French mirrors, its ornate pris-matic chandeliers imported from Paris, and the first "spring floor" in America. Escorted here by Charles Sumner, Dickens was received, in the midst of a terrific jam, by Mayor Jonathan Chapman, introduced to countless pretty young ladies, and regaled on oysters, ices, charlotte russe, and champagne.[82]

Perhaps it was at this ball that Mayor Chapman had the conver-sation with Dickens reported by Mrs. John Lothrop Motley, the wife of the historian.

"Mr. Dickens, will you dine with me?" "I am sorry, I am engaged." "Will you sup with me?" "I am engaged." "Will you lunch with me?" "I am engaged." "Will you breakfast with me?" "I am engaged." "Well, will you sleep with me?" "Thank you, with the greatest pleas-ure; nothing could gratify me more than to accept an invitation to sleep." [83]

Indeed, in the course of the week that followed Dickens and Kate found themselves obliged by sheer fatigue to break several engage-ments they had made. Instead of dining with George Hillard, a promi-nent lawyer, they sent word that both were ill, and dined in their suite. The Paiges, who had prepared a magnificent dinner for them, re-ceived an apology half an hour after the time they should have been there. And instead of arriving at Mrs. Peabody's, Dickens sent another apology, and collapsed in bed. But even at his hotel he was not left alone. One man, in spite of repeated refusals to receive him, forced his way into the parlor, where Dickens was stretched on a sofa, and remained an hour. Dickens, pleading illness, went to his room, and threw himself on his bed, but in spite of this the man brought up his wife and passed another hour with Kate. "This is one of the million things I could tell you," Mrs. Motley wrote her husband, "which make me feel sometimes as if I could cry with mortification." [84]

Within three days of his arrival Dickens was snowed under by let-ters and decided he must have a secretary. Francis Alexander recom-mended for the post a young pupil of his, George W. Putnam, who was hired at ten dollars a month and his board for the duration of Dickens's stay in America.[85] Putnam speedily settled down to a rou-tine. Arriving at nine o'clock, he would start working at a side table while Dickens and Mrs. Dickens had breakfast. Dickens autographed small cards while he ate, and Putnam wrote "With the compliments of Mr. Dickens" and the name of the recipient on the back. No request for an autograph was refused, but Dickens drew the line at gratifying the numerous young ladies who wanted locks of his hair.[86]

In one corner of the breakfast room Alexander made sketches of Dickens's head for the portrait he was painting in his studio; in another Henry Dexter worked on the moist clay of the bust. Dexter repeatedly came forward, stooped down solemnly, looked at one side of Dickens's face, passed around to look at the other. With his calipers he measured the width of Dickens's temples; then, waiting politely for him to set down his cup, tried the distance from nose to chin or came again to get the length of the nose.[87]

Forster could have no idea, Dickens wrote him, of all the communications he received, "copies of verses, letters of congratulations, welcomes of all kinds." "Authorities from nearly all the states have written to me. I have heard from the universities, congress, senate, and bodies, public and private, of every sort and kind." [88] There were also more eccentric epistles. One requested an original epitaph for the tombstone of an infant, another an autograph copy of Mrs. Leo Hunter's "Ode to an Expiring Frog." Authors sent voluminous manuscripts for Dickens to read, revise, and superintend through publication in England. A New Jersey lady had family records of one hundred years, interesting and tragic, which she would allow Dickens to rewrite and publish for a half share of the profits.[89]

"I can give you no conception of my welcome here," Dickens wrote to Mitton. "There never was a king or emperor upon the earth so cheered and followed by crowds, and entertained in public at splendid balls and dinners . . ." [90] And to Forster: "I have had deputations from the Far West, who have come more than two thousand miles distance: from the lakes, the rivers, the backwoods, the log-houses, the cities, factories, villages, and towns. . . . 'It is no nonsense, and no common feeling,' wrote Dr. Channing to me yesterday. 'It is all heart. There never was, and never will be such a triumph.' " [91]

* * * * *

Not all who saw Dickens, however, were completely carried away by enthusiasm. In restrained Boston, where gentlemen invariably wore black-satin waistcoats in the evening, his velvet waistcoats in vivid green and brilliant crimson were looked on as startling and even vulgar.[92] Nor did his personal appearance and manner please everyone. Tom Appleton said that if one took the genius from his face he looked exactly like a cockney. The first response of the younger Dana, author of *Two Years Before the Mast*, was also one of disappointment. Dickens had, Dana said, "a dissipated looking mouth with a vulgar draw to it, a muddy olive complexion, stubby fingers, and a hand by no means patrician. A hearty off hand manner, far from well bred, and a rapid, dashing way of talking." [93]

Nevertheless, Dana admitted a fascination, and later, at the Wednesday Evening Club, seeing Dickens with Prescott, Sparks, and Ticknor, revised his estimate. "The gentlemen all talking their best, but Dickens perfectly natural and unpretending. He couldn't have behaved better. He did not say a single word for display." [94] And finally, won over completely, "He is full of life," Dana wrote William Cullen Bryant. "And with him life does not appear to be according to the Brunonian theory—a forced state—but a truly *natural* one. I never saw a face fuller of light." [95] Dana's father made the same observations: "He has the finest of eyes; and his whole countenance speaks *life* and *action*—the face seems to flicker with the *heart's* and *mind's* activity. You cannot tell how dead the faces near him seemed." [96]

Everyone noticed this flashing animation. "Dickens himself is frank and hearty," William Wetmore Story wrote his father, "and with a considerable touch of rowdyism in his manner. But his eyes are fine, and the whole muscular action of the mouth and lower part of the face beautifully free and vibratory. People eat him here! never was there such a revolution; Lafayette was nothing to it." And later, "Dickens let off so much of the gas of enthusiasm here," Story said, "that people have been quiet since his departure." [97]

There were continued criticisms, however, of Dickens's breeding. At one great family mansion, observing in a mirror that his hair was disarranged, he calmly combed it at the dinner table.[98] A young lady visitor at the Ticknors', meeting him at several evening parties, thought these famous locks looked as if they "had not yet recovered from the tangle incident to days of sea-misery." Mrs. Dickens, she felt, seemed embarrassed by the limelight that beat upon them, and was clearly "born and bred her husband's social superior." At dinner in the Prescotts' quaint old family residence in Bedford Street, during a discussion about whether the Duchess of Sunderland or Mrs. Caroline Norton were the more beautiful, she heard Dickens drop a social bombshell among the staid Bostonians. "Mrs. Norton is perhaps the most beautiful," he nonchalantly remarked, "but the Duchess, to my mind, is the more kissable." [99]

Not all cultivated Boston even admired Dickens as a writer. At the Andrews Nortons' it was argued that he showed but little knowledge of human nature, that the character of Oliver Twist was an impossibility, and that it was a wonder he should be received with such enthusiasm. Mrs. Norton would grant no more than that his books "were well, some of them *very well*." The enthusiastic Felton, however, replied that they were much more than that. "I had been convinced since the first number of Pickwick, that one of the greatest minds of the age was coming out and . . . that Dickens was the most original and inventive genius since Shakespeare!" [100]

In spite of the mauling and mobbing to which he was subjected, Dickens's enthusiasm for America was high. There were, no doubt, a few drawbacks, like the bareness of the bedrooms in their hotel, the lack of curtains on the beds and the bedroom windows, and the furnaces supplying all the rooms and corridors with a positively infernal heat. But the women were beautiful, the behavior neither stiff nor forward, the good nature universal. "If you ask the way to a place—of some common waterside man, who don't know you from Adam—he turns and goes with you." [101] "The American poor, the American factories, the institutions of all kinds—I have a book, already. There is no man in this town, or in this State of New England, who has not a blazing fire and a meat dinner every day of his life. A flaming sword in the air would not attract so much attention as a beggar in the streets." [102]

As Dickens penned these words to Forster, nothing seemed clearer to him than that *his* book on America would be keyed to a very much more laudatory note than those of his predecessors. Had he not that very day been taken by Sumner and Mayor Chapman on a tour of the public institutions of Boston and heartily approved of what he had seen everywhere? At the Perkins Institute for the Blind he had warmed to the happy faces of the children, been pleased by the pleasant, orderly rooms and by the fact that the inmates of this charity school wore no ugly uniforms but followed their own tastes. He was deeply moved by the loving success with which Dr. Samuel Gridley Howe and his helpers taught blind, deaf, and dumb children like Laura Bridgman to communicate with their fellows and develop into intelligent and cheerful human beings. He was strongly impressed by the use of kindness and of occupational therapy in the State Hospital for the Insane. He remembered little potted plants on the window sills of the paupers, and stairs suited to the little legs of orphans, and noted that it was not assumed that they were evilly disposed people who must be there because of their inherent viciousness. He liked the regulations in the Reform School for Juvenile Offenders, and the varied occupations going on in the House of Correction.[103]

When he visited the carpet factories and woolen and cotton mills of Lowell, he was equally delighted. The town was neat and cheerful with its red-brick buildings and brisk young river. The working girls wore neat dresses with a show of little trinkets and worked in bright rooms with green plants. There was comparatively little child labor, and that regulated by state law. The young women had accounts in the Lowell Savings Bank, shared the use of a piano in many of their boarding-houses, belonged to circulating libraries, and published a periodical called the *Lowell Offering* written by themselves.[104]

Many people might exclaim, "How very preposterous!" Dickens remarks, and say, "These things are above their station." To which he responds, what *is* their station? "It is their station to work. And they *do* work. They labour in these mills, upon an average, twelve hours a day, which is unquestionably work, and pretty tight work too." [105] It is only the novelty of the pianos, libraries, and even the *Lowell Offering*, that startles, not anything wrong about them. "I know no station which has a right to monopolize the means of mutual instruction, improvement, and rational entertainment . . ." [106] And if these young ladies of Lowell even buy parasols and silk stockings, he concludes, he is not aware of any evil consequences. To Dickens himself this revelation that industry could be carried on without cruelty and degradation was deeply gratifying. He said this day was the happiest he had passed in America, and Samuel Lawrence promised to give a party if he visited the mills again, and invite twelve hundred of the mill girls to meet him.[107]

For "the University of Cambridge," as Dickens called Harvard, and many of the dwellers in that small village, he expressed warm admiration. The American universities, he said, "disseminate no prejudices; rear no bigots; dig up the buried ashes of no old superstitions; . . . exclude no man because of his religious opinions; above all, in their whole course of study and instruction, recognize a world, and a broad one too, lying beyond the college walls." [108] "Dana, the author of that Two Years Before the Mast," he wrote Forster, "is a very nice fellow indeed; and in appearance not at all the man you would expect. He is short, mild-looking, and has a care-worn face. His father is exactly like George Cruikshank after a night's jollity—only shorter. The professors of the Cambridge university, Longfellow, Felton, Jared Sparks, are noble fellows. So is Kenyon's friend, Ticknor. Bancroft is a famous man; a straightforward, manly, earnest heart; and talks much of you, which is a great comfort." [109]

With Longfellow, Dickens swiftly headed toward a cordial intimacy. Though the poet was five years older than Dickens, they strikingly resembled each other. Longfellow's hair, though less long and abundant, waved like Dickens's around a broad brow; he had the same liquid, full-orbed eyes, perhaps a shade more pensive; his nose was as straight, but narrower, less sensuous; his lips as sensitive, but with a faint touch of primness.[110]. He had fun enough in him, however, and immediately responded to Dickens. "Gay, free and easy," Longfellow found him, "fine bright face; blue eyes, long black hair, and with a slight dash of the Dick Swiveller about him." [111] Four days after their first meeting, Longfellow joined with Sumner to take Dickens off for a long Sunday walk around Boston.[112]

They visited the waterfront and the wharves where the Boston Tea Party had taken place. At the Seamen's Bethel near North Square they heard Father Taylor, the evangelist, preach a sermon that reminded Dickens of John Bunyan.[113] Emerging from the church, they walked up Moon Street to North Square and Paul Revere's house, entered Prince Street, and then proceeded to Snow Hill, where they turned right to Copp's Burying Ground, with its view of the Old North Church and the Bunker Hill Monument.[114] Down the hill again, Longfellow and Sumner conducted Dickens across the wooden bridge to Charlestown, and thence to Breed's Hill and the Monument, still unfinished and surrounded by scaffolding, but already 221 feet high.[115] At the end of their jaunt, the three men parted the warmest of friends, and Longfellow invited Dickens to breakfast with him at Craigie House and visit Harvard on the following Friday. "Dickens is a glorious fellow," he exclaimed in a letter to his friend Sam Ward.[116]

* * * * *

The great dinner of Tuesday, February 1st, was the public climax of Dickens's reception at Boston. Held at Papanti's under the superintendence of Major Barton, the proprietor of the Albion Hotel, the fifteen dollars a head charged for the tickets ("three pounds sterling," Dickens explained to Forster [117]) gave great dissatisfaction to many.[118] For that sum, however, a choice of more than forty dishes was provided. By five in the afternoon a full band was playing in the balcony, and the invited guests were beginning to assemble in front of the black-marble fireplace in the second-floor reception room, where they were received by a dinner committee with Josiah Quincy, Jr., at its head and including Dr. Oliver Wendell Holmes, Nathan Hale, Jr., and William Wetmore Story. The most prominent of the invited guests were Josiah Quincy, Sr., the President of Harvard, Washington Allston, the poet and artist, George Bancroft, the historian, and Richard Henry Dana, Jr.[119] The band played "Washington's March" as the hundred and fifty subscribers made their way into the hall, then it struck up "God Save the Queen," and the doors of the reception room swung open, when Dickens, the other guests, and the officers of the banquet were shown to the seats reserved for them.[120]

The speaking began with an eloquent introduction by Josiah Quincy, Jr. Quoting Falstaff, he said, " 'If the rascal have not given me medicines to make me love him, I'll be hanged: it could not be else—I have drunk medicines.' " Had they not all investigated with Mr. Pickwick the theory of tittlebats? Had they not all played cribbage with the Marchioness and quaffed "the rosy" with Dick Swiveller? How, then, could anyone think of Boz as a stranger! " 'D'ye think we didn't know ye?—We know ye as well as him that made ye.' " But Dickens had higher qualities, Quincy continued; in his magic mirror men saw the cruel abuses of public institutions, the poorhouse, the jail, the courts. They saw the goodness that could survive even the most polluted surroundings.[121]

Dickens expressed heartfelt gratitude for the cordial welcome they had rained down on his head.[122] Moved by a secret sympathy for the ideals of America, and for "a certain stately tree that has its being hereabout, and spreads its broad branches far and wide," he had "dreamed by day and night, for years, of setting foot upon this shore, and breathing this pure air." [123] Even if he had wandered among them unknown, instead of so honored, he would have come with his sympathies clustered as richly around them, with his sense of justice alive to their high claims, with his energies bent on judging and speaking out and telling the truth.

It was not easy for an author, he said, to speak of his own work. But his purposes were plain and simple. "I believe that virtue shows quite as well in rags and patches as she does in purple and fine linen. . . . I believe that she goes barefoot as well as shod. I believe that she dwells rather oftener in alleys and by-ways than she does in courts and palaces . . ." [124] and that the rejected and forgotten and misused of the world "are moulded in the same form and made of the same clay" as their more fortunate fellow creatures. That this feeling was alive in all the world was shown by those letters he had received from log cabins in solitudes and swamps and from browned hands readier with the ax than the pen.[125]

Before he sat down, there was one more topic on which he desired to lay stress. There were great writers in America, who were already "as familiar to our lips as household words." "I hope the time is not far distant when they, in America, will receive of right some substantial profit and return in England from their labours; and when we, in England, shall receive some substantial profit and return in America from ours. Pray do not misunderstand me. . . . I would rather have the affectionate regard of my fellowmen than I would have heaps and mines of gold." But the two were not incompatible, for nothing good was incompatible with justice. He was sure the time was not far distant when America would act with the justice that became the character of a great country. He concluded by giving the toast: "*America and England*—and may they never have any division but the Atlantic between them!" [126]

The applause that followed was tumultuous. No later speaker, however, deviated from his prepared remarks or left the safe regions of eloquent platitude by referring to the subject of international copyright that Dickens had thus brought up. Newspapers the next day screamed that he had been guilty of bad taste in introducing it before a social gathering having no other purpose than to do him honor, and charged that he had "created huge dissonance where all else was triumphant unison." [127]

The enormous furore ultimately created on this theme, and Dickens's refusal to be silenced, either by abusive anonymous letters or by vituperation in the press, make it one of the excited controversies of his visit. Much of the anger was no doubt whipped up by the newspapers, who were themselves often among the worst offenders against the rights of authors—which was much as if a burglar should object to the ill-breeding of a reference to housebreaking. No objections had been made when Joe Field mentioned the topic in the *Boz* Masque at the Tremont Theatre only a week earlier. (It may, indeed, have been this production that gave Dickens the idea of making his own allusion to international copyright.) Apparently, though, to newspapers and publishers, it was bad manners for the victim of an abuse to voice any plaint, even when he did so, as Dickens had done, with moderation, good temper, and justice.

Doubtless there were some idealists in his audience who deplored his selfishness and indelicacy in speaking of being done out of money. Such people may think, as Chesterton says, that "A beautiful young dreamer, with flowing brown hair, ought not to be even conscious of copyright." [128] But Dickens did not ask whether his claim was selfish, but whether it was just. If they thought "that he, of all men, ought not to speak" [129] because he was interested, he thought that he, of all men, ought to speak because he was wronged. As for the occasion, it was a public event, and all the more fitting therefore as a sounding board for the voice of truth. And, however some of the dinner guests may have felt, there were many who did feel that he had the right on his side and that there was nothing objectionable in either his manner or his matter. James T. Fields, sitting at the foot of one of the tables, among the youngest of the young men, evidently remembered no flaws in the occasion:

"It was a glorious episode in all our lives . . . We younger members of the dinner-party sat in the seventh heaven of happiness and were translated to other spheres. . . . And when Dickens stood up at last to answer for himself, so fresh and so handsome with his beautiful eyes moist with feeling and his whole frame aglow with excitement, how we did hurrah, we young fellows. Trust me it was a great night, and we must have made a great noise at our end of the table, for I remember frequent messages came down to us from the 'Chair' begging that we hold up a little and moderate if possible the rapture of our applause." [130]

The toasts went on. Letters were read from Prescott, Washington Irving, William Ellery Channing, Judge Story, and others, regretting their inability to be there.[131] Joe Field sang a comic song, entitled "The Wery Last Obserwations of Weller, Senior," in one stanza of which there was another reference to book piracies:

> "Remember vot I says, Boz—
>   You're going to cross the sea;
> A blessed vay avays, Boz,
>   To vild Amerikey;
> A blessed set of savages,
>   As books of travels tells;
> No guv'ner's eye to vatch you, Boz,
>   Nor even Samivel's.

>   . . . . . .

> "Just think of all of yours, Boz,
>   Devoured by them already;
> Avoid their greedy lures, Boz,
>   Their appetites is steady;
> For years they've been a feastin', Boz,
>   Nor paid for their repast;
> And von't they make a blessed feast
>   Ven they catches you at last!" [132]

Peals of laughter greeted every line of this song, and at the end there was a wild outburst. Finally, at one o'clock President Quincy announced that he was leaving the chair. After the parting sentiment, "A speedy return to Charles Dickens," he and Dickens left the hall.[133] "Was there ever," asked James T. Fields, "such a night before in our staid city?" [134]

CHAPTER TWO

Conquest—With Undertones

Four days later Dickens left Boston. The morning after the banquet he had breakfast in Mount Vernon Street with the elderly William Ellery Channing, whom he pronounced to be "just the man he ought to be," and who stimulated his interest in Unitarianism.[1] The breakfast at Longfellow's on the day before his departure firmly cemented the friendship established during their walk the preceding Sunday. With Cornelius Felton, who dropped by for him at the Tremont House, Dickens strode briskly to Bowdoin Square, where they took Morse's stage over the West Boston Bridge through open country to Cambridgeport, and alighted at the "Village," as Harvard Square was then called. Going up Brattle Street past the village smithy and its spreading chestnut tree, they reached the beautiful old colonial house with its yellow clapboards and classical pilasters, where Washington had made his headquarters during the first year of the Revolution. Here Longfellow welcomed them at the front door.

The two front rooms on the second floor he used as his dining room and study, and behind the study on the east was his bedroom. To these sunny rooms, with their fourteen windows looking out on the elm trees and the fields and flowers, Longfellow now led his guests.[2] At the round breakfast table Dickens met the solemn Andrews Norton, former Professor of Sacred Literature, and Longfellow's brother Samuel, who said they then sat down to "a bright little breakfast, at which Felton's mirthfulness helped, and Andrews Norton's gravity did not in the least hinder, the exuberant liveliness of the author of Pickwick." [3]

After breakfast Dickens was shown about the College and taken to the Harvard College Library in the newly built Victorian-Gothic

[378]

Gore Hall, where he was introduced to other Cambridge worthies. On his way back to Boston, he dropped in at the picturesque ivy-clad studio of Washington Allston, the painter, to say farewell to that "glorious old genius." [4] Then he returned to the Tremont House, where their maid had been packing steadily in preparation for their departure the following day. [5]

The leave-taking was a grand turmoil. Dickens's party descended the marble staircase for the last time. The entire management was in the lobby to say farewell. Twenty-five gentlemen who happened to be there had to be shaken hands with. Crowds shouted in the streets as they drove to the Worcester Railroad Station; the Alexanders were in the waiting room to see them off; Putnam hurried to get their luggage on the train; Governor Davis, with whom the Dickenses were to stay in Worcester, arrived with his party; and they boarded the three o'clock train. Felton accompanied them, his gold spectacles glittering and his face beaming. [6] At every station there were surging crowds: "Wherever the cars stopped," Felton said, "heads were incontinently thrust in bawling out, 'Is Mr. Dickens here?' . . . No less than six people came within a hair's breadth of losing their heads, by keeping them thrust in too long—not taking them out until the cars had been in motion several seconds." [7]

Dickens liked the New England towns and villages, with their white frame houses and green blinds crisp in the nipping winter air. [8] That night Governor Davis introduced him to his "general friends," a term that seemed to mean practically everybody, and Dickens shook hands and made a speech from his chamber window under the two-story Doric porch to the throng overflowing the snow-covered lawn outside. Sunday he met the Governor's "particular friends." [9] Felton reported a conversation between Dickens and the Governor at dinner. Dickens had remarked on a few peculiarities of pronunciation he had noticed in Boston.

"Did they sound *hash?*" inquired the Governor. "I beg your pardon, what did you say?" asked Dickens. "Did the Boston pronunciation sound *hash* to you?" the Governor repeated. "Excuse me, but I do not understand your Excellency's question." "I asked," the Executive persisted, "if those peculiarities . . . sounded *hash* to your ears?" "He means," interposed Mrs. Davis, "to ask, if they grated on your ears, if they were disagreeable to you." [10]

Dickens later joked about this lady and the parsimonious hospitality of her table. "She is too good a housekeeper and has a hungry eye," he wrote Charles Sumner. If Sumner cared for anybody invited there, he should "write an anonymous letter, and tell him not to go." [11] And William Prescott told his wife that Dickens "laughed about the short commons at the Governor's, where I believe they got tea and roast apples." [12]

Monday morning, Dickens and Kate went on by rail to Springfield, and then by a tiny shallow steamboat down through the crunching ice of the Connecticut River to Hartford. Kate's face was swollen again, so they remained four days at the City Hotel, while Dickens visited the Institute for the Deaf and Blind, the Insane Asylum and the State House, and saw the Charter Oak. [13]

Late one evening, after they had retired for the night, they were serenaded outside their chamber door by a nephew of John Quincy Adams and a friend with songs of home and absent friends. Suddenly Dickens had a ludicrous thought. How absurd their shoes must look outside their door in the hotel corridor while those two young men sentimentally strummed their guitars! The idea overwhelmed him with such hilarity that he was obliged to cover his face with the bedclothes to stifle his shouts of laughter. [14]

At Hartford there was another dinner, of seventy persons, and the bill of fare outdid that of the Boston dinner by listing over seventy dishes. [15] Dickens, determined to be bullied by no newspaper outcry, spoke again on the subject of international copyright. He had been shocked by the fact that even those who favored it seemed afraid to speak for it. "Washington Irving, Prescott, Hoffman, Bryant, Halleck, Dana, Washington Allston—every man who writes in this country is devoted to the question," he wrote Forster, "and not one of them *dares* to raise his voice and complain of the atrocious state of the law." When Dickens had done so at Boston, his friends "were paralyzed with wonder at such audacious daring. The notion that I, a man alone by himself, in America, should venture to suggest to the Americans that there was one point on which they were neither just to their own countrymen nor to us, actually struck the boldest dumb!" [16]

As if to emphasize the fact that *he* could not be gagged or frightened, therefore, Dickens amplified the mild remarks he had made at

Boston. He had made a compact with himself, he told his audience, that while he was in America he would omit no opportunity of referring to the subject. "I would beg leave to whisper in your ear two words: *International Copyright*." He used them, he insisted, in no sordid sense. He would rather his children trudged in mud and knew their father was beloved than have them ride in carriages and know only that he was rich. But there was no necessity for the choice.

If Scott had been aided in his labors by the existence of such a law, he "might not have sunk beneath the mighty pressure on his brain." And Dickens reminded his listeners of that touching scene when the great man was dying, listening on his couch through the open window to the rippling of the Tweed that he had loved. Think of the shame and the sorrow that even as he lay crushed by financial struggle the phantoms of his imagination—Jeanie Deans, Rob Roy, Caleb Balderstone, Dominie Sampson—should have brought him no aid from those foreign lands where they had carried delight to millions, no friendly hand to raise him from that sad bed, not even "one grateful dollarpiece to buy a garland for his grave." Let those who went to look on that tomb at Dryburgh Abbey remember it, "and bring the recollection home." [17]

"It is nothing," Dickens wrote Forster in telling him of the scene that ensued, "that of all men living I am the greatest loser . . . It is nothing that I have a claim to speak and be heard. The wonder is that a breathing man can be found with temerity enough to suggest to the Americans the possibility of their having done wrong. I wish you could have seen the faces that I saw, down both sides of the table at Hartford, when I began to speak about Scott. I wish you could have heard how I gave it out. My blood so boiled as I thought of the monstrous injustice that I felt as if I were twelve feet high when I thrust it down their throats." [18]

But even the faces of his audience gave Dickens no intimation of what was to follow this speech. The amenities of the occasion restrained the dinner guests. But afterwards, friendly persons tried to dissuade him from pursuing the subject any further. And then the howl in the press began. The Hartford *Times* said, "It happens that we want no advice on the subject and it will be better for Mr. Dickens if he refrains from introducing the subject hereafter . . ." Other newspapers asserted that he was no gentleman, that he was a mercenary scoundrel, that he was abusing the hospitality of the United States by uttering any such criticism of his hosts, that he had malignantly come to the country with that low purpose, that in comparison with Dickens a notorious murderer named Colt was an angel.[19] Anonymous letters echoed all these attacks in every key of scurrility. Dickens burned with scorn and indignation. But he did not give way. What had happened, he wrote to Jonathan Chapman in Boston, had "had the one good effect of making me iron upon this theme, and iron I will be here and at home, by word of mouth and in writing as long as I can articulate a syllable or hold a pen." [20]

Opposition had had its usual effect of making Dickens more adamantine in his determination than before. But it had, this time, other and more sweeping results as well. The anonymous insults and the yelpings of the yellow press altered the visionary image he had entertained of America as a land of freedom and changed the attitude he brought to all the later experiences of his visit.

"I believe," he wrote Forster, "that there is no country, on the face of the earth, where there is less freedom of opinion on any subject in reference to which there is a broad difference of opinion than in this. . . . There! I write the words with reluctance, disappointment, and sorrow; but I believe it from the bottom of my soul." [21] And in the same letter he noted that he reserved his opinion "of the national character—just whispering that I tremble for a radical coming here, unless he is a radical on principle, by reason and reflection, and from the sense of right. I fear that if he were anything else, he would return home a tory. . . . I say no more on that head . . . save that I do fear that the heaviest blow ever dealt at liberty will be dealt by this country, in the failure of its example to the earth." [22]

It was not merely that the great dream of America as the shining citadel of liberty had burst as if it were an iridescent bubble. It left behind a disillusion like an ugly smear coloring the scene. Things he had previously regarded as mere flaws in the grand achievement of the country moved into prominence; the shadows and the shortcomings became characteristic. Dickens granted that "the respectable newspapers and reviews" took up "the cudgel as strongly in my favour, as the others have done against me," [23] but the ruffian outcries seemed to him to drown the voices of decency and justice. To the courtesy and cultivation of many Americans whom he met he responded with warm appreciation, and he praised the warm-heartedness and kindliness of intention that greeted him almost everywhere. But the general crudity and the ill-breeding of the intrusions that at first he had regarded as an amusing excess of lionization came to rasp him more and more.

"I can do nothing that I want to do," he said, "go nowhere where I want to go, and see nothing that I want to see. If I turn into the street, I am followed by a multitude. If I stay at home, the house becomes, with callers, like a fair. If I visit a public institution, with only one friend, the directors come down incontinently, waylay me in the yard, and address me in a long speech. I go to a party in the evening, and am so enclosed and hedged about by people, stand where I will, that I am exhausted for want of air. I go to church for quiet, and there is a violent rush to the neighborhood of the pew I sit in, and the clergyman preaches at *me*. I take my seat in a railroad car, and the very conductor won't leave me alone. I get out at a station, and can't drink a glass of water, without having a hundred people looking down my throat when I open my mouth to swallow. . . . Then by every post, letters on letters arrive, all about nothing, and all demanding an immediate answer. This man is offended because I won't live in his house; and that man is disgusted because I won't go out more than four times in one evening. I have no peace, and am in a perpetual worry." 24

Consequently Dickens determined that, aside from two invitations in New York, to a ball and to a dinner, that he had already accepted while he was still at Boston, he would accept no further public entertainments during his stay in the United States. He would try to visit Philadelphia, Baltimore, Washington, and the South as a private individual, and then head west "through the wilds of Kentucky and Tennessee" and the Alleghenies to the Great Lakes and Canada. To be sure, he was told that the roads were bad, "the country a tremendous waste, the inns log-houses, and the journey one that would play the very devil with Kate." But only by "some such dash" could he "be a free agent, or see anything worth the telling." 25

As for the copyright controversy, he would *not* let it drop. He requested Forster to obtain for him a short letter from the principal English authors, supporting his position; its publication in the best American journals would unquestionably do great good. Henry Clay had sent to him from Washington "to declare his strong interest in the matter, his cordial approval of the 'manly' course I have held in reference to it, and his desire to stir in it if possible." It would be "a thousand pities if we did not strike as hard as we can, now that the iron is so hot." [26]

*   *   *   *   *

Meanwhile Dickens had moved on from Hartford, and taken the boat down Long Island Sound to New York. At New Haven he was serenaded by the Yale students in force, and the crowd assembled to see him at the Tontine Hotel was so numerous that the landlord placed two stout porters to lock their hands across the main staircase to the reception room and keep the throng at bay. These huskies admitted people only in successive waves that kept pouring in to wring the aching hand of their visitor until eleven o'clock. It was nearly midnight before he could retire to his room.[27] One citizen, in a letter to the press, commented that Dickens must despise such adulation as the behavior of a nation of silly parasites, and satirically asked why "some shrewd enterprising Yankee" did not "put him in a cage, and take him about the country for a *show?*" [28] Subscriptions had been taken, at both Hartford and New Haven, to pay all Dickens's expenses, but he refused to budge until Putnam had "received the bills from the landlords' own hands, and paid them to the last farthing." [29]

On the boat down the Sound Dickens had a rest from these excitements. Felton was with him, "unaffected, hearty, genial, jolly," and the two "drank all the porter on board, ate all the cold pork and cheese, and were very merry indeed." [30] Presently they were passing through Hell Gate, the Hog's Back, and the Frying Pan, familiar to Dickens from Diedrich Knickerbocker's *History of New York.* Sloping banks with trees and pleasant villas were succeeded by the sparkling waters of the Bay, and Dickens saw the buildings, spires, steeples, ships' masts, flapping sails, waving flags, and crowded ferries that clustered around the Battery.[31] Soon he was driving up Broadway, noting the ladies in rainbow silks and satins who thronged the sidewalks beneath the Lombardy poplars, their blue and pink parasols, their fluttering ribbons and richly lined cloaks and hoods, the beaux in Byronic collars and tasseled cloaks, the great blocks of ice being carried into shops and bars, and the gentlemanly pigs rooting in the gutters.[32]

New York had then a population of around three hundred thousand mostly concentrated on the lower tip of Manhattan Island. Fifth Avenue at Tenth Street was uptown, fashionable people lived in houses with hand-wrought iron fences around Park Place, Chambers Street, and St. John's Park, bolder pioneers were pressing up to Lafayette Street and Washington Square, and the Madison Cottage at Twenty-fourth Street was a roadhouse. Bloomingdale and even Murray Hill were summer resorts, and so was Hoboken, with its sweeping view up and down the Hudson, bathing in the river, rustic arbors, swings, and a menagerie that included a kangaroo, an anaconda, and a boa constrictor.[33]

At the Carlton House, Dickens was accommodated with "a very splendid suite of rooms" which he feared was also "(as at Boston) *enormously* dear." [34] David Colden, a man of forty-five and a lover of literature, who was a member of both the New York committees, for the ball and for the banquet, joined Dickens and Kate at dinner.[35] Colden had no sooner departed, leaving them sipping their wine, than Washington Irving's card was brought in. Dickens dashed in to the reception room, napkin still in hand, and the two met with open arms. "Irving!" Dickens cried. "I am delighted to see you!" And, dragging his guest into the room where they were still at the dinner table, "What will you have to drink," he went on enthusiastically, "a mint julep or a gin-cocktail?" Irving remained until ten o'clock.[36]

The following evening the Boz Ball took place at the Park Theatre. The interior was decorated in an extraordinary manner, the dome covered by festoons of bunting hanging from a central golden rosette, the galleries and tiers of boxes also draped in white muslin trimmed with gold, all serving as a background for statues of Cupid and Psyche, Apollo and the Nine Muses, portraits of the Presidents of the United States, the arms of all the states under a trophy of English and American flags, medallions representing Dickens's works interspersed with rosettes and silver stars, and, in the center, a portrait of Dickens brooded over by a golden eagle with a crown of laurel in its beak. In addition, there were "fourteen figures after the antique," a row of guitars and tambourines above the orchestra, and a large golden Maypole with an eagle at the top and pendant wreaths above golden

pillars on each side. All these splendors were illumined by a blaze
of five hundred lights, emanating from two chandeliers suspended
by golden ropes, from lamps and candelabra on golden columns at
the entrance of every box, and from six astral lamps hanging from
the proscenium pillars.

The stage, which was to be the scene of a series of twelve *tableaux
vivants,* had been widened to sixty feet and thrown open all the way
back to Theatre Alley to permit the erection of "a large and magnificent chamber of carved and gilded oak, with deep Gothic windows on
each side, and a lofty, fretted ceiling." Embellishing the walls were
twenty medallions representing scenes from the works of Boz, including no fewer than four devoted to Little Nell. On these poured the
light of six golden chandeliers, sixteen bracket candelabra, and one
hundred and ten gaslights with silk shades.[37] The entire amazing concoction, seen amid "light, glitter, glare, show, noise, and cheering,"
Dickens found "very striking"; from the roof to the floor, he added,
"the theatre was magnificently decorated." [38]

The doors of the theater were thrown open at seven-thirty, and
within half an hour the entire building was densely crowded.[39] Three
thousand people who had tickets that five thousand more had been
unable to obtain at any price milled around and trod on each other's
toes, waiting for a glimpse of Dickens, who was not slated to appear
until the formal opening of the ball at nine o'clock. Everyone was in
roaring good humor.[40] When the curtain went up on one of the
tableaux and revealed a silly-looking short gentleman in a green-velvet
suit, someone screamed, "there he is! There's Boz!" and the audience
shrieked with laughter.[41]

Finally, a little after nine, there was a persistent ringing of the
gong that had signalized the *tableaux,* the band burst into "See the
Conquering Hero Comes," and Dickens made his appearance escorted
by General George Morris in full-dress military uniform, and followed
by Kate under the escort of David Colden. Dickens was in black,
with a gay waistcoat; Kate in white with mazarine blue flowers and
a pearl necklace and earrings. The house rang with cheers, and handkerchiefs waved from the floor to all the boxes and tiers.[42] The Mayor
made a speech that nobody heard, the committee gave Kate a huge
bouquet arranged according to the language of the flowers, and

Dickens "breathed heavily, and cast one look up at the house, partly curious, partly bewildered, partly satiric, and a good deal humorous." [43]

Then came the Grand March, twice around the enormous ballroom, with members of the committee plunging into the crush and clearing a precarious path while Dickens escorted the Mayoress and the Mayor escorted Kate, and two-thirds of the audience complained that they couldn't see him through the crowd, and the rest fell in behind cheering and hurrahing. There were more *tableaux*, and, in between them, quadrilles and waltzes, although there was hardly room even to stand. "It was like dancing in a canebrake," wrote one spectator, "the poor girls clinging to their partners to avoid being swept beyond their power to protect them." [44] The bill of fare for supper, even after his experiences at Boston and Hartford, Dickens found, "in its amount and extent, quite a curiosity." At last, "being no longer able even to stand," he wrote Forster, "we slipped away quietly, and came back to the hotel." [45]

The evening after this exhausting affair Dickens attended a quiet family dinner at Colden's residence in Laight Street,[46] and during the following two days he was confined to his rooms in the Carlton House by a bad cold. Snuffling uncomfortably in the overheated rooms, he was at once amused and exasperated by the newspaper reports of his activities, which mingled "all manner of lies" with an occasional truth "so twisted and distorted that it has as much resemblance to the real facts as Quilp's leg to Taglioni's." "Another paper, coming after the ball, dwells upon its splendour and brilliancy; hugs itself and its readers upon all that Dickens saw; and winds up by gravely expressing its conviction that Dickens was never in such society in England as he has seen in New York, and that its high and striking tone cannot fail to make an indelible impression on his mind! For the same reason I am always represented, whenever I appear in public, as being 'very pale'; 'apparently thunderstruck'; and utterly confounded by all I see. . . . You recognize the queer vanity which is at the root of all this?" he asked Forster. "I have plenty of stories in connection with it to amuse you with when I return." [47]

Hard upon the Boz Ball came the great Dickens Dinner on Friday, the 18th.[48] Washington Irving, who was to preside, dreaded the dire necessity of making a speech with nearly as much dismay as Mr. Pickwick felt at the prospect of having to lead that "dreadful horse" around all day. Almost daily, to Dickens and other friends, he lamented in half-ludicrous, half-melancholy tones, "I shall certainly break down!" [49] The dinner committee, "composed," Dickens reminded Forster, "of the first gentlemen in America," were also dismayed by the hornets' nest Dickens had stirred up over copyright, and besought him "not to pursue the subject, *although they every one agreed with me.*" But Dickens was unmoved. "I answered that I would. That nothing should deter me. . . . That the shame was theirs, not mine; and that as I would not spare them when I got home, I would not be silenced here." [50] Accordingly, putting the best face they could upon it, the committee resolved to support him by having Irving propose the sentiment "International Copyright" and Cornelius Mathews, the Editor of the *Arcturus*, reply with a speech defending it.

At the City Hotel, where the dinner was held, outsiders pressed into the reception room to "have a look" at the guest of honor, and were surprised, Lewis Gaylord Clark reported, to see that Dickens "was only a bright-eyed young man with 'lots' of long, curly, brown hair, and big, laughing blue eyes." "I noticed especially," Dickens commented, "one young fellow, who, after examining me from a near 'stand-point' very attentively, retired to take a distant or bird's-eye view, surveying me from top to toe . . . making an inventory of my 'pints,' as if I had been *a building,* and he was anxious to secure in his mind my architectural proportions." [51]

An unusual feature marking the dinner was the presence of a small coterie of ladies, Mrs. Colden, her sister Miss Wilkes, Kate and others, in a room adjoining the banquet hall. These edged their way in to the main room and, by the time the speechmaking began, had taken possession of the stage behind the speakers' table. Irving, still dismally repeating, "I shall certainly break down," had brought the manuscript of his speech and laid it under his plate. He began in his pleasant voice with two or three sentences comparing the other more able speakers, waiting their turns, to mounted knights eager for the tournament, and then went on to speak of this enthusiastic welcome to Dickens as representing a national homage to intellect. At this point one of his listeners broke in with a loud "Admirable! excellent!" which so threw him off his balance that he lost what he was going to say, stumbled, forgot that he had his speech with him, and gave up, concluding only with the words, "*Charles Dickens,* the literary guest of the nation." "There!" he said, as he fell back into his seat, "there! I told you I should break down, and I've done it." [52]

Dickens, completely cool, made only a brief and mild allusion to the theme that had so worried the committee. "As I come here, and am here," he said, "without the least admixture of one hundredth part of one grain of base alloy, without one feeling of unworthy reference to self in any respect, I claim . . . for the last time, my right in reason, in truth and in justice, to approach as I have done on two former occasions, a question of literary interest. I claim that justice be done, and I prefer this claim as one who has a right to speak and be heard."

Then he went on to speak in the warmest terms of Washington Irving. "Why, gentlemen, I don't go upstairs to bed two nights out of seven—as a very reputable witness near at hand can testify—I say I do not go to bed two nights out of seven without taking Washington Irving under my arm." Was there an English farm, an English city, or an English country seat where Knickerbocker and Geoffrey Crayon had not been? Who could travel among the Italian peasants or the bandits of the Pyrenees without remembering Irving? "Go farther still—go to the Moorish fountains, sparkling full in the moonlight," and would it not be found that he had "peopled the Alhambra, and made eloquent its shadows?" Who but Irving, again, had crossed the dark Atlantic with Columbus, and what pen but his had made Rip Van Winkle, playing at ninepins, a part of the Catskill Mountains? Dickens ended the speech with a graceful reference to Irving's having just been appointed Minister to Spain. America well knew, he said, "how to do honour to her own literature, and that of other lands," when she chose "Washington Irving for her representative in the country of Cervantes." [53]

Cornelius Mathews, in his copyright speech, argued primarily for the welfare of American literature and American authors. That the profits on pirated books were stolen was too miserably obvious to need demonstration. But what was the effect on native letters, he asked, when unscrupulous publishers could snatch the writings of Ainsworth, Bulwer, Lever, and Dickens without the payment of a single penny? What hope was there for the young native writer? The "enormous fraud practised upon their British brethren" was also a blight upon a national literature. Did an author's "brood of speckled fancies" not deserve as honest a price as a poultry farmer's parti-colored capons? No one, therefore, should have been surprised or indignant that Dickens, "among brethren, in his own younger brother's house," should have ventured "to speak of a patrimony" he held in common with American authors. Statesmen should be willing to devise provisions to give both British and American writers their just due. When they did, then "the two sections of Anglo-Saxon Literature on either side of the great ocean" might move forward harmoniously, and America have a majestic literature of her own, "self-reared, self-sustained, self-vindicating!" [54]

This part of the proceedings went almost entirely ignored in the New York newspapers, which simply dropped the speech out of their reports. An exception was Horace Greeley's New York *Tribune*. On the very day of the Boz Ball, Greeley had come to Dickens's defense in a vigorous editorial. "We trust he will not be deterred from speaking the frank, round truth by any mistaken courtesy, diffidence, or misapprehension of public sentiment." Who should protest against robbery if not those robbed? Did America look well offering Dickens "toasts, compliments, and other syllabub, while we refuse him naked justice?" It was all very well "in a dinner speech to say that fame and popularity and all that are more than sordid gold," but the argument that Dickens should be disinterested came ill from publishers grown rich on his writings and readers who had never returned him a farthing for all the pleasure he had given them. Let the American people first be just, and then generous. Let them put their names to a petition for an international copyright law, and then they could honestly take Dickens's hand, instead of laying themselves open to the charge of trying to bribe him from criticism with "acres of inflated compliments soaked in hogsheads of champagne." [55]

On the Monday following the dinner, the *Tribune* not only printed Mathews's speech in full, but supported it in a further editorial. No unwarped mind could deny, the *Tribune* declared, that the author had the same rights in his books as the farmer in his wheat, the blacksmith in his axes, or the grazier in his ox. The robbery of foreign authors also meant the indigence of the American. "Copyright is at best a grudging restoration of part of what society had unjustly taken." And once again the *Tribune* appealed to its readers "to petition Congress for Justice to Authors." [56] The agitation Dickens had started progressed to such effect that before he was ready to leave New York he had in his portmanteau "a petition for an international copyright law, signed by all the best American writers with Washington Irving at their head. They have requested me to hand it to Clay," he reported to Forster in considerable satisfaction, "and to back it with any remarks I may think proper to offer. So 'Hoo-roar for the principle, as the money-lender said, ven he vouldn't renoo the bill.' " [57]

* * * * *

Dickens spent a total of three weeks in New York. Irving was an almost daily visitor, and Dickens paid a visit to Sunnyside, Irving's pleasant home in Tarrytown.[58] At Lewis Gaylord Clark's dinner table Dickens and Irving were loquacious with each other.[59] "Washington Irving is *a great* fellow," Dickens declared to Forster. "We have laughed together most heartily." [60] "It was delightful," said Felton, "to witness the cordial intercourse of the young man, in the flush and glory of his fervent genius, and his older compeer, then in the assured possession of immortal renown." [61] On one occasion, Irving came to breakfast, together with Bryant and Halleck. "Good Heaven!" exclaimed the clerk at the Carlton, "to think what the four walls of that room now contain! Washington Irving, William Cullen Bryant, Fitz-Greene Halleck, and Charles Dickens!" [62]

Theaters were not omitted from Dickens's round of New York amusements. On Saturday the 19th he saw Sheridan Knowles's *The Love Chase* and the farce of *The Young Widow* at the Bowery Theatre, and he may have witnessed some of the repertory with which the Park Theatre reopened on the 21st. At the Boz Ball he had been delighted to run into William Mitchell, an English comedian Dickens had warmly admired since his shorthand-writing days. Mitchell was now enormously popular in New York both as an actor and as manager of the tiny Olympic Theatre, near Niblo's Gardens. He followed up their meeting by a letter inviting Dickens to visit the theater, where a travesty of Shakespeare entitled *Richard Number III* had opened on the 16th. Dickens probably saw this and he was certainly a welcome backstage guest.[63]

The devoted Felton, who had not been able to tear himself away from Dickens's side, was still in New York. The two were together "daily and almost hourly," wrote Felton's friend Sam Ward, in a letter to Longfellow; "they have walked, laughed, talked, eaten Oysters and drunk Champagne together until they have almost grown together —in fact nothing but the interference of Madame D prevented their being attached to each other like the Siamese Twins, *a volume of Pickwick serving as connecting membrane*. Imagine them strolling up Broadway—the grave Eliot Professor and the *swelling*, theatrical Boz— the little man with the red waistcoat—talking Pickwickian and Barnaby . . ." [64] And frequently descending, Ward might have added, the steps of oyster cellars, to gorge on oysters, Felton's favorite delicacy, fried, and as large as cheese plates.[65]

Not until almost the end of February did Felton return to Cambridge from this "roistering and oystering," [66] bubbling over with the enthusiasm of his golden visit. He bore with him an invitation for Longfellow, who was going abroad that summer, to return to America by way of England and make his home in London with Dickens. "Write to me from the continent," Dickens commanded, "and tell me when to expect you. . . . Have no home but mine—see nothing in town on your way towards Germany—and let me be your London host and cicerone. Is this a bargain?" [67]

Neither theatergoing nor these oysterish dissipations with Felton had prevented Dickens from continuing his observation of American institutions. He was not as favorably impressed by those in New York as he had been by those in New England. The Lunatic Asylum was dirty, listless, bleak, and horribly overcrowded; the Alms House badly ventilated, badly lighted, and not too clean; the Island Jail, which he saw on a rainy day when the convicts could not work in the stone quarries,[68] was filled with an odor like that of "a thousand old mildewed umbrellas wet through, and a thousand dirty clothes-bags, musty, moist, and fusty." [69]

Escorted by two police officers, Dickens also made a night visit to the Five Points and its haunts of drunkenness, poverty, and vice. He noted rotten beams, broken windows, leprous houses sometimes attainable only by crazy outside steps, sometimes with pitch-dark stairs of trembling boards half revealed by candlelight flickering in the foul air. There were black caverns of rooms with the floors covered by what at first seemed mounds of dusky rags; the rags stirred at the flaring taper and were seen to be heaps of Negro women, waking from their slumber with white teeth chattering and eyes glistening in fear, "like the countless repetition of one astonished African face in some strange mirror." There were other interiors suffocating with the stench of clothes and human flesh; alleys knee-deep in mud; dens where sailors and mulatto girls, even as they drank and danced, rubbed shoulders with robbery and murder.[70]

The dismal-fronted prison-pile of The Tombs, with its bastard Egyptian architecture, however, affected Dickens even more painfully than the slums.[71] The noisome vapors and foul smell of the underground cells where drunkards were thrown overnight, the vaulted corridors without a ray of light, the iron doors within which there was not even a drop of water, the rats that sometimes attacked those too weak or sodden to defend themselves, filled him with a disgust he found it impossible to repress. In a cell no larger than the wine cellar at Devonshire Terrace there were often, the night policeman told him, as many as twenty-six young women locked up together, "beautiful ones too, and that's a fact." Prisoners waiting trial were sometimes confined in these filthy holes for months, Dickens learned, without even being permitted to walk out in a yard for exercise. In one cell Dickens saw a miserable-looking boy of ten or twelve. "What's *he* been doing?" he asked. "Nothing," said his guide. "Nothing!" said Dickens. "No," replied the other. "He's here for safe keeping. He saw his father kill his mother, and is detained to give evidence." "But that's rather hard treatment for a witness, isn't it?"—"Well! I don't know. It ain't a very rowdy life, and *that's* a fact." [72]

Dickens had heard American prison discipline lauded in England, but if what he had now seen in New York was characteristic he felt that his homeland had little to learn about prison reform from America. Even the more praiseworthy establishments he had seen in Massachusetts and Connecticut were not superior to those governed by Tracey and Chesterton in London.[73] The glories Dickens had come to see were beginning to seem like those legendary inns mentioned by earlier travelers in America, "where they undercharge literary people for the love the landlords bear them." [74] His own experience was one of monstrous and violent overcharge—£70 for two weeks at the Carlton House, though he had dined there only once and had in no more than four bottles of wine.[75] A faint tarnish, indeed, was gradually staining all his radiant first impressions. American hotels and hospi-

tality, American abolition of a degraded poverty, American enlightenment in public institutions, American freedom of opinion—none
were quite so admirable upon further knowledge as they had seemed
to the eye of inexperienced enthusiasm. America had shown Dickens
her most glowing face during the triumphant first two weeks at Boston.
Slowly the shining dream was darkening into shapes of prison cruelty,
slums as foul as Seven Dials at home, rude mobs, vulgar intruders,
malignant newspaper abuse, and intolerance of criticism.

CHAPTER THREE

"Not the Republic of My Imagination"

From New York to Philadelphia took six hours by railroad, and involved two changes to ferries.[1] Dickens sent Putnam on ahead with some of the baggage,[2] but was then detained six days in New York by another of Kate's ulcerated sore throats to which, he explained to Putnam, she was subject every spring. The doctor forbade her getting up, and Dickens feared that "alone in sickness and such a great distance from home, she would feel distressed after I had gone." [3] Consequently Dickens remained with her until the morning of March 6th, when she was again able to travel.

By this time poor Kate was also miserably homesick. Her only comfort was the portrait of the children, which was set up on a table or mantelpiece wherever they stayed. She became highly indignant at Nathaniel Parker Willis's persistently begging her to give him the picture as a souvenir. "Imagine!" she exclaimed in a letter to Maclise, "the impudence and audacity of such a request!" [4] Her heart-heaviness was deepened by not having heard from the children. The *Caledonia*, on which they had expected letters, had been twenty-four days at sea and there was still no news of her. Terrible gales had been strewing the coast with wrecks. Dickens was less distressed than Kate, but he too longed for word from England, and shared her fears that the ship had gone down. "Oh for news from home!" he exclaimed to Forster, "I think of your letters so full of heart and friendship, with perhaps a little scrawl of Charley's or Mamey's lying at the bottom of the deep sea, and am as full of horror as if they had once been living creatures." [5]

The trip to Philadelphia was Dickens's first considerable experience of American railway travel. He thought it neither as safe nor as comfortable as in England. The unguarded tracks drove right through the main street of a large town, "with pigs burrowing, and boys flying kites and playing marbles, and men smoking, and women talking, and children crawling, close to the very rails." Then, "slap-dash, headlong, pell-mell, down the middle of the street" there came "tearing along a mad locomotive with its train of cars, scattering a red-hot shower of sparks (from its *wood* fire) in all directions; screeching, hissing, yelling, and panting; and nobody any more concerned than if it were a hundred miles away." [6]

Inside the coaches, Dickens noted, the windows were "usually all closed," and "a hot, close, most intolerable charcoal stove in a red-hot glow" rendered the heat so insupportable that he had a "headache, morning, noon, and night." No smoking was allowed in the ladies' car where he sat with Kate, but there was a car for gentlemen directly ahead. "The flashes of saliva" from this car, he said, "flew so perpetually and incessantly out of the windows all the way, that it looked as though they were ripping open feather-beds inside, and letting the wind dispose of the feathers." [7]

Spitting was revoltingly universal all over America. "In the courts of law, the judge has his spittoon on the bench, the counsel have theirs, the witness has his, the prisoner his, and the crier his. The jury are accommodated at the rate of three men to a spittoon (or spit-box as they call it here); and the spectators in the gallery are provided for, as so many men who in the course of nature expectorate without cessation. . . . I have twice seen gentlemen at evening parties in New York, turn aside when they were not engaged in conversation, and spit upon the drawing-room carpet. And in every bar-room and hotel passage the stone floor looks as if it were paved with open oysters— from the quantity of this kind of deposit which tesselates it all over." [8]

Philadelphia Dickens found more provincial than either Boston or New York, and its brick pavements so distractingly regular that he longed for a crooked street.[9] He made his usual survey of public institutions, attended an evening party given by Leslie's brother-in-law, the publisher Henry Carey, and met the three Miss Leslies, accomplished young ladies, one of whom had copied all her brother's principal paintings.[10] Edgar Allan Poe, who sent Dickens a copy of his *Tales of the Grotesque and Arabesque,* was invited to call at the United States Hotel. The strain in Dickens that gave rise to the eerie delusions of Barnaby Rudge and the "Madman's Manuscript" in *Pickwick* was not alien to the lunar, demon-ridden imagination of Poe, and Dickens had that in him too which responded to the melancholy spell of Poe's lost maidens. Impressed and moved by something in this American poet with the brilliant mind and haunted eyes, Dickens undertook to seek an English publisher for Poe on his return to London in July.[11]

Two occurrences in Philadelphia sounded the discordant note that was beginning to reverberate through this American tour. Some gentlemen had written to ask if Dickens would receive their greetings; and on obtaining his assent, their spokesman, a local politician named Colonel Florence, promptly inserted a notice in the newspapers that Dickens would be "gratified to shake hands with his friends" for an hour on the Tuesday before he went south.[12] Six hundred people next morning besieged the street in front of the hotel, and Dickens indignantly found he was expected to hold a "levee." There would be a riot, his terrified landlord told him, if he refused. For two mortal hours, therefore, he was forced to let his arm be almost shaken off.[13] With a touch of comic effrontery at which Dickens could not help smiling even in the midst of his annoyance, Colonel Florence, "a little hatter with black whiskers,"[14] blandly constituted himself master of ceremonies and pompously introduced a series of strangers whose names he had to inquire one by one.[15] As a parting shot of American hospitality, the landlord of the United States Hotel not only charged for the entire time during which their rooms had been reserved for them—which Dickens thought quite right—but also billed him nine dollars a day for the meals he, Kate, and Anne had not eaten there.[16]

The train to Washington stopped for a short time in the market place at Baltimore. Instantly the windows were dark with staring heads thrust in and conveniently hooked on to the sills by elbows. "I never gained so much uncompromising information with reference to my own nose and eyes," wrote Dickens, "and various impressions wrought by my mouth and chin on different minds, and how my head looks when it is viewed from behind . . ."[17] A market woman began bawling to a friend, "What's the matter? What is it all about?" "Why," he replied, "they've got Boz here!" "Got Boz? What's Boz?" "Why," said the man, "it's Dickens. They've got him here!" "Well, what has he been doing?" said she. "He ain't been doing nothin'," an-

swered her friend; "he writes books." "Oh!" responded the woman
indignantly. "Is that all? What do they make such a row about that
for, I'd like to know!" 18

*　　*　　*　　*　　*

Dickens found the climate of Washington trying, and was no more
impressed by its legislators than by those at Westminster. "One day
it is hot summer," he wrote, "without a breath of air; the next, twenty
degrees below freezing, with a wind blowing that cuts your skin like
steel." 19 As for his coldness to Congress, he was to remind the readers
of *American Notes* that he had never "fainted away" or "even been
moved to tears of joyful pride, at the sight of any legislative body."
He had borne the House of Commons "like a man" and "yielded to
no weakness but slumber" in the House of Lords; had seen elections
without ever having "been impelled (no matter which party won) to
damage my hat by throwing it up into the air in triumph." 20

There were, to be sure, "a great many very remarkable men" in
Congress: John Quincy Adams, Clay, Preston, Calhoun. "Adams is
a fine old fellow—seventy-six years old, but with the most surprising
vigour, memory, readiness, and pluck. Clay is perfectly enchanting;
an irresistible man. There are some very noble specimens, too, out of
the West. Splendid men to look at, hard to deceive, prompt to act,
lions in energy, Crichtons in varied accomplishments, Indians in
quickness of eye and gesture, Americans in affectionate and generous
impulse. It would be difficult to exaggerate the nobility of some of
these glorious fellows." 21

But what a contrast were some of the others. Daniel Webster
feigned "abstraction in the dreadful pressure of affairs of state" and
rubbed his forehead wearily in "a sublime caricature of Lord Bur-
leigh." 22 A member of the House of Representatives, who had emphasized a violent speech attacking England by pointing at Lord
Morpeth, who happened to be present, was an evil-visaged man looking "as if he had been suckled, Romulus-like, by a wolf," and "with
a great ball of tobacco in his left cheek." 23 Another member, when
called to order, replied, "Damn your eyes, Sir, if you presume to call
me to order, I'll cut your damnation throat from ear to ear." The
speaking was a combination of "stump oratory" and "a dry and prosy
chopping of very small logic into very small mincemeat," no worse

than Parliament and no better. "One gentleman being interrupted by a laugh from the opposition," Dickens said, "mimicked the laugh, as a child would in quarrelling with another child, and said that 'before long he'd make honorable Members sing out, a little more on the other side of their mouths.' "²⁴

Dickens failed to understand the significance of some things he saw, through ignorance of their background. He was shocked, for example, at the hard words and contumely that assailed John Quincy Adams for presenting petitions against slavery to Congress.²⁵ He did not know that the House of Representatives had in 1836 refused to receive any further petitions about slavery, and that Adams, regarding this "gagging" resolution as unconstitutional, was rousing a tremendous storm of public approval by his calculated policy of defiance. During this period Adams presented "all petitions he received, from any quarter, including a letter advocating his own assassination." Dickens knew none of this, as T. A. Jackson points out. "He could only see an old gentleman, whose grey hairs and past record (as an ex-President) should have commanded a respectful hearing even from opponents, met with affronts, interruptions, insults, and savage denunciations. He didn't realize that the old gentleman, for all his grey hairs, was fighting a winning fight; and was deliberately provoking the bad manners of his opponents because of their propaganda value with the electorate at large." ²⁶

The morning after Dickens's arrival in Washington, he had a private audience with President John Tyler. The Secretary to the Senate took him to the White House. In the reception hall and in the blue-and-silver drawing room a number of gentlemen—"mostly with their hats on, and their hands in their pockets," Dickens observed—were strolling about, some of them showing the premises to ladies; others "lounging on the chairs and sofas; others, yawning and picking their teeth. . . . A few were eyeing the movables as if to make quite sure that the President (who is not popular) hadn't made away with any of the furniture, or sold the fixtures for his private benefit." ²⁷

Upstairs a more favored group waited for audiences. A tall, sunburnt old man from the West, with a brown-white hat and a giant umbrella, sat bolt upright, frowning shadily, like one who "had made up his mind that he was going to 'fix' the President in what he had to say, and wouldn't bate him a grain." A Kentucky farmer nearly seven feet high leaned against the wall and kicked the floor with his heel. A round-faced man with his beard "shaved down into blue dots . . . sucked the head of a big stick, and from time to time took it out of his mouth to see how it was getting on. A fourth did nothing but whistle. The rest balanced themselves, now on one leg, and now on the other, and chewed mighty quids of tobacco—such mighty quids, that they all looked as if their faces were swoln with erisypelas. They all constantly squirted forth upon the carpet a yellow saliva which quite altered its pattern; and even the few who did not indulge in this recreation, expectorated abundantly." 28

A Negro servant in plain clothes and yellow slippers who was gliding noiselessly about disappeared to announce Dickens and his guide to the President, and returned in five minutes to conduct them into his office. Here, "by the side of a hot stove, though it was a very hot day, sat the President—all alone; and close to him a great spit box . . ." The President rose, and said, "Is *this* Mr. Dickens?" "Sir, it is." "I am astonished to see so young a man, Sir," said the President. Dickens smiled, and thought of returning the compliment, but the President looked so worn and jaded "that it stuck in my throat like Macbeth's amen." "I am happy to join with my fellow citizens, warmly, in welcoming you to this country," said the President. The two men shook hands. Then they sat and looked at each other until Dickens rose, observing that doubtless the President's time was fully occupied and that he had better go.29

On Sunday, Dickens and Kate had dinner with ex-President John Quincy Adams,30 and the courtly old man gave Kate his word to send her a "sentiment" written in his own hand, a promise that he kept three days later:

> *"There is a greeting of the heart*
> *Which words cannot reveal—*
> *How, Lady, shall I then impart*
> *The sentiment I feel?*
> *How, in one word combine the spell*
> *Of joy and sorrow too?*
> *And mark the bosom's mingled swell*
> *Of welcome! and Adieu!"* 31

The next night Dickens, the ex-President, and General Van Ness were the guests of a club at a dinner given in Boulanger's Restaurant.

It was an informal occasion. Dickens excused himself from making a speech. To "gentlemen whose position in public life rendered it unavoidable that they should either speak themselves or listen to the speeches of others every day," he said laughingly, this must be more welcome and more novel than any remarks he could make. "He would, however, say that, like the Prince in the Arabian Tales, he had been doomed, since he arrived in this hospitable country, to make new friendships every night, and cut their heads off on the following morning." [32]

The previous evening at dinner Putnam had brought news that the long-awaited *Caledonia* had finally arrived, and now Kate sent Dickens word that their letters from home had come. At eleven o'clock, therefore, unable to control his impatience any longer, he rose to bid his hosts good night,[33] "Since I have been seated at this table I have received the welcome intelligence that the news from the dear ones has come at last—that the long-expected letters have arrived. Among them are certain scrawls from little beings across the ocean, of great interest to me, and I thought of them for many days past in connection with drowned men and a noble ship, broken up and lying in fragments upon the bottom of the ocean. But they are here, and you will appreciate the anxiety I feel to read them." [34]

With heroic fortitude Kate had refrained from opening the letters until Dickens was there to share them with her. They read exultantly until nearly two in the morning. They decided, he told Forster, "that humorous narrative is your forte, and not statesmen of the commonwealth." [35] And what marvelous tales there were of Charley's precocity at a Twelfth-Night party for children at Macready's, and the governess's dark hints that he had got out of pothooks and hangers and might write a letter any day now, and similar predictions about his sisters, "very gladdening to their mother's heart, and not at all depressing to their father's." The doctor's report gave the children a clean bill of health, and the nurse's report contained the electrifying news that Master Walter had cut a double tooth, "and done many other extraordinary things, quite worthy of his high descent. In short," Dickens concluded exuberantly to Felton, "we were made very happy and grateful; and felt as if the prodigal father and mother had got home again." [36]

*   *   *   *   *

Henry Clay had dissuaded Dickens from his original plan of going on to Charleston. The country, Clay told him, was nothing but dismal swamp, the equinoctial gales were blowing hard, the weather was intensely hot there, and the spring fever was coming on. Dickens had determined, however, that he must see Richmond and some of the tobacco plantations before he turned his face west across the Alleghenies.[37] Washington Irving, who had come to the Capital to receive his instructions as Minister to Spain, and who did not expect to see Dickens again before setting sail, saw him in a farewell meeting, "and *wept heartily* at parting." [38]

A resolute abolitionist, Dickens had recoiled from having to accept the services of slaves even in Baltimore, where slavery existed, he said, "in its least repulsive and most mitigated form." The mere feeling of being, however innocently, a party to the servitude of the Negroes filled him "with a sense of shame and self-reproach." [39] His flesh crawled with moral revulsion during the entire three days that he spent in Virginia, and everything that he saw and heard during that brief time confirmed him in his emotions. As they passed deserted plantations on their way to Richmond, with rotting barns and decaying houses bleak among vast pine barrens where there had formerly been rich fields, Putnam explained that this barren ground was once "the garden of America." "Great God!" Dickens exclaimed. "Kate, just hear what Mr. Putnam says! These lands were once cultivated and have been abandoned because they were worn out by slave labor!" [40]

In the black car on the train that conveyed them from Fredericksburg to Richmond there were a Negro mother and children who were weeping the whole way. "Them damn niggers," said a bluff, well-dressed man; "somebody has bought them and is taking them down to Richmond, and they are making a fuss about it." They were being sold away from the husband and father. On the toll bridge over the James at Richmond, a rotten and crazy structure, there was a notice against fast driving: "penalty—for whites, five dollars; for slaves, fifteen stripes." [41] No wonder, Dickens felt, that under so hideous and accursed a system Richmond had an atmosphere "of decay and gloom" that the planters themselves admitted to be characteristic of towns in the slave district, "deplorable tenements, fences unrepaired, walls crumbling into ruinous heaps." [42]

He was glad to turn his back on it. "I really don't think I could have borne it any longer," he wrote Forster. "It is all very well to say 'be silent on the subject.' They won't let you be silent. They *will* ask you what you think of it; and *will* expatiate on slavery as if it were one of the greatest blessings of mankind. 'It's not,' said a hard, bad-looking fellow to me the other day, 'it's not the interest of a man to use his slaves ill. It's damned nonsense you hear in England." [43]

"—I told him quietly," Dickens went on—and no doubt he believed that he said it quietly, feeling twelve feet tall—"that it was not a man's interest to get drunk, or to steal, or to game, or to indulge in any other vice, but he did indulge in it for all that. That cruelty, and the abuse of irresponsible power, were two of the bad passions of human nature, with the gratification of which, considerations of interest or of ruin had nothing whatever to do; and that, while every candid man must admit that even a slave might be happy enough with a good master, all human beings knew that bad masters, cruel masters, and masters who disgraced the form they bore, were matters of experience and history, whose existence was as undisputed as that of slaves themselves." [44]

Taken aback by this quiet diatribe, the man asked Dickens if he believed in the Bible. "Yes, I said, but if any man could prove to me that it sanctioned slavery, I would place no further credence in it. 'Well, then,' he said, 'by God, sir, the niggers must be kept down, and the whites have put down the coloured people wherever they have found them.' 'That's the whole question,' said I. 'Yes, and by God,' says he, 'the British had better not stand out on that point . . . for I never felt so warlike as I do now—and that's a fact.' I was obliged to accept a public supper in this Richmond, and I saw plainly enough, there, . . . the hatred which these Southern States bear to us as a nation . . ." [45]

Pausing in Baltimore before proceeding on the Western part of his journey, Dickens relieved his mind of all his accumulated impressions in a long letter to Macready. The actor had written to counsel him against leaping rashly at hasty conclusions; was Macready sure, Dickens demanded, that he himself did not view America through a pleasant mirage of memory? "The early spring birds, Mr. Macready, *do* sing that you were, very often, not over well pleased with many of the new country's social aspects. Are the birds to be trusted?" As for Dickens, he had burned up a preceding letter, he told Macready, lest he should be unjust to those who had welcomed him so enthusiastically. But he could not pretend. "This is not the republic I came to see; this is not the republic of my imagination. . . . The more I think of its youth and strength, the poorer and more trifling in a thousand aspects it appears in my eyes. In everything of which it has made a boast— excepting its education of the people and its care for poor children— it sinks immeasurably below the level I had placed it upon; and England, even England, bad and faulty as the old land is, and miserable as millions of her people are, rises in comparison. Strike down the established church, and I would take her to my heart, for better or worse, and reject this new love without a pang or moment's hesitation." [46]

Where was freedom of opinion in America? "I see a press more mean, and paltry, and silly, and disgraceful than any country I ever knew. . . . I speak of Bancroft, and am advised to be silent on that subject, for he is 'a black sheep—a democrat.' I speak of Bryant, and am entreated to be more careful—for the same reason. I speak of international copyright, and am implored not to ruin myself outright. I speak of Miss Martineau, and all parties—Slave Upholders and Abolitionists, Whigs, Tyler Whigs, and Democrats, shower down upon her a perfect cataract of abuse. 'But what has she done? Surely she praised America enough!'" (Miss Martineau's praises of America, it will be noticed, no longer seem to Dickens insufficient and grudging.) "'Yes, but she told us some of our faults, and Americans can't bear to be told of their faults. Don't split on that rock, Mr. Dickens . . .'" [47]

Macready should not think his observations had been one-sided. "The people are affectionate, generous, open-hearted, hospitable, enthusiastic, good-humoured, polite to women, frank and candid to all strangers, anxious to oblige, far less prejudiced than they have been described to be, frequently polished and refined, very seldom rude or disagreeable. . . . I have seen none of that greediness and indecorum on which travellers have laid so much emphasis. I have . . . not spoken to one man, woman, or child of any degree who has not grown positively affectionate before we parted. In the respects of not being left alone, and of being horribly disgusted by tobacco chewing and tobacco spittle, I have suffered considerably. The sight of slavery in Virginia; the hatred of British feeling on the subject; and the miserable hints of the impotent indignation of the South have pained me very much . . ." [48]

Macready must not imagine Dickens's attitude any snobbish recoil from the unvarnished freedom of American manners. "I have not had greater pleasure in the company of any set of men among the thousands I have received . . . than in that of the carmen of Hartford, who presented themselves in a body in their blue frocks, among a crowd of well-dressed ladies and gentlemen, and bade me welcome through their spokesman." "You know that I am, *truly*, a Liberal." "It is not these things I have in mind when I say that the man who comes to this country a Radical and goes home again with his opinions unchanged, must be a Radical on reason, sympathy, and reflection, and one who has so well considered the subject that he has no chance of wavering." [49]

Though Dickens had formed a warm attachment, as he gladly admitted, to many Americans, and though he had been given a public progress through the land unequaled even by Lafayette's, he had discovered that he was an Englishman after all with "a yearning after our English customs and English manners." [50] He had bought an accordion to take the place of the one the steward on the *Britannia* had lent him, and played "Home, Sweet Home" every night now, to himself and Kate, with great expression and a pleasant feeling of sadness. He thought tenderly of Forster and all his kindnesses. "What an unspeakable source of delight" was the pocket Shakespeare his friend had given him in parting at Liverpool! And he reflected on "the terrible folly of ever quarrelling with a true friend, on good for nothing trifles! Every little hasty word that has ever passed between us," he wrote remorsefully to Forster, "rose up before me like a reproachful ghost." [51]

A small delay in Baltimore, while Dickens was sending back to New York all the luggage he could possibly dispense with in the West,[52] enabled Washington Irving to join him for another farewell.[53] The two men dined together in Dickens's rooms at Barnum's Hotel, "the most comfortable of all the hotels" he had known in the United States, Dickens said, and the only one "where the English traveller will find curtains to his bed." [54] Afterward they sat over "a most enormous mint julep, wreathed with flowers," which had been sent Dickens that day by a Philadelphia admirer. "We sat on either side of it, with great solemnity, but the solemnity was of very short duration. It was quite an enchanting julep, and carried us among innumerable people and places that we both knew. The julep held out far into the night," and Dickens always remembered Irving "bending over it, with his straw, with an attempted gravity (after some anecdote, involving some wonderfully droll and delicate observation of character) and then as his eye caught mine, melting into that captivating laugh of his, which was the brightest and best that I have ever heard." [55]

* * * * *

Early next morning Dickens and his party were on the train for York. Kate's face was still swelling every other day,[56] and she looked forward with mute despair to the rough traveling that lay ahead of them. Anne, who had proved a very good traveler so far, and indispensably helpful to Kate, began now that they were heading into the wilds to have dismal apprehensions of being scalped by Indians.[57] At York they all transferred into a tremendous rumbling stagecoach drawn by four horses, "a kind of barge on wheels," "shaking its sides like a corpulent giant." [58] During one of the changes of horses, Dickens got down from the box in the midst of a heavy rain, to warm himself with a glass of whiskey and water, and when he returned observed something lying on the roof that he took to be a large fiddle in a brown bag. Presently he discovered "that it had a pair of dirty shoes at one end, and a glazed cap at the other," and it proved to be "a small boy, in a snuff-coloured coat, with his arms quite pinioned to his sides by deep forcing into his pockets." "Sir, when we stopped to water the horses, about two miles from Harrisburg, this thing slowly upreared itself to the height of three feet eight, and fixing its eyes on me with a mingled expression of complacency, patronage, national independence, and sympathy for all outer barbarians and foreigners, said, in shrill piping accents, "Well now, stranger, I guess you find this, a-most like an English a'ternoon,—hey?' " [59]

The innkeeper at Harrisburg generously desired to make no charge for their stay, but Dickens would not hear of it and insisted that, traveling four strong, he must pay his way.[60] From here they went on to Pittsburgh by canal boat. At night the cabin was separated by a red curtain into a ladies' section and a gentlemen's section. Dickens slept on a shelf sixteen inches wide, with one man below him and another above, twenty-eight of them packed into a tiny room too low to stand upright in with a hat on, and foul enough in its atmosphere before morning. "You can never conceive," Dickens wrote Forster, "what the hawking and spitting is, the whole night through. *Upon my honour and word* I was obliged, this morning, to lay my fur-coat on the deck, and wipe the half-dried flakes of spittle from it with my handkerchief: and the only surprise seemed to be, that I should consider it necessary to do so. When I turned in last night, I put it on a stool beside me, and there it lay, under a cross fire from five men—three opposite; one above; and one below." [61]

"I am looked upon as highly facetious at night, for I crack jokes with everybody near me until we fall asleep. I am considered very hardy in the morning, for I run up, bare-necked, and plunge my head into the half-frozen water, by half-past five o'clock. I am respected for my activity, inasmuch as I jump from the boat to the towing-path, and walk five or six miles before breakfast; keeping up with the horses all the time. In a word, they are quite astonished to find a sedentary Englishman roughing it so well, and taking so much exercise; and question me very much on that head. The greater part of the men will sit and shiver round the stove all day rather than put one foot before the other. As to having a window open, that's not to be thought of." [62]

The scenery of southern Pennsylvania, Dickens thought, was very grand, with the canal winding through deep and sullen moonlit gorges, though it did not approach the terror of Glencoe.[63] But the forlorn poverty of the new settlements and the detached log houses depressed him. "I have not seen six cabins out of six hundred, where the windows have been whole. Old hats, old clothes, old boards, old fragments of blanket and paper, are stuffed into the broken glass; and their air is misery and desolation." [64] It pained his eye to see the never-ending morass and swamp, with rotting stumps and trunks steeped in the unwholesome water, and the great tracts where settlers had burned down the trees, leaving their wounded bodies lying about like murdered creatures, with here and there some charred giant writhing two bare blackened arms aloft.

Pittsburgh, its townsfolk said, was like Birmingham, and Dickens did not contradict them, for it was indeed dark with smoke. At the "levee" to which he and Kate were now subjected wherever they went, as if they were royalty, one man with his trousers imperfectly buttoned stood behind the door and another "with one eye and one fixed gooseberry" stood in a corner "like an eight-day clock" and glared throughout the entire reception.[65]

They were going on by river steamer, down the Ohio and thence up the Mississippi to St. Louis, and Kate expressed alarm at the danger of a boiler explosion.[66] The steamboats were hardly more than long low barges with paddle-wheels and exposed furnaces and machinery glaring and roaring in the midst of a frail jumble of staterooms whose roofs were black with burnt-out sparks falling red-hot from the high chimneys. Fires and bursting boilers were frequent. It is dubious whether Kate felt much comforted to learn that the tiny stateroom they had in the stern of the *Messenger* was in the safest location "because the steamboats generally blew up forward." Dickens, however, was delighted to find that it opened on a narrow gallery where he could sit undisturbed by the other passengers and gaze upon the scenery.[67]

"The washing department" was a little better than it had been on the canal boat, where there was only dirty water dipped out of the canal by a tin ladle and where most of the men went "in foul linen, with yellow streams from half-chewed tobacco trickling down their chins." [68] But even on the steamer, it seemed to Dickens, the ladies were "content with smearing their hands and faces in a very small quantity of water." So were the men, who added to that skimpy mode of washing "a hasty use of the common brush and comb. It is quite a practice, too, to wear but one cotton shirt a week, and three or four fine linen *fronts*." [69]

Dickens could not spend all his time in the privacy of his stateroom, and the periods when he had to mingle with his fellow passengers convinced him that there were not on all the rest of the earth "so many intensified bores as in these United States." [70] There was "a horrible New Englander with a droning voice like a gigantic bee" [71] who insisted, when Dickens wanted to write, on sitting by him, droning and snuffling poetry, small philosophy, and metaphysics, and who never would be quiet. There was a doctor who, in addition to having all the dreadful qualities of the New Englander, was a phrenologist besides.[72] There was a weazen-faced, pigeon-breasted old general, acutely gentlemanly and officerlike, who was even worse than these two and was "perhaps *the* most horrible bore in this country." [73]

Dickens was kept dodging around the boat by these pests, beating a hasty retreat whenever he saw them bearing down upon him. The dread New Englander was very insistent that Dickens join them to "form a magnetic chain" and magnetize the doctor, but Dickens declined on a plea of tremendous absorption in letter-writing, although he had successfully experimented in that way on Kate only a few days before at Pittsburgh. He had been holding forth on the subject and Kate laughingly offered herself as a victim. Elliotson would doubtless be interested to know that in "six minutes, I magnetized her into hysterics, and then into the magnetic sleep. I tried again next night, and she fell into the slumber in little more than two minutes." [74]

Meanwhile the *Messenger* glided dreamily down the Ohio, past green islands and deep solitudes overgrown with trees, unbroken by any sign of human life, motionless save for the bright flash of the blue jay. At long intervals a log cabin sent a thread of smoke into the sky. On the river's banks fallen trees bathed their green heads in the stream and put forth new shoots and branches. At night sometimes there would be a place where tall trees were burning, seeming to vegetate in fire against the dark. [75]

"Think what rivers are in this country!" Dickens wrote to Fred. "The Ohio is nine hundred miles long; virtually as broad as the Thames at Greenwich,—very often much wider." [76] Throughout all this part of his journey Dickens was impressed by the solitudes and the distances. Writing to Mitton from Baltimore on the eve of starting west, he remarked of St. Louis, his goal on the borders of the Indian territory, that it was "a trifling distance from this place—only two thousand miles!" [77] Possibly American tall talk sometimes deceived him about distances, but here he may have been thinking of the journey as it had to be made by stage, canal, and coiling river rather than as the crow flies.

Cincinnati was a beautiful place, Dickens said, that had risen out of the forest like an Arabian Nights city, with pretty villas, turf-plots, and well-kept gardens. [78] He liked Judge Timothy Walker, [79] who gave an evening party for him there, but the party consisted of "at least one hundred and fifty first-rate bores. . . . I really think my face has acquired a fixed expression of sadness from the constant and unmitigated boring I endure. . . . There is a line in my chin (on the right side of the under-lip) indelibly fixed there by the New Englander . . . A dimple has vanished from my cheek, which I felt myself robbed of at the time by a wise legislator." [80]

A young lady among these bores at Judge Walker's thought Dickens foppish in dress and negligent rather than elegant in manner. His black waistcoat was embroidered with colored flowers and he wore too much jewelry; Mrs. Dickens, said the same young lady, was a large, highly colored, rather coarse but amiable-looking woman in a pink-silk dress with a white flounce. Dickens seemed tired and originated no remarks, but answered those made to him in an agreeable manner. One of the ladies asked for the large red rose he wore in his buttonhole, and in the end there was a scramble for its separate petals, ladies stooping for them as they fell upon the floor.[81]

The *Messenger* had gone on while Dickens stayed overnight at the Broadway Hotel in Cincinnati, and next morning they took the *Pike* on to Louisville.[82] Here they slept at the Galt House, "a splendid hotel," said Dickens, where they "were as handsomely lodged as though we had been in Paris, rather than hundreds of miles beyond the Alleghanies." [83] The following day they left on the *Fulton,* and two mornings later they were nearing the junction of the Ohio and the Mississippi.[84] Passing the swampy and fever-plagued hamlet of Cairo— on which Dickens later drew for the creation of "Eden" in *Martin Chuzzlewit*—they came upon the slimy Mississippi eddying its strong current of liquid mud through an enormous tree-choked ditch three miles across. For two days they toiled up this monstrous stream, striking constantly against floating timbers, and stopping repeatedly at night, whenever the lookout rang a bell, to avoid the dangerous snags that might rip a hole in the hull.[85] On the fourth night after leaving Louisville, they reached St. Louis, the westernmost point of Dickens's journey.[86]

Return Journey

THE Planters House, in St. Louis, Dickens found as large as London's Middlesex Hospital, and built very much on the plan of a hospital, with long corridors and plain whitewashed walls, and transoms above the doors to aid in the circulation of air. "They had a famous notion," he wrote Forster, "of sending up at breakfast time large glasses of new milk with blocks of ice in them as clear as crystal. Our table was abundantly supplied indeed at every meal. One day when Kate and I were dining alone together, in our own room, we counted sixteen dishes on the table at the same time." [1]

After a day of sightseeing among the gables, blinking casements, and tumbledown galleries of the French quarter of St. Louis, and the wharves, warehouses, and new buildings in the American sections,[2] Dickens desired to see the prairie, or, as it was variously pronounced, paraᵓrer, parearer, and paroᵓrer.[3] His hosts accordingly arranged an overnight expedition to Looking Glass Prairie for the following day. Starting out at seven in the morning, they ferried across the river into Illinois. All morning their vehicles wallowed through the deep mud of the American bottom, past French Village, where a wandering painter had recently made almost all the doors bright with red and yellow. Around noon they reached the village of Belleville.

This was a flourishing town with brick and stone houses fully one hundred feet above the river, whose inhabitants were mightily to resent Dickens's describing it in *American Notes* as "a small collection of wooden houses, huddled in the very heart of the bush and swamp." What Dickens saw as a forest path, with hitching posts for their horses, was the public square opposite the courthouse; and the hotel was no shambling compromise between a cowshed and a kitchen, as he called it, but the Mansion House, a two-story brick structure with a long wooden addition only three years old at the time. And the road from Belleville to Lebanon, local pride insisted, did not run through wasteland loud with the chirping of bullfrogs, but over high and undulating country.[4]

At Belleville there was an impromptu reception lasting half an hour while they waited for dinner. The curious citizens were disappointed in the unpretentious appearance Dickens made in a linen blouse and a great straw hat with green ribbons, with his "face and nose profusely ornamented with the stings of mosquitoes and the bites of bugs." Dickens gave only curt and commonplace answers to their remarks, and it was plain that he was bored with them. After a meal of "wheat-bread and chicken fixings," they left Belleville for Lebanon and from there rode on in time to see the prairie at sunset.[5]

The great plain, Dickens said, was like a sea without water, unbroken save by one thin line of trees, bare and lonely, with only a few birds wheeling in the empty sky, stretching on until it melted into the horizon in a distant blue.[6] The sun was descending, red and bright, in a glowing sky, and, remembering the scene later, Dickens imagined that he had been gazing toward the sunset, although at Lebanon the prairie stretches east.[7] Here, as the colors of the twilight mingled richly, they encamped and enjoyed a picnic dinner on the plain: "roast fowls, buffalo's tongue, ham, bread, cheese, butter, biscuits," Dickens wrote Forster, and "sherry, champagne, lemons, and sugar for punch, and abundance of ice." [8]

In St. Louis, as the most remote Western point of his travels, Dickens made an exception to his rule of not accepting any public entertainment.[9] On the evening of his return from Looking Glass Prairie, consequently, there was a soirée at the Planters House. "Of course the paper had an account of it," Dickens wrote Forster. "If I were to drop a letter in the street, it would be in the newspaper the next day, and nobody would think its publication an outrage. The editor objected to my hair, as not curling sufficiently. He admitted an eye; but objected again to dress, as being somewhat foppish, 'and indeed perhaps rather flash.—But such,'" the editor benevolently added, were the differences between American and English taste, rendered more striking by all the gentlemen except Dickens being in black. "Oh, that you could have seen the other gentlemen!" Dickens exclaims.[10]

Kate also shared in this rather exasperating patronage. One St. Louis lady assured her that nobody would ever have suspected that she was Scotch or even English, and paid her the compliment of adding that she would have been taken for an American anywhere. "I need not tell you," Dickens remarked to Forster, "that out of Boston and New York a nasal drawl is universal"; and as for the Southern accent, "all the women who have been bred in the slave-states speak more or less like negroes, from having been constantly in their childhood with black nurses." [11]

Missouri being a slave state, Dickens found himself embroiled in arguments about slavery once more. They wouldn't let him alone about it, he exclaimed. A St. Louis judge went so far "that I fell upon him (to the indescribable horror of the man who brought him) and told him a piece of my mind." The judge "pitied our national ignorance of the truths of slavery"; Dickens reminded him that England had abolished slavery upon the evidence of indisputable records gathered through years of careful investigation. He could sympathize, Dickens said, with men who admitted it to be a dreadful evil, but confessed their inability to devise a means of getting rid of it. For men to speak of it as a blessing, though, was beyond the pale of reason; and for such men to speak of ignorance or prejudice, a ridiculous absurdity.[12]

"They say the slaves are fond of their masters," Dickens went on to Forster. That, of course, was why the newspapers were full of advertisements for runaway slaves. That was why nine out of ten of these advertisements described the runaway as chained, manacled, mutilated, maimed, or branded. The Negroes worshiped England because of her leadership in emancipation; "and *of course* their attachment to us grows out of their deep devotion to their owners." "I know something," Dr. Elisha Bartlett told Dickens, "of their fondness for their masters. I live in Kentucky; and I can assert upon my honour, that, in my neighbourhood, it is as common for a runaway slave, retaken, to draw his bowie knife and rip his owner's bowels open, as it is for you to see a drunken fight in London." [13]

*   *   *   *   *

On the evening of April 14th, Dickens gladly embarked on the *Messenger* for his return east, and the next morning even more gladly passed the yellow line where the slimy Mississippi absorbed the clear Ohio.[14] Three nights later they were again at the Galt House in Louisville, and the following night around one o'clock the mail steamer *Ben Franklin* brought them to Cincinnati, where they groped through the darkness among labyrinths of engine machinery and leaking molasses barrels. Stumbling among these obstacles, and making their way over broken pavements, Kate had troubles evidently not unfamiliar to her even in more acccustomed surroundings, and multiplied many times by the strange hazards of her American experiences:

"—You recollect her propensity?" Dickens asked Forster. "She falls into, or out of, every coach or boat we enter; scrapes the skin off her legs; brings great sores and swellings on her feet; chips large fragments out of her ankle-bones; and makes herself blue with bruises." There is a faint hint of suppressed exasperation in the comic extravagance of this outburst, of which Dickens may have been aware, for immediately following it he pays tribute to Kate's endeavors to deal with her difficulties: "She really has, however, since we got over the first trial of being among circumstances so new and so fatiguing, made a *most admirable* traveller in every respect. She has never screamed or expressed alarm under circumstances that would have fully justified her in doing so, even in my eyes;"—this last phrase is significant—"has never given way to despondency or fatigue, though we have now been travelling incessantly, through a very rough country, for more than a month, and have been at times, as you may readily suppose, most thoroughly tired; has always accommodated herself, well and cheerfully, to everything; and has pleased me very much, and proved herself perfectly game." [15]

Kate's gameness was soon subjected to more painful trials. All the next day and night they traveled by stagecoach the hundred and twenty miles from Cincinnati to Columbus, Kate sitting on the back seat and being showered all night, in spite of Putnam's efforts to screen her, by flying tobacco spittle from a well-dressed man in the middle.[16] At Columbus they had breakfast at the Neill House and went to bed until dinnertime, after which they were obliged to hold a reception in their black-walnut suite. At this ceremony all the guests

paraded in, stood about, wore their clothes, and shook hands as if
they were a chorus at the Adelphi or the Haymarket, and received
each facetiousness Dickens uttered as if there had been a stage direction, "all laugh." [17]

There being no stagecoach next day, Dickens hired for their private
use one of the regular four-horse coaches, "an extra," to convey them
on their way toward Sandusky.[18] The landlord of the Neill House
put up a basket lunch of cold meats, fruit, and wine, and they all set
out in high spirits at being by themselves. The road, however, unlike
the macadamized highway they had traveled the day before, was a
track through swamp and forest, a great portion of it a "corduroy
road" of tree trunks left to settle down in the bog.[19] "Good Heaven!"
Dickens exclaimed, "if you had only felt one of the least of the jolts
with which the coach falls from log to log! It is like nothing but going
up a steep flight of stairs in an omnibus." [20]

Dickens tied a handkerchief to the doorpost on each side for Kate to
hang on to and brace herself. Dickens and Putnam kept a lookout
with their arms wound tightly around each other, letting out a
warning yell of "Corduroy!" at each yawning hole that they saw.[21]
In spite of these precautions the ride was harrowing. "Now the coach
flung us in a heap on its floor, and now crushed our heads against
its roof. Now one side of it was deep in the mire, and we were holding on to the other. Now it was lying on the horses' tails, and now
again upon its own back. . . . . Still, the day was beautiful, the air delicious, and we were *alone*, with no tobacco spittle, or eternal prosy
conversation about dollars and politics (the only two subjects they
ever converse about, or can converse about) to bore us. We really
enjoyed it; made a joke of the being knocked about; and were quite
merry." [22]

At two o'clock they stopped in the forest to open their hamper and
dine; "and we drank to our darlings and all friends at home." Before
they dined, Dickens heaped up a large quantity of oranges, apples,
nuts, and raisins, together with a bottle of the wine, and sent them to
the driver and his companion. After lunch there was more of the terrific bumping to be endured, but at last they got through the swamp
and left the corduroy road behind.[23] With the darkness there came on
a smart thundershower, with lightning flashes vivid blue between
branches that rattled and broke against the coach on each side of the

track.[24] Toward eleven o'clock the guard began to sound his horn to arouse the people at the log tavern in Lower Sandusky where they were to spend the night.[25]

The doors of their room, opening on opposite sides to the black wild country, had neither locks nor bolts and were constantly blowing each other open.[26] Kate was alarmed to hear that there had recently been an Indian pow-wow in a near-by lodge;[27] Dickens was concerned because he had £250 in gold in his dressing case, a sum for a small fraction of which he had been told there were "men in the West who would murder their fathers." Forster should have seen him, he said, in his nightshirt, trying to blockade the doors with portmanteaus![28]

Putnam went to bed under the rafters, where another man was already snoring loudly. He was too tired with the jolting he had endured to mind that, but he found his mattress swarming with bedbugs and the night grew piercingly cold.[29] But all the wraps were in Dickens's barricaded room, so at last he took refuge in the coach. It was not very warm, and the pigs, smelling him, "and looking upon the coach as a kind of pie with some manner of meat inside, grunted round it so hideously that he was afraid to come out again, and lay there shivering, til morning." When Kate emerged to wash in the tin basin standing upon a stump near the door, "Oh, Mr. Putnam," she exclaimed, "I have been almost devoured by the bugs!" Putnam then told his own experience. "Charles! Charles! just come here," Kate called, "and listen to what Mr. Putnam suffered last night!" and Putnam repeated his story while at the image of him besieged by the pigs they were torn between sympathy and helpless laughter.[30]

To Dickens, in fact, his solemn New England secretary was a source of endless amusement, although "Kate, of course," he reported to Fred, "don't like him." [31] Putnam wore a cloak, "like Hamlet; and a very tall, big, limp, dusty black hat, which he exchanges on long journeys for a cap like Harlequin's." Putnam sang, and could often be heard "grunting bass notes through the keyhole" to attract their attention. He made endless absurd efforts to be asked to sing for them by suggesting that they might call on this talent if they felt the need of *a little soothing.*" He imitated cows and pigs, and was in the habit of telling "the most notorious and patriarchal Joe Miller, as something that happened in his family." He felt it polite to inquire if they didn't "suffer for sleep" even if they had just risen from a nap of fourteen hours. He painted, blazing away for hours from an enormous box of oil colors, and produced a "big-headed, pot-bellied" sketch of Dickens in his fur coat "which brings the tears into my eyes at this minute." He was sentimental, and told Anne, with a languishing air, that he hoped they would "sometimes think of him" in their own country.[32]

Nevertheless Dickens also found Putnam indispensably useful. He took care of all the tremendous mass of correspondence from strangers, sifting out for Dickens's attention only those that required a personal reply.[33] He made advance arrangements for transportation and lodgings, settled with landlords, and took "such care of the luggage and all other matters," Dickens wrote, "that I walk into and out of every coach, car, wagon, boat, and barge, as if I had nothing with me but one shirt, and that were in my pocket." [34] Apart from "the amusement he gives us, I could not by possibility have lighted on any one who would have suited my purposes so well. I have raised his ten dollars per month to twenty; and mean to make it up for six months." [35]

Putnam was quite unaware of these responses to his personality. Mrs. Dickens, with her graceful brown hair waving over her high forehead, her blue eyes melting into violet, and her small sweet mouth, he thought beautiful, and felt in her a gentle dignity strikingly different from the "quick, earnest, always cheerful, but keen and nervous temperament of her husband." He was touched, too, by her anxiety for her children, her worship of the children's portrait, which it was one of his duties to remove from its traveling case and display in their rooms wherever they went, and her talk of those dear ones at home.[36] He had unbounded admiration for his generous, volatile, brilliant, and high-spirited employer, and never ceased to wonder at Dickens's capacity for transforming the vexations of travel into hilarity. While Dickens was writing to his friends at home, Putnam noted, his "face would be convulsed with laughter at his own fun"; then he would show Mrs. Dickens what he had written—perhaps, unknown to the secretary, an account of the pig imitations—and she would join in his mirth.[37]

Irritations did not cease, however, to press upon the very end of their journey. When the boat conveying them from Sandusky to Buffalo stopped overnight at Cleveland, among those who streamed on board to see them was "a party of 'gentlemen' " who planted their elbows on the window sill of the Dickens cabin and stared in *"while I was washing, and Kate lay in bed."* A flamingly patriotic Cleveland newspaper said that America had "whipped" England in her infancy, whipped her again in her youth, and must whip her once more in her maturity, and promised "all True Americans that within two years they should sing 'Yankee Doodle in Hyde Park, and Hail Columbia in the scarlet courts of Westminster.' " Incensed by these things, when the Mayor came on board to present himself, Dickens refused to see him, and bade Putnam explain why. "His honour took it very coolly, and retired to the top of the wharf," where he whittled lustily at a stick, "staring at the closed door of our cabin all the time." [38]

During the two-hour train ride from Buffalo to Niagara, Dickens was tense with excitement to come within sound and sight of the Falls. "At last, when the train stopped, I saw two great white clouds rising up from the depths of the earth—nothing more. They rose up slowly, gently, majestically, into the air." [39] Not until he alighted did he hear the rush of the waters and feel the ground tremble beneath his feet. They clambered down a steep path to the ferry, slippery with rain and half-melted ice, and were soon blinded by the spray and wet to the skin.[40] "I saw the water tearing madly down from some immense height, but could get no idea of shape, or situation, or anything but vague immensity." Only in the very basin did his imagination begin to take in the enormous spectacle. "The broad, deep, mighty stream seems to die in the act of falling; and, from its unfathomable grave, arises that tremendous ghost of spray and mist which is never laid, and has been haunting this place with the same dread solemnity— perhaps from the creation of the world." [41]

From their rooms at the Clifton House, which was so near the Falls that the windows were always wet and dim with spray, Dickens continued during their stay to gaze with awe at those waters "rolling and tumbling, and roaring and leaping, all day long, with bright rainbows making fiery arches down a hundred feet below us. When the day is gloomy, the water falls like snow, or sometimes it seems to crumble away like the face of a great chalk cliff, or sometimes again to roll along the front of the rock like white smoke. . . . From the bottom of both Falls, there is always rising up a solemn ghostly cloud, which hides the boiling cauldron from human sight, and makes it in its mystery a hundred times more grand than if you could see all the secrets that lie hidden in its tremendous depth." [42]

With one of his volatile changes from grave to gay, Dickens was amused to note the unimpressed indifference of Kate's maid. Neither Niagara nor, indeed, any scene in all America had excited her in any way. "I don't think Anne has so much as seen an American tree," Dickens wrote his brother-in-law Henry Austin. "She never looks at any prospect by any chance, or displays the smallest emotion at any sight whatever. She objects to Niagara that 'it's nothing but water,' and considers that 'there is too much of that.' " [43] Unmoved by an entire continent, Anne merely maintained her calm level of efficiency, and sustained Kate through all the afflictions of traveling, including the seven hundred and forty-three falls that Dickens estimated she had had in landing and going aboard boats and getting in and out of coaches.

*   *   *   *   *

At Buffalo Dickens had received the memorial in support of his copyright stand that he had asked Forster to obtain for him from a representative group of English authors.[44] Signed by a dozen distinguished names, including Bulwer, Tennyson, Talfourd, Rogers, Leigh Hunt, and Sydney Smith, it made a dignified appeal for protecting American men of letters from piratical competition, and argued that such a course would ultimately serve in every way the best interests of the American reading public.[45] Carlyle wrote a separate letter emphasizing the commandment, "Thou shalt not steal. That thou belongest to a different 'nation' and can steal without being certainly hanged for it gives thee no permission to steal." Doubtless publishers found it more convenient to take without paying. Rob Roy had found it more convenient to steal cattle from the glens than to buy beef from the Stirling markets. But both were stealing, for all that.[46]

Dickens wrote to Felton in Boston, asking his advice on the publication of these documents. Would it be a good idea to send one copy to a Boston newspaper, one to Bryant's New York *Evening Post,* another to the New York *Herald* (because of its large circulation), and a fourth to the *National Intelligencer* in Washington, whose editor, W. W. Seaton, had expressed sympathetic interest? He had also thought, Dickens said, of the *Knickerbocker* and the *North American Review.* Would Felton consult Sumner and see what he advised? [47] At the same time Dickens wrote to Seaton and the *Evening Post*.[48] On May 9th, whether with Felton's and Sumner's concurrence or not, the memorial and its accompanying letters appeared in the New York *Evening Post* and around the same time in other papers.[49]

As Dickens thought of the abuse and intimidations that had sought to prevent his even speaking on the subject, and how he had refused to be silenced, his heart swelled with pugnacious exultation. Was it not "a horrible thing that scoundrel booksellers should grow rich" from books whose authors received not a farthing, and that every "detestable newspaper, so filthy and bestial that no honest man would admit one into his house for a water-closet door-mat," might publish these stolen writings cheek by jowl with its own obscenities? Was it tolerable that they should be able to distort a writer's text and make him a party to cheating the best men in America out of the just rewards of their writings? His blood so boiled at these enormities that he felt eight feet taller than he had been when he previously denounced them, and seemed "to grow twenty feet high, and to swell out in proportion. 'Robbers that ye are,' I think to myself when I get upon my legs, 'here goes!' " [50]

Meanwhile the book-publishing interests had grown alarmed at the agitation Dickens had aroused. At a convention in Boston on April 26th they had memorialized Congress, not only protesting against the passage of any international copyright law, but asking that a duty be imposed on foreign books. There was not less than $27,000,-000, they said, involved in printing and publishing, and the interests of no fewer than 160,000 people were at stake.[51] Furthermore, defending the mutilations Dickens had denounced, they coolly remarked that to give English authors control over the republication of their own books in America would render it impossible "for American editors to *alter and adapt them to American taste.*"[52] Cornelius Mathews, in his speech at the Dickens dinner, had made a scathing indictment of this practice as an "outrageous wrong by which a noble English writer, speaking truths in London dear to him as life, is made to say in New York that which his soul abhors." [53] No attempt was made to answer these words.

Flagrantly dishonest though the booksellers' arguments were, Dickens speedily realized that they were going to win the day. (It was not in fact until he had been twenty-one years in his grave that the United States entered into an international copyright agreement with Great Britain.) Smarting at his defeat and the abuse he had endured, Dickens relieved his feelings in a final angry outburst to Forster. "I'll tell you what the two obstacles to the passing of an international copyright law with England are: firstly, the national love of 'doing' a man in any bargain or matter of business; secondly the national vanity." Successful knavery was admired as such. "It is so dar-nation 'cute— so knowing in Jonathan to get his reading on those terms. He has the Englishman so regularly on the hip that his eye twinkles with slyness, cunning and delight . . ." And those who were above such dishonesty were reconciled by the belief that an author should take pride in the mere fact of being liked in America. "The Americans read him; the free, enlightened, independent Americans; and what more *would* he have? Here's reward enough for any man. The national vanity swallows up all other countries on the face of the earth, and leaves but this above the ocean." "As to telling them they will have no literature of their own, the universal answer (out of Boston) is, 'We don't want one. Why should we pay for one when we can get it for nothing. Our people don't think of poetry, sir. Dollars, banks, and cotton are *our* books, sir.' And they certainly are in one sense; for a lower average of general information than exists in this country on all other topics, it would be very hard to find." [54]

* * * * *

For all his disappointment, though, how much there still was that he could praise about America, and how many noble friends he had made! Longfellow, Prescott, Jonathan Chapman, Sumner, Irving, and dear Felton! "Come to England! Come to England!" he wrote Felton. "Our oysters are small, I know; they are said by Americans to be coppery; but our hearts are of the largest size." [55] "David Colden is as good a fellow as ever lived," he wrote Macready; "and I am deeply in love with his wife. Indeed we have received the greatest and most earnest and zealous kindness from the whole family, and quite love them all." [56] To Colden himself, from Niagara, Dickens sent "all manner of loves to you and yours," [57] and enclosed a burlesque love-letter for Mrs. Colden—who was forty-six, a few months older than her husband and sixteen years older than Dickens—addressing her as 'My Better Angel.' [57a]

"If this should meet HIS eye, I trust you to throw dust in the same. HIS suspicions must not be aroused. HE says that I have applied tender epithets to a certain Mrs. D. I repel the charge with indignation. Alas his motive is but too apparent!" He was seeking to disrupt the bond between them by arousing her vanity. "HE IS A SERPENT. You are the Bride of a Scorpion." Working up to a fine frenzy, Dickens explained that it was hard "to be coherent, with a bosom full of arrows. Inclosed is a groan. I shall not miss it. I have a great many left." "When I think of futile attempts to tear two hearts asunder that are so closely knit together," Dickens concluded, "I laugh like a Fiend.

"Ha! ha! ha!
"C upi D"

To this impassioned effusion was added a love song in three stanzas opening:

> "Sweet woman is of many kinds;
> She sometimes is propi-tious;
> She sometimes has a Thousand minds;
> Sometimes is rayther wi-cious.
> Above her sex my love doth shine,
> Though by no means a bold 'un,
> 'I'd crowns resign to call her mine'
> —Her name is Missis . . . . . ." [58]

Despite the affectionate gaiety of these letters to American friends, as Dickens started for Montreal, on the last leg of his tour, he was undeniably glad to find himself on Canadian soil. He felt more at home even among the French villages of Quebec than he had in Pittsburgh, with all its supposed resemblance to Birmingham. "English kindness is very different from American," he wrote. "People send their horses and carriages for your use, but they don't exact as payment the right of being always under your nose." [59] "You cannot conceive with what transports of joy, I beheld an English Sentinel,—though he didn't look much like one, I confess, with his boots outside his trousers, and a great fur cap on his head. I was taken dreadfully loyal after dinner, and drank the Queen's health in a bumper . . ." [60]

Nevertheless Dickens did not blind himself to the fact that there were defects north as well as south of the border. He was shocked to find that albums carefully preserved at Table Rock, in which visitors inscribed "remarks and poetical effusions," were scrawled with filthy ribaldries and obscenity.[61] He was appalled by the rabid toryism in Toronto, and by political animosities so violent that the successful candidates in a recent election had been shot at. Kingston, the seat of government, was a poor town with mean and unimpressive public buildings.[62] Unlike the inns in the United States, so many of which even in the wilderness were surprisingly good, those in Canada were generally vile;[63] indeed, Rasco's Hotel, in Montreal, was "the worst in the whole wide world." [64]

After a trip through the Thousand Islands, shooting the rapids of the river, and proceeding down the broadening stream past gigantic rafts of lumber, Dickens reached Lachine by the afternoon of May 11th, and thence proceeded by land the last nine miles to Montreal.[65] Here there was a reunion with the Earl of Mulgrave, who on leaving Boston had gone on to Canada, where he was aide-de-camp to Lieutenant General Sir Richard Jackson, the Commander of the Forces.[66] Arrangements had been made for Dickens to join Lord Mulgrave and the officers of the garrison in a theatrical performance for the benefit of a local charity.[67] Dickens promptly became stage manager of the company and started rehearsals with a violence of enthusiasm.

"Everybody was told they would have to submit to the most iron despotism," he wrote Forster; "and didn't I come Macready over them? Oh no. By no means. Certainly not. The pains I have taken with them, and the perspiration I have expended, during the last ten days, exceed in amount anything you can imagine. I had regular plots of the scenery made out, and lists of the properties wanted; and had them nailed up by the prompter's chair. Every letter that was to be delivered, was written; every piece of money that had to be given, provided; and not a single thing lost sight of. I prompted, myself, when I was not on . . . The bedroom scene in the interlude was well furnished as Vestris had it; with a 'practicable' fireplace blazing away like mad, and everything in a concatenation accordingly." [68]

Dickens too blazed away like mad as manager and universal director. If Felton could only see him, he wrote, in that dark and dusty theater, "urging impracticable ladies and impossible gentlemen on to the very

confines of insanity, shouting and driving about, to an extent which
would justify any philanthropic stranger in clapping me into a strait-
waistcoat without further inquiry, endeavoring to goad Putnam into
some dim and faint understanding of a prompter's duties, and struggling in such a vortex of noise, dirt, bustle, confusion, and inextricable
entanglement as you would grow giddy in contemplating." Once
again, the magnetic attraction of the stage drew him, and he wondered
if pen, ink, and paper had not diverted a born stage manager.[69]

The comedy they were doing was Morton's A Roland for an Oliver,
followed by Mathew's interlude Past Two O'Clock in the Morning,
and Poole's farce Deaf as a Post. Dickens played in all three, taking
successively the parts of Alfred Highflyer, Mr. Snobbington, and
Gallop.[70] At Niagara he had suddenly fallen into a cold perspiration
at the thought that Montreal might not be able to supply the flaxen
wig and eyebrows he would need as Snobbington. He immediately
wrote to his actor friend William Mitchell in New York appealing
for help,[71] and Mitchell now sent him a hilariously comical arrangement of light flaxen hair with small side whiskers halfway down the
cheek.[72] Over this Dickens planned "to wear two night-caps, one with
a tassel and one of flannel; a flannel wrapper, drab tights and slippers." [73]

"The play comes off next Wednesday night, the twenty-fifth," he
wrote to Felton. "What would I give to see you in the front row of
the centre box, your spectacles gleaming not unlike those of my dear
friend Pickwick, your face radiant with as broad a grin as a staid professor may indulge in, and your very coat, waistcoat, and shoulders
expressive of what we should take together when the performance
was over." [74]

The performance took place at the Theatre Royal, renamed for this
one night only the Queen's Theatre.[75] The evening was a brilliant
success. "The audience, between five and six hundred, were invited
as to a party; a regular table with refreshments being spread in the
lobby and saloon." [76] Sir Charles Bagot, the Governor General, Sir
Richard Jackson, and their staffs were there, the bright gaslight making
a colorful spectacle of the military uniforms. Dickens was so well
made up that Sir Charles had no idea who was playing Snobbington
until the piece was over. "I really do believe that I was very funny,"
Dickens wrote Forster: "at least I know that I laughed heartily at

myself"; and everything "went with a roar." To prevent heartburnings, "in a very heartburning town," the private performance was followed on Saturday by a public one, before a paying audience, substituting professional actresses for the ladies who had taken part.[77]

One aspect of the evening's triumph occasioned Dickens considerable surprise. "Only think of Kate playing!" he exclaimed in a letter to Forster, "and playing devilish well, I assure you!" [78] In the playbill that he sent Forster, Dickens inscribed the names of the actors opposite those of the roles they played, and when he came to Amy Templeton in *Deaf as a Post* wrote in "Mrs. Charles Dickens" and slapped down no fewer than eight exclamation points after it.[79]

*   *   *   *   *

Their experiences on the *Britannia* had determined Dickens to return to England by a sailing packet, not a steamship. At night, on the steamers, you saw solid fire two or three feet above the top of the funnel; if it were blown down by a gale the entire boat "must instantly be on fire, from stem to stern." In addition, the rolling and pitching of the vessel was absolutely fearful; and "the struggling of that enormous machinery in a heavy sea seems as though it would rend her into fragments." [80] Dickens had consequently engaged passage on the *George Washington*, sailing from New York on June 7th and he now gratefully accepted David Colden's offer to see that he had two connecting staterooms on that ship.[81]

Dickens arrived in New York quivering with anticipation. From there he sent an affectionate letter of farewell to Jonathan Chapman in Boston. "The ocean can no more divide you and me than darkness can shut out heaven from a blind man. Were it twenty times as broad as it is, one could send a warm pressure of the hand across it . . ." [82] There was a final excursion, to the Shaker Village at Lebanon and to West Point on its heights above the Hudson, returning through those landmarks that Washington Irving had endeared to Dickens's imagination, the Catskill Mountains, Sleepy Hollow, and the Tappan Zee.[83] On the bright, breezy morning of June 7th, the Coldens gave him and Kate a farewell breakfast.[84] Then, with all the luggage that Putnam had taken care of so faithfully during their wanderings, and a little white Havana spaniel named "Timber Doodle," which had been presented to Dickens by Mitchell, the actor,[85] they drove to Jersey City.

An entire party went with them and accompanied them on board the steamer that was to convey them to the *George Washington*, lying off Sandy Hook. Between decks on this vessel they joined a large company in a cold collation, champagne, and farewell speeches.[86]

From Montreal Dickens had dispatched a last letter to Forster. "I have hardly spoken of our letters, which reached us yesterday, shortly before the play began. A hundred thousand thanks for your delightful mainsail of that gallant little packet. I read it again and again . . . I heard also, by the same ship, from Talfourd, Miss Coutts, Brougham, Rogers, and others. A delicious letter from Mac too, as good as his painting I swear. Give my hearty love to him. . . . God bless you, my dear friend. As the time draws nearer, we get FEVERED with anxiety for home. . . . Kiss our darlings for us. We shall soon meet, please God, and be happier and merrier than ever we were, in all our lives. . . . Oh home—home—home—home—home—home—HOME!!!!!!!!! !!" [87]

CHAPTER FIVE

Home Again: Valedictory
on America

DURING the whole of the voyage home Dickens was uproarious with hilarity. He established with three lively companions a maniacal association called the United Vagabonds, at whose antics their Negro steward lived for the entire three weeks in one broad grin. He soulfully played the accordion at all hours, while another played the violin, and another the key bugle, all rendering different tunes in different parts of the ship with intense expressiveness.[1] The captain being ill when they were a few days out, Dickens solemnly produced his medicine chest and "recovered" him. After that Dickens roamed "the wards" every day, accompanied by two Vagabonds, dressed as Ben Allen and Bob Sawyer, "bearing enormous rolls of plaster and huge pairs of scissors." [2]

How Dickens exulted as the ship slashed on through the water with every stitch of canvas set, now proudly riding a crest, now plunging down into a foaming valley, with the changing lights upon the white-bordered green waves! On the twentieth morning they passed Cape Clear and began sailing along the coast of Ireland; the next evening they sighted the revolving light glimmering on the rock of Holyhead. By early morning they were in the harbor of Liverpool, there was a farewell breakfast on shore, and then Dickens was on the railroad tearing through the small green fields and leafy hedgerows.[3]

The children were in bed when they arrived at Devonshire Terrace, brought back from the Macreadys' by their uncle Frederick, but Mamey in later years had a confused memory of seeing a hackney coach drive up after dark and kissing her father ecstatically through the bars of the gate. Perhaps she had merely been told about the coach, and really remembered leaping up behind the rails of a crib. All the children were wild with joy, for although Macready was the kindest of the kind, his solemn earnestness enforced a strict discipline in "the prim, gloomy, unjoyful house" that they were not used to at home.[4] Little Katey, indeed, while she was being dressed to be taken there, had cried and sobbed that she would "not doe"; [5] and during the weeks at "Creedy's" all the children had pined for Devonshire Terrace, with its raven, its guinea pigs and rabbits, the swing in the garden, and the laughing, joking father who sang funny songs. Charley's head was perfectly turned by joy. He fell into violent convulsions from being, as he told his mother, "too glad," and after he had recovered Dr. Elliotson informed the parents he had never seen the like in a child.[6]

From these excitements with the children, Dickens hurried off to see Macready in Clarence Terrace, and found him sitting on a sofa by the open window in a dark room. The two friends were immediately in each other's arms in a transport of delight. Thence Dickens rushed away to see Forster, who was dining out, but who guessed at once what it was when Dickens drove there and sent up word that a gentleman wished to speak to him. Forster came flying out of the house, leaped into the carriage, and began to cry, and did not remember until they had driven several miles on their way to see Maclise that he had left his hat behind him.[7]

Saturday of the following week there was a festive reunion dinner at Greenwich, with Captain Marryat in the chair and Jerdan as vice-chairman. Talfourd and Macready were unable to be there, but Ainsworth, Forster, Maclise, Stanfield, Cruikshank, and Cattermole gathered together with Procter, Barham, Father Prout, Monckton Milnes, Tom Hood, and a number of others to welcome Dickens home. Dr. Elliotson was also there, looking, with his long jet-black locks, Hood said, like someone of Cromwell's time, but placing no damper on the jollity of the occasion.[8] Songs and healths followed each other in such numbers that "Cruikshank came home in my phaeton on his head," Dickens reported, "—to the great delight of the loose midnight loungers in Regent Street," and "was last seen, taking Gin with a Waterman." [9]

During the next fortnight Dickens buoyantly renewed relations with scores of friends and acquaintances: Brougham, Landor, Jeffrey, Rogers, now grown a trifle deafer than he had been, Mrs. Norton and her sister Lady Seymour, "both sights for the Gods, as they have always been," Lady Blessington, wearing brilliantly and with "the gloss upon her, yet," Sydney Smith, "in greater force than ever, though waxing gouty." [10] Dickens also wrote Lady Holland, sending her a volume of American poetry and an eagle's feather from Niagara Falls, and called on her in the middle of July.[11] Lord Holland was dead now, but the dauntless old creature had fitted up some rooms on the lower floor and gave dinners as of yore. The old rooms on the floor above, though, where they had entertained together, she never entered, and when Dickens dined at Holland House, he "had a strange sense of their being dark and vacant, overhead." [12]

On his return to London, Dickens had learned that one of the old Whig newspapers, the *Courier*, had suspended publication and was merged with the *Globe*. Had he known in time, he wrote Lady Holland, he would have proposed to the leaders of the Liberal party that they save the paper, "nailing the true colors to the mast, and fighting the battle staunchly," with himself as editor. Perhaps it was not yet too late; the premises and types were still to be disposed of. Would Lady Holland like to ask Lord Melbourne and Lord Lansdowne if the Liberals would give financial backing to such an enterprise? He felt certain he could establish an organ that would serve the welfare of the people.[13]

But the statesmen Lady Holland spoke to said no, and Dickens reluctantly agreed that they might be right, although the Liberal party, he remarked, had seldom erred on the side of boldness. Certainly it would have meant, for him, not only a financial sacrifice, but a heavy burden of mental labor, since he could not have afforded to give up his other pursuits. Nevertheless, he regretted it when he thought of what a newspaper he might have created, and saw how the editorial writers "(except Fonblanque who is another Swift)" left untouched the very issues that concerned people's "business and bosoms most." [14]

*   *   *   *   *

Putting aside these reflections, however, Dickens was soon industriously at work on his *American Notes*.[15] He borrowed from Forster, Maclise, Beard, Mitton, and Fonblanque the letters that he had written them during his journey, to supplement his journal with their mass of details and profit from their spontaneity of observation.[16] Rapidly he dashed off an opening chapter and an impressionistic description of that wild January voyage across the Atlantic.[17] Before the end of July the "Boston" chapter was written.[18] It was a wonderful relief to be in his old room, with his books, surrounded by battledores and shuttlecocks, bats and balls, dumbbells, the raven, and little Timber Doodle, looking out with bright eyes from an ambush of white hair.[19]

"The raven, I am sorry to say," Dickens wrote Sumner, "has become a maniac. He falls into fits periodically; throws himself wildly on his back; and plucks his own feathers up, by the roots." The bird fancier thought it might be the weather; Topping, the groom, said it was "aggerawation." "I," Dickens darkly said, "suspect poison. A malicious butcher was heard to threaten some months since. He said that 'he worn't a goin' to have pieces took out of his leg ev'ry time he come down them mews, at no price. And that if the very dove as come out o' the Hark interfered vith him, he vished he might be busted if he wouldn't scrag him.' " [20]

Nothing could exceed Dickens's delight in his children or their delight in him. When he felt like defying his after-breakfast schedule of work, they played long riotous games of trap-bat and ball in the garden.[21] And before they went to bed Dickens would sit rocking in the American rocking chair he had brought back from the States, singing comic songs to a giggling childish audience: "The Loving Ballad of Lord Bateman" and one about "Guy Fawkes, that prince of sinisters, who once blew up the House of Lords, the King, and all his ministers." Each verse of the latter ballad contained some startling statement of this kind, which was then artfully explained away.

> "Crossing over Vauxhall Bridge,
> He that way came to London.
> That is he would have come that way
> To perpetrate his guilt, Sir,
> But a little thing prevented him,
> The bridge it wasn't built, Sir."

Then came a chorus of "Oh, oh, oh, ri fol de riddy oddy bow wow," delivered with great expression as the singer rocked with one child on his knee and the others clustered round.[22]

His American friends were not forgotten in the joy of home-coming. To Colden, Chapman, Felton, and others, Dickens sent lively letters. Felton he addressed as the American Dando; "but perhaps you don't know who Dando was. He was an oyster-eater, my dear Felton. He used to go into oyster-shops, without a farthing of money, and stand at the counter eating natives, until the man who opened them grew pale, cast down his knife, staggered backward, struck his white forehead with his open hand, and cried, 'You are Dando!!!' He had been known to eat twenty dozen at one sitting, and would have eaten forty, if the truth had not flashed upon the shopkeeper." [23]

To Mrs. Colden, Dickens wrote, "It is more clear to me than ever that Kate is as near being a Donkey as one of that sex whose luminary and sun you are, *can* be." For had she not written about the *Great Western* sailing for England on the fourteenth in a letter that could not possibly reach the Coldens before the sixteenth? Nevertheless, he added at the end of the letter, he wished, "sweet Foreigner," that "you would come and live next door; for the best part of my heart is in Laight Street, and I find it difficult to get on without it." "God bless you," he concluded, "—and—yes—and even—*Him*." [24]

During all this correspondence Dickens toiled steadily at *American Notes*. By the middle of August, in Broadstairs, he was blazing away at New York.[25] From the window where he wrote, he could see little Charley "digging up the sand on the shore with a small spade, and compressing it into a perfectly impossible wheelbarrow. The cliffs being high and the sea pretty cold, he looks a mere dot in creation." [26] The little dog was being taught to leap over a stick, "and jumps, as Mr. Kenwigs would say, perpetivally." [27] His name had been changed to Snittle Timbery,[28] and all the children had been fitted out with new nicknames. Charley was "Flaster Floby," a corruption of Master Toby; quiet Mamey was "Mild Glo'ster"; the fiery-tempered Katey "Lucifer Box"; and baby Walter, from his high cheekbones, "Young Skull"—each pronounced, Dickens wrote Henry Austin, with a peculiar howl, which I shall have great pleasure in illustrating." [29]

The seductions of these warm summer days often made it difficult for Dickens to work. "I have been reading Tennyson all the morning on the seashore," he wrote. "Among other trifling effects, the waters have dried up as they did of old, and shown me all the mermen and mermaids at the bottom of the ocean; together with millions of queer creatures, half fish and half-fungus, looking down into all manner of coral caves and seaweed conservatories; and staring in with their great dull eyes at every open nook and loophole." [30] And, again, "Today I had not written twenty lines before I rushed out (the weather being gorgeous) to bathe. And when I have done that, it is all up with me in the way of authorship until to-morrow." [31] But in spite of these distractions, by the last week in September Dickens had only the two final chapters to write, and was already receiving proofs through the description of Niagara Falls. [32]

*　　*　　*　　*　　*

The bulk of the book was devoted to vivid impressions, in the manner of some of the *Sketches by Boz*, of the scenes through which he had passed. Save, perhaps, in the chapter dealing with slavery, he had avoided the sharpness of tone that had crept into his letters, but he had painted no idyllic picture of America, and he well knew that that oversensitive country could not bear the faintest whisper of dispraise. The hornets' nest he had stirred up across the Atlantic was still buzzing furiously. The New York newspapers had published in July a spurious letter in which Dickens was made to say that the entertainment he had received in the United States was officiously forced upon him, and that he had met uncouth manners and gross selfishness throughout his entire journey. "DICKENS IS A FOOL, AND A LIAR," flared across newspaper headlines, and everywhere in the country the malignant forgery was received with credulous fury. [33]

To his personal correspondents Dickens denounced the letter, but although he felt "a vague desire to take somebody by the throat," he refused to engage in public controversy with the "unhung scoundrel" who invented it. [34] "When I tilt at such wringings-out of the dirtiest mortality, I shall be another man—indeed, almost the creature they would make me." [35] He was concerned, however, to assert his freedom of opinion without seeming unappreciative of the enthusiastic reception he had been given. With Forster's aid and advice he therefore worked out a dedication to the two volumes, which finally read: "I dedicate this Book to those friends of mine in America who, giving me a welcome I must ever gratefully and proudly remember, left my judgment free; and who, loving their country, can bear the truth, when it is told good-humouredly, and in a kind spirit." [36]

Among his American friends, nevertheless, there were some who were seriously perturbed at what Dickens might write. Jonathan Chapman counseled moderation; Dickens replied that Chapman's fears were dictated by a "tenderness for me . . . keener and less bold than any anxiety you would ever entertain for yourself." Suppose America were a man, he said, instead of a nation; was a friendship worth having that could be retained only by a timid silence, by debating at every turn, "Will he take this? Will he be angry if I say that? Will he find out that I am not a toy for his amusement if I do the other?" Clearly not. "And as I have never been deterred by hopes of approbation or visions of greatness, from pointing out abuses at home, so no amount of popular breath shall blow me from my purpose, if I see fit to point out what, in my judgment, are abuses abroad," and if this "bring down caprice and weather-cock fickleness . . . on my head," what can this matter "to any man who is worth the name"? He was convinced, Dickens wrote, that there was not in his book "one solitary line" that was not true or with which Chapman would not concur, and that he had never been betrayed into an unfair expression. "My dear Chapman, if we yielded to such reasons or such men as these, in five years' time there would be no such thing as truth in the world . . ." [37]

But warnings like Chapman's made Dickens keenly aware of the angry reception the book would have throughout most of the American press. He therefore planned to cut the ground from under some of this resentment, at least as far as the more thoughtful body of readers were concerned, by an introductory chapter outlining his position.[38] The book, it explained, was not statistical. It avoided personalities. It was not political. It contained no description of the reception "a most affectionate and generous-hearted people" had given him, because he could not well flourish before his readers matter involving so much of his own praise. It was simply a day-by-day record of things that had passed under his eye, with some of his reflections upon them.[39]

He knew, he said, that he would be accused of malice and ingratitude by journalists and by people so delicately made that they could not bear the imperfections of truth. But he did not believe the warm welcome he had received was a vulgar attempt to flatter him into turning a blind eye upon any blemishes in the nation. "From first to last

I saw, in those hospitable hands, a home-made wreath of laurel; and not an iron muzzle disguised beneath a flower or two." And consequently he had no more praised the abuses he had observed than he ever had those he saw at home. Since he had gone to America "expecting greater things than I found," and resolved to correct the prejudiced disparagements of previous writers, he was no less bound, when his sobered judgment confirmed theirs, to bear witness to the truth.[40]

Unfortunately, Forster strongly opposed printing this introduction. It might arouse, he thought, the suspicion that Dickens feared hostile judgments and was trying to deprecate them in advance. Much better to let the book stand on the strength of its own accuracy and truth. Dickens disagreed, but at last allowed himself to be won over, so reluctantly, however, that Forster had to promise that the suppressed chapter should be published at some more fitting time in the future. That time did not arrive, in Forster's estimation, until two years after Dickens's death, when he included the chapter in his biography.[41]

It seems likely that Forster's advice was tactically mistaken. Dickens's courteously worded separation of his freedom of utterance from the friendly welcome with which he had been greeted was entirely sound. His statement that he had never softened or glozed over the evils he had found at home was also cogent, and indeed he might have added that on the whole he treated America with a gentler hand than he did England. None of the introduction was liable to have done harm, and much of it might have been useful, although nothing but the most shameless flattery would have satisfied the more touchy element in American opinion.

*　　*　　*　　*　　*

The summer weather at Broadstairs had been followed by tremendous northeast gales rolling in heavy seas that drowned the pier in waves twelve feet high.[42] From these Dickens returned to London eagerly anticipating the promised visit from Longfellow. Every foreign steamer that had passed his windows since the beginning of August, he wrote, had filled him with horrible misgivings that Longfellow might have shipped himself back to Boston from Germany in gloomy desperation; and he had undergone tortures imagining Longfellow knocking at his door in London without notice, "and finding nobody there, but an old woman who is remarkable for nothing but a face of unchangeable dirtiness." But now a letter from the American poet arrived, and Dickens answered it at once. "How stands it about your visit, do you say? Thus.—Your bed is waiting to be slept in, the door is gaping hospitably to receive you, I am ready to spring towards it at the first indication of a Longfellow knock or ring; and the door, the bed, I, and everybody else who is in the secret, have been expecting you for the last month." [43]

Longfellow reached London on October 6th and came at once to Devonshire Terrace. "I write this from Dickens' study," he told Sumner. "The raven croaks in the garden; and the ceaseless roar of London fills my ears." [44] He spent the mornings replenishing his wardrobe from the fashionable tailors, bootmakers, and hatters of Piccadilly and Bond Street, but in the afternoons and evenings Dickens involved him in a round of entertainment.[45] The very evening of his arrival Dickens took him to see Macready in *As You Like It* and they visited Macready in his dressing room after the performance.[46] With Cruikshank, Maclise, and Macready there were "mad" dinners in Devonshire Terrace, at which they drank Schloss-Johannisberger and cold punch, and other evenings equally merry beneath Forster's bright dinner lamps in Lincoln's Inn Fields.[47] Dickens carried his guest off to meet the author of "The Song of the Shirt"—"dear Hood," Longfellow called him, and he long remembered "the pale face of the poet, and the house in St. John's Wood." [48] Longfellow breakfasted and dined at the table of Samuel Rogers, where he met Moxon, the publisher, and the poet Tom Campbell, shrunken and frost-nipped with age, and wearing a foxy wig.[49] At Gore House, Longfellow was received by Lady Blessington, and saw Count D'Orsay, who was confined withindoors "by a severe attack of *bum-bailiffs*" and could venture out only on Sundays.[50] At one of their few quiet evenings in Devonshire Terrace, "the phlegmatic poet," as Dickens jocosely called him, shared a plump brace of partridges and a stewed steak with his host and Henry Austin.[51]

In contrast to London's artistic and fashionable circles, Dickens gave Longfellow a lurid nocturnal glimpse of its criminal slums. Accompanied by Forster and Maclise, and guided by officers supplied through the courtesy of Chesterton and Lieutenant Tracey, they explored the foulest and most dangerous thieves' dens of the Borough.

On entering the very first of the Mint lodginghouses there, Maclise's stomach was so turned by the filth and stench that he was taken with a violent fit of vomiting and had to remain outside under the guardianship of the police while the others subjected themselves to the full horrors within.[52]

Another day Dickens and Forster carried Longfellow down into Kent to show him the Leather Bottle at Cobham, the Bull at Rochester, and all the other scenes among which Dickens had passed his childhood. The old Castle was barred to visitors, and a surly custodian threatened them with the law when they appealed to him. Defying his prohibition, they recklessly overleaped the gates and barriers, clambered up over piles of débris, across treacherous galleries, and climbed the gap-toothed circular stairs to the loftiest battlements of the ruinous structure, to look down on the Medway and over the clustered houses around the Cathedral to Fort Pitt and the heights of Chatham Lines.[53]

At the end of two weeks Longfellow set out for Bristol, where he was taking the steamship *Great Western* on the 21st.[54] Forster wanted to give him some bottled port wine to take back to America, but Dickens, remembering the *Britannia* plunging and shuddering through the waves, vetoed the suggestion. "No—no!—the Port will be shaken to the devil before it gets there." [55] Longfellow was entrusted, however, with some Johannisberger and punch for Dickens's friends across the Atlantic. With this he took copies of *American Notes*, which was just off the press, for Felton, Sumner, the elder Dana, Washington Allston, Bancroft, Prescott, and Chapman.[56] With Dickens and Forster he set off by rail for Bath, where he dined and spent the evening with Landor. Next morning he went on to Bristol.[57]

"I was but poorly received," Dickens reported, "when I came home from Bristol that night, in consequence of my inability to report that I had left you actually on board the Great Western; and that I had seen the chimney smoking." "After you left us, Charley invented and rehearsed with his sisters a dramatic scene in your honour . . ." It consisted of a ceremony of drinking healths. "The three small glasses are all raised together, and they look at each other very hard. Then Charley cries 'Mr. Longfellow! Hoo-ra-a-a-a-a-a-e!' Two other shrill voices repeat the sentiment, and the little glasses are drained to the bottom.

The whole concludes with a violent rapping of the table, and a hideous barking from the little dog, who wakes up for the purpose." [58]

*   *   *   *   *

Hardly was Longfellow gone when Dickens set off, with Forster, Maclise, and Clarkson Stanfield, for a holiday trip.[59] "I think of opening my new book," he had written Forster, "on the coast of Cornwall, in some terrible dreary iron-bound spot." [60] They would descend into a mine; he would obtain letters for that purpose from Dr. Southwood Smith, and information about what was the bleakest and most barren part. To Tintagel, with its legends of King Arthur, they accordingly went, and to St. Michael's Mount and Land's End.[61]

"Blessed star of morning!" Dickens wrote Felton. "Such a trip as we had into Cornwall just after Longfellow went away! . . . Heavens! If you could have seen the necks of bottles, distracting in their immense varieties of shape, peering out of the carriage pockets! If you could have witnessed the deep devotion of the postboys, the wild attachment of the hostlers, the maniac glee of the waiters! If you could have followed us into the earthy old churches we visited, and into the strange caverns on the gloomy sea-shore, and down into the depths of mines, and up to the tops of giddy heights where the unspeakably green water was roaring, I don't know how many hundred feet below!" [62]

"Don't I still see the Logan Stone," Maclise wrote to Forster, "and you perched on the giddy top, while we, rocking it on its pivot, shrank from all that lay concealed below! . . . And don't I recall you again, sitting on the tip-top stone of the cradle-turret over the highest battlement of the castle of St. Michael's Mount, with not a ledge or coigne of vantage 'twixt you and the fathomless ocean under you, distant three thousand feet? Last, do I forget you clambering up the goat-path to King Arthur's castle of Tintagel, when, in my vain wish to follow, I grovelled and clung to the soil like a Caliban, and you, in the manner of a tricky spirit and stout Ariel, actually danced up and down before me!" [63]

"I never laughed in my life," Dickens wrote, "as I did on this journey. It would have done you good to hear me. I was choking and gasping and bursting the buckle off the back of my stock, all the way.

And Stanfield got into such apoplectic entanglements that we were often obliged to beat him on the back with portmanteaus before we could recover him. Seriously, I do believe there never was such a trip. And they made such sketches, those two men, in the most romantic of our halting-places, that you would have sworn we had the Spirit of Beauty with us, as well as the Spirit of Fun." [64]

Into one of the paintings inspired by this holiday, *The Girl at the Waterfall*, Maclise introduced the figure of Kate's young sister Georgina,[65] who was fifteen years old at this time.[66] She had seen much of the children while their parents were in America and won their infant hearts to such a degree that they constantly chattered of "Aunt Georgy." Not long after, she was invited to stay at Devonshire Terrace and gradually slid into a place in the household very much like that which Mary had once filled. Dickens traced "a strong resemblance" between her and her dead sister, "so strange a one, at times," he wrote to Mrs. Hogarth, "that when she and Kate and I are sitting together, I seem to think that what has happened is a melancholy dream from which I am just awakening. The perfect likeness of what she was, will never be again, but so much of her spirit shines out" in Georgina "that the old time comes back again at some seasons, and I can hardly separate it from the present." [67]

So very anxious was Dickens to have the little picture in which Georgina appeared that he enlisted Beard's aid in a pious fraud to obtain it. If he hinted his desire to possess it, Maclise in his generosity would either insist on giving it to him outright or "set some preposterous price upon it, which he can by no means afford to take." Consequently Beard was to purchase it in the name of an imaginary friend in Sussex, offering whatever sum Maclise might ask. "A hundred, or a hundred and fifty guineas, will most likely be the mark." [68]

Mightily indignant was Maclise when he discovered the deception. "May I not be permitted to give some proof of the value I attach to your friendship?" he asked, and insisted on returning the money. Dickens refused to take it back, but begged him not to be offended. "If I could have contemplated the selfish engrossment of so much of your time, and extraordinary power, I should have had no need (knowing you, I knew that well) to resort to the little artifice I played off. I will take anything else from you at any time that you will give me any scrap from your hand; but I entreat you not to disturb this matter." [69]

Later, Maclise insisted on giving Dickens a portrait of Kate equal in size to his 1839 painting of her husband.[70]

*   *   *   *   *

Back in London, after the Cornwall holiday, Dickens made a determined onslaught on the opening of his new book. The writing of *American Notes* had delayed its commencement and forced postponing its publication date from November to January. Now Dickens forced himself to the task, an endeavor that involved shutting himself up, "obstinately and sullenly," in his own room "for a great many days without writing a word." During these agonies of plotting and contriving, he wrote Miss Coutts, he walked up and down the house, "smiting my forehead dejectedly," and "so horribly cross . . . that the boldest fly at my approach" and "my publishers always come two together, lest I should fall upon a single invader and do murder on his intrusive body." [71]

His lingering wish to begin the story in a lighthouse or mine in Cornwall was ultimately abandoned, and the tale opened in a little Wiltshire village on a windy autumn evening. Dickens had much trouble finding a name for the book and for his hero. Sweezleden, Sweezlewag, Chuzzletoe, Chuzzleboy, Chubblewig, and Chuzzlewig were among those he tried before he finally settled on Martin Chuzzlewit.[72]

The design of the book was to portray through Pecksniff and the other characters the numerous humors and vices that have their roots in selfishness, and by the third number Dickens had drawn up "old Martin's plot to degrade and punish Pecksniff." That *Martin Chuzzlewit* had a theme as well as a plot is a sign of Dickens's development as a writer. His previous novels, although they have much more structure than they are usually credited with, are still glorious improvisations. *Oliver Twist* is not so completely dominated by the campaign against the Poor Law, nor *Nicholas Nickleby* by the attack on the Yorkshire schools, as *Martin Chuzzlewit* is by the revelation of selfishness. Though Dickens deviated widely from parts of his original scheme, he never lost sight of his dominating intent.

During this arduous planning of *Martin Chuzzlewit*, Dickens heard from Maclise that a youthful artist named Frith had made some delightful sketches of Dolly Varden and Emma Haredale, the two heroines of *Barnaby Rudge*. Promptly he wrote asking Frith to paint two companion pictures for him, a Dolly Varden and a Kate Nickleby.[73] Thrilled by the commission, Frith produced a picture of Dolly Varden tripping through the woods and looking saucily back at her lover, and one of Kate with her thoughts wandering from her work as she sewed on a ball dress at Mme. Mantalini's. When they were done Frith was "in hourly and trembling expectation" for Dickens to come and see them.

The great day arrived. Frith saw "a pale young man with long hair, a white hat, and a formidable stick in his left hand," extending his right in a friendly clasp. The artist waited his verdict in an agony quickly ended by the cheery words, "All I can say is they are exactly what I meant, and I am very much obliged to you for painting them for me." Frith muttered something, feeling very foolish, and Dickens asked permission to bring his wife and her sister to see the pictures on the following Sunday. The artist was standing at his door Sunday afternoon as Dickens drove up to the curb in a dashing curricle with a bright steel bar. Rustling into the studio, Kate and Georgina exclaimed admiringly over the two paintings, while Dickens bestowed on the youthful artist a check for forty pounds.[74]

Despite the demands of his own work, Dickens found time to write a verse prologue for Macready's new production at Drury Lane. The first play of a twenty-three-year-old author named Westland Marston, *The Patrician's Daughter*, instead of being staged as costume drama, was courageously presented as a poetic tragedy of current life. Sympathizing warmly with the innovation, Dickens thought a prologue would help, "Get the curtain up with a dash—and begin the play with a sledge-hammer blow": [75]

> "No tale of streaming plume and harness bright
> Dwells on the poet's maiden harp tonight;
> No trumpet's clamour and no battle's fire
> Breathes in the trembling accents of his lyre . . .
>
> . . . .
>
> Awake the Present! Though the steel-clad age
> Find life alone within its storied page,
> Iron is worn, at heart, by many still—
> The tyrant Custom binds the serf-like will;
> If sharp rack, and screw, and chain be gone
> These later days have tortures of their own. . . ." [76]

Another poetic drama by which Dickens was deeply moved at this time was Browning's *A Blot on the 'Scutcheon*. The poet had confided the manuscript of the play to Forster, and Forster lent it to Dickens, from whom it compelled "a perfect passion of sorrow." "I know nothing that is so affecting, nothing in any book I have ever read, as Mildred's recurrence to that 'I was so young—I had no mother.' I know no love like it, no passion like it, no moulding of a splendid thing after its conception, like it. And I swear it is a tragedy that MUST be played; and must be played, moreover by Macready. . . . If you tell Browning that I have seen it, tell him that I believe from my soul there is no man living (and not many dead) who could produce such a work." [77]

* * * * *

From Longfellow now came word of his arrival home.[78] Dickens had tried to prevent any copies of *American Notes* reaching the United States before those carried by his friend,[79] but his efforts had failed. While the book was being set up in type a smart American journalist had bribed one of the pressmen at Bradbury and Evans, the printers, and stolen proof sheets had crossed the Atlantic before Longfellow.[80] By the time he reached home three or four publishers were hurriedly printing cheap editions that flooded the country at six cents a copy.[81] The New York *Herald* printed the work in nineteen hours after the arrival of copy from England and sold fifty thousand in two days. In Philadelphia three thousand copies went in half an hour.[82]

Among Dickens's friends in America, its reception was favorable. Longfellow said it was "jovial and good-natured," though "at times very severe." "He has a grand chapter on Slavery," Longfellow wrote Sumner. "*Spitting* and *politics* at Washington are the other topics of censure. Both you and I would censure them with equal severity to say the least." [83] "Opinions are various," Felton said; "but we agree pretty well here, in thinking it a capital book; lively, spirited, true and good humored." [84] Emerson was less laudatory. He thought it lively and readable, but as an account of American manners "too narrow, too superficial, and too ignorant, too slight, and too fabulous," full of exaggeration and caricature.[85]

The American press, of course, let out a howl of superheated rage. The New York *Herald* warned readers that it would "cause a sensation throughout the United States," and counseled them, "Don't burst, keep cool—be quiet." [86] But then, after reproducing extracts on its front page for two days—and paying the author not a penny—in a fit of virtuous resentment it burst itself. The book was "all leather and prunella," it said, not worth any sensible man's perusal, and Dickens, "that famous penny-a-liner," had "the most coarse, vulgar, impudent, and superficial" mind "that ever had the courage to write about . . . this original and remarkable country." His view "of the fermentative character of this land" was that of "a narrow-minded, conceited cockney." Of all its visitors he was "the most flimsy—the most childish— the most trashy—the most contemptible . . . the essence of balderdash, reduced to the last drop of silliness and inanity." [87]

Another newspaper said Dickens was a "flash reporter," with the feelings of "a low-bred scullion unexpectedly advanced from the kitchen to the parlour." Still another American paper sneered that he could extol Niagara Falls "when viewed from the British side" and find excuses if Canadian hotels were unfit to use, while the Toronto *Herald* was furious at his remarks on political violence in Toronto. Another American newspaper printed a letter from an angry citizen of St. Louis, saying that Dickens had spent his life "in the stews of London" and was "fit to associate only with the dancing monkeys and mulatto girls of Five Points." [88]

Thoughtful readers in England indulged in no such tantrums, but they did not care much for the book. Macready did not like it. Macaulay, who had demanded that it be set aside for him at the *Edinburgh Review,* sent it back. "It is impossible for me to review it, I cannot praise it, and I will not cut it up." He had eaten salt with Dickens, and furthermore, Dickens, "in spite of some faults of taste," was "a man of genius" and "a great man." Though it contained "a few lively descriptions and dialogues," it seemed to Macaulay "on the whole a failure. It is written like the worst parts of *Humphrey's Clock.* What is meant to be fine is a great deal too fine for me, as the description of Niagara." [89]

Captain Marryat, on the other hand, liked the book, and so did Mrs. Trollope. "Let me thank you most cordially," Dickens wrote her, "for your kind note, in reference to my Notes, which has given me true pleasure and gratification." Her praise was the more valuable to him, he now said, because he thought no writer had described America more entertainingly and truthfully than she had. The cry of exaggeration that had been raised against both of them only proved the truth of their observations. It was a charge he had never seen "made against a feeble performance," however untrue, and was what common observers might be expected to say of uncommon ones.[90]

More important in practical ways than these disagreements on the merits of *American Notes* was the fact that the public bought it. Three thousand copies were sold in the first week, and four large editions before the end of the year. It brought Dickens in a profit of £1,000 which he could readily use after the high expenses of the tour it celebrated.

Most American readers today will find little in *American Notes* to rouse their ire. The descriptions are colorful, often brilliant, the tone on the whole one of courteous moderation. In his desire, indeed, to give no unnecessary offense, Dickens omitted many of those personal observations and all the comments on well-known figures that add spice to his letters. He omitted any account of the copyright irritations that had simmered throughout his journey. He warmly praised many features of American life. He paid generous tribute to the American people. "They are, by nature, frank, brave, cordial, hospitable, and affectionate. Cultivation and refinement seem but to enhance their warmth of heart and ardent enthusiasm . . ." Individually, the average American citizen was prevailingly courteous and helpful, and many educated Americans had endeared themselves to him in a way he had never known before.[91]

Surely here was praise enough to satisfy even the most captious. Few people now would take exception to Dickens's feelings about spitting and tobacco-chewing, and even in 1842 there were many Americans who shared his revulsion. The indignation with which he lashed slavery was applauded then by many enlightened Americans, and would be resented by none today. On the other hand, his repeated accounts of prisons, workhouses, hospitals, and orphanages, grow tiresome after the first two or three. And, for all his studied moderation, Dickens's disappointment in America gradually emerges as a dislike of the country as a whole which becomes unmistakable before the end of the book.

This dislike is especially clear in Dickens's strictures on American "smartness," the excesses of the trading spirit, and the licentiousness

of the American press. He quotes a dialogue which, he says, "I have
held a hundred times": " 'Is it not a very disgraceful circumstance that
such a man as So and So should be acquiring a large property by the
most odious and infamous means, and notwithstanding all the crimes
of which he has been guilty, should be tolerated and abetted by your
Citizens? He is a public nuisance, is he not?' 'Yes, sir.' 'A convicted
liar?' 'Yes, sir.' 'He has been kicked, and cuffed, and caned?' 'Yes, sir.'
'And he is utterly dishonourable, debased, and profligate?' 'Yes, sir.'
'In the name of wonder, then, what is his merit?' 'Well, sir, he is a
smart man.' " [92]

In surrender to the love of trade American literature was "to remain
for ever unprotected," even though Americans professed to be very
proud of their poets; "before the stern utilitarian joys of trade" all
healthful amusements and cheerful recreations were obliged to give
way.[93] The vicious press was a constant moral poison in the public
life of the nation, corrupting politics with its venal hand, smearing
every decent opponent with its filthy slanders. Even those good men
who loathed and despised it in their hearts dared take no step to defy
its tyranny. But until they set their heels upon it to crush it, so long
would "the evil it works, be plainly visible in the Republic." [94]

The emotional revulsion behind these criticisms had three inter-
twining roots: Dickens's own limitations, the distortions inevitable
in the only view of America he was given, and the actual character of
the nation in the mid-nineteenth century. For all his sharpness and
penetration, for all the power of genius, Dickens was still a young man
—not yet quite thirty when he stepped ashore at the Custom House
in Boston. Beyond a few weeks' holiday in France and Belgium he had
had no experience of any country but his own. He had no cosmopolitan standard with which to measure America, no knowledge except
knowledge of England to apply, no acquaintance with any other national character. It is significant that he thought Americans a sad
rather than a humorous people, taking their straight-faced jests as
sober earnest, and reading their wild hyperbole as either mendacity
or windy boastfulness. Some of the things Dickens reports as serious
fact suggest a strong suspicion that his leg was being pulled by some
melancholy joker; even then the tall tale had long been a favorite
sport of the trader, the pioneer, and the flatboatman.

Furthermore, what Dickens saw of America was distorted by the extraordinary furore accompanying his progress. Everywhere he went there were goggling eyes, heads poked in through windows, a raw curiosity mingling with the genuine warmth, that left him less privacy than a side-show freak. He was always surrounded by milling crowds and being intruded on by crashing bores. What the flavor of American life was like for a farmer in the Genesee or the Ohio valley, a hardware dealer in Hartford, a merchant on Beacon Hill, he could no more experience than if he had been a parade or a five-alarm fire. It is remarkable under the circumstances that in the space of less than five months he hit on so much that was shrewd and true.

For of course most of what Dickens said about America, if sometimes exaggerated in detail, was true in essence. That was why it hurt, and why Americans resented it in a way incomprehensible to Dickens. He had never been given to immoderate panegyric on the state of civilization in England; why should he be in America? His own youthful intolerance did not understand the gawky adolescence of a country still awkwardly uncertain of its position in the comity of nations. Americans were proud of the conquests they had carved out of a virgin continent in so short a span of generations. But the effort had made them primarily a utilitarian people, with few artists or writers of distinction. Dickens saw the paucity of cultural achievement; he did not realize the resistance the big-boned continent had given to the plow and the forge, or the way the struggle to subdue it had formed the American character.

That struggle made Americans a tissue of contradictions. They deified the dollar, and sowed the land thickly with schools and seats of learning. They adulated the sharp dealer, and gave generously to every noble cause. Their raucous indifference to literature and art contrasted with their loud pride in Washington Irving and Fenimore Cooper, and with the fantastic triumph they gave to Dickens himself. They boasted windily because so many of their foreign visitors were supercilious to their desire for praise. They talked big, and felt smaller than they could bear to admit. They were oversensitive and bumptious at the same time.

Such a desperate longing to be loved and admired, and the deep-seated diffidence beneath the bluster and swagger, was a paradox incomprehensible to the insular complacence of most Europeans. It did not yield its secret to Dickens, although he had imagined he would understand the republican character, and although there were many elements in its pattern that he shared. But Dickens had little awareness of historical causes, and no tendency to relate them to psychological causes. He did not clearly perceive many of the ways in which his own aggressive self-respect and sensitivity had been shaped by his environment. He did not see the American character as the product of its world.

PART SIX

Crescendo of Restlessness

1843–1846

CHAPTER ONE

Year of Disappointment

URING 1843 Dickens worked and worried over *Martin Chuzzlewit*.
D But the year began gaily with a Twelfth-Night party for Charley,
at which Leigh Hunt, Edwin Landseer, and other "children of larger
growth" made merry.[1] There was a magic lantern, and Dickens had
bought the stock in trade of a conjurer, with which he entertained the
guests, aided by Stanfield, "who always does his part exactly the wrong
way, to the unspeakable delight of all beholders." "And O my dear
eyes, Felton, if you could see me conjuring the company's watches into
impossible tea-caddies, and causing pieces of money to fly, and burning pocket-handkerchiefs without hurting 'em . . . you would never
forget it as long as you live." [2] The show was such a success that Dickens had to repeat it for Mrs. Caroline Norton's children a little later.[3]

Since his return from America, Dickens had made no public reference to international copyright, except for a printed letter addressed
to the *Athenaeum*, the *Examiner*, and a number of other journals, in
which he stated his resolve to forgo all profits from the sale of early
proofs to American publishers, and urged others to refuse all correspondence with those engaged in piracy and to deal only with reputable houses.[4] In accordance with this principle he had rejected offers
from Lea and Blanchard, in Philadelphia, of £100 for advance sheets
of *American Notes* and £440 for *Martin Chuzzlewit*. His feelings toward them personlly, he wrote them, were of the friendliest, but he
had determined that he "would have nothing blown to me by a side
wind" which this legislative iniquity denied him, and would let "the
American people . . . have the full pride, honour, glory and profit
of it." [5]

Now, in January, the subject flared into the press again. An article

[449]

on *American Notes* in the *Edinburgh Review* repeated, from "some cut-throat American paper," Dickens had no doubt, the assertion that he had gone to America "as a kind of missionary in the cause of international copyright." Dickens strongly protested the careless acceptance of this falsehood, which portrayed him "as a traveller under false pretences, and a disappointed intriguer." He readily agreed, however, to the offer of a retraction made to him by Macvey Napier, the editor.[6] When the London *Times* referred to the same article, he wrote a denial to that paper also. It had occurred to him, he said, as it had to other English travelers in America, to speak of the existing state of the law, simply because he had never hesitated to denounce it at home, and because, "inexperienced at that time in the American people," he believed that they "would not refuse to recognize a principle of common honesty." But the statement that he had gone there for that purpose could only be characterized "by one of the shortest and strongest words in the language." [7]

Three months later, in early April, Dickens presided over a meeting called in Cockspur Street for the establishment of a Society of Authors. Its main purposes were to protect authors' rights, to work for the enactment of more satisfactory laws, both national and international, and to give legal advice and aid to its members. [8] But, Dickens wrote to Charles Babbage, the mathematician, "I am as well convinced of its invincible hopelessness as if I saw it written by a celestial penman in the Book of Fate." It was not merely that authors were the kind of men they were, but that without the co-operation of publishers their aims were unattainable.[9] To this end Dickens responded to suggestions from the two publishers Longman and Murray that an association of authors, publishers, printers, and stationers be formed to protect their mutual interests, and took the chair at a meeting held in the Longmans' offices on May 17th. From it emerged an association whose subscribers included more than a dozen of the leading publishers and printers and listed among its authors the names of Bulwer, Dickens, Forster, Lockhart, Macaulay, and Marryat.[10]

Dickens had hopes that this organization might accomplish some of its objects, but he was convinced that American piracy would outlast his time. "I quite agree with you," he wrote Longfellow, "that we shall never live to see the passing of an international Law." [11] And to Lewis Gaylord Clark, "What impossible odds shall I set . . . that we shall be in our graves and out of them again in particles of dust impalpable, before those honest men at Washington, in their earthy riots, care one miserable damn for Mind?" [12] But one might cry " 'Stop thief!' nevertheless, especially as they wince and smart under it." [13]

Indignant though he might be about such grievances, however, the injustices from which Dickens suffered himself never absorbed more than a small part of his sympathies. Instead of narrowing his mood to gloomy self-pity, they only quickened his sensitivity to the harsher misfortunes of others and made him a spokesman for the unhappy everywhere. His heart was wrung by the figures Dr. Southwood Smith gave him on the hours and wages of labor, although, like many good men, he was baffled to find a solution for the suffering they disclosed. In these hungry times, he told the doctor, it seemed almost a cruelty, by limiting "even the dreadful hours" that prevailed, to deprive the poor of the smallest fraction of their scanty wage. "Want is so general," he wrote, "distress so great, and Poverty so rampant,—it is, in a word, so hard for the million to live by any means—that I scarcely know how we can step between them and one weekly farthing. The necessity of a mighty change, I clearly see . . ." [14]

The Government blue book on sanitary conditions among the laboring population which Southwood Smith also sent him left Dickens stricken down with horror. He rose determined that he must strike a great blow against this massacre of the innocents. "Rest assured," he wrote Smith, "that when you . . . see what I do, and where, and how, you will certainly feel that a sledge-hammer has come down with twenty times the force—twenty thousand times the force" that could be exerted by any pamphlet. "Even so recently as when I wrote to you the other day I had not contemplated the means I shall now, please God, use. But they have been suggested to me; and I have girded myself for their seizure—as you shall see in due time." [15] The fierce polemic of *The Chimes*, published at the end of the following year, was one of the sledge-hammer blows animated by this determination.

These emotions made him wrathful against the selfish complacency that opposes social legislation and extols the good old times. "Oh Heaven," he wrote Douglas Jerrold, "if you could have been with me at a hospital dinner last Monday! There were men there—your City aristocracy—who made such speeches and expressed such sentiments as any moderately intelligent dustman would have blushed through his cindery bloom to have thought of. Sleek, slobbering, bow-paunched, over-fed, apoplectic, snorting cattle, and the auditory leaping up in their delight! I never saw such an illustration of the power of the purse, or felt so degraded and debased by its contemplation . . ." The spectacle made him no less furious against "the parrots of society" than against "its birds of prey." That was why, he told Jerrold, he was "writing a little history of England" for his boy. "I don't know what I should do if he were to get hold of any Conservative or High Church notions"; the best way of guarding against the horror was "to wring the parrots' necks in his very cradle." [16]

His father's irresponsibility and the careers of his brothers gave him worries more troublesome, however, than these fears about the future sentiments of his children. Even in America he had been vexed by news from Mitton about "that father of mine," and exclaimed, "How long he is, growing up." [17] On his return to England his parents bitterly renewed their complaints about being immured in the doll's house at Alphington; "family business (not the most pleasant in its nature)," Dickens wrote, "obliges me to leave town by railroad." [18] Dickens evidently yielded to their demand to be brought up to London, for at the same time he authorized Mitton to offer £70 for "that little house on Blackheath." [19] Not long after, he was writing Miss Coutts to ask if she could help him procure suitable employment for his brother Alfred, who was a civil engineer.[20] And Fred, although his Treasury salary had been increased, was falling into his father's extravagant ways. A creditor at Gray's Inn sent Dickens "for the second time a bill which I think is Frederick's," [21] and the younger brother, evidently resenting whatever Dickens did or said about it, angrily stayed away from Devonshire Terrace. "Your absence from here," Dickens wrote him, "has been your own act always. I shall be perfectly glad to see you; and should have been, at any time." [22]

Under these circumstances, it is no wonder that Dickens sometimes had difficulty in concentrating on his work. "I couldn't write a line yesterday," he told Forster; "not a word, though I really tried hard. In a kind of despair I started off at half-past two with my pair of petticoats to Richmond; and dined there! ! Oh what a lovely day it was in those parts." [23] And at the end of March, in order to immerse himself more completely in his story, he withdrew to Cobley's Farm, a lonely retreat at Finchley, five miles north of the Regent's Park, from which he revisited London only at intervals.[24]

Here he was joined by Forster, who had been ill in his chambers at Lincoln's Inn Fields, and the two men talked about *Martin Chuzzlewit* as they strolled in the green lanes.[25] While he was at Finchley, Dickens conceived the character of Sairey Gamp. During this time a lady who lived with Miss Coutts as her friend and companion, a Miss Hannah Meredith, had a serious illness and was under the care of a nurse whose oddities were communicated to Dickens. From this person he derived Mrs. Gamp's yellow nightcap, her habit of rubbing her nose along the top of the fender and supping up vinegar with a knife, her addiction to snuff and to tilting the bottle on the "chimley piece" when she felt "so dispoged," although her legendary friend Mrs. Harris seems to have been Dickens's own inspired addition.[26]

Despite the fact, however, that *Martin Chuzzlewit* was indeed, as Dickens himself said, "in a hundred points immeasurably the best" of the novels he had yet written,[27] sales were not going well. *Pickwick* and *Nickleby* had sold forty and fifty thousand; *The Old Curiosity Shop* had gone as high as one hundred thousand; but the sales of *Chuzzlewit* fell to little over twenty thousand.[28] What was wrong? A conference was held at Chapman and Hall's. Forster believed the public had got used to Dickens in weekly installments and didn't care to wait so long as a month to continue the story. But the mode of publication could hardly be changed now. Somebody else thought, possibly with some truth, that during the year in which there had been no story from him he had lost his conspicuous position in the public eye.[29] Any great popular reputation, however, is subject to lulls too capricious for explanation. But something clearly had to be done, and at the end of the fifth number Dickens had Martin announce that he'd "go to America." [30]

The success of *American Notes* was partly responsible for this decision.[31] It seemed likely that there was an audience for sharp comment on America. And with the uproar still going on in America, that was just what Dickens felt inclined to write. The polite restraints he had imposed on himself in that book had left him with a seething head of steam not yet blown off. Every post brought him scurrilous letters and marked copies of abusive articles in American periodicals which went into the fire unread.[32] He had abstained since 1838 from reading comments on himself, but he knew enough from general report to be aware of what these anonymous communications would be like. "I have a strong spice of the Devil in me," he wrote; "and when I am assailed, as I think falsely or unjustly, my red hot anger carries me through it bravely . . ." [33] It did more than that. Even as tongued by rumor, it aroused the old determination to say all over again what had been objected to, and say it with redoubled violence.

*   *   *   *   *

A more cheerful note at this time was a visit from Captain Hewett, of the *Britannia,* whom Dickens put up in Devonshire Terrace and took around to see the lions of London. In the morning the Captain would be called for by "other mahogany-faced men" and borne off to the docks, "whence he always returned late at night, with rum-and-water tear-drops in his eyes, and a complication of punchy smells in his mouth." He had "marvellous ways of tying his pocket-handkerchief round his neck at dinner-time in a sort of jolly embarrassment, and then forgetting what he had done with it; also of singing songs to wrong tunes, and calling land objects by sea names, and never knowing what o'clock it was . . ." [34]

In May, "good old John Black" was retired from the *Chronicle,* where he had served as editor for thirty years. Black was only sixty, but his enforced resignation was one of Sir John Easthope's typically peremptory acts. It aroused Dickens's indignation. "I am deeply grieved about Black," he wrote Forster. "Sorry from my heart's core." [35] With Albany Fonblanque Dickens planned a dinner to show their esteem, asking Professor Wilson to be among the guests, as one who could "carry an old Scotchman home again by one sound of your voice." [36] The dinner was postponed from May 20th because some negotiations were pending between Black and Easthope, and such a testimonial, "however private and friendly," Dickens said, "might give offense to the latter Potentate, whose sickly soul was cradled in the Stock Exchange." [37] Later it took place at Greenwich, where Thackeray, Forster, Southwood Smith, Macready, Maclise, and a group of Black's fellow journalists were among those united to do him honor.[38]

Another dinner was that of the Deaf and Dumb Provident Society, which Dr. Samuel Gridley Howe had come all the way from Boston to attend.[39] The preceding fall Dr. Howe had married Julia Ward,[40] and he brought his bride with him. At the Dickens dinner table the young wife, to Dickens's vast amusement, addressed her husband as "darling," an endearment then seldom used except in private. Dickens flung himself back in such an explosion of amusement that his chair fell over, depositing him on the floor, partly under the table, waving his legs in the air, laughing and gasping, "Did she call him darling?" [41]

Meanwhile, the device of taking Martin across the Atlantic had admirably succeeded in rousing the Americans to fury. "All Yankee-Doodle-dum," wrote Carlyle, blazed "up like one universal soda bottle," [42] and Dickens told Forster "that Martin has made them all stark staring raving mad across the water." [43] On the stage of a New York theater, to the savage delight of the audience, a copy of the book was destroyed by being thrown into the witches' cauldron in a burlesque of *Macbeth*. Readers in England, naturally, were amused. "You must settle it with the Americans as you can," Sydney Smith wrote Dickens. "I have only to testify to the humour and power of description." [44]

The enjoyment his American caricatures gave English readers forced up the sales, however, only by another three thousand.[45] And that discouraging fact had serious consequences. The agreement of September, 1841, contained a proviso that in the improbable event of the profits being insufficient to repay the advances Chapman and Hall had made Dickens throughout 1842 they might, after the first five numbers, deduct £50 monthly out of the £200 he was being paid.[46] Forster had objected to this detail at the time, but Hall had defended it as mere lawyer's verbiage that would never "be needed." "Mr. Dickens need have no concern on that score." And unfortunately Forster had let the matter drop.[47]

One June afternoon Dickens turned up in the Strand to superintend some detail in the number where Mrs. Gamp made her first appearance. And, worrying out loud, William Hall was so indiscreet as to refer to the disappointing sales. Worse yet, by a luckless slip of the tongue, he added that he hoped they would not have to put the repayment clause into effect.[48] It is unlikely that Hall would have advanced this "inconsiderate hint" as a deliberate judgment, even more unlikely that the partners would have insisted upon it. Hall was "a kind well-disposed man," [49] and a shrewd one; he simply let a half-digested thought escape him. But the effect was disastrous. "Dickens promptly went through at least two ceilings, the roof, and well into mid-air." [50] Flinging out of the office, he fumed home, blowing poor Hall's blunder up to gigantic proportions. "Publishers," commented Forster dryly, "are bitter bad judges of an author." [51]

"I am so irritated," Dickens wrote on the 28th, "so rubbed in the tenderest part of my eyelids with bay-salt, by what I told you yesterday that a wrong kind of fire is burning in my head, and I don't think I *can* write." [52] "The scaly-headed vultures might be within their strictly legal rights," [53] but when he remembered that they owed everything to him, that his writings had transformed them from petty booksellers to one of the richest and most influential publishing houses in London, his blood boiled as in a furnace. Before this he had received proposals from Bradbury and Evans urging that Dickens consider them if he ever thought of altering his plans. He would see what they had to offer before approaching anybody else. "A printer is better than a bookseller, and it is quite as much the interest of one (if not more) to join me. But whoever it is, or whatever, I am bent upon paying Chapman and Hall *down*. And when I have done that, Mr. Hall shall have a piece of my mind." [54]

Forster sympathized, but he counseled reflection. He prevailed upon Dickens to defer action until he came back from Broadstairs in October. Meanwhile Forster would sound Bradbury and Evans, as Dickens desired.[55] Forster was in a difficult position, for he was not only Dickens's friend but literary adviser to Chapman and Hall.[56] However, there was no real conflict, for it was clearly to Dickens's advantage to take no precipitate steps. Dickens forced himself back to his writing table again and was presently "working like a dragon." But Chapman and Hall must have had some intimation of his temperature; the £50 poor little Hall had only worried about must, Dickens fiercely insisted, and from this very moment, be deducted from his monthly payments. "I will not exceed by sixpence the reduced mouths of C. and H." This involved a financial pinch, for many expenses were crowding on him all at once, and he did not like to overdraw his bank account at Coutts's when Miss Coutts was "exerting herself in behalf of Alfred." He consequently asked Mitton to obtain £70 from *his* banker until September, when Dickens would repay it with interest.[57]

But his resentment gradually subsided. In Yorkshire, where he and

Kate visited the Smithsons in July, he rambled through the green woods and cantered over moss and turf so soft "that the horses' feet scarcely made a sound." The Smithsons were "the jolliest of the jolly, keeping a big old country house, with an ale cellar something larger than a reasonable church . . . Just the place for you, Felton! We performed some madnesses there in the way of forfeits, picnics, rustic games, inspections of ancient monasteries at midnight, when the moon was shining, that would have gone to your heart, and as Mr. Weller says, 'come out on the other side.' " [58]

During this same visit Dickens wrote to Forster: "Tell me what you think of Mrs. Gamp? You'll not find it easy to get through hundreds of misprints in her conversation, but I want your opinion at once. . . . I mean to make a mark with her." [59] And to Beard, who had been ill, Dickens insisted that he must spend no less than "eight undisturbed weeks" with them at Broadstairs. "The bedroom you had last year is ready for you. The bathing machine beckons with its wooden finger, and cocks its preposterous eye on the sands. . . . Forster asserts with dignified emphasis that 'it is the very sort of thing, my dear boy, that Beard requires to set him on his legs.' Timber makes himself as unlike a dog as possible, in confirmation of these sentiments." [60]

In London for a few weeks before proceeding down to Broadstairs, Dickens plunged into the task of raising money to help the children of Edward Elton, an actor drowned when the *Pegasus* went down in the Irish Sea. "He was a struggling man through his whole existence," Dickens wrote Miss Coutts, "always very poor, and never extravagant. His wife died mad, three years ago, and he was left a widower with seven children—who were expecting his knock at the door, when a friend arrived with the terrible news of his Death." [61] Miss Coutts responded at once in a "noble letter," [62] and so did scores of others. Dickens arranged a benefit performance of *Hamlet* at the Haymarket, to which Macready and other actors donated their services. Poor Tom Hood, who had no money to give, wrote a moving elegiac poem which Mrs. Warner, one of the actresses, recited from the stage.[63] From these and other sources well over a thousand pounds was raised, and subscriptions continued to pour in for a fund of which Dickens became one of the three trustees.[64]

Broadstairs was bright and beautiful as always. This year, though, there was a piano next door, close to the very bay window in which

Dickens wrote; and when he took refuge on the other side of the house, that turned out to look "into a street where the 'Flies' stand, and where there are donkeys and drivers out of number" making a noise almost as bad as the piano.[65] But it was not only the donkeys and the piano that disturbed him. The bay-salt of his irritation with Chapman and Hall still stung his eyelids, and he struggled furiously to subdue these fits of spleen, striding fiercely for hours along the cliffs with a seething intensity that disturbed both his work and his rest. "I performed an insane match against time," he wrote Forster, "of eighteen miles by the milestones in four hours and a half, under a burning sun the whole way. I could get no sleep at night, and really began to be afraid I was going to have a fever. You may judge in what kind of authorship-training I am today. I could as soon eat the cliffs as write about anything." [66]

A few days later he regained his spirits with a rush as he described the little village and its summer routine to Felton. "Seven miles out are the Goodwin Sands . . . whence floating lights perpetually wink after dark, as if they were carrying on intrigues with the servants. . . . Under the cliffs are rare good sands, where all the children assemble every morning and throw up impossible fortifications, which the sea throws down again at high water. Old gentlemen and ancient ladies flirt after their own manner in two reading-rooms and on a great many scattered seats in the open air. . . . In a bay-window in a one-pair sits, from 9 o'clock to 1, a gentleman with rather long hair and no neck-cloth, who writes and grins as if he thought he were very funny indeed. . . . At one he disappears, and presently emerges from a bathing-machine, and may be seen—a kind of salmon-coloured porpoise—splashing about in the ocean. After that he may be seen in another bay-window on the ground-floor, eating a strong lunch—after that, walking a dozen miles or so, or lying on his back in the sand reading a book. . . . He's as brown as a berry, and they *do* say is a small fortune to the inn-keeper who sells beer and cold punch. But this is mere rumour. Sometimes he goes up to London (eighty miles, or so, away), and then I'm told there is a sound in Lincoln's Inn Fields at night, as of men laughing together with a clinking of knives and forks and wineglasses." [67]

Longfellow had sent news on which Dickens commented in this letter. "And so Longfellow is married. I remember *her* well, and could draw her portrait, in words to the life. A very beautiful and gentle creature, and a proper love for a poet. My cordial remembrances and congratulations. Do they live in the house where we breakfasted?" "Our domestic news is slight, but portentous. Coming events cast their shadows before. I have visions of a fifth child . . ." [68]

Toward the close of August, Dickens went up to London to attend a farewell to Macready, who was going on a theatrical tour in America. There was a splendid dinner at the Star and Garter at Richmond, and Dickens proposed the only toast, Macready's health, in words so moving that Macready could hardly speak for tears.[69] It was planned that Dickens, Forster, Maclise, and Stanfield should accompany Macready to Liverpool when he sailed on September 5th, and bring his wife home from their leave-taking.[70] Forster, however, felt that it might injure Macready's prospects if any of the numerous Americans sailing at the same time were to spread the rumor that Dickens was among those who went to see him off.[71] Captain Marryat, to whom Stanfield chanced to mention the project, emphatically confirmed Forster by writing Dickens a letter imploring him not to go.

"If I were to go on board with him," Dickens admitted to Forster, "I have not the least doubt that the fact would be placarded all over New York before he had shaved himself in Boston." Thousands of men in America "would pick a quarrel with him on the mere statement of his being my friend." Although Forster had been the first one to raise the issue, he now thought Marryat and Dickens were hysterically exaggerating. Dickens insisted that this was not so. "You have only doubted Marryat because it is impossible for *any man* to know what they are in their own country, who has not seen them there." [72] Dickens therefore wrote Macready:

"So strongly have I felt that my accompanying you on board, would be, after the last Chuzzlewit, *fatal* to your success, and certain to bring down upon you every species of insult and outrage, that I have all along determined within myself to remain in the Hotel, and charge the Landlord to keep my being there, a secret." Marryat's urgent plea had strengthened this resolve into a determination not to leave London. "If you but knew one hundredth part of the malignity, the monstrous falsehood, the beastly attacks even upon Catherine, which were published all over America, even while I was there, on my mere confession that the country had disappointed me—confessions wrung from me in private society before I had written a word upon the people—you would question all this as little as I do." He begged Macready never, while he was in America, to mention their being friends, not even to write him, except by enclosures in letters to others. And in a postscript, "I wish to Heaven," Dickens groaned, "I could un-dedicate Nickleby until you come home again." [73]

Hard upon the receipt of this letter in Clarence Terrace came Dickens himself for a final shake of Macready's hand,[74] and then returned to Broadstairs for the remainder of the month. Here he pegged away "tooth and nail at Chuzzlewit." [75] "It gives me great pleasure," he wrote Marryat, "to find that you like the tickling." Despite the fury of the Americans, he intended before he had done to go in again "and give the eagle a final poke under the fifth rib." [76]

*   *   *   *   *

No sooner had Dickens returned to London than he hurried up to Manchester, where at a meeting of the Athenaeum he sat on the platform with Disraeli and Cobden.[77] It was inspiring to see this institution, he told his audience, with its lectures, its opportunities for bodily exercise and rational enjoyment, and know that amid clanking engines and whirling machinery the mind was not forgotten. He had no patience with the maxim that "a little knowledge is a dangerous thing." A little hanging was once considered a dangerous thing, "with this difference, that, because a little hanging was dangerous, we had a great deal of it; and, because a little knowledge was dangerous, we were to have none at all." And recalling the jails and criminal dives he had visited with Longfellow and many times since then, he confessed his heart died within him to see how thousands were condemned to walk a path "of jagged flints and stones, laid down by brutal ignorance, and held together, like the solid rocks, by years of this most wicked axiom." [78]

In the course of these roamings through the slums Dickens had seen the Ragged Schools conducted in some of them by earnest workers.[79] Founded some twenty years before by a shoemaker and a chimney sweep, these volunteer institutions for giving free instruction to poor children had been slowly spreading throughout the country.[80] In the unsavory neighborhood of Field Lane, Holborn, subjected to raids from young hoodlums who pelted the teachers with filth

and smashed the furniture, one of these schools was under the guidance
of a lawyer's clerk named Samuel Starey. This young man appealed to
Miss Coutts for support, and in response to her request Dickens had
arranged to visit the school.[81] Deeply moved and excited by the experience, he wrote her a long letter praising the work it did.[82]

Located among the very scenes described in *Oliver Twist*, the
school, he said, was "an awful sight." It was "held in three most
wretched rooms on the first floor of a rotten house: every plank, and
timber, and brick, and lath, and piece of plaster in which shakes as you
walk. One room is devoted to the girls; two to the boys. The former are
much the better-looking—I cannot say better dressed, for there is no
such thing as dress among the seventy pupils; certainly not the elements of a whole suit of clothes, among them all. I have very seldom
seen, in all the strange and dreadful things I have seen in London and
elsewhere, anything so shocking as the dire neglect of soul and body
exhibited among these children. And although I know; and am as
sure as it is possible for one to be of anything which has not happened,
that in the prodigious misery and ignorance of the swarming masses
of mankind in England, the seeds of its certain ruin are sown, I never
saw that Truth so staring out in hopeless characters, as it does from
the walls of this place. The children in the Jails are almost as common
sights to me as my own; but these are worse, for they have not yet
arrived there, but are as plainly and as certainly traveling there, as
they are to their graves.

"The Masters are extremely quiet, honest, good men. You may
suppose they are, to be there at all. It is enough to break one's heart
to get at the place: to say nothing of getting at the children's minds
afterwards. They are well-grounded in the Scotch—the Glasgow—
system of elementary instruction, which is an excellent one; and they
try to reach the boys by kindness. To gain their attention in any way,
is a difficulty, quite gigantic. To impress them, even with the idea
of a God, when their own condition is so desolate, becomes a monstrous task. To find anything within them—who know nothing of affection, care, love, or kindness of any sort—to which it is possible to
appeal, is, at first, like a search for the philosopher's stone. . . .

"The Masters examined them, however, on these points, and they
answered very well—sometimes in a shout all at once, sometimes
only one boy, sometimes half a dozen. I put a great many questions

to them upon their answers which they all answered very well. There was one boy, who had been selling Lucifer matches all day in the street—not much older than Charley—clad in a bit of a sack—really a clever child, and handsome too, who gave some excellent replies, though, of course, in language that would be very strange to your ears. Hardly any of them can read yet. For the Masters think it most important to impress them at first with some distinction (communicated in dialogue) between right and wrong, and I quite agree with them. They sell trifles in the streets, or beg (or some, I dare say, steal) all day; and coming tired to this place at night, are very slow to pick up any knowledge. That they *do* come at all, is *I* think, a Victory. . . .

"I am happy to say I afforded great amusement at first—in particular by having a pair of white trousers on, and very bright boots. The latter articles of dress gave immense satisfaction, and were loudly laughed at. Mr. Stanfield, who was with me,—in consequence of looking rather burly and fat in the small room—was received with a perfect cheer; and his sudden retirement in consequence of being overcome by the closeness of the atmosphere, and the dread of Typhus Fever, was much regretted. When they saw that I was quite serious, and had an interest in their answers, they became quiet, and took pains. They were still better-behaved on seeing that I stood with my hat off, before the Master (though I heard one boy express his opinion that I certainly wasn't a barber, or I should have cut my hair); and so far as their behaviour is concerned, I should not have the least doubt of my ability or that of anybody else who went the right way to work—to reduce them to order in five minutes at any time.

"The school is miserably poor, you may believe, and is almost entirely supported by the teachers themselves. If they could get a better room (the house they are in, is like an ugly dream); above all, if they could provide some convenience for washing; it would be an immense advantage. The moral courage of the teachers is beyond all praise. They are surrounded by every possible adversity, and every disheartening circumstance that can be imagined. Their office is worthy of the apostles.

"My heart so sinks within me when I go into these scenes, that I almost lose the hope of ever seeing them changed. Whether this effort will succeed, it is quite impossible to say. But that it is a great one, beginning at the right end, among thousands of immortal crea-

tures, who cannot, in their present state, be held accountable for
what they do, it is *as* impossible to doubt. That it is much too squalid
and terrible to meet with any wide encouragement, I greatly fear.
There is a kind of delicacy which is not at all shocked by the existence
of such things, but is excessively shocked to know of them; and I am
afraid it will shut its eyes on Ragged Schools until the Ragged Scholars
are perfect in their learning out of doors, when woe to whole garments.

"I need not say, I am sure, that I deem it an experiment most worthy
of your charitable hand. The reasons I have, for doubting its being
generally assisted, all assure me that it will have an interest for you.
For I know you to be very, very far-removed from all the Givers in all
the Court Guides between this, and China."

Dickens's mind immediately busied himself with plans for improving the institution. It needed larger and more satisfactory quarters.
Did Starey, he asked, know of "any one or two good spacious lofts of
rooms" in the neighborhood, and at what charge they could be rented?
The poor little dirty youngsters needed, as his letter to Miss Coutts
pointed out, some means of washing themselves before beginning
their tasks. Would Starey find out how much it would cost to install a
large trough or sink, with a good supply of running water, soap, and
towels? [83] All these ideas Dickens communicated to Miss Coutts in
"a sledge-hammer account." She wrote back to ask "what the rent of
some large airy premises would be, and what the expense of erecting
a regular bathing or purifying place." "I have no doubt," Dickens told
Forster, "she will do whatever I ask her in the matter. She is a most
excellent creature, I protest to God, and I have a most perfect affection and respect for her." [84]

For the *Edinburgh Review*, Dickens offered to write a description
of the Ragged Schools. If he did so, he told Macvey Napier, the editor,
he would have "to come out strongly against any system of education
based exclusively on the principles of the Established Church." For
"the dangerous classes of society," people "in a state so miserable and
so neglected, that their very nature rebels against the simplest religion," "mysteries and squabbles for forms *must* give way" to broad instruction in religious principles so general "as to include all creeds." It
was an absurd irrelevance for well-meaning ladies to ask theological
questions about the "Lamb of God" of youngsters who did not know
the meaning of honesty.[85] Napier accepted the offer, but hinted cau-

tiously that it seemed to him "bad policy to hit the church unneces-sarily in any tender place"; and Dickens agreed not to do so.[86] Confu-sions arose, however, about the date when the article should be delivered, and by the time they were straightened out Dickens was too busy in other work to write it.[87]

The dislike of theological dogma Dickens voiced in this exchange of letters was one that had been growing upon him steadily. Though he had been brought up in the Church of England, his family were not devout, and his heart did not warm to the conventionally pious. His antagonism to the evangelical churches and their shepherds emerges clearly in *Sunday Under Three Heads*, *Pickwick*, and Kit's sentiments on his mother's chapel-going in *The Old Curiosity Shop*. Dickens had been interested to find that many of his American friends in Cam-bridge and Boston belonged, as Forster did, to the Unitarian faith.[88] Dickens did not believe in the virgin birth of Christ, and was able to sympathize with the leading features of the Unitarian creed, which his friend W. J. Fox stated as "Belief in the supremacy of God the Father, and in the humanity and divine mission of Jesus of Nazareth." [89] After his return from America, for a few Sundays Dickens attended services in Essex Street Chapel under the Reverend Thomas Madge. In No-vember of that year he had heard the Reverend Edward Tagart preach a funeral service on Dr. Channing at the chapel in Little Portland Street, the leading West End place of worship of the Unitarians. Soon after, Dickens took sittings in the chapel and inaugurated a lasting friendship with Tagart.[90]

The task that prevented Dickens's writing the Ragged School ar-ticle for the *Edinburgh Review* was a tale that came to be called *A Christmas Carol*. Something about "the bright eyes and beaming faces" [91] on which he looked down at the Manchester Athenaeum had given him the inspiration for a cheerful, glowing, heart-moving story in which he would appeal to all of people's warmest feelings. But the story also had other and more immediately practical reasons for being written.

For, although *Martin Chuzzlewit* had "forced itself up in people's opinion," [92] it had not forced itself up in sales. And Bradbury and Evans, though they had invited a proposition from Dickens, were rather alarmed, when Forster sounded them on the subject, by the magnitude of the undertaking they had suggested.[93] From them there emanated only the disappointing notion of bringing out a cheap edition of the works already published and establishing a new magazine edited by Dickens.

"I am afraid of a magazine—just now," Dickens wrote Forster. "I don't think the time a good one, or the chances favourable. I am afraid of putting myself before the town as writing tooth and nail for bread, headlong, after the close of a book taking so much out of one as Chuzzlewit. I am afraid I could not do it, with justice to myself. I know that whatever we may say at first, a new magazine, or a new anything, would require so much propping, that I should be *forced* (as in the Clock) to put myself into it, in my old shape." [94]

In addition to this, he feared that the idea of a cheap edition of the books was premature. "I am sure if it took place yet awhile, it would damage me and damage the property, *enormously*. It is very natural in them to want it; but, since they do want it, I have no faith in their regarding me in any other respect than they would regard any other man in a speculation. I see that this is really your opinion as well; and I don't see what I gain, in such a case, by leaving Chapman and Hall." [95]

What he would really like to do was to "fade away from the public eye for a year, and enlarge my stock of description and observation by seeing countries new to me." If he had made money by *Martin Chuzzlewit*, this is what he would have done. But he thought he could do it anyway. "At the close of Chuzzlewit (by which time the debt will have been materially reduced)," he would draw all his share of the profits from Chapman and Hall and tell them that he would make no new arrangements for a year. Then he would let Devonshire Terrace, and go abroad to some cheap place in Normandy or Brittany, and later on travel in France and Italy. Perhaps, while he was turning over the new book he had in mind, he would write letters that would make another travel book, as he had in America. He had been taking lessons in Italian, and could perfect his knowledge of the language in Italy. He could live twice as cheaply as at home, and finance the entire year without binding himself to anyone, simply by giving as security one of his £5,000 insurance policies.[96]

Forster was startled, and inclined to attribute the scheme to that restlessness he had seen growing in Dickens recently.[97] But Dickens returned to the idea vehemently. This project of foreign travel had

got into his head "MONTHS AGO." Forster had seen Dickens working for eight years without leaving off, and thought two or three
months' rest would be enough. But Dickens insisted it was not enough.
"It is impossible to go on working the brain to that extent for ever."
"What would poor Scott have given to have gone abroad, of his own
free will, a young man, instead of creeping there, a driveller, in his
miserable decay!" [98] Forster must, consequently, look upon the project
"*as a settled thing*," and Chapman and Hall must be told. "If you
object to see them, I must write to them." [99]

This last Forster made Dickens defer doing on tactical grounds.
Chapman and Hall were publishing the *Christmas Carol* on commission for Dickens; the announcement that Dickens was quitting
them at such a time would foolishly jeopardize the little book's
chances. Its profits might help to meet some of those endless financial
demands by which his family harassed him. Added to his own domestic expenses, they were a serious drain, which he felt with increasing bitterness.[100] Worried by one of these in November, Forster says,
Dickens was quite put out of his work, and then blazed away until
nine o'clock that night to make up, stopping only ten minutes for his
dinner.[101] And the very next day there was another and worse repetition of precisely the same trouble.[102] Oh, to be abroad beyond the
reach of such daily exasperations! "I am quite serious and sober
when I say, that I have very grave thoughts of keeping my whole
menagerie in Italy, three years." [103]

*   *   *   *   *

Nevertheless, in the midst of these irritations, worries, and distractions, and even as "Chuzzlewit agonies" made their unending demands upon him, he felt his power more than ever, and threw himself
with intensity into the writing of his *Christmas Carol*. Though he had
not begun it until a week after his return from Manchester early in
October, the little book established over him a strange mastery that
drove it on to completion before the end of November.[104] None of his
stories did he more utterly live as it poured itself out of him. Over it,
he said, he "wept and laughed, and wept again, and excited himself in
a most extraordinary manner in the composition; and thinking
whereof he walked about the black streets of London fifteen and
twenty miles many a night when all sober folks had gone to bed." [105]

The *Carol* was certainly intended to relieve Dickens of some of his monetary difficulties, and to this end he had insisted upon its being sold at five shillings, to encourage the largest possible number of purchasers. But at the same time, the manuscript, scored with corrections and deletions, and with entire redrafts of many pages, to a degree unusual with Dickens at this stage in his career, shows the loving care with which the book was composed. And although Chapman and Hall were publishing it on commission, with Dickens paying all the costs of publication, he insisted on an elaborate and expensive format, with gilt edges, colored end papers, a title page printed in blue and red, and four hand-colored plates by John Leech. Mercenary hopes were far from dominating the production of the book.[106]

When it was done at last, as Dickens said, he "broke out like a madman." During the Christmas season his spirits demanded a release. "Forster is out again," he wrote Felton; "and if he don't go in again, after the manner in which we have been keeping Christmas, he must be very strong indeed. Such dinings, such dancings, such conjurings, such blind-man's-buffings, such theatre-goings, such kissings-out of old years and kissings-in of new ones never took place in these parts before. . . . And if you could have seen me at a children's party at Macready's the other night, going down a country dance with Mrs. M., you would have thought I was a country gentleman of independent property, residing on a tiptop farm, with the wind blowing straight in my face every day." [107]

"Good God, how we missed you," he wrote Macready, "talked of you, drank your health, and wondered what you were doing! Perhaps you are Falkland enough . . . to feel rather sore—just a little bit, you know, the merest trifle in the world—on hearing that Mrs. Macready looked brilliant, blooming, young, and handsome, and that she danced a country dance with the writer hereof (Acres to your Falkland). . . . Now you don't like to be told that? Nor do you quite like to hear that Forster and I conjured bravely, that a plum-pudding was produced from an empty saucepan, held over a blazing fire kindled in Stanfield's hat without damage to the lining; that a box of bran was changed into a live guinea-pig, which ran between my godchild's feet, and was the cause of such a shrill uproar and clapping of hands that you might have heard it (and I daresay did) in America . . ." [108]

Jane Welsh Carlyle bore testimony to the mad hilarity of this party.

"Dickens and Forster," she said, "above all exerted themselves till the
perspiration was pouring down and they seemed *drunk* with their
efforts. Only think of that excellent Dickens playing the *conjuror* for
one whole hour—the *best* conjuror I ever saw . . . Then the dancing
. . . the gigantic Thackeray &c &c all capering like *Maenades*!! . . .
after supper when we were all madder than ever with the pulling of
crackers, the drinking of champagne, and the making of speeches; a
universal country dance was proposed—and Forster *seizing me round
the waist*, whirled me into the thick of it, and *made* me dance!! like
a person in the tread-mill who must move forward or be crushed to
death! Once I cried out, 'Oh for the love of Heaven let me go! you are
going to dash my brains out against the folding doors!' 'Your *brains*!!'
he answered, 'who cares about their brains *here*? Let *them* go!' "

By midnight the scene was rising, the delirious Jane said, "to something not unlike the *rape of the Sabines*!" Dickens took Thackeray
and Forster home with him " '*to finish the night there*' and a *royal*
night they would have of it I fancy!" All in all, Jane Carlyle doubted
that "there was as much witty speech uttered in all the aristocratic,
conventional drawing rooms thro' out London that night as among
us little knot of blackguardist literary people who felt ourselves above
all rules, and independent of the universe!" Truly, "the pleasantest
company . . . *are* the *blackguards*!" [109]

CHAPTER TWO

Selfishness and the Economic Man

CRITICISM: *Martin Chuzzlewit*
and *A Christmas Carol*

"I FEEL my power now," Dickens wrote Forster in November, 1843, "more than I ever did." [1] It was no idle boast, despite the fact that *Martin Chuzzlewit* still lagged disappointingly in sales. His imaginative energy had never been more electric. New characters swarmed from his mind with a profusion and variety surpassing his achievement in any book since *Pickwick*. Towering above the rest are those two marvelous feats of satiric creation, the bland and unctuous Pecksniff, with his moral throat smooth between its celestial wings of collar, and the bulging Mrs. Gamp, fusty, snuffy, smelling of spirits, and overflowingly garrulous. Surrounding these crowd all the others—grasping old Anthony Chuzzlewit and his brutal son Jonas, the raffishly leering Montague Tigg, Mark Tapley with his eagerness to "come out strong," Betsey Prig, pretty little Ruth Pinch, and the denizens of Todgers's commercial Boarding House—impudent and swaggering young Bailey junior, Mrs. Todgers immersed in the anxieties of gravy, Mr. Jinkins, the oldest boarder, the oppressed and unhappy Moddle, literally dozens more. And when, on a spur-of-the-moment decision, Dickens sweeps young Martin off to America, he exuberantly brings into being an entire additional gallery of brilliantly drawn figures. In sheer fertility of invention *Martin Chuzzlewit* almost constitutes a world in itself.

Nor is this enormous cast of characters a random assemblage only loosely connected by mechanical ingenuities of plot. With the exception of the rather digressive American episodes (and a little special pleading might bring even them into the pattern), all the characters are linked by their relationship to the theme of selfishness. In a curious way this rendition of a generalized vice gives *Martin Chuzzlewit* affinities with novels otherwise so different as George Meredith's *The Egoist* and Jane Austen's *Pride and Prejudice*. Dickens has none of Meredith's ornately coruscating style and labyrinthine intricacy of analysis, of course, and none of his wire-drawn wit; he is determined to be clear to the common reader, and though he is witty, his wit is not that of the poisoned needle but the sword. He has none of Jane Austen's amused detachment; his feelings about his characters are undisguisedly partisan. But his exposure of selfishness is as sharp, if not as subtle, as Meredith's dissection of egoism, and his method is identical with Jane Austen's, whose characters are all mutations on pride and prejudice.

In this vast series of multiple perspectives on selfishness, what a panorama *Martin Chuzzlewit* extends before us!—Young Martin, thoughtless and self-indulgent, youthfully defying his grandfather in pure obstinacy; old Martin, domineering and distrustful, seeing selfishness in others everywhere; all the other Chuzzlewits and Spottletoes snarling savagely in their rival hopes for the old man's fortune. Pecksniff oozes hypocritical eloquence while he exploits his pupils and weeps tears of pious joy as he marries off his daughter Merry to the ruffianly Jonas; Cherry is sharp-nosed with jealous fury at the sister for whom she has been slighted, and Merry flippantly and shallowly amuses herself by tormenting the lover who secretly swears to revenge himself when they are married. Old Anthony Chuzzlewit, deliberately inculcating in his son the ugliest rapacity, comes to realize that Jonas is capable of trying to hasten his own father's death. And finally, in deliberate contrast to all these, there are Mark Tapley's humorous and cheerful generosity, the kindliness of Mrs. Lupin, the loving simplicity of Ruth Pinch, and her brother Tom's unsuspicious purity of heart.

Both in structure and in vividness of character portrayal, *Martin Chuzzlewit* reveals Dickens in the fullness of his powers. Nevertheless, although not an absolute failure with the public, it met with the poorest reception of any of his novels. Nor is the reason hard to find. Dickens had returned from America with a grimmer gaze for human shortcomings than he had taken there. His very opening chapter establishes an atmosphere of harsh jeering, and throughout the first half of the book there is little of the genial warmth, the playful high spirits, the affectionate comedy, that had previously mellowed even the bitterest of Dickens's satire. The comedy, though plentiful, is subacid; the characters are sharply observed, but drawn for the most part with a soiled and grimy realism that makes them predominantly unattractive. Power the opening certainly has, but of a biting quality that temporarily submerges the glow Dickens's readers desired to find.

The few amiable characters play but a slight part in the beginning of the story and fail to arouse much sympathy. We have no more than brief early glimpses of the kindly Mrs. Lupin and the cheerfully generous Mark Tapley. Old Martin Chuzzlewit's protégée Mary Graham remains a mere cipher like Madeline Bray. Tom Pinch seems for a long while only a foolish puppet duped and imposed upon by Pecksniff. The departing pupil, John Westlock, who displays some sense and force, appears and then promptly disappears. Almost all the other characters are repulsive and unsavory, as if they had been rummaged out of a gritty dustbin. Momentarily Dickens seems in no mood for the joyful excess that gleamed in Bumble's fat-witted pomposity and made Sampson Brass preposterous even in his servile nastiness. And, although filled with fun and relish, the very hilarity with which Dickens elaborates that prodigious caricature Pecksniff is strongly tinged with astringency. The dominant tone of all the earlier part of the story is set by the acrimonious wranglings of the Chuzzlewit clan, Pecksniff's mellifluous and hypocritical moralizing, and old Martin's bitterness as he crouches in bed, peering suspiciously over his shoulder.

The same tart flavor is sharpened in the American episodes. The scurrilous howlings aroused across the Atlantic by his *American Notes* irritated in Dickens a defiant truculence that never slept without keeping one eye open, and he sprang exultantly into battle. If the filthily slanderous American press resented the polite criticisms to which he had previously restrained himself, let them see what a mauling he could inflict when he really set his mind to it! The Jefferson Bricks and LaFayette Kettles were forever twisting the British Lion's tail; by the time Charles Dickens had finished, the American Eagle should be a bedraggled bird. Fierce as Dickens had been in his onslaughts upon Bumble's workhouse and Dotheboys Hall, he had never been so controversially clever, so challengingly witty, so pugnaciously cutting as in these American scenes.

His own enjoyment in exercising this startling brilliance may, in-

deed, have led him to indulge it to a greater extent than was warranted
by the structural importance of the American interlude. It is not
strictly digressive; Martin has to be kept out of the way during the
development of his grandfather's plot against Pecksniff (just as, for
different reasons, Nicholas had to be away from London while Ralph
Nickleby used Kate as a decoy). And it is still more closely knit to the
scheme of the story by the fact that Martin's sufferings in Eden and
his grateful appreciation of Mark Tapley are needed to drive home his
awareness of his own conceit and self-absorption. Nevertheless,
throughout a large part of their American adventures the spotlight
slides away from Mark and Martin altogether and beats instead upon
America itself with a sharp satiric glare.

To complain, however, that this blaze of wit has little to do with its
setting is as if one were to quarrel at the irrelevance of a ten-acre dia-
mond blinding Tottenham Court Road with its glitter. Never had
Dickens's use of burlesque been more dazzling. Colonel Diver and
Mr. Jefferson Brick drinking the libations of freedom in blood; Mr.
LaFayette Kettle, General Choke, and the Honorable Elijah Pogram,
each "one of the most remarkable men in our country, sir"; [2] Zephaniah Scadder, with his one blank profile and his other grinning one;
Mrs. Hominy, "talking deep truths in a melodious snuffle"; [3] the
Watertoast Association of United Sympathizers; Hannibal Chollop,
flourishing his "ripper" and his "tickler" and gouging out people's
eyes, "a splendid example of our na-tive raw material, sir" [4]—what a
set of glorified freaks they are in a gigantic national circus! And how
annihilatingly they caricature the America of the 1840's in all its wild
boastfulness, illiteracy, and greed, its corruptions of politics, journalism, and business, and its intolerant resentment of the slightest
criticism!

Throughout page after page the farce never slackens. "Here's this
morning's New York Sewer!" cry the newsboys on the wharves. "Here's
the New York Keyhole Reporter! Here's the New York Rowdy Journal!" [5] And when Martin tells Colonel Diver he has never heard of
that famous war correspondent Jefferson Brick, "Keep cool, Jefferson," says the colonel, echoing the actual New York *Herald*, "Don't
bust!" [6] Hearing the Irish servant girl at Major Pawkins's boarding-
house speak of "the master," "Oh! The depressing institutions of that
British empire, colonel!" exclaims Brick. The word is never heard in

America, Colonel Diver explains, except when "used by some degraded Help" "new to the blessings of our form of government." "There are no masters here." "All 'owners,' are they?" retorts Martin.[7]

Mutilated slaves fit in grotesquely enough with such pretensions. But the only abolitionists Martin discovers during his American experiences, the genteel Norrises, ridicule the entire Negro people as an absurd and inferior part of creation. These same Norrises are also the only people of cultivation he finds. The two pretty Miss Norrises sing in German, French, Italian, Spanish, Portuguese, Swiss, "all languages —except their own." [8] (Learned readers have solemnly pointed out that Dickens made a slip in endowing the Swiss with a language of their own, overlooking the possibility that it may have been deliberate.) The Norrises enlarge upon the inestimable advantage of democracy in having "no noblemen but nature's noblemen," and simultaneously make exhilarated display of a large acquaintance among the British peerage.[9] Their friend General Fladdock, returning from abroad swollen with pride at the figure he has cut among the dukes and lords of these benighted countries, greets the family with enthusiasm. "And do I then," he cries, "once again behold the choicest spirits of my country!" "Yes," replies Mr. Norris modestly, "here we are, General." [10]

Americans everywhere are blandly sure they know more than Martin does himself about his native country. "When you say, sir," General Choke informs him, "that your Queen does not reside in the Tower of London, you fall into an error, not uncommon to your countrymen." [11] When Martin denies that the word "start" is unused in England, "You air mistaken, sir," is the decisive answer, "but we will not pursue the subject, lest it should awaken your prĕjŭ-dīce." [12] "Well, how's the unnat'ral old parent by this time?" an entire stranger says, asking for news of England, "Progressing back'ards, I expect, as usual?" [13] Mingled with such courtesies—and in men addicted to lynch law with a garnishing of tar and feathers—is a dogmatic conviction that British courts still invoke the stake, the block, the thumbscrew, and the rack.

The same infatuated conceit and ignorant pretentiousness are revealed in the floundering symposium in which the Honorable Elijah Pogram, the two Literary Ladies, and the Mother of the Modern Gracchi all wallow out of their intellectual depth, splashing transcendental nonsense into billows of words that they and their audience mistake for poetry and philosophy. "Mind and matter," one of these remarks, "glide swift into the vortex of immensity. Howls the sublime, and softly sleeps the calm Ideal, in the whispering chambers of Imagination. To hear it, sweet it is. But then outlaughs the stern philosopher, and saith to the Grotesque, 'What ho! arrest for me that Agency. Go, bring it here!' and so the vision fadeth." [14]

In such an atmosphere it is no wonder to find jingoism and bad manners pluming themselves on being the natural behavior of freedom and integrity. When Martin ventures to express distaste for an unusually ill-bred and belligerent specimen, the magniloquent reply assails him: "He is a true born child of this free hemisphere; bright and flowing as our mineral drinks; unspoiled by withering conventionalities as are our broad and boundless Perearers! Rough he may be. So are our Barrs. Wild he may be. So are our Buffaloes. But he is a child of nature, and a child of freedom, and his boastful answer to the Despot and the Tyrant is, that his bright home is in the Settin' Sun." [15]

What wonder, finally, that these rough diamonds everywhere display a fierce intolerance of criticism which they masquerade as freedom of speech. "We must be cracked-up, sir," the egregious Hannibal Chollop tells Mark Tapley in a tone of menace. "You are not now in A despotic land." "What, I speak too free, do I?" cries Mark. "I have know'd men Lynched for less," responds Chollop, "and beaten into punkin'-sarse for less, by an enlightened people. We are the intellect and virtue of the airth, the cream Of human natur', and the flower Of moral force. Our backs is easy ris. We must be cracked-up, or they rises, and we snarls." [16]

The wild burlesque of all this is executed with a cruel and comic gusto. It is completely external; it makes no endeavor to see its victims from within. Nothing ever gives us the faintest conception of what Major Pawkins or Dr. Ginery Dunkel or the Mother of the Modern Gracchi must seem like to themselves. It is satire that is not so much dissection as a massacre with a meat ax. The only American character delineated with any gentleness is the amiable Mr. Bevan of Massachusetts, and he is a mere blank designed mainly to show that there *are* Americans aware of the national deficiencies. "If another Juvenal or Swift," he says, "could rise up among us tomorrow, he would be hunted down." And, apologizing for the snobbery of his friends, the Norrises, "I dare say," he asks Martin pleadingly, "you might have such a scene as that in an English comedy, and not detect any gross improbability or anomaly in the matter of it?" "Yes indeed!" [17] Martin replies heartily. But Mr. Bevan rightly perceives that all these shortcomings are made more ridiculous by the high-flown American professions of republican superiority and free-born integrity.

Save for this gentleman, however, *Martin Chuzzlewit* has no hint of the virtues Dickens had praised in his letters and none of the warm commendations of *American Notes*. Its menagerie of grotesques paints only the vices and crudities in the loudest of colors. And yet its very omissions and distortions are vehicles of truth. America had, and has, nobler aspects than those Dickens derided; but it had, and has, the faults he found as well. The wincing and the howls of American readers only showed how every blow struck home. "A man is angry at a libel," G. K. Chesterton shrewdly remarks, "because it is false, but at a satire because it is true." [18]

Perhaps Americans today believe we have outgrown that gawky and raucous national adolescence to which Dickens held up such a devastating mirror, and can take the terrific walloping he inflicted on our forebears with a certain amused detachment. It may even be that during the intervening years native satirists have taught us to realize that some of the things Dickens saw are still true. Theodore Roosevelt certainly thought so: "Jefferson Brick and Elijah Pogram and Hannibal Chollop," he wrote his children, "are all real personifications of certain bad tendencies in American life, and I am continually thinking of and alluding to some newspaper editor or Senator or homicidal rowdy by one of these three names." [19]

Not much search is needed to find contemporary newspapers like the New York Rowdy Journal and journalists who might well write for the Keyhole Reporter. The Eden Land Corporation will not seem scandalously overdrawn to some of those who bought Florida real estate that high tide covered with water. Nor is Elijah Pogram more fantastic than McCarthy and the late Senator Bilbo, or Hannibal Chollop than those firebrand legislators who scream that freedom of speech is gagged unless they may talk to death every danger of their being defeated by majority vote. Does not Sinclair Lewis in *Babbitt* substantiate eighty years later the comment Dickens makes on the conversation of businessmen and politicians: "Whatever the chance contributions that fell into the slow cauldron of their talk, they made the gruel thick and slab with dollars. Men were weighed by their dollars, measures gauged by their dollars; life was auctioneered, appraised, put up, and knocked down for its dollars. . . . Make commerce one huge lie and mighty theft. Deface the banner of the nation for an idle rag; pollute it star by star; and cut out stripe by stripe as from the arm of a degraded soldier. Do anything for dollars!" [20]

* * * * *

If the reader still feels a trace of British "prĕjŭ-dīce" in Dickens's American scenes, it should be noted that he bestowed an even fiercer scorn on evils at home. He shows nothing in America to equal the frowzy and whining insolence of Chevy Slyme or the greedy meanness of the whole Chuzzlewit clan. No American dissimulation surpasses the oleaginous insincerity of that holy hypocrite Pecksniff. The Eden Land Corporation is no more disreputable a swindle than the Anglo-Bengalee Disinterested Loan and Life Assurance Company, and Zephaniah Scadder no worse a scoundrel than the jauntily grimy Montague Tigg transformed into the brassily glittering Tigg Montague. And the backwoods bullies and blustering American patriots, with their "ticklers," "rippers," revolvers, and bowie knives, do not come up to the brutal and cowardly Jonas Chuzzlewit maltreating his wife, poisoning his father's cough medicine, and leaving his bloodstained cudgel in the gloomy wood.

Few parts of *Martin Chuzzlewit* are more brilliantly done than the scenes in which the swindler Montague baits his hook for the knavish Jonas and the ominous melodramatic tension slowly builds up to murder. No pretensions of rectitude could entangle Jonas so utterly as the cynical avowal of chicanery: "We companies are all birds of prey: mere birds of prey. The only question is . . . whether in double-lining our own nest, we can put a single lining in yours," And when Jonas begins, "The truth is—" "Don't say the truth," Tigg grins. "It's so like humbug." "The long and short of it is—" Jonas begins again. "Better," Tigg interrupts, "Much better!" [21] And once the sharper rogue has got the blundering cheat into his power, with what cat-and-mouse cruelty he plays upon his victim's guilty fears until at last he comes close and whispers in Jonas's ear the secret of the cough medicine that turns his face "From red to white; from white to red again; from red to yellow; then to a cold, dull, awful, sweat-bedabbled blue." [22]

The doomed journey by night from which one of the two will never return is haunted by a foreboding more awful than the terror in which Sikes flees after he has beaten in Nancy's face. The uneasy slumbers of Jonas and Montague and their dark dreams are subtly revelatory; the tormented nightmares of Raskolnikov in *Crime and Punishment* are not more steeped in coagulated horror than these fevered visions that link murderer and victim in a hideous awareness of each other coiling even below the level of consciousness. From Montague's troubled memory of the chamber door opening he knows not where, and the suppressed fears disturbing him, rises the dream of the door and the secret thing lurking behind it, with his frenzied endeavors to bar it out with iron plates that turn to paper and nails that change to worms while the wood of the door crumbles and he feels the creature on the other side gaining on him.[23] And then, following hard on this, comes Jonas's dream of a journey through a strange city of streets so precipitous that he must descend great heights from one to another by ladders that are too short and by swaying ropes that move deep bells, and of the livid head that struggles up to denounce him—and his waking in the very act of striving to strike it down with a club.[24] The same occult and mysterious kinship that Dostoevski was to explore in the relation between Myshkin and Rogozhin is foreshadowed in these deadly chains Dickens reveals riveting murderer-victim and black-mailer-prey together in indissoluble embrace.

It is this deeper inwardness of vision that distinguishes Dickens's handling of evil in his native land from his pictures of trickery and folly in America. Despite the extraordinary vividness with which he snapshots a wide range of American types and their mannerisms, and despite his wit in parodying their idiom, he never gets inside them, perhaps never tries to do so. Nor would success have been easy even for Dickens; to pierce into the heart of a foreign people is no light task. British readers sometimes have reservations about whether Henry James accomplished it, for all his subtle sensitivity and prolonged observation. It is startling enough that from an experience of less than five months Dickens was able to create such triumphant caricatures.

But the British figures in *Martin Chuzzlewit*, even when they are lurid with melodrama or outrageously burlesqued, are seen to some degree from within as well as from without, and this endows them with a certain imaginative sympathy that the American ones lack. Dickens has no love for Jonas and Montague, but he knows their thoughts; and though he never tells the thoughts of Pecksniff, he knows that ineffable and oily dissembler, too, in his very depths. It is for these reasons that the hilarious travesty of the American scenes presents the appearance of a sharper hostility than what is in fact the far deeper condemnation with which he surveys corruption at home.

Furthermore, as the story moves past its midpoint the more amiable characters grow in importance and even in vitality, and Dickens responds to them with a sun-warmed glow of sympathy. From the moment Tom Pinch is forced to see through Pecksniff, he begins to take on dignity and stature. He "comes out strong," as Mark Tapley would say, when he finds his sister being ill-used in the brass founder's family where she has been a governess, and lets go with some home truths. "Pretty well!" exclaims her employer. "Upon my word, this is pretty well!" "It is very ill, sir," Tom rejoins. "It is very bad and mean, and wrong and cruel. Respect! I believe young people are quick enough to observe and imitate; and why or how should they respect whom no one else respects, and everybody slights? And very partial they must grow—oh, very partial!—to their studies when they see to what a pass proficiency in those same tasks has brought their governess!" "Ruth, my dear, get your bonnet on!" [25]

As Tom and his sister settle down in the triangular parlor of their three rooms at Islington, what an enchanting happiness irradiates their housekeeping! Ruth's timid decision to try making a beefsteak pudding, their visit to the butcher, and the experimental concocting of the pudding are all an idyl of affectionate humor. "But if it should happen . . . not to be a pudding exactly," Ruth falters, "but should turn out a stew, or a soup, or something of that kind, you'll not be vexed, Tom, will you?" [26] And when the butcher wraps the steak in a green cabbage leaf and sees Tom awkwardly trying to force it into his pocket, he begs "to be allowed to do it for him; 'for meat,' he said with some emotion, 'must be humoured, not drove.'" [27] Then comes the agitation of preparing the crust, with Ruth getting herself deliciously floury, and her palpitations when Tom has the indiscretion to invite John Westlock to stay for dinner and help eat it, and the triumphant success of that initial dish—all alight with a veritable sunshine of the heart.

Meanwhile there has been an increasing warmth in all the other corners of the story. Mark Tapley had thought Martin a pupil "so low down in the school of life" that, in his primary devotion to himself, he was "always a-making figures of one in his copy-book." [28] But by the end of their American experiences Mark is astonished at the change wrought in Martin by misfortune and his own bright example. There was some credit, Mark had thought, in being jolly with "a man as is his own great coat and cloak, and is always a-wrapping himself up in himself." But now: "I'm reg'larly defrauded," Mark thinks with a happy face. "It's a swindle. I never entered for this sort of service. There'll be no credit in being jolly with *him!*" [29] And Mrs. Todgers, for all the trials on her temper of commercial gentlemen and gravy, has gradually been revealed to have a tender heart, and comfortable Mrs. Lupin has reappeared, and all the sunlit dimples in the fountain of the Temple swell into a general smile as Ruth Pinch bashfully lingers by its basin with John Westlock. Even poor Merry Pecksniff has learned from adversity, and is no longer the shallow flippant creature who carelessly bestowed her hand upon the brutal Jonas. Old Martin's scheme to lead Pecksniff on to a full display of his self-seeking meanness and duplicity by pretending to be his feeble-minded dupe has ripened to its consummation, and the reader looks forward with tickled anticipation to the hilarious dénouement of Pecksniff's discomfiture.

Psychologically, of course, this is one of those happy incredibilities that only the sheer fun with which Dickens portrays it could make us swallow. Jonson's *Volpone* handles with much more plausibility its theme of the deceiver gulled; his two rascals, Volpone and Mosca, preying upon the greed of Corbaccio, Corvino, and the rest, have the believable motivation of a scheming rapacity that old Martin lacks. With his usual enormous cleverness, to be sure, Dickens has planted early and numerous hints of the old man's continuing love for his grandson and insinuations that he is not the senile tool he seems, and all these we recall as his purpose begins to clear. None of these ingenuities, however, quite disguise the underlying flaw. Old Martin has been so outspoken in his scornful distrust of his entire family and his disgust with all mankind, so headstrong in his willfulness, that we cannot credit this unnatural self-restraint controlling itself, in a world filled with hypocrisy, for the one sole purpose of humiliating a single hypocrite. Old Martin's shell of morose senility cracks, and the entire story bursts into a series of hearty transformation scenes in which he becomes a comic Prospero, the kindly wizard of a Christmas pantomime. We smother our skepticism in a pure frolic of willing make-believe.

But no such suspension of disbelief is needed for the enjoyment of Mrs. Gamp. The divine Sairey, with her snuff-stained musty black gown, the upturned whites of her eyes, her thick and gurgling flux of speech and its tortured syntax, inspired mispronunciations, and fulsome tributes to her own virtues, always quoted from the invisible Mrs. Harris, her weakness for putting her lips to the bottle on the "chimley-piece" when she feels so "dispoged," is a solidly triumphant reality from beginning to end. " 'Mrs. Gamp,' " Sairey quotes her friend, " 'if ever there was a sober creetur to be got at eighteen pence a day for working people, and three and six for gentlefolks—night watching,' " she emphasizes the words, " 'being a extra charge—you are that inwallable person.' 'Mrs. Harris,' I says to her, 'don't name the charge, for if I could afford to lay all my fellow creeturs out for nothink, I would gladly do it, sich is the love I bears 'em.' " [30]

Inexhaustible in comic resource, Mrs. Gamp is not only great in herself, she is still greater as the creator of Mrs. Harris. "I says to Mrs. Harris only t'other day, the last Monday evening fortnight as ever dawned upon this Piljian's Projiss of a mortal wale—" [31] And with what a fervor of ungrammatical fury she resents Betsey Prig's awful revelation of disbelief in Mrs. Harris's existence, "which her own sweet picter hanging up afore you all the time to shame your Bragian words!" [32] Or observe the gasping parentheses with which she jumbles together scenes of Mrs. Harris's domestic life, "with little Tommy Harris in her arms, as calls me his own Gammy, and truly calls, for bless the mottled little legs of that there precious child (like Canterbury brawn his own dear father says, which so they are) his own I have been, ever since I found him, Mr. Westlock, with his small red worsted shoe a gurglin' in his throat, where he had put it in his play, a chick, while they was leavin' of him on the floor a looking for it through the ouse and him a-choakin' sweetly in the parlour!" [33] Nothing like this amorphous flow of words was to appear in literature until

Joyce's *Ulysses* poured forth the endless soliloquy of Marion Bloom.

The supreme achievement of *Martin Chuzzlewit*, however, is Mr. Pecksniff.[34] He is a prodigious achievement of imaginative energy, a Tartuffe despoiled of his terrifying and satanic power and translated into the world of Mrs. Grundy, an embodiment of all the bourgeois hypocrisy of Victorian England. And Dickens builds him up with an elaborate virtuosity far transcending in richness the few sharp lines of Molière's powerful sketch, illustrating him from a thousand angles in which he is always outrageous and always himself, forever the same and forever a splendid surprise. We never anticipate what Pecksniff is going to say or do next, but whenever he appears he is superbly, ludicrously, convincingly true to his own essence. With what dazzling ingenuity of language and joyful zest Dickens describes him, with what inspired absurdity of grandiose humility endows his speech!

Pecksniff is a triumph from our first glimpse of his moral throat beheld "over a very low fence of white cravat," "a valley between two jutting heights of collar, serene and whiskerless." "It seemed to say, on the part of Mr. Pecksniff, 'There is no deception, ladies and gentlemen, all is peace, a holy calm pervades me.' " [35] He indulges in playful moral reflections "with a sort of saintly waggishness" [36] while his daughters laugh knowingly; in his tender reception of his wealthy kinsman he looks not "as if butter wouldn't melt in his mouth," but rather "as if any quantity of butter might have been made out of him, by churning the milk of human kindness, as it spouted upwards from his heart." [37] He makes himself a pious chorus to the interview between old Martin and his grandson when the latter has returned from America: "Beautiful Truth!" he exclaims, looking upward, "How is your name profaned by vicious persons! You don't live in a well, my holy principle, but on the lips of false mankind." [38]

Finally, magnificent in defeat, behold him meekly forgiving old Martin and all the others who have witnessed his discomfiture: "I have been struck this day with a walking-stick (which I have every reason to believe has knobs upon it) on that delicate and exquisite portion of the human anatomy, the brain. Several blows have been inflicted, sir, without a walking-stick, upon that tenderer portion of my frame: my heart. . . . If you should wish to have anything inscribed upon your silent tomb, sir, let it be, that I—ah, my remorseful sir! that

Truth prevails and Virtue is triumphant

I—the humble individual who has now the honour of reproaching you, forgave you." [39]

The solitary flaw in the artistry of this marvelous characterization appears only in the aftermath to the story, when Pecksniff is exposed and ruined. Then, contrary to all probability, Dickens makes the moral gesture of depicting him as hopelessly undone; turned into "a drunken, squalid, begging-letter-writing man" [40] haunting his erstwhile dupe Tom Pinch with appeals for cash and whimpering reproaches of his ingratitude. Molière's Tartuffe, exposed, merely goes to jail. He will find other dupes when he emerges, and so would Pecksniff. So much oil would never remain permanently submerged.

Pecksniff and Mrs. Gamp, like all great character creations, imply much more than they seem to mean. They stand, as Gissing pointed out, for powerful forces in society. In a social order devoted to material ends but professing moral standards, Pecksniff is bound to appear, and Mrs. Gamp "lower down, where the atmosphere is thicker and fouler." [41] They represent mere respectability in all its concern with the main chance, all its vulgar obsession with physical good things, all its indifference to more than the show of ideal principles. As symbols of the ego disguised in propriety they are far more profoundly characteristic of society than Meredith's subtle and quiveringly sensitized Sir Willoughby Patterne. They are the norms of success. In life, as distinguished from art, they are seldom shown up.

*   *   *   *   *

A growing warmth in the second half of *Martin Chuzzlewit* reflects a change in its author. In Dickens himself that "wrong kind of fire" kindled by his irritation with Chapman and Hall had burned itself out (for the time being, at least) and he looked forward to the winter holidays with all his old feelings of genial cheer. It was in this mood that he began *A Christmas Carol*, the most widely known and best beloved of all his stories.

Not even the Christmas festivities at Dingley Dell, in *Pickwick*, were suffused in such an intensity of sentiment about the Christmas season as Dickens poured into the laughter and tenderness and jollity of the *Carol*. It is full of the tang of snow and cold air and crisp green holly leaves, and warm with the glow of crimson holly berries, blazing hearths, and human hearts. More than this, however, Dickens makes of the Christmas spirit a symbolic criticism of the relations that throughout almost all the rest of the year subsist between men and their fellow men. It is a touchstone revealing and drawing forth the gold of generosity ordinarily crusted over with selfish habit, an earnest of the truth that our natures are not entirely and essentially devoted to competitive struggle. Dickens is certain that the enjoyment most men are able to feel in the happiness of others can play a larger part than it does in the tenor of their lives. The sense of brotherhood, he feels, can be broadened to a deeper and more active concern for the welfare of all mankind. It is in this light that Dickens sees the spirit of Christmas, and so understood, as Professor Cazamian has pointed out, it becomes the very core of his philosophy.

It should not be imagined that Christmas has for Dickens more than the very smallest connection with Christian dogma or theology. For Dickens Christmas is primarily a human not a supernatural feast, with a glowing emphasis on goose and gravy, plum pudding and punch, mistletoe and kissing-games, dancing and frolic, as well as on open-handedness, sympathy, and warmth of heart. Dickens does not believe that love of others demands utter abnegation or mortification of the flesh; it is not sadness but joyful fellowship. The triumphal meaning of Christmas peals in those angel voices ringing through the sky: "On earth peace, good will toward men." It is a sign and an affirmation that men do not live by bread alone, that they do not live for barter and sale alone. No way of life is either true or rewarding that leaves out men's need of loving and of being loved.

The theme of the *Christmas Carol* is thus closely linked to the theme of *Martin Chuzzlewit*. The selfishness portrayed in so many ways in the one is limited in the other to the selfishness of financial gain. For an acquisitive society the form that selfishness predominantly takes is monetary greed. The purpose of such a society is the protection of property rights. Its rules are created by those who have money and power, and are designed, to the extent that they are consistent, for the perpetuation of money and power. With the growing importance of commerce in the eighteenth century, and of industry in the nineteenth, political economists—the "philosophers" Dickens detested—rationalized the spirit of ruthless greed into a system claiming authority throughout society.

Services as well as goods, they said, were subject only to the laws of profitable trade. There was no just price. One bought in the cheapest market and sold in the dearest. There was no just wage. The mill owner paid the mill hand what competition decreed under the determination of the "iron law of wage." If the poor, the insufficiently aggressive, and the mediocre in ability were unable to live on what they could get, they must starve—or put up with the treadmill and the workhouse—and even these institutions represented concessions to mere humanity that must be made as forbidding as possible. Ideally, no sentimental conceptions must be allowed to obstruct the workings of the law of supply and demand. "Cash-nexus" was the sole bond between man and man. The supreme embodiment of this social theory was that curiously fragmentary picture of human nature, "economic man," who never performed any action except at the dictates of monetary gain. And Scrooge, in the *Christmas Carol*, is nothing other than a personification of economic man.

Scrooge's entire life is limited to cashboxes, ledgers, and bills of sale. He underpays and bullies and terrifies his clerk, and grudges him even enough coal in his office fire to keep warm. All sentiment, kindness, generosity, tenderness, he dismisses as humbug. All imagination he regards as a species of mental indigestion. He feels that he has discharged his full duty to society in contributing his share of the taxes that pay for the prison, the workhouse, the operation of the treadmill and the Poor Law, and he bitterly resents having his pocket picked to keep even them going. The out-of-work and the indigent sick are merely the idle and useless; they had better die and decrease the surplus population. So entirely does Scrooge exemplify the economic man that, like that abstraction, his grasping rapacity has ceased to have any purpose beyond itself: when he closes up his office for the night he takes his pinched heart off to a solitary dinner at a tavern and then to his bleak chambers, where he sits alone over his gruel.

Now from one angle, of course, *A Christmas Carol* indicts the economic philosophy represented by Scrooge for its unhappy influence on society. England's prosperity was not so uncertain—if, indeed, any nation's ever is—that she needed to be parsimonious and cruel to her waifs and strays, or even to the incompetents and casualties of life. To neglect the poor, to deny them education, to give them no protection from covetous employers, to let them be thrown out of work and fall ill and die in filthy surroundings that then engender spreading pestilence, to allow them to be harried by misery into crime—all these turned out in the long run to be the most disastrous shortsightedness.

That is what the Ghost of Christmas Present means in showing Scrooge the two ragged and wolfish children glaring from beneath its robes. "They are Man's," says the Spirit. "And they cling to me, appealing from their fathers. This boy is Ignorance. This girl is Want. Beware them both, and all of their degree, but most of all beware this boy, for on his brow I see that written which is Doom, unless the writing be erased." And when Scrooge asks if they have no refuge, the Spirit ironically echoes his own words: "Are there no prisons? Are there no workhouses?" [42]

Scrooge's relation with his clerk Bob Cratchit is another illustration of the same point. To say, as some commentators have done, that Scrooge is paying Cratchit all he is worth on the open market (or he would get another job) is to take for granted the very conditions Dickens is attacking. It is not only that timid, uncompetitive people like Bob Cratchit may lack the courage to bargain for their rights. But, as Dickens knows well, there are many things other than the usefulness of a man's work that determine his wage—the existence, for example, of a large body of other men able to do the same job. And if Cratchit is getting the established remuneration for his work, that makes the situation worse, not better; for instead of an isolated his is a general case. What Dickens has at heart is not any economic conception like Marx's labor theory of value, but a feeling of the human value of human beings. Unless a man is a noxious danger to society, Dickens feels, a beast of prey to be segregated or destroyed, if he is able and willing to work, whatever the work may be, he is entitled at least to enough to live on, by mere virtue of his humanity alone.

But the actual organization that Dickens saw in society callously disregarded all such humane principles. The hardened criminal was maintained in jail with more care than the helpless debtor who had broken no law. The pauper who owed nobody, but whom age, illness, or industrial change might have thrown out of work, was treated more severely than many a debtor and jailbird. And the poor clerk or laborer, rendered powerless by his need or the number of others like him, could be held to a pittance barely sufficient to keep him and his family from starvation.

Against such inequities Dickens maintains that any work worth doing should be paid enough to maintain a man and his family without grinding worry. Or are we to let the crippled Tiny Tims die and decrease the surplus population? "Man," says the Ghost, "if man you be in heart, not adamant, forbear that wicked cant until you have discovered What the surplus is and Where it is. . . . It may be, that in the sight of Heaven, you are more worthless and less fit to live than millions like this poor man's child. Oh God! to hear the Insect on the leaf pronouncing on the too much life among his hungry brothers in the dust!" [43]

Cold-hearted arrogance and injustice storing up a dangerous heritage of poverty and ignorance—such is Dickens's judgment of the economic system that Scrooge exemplifies. But its consequences do not end with the cruelties it inflicts upon the masses of the people or the evils it works in society. It injures Scrooge as well. All the more generous impulses of humanity he has stifled and mutilated in himself. All natural affection he has crushed. The lonely boy he used to be, weeping in school, the tender brother, the eager youth, the young man who once fell disinterestedly in love with a dowerless girl—what has he done to them in making himself into a money-making machine, as hard and sharp as flint, and frozen with the internal ice that clutches his shriveled heart? That dismal cell, his office, and his gloomy rooms, are only a prison within which he dwells self-confined, barred and close-locked as he drags a chain of his own cashboxes and dusty ledgers. Acting on a distortedly inadequate conception of self-interest, Scrooge has deformed and crippled himself to bitter sterility.

And Scrooge's fallacy is the fallacy of organized society. Like his house, which Dickens fancifully imagines playing hide-and-seek with other houses when it was a young house, and losing its way in a blind alley it has forgotten how to get out of, Scrooge has lost his way between youth and maturity. Society too in the course of its development has gone astray and then hardened itself in obdurate error with a heartless economic theory. Scrooge's conversion is more than the transformation of a single human being. It is a plea for society itself to undergo a change of heart.

Dickens does not, it should be noticed, take the uncompromising position that the self-regarding emotions are to be eradicated altogether. He is not one of those austere theorists who hold that the individual must be subordinated to the state or immolate himself to the service of an abstract humanity. Concern for one's self and one's own welfare is necessary and right, but true self-love cannot be severed from love of others without growing barren and diseased. Only in the communion of brotherhood is it healthy and fruitful. When Scrooge has truly changed, and has dispatched the anonymous gift of the turkey to Bob Cratchit as an earnest of repentance, he may go to his nephew's house and ask wistfully, "Will you let me in, Fred?" With love reanimated in his heart, he may hope for love.

There have been readers who objected to Scrooge's conversion as too sudden and radical to be psychologically convincing. But this is to mistake a semi-serious fantasy for a piece of prosaic realism. Even so, the emotions in Scrooge to which the Ghosts appeal are no unsound means to the intended end: the awakened memories of a past when he had known gentler and warmer ties than any of his later years, the realization of his exclusion from all kindness and affection in others now, the fears of a future when he may be lonelier and more unloved still. And William James in *The Varieties of Religious Experience* provides scores of case histories that parallel both the suddenness of Scrooge's conversion and the sense of radiant joy he feels in the world around him after it has taken place. It may be that what really gives the skeptics pause is that Scrooge is converted to a gospel of good cheer. They could probably believe easily enough if he espoused some gloomy doctrine of intolerance.

It is doubtful whether such questions ever arise when people are actually reading the *Christmas Carol*. From the very beginning Dickens strikes a tone of playful exaggeration that warns us this is no exercise in naturalism. Scrooge carries "his own low temperature always about with him; he iced his office in the dog-days." [44] The entire world of the story is an animistic one: houses play hide-and-seek, door knockers come to life as human heads, the tuning of a fiddle is "like fifty stomach aches," [45] old Fezziwig's legs wink as he dances, potatoes bubbling in a saucepan knock loudly at the lid "to be let out and peeled." [46] Scrooge's own language has a jocose hyperbole, even when he is supposed to be most ferocious or most terrified, that makes his very utterance seem half a masquerade. "If I could work my will," he snarls, "every idiot who goes about with 'Merry Christmas' on his lips, should be boiled with his own pudding, and buried with a stake of holly through his heart. He should!" [47] Is that the accent of a genuine curmudgeon or of a man trying to sound more violent than he feels? And to Marley's Ghost, despite his disquiet, he remarks, "You may be an undigested bit of beef, a blob of mustard, a crumb of cheese, a fragment of an underdone potato. There's more of gravy than of grave about you, whatever you are!" [48]

All these things make it clear that Dickens—as always when he is most deeply moved and most profound—is speaking in terms of unavowed allegory. But the allegory of Dickens is in one way subtler than the allegory of writers like Kafka and Melville. Kafka is always hinting the existence of hidden meanings by making the experiences of his characters so baffling and irrational on a merely realistic level that we are obliged to search for symbolic significances. And Melville, too, by a score of devices, from those rolling, darkly magnificent, and extraordinary soliloquies to the mystery of Ahab's intense and impassioned pursuit of the White Whale, forces us to realize that this is a more metaphysical duel than one with a mere deep-sea beast.

Dickens, however, leaves his surface action so entirely clear and the behavior of his characters so plain that they do not puzzle us into groping for gnomic meanings. The grotesque and comic animism and the supernatural action make the reader emotionally receptive to a symbolic significance he is not even obliged to recognize as symbolism: he can take the runaway house and the potatoes knocking in the pot as mere playfulness and the fantastic events as dream hallucination. Scrooge is just the miser he seems, his nephew a warm-hearted fellow, Bob Cratchit a poor clerk—what could be simpler? If there is a touch of oddity in the details, why, that is merely Dickens's exuberant fancy; if Scrooge's change of heart is sharply antithetical, that is only Dickens's melodramatic sentimentality—it is an established fact that Dickens is never profound.

But the truth is that Dickens has so fused his abstract thought and its imaginative rendering that one melts almost entirely into the other, and only a critical dissection can separate them again. Nothing in his handling thrusts upon us the need of perceiving what *A Christmas Carol* is in reality—a serio-comic parable of social redemption. Marley's Ghost is the symbol of divine grace, and the three Christmas Spirits are the working of that grace through the agencies of memory, example, and fear. And Scrooge, although of course he is himself too, is not himself alone: he is the embodiment of all that concentration upon material power and callous indifference to the welfare of human beings that the economists had erected into a system, businessmen and industrialists pursued relentlessly, and society taken for granted as inevitable and proper. The conversion of Scrooge is an image of the conversion for which Dickens hopes among mankind.

CHAPTER THREE

Battles and Italian Air-Castles

O N NEW YEAR'S morning, 1844, Dickens greeted the postman bearing a letter from Felton "with a moist and oystery twinkle" of the eye, a glass of whiskey, and a cheery blessing.[1] His spirits were buoyant with the success of the *Christmas Carol*: six thousand copies of the first edition sold on the very day of publication, two thousand of the second and third already taken by the trade, and letters of enthusiastic delight from complete strangers pouring in daily.[2] Never had a little book had so brilliant a reception.

Nor was the chorus of praise only a popular one. "Blessings on your kind heart," wrote Jeffrey. "You should be happy yourself, for you may be sure you have done more good by this little publication, fostered more kind feelings, and prompted more positive acts of beneficence, than can be traced to all the pulpits and confessionals in Christendom since Christmas 1842." "Who can listen," exclaimed Thackeray, "to objections regarding such a book as this? It seems to me a national benefit, and to every man or woman who reads it a personal kindness." [3]

The burden of worry under which Dickens had felt weighed down melted into air. He would be able to clear off the nagging debts and family demands, and then for a glorious year of freedom, in France, Italy, perhaps Germany! Bag and baggage, little ones and all, he would leave England at midsummer and bathe in the luxurious idleness of the southern sun. And at last he would indulge the long-deferred dream of meditating and turning out a book with no presses thundering their deadline at him, "*such* a story, Felton, all at once, no parts, sledge-hammer blow." [4]

His genial warmth did not embrace Chapman and Hall, however. For those unhappy booksellers had not even advertised the *Carol* in any of the December magazines except *Blackwood's*. "Bradbury would not believe it when I told him," and said that only an extraordinary push could atone for their fatal negligence. Dickens had been "obliged to write them a most tremendous letter," telling them "not to answer it, or to come near me, but simply to do what I have ordered them." "Do this—Do that—Do the other—Keep away from me—and be damned." [5] Once "the best of booksellers" and his "trusty friends," [6] Chapman and Hall had fallen (since the junior partner's blunder the preceding June) to the point where they were now "preposterously ignorant of all the essentials of their business." The resounding triumph of the *Christmas Carol* was none of their doing; they were summarily directed to submit the accounts as soon after the New Year as possible.[7]

Pending the profits of the Christmas book, however, Dickens found himself hard pressed for cash. His expenses had been high, there would soon be another baby, and in December he had discovered to his horror that he was already overdrawn at Coutts's. That month's money had to go to insurance and "Next month's is bespoke." Of course he could have any sum he wanted from his publishers, but nothing would induce him to appeal to them. The only thing was to obtain another £200 from Mitton, leave the rest of the bills unpaid, and wait for his *Carol* earnings to come in.[8]

Splendid as these ought to be, the slackness of Chapman and Hall was not the only reason for thinking they might have been better still. For if Dickens was exasperated by American pirates, he was hardly less plagued at home by plagiarists and imitators. *The Posthumous Notes of the Pickwickian Club, Nichelas Nickleberry, Oliver Twiss*—there had been an endless series of imitations.[9] Hack dramatists rushed mutilated versions of all his stories to the stage. One of these, W. T. Moncrieff, calling himself "an universal Robber of Romance," who had dramatized "no less than *two hundred and forty-seven Novels*, as fast as they came out" and faster,[10] impudently boasted that his *Sam Weller, or The Pickwickians* had vastly increased the popularity and sales of *Pickwick*, and upbraided Dickens's "injudicious friends" for displaying "soreness" at his thievery.[11] Later he pathetically lamented Dickens's annoyance at his dramatization of

Nicholas Nickleby, "which he declared he never would have written, had Dickens sent him a note to say it would be disagreeable to him." [12]

Unable to prevent these plagiarisms, Dickens had given his assistance to actor friends like Frederick Yates in their productions. But he had never ceased to resent the fact that such liberties could be taken with his creations, and repeatedly refused appeals to give them his official sanction. Into *Nicholas Nickleby* he dragged two lengthy and gratuitous outbursts against pilfering the property of authors and garbling their work by crude distortions.[13] And now, in a twopenny weekly called *Parley's Illuminated Library,* appeared a peculiarly flagrant plagiarism of *A Christmas Carol,* with the claim that it was "re-originated from the original by Charles Dickens, Esq., and analytically condensed expressly for this work." [14]

"The story," Dickens exploded, "is practically the same, and the characters the same; and the names the same; with the exception of the name Fezziwig, which is printed Fuzziwig." The incidents were the same, and in the same order. The language was often the same, and where it was not was made "vile, ignorant, and mawkish." [15] Would the law really allow such thieves to use his ideas "as gipsies do stolen children; disfigure them and then make them pass for their own"? [16] "If these Vagabonds can be stopped," Dickens swore, "they must be." [17]

With Talfourd as his counsel, Dickens moved for an injunction to stop publication. Lee and Haddock, the publishers, moved to dissolve the injunction, arguing that when they had "re-originated" *The Old Curiosity Shop* and *Barnaby Rudge* Dickens had made no protest, and claiming that they had made great improvements and important additions to the *Carol,* including a song of sixty lines for Tiny Tim.[18] But the Vice-Chancellor, Sir J. Knight Bruce, would have nothing of either defense. He demanded that Lee and Haddock's counsel cite a single passage that was not contracted or expanded from Dickens's book. "And at every successive passage he cried out, 'That is Mr. Dickens's case. Find another!' He said that there was not a shadow of doubt upon the matter. That there was no authority which would bear a construction in their favour; the piracy going beyond all previous instances." [19]

"The Pirates are beaten flat," Dickens reported exultantly. "They are bruised, bloody, battered, smashed, squelched, and utterly undone." [20] The Vice-Chancellor had not even required to hear Dickens's counsel, but instantly gave judgment without it. "Oh! the agony of Talfourd at Knight Bruce's not hearing him! He had sat up till three in the morning, he says, preparing his speech . . ." [21] The way was consequently clear for Dickens to plunge into no fewer than six chancery suits, against the publishers, booksellers, printers, and "author."

Talfourd strongly advocated no compromise. The case should be referred to the Court "to ascertain what profits had been made by the piracy," [22] and to order the entire profits paid to Dickens. But Dickens was willing to let the printers off with an apology and their costs, and the booksellers who had merely handled the book might get out with their costs. From the publishers and author, however, he demanded £1,000 damages. "I am in for it now," he announced; "and I dare say (through the villainy of the law, which after declaring me robbed, obliges me to bring an action against men from whom it demands no security for the expences to which I shall be put) am in a fair way to lose Three Hundred Pounds or so. Never mind. I declare war against the Black Flag; and down it shall come, if strong and constant hauling will do it." [23]

The defendants tried every conceivable dodge. Lee and Haddock, the principal offenders, took refuge in bankruptcy, and Dickens was obliged to initiate an action against their assignees.[24] One of the booksellers, a Mr. Strange, tried to intimidate him by sending "a literary gentleman" who warned Dickens of an intended advertisement "which would have a dreadful effect on any man," hinted darkly at horrendous legal strokes under way, and recommended that for his own sake he had better "let Mr. Strange off, scot free." His hand on the bell rope, Dickens told the emissary that he regarded his character as beyond Mr. Strange's assailment, and was determined to stop the piracy even should all London be sent to him.[25]

Ultimately the four booksellers compounded their cases and paid their costs. "So that I lose nothing by them." But the publishers had proved too wily for him. "We have had communcation with the assignees, and found their case quite desperate." Instead of the damages and the ample public apology that he might reasonably have expected, Dickens found himself bogged in a legal morass from which he was able to withdraw only with the loss of all the costs of bringing suit. "I have dropped—dropped!—the action and the chancery suit against the bankrupt Pirates," he wrote in May. ". . . But it is something to know the worst of it and to be rid of Knight Bruce, whom I should call . . . a pragmatical donkey—judicially speaking." "By Lee and Haddock (the vagabonds) I . . . lose of course, all my expenses, costs and charges in those suits." [26]

The blow that was to have annihilated the pirates cost Dickens £700. So little intimidated were publishers who lived by such means that only two years later he was again their victim.[27] But this time he decided to suffer in silence. "I shall not easily forget the expense, and anxiety, and horrible injustice of the Carol case, wherein, asserting the plainest right on earth, I was really treated as if I were the robber instead of the robbed." "It is better to suffer a great wrong than to have recourse to the much greater wrong of the law." [28]

*   *   *   *   *

The indignation with which Dickens saw himself left without redress and out of pocket for his pains was not lessened by the fact that the expected baby had arrived and that he now had five dependent children. He was a devoted father, but with the four he already had he felt his family, and his expenses, large enough, and he had no enthusiasm for the domestic disruptions following a childbirth. The baby was born on January 15th, and two days later Maclise, Stanfield, and Forster invited Dickens to celebrate by dining with them at Richmond. He accepted in a burlesque reply that jests with these sentiments: "Nurses, wet and dry; apothecaries; mothers-in-law; babies; with all the sweet (and chaste) delights of private life; these, my countrymen, are hard to leave. But you have called me forth, and I will come." [29] And, a month later, "Kate is all right again," he wrote; "and so, they tell me, is the Baby. But I decline (on principle) to look at the latter object." [30] Though both comments were intended facetiously, Dickens had made no such jokes about his previous children.

His youngest brother, Augustus, whose nickname "Boses" had suggested the pseudonym of Boz, was now seventeen, and of course it fell upon Dickens to settle him in a means of earning a livelihood. Dickens sought the aid of Thomas Chapman, a wealthy merchant in the City, senior proprietor of John Chapman and Company, of Leadenhall Street, and Chairman of Lloyd's Registry of Shipping. Augustus, he explained, had lately come from a good school at Exeter and was living with his parents at Greenwich. He was quick and clever, and Dickens had "no reason to suppose that he is addicted to authorship, or any bad habits of that nature." [31] Chapman obligingly took Augustus into his office.

On February 10th the eagerly awaited *Christmas Carol* accounts reached Dickens's hands. He opened them with a pleased anticipation of learning that he had made a clear £1,000, and being able to straighten out all his financial affairs. A glance supplied him with the truth. "Such a night as I have passed!" he wrote Forster. "I really believed I should never get up again, until I had passed through all the horrors of a fever. . . . The first six thousand copies show a profit of £230! And the last four will yield as much more." As he wondered what he was to do, Dickens fell into a hysteria little short of panic. "My year's bills, unpaid, are so terrific, that all the energy and determination I can possibly exert will be required to clear me before I go abroad; which, if next June come and find me alive, I shall do." [32]

As he looked at the disastrous figures, Dickens was "utterly knocked down." But during the night, although he "slept as badly as Macbeth." [33] he recovered his courage. "If I can let the house for this season, I will be off to some seaside place as soon as a tenant offers. I am not afraid, if I reduce my expenses; but if I do not, I shall be ruined past all mortal hope of redemption." "What a wonderful thing it is, that such a great success should occasion me such intolerable anxiety and disappointment." [34] The only thing that upheld him was "the very circumstance that makes it so tremendous—the wonderful success of the book." [35]

Though he was fierce in his refusal to allow himself to be crushed by the blow, he did not know what to do. He was, he told Mitton, "not only on my beam-ends, but tilted over on the other side." The £200 Mitton had obtained for him in December "*must* be provided for. To that I must plan to devote this previous balance. The rest must be worked round somehow. I wish I could say that I see how (I am thunderstruck by the amount), but I have been on the other side with you often, and you must do your best for me." [36]

Against Chapman and Hall he felt relentlessly bitter. Nothing could persuade him to return to them now. "I have not the least doubt that they have run the expenses up anyhow purposely to bring me back and disgust me with the charges." Why, the different charges for the plates alone, engraving, printing, coloring, came to more than his profits did! Nor did he like the tone Chapman and Hall took in their correspondence with him. "Observe little Hall's note with the allusion to the American book. Oh, Heaven!" Dickens plainly saw "the shadow of war" before him.[37]

He would reopen negotiations with Bradbury and Evans at once. They must not be told anything of this quarrel or its causes, "as I think it highly important not to dash the triumph of the book." [38] The printers were more alert this time than they had been when Forster approached them in October, and now professed themselves eager to serve Dickens in any way. Dickens obtained £500 from them, which relieved his immediate needs. He explained that in addition he wanted to pay off the remainder of the £150 monthly he had received from Chapman and Hall throughout 1842, and to have enough to meet his expenses during the year he proposed to spend abroad. To balance these demands there were whatever new books he might produce, the republication of those he had already written, and possibly the new magazine that had been suggested.[39] Whatever the details, it was obvious that Bradbury and Evans would be mad not to secure Dickens. His future writings alone ought to be worth enough to guarantee any sum they advanced to him. The amount required and the precise terms could all be settled in the course of the spring.

Chapman and Hall were notified that Dickens intended to have no further dealings with them after the bound volumes of *Chuzzlewit* came out in July. That was a dark day at 186 Strand; and William Hall must have smote his brow and gone in sackcloth and ashes for weeks thereafter. He knew that it was his thoughtless remark that had set the first match to the blaze of Dickens's wrath.[40] But in truth the partners were not in any other ways very much to blame. Dickens's expectations for the *Carol* had been oversanguine. The £1,000 he had expected to clear—and apparently on the first ten thousand copies—was an unreasonably high profit on any book selling to the customer at five shillings.[41] And he had himself insisted upon colored plates and an unusually luxurious format. Though Forster criticized the "want of judgment . . . in not adjusting the expenses of production" [42] to the price, it was also Dickens, not Chapman and Hall, who had determined the book's selling price. Perhaps they had made no strenuous endeavor to keep down costs, but there is little support for Dickens's belief that they had deliberately run them up. Only the price of coloring the plates seems extraordinarily high. And when the final accounts came in, the profits on editions totaling fifteen thousand amounted to £726.[43] It would have been judicious had Chapman and Hall included with their February statement some forecast of this outcome.

* * * * *

But the damage was done, and by the time Dickens went off, near the end of February, to preside at a soirée of the Liverpool Mechanics' Institute, his ties with his old publishers were already severed. When he arrived in Liverpool he found his friend T. J. Thompson and a pleasant dinner awaiting him at Radley's Hotel. The next morning he inspected the great lecture hall, with it seats rising in semicircular tiers, where the meeting was to be held. Before returning to the hotel he was joined by Captain Hewett, who carried him off to the *Britannia* for champagne chilled with a fifty-pound block of Boston ice and gave him an account of Macready playing *Macbeth* in Boston.[44]

Tremendous applause greeted Dickens when he took the chair that evening. His "white-and-black or magpie waistcoat" also created a sensation; he was later gratified to hear people exclaiming, "What is it? *Is* it a waistcoat? No, it's a shirt." [45] In his speech, he praised the city of Liverpool and the founders of the Institute for their noble work in making education and enlightenment available to laboring people. He spoke warmly of the decision to add a girls' school to the institution and extend education to "those who are our best teachers, and whose lessons are oftenest heeded in after life." All society, he concluded, had one common goal of human improvement, transcending differences of rank and wealth. "True hearts are more than coronets," he quoted Tennyson, "And simple faith than Norman blood." [46] At these words the thirteen hundred people in the audience cheered, clapped, and stamped their feet in a way "thundering and awful." [47]

In the entertainment that followed, Dickens, referring to the program, said, "I am requested to introduce to you a young lady whom I have some difficulty and tenderness in announcing—Miss Weller, who will play a fantasia on the piano." The whole audience, with happy memories of Mr. Pickwick's faithful follower, exploded into laughter; and, looking around, Dickens saw a young girl, painfully embarrassed, frail and ethereally beautiful, looking at him beseechingly.[48] His heart leaped in his breast. Such loveliness implied a nature not for this world; [49] it seemed to him that he "saw an angel's message in her face . . . that smote me to the heart." [50]

Recovering his self-control, he led her to the piano, whispering that he hoped some day she would change her name and be very happy.[51] Her playing did not dim the shining impression she had made. What a high and unusual nature was implied "in every look and gesture"! How she "started out alone from the whole crowd" the instant he saw her! [52] Her name was Christiana Weller, he learned, amazed by his own interest in her and startled by his feelings. At the end of the evening he asked her to bring her father to lunch with him the next day. Going back to his hotel, he was haunted by that angel face and by shadowy images of her green dress trimmed with fur.[53]

Riding out to see her again the day after, he composed a piece of doggerel for her album:

> "I put in a book, once, by hook and by crook,
> The whole race (as I thought) of a 'feller,'
> Who happily pleased the town's taste, much diseas'd,
> —And the name of this person was Weller.
>
> "I find to my cost that One Weller I lost—
> Cruel Destiny so to arrange it!
> I love her dear name, which has won me some fame,
> But, Great Heaven! how gladly I'd change it." [54]

The next day obliged him to leave for Birmingham, where he had agreed to speak for the Polytechnic Institution that night, and he tore himself away promising to send her Tennyson's poems, which he learned that she had not read. The copy he then dispatched, he wrote her father, was not new, "hoping she may like it none the worse for having been my companion often, and for having been given to me by Tennyson himself." [55] And to Thompson, who had also met her, he wrote, "I cannot joke about Miss Weller. . . . Good God, what a madman I should seem, if the incredible feeling I have conceived for that girl could be made plain to anyone!" [56]

The reception at Birmingham was even more brilliant than that at Liverpool. Ladies had decorated the entire auditorium of the Town Hall with artificial flowers, so that it looked like a vast garden. Facing the platform, in front of the gallery, the words "Welcome Boz" appeared in letters of flowers six feet high. Over the platform and about the great organ were transparencies "representing several fames in the act of crowning a corresponding number of Dicks—at which Victoria (taking out a poetic license) was highly delighted." [57] Made rather nervous by these preparations, Dickens dined alone, "in the Magpie waistcoat—" "took a pint of champagne, and a pint of sherry . . . and was as hard as iron and as cool as a cucumber again." [58]

At ten minutes to eight he was brought to the Hall, crammed to the roof with two thousand people. "The ladies were in full dress and immense numbers," he wrote Thompson; "and when Dick showed himself the whole company stood up; rustling like the leaves of a wood. Tar-nation grand it was, and rather unbalancing, but Dick with the heart of a lion dashed in bravely and made decidedly the best speech I ever heard him achieve. Sir, he was jocular, pathetic, eloquent, conversational, illustrative, and wise—always wise. He introduced that about the Genie in the casket with marvellous effect; and was applauded to the echo which did applaud again." [59]

On March 11th, a little more than a week after his return to London, Dickens found in his morning mail a letter postmarked from Liverpool and in Thompson's handwriting. As he broke the seal and looked at its opening lines, he had an intuition of its entire contents. Thompson had fallen in love with Christiana Weller. "I felt the blood go from my face to I don't know where," Dickens responded, "and my very lips turn white. I never in my life . . . had the whole current of my life so stopped, for the instant, as when I felt, at a glance, what your letter said. Which I did, correctly. For when I came to read it attentively, and several times over, I found nothing new in it." [60]

Thompson was worried by the fact that he himself was a widower and considerably older than Christiana. What should he do? Dickens's answer came in a rush: "If I had your independent means . . . I would not hesitate . . . But would win her if I could, by God. I would answer it to myself, if my world's breath whispered me that I had known her but a few days, that hours of hers are years in the lives of common women. That it is in such a face and such a spirit, as parts of its high nature, to do at once what less ethereal creatures must be long in doing." [61]

To her father, Dickens urged, Thompson should point out that the musical career to which he was bent on devoting her "should not be called her life but Death"; only repose, a mind at rest, a foreign climate, might possibly save her from an end that otherwise was speedy and certain. But even without this hope, Dickens added passionately, "I could bear better her passing from my arms to Heaven than I could endure the thought of coldly passing into the World again to see her no more"; to lose her memory save "at odd times and in remorseful glances backwards," and only be reminded of her at last by hearing someone say, " 'You recollect her? Ah! She's dead.'

"As I live, I write the Truth and feel it." [62]

Two days later he was urging Thompson not to tarry, but dash in at once; and then—"Think of Italy!" [63] For of course Thompson must bring her to Italy, where they might all be together "in some delicious nook." [64] "At the father I snap my fingers. I would leap over the head of the tallest father in Europe, if his daughter's heart lay on the other side . . ." [65] "Such Italian Castles, bright in sunny days, and pale in moonlight nights, as I am building in the air!" [66]

*　*　*　*　*

Dickens's own plans for departure were shaping up rapidly. Renting agents had Devonshire Terrace listed as to let, and his letter of credit was ready at Coutts's.[67] He had asked Lady Blessington what she thought of Nice, but she and Count D'Orsay insisted there was no place to equal Pisa. To Angus Fletcher, who was in Italy, Dickens wrote suggesting that Fletcher join them in Pisa and asking his help in finding a *palazzo* for them to rent. "Here is a list of the caravan:

"(1) The inimitable Boz.

"(2) The other half ditto.

"(3) The sister of ditto ditto.

"(4) Four babies, ranging from two years and a half to seven and a half.

"(5) Three women servants, commanded by Anne of Broadstairs." [68] The baby, Francis Jeffrey, they would leave in the care of Mrs. Hogarth.

About his financial situation Dickens had become less agitated. "The half year's account," he wrote Mitton, "is GOOD. Deducting £50 a month from Chuzzlewit up to the end, the debt is reduced to £1,900. There will then be the half year's profits to deduct, and the whole subscription. So please God it will have come down bravely by the time I start." [69] Nevertheless, he was still so pinched that in April he was obliged to tell Mitton that he had pressing need of another £100 until June: "my father's debts, two quarters income tax etc., coming all at once, drive me, sailing so near the wind, into a most uncomfortable corner." [70] Fortunately, Bradbury and Evans had decided that the entire remainder of this debt to Chapman and Hall should be paid before he left, and all matters settled concerning the stock of books in which Dickens had an interest. All the documents dealing with these books must be gone over.[71]

From the examination of these papers the final details of his arrangement with Bradbury and Evans were worked out. The debt to Chapman and Hall amounted to no more than £1,500. From the book sale of *Martin Chuzzlewit* he was able to repay Bradbury and Evans the £500 they had advanced him. He estimated that he would need £1,500 for his year abroad, with possibly another £500 in the spring of next year. The agreements with Chapman and Hall left only *Oliver Twist* and *American Notes* available for immediate republication, but possibly Chapman and Hall would be favorable to a general reissue of the others in volumes, under the auspices of Bradbury and Evans, with new prefaces and notes. The money, Dickens said, he would need on the first of June.[72]

Ultimately, in an agreement of this date, Bradbury and Evans advanced Dickens £2,800, secured by a fourth share of whatever he might write during the ensuing eight years. No interest was to be paid on this sum, and no obligations imposed about what works were to be written, though it was understood that a successor to the *Carol* would be ready for Christmas, 1844. No arrangements were made about the Italian travel book. If the magazine that had been discussed were initiated, and Dickens were "only partially editor or author," he was to own two-thirds of its copyright and profits, instead of the three-quarters that would otherwise be his.[73]

In the weeks immediately before and after working out this arrangement, Dickens was as busy as ever. He wrote several leading articles for the *Morning Chronicle* which aroused so much interest that Richard Doyle, Black's successor in the editorial chair of that paper, asked him if he would not send a weekly travel letter from Italy; "for such contributions Easthope would pay anything." [74] But Easthope was "such a damned screw," Dickens told Mitton, that "that wouldn't do," though he gave no definite refusal. "I said to Doyle, 'I won't make any bargain with him at all, or haggle like a peddler, but I'll write a leader now and then and leave him in June to send me a cheque for the whole. He shall set his own value on them; and if he sets too little, the shame is his, and not mine.' " [75]

John Overs, the carpenter, was now hopelessly ill, and striving desperately to make some provision for his family before he died. He asked Dickens's aid in getting one of his little boys into Christ's Hospital, the famous Blue Coat School where Lamb and Coleridge had been scholars, and Dickens gave him the names of several gentlemen whose influence might help.[76] He also gave Overs a letter to a number of publishers who might be induced to bring out a volume of his collected pieces.[77] One of these did accept the little book. When it came out, toward the close of the year, under the title, *Evenings of a Working Man*,[78] it was dedicated to Dr. Elliotson and had an introduction that Dickens wrote for it during these last hurried weeks before his departure.

Walks and dinners with Forster, Maclise, and Stanfield were wedged into the programs of such busied days where time could be found for them. "Sir, I will—he—he—he—he—he—he—I will NOT eat with you . . . But the morning looks bright, and a walk to Hampstead would suit me marvellously. If you should present yourself at my gate (bringing the R. A.'s along with you) I shall not be sapparized. So no more at this writing from poor Mr. Dickens." [79] And again, "November blasts! Why, it's the warmest, most genial, most intensely bland, delicious, growing, springy, songster-of-the-grovy, bursting-forth-of-the-buddy, day as ever was. At half-past four I shall expect you.—Ever, MODDLE." [80]

Late in March Thompson sent Dickens a letter announcing his engagement to Miss Weller. "It is a noble prize you have won," Dickens replied. ". . . Good Heavens, what a dream it appears! Shall we ever forget that night when she came up to the piano—that morning when Dick, the energetic Dick, devised the visit!" The dress— "the dress with fur on it"—should be saved, and remain "a household God, Immortally Young and Perpetually Green." Of Mr. Weller's apparent opposition, now withdrawn, Dickens commented, "The father seems to have acted like a man. I had my fears of that, I confess; for the greater part of my observation of Parents and children had shown selfishness in the first, almost invariably." [81]

Unexpectedly, within the course of the next few days, Thompson's brother-in-law Charles Smithson died. Dickens hurried down to Yorkshire to give what help and comfort he could.[82] Smithson had always appeared to be a prosperous, even a wealthy, man, but he left his affairs as badly confused as those of Mr. Spenlow, in *David Copperfield*. There was no doubt whatever, Dickens wrote home to Kate, that he had died without a will. "Every place has been searched that could be thought of: and nothing has been found. He has even dropped a certain Life Insurance for £3000 which in a man of business is extremely strange." It looked as if the entire estate would shrink to a few thousand pounds.[83]

At the funeral Dickens was surprised to find Thompson again despairing of his courtship, "acting as chief mourner to his own hopes, and attending them to an early grave." [84] The obstacles to his success, it turned out, had not been the father after all, but "exactly what I predicted," Dickens exclaimed, a prior attachment, "—kept secret by her—and the parents *with* Thompson." [85] "She" told Thompson "he had been a little premature, and that there were other footprints in the field—and so forth." [86]

But Dickens counseled Thompson not to give up hope—"There might be a host, and yet the best flowers might grow up at last in the steps of the last man, if he were True . . ." [87] And on returning to London, Dickens wrote Miss Weller in his friend's behalf. He could not find it in his heart, he said, to remonstrate with Thompson's folly. "Indeed I rather encouraged him in it than otherwise; for I had that amount of sympathy with his condition, which, but that I am beyond the reach—the lawful reach—of the Wings that fanned his fire, would have rendered it the greatest happiness and pleasure of my life to have run him through the body. In no poetical or tender sense, I assure you, but with good sharp Steel." [88]

And so, he concluded, he had resumed hoping for Thompson, and meant to keep on, "unless you hold my hands; and that you won't do, I believe. Whatever happens in this case, of this I am quite sure—it will all happen Wrong, and cannot happen otherwise than Wrong, the undersigned being excluded from all chance of competition, and only throwing up his cap for other men, instead of cutting it up into Favors for himself." [89]

*   *   *   *   *

Meanwhile, preparations for the journey to Italy went forward. Landor had told Dickens that Genoa was preferable to Pisa, and suggested that he try to rent Lord Byron's villa, Casa Saluzzi, at Albaro, on the seacoast near the city. It turned out, however, that this house had fallen into ruinous condition and had a cheap wineshop in its ground floor. Dickens had consequently written Fletcher, asking him to find another house, preferably at Albaro. Fletcher wrote back that he had turned up a house named the Villa di Bella Vista, belonging to a local butcher.[90] Dickens did not like to bind himself to rent for an entire year a place that he had not seen and tried out. "Take the illustrious abiding place for the illustrious man *for three months*," he instructed Fletcher, with the stipulation that he should be able to extend the time to a year if he wished. "Of course you will get it as cheap as you can." [91]

It now occurred to Dickens that he might purchase cheaply "some good old shabby devil of a coach—one of those vast phantoms that hide themselves in a corner of the Pantechnicon," and have the convenience of traveling in his own conveyance. "Exactly such a one he found there," Forster says, "sitting himself inside it, a perfect Sentimental Traveller, while the managing man told him its history." "As for comfort," Dickens wrote Forster, "—let me see—it is about the size of your library; with night-lamps and day-lamps and pockets and imperials and leathern cellars, and the most extraordinary contrivances." When Forster saw it, he would "roar at it," and then "proclaim it to be 'perfectly brilliant, my dear fellow.' " Marked £60, this prodigy was obtained for £45; and when Forster beheld it he roared as predicted.[92] At the same time Dickens engaged as courier one Louis Roche, a beaming and vigorously bustling native of Avignon.[93]

Devonshire Terrace was expeditiously rented. "A most desirable widow (as a tenant I mean) proposed, only last Saturday," Dickens wrote Southwood Smith, "to take our house for the whole time of our intended absence abroad—on condition that she had possession of it today." [94] The family therefore went into temporary lodgings at 9

Osnaburgh Terrace from May 28th until their departure in early July. This unexpected move produced a small domestic crisis: the kitchen was inadequate to handle a dinner Dickens had planned. "Investigation below stairs," he explained to Forster, "renders it, as my father would say, 'manifest to any person of ordinary intelligence, if the term may be considered allowable,' that the Saturday's dinner cannot come off here with safety." What on earth was to be done, with all the invitations issued, to Lord Denman, to Sydney Smith, Lord Normanby, Easthope, Southwood Smith, Thomas Chapman, and almost a dozen others? [95] Forster's advice was to throw over the party altogether, but additional help was obtained, and the dinner went off pleasantly in the temporary quarters.[96]

Three days later, on June 4th, Dickens presided at the London Tavern over a dinner in aid of the Sanatorium at Devonshire Place House established by Dr. Southwood Smith as the first nursing home in London.[97] There was also, just before Dickens's departure, a farewell dinner at Greenwich to celebrate the completion of *Martin Chuzzlewit*. Over this dinner presided the Marquess of Normanby, whose son, Lord Mulgrave, had been with Dickens on the *Britannia*. Among the other guests came, in the tow of Stanfield, the great painter Turner, enveloping his old throat that sultry June day in a huge red belcher-handkerchief, and paying more attention to the changing lights on the river than to the speeches.[98] Carlyle, though invited, did not come. The thought of "dinner, at Greenwich,—in the dog-days,—under Lord Normanby," with "leg-of-mutton eloquence," was too much: "my soul dies away at the idea. . . ." But, he told Forster, he would have been glad to honor Dickens in some good way. "I truly love Dickens," he wrote; "and discern in the inner man of him a tone of real music . . ." [99]

At last, on July 2nd, Dickens and his entourage started out. Lady Holland had been thanked for letters of introduction she had procured for him.[100] The raven had been left with Edwin Landseer.[101] With that "vast phantom" of a traveling coach, however, went Dickens and Kate, Georgina, Charley, Mamey, Katey, Walter, and the baby, who was coming after all, instead of being left with his grandmother. With them came Anne, the faithful maid of their American trip, and the domestic staff that she commanded. With them came Roche, the courier. With them came Timber, leaping and barking excitedly.

Dickens also was excited. He was glad to get away from England, and fed up with the way its social system was dominated by the aristocracy. "I declare I never go into what is called 'society' that I am not aweary of it, despise it, hate it, and reject it. The more I see of its extraordinary conceit, and its stupendous ignorance of what is passing out of doors, the more certain I am that it is approaching the period when, being incapable of reforming itself, it will have to submit to be reformed by others off the face of the earth." [102]

Meanwhile, all enthusiasm for the "gallant holiday" in Italy, he pictured himself "in a striped shirt, moustache, blouse, red sash, straw hat, and white trousers, sitting astride a mule, and not caring for the clock, the day of the month or the day of the week." [103]

CHAPTER FOUR

From the Bells of Genoa . . .

THE Channel crossing was uneventful. In Boulogne, going into the bank for money, Dickens delivered laboriously a rather long address in French to the clerk behind the counter, only to hear the latter say in English, "How would you like to take it, Sir?" He took it, as everyone had to, in five-franc pieces, an inconveniently bulky coinage that forced him to carry it in two small sacks.[1]

Five days after their departure from England, on Sunday, July 7th, the party left Paris. The postilion hoisted himself into his tall jackboots, adjusted the rope harness on the four horses, making them kick and plunge, cracked his whip like a madman, shouted "En route! Hi!" and they were off, through the gate of the Hôtel Meurice, rumbling over the cobblestones near the Morgue, and across the Pont Neuf on the road to Marseilles.[2]

For two days the conveyance rolled through dreary plains, the bells on the horses jingling monotonously, past walled towns, châteaux with candle-snuffer towers, wagons loaded with Swiss cheeses, bony women holding cows by ropes. At sunset it would rattle into a market town, bumping, whip-cracking, shouting, and heave under the wooden arch of a rambling inn amid a dementia of excitement. Idlers stared awestruck at the enormous vehicle, landlord and landlady shouted rapturously over the children, Roche the courier rushed around looking after beds and eating cucumbers, one in each hand. Early next morning, after a violent dispute over the bill between Roche and the landlord, they were off again, past the lace sellers, and the butter and egg sellers, the fruit sellers swarming in the square.[3]

At Lyons, scorching and chaotic, with garbage rotting in the gutters, the stone pavement in the Cathedral was as dirty as the streets, and the building empty except for some old women and a few dogs engaged in contemplation. The sacristan set in motion for the English visitors the mechanism of the famous clock: hosts of small doors flew open, little figures staggered out and jerked back unsteadily. From a pigeonhole near the Virgin Mary, in the center, one evil-looking puppet, Dickens wrote, "made one of the most sudden plunges I ever saw accomplished: instantly flopping back again at the sight of her, and banging his little door after him. Taking this to be emblematic of the victory over Sin and Death . . . I rashly said, 'Aha! The Evil Spirit. To be sure. He is very soon disposed of.' 'Pardon, Monsieur,' said the Sacristan, with a polite motion of his hand towards the little door, as if introducing somebody—'The Angel Gabriel!' " [4]

Daybreak of the 11th saw the carriage and the entire party loaded on a dirty merchandise vessel and steaming down the arrowy Rhône. The Alps, distant sullen hills during the preceding two days, were now close at hand, with ruined castles perched on every eminence and tiny houses white amid the dull green of the olive trees. By afternoon they sighted the bridge of Avignon and all the underdone-piecrust battlements of the city baking in the sun.[5]

The old city of the Popes was cleaner than Lyons, brilliant with oleanders in bloom and clustered grapes, but shadowed for Dickens by the ancient palace with its funnel-roofed torture chamber, the dismal tower where Rienzi was chained to a wall, and the dark oubliettes where the prisoners of the Inquisition were lost to the world.[6] As Dickens gazed on the hammers that mashed the victims' limbs, the sharp stake, the irons once heated red-hot, the stone trough of the water torture, and the trap door for disposing of the mangled remains, his heart sickened at the image of those cruelties. "Gurgle, swill, bloat, burst, for the Redeemer's honour! Suck the bloody rag, deep down into your unbelieving body, Heretic, at every breath you draw!" [7] One sight that he saw in the room where the tribunal sat struck him with bitter irony. "Conceive the parable of the Good Samaritan having been painted on the wall of one of these Inquisition chambers!" [8]

Jolting in the unwieldy carriage again, over roads lined with burnt-up trees and vines powdered white with dust, under a sun that made the noonday air like crisp blue fire, the party passed through Aix and presently reached the dirty suburbs of Marseilles and the dirty city foul with the stench of its stagnant harbor. Here a gay-awninged little boat took them out to the *Marie Antoinette*, lying near the mouth of the harbor. Their carriage was hoisted on board from a flat barge, bumping into everything amid a Vesuvius of profanity. Under a clear afternoon sky they steamed out into the blue Mediterranean on their way to Genoa.[9]

Early next morning they were off Nice. Before three, Genoa was in view, and they saw it rise, terrace above terrace, garden above garden, palace above palace, height upon height. Ashore, the bulging carriage was provided with horses to take them the last short stage of the journey, the two-mile drive to Albaro. Dickens was dismayed by his first glimpses of the city. The Strada Nuova and the Strada Balbi, the famous streets of palaces, were a disorderly jumble of grimy houses, full of filth and sickening smells, the passages narrower and more squalid than any in the rookeries of St. Giles. As they dragged uphill, past fruit stalls with lemons and oranges hanging in garlands, through mournful and neglected lanes, Dickens fell into a dismal reverie. The way grew still narrower; the carriage had to be measured to see whether it would squeeze through between the walls, and was so tight a fit that it scraped holes in the plastered walls on either side as it swayed along. At last they came to a stop before an archway with a rusty and sagging gate opening on a rank, dull, weedy courtyard attached to a building that looked, Dickens reflected, like a pink jail.[10] His heart sank. This "lonely, rusty, stagnant old staggerer of a domain" was the Villa di Bella Vista![11]

He and Kate did not feel more cheerful as he yanked repeatedly on a bell-pull and no one came to let them in. He tried a crumbling old knocker that slid round when he touched it, and at last Roche appeared and opened the gate.[12] They walked through the seedy little garden, into a bleak square hall like a cellar, up a cracked marble staircase, and through the doors of an enormous conical-vaulted *sala* with white-washed walls, time-blackened pictures, and monumental furniture in red brocade.[13] "All the chairs are immovable," Dickens noted later, "and the sofa weighs several tons." On the same floor and upstairs and downstairs were innumerable other gaunt apartments, drawing room, dining room, bedchambers, some half dozen small sitting rooms, and kitchens looking like alchemical laboratories. "A mighty old, wandering, ghostly, echoing, grim, bare house . . . as ever I beheld or thought of."[14]

In a state of lugubrious discouragement, the tired parents saw that the children were given supper and put to bed. How had Angus Fletcher happened to choose a bleak mausoleum like this pink monstrosity? And in fact, as Dickens came to learn, the kind-hearted but inefficient sculptor, no businessman, had made a very poor bargain. M. De la Rue, the Swiss banker in Genoa whom he had consulted, had urged him to take the magnificent Doria Palace, which was to be had at ₤40 a year. Located only six miles outside Genoa on the seacoast, it was splendidly furnished, and had beautiful gardens, terraces, and a wood of great trees. But Fletcher had been instructed to rent a villa at Albaro, and this pink elephant of a house being the only one available there, he had taken it at four times the price of the Palazzo Doria.[15]

*   *   *   *   *

Next morning, though, Dickens felt more cheerful. The sun was shining brilliantly in a clear blue sky on the deep ultramarine of the Mediterranean. To the right, beyond the bay of Genoa, the Alps stretched to the far horizon; on the other side, three or four miles away, were mountains crowned with forts; in between, a dotting of villas, "some green, some red, some yellow, some blue, some (and ours among the number) pink." Below the terrace outside the French windows of the *sala*, the vineyard was bursting with grapes and figs. From the courtyard gate a narrow lane led down to the sea.[16] And "such green, green, green, as flutters in the vineyard down below," Dickens wrote to Maclise, "*that* I never saw; nor yet such lilac and such purple as float between me and the distant hills; nor yet in anything . . . such awful, solemn, impenetrable blue, as in that same sea. . . . It looks as if a draught of it, only so much as you could scoop up on the beach in the hollow of your hand, would wash out everything else, and make a great blue blank of your intellect." [17]

Everything was in extremes. "There is an insect here that chirps all day . . . something like a Brobdingnagian grasshopper. The creature is born to chirp; to progress in chirping; to chirp louder, louder, louder, till it gives one tremendous chirp and bursts itself. . . . The summer gets hotter, hotter, hotter, till it explodes. The fruit gets riper, riper, riper, till it falls down and rots." "The day gets brighter, brighter, brighter, till it's night." Suddenly the impatient sun would plunge down head-long, and then "you may behold the broad sea, villas, houses, mountains, forts, strewn with rose leaves. Strewn with them? Steeped in them! Dyed, through and through and through. For a moment. No more." [18] In one rush there would be the star-sprinkled dark.

In the heat of the day, though, Dickens discovered, the lattice-blinds had to be close-shut against the view, "or the sun would drive you mad"; and after sunset the windows had to be shut, "or the mosquitoes would tempt you to commit suicide." [19] The stable was "so full of 'vermin and swarmers,'" he wrote Forster, "that I always expect to see the carriage going out bodily, with legions of industrious fleas harnessed to and drawing it off, on their own account." [20] Poor little Timber was driven so frantic by them that Dickens transformed him into a lion dog by having most of his hair clipped off, so that he looked "like the ghost of a drowned dog come out of a pond after a week or so. It is very awful to see him slide into a room. He knows the change upon him, and is always turning round and round to look for himself. I think he'll die of grief." [21]

In comparison with the fleas, other afflictions were trivial. "As for the flies, you don't mind them. . . . The rats are kept away, quite comfortably, by scores of lean cats, who roam about the garden for that purpose. The lizards, of course, nobody cares for; they play in the sun, and don't bite. The little scorpions are merely curious. The beetles are rather late, and have not appeared yet. The frogs are company. There is a preserve of them in the next villa; and after nightfall, one would think that scores upon scores of women in pattens were going up and down a wet stone pavement without a moment's cessation." [22]

Dickens rapidly set about solving all the problems of adjustment to this strange environment. It was clear that the Villa Bagnarello, as he called it, after the name of its owner, would not do for the winter. Luckily, he had bound himself only for the three summer months, and he could look around for something else meanwhile. The children were all well except for Katey, who had a sore throat from sitting in drafts.[23] They could play in the garden and the vineyard; and under the terrace there was a stable where three cows lazily chewed vine leaves all day and supplied milk by the bucketful.[24] Fruit and vegetables were abundant. "Green figs I have already learnt to like. Green almonds (we have them at dessert every day) are the most delicious fruit in the world. And green lemons, combined with some rare hollands that is to be got here, make prodigious punch, I assure you." [25]

For better air Dickens transformed the dining room, alongside the *sala*, into a nursery. The corner room, adjoining, which was the best bedroom, he took as his and Kate's, and determined it should be the room in which he wrote.[26] After twelve the sun was off the corner window, and he could then "throw the blinds open, and look up from my paper, at the sea, the mountains, the washed-out villas, the vineyards, at the blistering white fort with a sentry on the drawbridge standing in a bit of shadow no broader than his own musket, and at the sky, as often as I like." [27] Around the corner were Georgina's room and another nursery.[28] Within a week Dickens had added a piano to the furniture of the *sala*, and they had all settled down to a regular routine.[29]

Breakfast was at half-past nine or ten, he said, dinner at four, bedtime at eleven. The servants they had brought with them were soon on cordial terms with the couple of Italian work-people who completed the establishment. "To hear one or other of them," Dickens wrote, "talking away to our servants with the utmost violence and volubility in Genoese, and our servants answering with great fluency in English (very loud: as if the others were only deaf, not Italian), is one of the most ridiculous things possible." [30]

Dickens's books and writing equipment had not yet arrived, but meanwhile he engaged "a little patient revolutionary officer, exiled in England during many years," [31] to read and speak Italian with him three times a week, and began Manzoni's *I Promessi Sposi*.[32] Within a month he could ask for whatever he wanted in any shop or coffee-house and read with a fair degree of fluency. "I wish you could see me without my knowing it," he wrote Forster, "walking about alone here. I am now as bold as a lion in the streets. The audacity with which one begins to speak when there is no help for it, is quite astonishing." [33]

When visitors came Dickens generally bolted, leaving Kate to entertain them.[34] Except for studying Italian, he led a lazy life, idling in the shade of the vineyard or underneath the rocks on the seashore. In the enervating heat, indeed, he found it difficult at first to force himself to the slightest physical exertion; he felt as if a blow behind the knees had so weakened his legs that he could neither walk nor stand. It was worst on first getting up, when it took a strong determination to keep on dressing, "one's tendency being to tumble down anywhere and lie there." [35]

Before long, though, his restlessness burst forth, and in spite of the hot sirocco blowing "like a gigantic oven out for a holiday," [36] he began exploring the surrounding countryside. Every lane crept between great villas, but they were nearly all faded and neglected. Mildew obliterated the paintings on their outer walls and their courtyards were overgrown with weeds. Patches stained the bases of the statues like a hideous skin disease. Fountains too tired to play gurgled with just enough sleeping memory of their function to keep the neighborhood damp. Iron bars flaked from the lower windows, gates were rusty, firewood dried in lordly halls.[37]

In Genoa a confused and noisy life elbowed the decayed magnificence. Gilded sedan chairs plied down tortuous alleys among blind beggars, jingling mules, and naked children. The peasant girls were not beautiful but carried themselves well; the old women were of an ugliness so stupendous that Dickens seemed to see the witches from *Macbeth* in every doorway. Bare-legged Cappucini were everywhere in the cramped streets that zigzagged beneath the towering walls of great structures. Palaces with terraces of orange trees thirty feet above the street had heavy stone balconies and immense public staircases leading to great frescoed halls moldering and blotting and rotting in the oozing corners. Buildings once noble residences were now crammed with miscellaneous occupants. There was a hatter's shop in one little room of the palace where the English Bank had its offices, and in the elaborately decorated hall a vendor sold walking sticks while a few loungers lay sleeping on the floor. Macaroni and polenta sellers established their stalls under the garbage-strewn arches of ruinous houses. Tumble-down tenements in the narrow by-ways smelled like cheese kept in hot blankets. Amid the refuse between them, greasy shops sprouted like parasitic fungus.[38]

Only the churches seemed free from the general squalor, although Dickens found much tasteless trash and tinsel mingled with their rich embellishments and too many "sprawling effigies of maudlin monks." [39] The Church of the Annunciata, in the process of restoration, with its innumerable small chapels and high dome, was so splendidly decorated and set in gold from the outer door to the utmost height of its cupola[40] that it looked, he said, "like a great enamelled snuff-box." [41] "But every sort of splendor is in perpetual enactment through the means of these churches. Gorgeous processions in the streets, illuminations of windows on feast nights, lighting up of lamps and clusterings of flowers before the shrines of saints; all manner of show and display. The doors of the churches stand wide open; and in this hot weather great red curtains wave in their places; and if you go and sit in one to get out of the sun, you see the queerest figures kneeling against the pillars . . . and vast streams of women in veils (they don't wear bonnets), with great fans in their hands, coming and going, that you are never tired of looking at." [42] But Dickens did not like the faces of the countless priests and monks. Their "repulsive countenances" seemed to him to bear the legible signs of "sloth, deceit, and intellectual torpor." [43] "The Jesuits, too," he wrote, "muster strong in the streets, and go slinking noiselessly about, in pairs, like black cats." [44]

By the 10th of August his paper and inkstand and the knickknacks he liked to have on his writing table had arrived from England, and he began to think about his Christmas story.[45] His books, however, had not yet passed the customhouse; he wanted Ruskin's *Seven Lamps of Architecture* and worried lest some volumes of Voltaire might be confiscated.[46] And although he had arranged to move from the unsatisfactory Villa Bagnarello to the Palazzo Peschiere in Genoa at the end of September, he felt unsettled until the change was actually made. Not a word, therefore, got on paper during the two and a half months at Albaro.[47]

Meanwhile Dickens had made the acquaintance of the French Consul-General, an enthusiastic admirer who had written on his books in one of the French reviews, and who lived with his English wife in the very next villa.[48] At a dinner there, Dickens met the Marquis di Negri, once the friend of Byron and a prodigious improviser in verse,[49] "a very fat and much older Jerdan, with the same thickness of speech and size of tongue." [50] After dinner the Consul proposed Dickens's health, and the Marquis, giving himself a great rap on the breast of his bright-buttoned blue coat, "turns up his fishy eyes, stretches out his arm like the living statue defying the lightning at Astley's and delivers four impromptu verses in my honour, at which everybody is enchanted, and I more than anybody—perhaps with the best reason, for I didn't understand a word of them." [51]

Shortly afterward, the Marquis invited Dickens to a great reception in his splendid residence with grounds carved in grottoed walks and lit by variegated lamps, all of which his host delightedly showed off by "diving out into dark corners and then among the lattice-work and flower pots, rubbing his hands and going round and round with explosive chuckles." [52] Suddenly Dickens remembered in horror that the gates of Genoa closed at midnight and realized that he must make a sudden bolt if he wished to get back to Albaro. He was running as hard as he could, over uneven ground, downhill, when he came to a pole fastened across the street breast-high, "without any light or watchman—quite in the Italian style. I went over it headlong, with such force that I rolled myself completely white in the dust; but although I tore my clothes to shreds, I hardly scratched myself except in one place on the knee. I had no time to think of it then, for I was up directly and off again to save the gate, but when I got outside the wall and saw the state I was in, I wondered I had not broken my neck." [53]

The lonely two miles home he "took it easy," but the misadventure brought on an attack of the old "unspeakable and agonizing pain in the side." [54] for which Bob Fagin had applied hot bottles in the blacking-warehouse days. For some time thereafter Dickens had to sit quietly in the shade of the ruined chapel on the seashore, or watch the peasants making wine, or listen to shooting parties blazing away at the rats who came out in strong detachments after dusk to eat the grapes. By this time, too, the mosquitoes were unbearable, and he had to sleep under gauze at night, "like cold meat in a safe." [55]

But it was not long before he had recovered from both his accident and his illness, and was swimming daily in the "little blue bay just below the house here, like a fish in high spirits," clad in a bathing costume, he wrote Stanfield, that made him resemble Yarnold in the opera *Masaniello*. "I enhanced the likeness very much, last Friday morning, by singing a barcarole in the rocks. I was a trifle too flesh-coloured (the stage knowing no medium between bright salmon and dirty yellow), but apart from that defect, not badly made up by any means." [56] Between plunges he made friends with the coastguard men, amiable fellows, startlingly innocent of maritime knowledge. "One of them asked me only yesterday, if it would take a year to get to England in a ship?" [57]

A delightful discovery was the marionette theater in Genoa. The puppet that played the comic parts had "prodigious" spirits, and was equipped, Dickens wrote, "with extra joints in his legs: and a practical eye, with which he winks at the pit in a manner that is absolutely insupportable." A miniature ballet brought the entertainment to a delirious climax: "the height to which they spring; the impossible and inhuman extent to which they pirouette; the revelation of their preposterous legs; the coming down with a pause, on the very tips of their toes, when the music requires it; . . . the final passion of a pas-de-deux; and the going off with a bound!—I shall never see a real ballet, with a composed countenance ¬gain." [58]

Another especially mind-shattering performance dealt with the death of Napoleon. The dethroned Emperor had sentimental eyes in a face that maintained a settled expression of melancholy while his feet sometimes dangled in the air and sometimes skated away with him in the middle of a long noble speech. The Governor of St. Helena, Sir Hudson Lowe (pronounced "Sir Yew ud se on Low"— the last as in "cow"), wore a great clump of a lower jaw "to express his tyrannical and obdurate nature," and wound up his speeches with the word "Yas!" as a proof that he was English.[59] In the death scene, with Napoleon pathetic in bed, the doctor, through "some derangement of his wires, hovered about the couch like a vulture, and gave medical opinions in the air." [60]

Early in September, Dickens went to Marseilles to meet his brother Fred, who was coming to pass a fortnight's holiday at Genoa.[61] They made the return journey over the Alps and along the Corniche Road, resting overnight at inns resembling ancient wine vaults and infested with mosquitoes and "fleas of elephantine dimensions . . . gambolling boldly in the dirty beds." [62] By Friday the 13th they reached Albaro. Swimming out the next morning too far, Fred was almost drowned in a strong current, and was rescued only by the chance of a fishing boat leaving the harbor at that time.[63] "It was a world of horror and anguish," Dickens wrote Forster, "crowded into four or five minutes of dreadful agitation; and, to complete the terror of it, Georgy, Charlotte" the nurse, "and the children were on a rock in full view of it all, crying, as you may suppose, like mad creatures." [64]

*   *   *   *   *

On Fred's return to England, near the end of September, Dickens moved from the Pink Jail to the Palazzo Peschiere, the Palace of the Fishponds.[65] He had taken the entire *piano nobile* of this famous building; on the floor below lived a Spanish duke. "The duchess was his mistress many years," Dickens told Forster, "and bore him (I think) six daughters. He always promised her that if she gave birth to a son, he would marry her; and when at last the boy arrived, he went into her bedroom, saying—'Duchess, I am charmed to salute you!' " [66]

The day the Dickens household left Albaro began with violent wind and driving rain,[67] but as they reached the stately terraces leading to the Palazzo the sun came out and shone brightly on its urns and sculptured figures, and on the groves of camellias and orange and lemon trees. Goldfish swam and dived in the glittering water of seven fountains, hedges of pink roses blushed in the greenery, vines clambered up the balconies, and, beyond the steep descending slope, Genoa stretched its panorama of steeples and towers in a bowl of harbor and hills encircled by the blue Mediterranean and the distant mountains sparkling with snow.[68]

Within was "the grand sala, fifty feet high, of an area larger than the dining room of the Academy," Dickens wrote Forster, "and painted, walls and ceiling, with frescoes" designed by Michelangelo, and "as fresh as if the colours had been laid on yesterday. On the same floor as this great hall are a drawing room and a dining-room, into which we might put your large room—I wish we could!—away in one corner, and dine without knowing it, both covered also with frescoes still bright enough to make them thoroughly cheerful, and both so nicely proportioned as to give their bigness all the effect of snugness. . . .

"Adjoining the sala right and left, are the two best bedrooms; in size and shape like those at Windsor Castle but greatly higher; both having altars, a range of three windows with stone balconies, floors tesselated in patterns of black and white stone, and walls painted every inch: on the left, nymphs pursued by satyrs as large as life and as wicked; on the right, Phaeton larger than life, with horses bigger than Meux and Co.'s, tumbling down into the best bed." [69] The right-hand room Dickens occupied with Kate; of the left he took posssession as a study, writing behind a big screen set up before a window whence he could look down into the gardens with the goldfish and the orange trees, and out over Genoa to the lighthouse a mile distant in the harbor.[70]

Dickens was now eager to begin his Christmas story. But in spite of the fact that he had chosen his subject, he still found it difficult to make a start. His hand was out; he was trying against the grain. He missed the London streets that he had paced at night in blazing excitement while the *Christmas Carol* seethed in his imagination. He had no title, and he had never found it possible to make headway in writing until a title was decided on. The bells of Genoa, clanging and clashing the hours from every tower, drove him almost mad with distraction, pouring into his ears, "a tuneless, grating, discordant, jerking, hideous vibration that made his ideas 'spin round and round till they lost themselves in a whirl of vexation and giddiness, and dropped down dead.' " [71]

Something was wrong. And with the emotional disturbance of his inability to break through the barrier, he dreamed of Mary again in the old heart-rending way. Just before they left Albaro he had had a return of rheumatism in his back and knotted around his waist "like a girdle of pain" that kept him awake nearly all night. At last he fell asleep and dreamed himself in an indistinct place of light with a spirit draped in blue like one of Raphael's Madonnas. Although he could not make out the face, he knew that it was Mary's spirit. Weeping with delight, he stretched out his arms, calling it "Dear," at which it recoiled, but with so much tenderness and compassion that he was cut to the heart. In an agony of entreaty lest the vision leave him, he asked questions: "Give me some token that you have really visited me!" and then, desperate that it might vanish, "What is the True religion?" The spirit hesitated. Dickens suggested that perhaps the forms of religion did not greatly matter, "if we try to do good?—or perhaps," he added, "the Roman Catholic is the best?" "For *you*," it said, with a heartbreaking, heavenly tenderness, "for *you*, it is the best!" Then he awoke, with the tears running down his face. [72]

A week passed by at the Palazzo Peschiere, and his work had not progressed an inch. "Never did I so stagger upon a threshold before," he lamented to Forster. "I seem as if I had plucked myself out of my proper soil when I left Devonshire Terrace; and could take root no more until I return to it." [73] Two days later he was longing for his London night walks again. "Put me down on Waterloo Bridge at eight o'clock in the evening, with leave to roam about as long as I like, and I would come home, as you know, panting to go on. I am sadly strange as it is, and can't settle." [74] The sun shone, the water sparkled in the fountains, the bells clamored with an intolerable resonance that hammered his brain empty. But suddenly the title came, and he announced it to Forster in a letter consisting only of a quotation from Falstaff: "We have heard THE CHIMES at midnight, Master Shallow!" [15]

The bells of the foreign city had evoked some reverberating chord within his imagination. "Let them clash upon me now from all the churches and convents in Genoa, I see nothing but the old London belfry I have set them in. In my mind's eye, Horatio, I like more and more my notion of making, in this little book, a great blow for the poor." [16] And so, in Italy, amid the marble and frescoes of the Palazzo Peschiere, there came to him the image of Trotty Veck, the "sorry old drudge of a London ticket-porter, who in his anxiety not to distrust or think hardly of the rich, has fallen into the opposite extreme of distrusting the poor," fearing them "irredeemably bad," and concluding "that his class and order have no business with a new year, and really are 'intruding.'" [17]

The story was to be a plea for charity and mercy no less than justice, an indictment of the hard-hearted views that made the almshouse a place of punishment as grim as the jail and that condemned the workers to a routine of toil unrelieved by any gleam of happiness or genial indulgence. Nineteenth-century political economy denied any outlook to the laboring classes save a dreary hovering on the edge of starvation. The Malthusian doctrine of population hung over England like a dark cloud. "Let the poor live hard lives," it said, "sober, celibate, and unamused, let them eat the plainest food, pinch to save, and save to lower the rates—then 'civilization' might win through. . . . Shut the gin shops, prevent travelling on the only day a workingman can travel, make copulation even in marriage seem a sin . . ." [18] Meanwhile let wages go lower, and "put down" suicide by harsh penalties against any poor creatures who have tried and failed to end their own misery. Such were the harsh doctrines against which Dickens raised his banner and sounded a trumpet of resistance.

On the verge of beginning, Dickens was disturbed to hear that he was expected to attend the levee of the Governor, who had just arrived in Genoa. He requested the English Consul to explain for him. " 'Where's the great poet?' said the Governor. 'I want to see the great poet.' 'The great poet, your excellency,' said the consul, 'is at work, writing a book, and begged me to make his excuses.' 'Excuses!' said the Governor, 'I wouldn't interfere with such an occupation for all the world. Pray tell him that my house is open to the honour of his presence when it is perfectly convenient to him; but not otherwise. And let no gentleman,' said the Governor, a surweyin' of his suite with a majestic eye, 'call upon Signor Dickens till he is understood to be disengaged.' " [79]

Soon Dickens was feverishly engrossed in tearing off the story. "With my steam very much up," he wrote Forster, "I find it a great trial to be so far off from you, and consequently to have no one (always excepting Kate and Georgy) to whom to expatiate on my day's work. And I want a crowded street to plunge into at night." [80] A few days later: "I am in a regular, ferocious excitement with the Chimes; get up at seven; have a cold bath before breakfast; and blaze away, wrathful and red-hot until three o'clock or so: when I usually knock off (unless it rains) for the day. . . . I am fierce to finish off in a spirit bearing some affinity to those of truth and mercy, and to shame the cruel and the canting." [81]

All through October the weather was wild and stormy, "worse than any November English weather I have ever beheld, or any weather I have had experience of anywhere. So horrible today that all power has been rained and gloomed out of me. Yesterday, in pure determination to get the better of it, I walked twelve miles in mountain rain. You never saw it rain. Scotland and America are nothing to it." [82]

Confinement to the house was rendered more trying by the fact that during the entire month Mrs. Macready's young sister, Susan Atkins, was staying with the family and proved to be an exasperating house guest. Dickens had constantly to curb the irritation that both Kate and Georgina were forever inclined to reveal, and remind them of the sacred duties of hospitality. And how could Kate dream of being rude to Susan, he was obliged to ask, when she remembered how generously the Macreadys had taken care of the children when Dickens and Kate were in America? Did he himself not repeatedly spare even Fletcher at his most foolishly annoying despite the strongest temptation to "put him down?" [83]

From these frictions it was even a relief to get back to the toilsome and nervous application of his study. There, despite the rain sweeping in gusts across the terrace and the wind worrying the orange trees,

Dickens plunged himself into the emotion of his story until he grew worn and gaunt. "My cheeks, which were beginning to fill out, have sunk again; my hair is very lank; my eyes have grown immensely large; and the head inside the hair is hot and giddy. . . . Since I conceived, at the beginning of the second part, what must happen in the third, I have undergone as much sorrow and agitation as if the thing were real; and have wakened up with it at night. I was obliged to lock myself in when I finished it yesterday, for my face was swollen for the time to twice its proper size, and was hugely ridiculous." [84]

On November 3rd, at half-past two in the afternoon, Dickens flung down his pen. "Thank God!" he wrote Forster, "I have finished the Chimes. This moment. I take up my pen again today, to say only that much; and to add that I have had what women call 'a real good cry.' " [85] And to Mitton he explained that he had not written because he had worn himself to death in this month of work. "None of my usual reliefs have been at hand; I have not been able to divest myself of the story—have suffered very much in my sleep in consequence—and am so shaken by such work in this trying climate that I am as nervous as a man who is dying of drink, and as haggard as a murderer." [86]

* * * * *

Under the efficient direction of Roche, the household was now running as smoothly as an oiled machine. "There never was such a fellow," Dickens exclaimed; the servants did their work perfectly and were "as quiet and well-behaved as at home." [87] Carpets were down on the floors, fires burning cheerfully on the autumn nights, curtains at the windows to be drawn cozily against the dark. Charley had a writing master and a French master every day, and he and the little girls were about to learn dancing. Dickens had a box at the opera, with his own key, and could go there when he pleased as if it were his own drawing room. He had made a number of pleasant acquaintances, among them M. De la Rue, the Swiss banker, who with his pretty little English wife had apartments in the Palazzo Rosso. With *The Chimes* off his hands, Dickens was now free to enjoy himself.

Nevertheless he felt tense, agitated, restless. It had not been easy to keep peace between Susan, Kate, and Georgina; and his nerves were frayed, besides, by the fierceness with which he had felt his story. He was keyed up and overwrought. He wanted distraction; he wanted to get away. He missed England.

The mood had been growing upon him as October drew to its close. On the 25th, Forster received a hint of his feelings. "I would give a hundred pounds (and think it cheap) to see you read it." [88] And hard on this Dickens rushed a proposal that he make the long return journey to England in the face of approaching winter, just to spend a few nights in London and read his story aloud to a group of friends there. "If I come," he told Forster, "I shall put up at Cuttris's"—the Piazza Hotel, in Covent Garden—"that I may be close to you." [89] Forster argued against the fatigue and the expense. But Dickens's resolve was already fixed. "Nothwithstanding what you say," he answered, "I am still in the same mind about coming to London." [90] The unspeakable restlessness that had possession of him would no more let him remain where he was than a full balloon could be prevented from tugging to go up, and there were no ropes that could hold him down.

"Shall I confess to you, I particularly want Carlyle above all to see it before the rest of the world, when it is done; and I should like to inflict the little story on him and on dear old gallant Macready with my own lips, and to have Stanny and the other Mac sitting by." And cajolingly he drew a picture of a little circle in Lincoln's Inn Fields on a wet evening, with Forster saying, "My boy, would you give us that little Christmas book (a little Christmas book of Dickens's, Macready, which I'm anxious you should hear); and don't slur it now, or be too fast, Dickens, please!" [91]

By the time the story was finished, Dickens had carried his point and suggested additional guests for the occasion. He was starting off at once, with Roche, on a fortnight's holiday tour that would take in Parma, Modena, Bologna, Venice, Verona, Brescia, and Milan. "Here is the brave Courier measuring bits of maps with a carving-fork, and going up mountains on a tea-spoon." [92] At Milan on the 18th he would be joined for a few days by Kate and Georgina, who would bring on all his letters. Thence he would proceed "across the wildest pass of the Alps that may be open, to Strasbourg," and so on to Paris, and from there to England.

"Now, you know my punctiwality," Dickens concluded. "Frost, ice, flooded rivers, steamers, horses, passports, and custom-houses may damage it. But my design is, to walk into Cuttris's coffee-room on

Sunday the 1st of December, in good time for dinner. I shall look for you at the farther table by the fire—where we generally go." [93]

The day before his departure Dickens had a dinner party of fourteen guests, including the English Consul and his wife, the English banker, and the De la Rues. Roche, as major-domo, was in a state of beaming excitement. At nine in the morning arrived "two men in immense paper caps," the Governor's cooks, and Roche's private friends, who announced that they had come to dress the dinner, but Dickens's cook refused to stand for this. Six other friends of his, however, "having the appearance of English clergymen," were allowed to wait on the table. Roche delightedly hovered behind Kate with a case of toothpicks in his pocket, looking at Dickens, and whispering to Georgina, whenever he handed her anything, "What does master think of datter 'rangement? Is he cŏntĕnt?" The climax of his joy came with the arrival of the dessert, over which, as a special distinction, he had been given supreme control, and he triumphantly produced ices frozen in the shapes of fruit. [94]

The next afternoon, November 6th, Dickens and Roche set off for Piacenza in a stagecoach like a traveling caravan, which also contained a lady with a large dog. The weather was very wet and cold, and the dog howled dolefully all night. The coach crept on at the rate of four miles an hour over bad roads through rain and mud. [95] It was a gloomy start, but ahead there were Parma, Ferrara, Venice, Milan, and at the end of the journey England and the longed-for reunion with his friends.

CHAPTER FIVE

...To the Chimes of London

ALL next day they drove through a cheerless rain, packed into a small coach with an old priest, a young Jesuit, a provincial lawyer, and a red-nosed gentleman with a very wet brown umbrella, and reached Stradella at ten that night. Here an inn consisting of "a series of queer galleries open to the night" gave them a supper of cabbage boiled with rice and cheese, fried pork and pigs' kidneys, stringy veal, and baby turkeys, all strongly impregnated with garlic.[1] Dickens's bedroom was bare and cold, but Roche, looking "like Birnam Wood taking a winter walk," [2] brought in a huge quantity of dried brush, kindled a roaring fire, and made Dickens a glass of scorching hot brandy.

At four the next morning "the brave Courier" was up again, "fresher than a new-blown rose," making blazing fires, producing mugs of scalding coffee, and roaring in the dark streets for fresh milk, "on the chance of somebody with a cow getting up to supply it." [3] By five they were off, and by eleven they were leaving Piacenza, a brown, decayed old town with streets of frowning houses and a solemn palace guarded by two colossal statues. Then along a road with vines festooning their red and gold foliage from tree to tree, until they came to Parma and its campanile with Correggio frescoes rotting in the cupola.[4] Within the Cathedral the worshipers listened "to the same drowsy chaunt" and whispered "in the selfsame dark confessionals" [5] he had seen everywhere; and in Modena, too, when he came to it, he found "this same Heart beating with the same monotonous pulsation, the centre of the same torpid, listless system." [6]

At Bologna, the waiter who attended Dickens was full of memories of Lord Byron, dead these twenty years. "Milor Beeron" had been fond of the kind of matting on the bedroom floor; Milor Beeron never touched milk; the Monte Pulciano wine served at dinner had come from vines on an estate Milor Beeron once owned; the road on which Dickens presently departed for Ferrara had been Milor Beeron's favorite ride.' Ferrara, next morning, seemed more solitary than any other city through which Dickens had passed, with Tasso's prison, the castle dungeons where Parisina and her lover were beheaded, and weeds creeping up the stairs of the dismantled palaces, gloomy in the grim town.[8]

Crossing the Po, they came into Austrian territory, and the brave Courier, hail fellow everywhere else, fell into his usual rage with the custom-house men who asked for bribes. In a letter to Forster, Dickens described the regularly repeated scene:

" 'Is there anything contraband in this carriage, signore?'—'No, no. There's nothing here. I am an Englishman, and this is my servant.' 'A buono mano, signore?' 'Roche,' (in English) 'give him something, and get rid of him.' " But Roche would sit unmoved, and the man would repeat his request. " 'A buono mano, signore?' 'Go along with you!' says the Brave C. 'Signore, I am a custom-house-officer!' 'Well, then, more shame for you!' " And, in English, to Dickens, "while the custom-house-officer's face is a portrait of anguish from his intense desire to know what is being told to his disparagement. 'Dattei chip,' shaking his fist at him, 'is greatest tief—and you know it you rascal—as never did en-razh me so, that I cannot bear myself!' I suppose chip to mean chap, but it may include the custom-house-officer's father and have some reference to the old block, for anything I distinctly know." [9]

On the road Dickens had felt it necessary to write Kate warning her again about Mrs. Macready's sister. No "natural dislike to her inanities" must be allowed to destroy the memory of their debt to the Macreadys. "You are too easily run away with—and Georgy is too—by the irritation and displeasure of the moment," Dickens wrote. And that there would be trouble he saw clearly, unless Kate was "as careful with that girl as if you were treading on hot ploughshares." "I should never forgive myself or you, if the smallest drop of coldness or misunderstanding were created between me and Macready, by means so monstrously absurd." After chitchat about little episodes of his journey, and affectionate messages to Kate, Georgina, and all the children—including the baby, who now bore the nickname Chickenstalker—

Dickens returned to giving injunctions: "Keep things in their places. I can't bear to picture them otherwise." [10]

Late in the evening of the 11th, Dickens's coach came to a stop by the waterside, and a black gondola conveyed him five miles over the dark sighing water to a great light lying in the distance on the sea. Presently the city rose like a huge ship, and then he came splashing through the silent and deserted canals, feeling as if the houses were reality but the water fever-madness.[11] Flitting shadows, branching lanes of mysterious water, painted pillars with boats moored to them, torchlit palace entries, bridges, and open spaces of ponderous arches and pillars frothing with a lace of decoration like "garlands of hoarfrost or gossamer," drifted in succession past him dreamlike in the night.[12]

But not until the cold, bright, bracing day, when he stood in the sunlight of the Piazza, did the glory of Venice burst around him. "The wildest visions of the Arabian Nights are nothing to the Piazza of Saint Mark, and the first impression of the inside of the church. The gorgeous and wonderful reality of Venice, is beyond the fancy of the wildest dreamer. Opium couldn't build such a place, and enchantment couldn't shadow it forth in vision." [13] Splendid domes and turrets, golden crosses glittering in the light, the majestic palace, the magnificent Cathedral fretted with traceries, the campanile, the red granite pillars with the Lion of St. Mark, the blue orb with the twelve signs of the zodiac and a mimic sun glowing upon it, the two bronze giants hammering out the hours upon a sounding bell, the white houses of the square, the graceful arcade, the masts with their bright flags, all lay floating with incredible buoyancy on the bosom of the green sea.[14]

But beneath all that iridescent glory there was a nightmare world of "wickedness and gloom—its awful prisons, deep below the water; its judgment chambers, secret doors, deadly nooks, where the torches you carry with you blink as if they couldn't bear the air." [15] There were the cells, Dickens wrote to Douglas Jerrold, "where the monk came at midnight to confess the political offender; the bench where he was strangled; the deadly little vault in which they tied him in a sack, and the stealthy crouching little door through which they hurried him in a boat, and bore him away to sink him where no fisherman dare cast his net." [16]

With the memory of these horrors burning in his brain, Dickens burst into a passionate denunciation of those witless worshipers of the good old times who always aroused his bitter scorn. That, in the face of these dungeons, and of that hideous museum he had just seen, "having a chamber full of such frightful instruments of torture as the devil in a brain fever could scarcely invent," there should be "hundreds of parrots," he exclaimed, "who will declaim to you in speech and print, by the hour together, on the degeneracy of the times in which a railroad is building across the water at Venice; instead of going down on their knees, the drivellers, and thanking Heaven that they live in a time when iron makes roads, instead of . . . engines for driving screws into the skulls of innocent men." [17]

From Venice, Dickens passed on to Verona and Mantua. Here the paintings impressed him less than those in Venice. Especially the Julio Romanos, in the Palazzo Té, he disliked; and he refused to give a canting admiration where none was felt. He found the Titans warring against Jove grotesque monsters "with swollen faces and cracked cheeks," distorted in look and limb, "staggering under the weight of falling buildings," "undergoing and doing every kind of mad and maniacal destruction," uncouth, harsh in coloring, all like "a violent rush of blood to the head." [18] Far different were the masterpieces of Titian and Tintoretto. "I have never yet seen any praise of Titian's great picture of the Assumption of the Virgin at Venice, which soared half as high as the beautiful and amazing reality. Tintoretto's picture too, of the Assembly of the Blest, . . . with all the lines in it (it is of immense size and the figures are countless) tending majestically and dutifully to Almighty God in the centre, is grand and noble in the extreme." [19]

However, in the battle pieces Dickens could not help noticing, with some amusement, that no matter how involved and slaughterous they might be, the generals were always rendered with a "surprising art" that made it impossible not to notice them, even though they were in the thick of a crowd. All told, he did not intend to be bullied into merely conventional judgments. "I have seen some delightful pictures; and some (at Verona and Mantua) really too absurd and ridiculous even to laugh at. Hampton Court is a fool to 'em—and oh there are some rum 'uns there, my friend." His general impressions Dickens summarized briefly and independently: "the rules of art are much too slavishly followed; making it a pain to you, when you go into the galleries day after day, to be so very precisely sure where this figure will be turning round, and that figure will be lying down, and that other will have a great lot of drapery twined about him, and so forth." [20]

He had been rather startled to discover that the distance of Romeo's banishment, from Verona to Mantua, was only twenty-five miles. The old palace of the Capulets, with the hat that was their heraldic device carved in stone upon a wall, had become a miserable inn, with its court full of crazy coaches, geese, and pigs, and ankle-deep in mud and dung.[21] But how impressive was the Roman amphitheater, with its entrances, passages, and staircases, its arches over some of which the old Roman numerals were still to be read, its subterranean ways for beasts, and those forty-four rows of seats, "as fresh and perfect as if their occupants had vacated them but yesterday." [22]

Two and a half days of further traveling brought Dickens, through Cremona and Lodi, to Milan. The inns, like all those at which he had stayed, were bare and comfortless. "The windows won't open," he wrote at Lodi, "and the doors won't shut; and these latter (a cat could get in, between them and the floor) have a windy command of a colonnade which is open to the night, so that my slippers positively blow off my feet, and make little circuits in the room—like leaves." The ashy wood-fires, burning on immense fenderless hearths, knew only two extremes, "an agony of heat when wood is put on, and an agony of cold when it has been on two minutes." [23]

Nevertheless, Dickens had enjoyed himself thoroughly. The beds were clean, the meals good, and the servants so quick and obliging "that you would be a beast not to look cheerful"; without being obsequious they were always amiably inventing little attentions that they supposed to be English, and their light-heartedness made it "a pleasure to have to do with them. But so it is with all the people." Sometimes, when he walked on ahead of the horses for two hours in the middle of the day, he would have to ask his way: "and the men are such gentlemen," he wrote Forster, "and the women such ladies, that it is quite an interchange of courtesies." [24] By November 18th, when he joined Kate and Georgy at Milan, he had shaken off all his nervousness, was red-faced from being in the open air, and slept soundly again.[25]

After three days in Milan, seeing Leonardo's *Last Supper* and the jeweled mummy of San Carlo Borromeo in its rich subterranean shrine, driving on the tree-shaded Corso, and attending a ballet at the Scala, Dickens left the city at five o'clock on the morning of the 21st.[26] Before the golden statue on the summit of the cathedral was lost in the blue sky, the stupendous confusion of the Alps towered ahead.[27] By sunset he reached Lago Maggiore and Isola Bella rising fantastically out of the blue water. Though it was ten at night when he came to Domo d'Ossola, at the foot of the Simplon Pass, the moon illumined the snow so brightly that he and the faithful Roche resolved to go on.[28]

Winding upward among dark trees over a track beaten five feet deep, between massive perpendiculars of rock, through a cave with a thunderous cataract deep below, across a dizzy bridge, they toiled all night to the bleak and lonely top of the pass, where the north wind, high and boisterous, cut their faces with sharp particles of snow and pierced into the very blood.[29] Here they saw the sun rise and turn the white wastes into a glory of rose.[30] From then on began the descent under everlasting glaciers arched with galleries of dripping icicles, under and over foaming waterfalls, across lofty bridges, and through horrible ravines, winding down until there glittered beneath them in the sunshine the red, green, and yellow roofs of a Swiss town, piled like playthings in the steep landscape.[31]

Then came Vevey beside the smooth lake of Geneva, Fribourg and its statue of St. Peter grasping his enormous key, Basle where the swollen Rhine ran swift and green, and Strasbourg's great mechanical clock with the crowing cock clapping his wings and straining his throat while his voice came from deep within the works.[32] Throughout all the journey the cold continued so intense that Dickens felt his eyes and face tingling like cymbals that had just been clashed.[33] It was a relief at Strasbourg to sit in his bedroom by the fire drinking scalding brandy and water and feeling "the preliminary agony of returning animation." [34]

The fifty-hour ride by diligence to Paris was a sea of mud.[35] Here Dickens hoped to find Macready, who had returned from America in October and was now about to open a season of Shakespearean and other plays.[36] What fun it would be to send in a card to Macready's dressing room at the Salle Ventadour, inscribed "Mr. G. S. Hancock Muggridge, United States," and then burst in upon his startled friend and wring his hand! [37] But the season had not yet begun, and although the porter at the Hôtel Brighton said that Macready was expected that night, he did not turn up. Reluctantly obliged to conclude that they would not see each other until he passed through Paris again on his way back to Italy, Dickens took a coach for Boulogne at eight the next morning.[38]

Hard frosts made the roads better during the remainder of the journey, the Channel crossing was quickly accomplished,[39] and on the wintry evening of Saturday, November 30th, Dickens strode eagerly into the coffeeroom of Cuttris's hotel. In a moment Forster had spied him, and the two men rushed into each other's arms.[40] Maclise, who was also there in welcome, gave him an equally hearty greeting.[41]

*　　*　　*　　*　　*

The eight days Dickens spent in London after the long journey from Genoa were jammed to overflowing with work and engagements. Forster's letters had objected to some of the satire in *The Chimes*. Filer, he thought was a too distorted caricature of the tenets of political economy, and the attack on the benevolent feudalism of the Young England movement was ineffective. Such exaggerated burlesque would lay Dickens open to the charge of not knowing what he was talking about. These details Dickens had consequently agreed to amend before the book went to press.

"As you dislike the Young England gentleman," he had written Forster from Genoa, "I shall knock him out, and replace him by a man (I can dash him in at your rooms in an hour) who recognizes no virtues in anything but the good old times, and talks of them, parrot-like, whatever the matter is. A real good old city tory, in a blue coat and bright buttons and a white cravat, and with a tendency of blood to the head. File away at Filer, as you please; but bear in mind that the Westminster Review considered Scrooge's presentation of the turkey to Bob Cratchit as grossly inconsistent with political economy." [42]

The revisions occupied Sunday and the completed manuscript was rushed into the hands of the printers on Monday. As Bradbury and Evans had not yet built up any machinery of distribution, they had arranged to use the facilities of Chapman and Hall, under whose imprint the volume consequently appeared. Dickens's heat against his former publishers, however, had cooled, and he was not displeased. With the form of the book and its illustrations he was delighted. One woodcut of Doyle's, to be sure, and another of Leech's, he found so unlike his idea that he invited the two artists to breakfast, he wrote Kate, "and with that winning manner which you know of, got them with the highest good humour to do both afresh." Stanfield's two illustrations were just right, and "Mac's frontispiece," he concluded, "is charming. The book is quite splendid . . ." [43]

After a busy day at the Whitechapel offices of Bradbury and Evans, Dickens dashed off to dine at Gore House with Lady Blessington and Count D'Orsay. [44] The next day he had a dinner engagement with Ainsworth. [45] And for the evening—Tuesday, December 3rd, was the date—there was scheduled the reading Dickens had so eagerly anticipated and come all the way from Italy to give. [46]

Forster had assembled a group of some ten friends at Lincoln's Inn Fields, under his painted ceiling "where Allegory, in Roman helmet and celestial linen," [47] sprawled among balustrades and billowing clouds. Dickens had originally suggested that Mrs. Carlyle be among the guests—"*her* judgment would be invaluable" [48]—but in the end Forster had included no ladies. Maclise sketched the scene and some of the auditors, rendering his own eager interest and that of Stanfield, "the grave attention of Carlyle," "the rapt look of poor Laman Blanchard" (who, a few months later, was to die by his own hand), "the rapt solemnity" of the journalist William Johnson Fox, "Jerrold's skyward gaze, and the tears of Harness and Dyce"—and, of course, Forster and Dickens, the latter drawn with rays of light surrounding his head. [49]

The evening turned out to be an overwhelming triumph. Dickens read eloquently, and all the guests were so moved and excited that rumors of the wonderful occasion spread over all London. [50] At Richard Barham's urgent persuasion, Dickens repeated the reading on a second evening with a number of new auditors, including Albany Fonblanque. [51] But *The Chimes* did not require Dickens's talents as a reader to sway the emotions of those who listened to it. "Anybody who has heard it," Dickens reported to Kate, "has been moved in the most extraordinary manner. Forster read it (for dramatic purposes) to A'Beckett"—one of the staff of *Punch*. "He cried so much and so painfully, that Forster didn't know whether to go on or stop; and he called next day to say that any expression of his feelings was beyond his power." The response of Macready, who had proved to be still in London, was no less conclusive. "If you had seen Macready last night," Dickens concluded the same letter to his wife, "undisguisedly sobbing, and crying on the sofa as I read, you would have felt, as I did, what a thing it is to have power." [52]

When the little book was published its success was tremendous. Twenty thousand copies were sold almost at once.[53] But among some of its readers its reception was more varied. Thackeray's friend the Reverend W. H. Brookfield told his wife that it was "as utter trash as was ever trodden under foot." [54] "Jeffrey," Dickens wrote Forster, "is most energetic and enthusiastic. Filer sticks in his throat rather, but all the rest is quivering in his heart." [55]

But Dickens had in fact delivered a telling thrust against the chill doctrine that the poor had no right to any save the harsh subsistence imposed by the iron law of wages and should resign themselves to a meager diet and a life of unrelieved toil. Filer's horrified condemnation of the wastefulness of a poor man's eating tripe was hardly more fantastic than the economist McCulloch's advice to laboring men that if they wished to improve their economic status they should tighten their belts and have fewer children, or the argument of another economist, Nassau Senior, that the workers had no cause of complaint: they were better off than primitive savages. The hated Poor Law that confined the indigent in workhouse bastilles where they were fed more sparsely than criminals in the jails was not so uncompromising as Malthus, who held that feeding paupers merely increased their numbers. The passages in *The Chimes* devoted to Alderman Cute are only a bitter parody of the sentiments of Sir Peter Laurie, a London alderman who had expressed the determination to put suicide down:

"There's a certain amount of cant in vogue about Starvation," says Alderman Cute, "and I intend to Put it Down." [56] Let Trotty Veck's daughter marry, and what will happen? She will quarrel with her husband and become a distressed wife. "Now, I give you fair warning, that I have made up my mind to Put distressed wives Down." Perhaps her husband will die young "(most likely)" and leave her to wander the streets with a baby. "Now, don't wander near me, my dear, for I am resolved to Put all wandering mothers Down." And if she attempts "desperately, and ungratefully, and impiously," to drown or hang herself, "I'll have no pity on you, for I have made up my mind to Put all suicide Down!" [57]

Through the benevolence of Sir Joseph Bowley, "the Poor Man's Friend," [58] Dickens neatly reveals the other side of the governing class's attitude toward the workers. "You needn't trouble yourself to think of anything. I will think for you, I know what is good for you; I am your perpetual parent." "Live hard and temperately, be respectful, exercise your self-denial, bring up your family on next to nothing, pay your rent as regularly as the clock strikes," says Sir Joseph, "and you may trust me to be your Friend and Father." [59] But if, letting themselves be misled by "wicked and designing persons," the poor "become impatient and discontented, and are guilty of insubordinate conduct and black-hearted ingratitude," [60] if, like Will Fern, they try to better themselves and reject his patronizing superiority, there is no limit to the vindictive anger with which Sir Joseph will join hands with Alderman Cute and persecute the rebel into vagabondage and jail.[61]

Only ignorance or blind prejudice could deny the existence of the attitudes Dickens portrays, and *The Chimes* denounces them impartially, whether they spring from selfish complacency or from the credulous acceptance of an economic dogma that denied the possibility of ameliorating human misery. Poor Trotty Veck, humbly deferring to the judgment of his betters, concludes in despair that the poor are wrong in every way, that they are born bad and have no right to exist.[62] For him to have a little dish of tripe was a waste that starved the widowed and the orphaned, but when the rich enjoyed the luxury of turtle soup they only made trade more prosperous. "Divide the lively turtles in the bills of mortality," Trotty reflects, "by the number of gentlefolks able to buy 'em; and whose share does he take but his own! As to snatching tripe from anybody's wife—he'd scorn it!" [63]

In Trotty's dream, the Chimes show him that Alderman Cute feels far more sympathetic about the suicide of Deedles the Banker than he does about a starving mother throwing herself into the Thames,[64] that even the kind-spoken Sir Joseph Bowley has left duties unperformed,[65] and that the best use Mr. Filer can make of his statistics is to feel indignant that Will Fern's jail sentences have exceeded the average.[66] And the Chimes show him "how the poor and wretched, at the worst—yes, even in the crimes that aldermen put down and he thought so horrible—have some deformed and hunch-backed goodness clinging to them," so that when his daughter Meg goes down to the water with her baby, she "adjusts its rags so as to make it pretty in its sleep, and hangs over it, and smooths its little limbs, and loves it." [67]

The social plea that Dickens has to make is put in the mouth of Will Fern, the rebellious farm laborer: "Give us . . . better homes when we're a-lying in our cradles; give us better food when we're a-working for our lives; give us kinder laws to bring us back when we're a-going wrong; and don't set Jail, Jail, Jail, afore us, everywhere we turn." [68] There is a more explicit sounding, too, of the same prophecy that Dickens had insinuated into both *The Old Curiosity Shop* and *Barnaby Rudge*, and that Disraeli was to make in his *Sybil* of the following year: If the upper classes persisted in dividing Eng-land into two nations, the rich and the poor, the time would come when the multitudes would make them regret it. Let the wealthy be-ware, Dickens says, the poor coming to read their Bibles with a change in the wording: "Whither thou goest, I can Not go; where thou lodgest, I do Not lodge; thy people are Not my people; Nor thy God my God!" [69] And through Will Fern again he voices the danger, the dark nights lit by fires, east, west, north, and south: "When you see the distant sky red, they'll be blazing. When you see the distant sky red, think of me no more; or, if you do, remember what a Hell was lighted up inside of me, and think you see its flames reflected in the clouds." [70]

The Chimes is evidence of Dickens's growing preoccupation with social problems and of his growing knowledge that they could not be explained in terms of individual villainy. Sympathy with the poor he had always had since his Parliamentary-reporting days, and impatience with those legislators and economists to whom people were mere sta-tistical abstractions. But the reports on child labor and on the hard toil and filth and long hours in the mines and factories that his friend Southwood Smith had put in his hands had broadened his horizons. He saw that the same forces that made the criminal dens of Saffron Hill and the slums of Bethnal Green were at work in the Black Coun-try, making hard and greedy men harder and greedier, and forcing men who were not naturally cruel or grasping to behave as if they were. And the hard times that had set in with the forties, the rick-burnings in the south, the labor violence in the industrial north, were ominous signs of the more catastrophic disorders that a ruthless system might generate.

This deepened understanding is reflected in a difference between *The Chimes* and the books that had preceded it. In those books the responsibility for evil was concentrated in the figures, hideous or grotesquely comic, that moved through them. Ralph Nickleby and Squeers, Quilp and Brass, Montague Tigg and Jonas Chuzzlewit, are hatefully or ludicrously bad in themselves; we do not think of the City or of England as filled with men like them. And although in *Oliver Twist* Dickens reveals quite clearly his awareness that the new Poor Laws starved their victims to save the pockets of the rate-payers, the reader's imagination easily stops short with deriding or loathing Bumble, Fagin, Sikes, and Fang instead of thinking of society at all. Even *Barnaby Rudge*, with its lurid awareness of public discontents so bitter that they might at any time blaze into fury, leaves privilege and injustice almost hidden in the black smoke of Newgate, and forgotten in comparison with the personal insolence of Sir John Chester and the wild figures of Hugh and Dennis.

But Filer and Sir Joseph Bowley, and even the egregious Alderman Cute, are not villains, and, instead of standing out from, they symbolize the social conditions of which they are a part. Although the Young England gentleman disappeared from the book in the process of revision, Bowley visibly embodies the spirit of a place-proud philanthropy asserting the aristocratic right to rule.[71] Filer's premature Malthusian arithmetic and exaggerated devotion to economic theory and the Alderman's pitiless determination to put down every timorous claim of the poor to be treated as human beings are representative of the link between material interests and political economy, "the tyranny of a narrow abstraction among the economists," as Professor Cazamian remarks, merely echoing "the hard-heartedness of the business men." [72] Against a callous self-seeking and a cold utilitarianism Dickens asserted the sense of justice, the generosity of the human heart, the virtue of sympathy, the need to extend the helping hand, not merely in relieving individual misfortune but in solving the problems of society.

* * * * *

For the few days Dickens remained in London after the second reading of *The Chimes,* his time was almost wholly occupied in one of those private endeavors to help others that for him represented the half of his social philosophy and that no striving for institutional reforms alone could quite replace. John Overs had died of the lung disease against which he had struggled, leaving a wife and six young children, one of them a cripple. His *Evenings of a Working Man,* for which Dickens had written the introduction and helped to find a publisher, had brought in some money, but the family were still left in "great distress and perplexity," and Dickens immediately plunged into the task of extricating them.[73]

In consequence, although he had promised himself the pleasure of seeing Miss Coutts, when he left for Italy again on Sunday night, December 8th, he had been unable to find even a few free hours in which to visit her. In the stress of making arrangements for the Overs children, he wrote her regretfully, "I have seen no one, and gone nowhere." [74] But at least he had been of some help to them. He left, furthermore, with what amounted to a promise from the Governors of the Orphan Workers School that the eldest boy, a youngster of nine, would be admitted to that institution in April.

It occurred to him, he continued, that Miss Coutts "might have an opportunity of presenting one of the Girls to some other school or charity, and as I know full well that . . . you would rather thank than blame me for making a real and strong case known to you," Dickens sent her the children's names and ages, from Amelia, aged eleven years, to the baby John, four months.[75] Nor did Miss Coutts ignore the suggestion. "Mrs. Overs tells me," Dickens wrote a few months later, "that Miss Coutts has sent her, at different times, sixteen pounds, has sent a doctor to her children, and has got one of the girls into an Orphan School. When I wrote her a word in the poor woman's behalf, she wrote me back . . . that it was a kindness to herself to have done so, 'for what is the use of my means but to try and do some good with them?' " [76]

On his way back to Italy, Dickens remembered a package that until then, in the distraction of travel, he had forgotten about. "When poor Overs was dying," he explained to Forster, "he suddenly asked for a pen and ink and some paper, and made up a little parcel for me which it was his last conscious act to direct. She (his wife) told me this and gave it me. I opened it last night. It was a copy of his little book in which he had written my name. 'With his devotion.' " [77]

Meanwhile, Dickens had stopped off for a busy three days with Macready in Paris. Macready was playing *Hamlet, Macbeth, King Lear, Othello*, Sheridan Knowles's *Virginius*, and the most famous of all his roles, *Werner*.[78] He introduced Dickens to his own Parisian friends, Théophile Gautier, Louis Blanc, Victor Hugo, and Alexandre Dumas.[79] From Dumas's box they saw his *Christine* played by Mme. St. George, "once Napoleon's mistress, now of an immense size, from dropsy, I suppose . . . Her age, withal, somewhere about 80 or 90. I never in my life beheld such a sight. Every stage conventionality she ever picked up (and she has them all) has got the dropsy too, and is swollen and bloated hideously." [80]

The following night, at the Salle Ventadour, where Macready was immediately to open, they saw Grisi in *Il Pirato*,[81] and Dickens was carried away by "the fire and passion of a scene between her, Mario, and Fornasari. They drew on one another, the two men—not like stage-players, but like Macready himself: and she, rushing in between them, now clinging to this one, now to that, now making a sheath for their naked swords with her arms, now tearing her hair in distraction as they broke away from her and plunged again at each other; was prodigious." [82]

And the very next day Dickens saw Macready rehearsing the scene before the doge and council in *Othello*.[83] Meanwhile he had also been a great deal in the company of Régnier of the Théâtre Français, and of Louis Bertin, editor of the *Journal des Débats*, made friends with the painters Delaroche and Delacroix, gossiped about Guizot with Michelet and Quinet, and made the acquaintance of the Comte de Vigny, the author of *Cinq-Mars*.[84] It was a wrench to forgo all this stimulation and tear himself away from the Macreadys, but Christmas was only twelve days off, and Dickens wished to spend it with his family. On the night of the 13th he left Paris by the *malle-poste*.[85]

Through three days and nights of roads deep in snow and churned into a horrible slush by a thaw they waded to Marseilles.[86] There freezing weather returned again, and Dickens was taken out of the coach, he wrote Mrs. Macready, "in a perfectly torpid state and was at first supposed to be luggage." But there were no directions on him, and further examination led to " 'the vital spark' " being "discovered under a remote corner" of his traveling shawl. Bad weather then delayed sailings at Marseilles for "three days of waking nightmare." [87] When the steam-packet *Charlemagne* was finally ready to weigh anchor Dickens was not on board; he had gotten into some confusion between it and a rival packet, and managed to get to the vessel just as it was moving out of the harbor more than an hour late from waiting for him.[88]

"As he went up the side," Forster says, "he saw a strange sensation among the angry travellers whom he had detained so long; heard a voice exclaim 'I am blamed if it ain't DICKENS!' and stood in the centre of a group of *Five Americans*!" Fortunately, they were all glad to see him; one of them had met him in New York, and introduced him to the rest with the remark, "Personally, our countrymen, and you, can fix it friendly, sir, I do expectuate." [89]

The passage to Genoa was so stormy that the vessel threatened now to run into Toulon, now into Nice.[90] Dickens was so ill in his cabin "that I should have made my will if I had had anything to leave, but I had only the basin and I couldn't leave that for the moment." [91] In the next cabin his American friend, seemingly the only one of his party with a traveling dictionary, refused to give it up though he was also deathly sick, and Dickens could hear his companions asking, "What's the French for pillow?" "Is there any Italian phrase for a lump of sugar?" "What does echo mean? The garsong says echo to everything!" They also wanted to know the population of every little town on the Corniche, the very last thing, Dickens remarked, that an Italian steward would be apt to know. But having some vague idea that they would like a large number, the steward would obligingly say at random "fifty thousand, ninety thousand, four hundred thousand, when they asked about the population of a place not larger than Lincoln's Inn Fields. And when they said, *Non Possible!* (which was the leader's invariable reply), he doubled or trebled the amount; to meet what he supposed to be their view, and make it quite satisfactory." [92]

Finally the wind moderated, and the vessel ran into Genoa Harbor, where the now familiar bells, Dickens wrote, "rang sweetly in my ears."[93] From shipboard he rushed into the arms of his expectant family. By the 22nd he had resumed his former Genoa routine, and was looking forward to celebrating his first Christmas season in Italy.[94]

"Miss Coutts had sent Charley, with the best of letters to me," he wrote Forster, "a Twelfth Cake weighing ninety pounds, magnificently decorated," which was "detained at the custom-house for Jesuitical surveillance!" [95] It was also exhibited at a Swiss pastry cook's in Genoa where it was sent to have some of its sugar ornaments repaired after its voyage. No Twelfth-Night confection had ever been seen in Genoa before, and the customers wondered mightily at its bonbons, crackers, and Twelfth-Night characters all wrought in a marvel of confectionery. [96]

CHAPTER SIX

Last Days in Italy

DICKENS had come abroad, six months before, glowing with the dream of writing a novel unharried by the tyranny of monthly deadlines. But the restlessness that perturbed the beginning of *The Chimes* had not been allayed either by his Italian sightseeing or by his impetuous trip to London, and he had returned to Genoa with his literary plans no more definite than they had been before.

Back in September, indeed, he had been distracting himself with the thought of further travels in the south of Italy,[1] and from Paris, on his way to England, he had written to Kate suggesting a trip to Naples, where they would be joined by Georgina and climb Vesuvius together.[2] This idea blossomed into an elaborate scheme of going to Rome for Holy Week, and at last winding back to Genoa through Perugia, Arezzo, and Florence. It would then be April and there would be little more than two months left of Dickens's year abroad.

An indubitable change had come over his habits of determined application. If he was just as vigorously energetic as ever, his energies were not being poured into literary channels. Though he had labored with fierce excitement over *The Chimes*, that little book had occupied him for only a month. Perhaps he had been exhausted by the unremitting toil of nine years in which he had written almost two million words, and his imaginative powers needed a rest. Perhaps he felt uprooted in these strange Italian scenes and had not assimilated their crowding exotic impressions. Perhaps, as he himself thought, he felt the loss of his accustomed walks in London streets and rural lanes and missed the stimulus of familiar companionship. Whatever the reasons, nothing is heard of any new book even conceived.

His feeling of separation from his friends was deepened early in

January by hearing that Forster had lost his only brother. All the warmth of his sympathy poured itself out for his friend's grief as he wished that he could be in London to say his words of comfort in person. "I feel the distance between us now, indeed. I would to Heaven, my dearest friend, that I could remind you in a manner more lively than this dull sheet of paper can put on, that you have a Brother left." Forster's bereavement stirred in Dickens's heart too the dormant pain of eight-years-past sorrow that had fallen on his own hearth "and made it dark and cold" with sudden anguish. Out of the fullness of that memory, "I know—I *know*, my dear friend," he wrote, "—that before the ground is green above him, you will be content that what was capable of death in him, should lie there." [3]

Meanwhile, in Genoa, Dickens had found his sympathies responding to another kind of appeal. His friendship with the De la Rues had grown steadily, and he often visited them in their apartment in the Palazzo Rosso, or the Brignole Rosso, as it was also called. Mme. De la Rue was a "most affectionate and excellent little woman"[4] who suffered so distressingly from a nervous tic that Dickens felt sorry for her and suggested to her husband that he might be able to relieve her by means of those magic powers he had successfully exerted upon both Kate and Georgina. Possibly her disorder would yield to hypnotic influences, as Kate's headaches had done. M. De la Rue gladly accepted Dickens's offer. Soon the experiment was under way.[5]

In the course of the sympathetic relationship thus established, Mme. De la Rue was presently making strange revelations. Her affliction, she told Dickens, was mysteriously rooted in terrifying hallucinations. She constantly found herself on a green hillside with a very blue sky above, sometimes surrounded by a crowd of men and women with invisible faces, sometimes alone but in great pain and terror, with stones hurled down upon her by some unseen people. But worst of all was a man haunting this place, its evil spirit, of whom she was so terrified that she dared not look upon him and trembled when she spoke of him. This phantom figure, the only one that spoke to her, was more horrible to her than all the others, and filled her with an agony of unending fear. What could she do?

Dickens felt convinced that he could banish the delusions by suggestion during the magnetic sleep, and was soon hearing Mme. De la Rue's descriptions of the hill, the crowds of faceless people, and the man she called her bad spirit during her very hallucinations themselves. In these séances he subjected her to the most searching and persistent questioning.[6] When she was awake, he urged her not to endanger the possibility of a cure by maintaining any reticences with him. The slightest secret withheld might be the clue that would enable him to overcome her malady.

The endeavor to exorcise these spectral forms necessitated prolonged meetings at all hours. They often took place, Kate was disturbed to observe, at the most unconventional times, and sometimes there was more than one in a day. Dickens had explained to her that "poor little Mrs. De la Rue"[7] was tortured by phantasms whose faces she could never see, and that he was sure he could help her dispel them, but Kate did not like the situation and began to feel a suppressed antagonism to Mme. De la Rue.

While Kate fretted over this undesirable intimacy and Dickens exulted over an improvement he believed he could already discern in his patient, the time of the Roman Carnival drew near. Mme. De la Rue, agitated by the impending withdrawal of his influence, was worried by hallucinatory fears for Dickens no less than for herself. Her devilish figure had frightened her by talking of Dickens; she begged him not to go upon a Monday. "It's not he who says that. I say it." [8] She also implored him under no circumstances while he was in Rome to go alone to Trinità dei Monti—it was there that she had undergone her first dreadful experience, and she feared that in treating her he might have rendered himself vulnerable to the same evil forces. It was probably a relief to Kate when on Sunday, the 19th of January, she and Dickens set out on their journey south.[9]

The day was gloomy with mist and wind-driven rain. The Mediterranean roared in hoarse invisibility on the crags below their road save when a sudden gust tore a clearing in which the agitated waves could be seen lashing the rocks.[10] Throughout the long tempestuous drive to Spezzia, Dickens remained silent and distraught. Kate presently learned that he was worrying lest his absence have a harmful effect on Mme. De la Rue and was concentrating his thoughts on giving her absent treatment.[11] The rains had swollen the River Magra to such dangerous violence that they had to remain a day at a ghostly inn at Spezzia and wait for the current to subside before they could cross by ferry.[12]

At the inn they chanced to find Angus Fletcher, who was visiting a marble merchant, a Yorkshireman established in business at Carrara. Fletcher too had been caught in the downpour and was eating his dinner in a blanket while his clothes were drying. Very red and warm before the fire, "and looking," Dickens wrote M. De la Rue, "like a new-born baby, suddenly grown-up," Fletcher ate another dinner with them, at the end of which his eyes were bulging. "You never saw such a human Prawn as he looked in your life." [13]

Next afternoon, together with Fletcher, they were ferried over the swirling Magra and drove on to Carrara.[14] Here they spent two nights at the home of Mr. Walton, Fletcher's Yorkshire friend. On the second of these evenings, in the marble theater, they heard a comic opera with a chorus consisting of laborers who sang entirely by ear. A great reception was held in their box, and later the orchestra turned out in a body to serenade them at Mr. Walton's.[15]

The sky had cleared next day when Dickens and Kate resumed their journey. From a lofty hill beyond Carrara they could see the fertile plain in which lay the towns of Pisa and Leghorn purple in the distance. As they drew near Pisa that evening, there was the famous tower leaning shadowily behind the wall in the moonlight. Dickens was startled by the curious view up the slanted inner tube of the tower and by the strange distorted perspective of the shaft receding from the summit to its base. He was moved, too, by the solemn beauty of the Campo Santo, with the delicate tracery of its cloisters etched by light and shadow on the stone pavements surrounding the grass-grown graves.[16]

From Pisa the two travelers proceeded to Leghorn, "made illustrious by Smollett's grave." [17] Here Dickens heard from the De la Rues that his patient was doing well. He hoped, Dickens replied, that they would be able to join them in Rome and meanwhile would "rely on the idea of her anxious Physician." "I see afar off, *how essential it is that this phantom should not regain its power for an instant*." [18]

In Pisa again, Dickens hired "a good-tempered Vetturíno and his four horses" [19] to drive them to Rome. Through the pleasant Tuscan villages they rolled, past countless roadside crosses garnished with little wooden models of the cock that crowed when Peter had denied his Master thrice, the dicebox with which the soldiers cast lots, the hammer that drove in the nails, the ladder that was set against the cross, the crown of thorns, "a perfect toy-shop" "of every possible object that can be connected with the Saviour's death." [20] In the evening their carriage reached the dreamy, fantastic city of Siena, "like a bit of Venice, without the water." [21]

They drove on next day over wild bleak moors bare and desolate as the heath in *Macbeth*. They stayed overnight in a lone *osteria* with a labyrinth of black, cutthroat-looking bedrooms and a staircase coming up abruptly through a trap door in the floor.[22] The sinister place was not improved by the rumor of robbers lurking in the neighborhood.[23] But Dickens dismissed these from his mind, and made a good meal of soup, boiled fowl, stewed pigeon, beef, Parmesan cheese, and coffee.[24]

His mind was still busy with Mme. De la Rue and her strange affliction. He had written M. De la Rue twice since leaving Genoa, and now wrote again. "I cannot yet quite make up my mind," he said, "whether the phantom originates in shattered nerves and a system broken by pain; or whether it is the representative of some great nerve or set of nerves on which her disease has preyed—and begins to loose its hold now, because the disease of those nerves is itself attacked by the inexplicable agent of the magnetism." But the phantom was clearly the clue to the whole problem, a symbol of painful causes that the sufferer could not face. "There the danger lies, so deep, that she herself can hardly probe it, even now." [25]

The country grew wilder, more barren, and more stony as they went on, and Dickens began to wonder if they might not have an encounter with bandits after all: "I had brought (like an ass) a bag of napoleons with me from Genoa," and "I called up all the theatrical ways of letting off pistols that I could call to mind." [26] At Radicofani, a gaunt hamlet hanging on the side of a hill, the inn was a "winding, creaking, wormy, rustling, door-opening, foot-on-staircase-falling" horror of a place that might have inspired "all the murdering and phantom tales that ever were written." [27] Despite its melodramatic appearance, however, and the uncomfortable whispers they had heard about it, nothing disturbed the peace of their night's lodging there.

On the following morning, though, a wet and blusterous one, when they had got started in their carriage, there darted down upon them from one of the steep alleys a fierce rabble of men and boys like a host of ragged birds of prey. Through the rain the wind was blowing so hard that Dickens could hardly keep his place on the box beside Roche and the *vetturino*.[28] At the head of the mob, staying them with his staff, still breathless with his dive, stood a figure in a frowzy brown cloak, white hair and white beard streaming in the air, importunately begging.[29]

"I had no small money," Dickens wrote Forster; "and the brave C. never has, when I want it for a beggar." The leader drew himself up with a wizard look, and said, "Do you know what you are doing, my lord? Do you mean to go on today?"—"Yes," Dickens said, "I do." "My lord, do you know that your vetturíno is unacquainted with this part of the country; that there is a wind raging on the mountain which will sweep you all away; that the courier, the coach, and all the passengers, were blown from the road last year; that the danger is great and almost certain?"—"No," Dickens said, "I don't."—"My lord, you don't understand me, I think?"—"Yes," said Dickens, nettled by this persistence, "I do, damn you! Speak to my servant. It's his business. Not mine."—"Santa Maria, these English lords! It's not their business if they're killed! They leave it to their servants!" But the old scarecrow drew off his followers and retreated a way up the hill. From here, however, as the carriage moved on, he shrieked a last word, pointing to Roche with his long staff: "It's *his* business if you're killed, is it, my lord? Ha! ha! ha! whose business is it when the English lords are born?" and the whole pack echoed his shrill yell of laughter.[30]

"I must confess," Dickens reported to Forster, "that I thought he had the best of it. And he had so far reason for what he urged, that when we got to the mountain pass the wind became terrific, so that we were obliged to take Kate out of the carriage lest she should be blown over, carriage and all, and had ourselves to hang on to it, on the windy side, to prevent its going Heaven knows where!"[31]

*   *   *   *   *

After they crossed the papal frontier they rolled on until dusk brought them to the melancholy Lake of Bolsena in a flat malarial country with not even a cottage or a stick for mile after mile. For another day it was the same, but after passing Viterbo and climbing a long slow hill, they came, near sunset, upon a solitary lake surrounded by bleak volcanic hills strange beneath a red sun. At Ronciglione, a little town like a large pigsty, they passed the night. They were now

on the Roman Campagna, and toward the next afternoon they began
to strain their eyes for the first glimpse of the Eternal City.[32] When
at length it appeared in the distance, "it looked," Dickens recorded,
"like—I am half afraid to write the word—like LONDON!!! There
it lay, under a thick cloud, with innumerable towers and steeples and
roofs of houses, rising up into the sky, and high above them all, one
Dome." [33]

They entered the city about four o'clock in the afternoon of January 30th. Though the Tiber "had looked as yellow as it ought to look,"
the muddy streets and the commonplace shops were a disappointment.[34] Where were the great ruins, the solemn tokens of antiquity?
"It was no more my Rome, degraded and fallen and lying asleep in
the sun among a heap of ruins, than Lincoln's Inn Fields is." [35] Dickens went to bed that night at the Hotel Meloni "in a very indifferent
humour." [36]

St. Peter's, next day, was also a disappointment. Though it had
looked immense in the distance, and though nothing could exaggerate
the beauty of the Piazza, with its exquisite columns and gushing fountains, or the first burst of the interior and its glorious dome, the structure looked small on a near approach and the red-and-yellow fripperies
swathing the marble pillars gave it the frivolous atmosphere of a lavish pantomime. "I have been infinitely more affected in many English
cathedrals when the organ has been playing, and in many English
country churches when the congregation have been singing. I had a
much greater sense of mystery and wonder in the Cathedral of San
Mark at Venice." [37]

The Colosseum, though, in its "solitude, its awful beauty, and its
utter desolation," was overwhelming. "To see it crumbling there, an
inch a year; its walls and arches overgrown with green; its corridors
open to the day; the long grass growing in its porches; young trees of
yesterday, springing up on its ragged parapets, and bearing fruits; . . . to
see its Pit of Fight filled up with earth, and the peaceful Cross planted
in its centre; to climb into its upper halls, and look down on ruin, ruin,
ruin, all about it; the triumphal arches of Constantine, Septimius
Severus, and Titus; the Roman Forum; the Palace of the Caesars; the
temples of the old religion, fallen down and gone; is to see the ghost
of old Rome, wicked wonderful old city, haunting the very ground

on which its people trod. It is the most impressive, the most stately, the most solemn, grand, majestic, mournful sight, conceivable." [38]

"Here was Rome indeed at last; and such a Rome as no one can imagine in its full and awful grandeur! We wandered out upon the Appian Way, and then went on, through miles of ruined tombs and broken walls . . . past the Circus of Romulus, where the course of the chariots, the stations of the judges, competitors, and spectators, are yet as plainly to be seen as in old time: past the tomb of Cecilia Metella: past all enclosure, hedge, or stake, wall or fence: away upon the open Campagna, where on that side of Rome, nothing is to be beheld but Ruin. . . . Broken aqueducts, left in the most picturesque and beautiful clusters of arches; broken temples; broken tombs. A desert of decay, sombre and desolated beyond all expression; and with a history in every stone that strews the ground." [39]

The Carnival Week was a delirium. Throughout the mile length of the Corso draperies of red, green, blue, white, and gold fluttered from balconies so innumerable that it looked as if the sky had rained and blown balconies, and rich streamers of the most sparkling colors floated from every window and parapet. The open fronts of shops were groves hung with flowers and evergreens; scaffoldings made temples radiant in silver, gold, and crimson. Carriages heaped with confetti, sugarplums, and nosegays crowded the way.[40] Everywhere women's eyes laughed and sparkled like light in water; everywhere graceful forms swam in every bewitching madness of dress: "Little preposterous scarlet jackets; quaint old stomachers more wicked than the smartest bodices; Polish pelisses, strained and tight as ripe gooseberries; tiny Greek caps, all awry, and clinging to the dark hair, Heaven knows how; every wild, quaint, bold, shy, pettish, madcap fancy . . ." [41]

Brigands and Harlequins surged in the street among Greek warriors, Policinelli laying about them with blown bladders, men-monkeys, and strange animals with pigs' faces and lions' tails. Showers of confetti descended from windows and balconies like clouds, making everyone as white as millers. Maskers in carriages pelted each other with bonbons and flowers.[42] "I wish you could have seen me," Dickens wrote Georgina, "catch a swell brigand on the nose with a handful of very large confetti every time we met him. It was the best thing I have ever done." [43] Another gentleman who had achieved a similar feat "was exchanging facetious remarks with a stout gentleman in a doorway—one-half black and one-half white, as if he had been peeled up the middle—" when "he received an orange from a house-top, full on his left ear," and was so much surprised that as his carriage suddenly moved forward he "staggered ignominiously, and buried himself among his flowers." [44] And throughout the entire mad, shouting turmoil the mood mounted to a riotous climax of illimitable hilarity, culminating in the horse races and, after nightfall, the bright scenes of blazing torches and multitudes of lanterns and candles.[45]

With the close of the Carnival, Dickens and Kate started south for Naples. Across the undulating Campagna they rolled to Albano, on for miles,[46] always with ruined aqueducts stalking their giant course in the distance.[47] The Pontine Marshes were flat and lonely beneath a shadowed sky, and the weather turned bad again as they went on,[48] so that they saw no sunshine until they reached the great robber crags and blue sea of Terracina. All night from there the narrow road wound under sharp points of rock, with the sea murmuring beneath the stars. Just at daybreak, far away, there came the first glimpse of Naples with its islands, and Vesuvius spouting fire. After another day's journey and a night on the road, they had a day's rest at Capua. There, at last, Mount Vesuvius seemed close at hand, its cone white with snow and a dense cloud of smoke hanging in the air. And so they rattled downhill into Naples.[49]

Dickens and Kate were joined at Naples by Georgina, arriving by sea from Genoa with eagerly awaited news of the children and an accumulation of letters from home. But Dickens was even more impatient to learn how Mme. De la Rue had been faring in his absence. After the vessel was sighted in the bay, he excitedly watched through a telescope the unloading of its mailbags. Feverishly he ripped open his mail and read M. De la Rue's journal, and was distressed to learn that his unhappy patient was sliding back fast. He was relieved, however, by the news that the De la Rues would join him in Rome, where the mesmeric treatments might be resumed during Holy Week. He tore off a letter to reach Genoa by return boat, giving the date of his expected arrival in Rome, and expressing his intense concern.[50]

Meanwhile, Dickens had been seeing Naples. "It is a fine place," he wrote to Mitton, "but nothing like so beautiful as people make it out to be." The famous bay was inferior to that of Genoa and there were no palaces as lovely as the Peschiere.[51] And, except for Fondi, Dickens had seen no place as dirty. The houses were like pigsties "heaped up story on story, and tumbled house on house." [52] He was shocked by the degraded condition of the poor. "What would I give," Dickens wrote Forster, "that you should see the lazzaroni as they really are— mere squalid, abject, miserable animals for vermin to batten on; slouching, slinking, ugly, shabby, scavenging scarecrows! And oh the raffish counts and more than doubtful countesses, the noodles and blacklegs, the good society! And oh the miles of miserable streets and wretched occupants, to which Saffron Hill or the Borough Mint is a kind of small gentility, which are found to be so picturesque by English lords and ladies, to whom the wretchedness left behind at home is lowest of the low, and vilest of the vile, and commonest of all common things." [53]

The burial place of the poor was "a great paved yard with three hundred and sixty-five pits in it: every one covered by a square stone which is fastened down. One of these pits is opened every night in the year; the bodies of the pauper dead are collected in the city; brought out in a cart . . . and flung in, uncoffined. Some lime is then cast down into the pit, and it is sealed up until a year is past, and its turn again comes round. . . . The cart has a red lamp attached, and about ten o'clock at night you see it glaring through the streets of Naples: stopping at the doors of hospitals and prisons, and such places, to increase its freight; and then rattling off again." [54]

The weather had become so atrocious—"rain, snow, wind, darkness, hail, and cold"—that Dickens gave up going over into Sicily.[55] But he explored all the curving Neapolitan shoreline to Miseno, past the Grotto of Posilipo and the Grotto del Cane, and around to Baia, with Capri always floating across the blue water like a vision of fairyland. He took the railroad along the sea beach to Sorrento, past Torre del Greco to Castellammare and the vineyards, olive trees, and groves of oranges and lemons sloping down from the summit of Sant' Agnello, and even ranged as far south as Paestum and its temples. And he wandered through the dead streets of Pompeii and Herculaneum, noting that the ashes of the gigantic eruption that had buried the two cities had forced their way even into the earthen vessels in the wine cellars, choking out the wine with dust. "In the tombs, they forced the ashes of the dead from the funeral urns, and rained new ruin even into them. The mouths, and eyes, and skulls of all the skeletons, were stuffed with this terrible hail." [56]

On the afternoon of February 21st, with Kate and Georgina, Dickens undertook the long-anticipated ascent of Vesuvius. They were in a party of six, accompanied by twenty-two guides. The weather, the severest in twenty years, had covered the steep sides of the mountain in deep snow "glazed with one smooth sheet of ice from the top of the cone to the bottom." Halfway up they caught the sunset, lovely in a cloudless sky, and a little later rose a nearly full moon, shining over the sea and the Bay of Naples. They rode on saddle horses to where the snow began, where Kate and Georgina were seated in sedan chairs and Dickens was accommodated with a stout stick for the almost perpendicular ascent. [57]

"By prodigious exertions," Dickens wrote in a letter to Mitton, "we passed the region of snow and came into that of fire—desolate and awful you may well suppose. It was like working one's way through a dry waterfall, with every mass of stone burnt and charred into enormous cinders, and smoke and sulphur bursting out of every chink and crevice, so that it was difficult to breathe. High before us, bursting out of a hill at the top of the mountain . . . the fire was pouring out, reddening the night with flames, blackening it with smoke, and spotting it with red-hot stones and cinders that fell down again in showers. At every step everybody fell, now into a bed of ashes, now over a mass of cindered iron," as they stumbled through a darkness of smoke that hid the moon. [58]

At the foot of the topmost cone Kate and Georgina, who were now on foot, were obliged to stop. Dickens, the head guide, and another gentleman resolved, however, in spite of the hoarse roaring of the mountain, to climb the hill to the brink and look into the crater. "You may form some notion of what is going on inside it," Dickens wrote Mitton, "when I tell you that it is a hundred feet higher than it was six weeks ago. The sensation of struggling up it, choked with the fire and smoke, and feeling at every step as if the crust of ground between one's feet and the gulf of fire would crumble in and swallow one up (which is the real danger), I shall remember for some little time, I think. But we did it. We looked down into the flaming bowels of the mountain and came back again, alight in half a dozen places, and burnt from head to foot. You never saw such devils. And *I* never saw anything so awful and terrible." [59]

The solid coating of ice made going down even harder than going up. But they formed a chain of hands, with half a dozen men each hanging on to Kate and Georgina, staggering and sliding, and driving sticks into the ice to prevent going sheer down the precipices every time they fell. Two of the men, one with a basket containing their spare cloaks, did fall, and plunged down into the black night five hundred feet below, and an Italian boy went shrieking after them. One of the men was recovered, a heap of rags and bruises, and the boy was brought in with his head in a bloody rag. But when they left the mountain at midnight the man with the cloaks had not yet been found, and Dickens does not report whether he ever was. "My ladies' clothes," Dickens concluded, "were so torn off their backs that they would not have been decent, if there could have been any thought of such things at such time." He himself was rather stiff, "but quite unhurt, except a slight scrape on my right hand. My clothes are burnt to pieces. My ladies are the wonder of Naples, and everybody is open-mouthed." [60]

* * * * *

A few mornings after this horrendous expedition, the three travelers started on the journey north to Rome, driven by the same cheerful *vetturino* who had brought Dickens and Kate from Pisa. After three days of winding byroads they came to the gray walls and towers of Monte Cassino vast on its steep and lofty hill, with raw vapors of early mist rolling through its cloisters. Hopping behind two of the black-clad figures walking in the quadrangle, in and out of the old arches, Dickens was amused to see a raven, croaking "in the purest Tuscan" and making the porter seem a dull-headed monk indeed by comparison with his sly and stealthy sharpness. "How like a Jesuit he looks!" Dickens exclaimed. Then there were more muddy roads, women in bright red bodices, dirty soldiers, hobgoblin inns with beds "of the liveliest kind," but always cheerful service, good red wine, and good food, and at last Rome again.[61]

Here Dickens received from Forster a letter telling of Laman Blanchard's suicide. Saddened by his wife's illness and death, pursued by ill-health and poverty, the unhappy man had slit his throat with a razor. "No philosophy will bear these dreadful things," Dickens wrote in reply, "or make a moment's head against them, but the practical one of doing all the good we can, in thought and deed. . . . Bulwer Lytton's conduct is that of a generous and noble-minded man, as I have ever thought him. Our dear good Procter too! And Thackeray— how earnest they have all been. . . . It says something for our pursuit, in the midst of all its miserable disputes and jealousies, that the common impulse of its followers, in such an instance as this, is surely and certainly of the noblest." [62]

At the Hotel Meloni Dickens found that the De la Rues had also reserved rooms, and as soon as they arrived he began mesmerizing Mme. De la Rue daily. Her worst times always came in the late hours of the night. Once Kate wakened to find Dickens striding up and down the bedroom with all the candles lit. He had just come from struggling with Mme. De la Rue's terrors and was still violently agitated with the experience. It was not until one o'clock that he subdued his own emotion and returned to bed. Some nights later M. De la Rue tapped on their door in great disturbance at one o'clock, and begged Dickens to come to his wife's assistance again. Dickens discovered her "rolled into an apparently insensible ball, by tic on the brain." He only found "where her head was by following her long hair to its source." Her state was so alarming that he had hardly any belief in his power to deal with it. But although such fits had always previously held possession of her for at least thirty hours, within half an hour Dickens had her peacefully asleep. The next morning she seemed quite well.[63] The fight against her affliction, however, continued to fluctuate desperately; on March 19th she was again very ill in the night and Dickens did not return to his own room until four in the morning.[64]

When Mme. De la Rue's health permitted, she and her husband now joined Dickens's party in all their sightseeing.[65] In the Vatican, Dickens assiduously gazed at paintings and sculpture. "There are portraits innumerable by Titian, Rubens, Rembrandt and Vandyke," he wrote Forster; "heads by Guido, and Domenichino, and Carlo Dolci; subjects by Raphael, and Correggio, and Murillo, and Paul Veronese, and Salvator; which it would be difficult indeed to praise too highly, or to praise enough. It is a happiness to me to think that they cannot be felt by the profound connoisseurs who fall into fits upon the longest notice and the most unreasonable terms. Such tenderness and grace, such noble elevation, purity, and beauty, so shine upon me from some well-remembered spots in the walls of these galleries, as to relieve my tortured memory from legions of whining friars and waxy holy families. I forgive, from the bottom of my soul, whole orchestras of earthly angels, and whole groves of St. Sebastians stuck as full of arrows according to pattern as a lying-in pincushion is stuck with pins." [66]

The ceremonies of Holy Week, Dickens found merely tedious and wearisome. The scene at the Sistine Chapel on the Wednesday was one of struggling confusion, with the chanting of the Miserere hardly audible through the heavy curtain of the doorway. At the Washing of the Feet, the favored thirteen all held great bouquets as large as cauliflowers, the Pope moved briskly from one to another, and the Cardinals smiled at each other as if they thought it all "a great farce," a judgment with which Dickens perfectly agreed. The shuffling progress up the Scala Sancta of numerous worshipers making the pious ascent on their knees struck him as ridiculous and unpleasant "in its senseless and unmeaning degradation." [67] "And the canopies, hangings, and carpets (of all sorts of reds and greens) now hung up, and put down . . . ," he confided to Miss Coutts, "have the effect of an enormous Bon-bon. Before which, and round which, and indeed out of which, they are perpetually carrying the poor old Pope about on men's shoulders, like a gorgeous Guy Faux." [68]

To Dickens, indeed, the entire ancient, magnificent, and solemn ritual was only a painted rigmarole, a humbug for which he could feel little except a contemptuous impatience. He was glad to emerge from its ornate glitter and make his way, as he did again and again, to the desolate grandeur of the Colosseum. "The open Campagna also," he wrote Angus Fletcher, he thought sublime; he had walked it all, "beyond the tomb of Cecilia Metella . . . and thence to Albano." [69] It was the ancient Rome of the Republic and the Caesars that burned in his imagination, not the medieval and Renaissance pomp of the wicked old city or the ecclesiastical traditions of a Church that seemed to him a mass of degraded superstitions.

On the Tuesday after Easter, the Dickenses left Rome.[70] With them in their carriage traveled the De la Rues, despite the growing tension created by Kate's dislike of Mme. De la Rue and her distrust of the strange relationship between Dickens and that lady. It was true that M. De la Rue seemed to entertain no objections, but Kate's doubts were not alleviated by his complaisance. Every day Dickens magnetized Mme. De la Rue, "sometimes under olive trees, sometimes in vineyards, sometimes in the travelling carriage, sometimes at wayside inns during the midday halt," [71] and her delusions gradually faded under the influence of these treatments. Kate's disturbance, however, did not diminish with the daily protraction of this enforced and unwelcome intimacy.

Meanwhile, they passed the Falls of Terni, dashing in rainbow spray from their rocky height, and presently saw the fortifications of Perugia rising abruptly from the plain. Leaving its somber Gothic buildings behind, they reached Castiglione by night, and Arezzo the following day. Next came the clear morning when they looked down from the summit of a hill on the sunlit valley of the Arno, where the domes and towers of Florence glittered like gold among the swelling hills.[72]

Dickens was enchanted with the magnificent and somber city, the prodigious palaces with their small distrustful windows, the Fountain of Neptune in the Piazza, the enormous overhanging battlements and great tower of the Palazzo Vecchio, the massive staircase rising from the ponderous gloom of the courtyard. He paced the Ponte Vecchio between the shops of the jewelers and goldsmiths, mused over Beatrice and Dante's bitter exile in the shadow of the Cathedral and its great Gothic companile, gazed on the wrought bronze doors of the Baptistery, saw the Chapel of the Medici, "the Good and Bad Angels of Florence," and reflected on the deaths of great men at the burial place of Michelangelo in Santa Croce.[73]

Beyond the walls, at Fiesole, he visited the convent, and Boccaccio's house, and saw the villa in which Landor had lived nestling among its vines and olive trees. When he left England he had asked Landor what he would most like to have in remembrance of Italy. "An ivy-leaf from Fiesole," Landor had replied.[74] Gazing now on the central tower of the house in the glowing landscape, Dickens recalled the splendid old man and his desire. "I plucked a leaf of ivy from the convent-garden as I looked," he wrote Forster; "and here it is. For Landor. With my love." [75]

While in Florence he heard from Forster of friends at home. "Poor Hood, poor Hood!" he commented. "I still look for his death, and he still lingers on. And Sydney Smith's brother gone after poor dear

Sydney himself! . . . Poor old Rogers will contradict some young man at dinner, every day for three weeks." He could still see Lady Holland, he wrote Forster in a later letter, "crying about dear Sydney Smith behind that green screen as we last saw her together." [76]

Lady Holland was especially present to Dickens's mind because in Florence he was entertained by young Lord and Lady Holland at their beautiful villa, Careggi de' Medici. A young English artist, George Watts, was decorating its rooms with frescoes, but he was so bashful that he retreated to a pavilion whenever visitors appeared.[77] The other members of the English colony at Florence, however, including Mrs. Trollope and her elder son Thomas Adolphus, were invited to meet Dickens, and he passed a "very pleasant and very merry day." Trollope thought him "a dandified pretty-boy-looking sort of figure, singularly young-looking, . . . with a slight flavor of the whipper-snapper." [78]

On April 9th Dickens was once more at home in the Palazzo Peschiere. Kate was miserably unhappy. Far from lessening, her resentment of the relationship with Mme. De la Rue had deepened to jealous certainty. The later part of the journey from Rome had seen such a growth of friction that she was no longer speaking to the De la Rues. When she and Dickens were alone together she expressed her agitation with anger and tears. Dickens tried in vain to persuade her that her suspicions had no foundation. The young wife remained hysterically unconvinced. If the intimacy was as innocent as he said, she could not see why he wouldn't give it up. This Dickens rigidly refused to do; he would not surrender the hope of a cure because Kate persisted in monstrous misconceptions. With the De la Rues he endeavored to excuse her conduct as a nervous breakdown, but her behavior was so undisguised that at last it forced him to make a "painful declaration of [her] state of mind" to them.[79] M. De la Rue received it with great delicacy, and considerately made no further allusions to it during the remainder of Dickens's stay in Genoa. The confession, though, was humiliating to his pride, and he did not forget having been obliged to make it.

*   *   *   *   *

Fortunately, the date of his departure from Italy was now less than two months away. The children were all well and happy and had flourished amazingly; they looked beautiful.[80] "Charley and his two sisters," he wrote Tom Beard, had learned to dance, and would "rather astonish you, I think, with sundry Polka, Mazurka, and other fine performances." [81] Katey, to be sure, had momentarily "been quite lamed by chilblains," but she was soon hobbling around, and was presently as agile again as the elder two. And the chilblains had "not affected her rosy looks." "Master Frank," the baby—otherwise Chickenstalker —now fourteen months old, was "a prodigious blade, and more full of queer tricks than any of his predecessors have been at his time of life." [82] Dickens boasted him "decidedly a success—a perpetual grin is on his face: and the spoon exercise is amazing." [83]

There was good news, too, from Bradbury and Evans. *The Chimes* had made a profit on the first twenty thousand of between £1,400 and £1,500, and if they had not been obliged to employ Chapman and Hall, they wrote, it would have been from £150 to £200 more. "They were very anxious to know what I thought of their management in general, under the disadvantageous circumstance of having C and H in the business at all. I wrote and told them that I was greatly pleased, and that I was quite certain it couldn't have been better done, as I am." In addition to these profits, Dickens found that his earnings on the books that Chapman and Hall still controlled amounted for the nine months ending in December, 1844, to £934 19s. 2d.—"which," he wrote Mitton, "they have received directions from Lincoln's Inn Fields, to pay into Coutts's. This is not so bad either?" [84]

There was certainly no longer any need to worry about money. Dickens accordingly sent Mitton directions about having Devonshire Terrace redecorated as soon as his tenant turned out. The doors and railings in the garden were to be a bright cheerful green, except for the staircases from the windows, which were to remain white. The hall and staircase inside, to the top of the house, were to be a good green, "not too decided, of course, to spoil the effect of the prints." The street door was to have a letter box constructed in it, with a glass back, "so that John may see when there are letters in the inside." [85]

For more elaborate improvements in the drawing room Dickens desired an estimate of the expense. These he designed as an affectionate surprise for Kate. The ugly handrail was to be ripped out, and the walls papered down to the skirting board in "blue and gold or purple and gold—to agree with the furniture and curtains." "I should like the skirting board to be painted in imitation of Satin-wood—the ceiling to have a faint pink blush in it—and a little wreath of flowers to be painted round the lamp. . . . I can safely trust your taste, if you will choose it," he told Mitton. Then, with a final inspiration of magnificence he added, "Gold moulding around the paper." [86]

Mitton's reply, in May, cast doubts upon the desirability of green for the hall and stairs. Dickens accordingly consulted Kate, who agreed with Mitton that it was quite out of the question. "So let it be," Dickens wrote cheerfully, "whatever you and the Decorator think best—not so cold as to be dull, and not so warm as to suffocate the prints.[87]

"The Drawing-room estimate is what Mr. Swiveller calls, a staggerer. I had no idea it would mount so high. It really should be done; for as it is, it is very poor and mean in comparison with the house— and I have been 'going' to do it these five years. But before I quite decide, will you let me know in one line, by return, *about* the cost of the other repairs in the lump." [88] The statement came,[89] and Dickens told Mitton to go ahead quickly so that the room could be done and the smell of paint evaporated before the family returned.

The last weeks of the Italian sojourn were delightful. "Seriously, it is a great pleasure to me," he wrote Forster, "to find that you are really pleased with these shadows in the water, and think them worth the looking at. Writing at such odd places, and in such odd seasons, I have been half savage with myself, very often, for not doing better. But d'Orsay, from whom I had a charming letter three days since, seems to think as you do . . . and says they remind him vividly of the real aspect of these scenes. . . . Well, if we should determine after we have sat in council, that the experiences they relate are to be used, we will call B and E to their share and voice in the matter." [90]

"Since our return," he wrote Forster on April 27th, "we have had charming spring days. The garden is one grove of roses; we have left off fires; and we breakfast and dine again in the great hall, with the windows open." [91] And, by June, "The fireflies at night now," he wrote, "are miraculously splendid; making another firmament among the rocks on the sea-shore, and the vines inland. They get into the bedrooms, and fly about, all night, like beautiful little lamps." [92]

As preparations for departure began to be made, Dickens discovered that one of the servants would not be returning with them. "Would you like to know a piece of domestic news that Forster don't know?"

he jocosely wrote Maclise. "Would you permit me to put you in the position of crushing him? I will do so. Forthwith. You recollect our cook, our nice cook, our good-looking cook; the best servant as ever trod (excuse my being nautical) 'twixt stem and stern, your Honour? Yesterday she came up to her mistress and announced that she was not going to return to England, but intended to be married and to settle here!!!" [93]

The bridegroom was the Governor's cook, a Frenchman whom she had been meeting at the weekly servants' balls. He spoke no English, and she no French; their courtship had taken place in Italian. The two intended to open a restaurant in Genoa. One of the nurses also had a suitor. "I am in daily expectation," Dickens went on, "of finding that Anne is secretly married to Roche and has a young family. I have interrogated Charley in private, but I believe he is still free, also his sisters. Chickenstalker (whom I think you will like—you always predicted well of him) is still heartwhole, I believe." [94]

The cook would have to go to Florence to be married in Lord Holland's house, and even then would be married only according to English law. "The man hasn't a penny. If there were an opening for a nice clean restaurant in Genoa—which I don't believe there is, for the Genoese have a natural enjoyment of dirt, garlic, and oil—it would still be a very hazardous venture, as the priests will certainly damage the man, if they can, for marrying a Protestant woman." All Dickens could do was to ensure, if a crisis came, that she should be able to get back to England. "As my father would observe, 'she has sown and must reap.' " [95]

By June 7th the Peschiere was in a turmoil of packing. Dickens himself had "fled the miseries of moving," [96] and was staying at the Brignole Rosso, with the De la Rues.[97] "They are all at sixes and sevens up at the Peschiere, as you may suppose," he wrote Forster; "and Roche is in a condition of tremendous excitement, engaged in settling the inventory with the house-agent, who has just told me he is the devil himself. I had been appealed to, and had contented myself with this expression of opinion, 'Signor Noli, you are an old impostor!' 'Illustrissimo,' said Signor Noli in reply, 'your servant is the devil himself: sent on earth to torture me.' I look occasionally towards the Peschiere (it is visible from this room) expecting to see one of them flying out of a window." [98]

The problem of loading the gigantic traveling carriage was complicated by the fact that the lane leading to the Peschiere grounds had
been torn up by pavers ever since April. Unless the work were finished
at once, everything would have to be brought down through the
gardens, piecemeal, and packed in the street. "To avoid this inconvenience, the Brave made proposals of bribery" and induced the pavers
"to pledge themselves that the carriage should come up at seven this
evening. The manner of doing that sort of paving work here, is to
take a pick or two with an axe, and then lie down to sleep for an hour.
When I came out, the Brave had issued forth to examine the ground;
and was standing alone in the sun among a heap of prostrate figures:
with a Great Despair depicted in his face, which it would be hard to
surpass. It was like a picture: 'After the Battle.'—Napoleon by the
Brave: Bodies by the Paviours." [99]

Although Mme. De la Rue had been much helped by Dickens's
ministrations, and was less haunted by her phantoms than she had
been, he feared that after his departure she might be troubled by their
return. In consequence he suggested that M. De la Rue endeavor to
acquire the mesmeric technique that had proved so useful in dealing
with his wife's seizures, and offered his own services in making a beginning. "Unless you have other plans for yourself and tell me so at
the opera tonight," he wrote, "perhaps you might as well make your
magnetic start, tomorrow instead of Monday." [100] While Kate, Georgina, Roche, and the servants wrestled with the packing, therefore,
Dickens was engaged in teaching M. De la Rue how to induce the
magnetic sleep.

At last all arrangements for departure were made. Farewells had
been said. Packing cases, large and small, were ready for dispatch to
England.[101] The traveling coach was loaded to bursting. Once again
Kate, Georgina, the children, and the maids were crammed within,
although the cook, of course, was left behind. Dickens and Roche took
their places on the box. With an unwieldy lurch, the vehicle started,
heading north for the St. Gothard pass.

The road over the Alps, when they reached it, had been open only
eight days, and curved between two massive walls of snow twenty feet
high. "Vast plains of snow," Dickens wrote, "range up the mountain-
sides above the road, itself seven thousand feet above the sea; and tremendous waterfalls, hewing out arches for themselves in the vast

drifts, go thundering down from precipices into deep chasms, here and there and everywhere: the blue water tearing through the white snow with an awful beauty that is most sublime." [102]

The descent from the Great St. Gothard with a carriage, four horses, and only one postilion, Dickens looked upon "as the most dangerous thing that a carriage and horses can do. We had two great wooden logs for drags, and snapped them both like matches. The road is like a geometrical staircase, with horrible depths beneath it; and at every turn it is a toss-up, or seems to be, whether the leaders shall go round or over. The lives of the whole party may depend upon a strap in the harness; and if we broke our rotten harness once yesterday, we broke it at least a dozen times." The horses "slip and slide, and get their legs over the traces, and are dragged up against the rocks; carriage, horses, harness, all a confused heap. The Brave, and I, and the postilion, were constantly at work, in extricating the whole concern from a tangle like a skein of thread. We broke two thick iron chains, and crushed the box of a wheel, as it was; and the carriage is now undergoing repair . . ." [103]

Gradually the descent from Andermatt to Altdorf, "William Tell's town," was achieved, and on June 14th they reached Lucerne. The Swiss villages, Dickens said, were even more beautiful in summer than in winter. "Shut in by high mountains capped with perpetual snow; and dotting a rich carpet of the softest turf, overshadowed by great trees; they seem so many little havens of refuge from the troubles and miseries of great towns. The cleanliness of the little baby-houses of inns is wonderful to those who come from Italy. But the beautiful Italian manners, the sweet language, the quick recognition of a pleasant look or cheerful word; the captivating expression of a desire to oblige in everything; these are left behind the Alps. Remembering them, I sigh for the dirt again: the brick floors, bare walls, unplastered ceilings, and broken windows." [104]

* * * * *

Indeed, Dickens had enjoyed Italy much more than he had America. He had relished the magnificence and the spacious leisure of the Peschiere, and even the unflagging energy of his sightseeing had not been the feverish scramble with which he had hastened over thousands of miles in the United States. There were no intrusive mobs treating him as a traveling freak-show, no throngs of damsels snipping fragments off his clothes for souvenirs, no angry snarlings from a noisy press. Although cultivated Italians already knew his name, to the bulk of the Italian people he was unknown. The upper classes gave him a courteous welcome when he came among them, but did not intrude upon him; and to the peasants, landlords of inns, shopkeepers, and servants whom he encountered he was merely another traveling English milord.

No doubt, also, Dickens had learned from his American adventures. He had resolved to make no public comments on Italian institutions or the governments of its states. Nor had he expected any such glorious things of Italian society as he had of the republic across the Atlantic. No nineteenth-century liberal who knew of the Italian political exiles, who had talked in London, as Dickens had, with Mazzini, entertained utopian pictures of the Papal States, the Venetian territories ruled by Austria, or the Neapolitan kingdom of Ferdinand II.

Dickens went to Italy, therefore, much more in the spirit of a tourist visiting a museum than in that of a social observer. And the beauty of the Italian landscape was a perpetual revelation and delight to him. But he responded no more profoundly than scores of other travelers to Italian art and architecture. His standards in painting were a bluff insistence on the facts of human anatomy and visual perspective, and a feeling of what facial expressions were "natural to certain passions." [105] The "rules of art" that were always on the tongues of connoisseurs he regarded as so much slavish cant.[106] Rather ostentatiously determined not to be intimidated into insincere aesthetic raptures, he made facile mockery—as Mark Twain was to do later in *The Innocents Abroad*—of the St. Sebastians stuck as full of arrows as animated pincushions and the other conventions of religious iconography.[107]

This crude honesty resulted in judgments sometimes shrewd and sometimes merely flippant. Dickens derided "jolly young watermen" masquerading as cherubim and brewers' draymen impersonating Evangelists, and grew facetious about "libellous Angels" playing on fiddles "for the delectation of sprawling monks apparently in liquor." [108] Sculpture he hardly mentioned at all, though he was very good on the exaggerated figures of Bernini, those "breezy maniacs, whose every fold of drapery is blown inside-out." [109] He lumped artists of very different degrees of merit together, and seldom said anything to suggest that he looked on painting with the eyes of an artist. Only occasionally, as in Tintoretto's *Assembly of the Blest*, did he note the organizing principle of a picture, "all the lines . . . tending majestically . . . to Almighty God in the centre." [110] But in general the grandeur and nobility he saw was less the flowering of glory in color or composition than a response to sentiment and the story subject matter of a picture.

The monuments of ancient Rome and the ruins of Pompeii struck a vibrant chord in his imagination. Romanesque and Gothic churches moved him with emotions like those he had known in English cathedrals. But although he could enjoy the splendor of the Renaissance and even the baroque in palaces and other secular buildings, those styles seemed frivolous and incongruous to him in ecclesiastical structures. Only when their ornate magnificence of gold, marble, mosaic, and glowing color blazed into the Byzantine gorgeousness of St. Mark's—an encrustation of jeweled pomp like one of the Arabian Nights fantasies of his childhood—could Dickens forget how different was this polychrome glitter from the cool spaces and gray stonework of Rochester or Canterbury.

Something of this same piety to the associations in which his own memory was steeped colored his feelings about the ceremonies of the Catholic Church. Although he had rejected the Church of England and detested the influence of its bishops in English politics, its services had for his imagination the authority of a familiar comeliness. The brilliant pageantry and processions of Rome, the colorful vestments, the incense, the elaborate symbolic rituals, all seemed to him only a theatrical mummery. He did not analyze *as* traditional what was traditional in his own feelings; where he recognized tradition at all he disliked it as obstructive and reactionary; and he made no endeavor to understand its emotional power when he found it embodied in strange and alien forms.

In addition, of course, he felt still more violently unsympathetic to the Church of Rome as an institution than he did to the Church of England or even to the bulk of the Dissenters. Although he deplored inflicting penalties on people for their religious affiliations, and hated all religious persecution, he thought the influence of the Roman Church almost altogether evil. In every state of Europe where it wielded power it seemed to him hand in glove with tyranny and oppression. Everywhere he thought it complaisant to privilege and corruption. Everywhere it riveted shackles on the hearts and minds of the poor whom it professed to succor, and wrung its wealth from their toil and misery. Everywhere it did its worst to keep them in degraded ignorance.

Holding such views, Dickens found it hard to believe that its prelates were not cynically pursuing their own aggrandisement and only pretending to a faith in the rites they solemnly performed. During the ceremonies of Holy Week he could not help regarding the Pope as a mere puppet going through a degrading chicanery which Dickens suspected that as a sensible man he must despise in his heart. In the glances of the Cardinals he imagined he read signs that they considered it all a great farce. To his impatient scorn it was incredible that any except the victims of superstition could find in such tiresome flimflam a sincere emotional beauty and a deep spiritual truth.

The lower clergy almost uniformly seemed to him sunk in "sloth, deceit, and intellectual torpor," [111] their faces "coarse and heavy," with a "dogged, stupid, monotonous stare." [112] The Cappuccini, ignorant as they were, perhaps did some good among the poor, but the other orders were constantly prying into secrets of families to establish a baleful ascendancy.[113] The Jesuits, above all, Dickens always saw in unfavorable lights, "skulking," [114] stealthily "creeping in and out," [115] "slinking noiselessly about, in pairs, like black cats" [116] or ugly birds of prey,[117] In the end, whenever Dickens saw paintings in which some of the faces were vulgar and degraded he immediately labeled them in his mind as having the "convent stamp."

But for the Italian people as a whole Dickens came to feel a warm regard and affection. From the upper classes he had largely kept aloof, not even presenting the greater part of the letters of introduction he had brought with him. "Not falling on very good specimens of the higher orders, in the beginning," he explained to Miss Coutts, "I have not pursued that Enquiry." He liked "the Neapolitans least of all," and "the Romans next, for they are fierce and brutal." "In the mass," though, he told Miss Coutts, "I like the common people of Italy very much." [118] Their cheerfulness, their beautiful manners, their swift response to friendly treatment, their captivating desire to please, brought a glow to his own heart. Saying his farewell to Italy, "with all its miseries and wrongs," he said it with an affectionate tenderness to "a people naturally well-disposed, and patient, and sweet-tempered."

On the closing page of *Pictures from Italy*, "Years of neglect, oppression, and misrule," he wrote, "have been at work, to change their nature and reduce their spirit, miserable jealousies, fomented by petty Princes to whom union was destruction and division strength, have been a canker at the root of their nationality . . . but the good that was in them ever, is in them yet, and a noble people may be, one day, raised up from these ashes. Let us entertain that hope!" [119]

CHAPTER SEVEN

Birth Pangs of the *Daily News*

SINCE 1842 Dickens's mind had recurred more than once to the idea of founding a great liberal newspaper with himself as editor. Nagged by nervous fears lest his popularity might wane, he worried about how he could support his large family if the public suddenly stopped buying his books. To be sure, he was doing well at present, but the periodical sales of *Martin Chuzzlewit* had been a frightening portent of uncertainty. Now, in 1845, he had five children to provide for, and there was another one on the way. A handsome editorial salary would be a comforting provision against future dangers.[1]

Moreover, the time seemed ripe for such an enterprise. During the later years of the Whig administration there had been nothing but annual deficits, universal stagnation in business, and acute misery in the laboring population; and in 1841 the Tories had been returned to power. Sir Robert Peel's annual budgets from 1842 to 1845 had re-animated trade by sweeping away duties on exported machinery and imported raw materials, but Peel had done little to help the working classes.[2] He could not make up his mind to regulations ameliorating the hideous conditions in mines and factories and was implacably opposed to the Ten Hours Bill.[3] Unable to refute the arguments against the Corn Laws that Cobden poured at him across the floor of the House of Commons in streams of lucid reasoning, he crumpled up his notes and whispered to a colleague, "You must answer this, I cannot." But he was afraid to break his election pledges of 1841 and split his party by announcing his conversion. Meanwhile the champions of factory reform never ceased agitation, and anti-Corn-Law orators, rubbing in the distress of agricultural labor, "pointed in triumphant pity to the hollow-cheeked serf of the fields, and produced him on

[565]

platforms in his smock frock to say, 'I be protected, and I be starving.' " [4] During the summer of 1845 the free-trade position was strengthened by the Irish potato blight and a month of rain in England that rotted the corn harvest on the ground.[5] The dangers of famine and disorder weakened the whole fabric of resistance to change.

What a moment for establishing a great new organ to sound the radical doctrines of reform! More than any weekly, a daily newspaper could be a very spearhead in the fight against all the entrenched forces of privilege. It might do incalculable good in exposing inefficiency and corruption, hammering away at reaction, arousing public sentiment, and advancing the welfare of the masses. To be in control of a leading paper in the nation's capital would be a source of enormous power. Parliament itself feared the voice of the London *Times*, the great "Thunderer," and it was not inconceivable that a brilliantly edited rival might wrest the leadership from the older paper. Dickens had refused more than one seat in the House of Commons, but how much more effective to wield a force that ministers could not ignore!

Memories of his old newspaper days doubtless had a part, too, in rendering the role of editor attractive. What a triumph it would be to show the proprietors of the *Chronicle* the way a newspaper should be run! How Sir John Easthope would rage and foam to see his own journal being overshadowed by a newcomer under the control of a former subordinate and one whom he had angrily rated! What trembling there might be even in the great *Times* editorial chambers in Printing House Square! There was a splendor, too, in the thought of sitting at the center of a vast web of authority directing the roar of the huge presses, deciding policies that must have weight in Whitehall and Westminster.

Before Dickens left for Italy in the spring of 1844 he and Forster had broached the idea to Bradbury and Evans at their offices in Whitefriars. No decision was then made, but the printing firm agreed to go into its financial aspects and renew their discussions when Dickens returned the following year.[6] Some steps were evidently taken even while Dickens remained abroad, for in Rome he tentatively secured Father Prout, the Reverend Francis Mahony, as Roman correspondent of the projected paper. "When you took leave of me at the Milvian bridge," the latter wrote him, ". . . you engaged me to enter upon this correspondence, and we ratified the solemn compact by your acceptance of that handful of cigars which I pressed on you under the pretext that they were 'blessed by the Pope,' whereas I had bought them freshly at the shop of his Highness Duke Torlonia in the Corso." [7] But that the entire plan was still very shadowy is shown by the fact that a few weeks after settling into Devonshire Terrace again, Dickens was asking Forster's opinion of a quite different sort of periodical.

"I have turned it over, the last two days, very much in my mind: and think it positively good. I incline still to weekly; price three half-pence, if possible; partly original, partly select; notices of books, notices of theatres, notices of all good things, notices of all bad ones; Carol philosophy, cheerful views, sharp anatomization of humbug, jolly good temper . . . And I would call it, sir,—

THE CRICKET

A Cheerful creature that chirrups on the Hearth.

Natural History

". . . And I would chirp, chirp, chirp away in every number until I chirped it up to—well, you shall say how many hundred thousand!" [8]

Forster, however, poured cold water on this scheme, and in a renewal of the newspaper project it was so swept away as to leave only one trace behind.[9] "What do you think," Dickens wrote in July, "of a notion that has occurred to me in connection with our abandoned little weekly? It would be a delicate and beautiful fancy for a Christmas book, making the Cricket a little household god—silent in the wrong and sorrow of the tale, and loud again when all went well and happy." [10] This grew into *The Cricket on the Hearth*, the Christmas book of 1845, which was so popular that it doubled the initial sale of both its predecessors.

By August Dickens was busily engaged in calculating the expenses of running a newspaper, and asking his friend Beard in confidence how much the *Herald* spent on its Foreign Department, "correspondents' salaries, and everything included." [11] But meanwhile he had also flung himself headlong into whipping up a private theatrical entertainment to which he had long been looking forward.

*   *   *   *   *

He had suggested the idea to Forster the preceding December, when he had traveled to England to read *The Chimes* in Lincoln's Inn Fields.[12] "ARE we to have that play???" he wrote from Genoa in June. "Have I spoken of it, ever since I came home from London, as a settled thing!" [13] Soon after his return from Italy he decided on Ben Jonson's *Every Man in His Humour*, and gaily began assembling a cast. "As I write to you now, not as a Private Friend, but as a Stage Manager," he informed Clarkson Stanfield, who was to handle the scenery, "I have half a mind to damn your eyes by way of beginning. . . . In the meantime merry rehearsals innumerable." [14]

Each of the players was to be allowed thirty to thirty-five guests, admitted by a printed card of invitation.[15] To accommodate this considerable audience, Dickens selected a private theater in Dean Street, Soho, where the retired actress Frances Kelly conducted a dramatic school. Once beloved by Charles Lamb, who praised her "divine plain face," she was now aging into a fussy eccentricity. "Heavens! such a scene as I have had with Miss Kelly here, this morning!" Dickens wrote Forster after his first interview with her. "She wanted us put off until the theatre should be cleaned and brushed up a bit, and she would and she would not, for she is eager to have us and alarmed when she thinks of us. By the foot of Pharaoh, it was a great scene! Especially when she choked and had the glass of water brought." *[16]*

Dickens had cast himself for the braggart Bobadil and Forster for Kiteley. Among the other actors were Frederick and Augustus Dickens, T. J. Thompson, the artist Frank Stone, Douglas Jerrold, Mark Lemon (the plump and beaming editor of *Punch*), and the caricaturist John Leech. Maclise had been one of them, but took fright on the eve of rehearsals, and Stanfield, after two terrified attempts to get through the part of Wellbred, pleaded to be allowed to confine himself to the scenery.[17]

Dickens took charge of everything. The dirt and confusion of Miss Kelly's theater gave way to cleanliness and order.[18] Scenery was new-painted. Bright costumes were designed from originals in seventeenth-century pictures. Rehearsals went on while Miss Kelly flitted anxiously about, and two mysterious pensioners of hers made fitful entrances and exits, a silent "Man in a Straw Hat" and a small girl whose starts and shrieks at the play earned her the nickname of "Fireworks." [19] Still other rehearsals were held in a ground-floor room at 90 Fleet Street, premises belonging to Bradbury and Evans, with whom Dickens was now deep in plans for the proposed newspaper.[20]

Beside these activities, Dickens had his little Christmas book to plan and write, and had also agreed to do an article on capital punishment for the *Edinburgh Review*. In a letter to Macvey Napier, the editor, he outlined his ideas on the subject. The death penalty, he thought, instead of serving as a deterrent, only aroused a diseased sympathy for the criminal and brutalized the feelings of those who witnessed it. Would it not be better for society, he asked, "to substitute a mean and shameful punishment, degrading the deed and the committer of the deed," and allowing the general compassion to remember what was too often forgotten, the murderer's victim? [21]

His youngest brother, Augustus, now eighteen, was in the throes of a love affair that reminded Dickens of his own early days. "Twice," he wrote, "I was very horribly in earnest; and once I really set upon the cast for six or seven long years, all the energy and determination of which I am owner. But it went the way of nearly all such things at last . . ." For Augustus, though, he was not much worried. The young lady probably entertained no designs on a youth who had "no possessions of any sort or kind"; in all likelihood it was only "a means of getting rid of spare time pleasantly. . . . I have sounded my brother Fred; and he seems to think the Virgin may be 'only joking.' She may be a Platonic Virgin perhaps. Who knows?" [22]

In the middle of August, Dickens took Kate and Georgina down to Broadstairs for a week-end and arranged for the children to stay there, though he was too busy with the play and the newspaper by now to pay more than flying visits.[23] "I went to a circus at Ramsgate on Saturday night," he wrote Forster, "where Mazeppa was played in three long acts without an H in it: as if for a wager. Evven, and edds, and orrors, and ands, were as plentiful as blackberries; but the letter H was neither whispered in Evven nor muttered in Ell . . ." [24] A little later, running down for another week-end to see how his young family were, he reported to Kate finding them all in a cornfield, looking very brown and healthy, and "Chickenstalker . . . beyond all question a size larger." [25]

As rehearsals continued, Dickens developed a low opinion of both the play and his fellow actors. "It is such a damned thing," he wrote Macready, "to have all the people perpetually coming on to say their parts, without any action to bring 'em in, or take 'em out, or keep 'em going." [26] And most of the players were "an utterly careless and un-business-like set of dogs"; "I don't except Forster: for so far as he is concerned, there is nothing in the world but Kitely—there is no world at all; only a something in its place that begins with a 'K' and ends with a 'Y.' " [27]

As the time for the performance drew near, Dickens lived in a turmoil of property lists, playbills, and rehearsal calls. "I am half dead with Managerial work," he wrote, "—and with actual work in shirt-sleeves; with a dirty face, a hammer, and a bag of nails." [28] On the morning of September 20th—the day of the performance—Dickens borrowed a young man from the skeleton office force already in the newspaper premises, and took him along to help out in Dean Street. On the stage, Jerrold prepared a theatrical fire of slacked lime and red tinsel; in the boxes and dress circle Lemon and Dickens, stripping off their coats, numbered the seats, Dickens stuffing the pockets of his puce-colored velvet waistcoat with bradawl and tin tacks.[29]

The curtain was to rise at seven-thirty.[30] By seven carriages crowded Dean Street; "it was as much as we could do with a strong body of Police," Dickens wrote Mme. De la Rue, "to keep the doors from being carried by force." Among the guests, Alfred Tennyson had traveled a couple of hundred miles in one direction to be present, and the Duke of Devonshire a couple of hundred in another. "It really was a brilliant sight. The audience so distinguished for one thing or another, everyone so elegantly dressed, all in such a state of excitement and expectation." [31] Jane Welsh Carlyle, as usual, described the scene more acidulously. The aristocratic guests, she thought, "looked rather a *rum set*"; adding that the Duke of Devonshire sat opposite her, "with his nose 'looking toward Damascus,' and old Lady Holland graced it (not the nose but the play) with her hideous presence." "*Oh how expensive!*" Jane summarized tartly. "The 'fule creturs' must have spent a mint of money . . ." [32]

She and her husband were equally contemptuous of the acting. Forster, said Carlyle, imitated Macready without ever ceasing to be Forster; and he was grimly patronizing about "poor little Dickens, all painted in black and red, and affecting the voice of a man of six feet." [33] Macready, however, though grumpy with a severe cold and professionally scornful of the enterprise, admitted that "several of the actors were very fine as amateurs" and praised Dickens and Lemon.[34] Most of the other guests lauded Dickens to the skies. He was "glorious in Bobadil," said one of them. "He literally floated in braggadocio. His air of supreme conceit and frothy pomp in the earlier scenes came out with prodigious force in contrast with the subsequent humiliation . . ." [35]

Dickens enjoyed it all hugely. "I wore real armour on my throat and heart," he wrote; "and most enormous boots and spurs—and looked like an old Spanish Portrait, I assure you." He had had a dresser from one of the large theaters make him up with a peaked black beard and a mustache fiercely curling skyward, stuck on hair by hair, which were replaced, after Bobadil was beaten, by a beard all disheveled and mustache drooping lankly down. And the triumph of his directing was resounding. "There are whispers of gold snuff-boxes for the indefatigable manager from the performers—Hem!" [36]

The evening ended with a supper for the players and their wives, to which the Macreadys, Count D'Orsay, George Cattermole, and a few others were invited.[37] Public furore about the performance was extravagant. People who had not seen it, said the *Times*, declared they would have given £5, £10, £20, to be present, and those who had behaved as if like Pythagoras they "had been initiated into all sorts of mysteries." [38] Invitations, applications, petitions, and memorials begged for a repetition. Ultimately Dickens and his colleagues decided on a benefit performance to raise a building fund for Dr. Southwood Smith's nursing home, which was then lodged in Devonshire Place House opposite Devonshire Terrace. They took the St. James's Theatre to provide more seats. An unexpected event set the date for the middle of November. "Here's a pretty kettle of Fish!" [39] Dickens exclaimed. "Prince Albert has written to say that he dies to see the amateur Performance on behalf of the Sanatorium, and can it be done on the fifteenth! Lord and Lady Lansdowne and the 'Tarnal Smash knows who, have taken boxes . . ." [40]

On the great night the entire theater glittered with celebrities.

There were the Duke of Wellington and Prince George of Cambridge, the Duke of Devonshire again, Lord Melbourne in a box with Mrs. Norton, Lady Duff Gordon, and Dwarkanauth Tagore, the last in gorgeous Indian costume, Baron de Rothschild, Macready, and innumerable others. When Prince Albert and his suite arrived, they were given white-satin playbills and the curtain rose. But though the *Times* reported that the actors were even better than they had been on the previous occasion, the second evening did not have the success of the first.[41] "The audience were as cold as ice," wrote Charles Greville in his diary; and between the acts Melbourne complained in a stentorian voice heard across the pit, "I knew this play would be dull, but that it would be so damnably dull as this I did not suppose!" [42]

Despite these less than rapturous comments the same amateur company, with a few changes of personnel, gave a benefit performance of Massinger and Fletcher's *The Elder Brother* for Miss Kelly at her theater on the third day of the new year.[43] Dickens's friend Thompson had dropped out after the first night of *Every Man in His Humour* and been replaced by George Cattermole.[44] During the entire preceding year and a half Thompson had been engaged to Christiana Weller, the delicate Liverpool beauty by whom Dickens had felt so deeply moved, and the marriage was to take place early in October. Suddenly, on the very eve of the ceremony, "the ring purchased, wedding dresses made," a strange crisis arose. The whole contract was "shattered like Glass," Dickens wrote, "in an instant, under the most inexplicable circumstances that ever distracted the head of 'a mutual friend.'" Dickens set himself to restore it. "If you could have seen me yesterday, as the acting manager of this drama (a domestic tragedy) you would have said that Miss Kelly's was nothing to it." [45]

Somehow, Dickens managed to smooth away Thompson's difficulties, whatever they were, and later in the month attended the wedding. He was magnificent in a waistcoat with "broad stripes of blue or purple" copied from one Macready had worn in Bulwer Lytton's *Money*. "Mr. Macready, Sir, are you a father?" he wrote. "If so, lend me that waistcoat for five minutes. I am bidden to a wedding (where fathers are made), and my artist cannot, I find (how should he?) imagine such a waistcoat. Let me show it to him as a sample of my tastes and wishes; and—ha, ha, ha, ha!—*eclipse* the bridegroom!" [46] From England the newly wedded couple were going to Genoa, where

Dickens predicted that Christiana would find an affectionate friend in Mme. De la Rue and Thompson "a resource in the most elegant and comfortable family there." [47]

*   *   *   *   *

Meanwhile Dickens had been so delayed by all these distractions that he did not begin writing his Christmas book until the middle of October.[48] The newspaper scheme had reached the point where Dickens was constantly making confidential inquiries of Beard and asking him to untangle little knots of journalistic procedure. "Resolve me this question," he asked. "Those small correspondents at Madras, Ceylon, and Aden,—do they make separate parcels of their newspapers, addressed to the agent at Malta; or do they open the parcel on its way from Calcutta and put them in? If so, how is the parcel addressed when it leaves Calcutta? To the agent at the next place? This seems to me a query essential to the right working of things." [49]

He was obliged to withdraw his acceptance of an invitation to a meeting of the Manchester Athenaeum, although he had intended to use the occasion as a means of looking into who were the best reporters in that town, for Kate was now very near the time of her confinement and feeling extremely miserable. "I cannot win any cheerful consent from her to my being absent from home," he wrote. "Apart from my own anxieties, it would be cruel, therefore, to attempt the Manchester flight." [50] Four days later, however, her labor had not yet begun. "I call her Joanna Southcote," he told Beard.[51] Not until thirty-six hours later still, on the morning of October 28th, did she give birth to "what is usually called (I don't know why) a strapping boy." [52]

Tennyson and Count D'Orsay stood as godfathers to this sixth child, who was christened Alfred D'Orsay Tennyson Dickens. The extraordinary name aroused a considerable amount of not altogether friendly comment. Edward Fitzgerald took it as evidence that Dickens was a snob. "For what is Snobbishness and Cockneyism," he asked, "but all such pretensions and parade?" [53] Even good-natured Robert Browning joked about it to Elizabeth Barrett: "You observe: Alfred is common to both the godfather and the devil-father. . . . When you remember what the form of sponsorship is, to what it pledges you in the Church of England—and then remember that Mr. Dickens is an enlightened Unitarian,—you will get a curious notion of the man, I fancy." [54]

The end of October saw the newspaper project rapidly taking shape. Bradbury and Evans were ready to put up a great block of capital. Associated with them was Joseph Paxton, who had begun his career as gardener to the Duke of Devonshire and made a fortune in railway shares.[55] "Paxton," wrote Dickens to Mitton, "has command of every railway influence in England and abroad except the Great Western, and he is in it heart and purse. One other large shareholder is to come in; and that is to be a house which has the power of bringing a whole volley of advertisements upon the paper always. The commercial influence that will come down on it with the whole might of its aid and energy; not only in the City of London, but in Liverpool, Manchester, Bristol, and Yorkshire, is quite stunning. I am trying to engage the best people right and left." [56]

Among the prospective backers from the north of England were Sir William Jackson and Sir Joshua Walmsley. Sir William was the leading champion of liberalism in the north. Sir Joshua had been President of the Liverpool Mechanics' Institute and Mayor of Liverpool, was closely connected with George Stephenson in railway schemes, and was now working actively with Cobden and Bright in the Anti-Corn-Law League. He had praised Dickens as "the best friend to progress and reform yet seen in English fiction." His vigorous endeavors to make the reform movement not a conflict of class interests but a joint concern for the welfare of the entire country became one of the cardinal principles of the new paper.[57]

Although Dickens had not yet absolutely committed himself to assuming the editorship, he began to assemble a formidable staff, striking terror among the older papers by offering salaries well above established rates and wresting away some of their ablest men.[58] There was much dread, Dickens reported, that this new venture represented "a powerful combination of energy, experience, and money"; [59] he had "certain knowledge that it had filled the Times people with dismay, and had been the cause of all sorts of councils and discussions in Printing-House Square." [60] Gloom lay heavy over the editorial chambers of the Strand and Shoe Lane.

Despite these encouraging signs, Dickens was disturbed by what seemed to him Paxton's "loose, flurried way" of doing business. To one financial associate the entire enterprise had "been prematurely broached, at a disadvantage, without a point the size of a pin's head being gained." [61] And a few days later, "It seems to me," Dickens exclaimed testily, "that Mr. Paxton's City man has broken down dead, in the very outset, if the assistance we got this morning be any criterion." [62] With these exasperations, and the struggle of working on his Christmas story at the same time, Dickens felt "sick, bothered and depressed," and was tempted to make off to Brighton.[63] "I have been so very unwell this morning," he wrote Forster, "with giddiness, headache, and botheration of one sort or another, that I didn't get up till noon: and, shunning Fleet Street, am now going for a country walk . . ." [64]

Forster doubted the wisdom of Dickens's taking the editorship at all. He had aided in the initial steps of founding the paper, but he now wrote trying to dissuade Dickens from his course, pointing out how little it could enhance his fame and genius, and warning against its party and political involvements.[65] But Dickens made light of these objections. The times were right for such an effort, he insisted; at worst he could retire unharmed. "And most of all I have, sometimes, that possibility of failing health or fading popularity before me, which beckons me to such a venture when it comes within my reach." [66] By the 3rd of November he announced his decision to Bradbury and Evans. "I will take that post of Editor which is marked in the little statement as having a salary of a Thousand Pounds attached to it— for double that salary." [67]

The printers raised no objection to these terms, but overnight came a rude setback. There was a failure of a great broker in the City, "which so affects two of my principal people," Dickens told Beard, "that the Paper *cannot be,* on any proper footing." [68] After laying aside all his "usual and dear pursuits for this object," Dickens was considerably shaken. He was convinced that Paxton had had a foreknowledge of the catastrophe for many days; "it stared him in the face (and looked out of his face too)," Dickens wrote, when they had last met in Fleet Street.[69] "But never say die is the Inimitable's motto: and I have already pumped up as much courage as will set me going on my old track, please God, in four-and-twenty hours." [70]

Bradbury and Evans, after the first shock, desired to proceed despite the loss. But Dickens was panicky with the conviction that the enterprise was "a doomed thing," its heart "broken and dead." There could no longer be any confidence in it; if they patched it up and tried to carry it out with curtailed means and inferior abilities, all the pre-eminence that would have assured it a great course would be destroyed. The advertising they had counted on was gone.[71] Some of the men who had been engaged had already asked to be taken back on the *Chronicle*; others had applied to the *Times*, and the *Herald*.[72] Those who had resigned the certain income of a lifetime for the chances of this paper would have to be compensated—an act of justice that might cost several thousand pounds, but that Bradbury and Evans would find better than having "the maimed hands of this wounded newspaper" dragging at them night and day.[73] If they felt committed to going on, Dickens would give them every assistance in his power, but he would not connect himself with it. "Nor can I conceal from you that I believe in my soul it would end in your Ruin." [74]

He consequently advised their calling together the gentlemen who had been engaged and asking on what terms they would compound for their engagements. "And lastly, let me say that my confidence in the Paper and my confidence in you, are as distinct and separate things as Heaven and Earth; and that while the first is gone utterly— the second is not affected by a hair's breadth or a feather's weight." [75] "My dear Bradbury and Evans," he reiterated in a further letter, "in a truly earnest and affectionate spirit, I assure you from my heart that I esteem and honour you the more for what I have known of you since these occurrences. I hope and believe that a long course of mutual confidence and friendship and mutual usefulness, is open to us." [76]

*   *   *   *   *

Meanwhile Dickens was trying desperately to finish *The Cricket on the Hearth* and arranging with no fewer than four artists for its illustrations.[77] To the editor of the *Edinburgh Review* he apologized for his inability to do the article on capital punishment. "I have been involved for the last fortnight in a maze of distractions which nothing could have enabled me to anticipate or prevent. Everything I have had to do, has been interfered with, and cast aside. I have never in my life had so many insuperable obstacles crowded into the way of my pursuits. It is as little my fault, believe me, as though I were ill and wrote to you from my bed." [78]

But within another week Dickens once again reversed his decision about the newspaper. Bradbury and Evans convinced him that the failure of the brokerage house was not the disaster for them that he had believed, and he agreed to remain as editor. On November 17th an agreement was signed establishing the paper, now named the *Daily News,* with a capital of £50,000, of which Bradbury and Evans subscribed £22,500, Paxton £25,000, and a third proprietor named Richard Wright the remaining £2,500.[79] Somewhat later Sir William Jackson and Sir Joshua Walmsley brought the raised or promised capital up to £100,000.[80]

Dickens promptly set about completing his editorial staff. Earlier in the fall he had chosen William Henry Wills as his personal secretary and general administrative assistant. Wills was a sharp-nosed man with a blotched complexion, who was so thin that Douglas Jerrold described him as having spent his life "in training to go up a gas-pipe." He had contributed to *Bentley's Miscellany* in 1837, had been a member of the literary staff of *Punch* at its founding in 1841, and had served since 1842 as assistant editor of *Chambers's Journal* in Edinburgh; [81] though not a man of great imagination, he was quick, efficient, and thoroughly dependable.

As subeditor, Dickens obtained a journalist named Powell, who had been subeditor of the *Morning Chronicle* and editor of the *Evening Chronicle,* [82] "the man of all others in London," Dickens wrote, "best qualified to act as one of the sub-editors of an enterprising paper." [83] For another unidentified subeditor, he exultantly said, "I have received a proposal which is likely to drive Easthope (when he knows it) raving mad." [84] Douglas Jerrold and Mark Lemon also joined the subeditorial staff. Thomas Hodgkinson, of the *Economist,* became assistant subeditor; Scott Russell was railway editor and William Weir wrote railway comments and information; Dudley Costello took charge of foreign news and Frederic Knight Hunt of provincial intelligence. Forster and Albany Fonblanque were among the leader writers, of whom the chief was William Johnson Fox, Unitarian minister and "golden-tongued apostle of untaxed bread," later member of Parliament for Oldham. Eyre Evans Crowe, previously the Paris correspondent of the *Chronicle,* took over that post for the *Daily News.* Military and naval news, sports, commerce, and clerical news were all in the hands of the ablest men Dickens could find.[85]

A curious footnote to these major appointments was that Dickens's father-in-law, George Hogarth, was made music critic with "a general liability to Theatres." [86] When Dickens was a youthful reporter Hogarth had been editor of the *Evening Chronicle*. Later he had left Easthope's employ and only recently returned to it. But now he was entirely willing to throw up his post and come to the *Daily News* for five guineas a week, a salary that Dickens had been earning eleven years before. It seems unmistakable that Hogarth had been during the intervening years no great success as a journalist.

Later, in January, Dickens requested Lady Blessington to write social gossip and literary and art news, inviting her to name her own remuneration. He was startled, however, when she demanded £800 a year, and felt obliged to retract his unwary generosity. Instead he offered £400 for a year, or £250 for six months, at the end of which time, if both wished, they might make another agreement.[87] The latter Lady Blessington promptly accepted.

The reporting staff included George Hodder, R. H. Horne, Joseph Archer Crowe, Blanchard Jerrold, Laman Blanchard, William Hazlitt, and Thomas Holcroft, the last three sons of the older writers of those names.[88] In charge of them Dickens placed his father, now an obese and bustling man of sixty, still full of fun and energy, and still fond of a glass of grog. Though so stout that he could no longer move with very great speed, John Dickens was a hard-working and efficient organizer. His difficulties had never arisen from lack of professional ability. He proceeded at once to arrange a system for the regular marking and orderly dispatch of copy to the printers, and above all of the pages that would stream in steadily from the men in the Gallery.[89]

The newspaper offices were tucked away in a block of tumble-down rookeries alongside Bradbury and Evans's establishment in Whitefriars, approached from Fleet Street through an archway into a narrow back lane parallel to Bouverie Street. Inside there were worn steps, grimy walls, soiled cocoa-matting, and wooden stairs leading to the upper floors. Next door, in the printing house, amid a gloom lit by flares of gas and a smell of oil and paper, the presses slid, revolved, and thundered in the basement, and ghostly men in paper caps and dirty shirt sleeves loomed through the foggy atmosphere.[90] Away from the other offices, high aloft on the third floor at Whitefriars, Dickens himself had two rooms with a carpet, a plain office table and armchair, a black horsehair sofa, and a small bookcase containing volumes of Hansard, the *Mirror of Parliament*, some dictionaries and reference books, Shakespeare and the Bible, and a collection of works that the office boy remembered in later years as "a complete set of the Classics." [91]

Near the middle of December, Dickens ran up to Liverpool, "to blow vague trumpets," he said, "for the Daily News," [92] and on the 27th it was publicly announced in *Punch* as an independent newspaper of liberal politics under his direction.[93] Simultaneously the *Times* printed a savage review of Dickens's Christmas book, *The Cricket on the Hearth*, which had just been published. To his friend Macready this looked "like the heavy and remorseless blow of an enemy, determined to disable his antagonist by striking to maim him or kill if he can," and the actor was "sorry to see in a newspaper so powerful as the *Times* an attack so ungenerous, so unworthy of itself." [94]

Forster agreed with Macready about the damage it would do, and shared his apprehensions that Dickens had rushed into an undertaking for which he was not fitted. But Dickens had become "so intensely fixed on his own opinions," Forster said, "and in his admiration of his own works" ("Who could have believed it?" Macready exclaimed) "that he, Forster, was useless to him as a counsel," and, "since he refused to see criticisms on himself, this partial passion would grow upon him, till it became an incurable evil." [95]

Dickens's confidence, however, in his hold upon the public proved to be justified. As if readers sensed the hostility behind the rival newspaper's onslaught, they only bought the little book in larger numbers. "The Times," Dickens remarked cheerfully, "has done it a great deal of service." [96] The Keeleys gave a dramatized adaptation at the Lyceum for Christmas, and a fortnight later there were versions playing at six London theaters.[97]

And yet, aside from a few glowing passages of domestic description, *The Cricket on the Hearth* is a weak book. The clumsiness of Tilly Slowboy, which sounds like a parody of Kate's tendency to stumble and gouge chunks out of her shins and elbows, makes but poor comedy. Tender-hearted little Dot Peerybingle's innocent plot to unite the lovers is tiresomely transparent to any reader less slow-witted than her husband. Caleb Plummer's loving deception in describing their bleak hovel to his blind daughter as a cheerful cottage, and portraying the snarling Tackleton as a benevolent eccentric, overflows with an excess of sentimental pathos. Tackleton, the cantankerous toy merchant, is a mere automaton. There is a forced quality of emotional exaggeration in the happy dénouement, with Dot sobbing joyfully and even the grumpy Tackleton converted to an improbably sudden joviality.

* * * * *

Dur..g the three weeks prior to publishing the first number of the *Daily News* Whitefriars was filled with a turmoil of bricklayers, carpenters, painters, and plasterers. On Saturday, January 17th, a party of ladies and gentlemen saw a "christening" ceremony in which a bottle of champagne was dashed against one of the printing machines named "Perseverance." In a full rehearsal a dummy paper dated January 19th was run off the presses, with a burlesque leading article commenting on an alleged indictment of Mr. Jones, the master printer, for having lured various workmen to Whitefriars and brought about their death by persuading them to supernatural exertions.[97a] Despite these high jinks there were friendly observers who had grave forebodings for the future of the paper. Coming away from a dinner on the eve of publication, at which Dickens had highly lauded its prospects, Henry Reeve, one of the guests, said to Charles Wentworth Dilke, the editor of the *Athenaeum*, "I foresee your knowledge will some day be invoked to remedy the mischief done by Dickens's genius to this new paper."[98]

It came out in a time of tremendous political excitement. Late in November, Lord John Russell had announced his conversion to free trade. Sir Robert Peel also saw the necessity of repealing the Corn Laws. His party, however, was stormy with dissension against the step, and, failing to unite his Cabinet behind him, Peel resigned. Russell was sent for by the Queen. Though the Whigs pretended to be the popular party and were the logical ones to carry out the measure, they shrank from the struggle of getting it through the House of Lords. They hoped that Peel would be able to pass the bill with the least disturbance. Lord John consequently did not complete the formation of a Ministry, and "handed back with courtesy the poisoned chalice to Sir Robert."[99] The entire country was waiting breathlessly for the speech in which Peel would indicate his plans when Parliament reconvened on January 20th.[100]

That night the turmoil at the *Daily News* offices was enormous. The debate in the House of Commons was a heavy one, and John Dickens had to make great efforts to keep his men moving swiftly and to see that their reports were handled smoothly. Again and again he descended from the reporters' room in the printing house, passed through the yard dividing it from the newspaper offices, and ascended to the subeditorial room, carrying his heavy bulk up and down the stairs.[101] He never walked down Fleet Street without the pickpockets stealing his silk handkerchief, a theft that he moved too slowly to prevent; and as he was always hot even in the frostiest weather, he lamented his loss while he tried to wipe the perspiration from his brow.[102]

During the night Mr. Bradbury wandered nervously through the establishment, Joseph Paxton and Douglas Jerrold were in and out of the printing house, and Mr. Evans and Mark Lemon were pressed into service as reader and reading-boy. Printers made blunders, some of them were said to be drunk, and only by superhuman efforts did they get out the first number, of Wednesday, January 21st, by three-forty of that morning.[103] "I cannot enter into all the dreadful worry that this affair has been," Paxton wrote his wife. "I have been up all night and all day . . ." [104] Dickens had made advance arrangements to have a second edition, containing the speech in which Peel announced his conversion to Cobden's views on the Corn Laws, dispatched "by special engines, to every town on every line in England." [105] When the paper went on sale in Fleet Street, there was a wild rush and ten thousand copies were sold across the counter.[106]

At first sight of the outer sheet, relief lighted the gloom of the other papers. It was ill-printed on poor paper and "badly made up." There were social rejoicings in editorial chambers that had been long beset by dread.[107] "I need not tell you," Dickens wrote William Johnson Fox, "how our Printer failed us last night. I hope for better things tonight, and am bent on a fight for it. If we can get a good paper tomorrow, I believe we are as safe as such a thing can be." [108]

But the first number of the *Daily News* was by no means as bad as the hostility of its rivals represented it. There was an eloquent leading article by Fox demanding repeal of the Corn Laws, and three others on that subject; nearly an entire page of railway news; [109] a spirited poem, "The Wants of the People," by Charles Mackay; two columns on music by Hogarth; the first of Dickens's brilliant *Travelling Letters Written on the Road*, made from his Italian letters of 1844; a total of eight pages, selling for fivepence instead of the established newspaper price of sevenpence. [110]

In an introductory article Dickens outlined the program of the paper: "The principles advocated by 'The Daily News' will be Principles of Progress and Improvement, of Education, Civil and Religious Liberty, and Equal Legislation—Principles such as its Conductors believe the advancing spirit of the time requires, the Condition of the country demands, and Justice, Reason, and Experience legitimately sanction." Much had to be done for the bodily and mental improvement of the English people. But social improvement was so inseparable from the well-doing of arts and commerce and the growth of public works, that the true interests of the people were not a class question. "Therefore it will be no part of our function to widen any breach . . . between Employer and Employed"; but rather to show their mutual dependence and power of adding to the general happiness. [111]

After the first curiosity about the *Daily News*, however, its sales subsided to less than four thousand, and although this did not compare unfavorably with most of the other morning papers, it did not challenge the overwhelming supremacy of the *Times*, with its twenty-five thousand. [112] Dickens continued to be exasperated by slipshod work in his subordinates. [113] In addition, although the members of his editorial staff were all free traders, they differed violently on foreign and colonial policy, and Dickens could not reconcile them to each other or subordinate their views to his own. [114] Worst of all, there developed administrative frictions between him and the proprietors of the *Daily News*.

Some of these grew out of the paper's railway connections. Though a source of financial advantage, they also limited the independence of its position in ways that Dickens considered dangerous. "I have already told Mr. Paxton," he wrote Bradbury and Evans, "and I have already warned you, that very sensible and far-seeing gentlemen all accustomed to newspapers regard the Railway policy of the D. N. as being too one-sided and as threatening to taint it, and I think if you could get beyond deposit men, and professional directors, and committee men, and the like, you would find this out, and have very little doubt if you do not, that the Times will discover it for you." [115] It is clear that Dickens now feared the newspaper would become tarred with the brush of railway corruption.

Perhaps less important in the long run, but more irritating at the moment, were a series of interferences in his powers as editor. Mr. Bradbury, a prey to worrisome fidget, was constantly countermanding Dickens's orders. "I consider," Dickens wrote stormily to Evans, "that his interposition between me and almost every act of mine at the newspaper office, was as disrespectful to me as injurious to the enterprise." Bradbury had written a violent note, incorrect even in its facts, about Dickens's sending a reporter to attend an important country election. By Bradbury's direction a minor employee Dickens had engaged was rudely refused his first week's salary and forced to apply to Dickens. Bradbury had been discourteous to Dickens's father, "than whom there is not a more zealous, disinterested, or useful gentleman attached to the paper." Finding greater difficulties and discouragements than he had anticipated at first, Bradbury seemed to Dickens to have become convinced that everyone receiving a salary on the paper was his natural enemy, to "be suspected and mistrusted accordingly." This had disturbed the entire working of the paper. In the worst times of Sir John Easthope, Dickens concluded, "I never saw anything approaching Mr. Bradbury." [116]

These areas of conflict expanded with startling rapidity. A week after the paper began publication, Bradbury and Evans informed Dickens, "on certain nameless authority," that his subeditor, Powell, was "quite unfit for the place he holds!" Dickens took violent umbrage. He demanded to know who had made the accusation. His own confidence in Powell was unabated. "When I tell you distinctly that I shall leave the Paper immediately if you do not give me this information, I think it but fair to add that it is extremely probable that I shall leave it when you have done so." [117] And to Forster, the same day, he wrote, "I have been revolving plans in my mind this morning for quitting the paper and going abroad again to write a new book in shilling numbers." [118]

During the week that followed there was no diminution in the tension between Dickens and his principals. On the 9th of February he cut the knot. He had been editor of the *Daily News* for just seventeen numbers. [119] His position on the paper he handed over to Forster, in somewhat the same way that he had handed over *Bentley's Miscellany* to Ainsworth. Indeed, in the whole of this brief interlude as a newspaper editor there is a strange, speeded-up resemblance to his prolonged battle with Bentley. But he did not sever his relations with Bradbury and Evans altogether; they were still to remain the publishers of his books. "Of Mr. Bradbury separated from the newspaper," Dickens wrote to his partner, "I entertain my old high opinion." [120]

In the few weeks following his resignation he was explaining to correspondents that his "connection with D. N." was not one of authority that could settle matters, and that he was forwarding their letters "to the Editor." [121] "I am not a party to the management of the Daily News (otherwise than as one who has an interest in the paper) and must therefore refer your letter and its enclosure to the *Powers* that be." [122] To personal friends he gave more detailed explanations. "I was not satisfied," he wrote Mme. De la Rue, "with the business managers of the newspaper. In the course of a little more time, I saw so much reason to believe that they would be the Ruin of what might otherwise have been made a very fine property . . . that I . . . walked bodily out of the concern. The result has been a steadily widening division among all the half hundred people connected with the Paper; and I am strongly inclined to believe it will *stop* abruptly." [123]

Indeed, the paper did almost go by the board. Mr. Bradbury proved as troublesome when Dickens was gone as he had been during Dickens's editorship. "I trust the new Printer *is* a Tartar," Dickens wrote Wills ferociously; "and I hope to God he will so proclaim and assert his Tartar breeding as to excommunicate [Bradbury] from the 'chapel' "—Whitechapel—"over which he presides." [124] The confusions prolonged themselves into April, while Dickens felt duty bound to Forster to stand by. "Every day we have expected that the squabbling body of proprietors would decide on their course, and so enable me to decide on mine." [125]

Even when Dickens had long retired from the scene the troubles of the paper continued. "A series of editors, transient and embarrassed phantoms, flitted across the stage. Matters grew from bad to worse, as Paxton's letters show." [126] Charles Wentworth Dilke became business manager in June, 1846; there was a financial reorganization of the paper in November, 1847; Dilke retired from its management in 1849. During the first ten years of its struggling life another £100,000 was sunk in it.[127] In the light of these later facts, Dickens's brief and violent connection with the paper is more intelligible.

No doubt he was touchy and arbitrary. But no doubt, too, the proprietors did trespass within the realm of his editorial authority. Successful businessmen who own the entire capital of an enterprise are not likely to defer completely to the demands of any executive, no matter how important, who has no money invested in its success. Dickens, on the other hand, was inclined to insist on powers almost as absolute as if he were in sole control. Even with Paxton, consequently, although to a lesser degree than with Bradbury and Evans, he had stormy contentions.[128] He did not fail to learn from the experience. When he next undertook the direction of a publication, he was careful to own one-half of it outright, and, through Forster and a sub-editor dependent on his own will, to control another quarter.

Notes

In abbreviating dates I have followed the American usage of giving month, day, and year: 1/20/56 for January 20, 1856. Dates later than the nineteenth century have the year in full: 10/27/1905. For the abbreviations used to identify quotations from or references to manuscript sources, the works of Dickens, and other printed books and articles, see the explanations in the three sections of the Bibliography.

PART ONE

Chapter 1 [pp. 3-10]

1. Forster, 23; R. P., U. T., "Travelling Abroad," 344-5.
2. Kitton, *Novels*, 64, says the sales of *The Old Curiosity Shop* reached as high as 100,000. The population of the British Isles in the 1840's was approximately 15,-000,000. Considering the size of Victorian families and book borrowing, it is not excessive to estimate fifteen readers to each copy.
3. Forster, 860.
4. D. C., XLIV, 641; *Let.*, II, 261, Mrs. Watson, 1/1/51; 340, Forster, 8/?/51; 382, Forster, 3/7/52; 735, Forster, 1/20/56; 765, Forster 4/?/56; etc.
5. Forster, 15, n. 1, gives the present address as 393 Commercial Road, Mile End, Landport.
6. The clock, certified as authentic by Georgina Hogarth, is now in the possession of Maggs Brothers. Fanny was born in the autumn of 1810 and baptized 11/23/10; Langton, 12.

7. Langton, 12, records the first quarter's rent as paid 9/29/09. Kitton, *Pen and Pencil*, 126, gives the landlord's name as William Pearce.
8. Storey, 40.
9. Langton, 17.
10. Storey, 34.
11. Langton, 11.
12. Storey, 34.
13. *Let.*, III, 717, James Orr Marples, 4/5/69. *Dick.*, XXVII, 236, quotes a correspondent as receiving a letter from the College of Heralds, 11/16/1921, stating that Dickens had never been authorized to use any crest.
14. *Dick.*, XLVI, 33-4; XLV, 65-6.
15. Kitton, *Life*, 64.
16. Langton, 11; Storey, 35.
17. Langton, 11; Wright, 23.
18. Kitton, *Life*, 2; Storey, 35.
19. Storey, 36-8.
20. *Dick.*, XLVI, 35.
21. Storey, 39.
22. Dent, 27, quoting Sir Wemyss Reid.
23. Storey, 33.
24. *Dick.*, XLVI, 35; XLV, 65-6.
25. *Let.*, I, 68, Thomas Culliford Barrow, 3/31/36.

26. Forster, 15, nn. 2, 3; Langton, 13-4.
27. Langton, 17; Storey, 40.
28. Forster, 2.
29. Storey, 40-2.
30. Trevelyan, *British History*, 113, 120, 128, 175.
31. Forster, 2; Kitton, *Life*, 4; Storey, 43. Norfolk Street is now called Cleveland Street.
32. Forster, 16, n. 6.

Chapter 2 [pp. 11-26]

1. Forster, 6, 19, n. 15.
2. Langton, 22.
3. Ibid., 40.
4. R. P., U. T., "Dullborough Town," 400; Langton, 36.
5. Langton, 23; S. by B., ii, 10-2.
6. Langton, 24, 52.
7. Forster, 2, fn.
8. R. P., U. T., "Dullborough Town," 402.
9. R. P., U. T., "Nurses' Tales," 435-42.
10. Forster, 3.
11. Ibid., 4.
12. R. P., "A Christmas Tree," 265; Forster, 4.
13. Langton, 25-6.
14. Forster, 4.
15. Ibid., 4 fn.; R. P., "Our School," 228.
16. Let., I, 807, Forster, 11/4/46; Forster, 27; Lindsay, 17.
17. Langton, 23; Kitton, *Life*, 4.
18. R. P., U. T., "Birthday Celebrations," 471.
19. R. P., U. T., "Dullborough Town," 401. Forster's *Life*, 7-8, confuses the field opposite the Dickens house with the school playground.
20. Langton, 25-6.
21. *Dick.*, XXIV, 208, 264.
22. Forster, 6.
23. Langton, 34-6.
24. Forster, 6.
25. Trevelyan, *British History*, 188-90.

26. R. P., U. T., "Dullborough Town," 401.
27. *Dick.*, VI, 62, Marcus Stone's recollections, March, 1910.
28. Langton, 21-2. It is doubtful whether Alfred Dickens, born 1813, was still alive. Alfred Lamert Dickens was born 4/3/22, and it would seem likely that there would be at least a short interval before another infant would be given the same Christian name.
29. Langton, 10.
30. Ibid., 43.
31. Forster, 2, 16, n. 7.
32. R. P., "A Child's Dream of a Star," 22; Langton, 47.
33. Langton, 44.
34. Ibid., 47-9.
35. R. P., U. T., "Chatham Dockyard," 528.
36. Ibid., 525-9.
37. Langton, 48-9; Gr. Ex., XII, 93.
38. Langton, 39; Forster, 8.
39. R. P., U. T., "Chatham Dockyard," 524-5.
40. Langton, 50; Gr. Ex., V, 37.
41. Langton, 49-50.
42. Forster, 8.
43. Langton, 60.
44. R. P., U. T., "Dullborough Town," 401; Langton, 218.
45. R. P., U. T., "Dullborough Town," 403-4; Langton, 218.
46. Forster, 9.
47. Langton, 158-62.
48. Forster, 2-3; R. P., U. T., "Traveling Abroad," 343-4.
49. Humphries, pamphlet; Langton, 56.
50. R. P., U. T., "City of London Churches," 366.
51. Humphries, pamphlet; Langton, 56.
52. Humphries, pamphlet; Langton, 56-9.
53. D. C., IV, 52, quoted by Forster, 4.
54. D. C., IV, 54-5, quoted by Forster, 5-6.

55. Forster, 8.
56. Ibid., 123 fn.; P. Fitzgerald, *Life,* 10.
57. *H. T.,* I, ii, 495.
58. *Coll, P.,* I, "Preface to *Grimaldi,*" 8-9.
59. Langton, 29-30.
60. *Coll. P.,* I, "Preface to *Grimaldi,*" 9.
61. Forster, 6.
62. Langton, 52-3; Forster, 6.
63. *R. P., U. T.,* "Dullborough Town," 404.
64. Forster, 8; Langton, 24, 62-3.
65. Forster, 21, nn. 20, 21.
66. Forster, 9; Langton, 64.
67. Langton, 65; *R. P., U. T.,* "Dullborough Town," 400, quoted by Forster, 9.

Chapter 3 [pp. 27-46]

1. Forster, 9-10; Dent, 48; Kitton, *Life,* 10; Langton, 63.
2. Forster, 10-1, 21, n. 26; *Notes and Queries,* VIII: 6, 251. Fanny was originally admitted 4/9/23 as a piano pupil on the recommendation of Thomas Tomkisson, a pianoforte maker, of 77 Dean Street, Soho. She left in Jan., 1827, was readmitted Jan., 1832, and finally left June, 1834. See also *Dick.,* XLVI, 33, on the musical background of the Barrow family.
3. Forster, 9.
4. Ibid., 10. If there were six children at this time, it is therefore evident that Alfred was now dead but Harriet not.
5. Forster, 9.
6. Storey, 53.
7. Forster, 11.
8. Ibid., 12.
9. Ibid., 12, 13.
10. Ibid., 12.
11. Ibid., 11.
12. Ibid., 23.

13. Ibid., 13; Kitton, *Life,* 14 fn.
14. *Dick.,* XXIV, 264.
15. Forster, 13.
16. Ibid.
17. *D. C.,* XI, 158.
18. Forster, 14-5.
19. Ibid., 24-6.
20. Ibid., 25; Storey, 52. Dickens's birthday was Saturday, 2/7/24; he started work 2/9/24.
21. Young, *Early Victorian England,* II, 464; Dent, 59.
22. Forster, 25-6.
23. Ibid., 26.
24. Ibid., 29; Dent, 61.
25. Forster, 26.
26. Ibid., 29.
27. Storey, 52, gives the date as 2/23/24; Pope-Hennessy, 9 fn., says a copy of the Register at the Record Office gives the date as 2/20/24. Probably the difference is represented by the period, mentioned by Forster, 23, elapsing between the time John Dickens was taken to the sponging house and the time he was committed to the Marshalsea.
28. Forster, 13.
29. Ibid.
30. Ibid., 14.
31. *L. D.,* I, vi., 62-3.
32. Storey, 53.
33. Forster, 15.
34. *E. D., Christmas Stories,* "The Haunted House," 461.
35. Forster, 15.
36. Ibid., 26-7.
37. Ibid., 27, 36, n. 37.
38. Forster, 31; Storey, 34.
39. Forster, 27.
40. Ibid., 30
41. Ibid., 27, 36, n. 38.
42. Ibid., 27.
43. Ibid., 28.
44. Ibid., 27.
45. Ibid., 29.
46. Ibid., 29-30.
47. Ibid., 30-1.
48. Ibid., 32.
49. Ibid., 33-4.

50. Ibid., 30.
51. Ibid., 33.
52. Ibid., 32-3.
53. Storey, 53-4.
54. Forster, 33.
55. Ibid., 34.
56. Ibid.
57. Ibid., 34-5.
58. Ibid., 35.
59. Ibid.
60. Ibid., 23.
61. Langton, 85; Storey, 56.
62. Wilson, *Wound and Bow*, 6.
63. Forster gives three seemingly contradictory times for the writing of the autobiographical fragment. On p. 23 he says it was written in 1847. On p. 24 he says it was written several months before Dickens conceived the idea of *David Copperfield*. On p. 32 he says that three or four years after it was written as fact the petition episode was included in the novel. Now Dickens first mentions *David Copperfield* in April, 1849, and he was in the habit of telling Forster his writing plans almost as soon as he formed them. Both 1847 and several months before the conception of *David Copperfield* are inconsistent with the episode being written three or four years before the writing of the novel. Since Dickens was in Italy in the first half of 1845 and on the Continent again from May, 1846, to almost the end of Feb., 1847, it is most probable that the autobiographical fragment was written between Sept., 1845, and May, 1846. This was when the *Daily News* project would have brought Dickens and Forster into contact with Charles Dilke and suggested Dilke's memory of seeing Dickens in the blacking warehouse.
64. Forster, 35.

Chapter 4 [pp. 47-66]

1. Langton, 93-4; Carlton, 20-1.
2. Storey, 49.
3. Forster, 51, n. 55.
4. Kitton, *Life*, 23.
5. Storey, 55.
6. Forster, 43.
7. Ibid., 39.
8. D. C., XVI, 228.
9. *Dick.*, VII, 229; Forster, 41; Langton, 85.
10. R. P., "Our School," 229.
11. Ibid., 232; Forster, 41, 51, n. 51. John Bowden in a letter to the *Daily News*, 12/21/71, in the Forster Collection, says Taylor left Jones to open his own school at "The Retreat," South Lambeth, and that Dickens went with him. But Owen Thomas is quoted by Kitton, *Pen and Pencil*, 127-8, as saying Dickens told him that in London he went to no other school than Wellington House Academy.
12. R. P., "Our School," 232; Langton, 86.
13. Forster, 41; R. P., "Our School," 233, 229.
14. Forster, 40; Langton, 87; R. P., "Our School," 232.
15. Forster, 44; *Dick.*, XLIII, 154. Van Amerongen, 172, gives the author of *The Dog of Montargis* as W. H. Arnold.
16. Forster, 43 fn.
17. Ibid., 51, n. 52; Langton, 89.
18. *Dick.*, VII, 229.
19. Forster, 42.
20. Ibid., 44.
21. Storey, 58.
22. Forster Coll., Bowden, letter to *Daily News*, 12/21/71.
23. Wright, *Life*, 4-5.
24. Lunn, 27.
25. Straus, 37; Wright, 46; Forster, 53, n. 66; Kitton, *Pen and Pencil*, 129; Forster, 46.
26. Forster, 45-6, 51, nn. 59, 60;

Langton, 93. Molloy did, as Forster says, have offices in New Square, but not at the time Dickens was with him.

27. Kitton, *Pen and Pencil*, 132, 129, 131.

28. Carlton, 20-1; Kitton, *Pen and Pencil*, 129.

29. Dent, 72; Kitton, *Life*, 52-4; Forster, 52, n. 6-; Kitton, *Pen and Pencil*, 130.

30. Wright, *Life*, 46; Straus, 38. Dickens would *not* have thought of becoming a Q.C.; Queen Victoria did not ascend the throne until 1837.

31. Forster, 47.

32. Storey, 57, 59.

33. Langton, 40.

34. Forster, 52, n. 65; Hall, *Retrospect*, 111.

35. Dent, 79.

36. Forster, 48.

37. Hall, *Retrospect*, 111.

38. Forster, 48.

39. Ibid., 48, 53, n. 67.

40. Collier, 12.

41. D. C., XXXVIII, 540; quoted by Forster, 48.

42. *Notes and Queries*, VIII: 6, 226.

43. Collier, 14.

44. *S. by B.*, passim.

45. Kitton, *Pen and Pencil*, 131.

46. Ibid., 131.

47. Forster, 46.

48. Kitton, *Pen and Pencil*, 132.

49. Forster, 47.

50. *S. by B.*, "Making a Night of It," 264.

51. S. J. A. Fitzgerald, 63.

52. Van Amerongen, 95.

53. Young, *Early Victorian England*, II, 265.

54. Van Amerongen, 98-9; *Early Victorian England*, II, 275, 277; *S. by B.*, "Miss Evans and the Eagle," 229.

55. Van Amerongen, 8, 158.

56. *S. by B.*, "Private Theatres," 119-24.

57. From around this time dates a play, *The Stratagems of Rozanza*, in the handwriting of Dickens's mother and with the name C. J. H. Dickens on the title page. Forster, 69, n. 74, establishes the fact that it is not by Dickens. It is a translation of a comedy by Goldoni; except for slight alterations in the names (which might be the result of mispronouncing the Italian) it tallies with the original even to the stage directions. Possibly it was intended for production in a toy theater or at home. Perhaps Dickens had admired it on the stage and desired to have a copy he could obtain in no other way, or perhaps it was a shorthand exercise dictated from his notes. His name on the title page may have been intended to indicate no more than the ownership of the manuscript.

58. *Dick.*, XLV, 187.

59. Langton, 93-4.

60. *S. by B.*, "Doctors' Commons," 86-7.

61. D. C., XXIII, 348; *S. by B.*, "Doctors' Commons," 86-7.

62. D. C., XXIII, 338-9.

63. Langton, 102; Forster, 53, n. 66.

64. Pope-Hennessy, 20 fn.

65. *Dick.*, XLIII, 83; Masson, 130; Storey, 59.

66. *Dick.*, XLIII, 83-4.

67. Forster, 48.

68. Kitton, *Pen and Pencil*, reproduced in Part IV.

69. *Dick.*, XXX, 151; XLV, 181; information in letter from R. F. R. Barrow to author.

70. Carlton, 47; Forster, 54, n. 68.

71. *S. by B.*, "Doctors' Commons," 88-9.

72. Forster, 59.

73. Langton, 100.

74. Forster, 54, n. 69; Payne and Harper, 23 passim.

75. Forster, 57, 67-8, n. 74.

76. *Let.*, I, 681, Forster, 6/?/45.
77. Ibid., II, 627, Maria Winter, 2/10/55.
78. Forster, 59-60; Nicoll, II, 329. *The Hunchback* was by James Sheridan Knowles. It opened 4/5/32.
79. Forster, 65-66, n. 72; Carlton, 75.
80. *Dick*, XXXVI, 211. Gerald Grubb suggests in this article that the date may have been as early as 1830, but it is unlikely that Dickens would have been seeking a trial in the theater if he already had the newspaper employment for which he had so laboriously prepared.
81. Ibid.
82. Forster, 59.
83. Ibid., 60.
84. Ibid., 69, n. 76; Grant, I, 295.
85. Carlton, 81.
86. *Coll. P.*, II, 484, speech, 5/20/65.
87. Forster, 49.
88. Trevelyan, *British History*, 226-39.
89. Kent, 369.
90. Carlton, 88.
91. Forster, 66, n. 72.
92. Carlton, 88.
93. Layard, *Brooks*, 61.
94. Forster, 62.
95. *Let.*, I, 7, Thomas Beard, 2/4/32. The family now resided at 70 Margaret Street.
96. Grant, I, 295-6.
97. Forster, 853, n. 607; *Let.*, I, 8, Henry Kolle, [1832].
98. *Let.*, I, 8, Henry Kolle, [1832], Longhurst, [7/30/32].
99. Ibid., 10, Thomas Beard, [1832], 17, Henry Kolle, [1833].
100. Ibid., 7-8, Henry Kolle, [1832.]
101. Ibid., 7-8, Henry Kolle, [1832].
102. Ibid., 8-11, to various correspondents.
103. Ibid., 7, Henry Kolle, [1832].
104. Ibid., 29, Henry Kolle, [1834].
105. Ibid., 10, H. G. Hartland, 12/9/[32].
106. *Dick.*, XXIX, 91, gives the date of Stanley's speech as 1/29/33, but there is no such speech on that date in either *Hansard* or *The Mirror of Parliament*. Stanley's long address on the condition of Ireland was delivered 2/27/33.
107. Fields, *Yesterdays*, 231.
108. *Let.*, I, 25, Earle, 6/6/[33].
109. Ibid., II, 716, Forster, 12/?/55.

Chapter 5 [pp. 67-83]

1. Wright, *Life*, 54. It is possible that Dickens did not meet Maria Beadnell until early 1830 when he was eighteen. His poem "The Bill of Fare," written in 1831, states that he had fallen in love with her twelve months earlier.
2. *Let.*, II, 634, Maria Winter, 2/22/55.
3. *D. C.*, XXVI, 387; *Coll. P.*, II, "The Bill of Fare," 285.
4. *Let.*, II, 180, George Beadnell, 10/17/49.
5. *Coll. P.*, II, "The Bill of Fare," 287, 290, 292.
6. Wright, *Life*, 55.
7. *Coll. P.*, II, "The Devil's Walk," 280.
8. *Let.*, II, 634, Maria Winter, 2/22/55.
9. Ibid., 628-9, Maria Winter, 2/15/55.
10. *Coll. P.*, II, "The Bill of Fare," 285-6.
11. *Let.*, II, 627, Maria Winter, 2/10/55.
12. *Coll. P.*, II, "The Bill of Fare," 291, 286, 287.
13. *Let.*, II, 628, Maria Winter, 2/15/55.
14. Straus, 45.
15. *D. C.*, XXVI, 393.
16. Ibid., XXXIII, 470.
17. *Coll. P.*, II, "The Bill of Fare," 289.
18. *Dick.*, XXXVI, 103, giving a letter to Marianne Leigh, 3/7/31.

19. *D. C.*, XXVI, 393.
20. *Let.*, II, 627, Maria Winter, 2/10/55.
21. Wright, *Life*, 55.
22. *Coll. P.*, II, "The Bill of Fare," 284-94.
23. Ibid.
24. *D. C.*, XXVI, 387.
25. *Let.*, II, 633, Maria Winter, 2/22/55.
26. Ibid., I, 16, Maria Beadnell, 3/18/33.
27. Ibid., II, 629, Maria Winter, 2/15/55.
28. Ibid.
29. Wright, *Life*, 56.
30. *Let.*, II, 627, Maria Winter, 2/20/55. Wright, *Life*, 63, believes that it was not until after May, 1833, that the Beadnells sent Maria to Paris. But Dickens's letters to her in 1833 make it clear that at this time she was breaking with him herself, and by the end of May she had written him the last "cold and reproachful" letter after which, as he writes her on 2/22/55, he "went his way." His distress at her being sent abroad must, therefore, have occurred at a date earlier than the final separation.
31. *Let.*, I, 7, Henry Kolle, [1832]. The reference to his leaving "the Sun" dates this letter around July-August. But if Kolle had introduced Dickens to the Beadnells in 1829, the acquaintance would hardly have been so slight three years later that Dickens would still not have known the correct spelling of his name.
32. *Let.*, II, 628, Maria Winter, 2/15/55.
33. Ibid., I, 9, Kolle, [1832].
34. Ibid., 10, Kolle, [1832].
35. Ibid., 15, Kolle, 1/5/33.
36. Ibid., 15, Thomas Beard, 2/2/33.
37. Ibid., 15 fn.
38. *R. P., U. T.*, "Birthday Parties." 474-5.
39. *Let.*, II, 635, Maria Winter, 2/22/55.
40. Ibid., I, 19, Maria Beadnell, 5/14/33.
41. Ibid., 20, Maria Beadnell, 5/16/33.
42. Ibid., 16-7, Maria Beadnell, 3/18/33.
43. Ibid., II, 629, Maria Winter, 2/15/55.
44. Ibid., I, 16-7, Maria Beadnell, 3/18/33.
45. *Dick.*, IX, 8. The music of *Clari* was by Henry R. Bishop. *The Married Bachelor* was by P. P. O'Callaghan. *Amateurs and Actors* was by R. Brinsley Peake.
46. *Dick.*, IX, 8; Berg MS., Dickens to Miss Austin, April, 1833; Morgan MS., Dickens to Miss Urquhart, n.d.
47. *Let.*, I, 21, Maria Beadnell, 5/16/33.
48. Ibid., II, 626, 634, Maria Winter, 2/15/55, 2/21/55.
49. Ibid., I, 17, Kolle, [April, 1833].
50. Ibid., 17, Kolle, [4/15/33].
51. Ibid.
52. Ibid., 18, Kolle, [4/23/33].
53. Ibid., 20, Maria Beadnell, 5/16/33.
54. Ibid., 19, Maria Beadnell, 5/14/33.
55. Ibid., 21, Maria Beadnell, 5/16/33.
56. Ibid., 19, Maria Beadnell, 5/14/33.
57. Ibid., 18, Kolle, 5/14/33.
58. Ibid., 20, Maria Beadnell, 5/14/33.
59. This paragraph is inferable from Dickens's letter to Maria Beadnell, *Let.*, I, 20, 5/16/33, par. 1.
60. *Let.*, I, 21, Maria Beadnell, 5/17/33.
61. Ibid., 22, Marianne Leigh, 5/17/33.
62. Ibid., 23, Kolle, 5/19/33.
63. Ibid.

64. Ibid., 24, Maria Beadnell, 5/19/33.
65. Ibid., II, 633, Maria Winter, 2/22/55.
66. Ibid., 628, Maria Winter, 2/15/55.
67. Forster, 38.
68. *Let.*, II, 633, Maria Winter, 2/22/55.
69. Ibid.

PART TWO

Chapter 1 [pp. 87-104]

1. *S. by B.*, "Parliamentary Sketches," 153.
2. Pugh, 5; Langton, 105. The latter quotes Sala as authority for the statement that Dickens reported Brougham's great speech at Edinburgh after he resigned the Chancellorship, perhaps Stanley's Irish Church oration, and certainly speeches by Grey, Peel, Denman, Lyndhurst, Ellenborough, Hume, Melbourne, and Grote.
3. Trevelyan, *British History*, 242, 247, 249.
4. *D. C.*, XLIII, 621. Cf. XLVIII, 684: "One joyful night, therefore, I noted down the music of the parliamentary bagpipes for the last time, and I have never heard it since; though I still recognize the old drone in the newspapers, without any substantial variation (except, perhaps, that there is more of it) all the livelong session."
5. Forster, 853, n. 507.
6. *Notes and Queries*, 8:6, 251.
7. *Let.*, I, 48 fn.
8. *Coll. P.*, II, 59.
9. *Let.*, I, 24, 29 passim.
10. *Let.*, I, 25, Earle, 6/6/[33], asking for such work.
11. Collier, 12-3, 7/24/33.

12. Mackay, *Recollections*, 69.
13. Collier, 13-4, 7/24/33.
14. Ibid., 14, 7/27/33. It should be noted, however, that Collier's diary is not invariably recorded at the time events occurred. Under this very date, for example, Collier made two later additions: that Dickens obtained a post on the *Chronicle* through the recommendation of someone more influential than himself, and the recollection of meeting Dickens still later, dashingly dressed, in Hungerford Market.
15. Stonehouse, 12.
16. *S. by B.*, "Dinner at Poplar Walk," 311-21.
17. *P. P.*, preface, xviii.
18. *Dick.*, III, 10, XXX, 61, 105. The name of this publication was not, as some writers give it, the *Old Monthly Magazine*, but the *Monthly Magazine*; it came to be identified by the adjective after a periodical called the *New Monthly Magazine* came into existence.
19. Forster, 64.
20. Waugh, *Hundred Years*, 12.
21. *P. P.*, preface, xviii; Forster, 60.
22. *Let.*, I, 29, Kolle, [1834].
23. Ibid., 25, [12/?/33].
24. Ibid., 29, [1834].
25. *Dick.*, XXX, 151.
26. *S. by B.*, 420-30; Stonehouse, 13.
27. Kitton, *Minor Writings*, 5; *S. by B.*, 356-71, 465-81, 275-311.
28. *P. P.*, preface, xix; Forster, 64.
29. Mackay, *Recollections*, 82, 94-6.
30. Carlton, 94.
31. Forster, 67, n. 73.
32. Collier, 15, 7/27/33. This event took place a full year after the date under which Collier records it. He does, however, note that it was some time later.
33. Grant, I, 280-3, 289; Mackay, *Recollections*, 72-3, 89-93.
34. Bourne, 13-4.

35. Ibid., 12, quoting from Robert Harrison article, "John Black," D. N. B., V, 108.
36. Mill, 63.
37. Bourne, 87.
38. Mackay, Recollections, 81.
39. Dick., XXXI, 5.
40. S. by B., 465-81.
41. Coll. P., I, 3-4; Morning Chronicle, 9/17/34.
42. Ibid., 6-7; Morning Chronicle, 9/18/34.
43. Ibid., 7.
44. Collier, 55, 10/15/33. There is some confusion here about dates, however; Collier speaks as if Dickens were already his colleague on the Chronicle at this time, whereas he did not join the reporting staff until September, 1834.
45. Froude, First Forty Years, II, 292.
46. Coll. P., II, 420-1, speech, 6/27/55.
47. Dick., XXX, 105; Let., I, 41 fn.
48. Mackay, Recollections, 80.
49. Dick., XXXI, 105.
50. Let., I, 32, Editor of the Monthly Magazine, [10/?/34].
51. Dick., XXX, 223.
52. Dick., III, 10, XXX, 105. Macrone had been a member of the partnership of Cochrane and Macrone, which acquired the Monthly Magazine in January, 1834. He set up as a publisher by himself, however, in September, 1834, and the Monthly then appeared under the imprint of James Cochrane and Company.
53. Collier, preface, viii.
54. Smith, Earliest Letters, 82.
55. Let., I, 32-3, Mitton, [1834].
56. Ibid., 33.
57. Ibid.
58. Ibid., 34.
59. Let., I, 34-5, Beard, 11/29/34.
60. Ibid., 35, [1834].
61. Ibid., 35, 11/29/34.

62. Ibid., [1834].
63. Ibid., 36, [12/16/34].
64. Mackenzie, 53.
65. Forster, 73 fn., says that Dickens laughed at Willis's anecdote, and claims that "hardly a word" of it was true, but it accords with all the known circumstances. Ley, in Forster, 80, n. 84, denounces the statement that there was a meeting as a fabrication, claiming that Willis was not even in England at the time. Beers, Willis, 130, 153-4, 179, however, shows that Willis landed at Dover 6/1/34 and arrived in London 11/1/34, where he remained for the next ten months. Both the dates and Dickens's momentary financial difficulties make Willis's story entirely probable.
66. Forster, 71, n. 78. The Ipswich election was reported in the Chronicle 1/6,7/35; the Sudbury election 1/7/35.
67. Let., I, 39, Austin, 1/7/35.
68. Ibid., 39, Beard, 1/11/35.
69. Ibid., 40, Hogarth, 1/20/35, 40 fn.
70. John Dickens's highest salary in the Navy Pay Office had been £350 a year; Dickens was now receiving £382 4s.
71. Christie, Ancestry; Dick., XIII, 106, XXII, 219, XLIII, 19.
72. Let., I, 44, Robert Hogarth, [1835].
73. Kitton, Minor Writings, 7.
74. Ibid., 5.
75. Pope-Hennessy, 33. Dent, 98, says Dickens and Beard spent only £84 and gives the Times outlay as £250.
76. Coll. P., II, 480, speech, 5/20/65.
77. Let., I, 42, Beard, [5/2/35].
78. Ibid., 43, [5/4/35].
79. Bourne, 88-89, gives the date of the Times and Chronicle exchange as 6/13/35, but does not date the others.
80. Dexter, Mr. and Mrs., 5 fn.

81. Ibid., 9; *Let.*, I, 44, W. Thomson, 7/14/35.
82. Kitton, *Minor Writings*, 7-8.
83. Ellis, *Ainsworth*, I, 273; *Dick.*, XXVIII, 182.
84. Kitton, *Minor Writings*, 9.
85. *Let.*, I, 46, Macrone, 10/28/[35].

Chapter 2 [pp. 105-120]

1. Forster, 72, n. 81.
2. *Dick.*, XXXV, 205.
3. *Let.*, I, 46-7, Macrone, 10/28/[35].
4. Ibid.
5. Ibid., 47-8, [10/29/35].
6. Ibid., 49, [11/7/35].
7. Ibid., 50, Fraser, [11/8/35].
8. Ibid., 51, [11/10/35].
9. Dexter, *Mr. and Mrs.*, 31, [11/8/35].
10. Ibid., 32-3, [11/9/35], 33 fn.
11. The dinner, according to Forster, 70, n. 77, was on 11/10/35; the *Morning Chronicle* report was published 11/11,12/35.
12. *Let.*, I, 54. Macrone, [11/?/35].
13. Ibid., 53, [11/28/35].
14. Ibid., 54-5, [12/8/35].
15. Ibid., 53, [11/23/35].
16. Ibid., 56, [12/9/35], 53, [11/20/35].
17. Ibid., 56, [12/17/35].
18. Dexter, *Mr. and Mrs.*, 45. Dickens also reported the spectacular fire at Hatfield House, 11/27/35, in which the Marchioness of Salisbury was burned to death (*Mr. and Mrs.*, 38, 38 fn.). The story appeared in the *Morning Chronicle*, 12/3/35.
19. Dexter, *Mr. and Mrs.*, 44-5.
20. Ibid., 44, 45 fn., quoting *Morning Chronicle*, 12/16/35, under date of 12/15/35.
21. Ibid., 46, 48.
22. Ibid., 50.
23. *Let.*, I, 48, Hullah, 11/6/35.
24. *Dick.*, XLIII, 22.
25. Dexter, *Mr. and Mrs.*, 51.
26. *Let.*, I, 61-2, Macrone (5 letters), 62 fn.

27. Dexter, *Mr. and Mrs.*, 55.
28. *Let.*, I, 63, Beard, [2/2/36]; Forster, 59. The strike was clearly against the *Chronicle*, however, not against the *True Sun*, as Forster mistakenly says.
29. *Let.*, I, 62 fn. The announcement in the *Morning Chronicle* appeared 2/2/36, heralding publication of the *Sketches* "at the end of the week." Saturday was 2/6/36.
30. Ibid., 64-5, Macrone, [2/9/36].
31. Ibid., 64, Stanley, 2/8/36.
32. Pope-Hennessy, 52.
33. *Let.*, I, 63, 65, Macrone, [2/7,11/36].
34. Dexter-Ley, 27.
35. *Let.*, I, 65, Macrone, 2/14/36.
36. Ibid., 2/11/36.
37. Dexter-Ley, 27-8.
38. *Let.*, I, 69, Macrone, [4/?/36], 69 fn. The *Morning Post* review appeared 3/12/36.
39. Ibid., 68, Barrow, 3/31/36.
40. Kitton, *Minor Writings*, 11.
41. *S. by B.*, "Horatio Sparkins," 356-70, "Watkins Tottle," 430-64, "The Boarding House," 275-310.
42. *Let.*, I, 263, Forster, [7/?/40].
43. Ibid., 768, 7/18/46.
44. *S. by B.*, "Meditations in Monmouth Street," 75-81, "Gin Shops," 180-4, "The River," 97-103, "The Steam Excursion," 382-402, "Greenwich Fair," 111-8, "Gin Shops," 180-4.
45. Ibid., 51, 56.
46. Ibid., 55.
47. Ibid., 58.
48. Ibid., "Shabby-Genteel People," 261.
49. Ibid., "The Prisoners' Van," 271, 272.
50. Ibid., "Gin Shops," 184.
51. Ibid., 53.
52. Ibid., 64.
53. Ibid., 111.
54. Ibid., 236.
55. Ibid., 338.
56. Ibid., 394.

57. Ibid., 72.
58. Ibid., 109.
59. Ibid., 79-80.
60. *Let.*, I, 65, Catherine Hogarth, [2/10/36].
61. Kitton, *Life*, 31.
62. *Let.*, I, 66, Macrone, [2/?/36].
63. Dexter-Ley, 22-3.
64. Ibid., 29.
65. *P. P.*, preface, xviii.
66. Waugh, *Hundred Years*, 15-7.
67. Dexter-Ley, 22-3.
68. Waugh, *Hundred Years*, 17.
69. Forster, 72, n. 80; *Let.*, I, 66, Chapman and Hall, 2/16/36.
70. Forster, 74; Waugh, *Hundred Years*, 18; *P. P.*, preface, xviii.
71. Forster, 75; *P. P.*, preface, xviii; *Coll. P.*, I, 108-10, "History of Pickwick," *Athenaeum*, 3/31/66. Seymour's suggestions were partly derived, of course, from Surtees's *Jorrocks's Jaunts and Jollities*, parts of which had appeared in the *New Sporting Magazine* from 1831 on, although it was not published as a book until 1838.
72. Forster, 75; Waugh, *Hundred Years*, 18; *P. P.*, preface, xviii. The last is especially revealing, in its phraseology, of Dickens's character: "my views having been *deferred to*" (my italics).
73. Waugh, *Hundred Years*, 18-9.
74. Phillips, 39-44.
75. Waugh, *Hundred Years*, 19.
76. Dexter-Ley, 30.
77. *Let.*, I, 66, Chapman and Hall, 2/16/36, gives the date of their letter outlining the terms agreed on as "Friday last," which was 2/12/36. Dickens had announced their proposal to Kate on the day it was made, *Let.*, I, 65, Catherine Hogarth, [2/10/36].
78. *P. P.*, preface, xviii.
79. *Let.*, I, 67, Chapman and Hall, [2/18/36].

80. Ibid., 68, Catherine Hogarth, 2/21/36.
81. Wright, *Life*, 80.
82. Waugh, *Hundred Years*, 21.
83. *P. P.*, preface, xviii; Forster, 75; *Coll. P.*, I, 108-10.
84. Waugh, *Hundred Years*, 21.
85. Forster, 76.
86. Dexter-Ley, 21.
87. Forster, 76, n. 80.
88. Dexter, *Mr. and Mrs.*, 66-7, 61, 63, 67. Various letters falling between [2/24/36] and [3/25/36].
89. Ibid., 66, [3/24/36].
90. Ibid., 63, [3/18/36].
91. Ibid., 64, [3/20/36?].
92. Ibid., 65, [3/21/36].
93. Ibid., 63, [3/18/36].
94. Ibid., 66, [3/24/36].
95. Waugh, *Hundred Years*, 22; Dexter-Ley, 65-6.
96. Waugh, *Hundred Years*, facsimile f. 26.

Chapter 3 [pp. 121-134]

1. There are portraits of Catherine Dickens by Daniel Maclise, 1836, 1842, and 1846.
2. Christian, 481.
3. Ibid., 486.
4. Wright, *Life*, 73; Dexter, *Mr. and Mrs.*, Dickens's letters to her, passim.
5. Dexter, *Mr. and Mrs.*, 66 fn., quoting Henry Burnett.
6. *Dick.*, XXII, 21.
7. Ibid., XLIII, 19-20.
8. Pope-Hennessy, 55, is in error, however, in attributing to the youthful Catherine a humorous comment on Adam and Eve in the Garden of Eden. According to Henry Fielding Dickens, this was an anecdote *quoting* a Scottish lady which he heard his mother tell when he was already a man. I have found no testimony contemporary with her

that she herself had a Scottish accent.

9. Wright, *Life*, 72-3. The Drummond portrait is reproduced as a separate plate in Kitton, *Pen and Pencil*.
10. Dexter, *Mr. and Mrs.*, 1-3, [5/?/35].
11. Ibid., 3-4, [1835].
12. Ibid., 5 fn.
13. Ibid., 5, [1835].
14. Ibid., 6, [1835].
15. Ibid., 8, [1835].
16. Mary Dickens, 28.
17. Dexter, *Mr. and Mrs.*, 11, [1835].
18. Ibid., 12, [1835].
19. Ibid., 11, [1835].
20. Ibid., 17-21, [1835].
21. Ibid., 20, 15, 52, 23, 24, [1835].
22. Ibid., 26, [1835].
23. Ibid., 25, [1835].
24. Ibid., 29, [1835].
25. Ibid., 30, [1835].
26. Ibid., 22, [1835].
27. Ibid., 25, [1835].
28. Ibid., 49, [1835].
29. Ibid., 22, [1835].
30. Ibid., 36, [1835].
31. Ibid., 49, [12/18/35].
32. Ibid., 29, [1835].
33. Ibid., 40, [1835].
34. Ibid., 35, [1835].
35. Ibid., 59-60, [3/6/36].
36. Ibid., 62-3, [3/11,18/36].
37. Ibid., 30, [1835].
38. Ibid., 34, [1835].
39. Ibid., 41, [1835].
40. Ibid., 37, [1835], 58, [1836]; *Let.*, I, 52, Hullah, [11/17/35], 52 fn. The operetta opening at the Olympic 11/16/35 was *Comfortable Service*. For Mme. Vestris, see Young, *Early Victorian England*, II, 272-3.
41. *Let.*, I, 63, Beard, [2/2/36].
42. Dexter, *Mr. and Mrs.*, 51-2, [1835], 62, [3/11/36].
43. *Let.*, I, 81, Hullah, [9/11/36].
44. Ibid., 52, Hullah, [11/17/35].
45. Dexter, *Mr. and Mrs.*, 42, [1835], 55, [1/21/36].

46. Ibid., 53, [1835]; *Let.*, I, 66; Chapman and Hall, [2/18/36].
47. Dexter, *Mr. and Mrs.*, 55, [1/21/36].
48. Ibid., 58, [1836].
49. Ibid., 63, [3/18/36].
50. Ibid., 55, [1/21/36].
51. Ibid., 58, [1836].
52. Ibid., 64, [3/20/36].
53. Ibid., 51, 58, 65, 62, 61, [1836].
54. *Let.*, I, 68; Barrow, 3/31/36.
55. Christie gives the date of Catherine's birth as 5/19/15.
56. *Dick.*, XLIII, 114, has a reproduction of the marriage license.
57. Forster, 79, n. 82.
58. Dexter, *Mr. and Mrs.*, 65 fn. This note is incorrect, however, in saying that Kingsley officiated.
59. Ibid., 65 fn.
60. *Let.*, I, 67, Macrone, 3/?/36.
61. Rylands MSS., John Dickens letter to John Pritt Harley, 4/2/37, shows that Henry Burnett and Fanny were engaged at that time.
62. Wright, *Life*, 83, quoting Burnett; also in Kitton, *Pen and Pencil*.
63. Dexter, *Mr. and Mrs.*, 66 fn.
64. Forster 74, 80, n. 85. The Craddock dwelling, at the corner of Thong Lane, was long mistakenly identified as the honeymoon cottage, but as Ley's note points out, this house was never let to lodgers. "Mrs. Nash's" is nearer Gravesend, on the opposite side of the road.
65. There has never been any recorded explanation of this rather strange domestic arrangement of Mary Hogarth's leaving the home of her parents to live with the newly married couple. It is not known whether Kate wished it or Dickens suggested it, nor what the Hogarths felt about it, nor how long Mary was supposed to remain as a member of Dickens's household, but she was at Furnival's Inn from

shortly after the marriage to the time they moved to Doughty Street, and stayed with them there until she died. And after Dickens returned from the American trip in 1842, Georgina Hogarth became a member of his household in the same way.

66. *Let.*, I, 106; passim; Wright, *Life*, 108.
67. *Let.*, I, 133, Mrs. Hogarth, 10/26/37.
68. Ibid., 109, Beard, [5/17/37].
69. Ibid., 120, Johns, 7/12/37, 109, Beard, [5/17/37].
70. Dexter, *Mr. and Mrs.*, 57, [1/28/36].
71. Ibid., 60, [3/6/36], 57, [1/28/36].
72. Wright, *Life*, 109, says that Cathrine "resented . . . being relegated to the background" by Mary. There is not only no evidence to support this statement, but the fact that Catherine was so distressed by her death that it brought on a miscarriage demonstrates a deep attachment.

Chesterton, *Charles Dickens*, 66-7, suggests that Dickens, "suddenly thrown into the society of a whole family of girls" and "intoxicated" by "an abstract femininity," really "fell in love with all" the Hogarth girls and "by a kind of accident . . . got hold of the wrong sister." But the implication that Dickens found himself surrounded by young girls for the first time when he met the Hogarth family is completely erroneous. He had already known the Beadnell girls and their friends, including Marianne Leigh; in *Clari* he had acted with Miss Austin and Miss Urquhart; and he had met the Ross girls and responded to the charms of at least one "very nice pair of blackeyes" (*Let.*, I, 29, Kolle, 1854). In a letter to Thomas Powell (*Let.*, I, 600,

8/2/45), Dickens wrote, "I broke my heart into the smallest pieces, many times between thirteen and three and twenty. Twice, I was very horribly in earnest . . ." The idea, furthermore, that Dickens was really in love, not with Catherine, but with the Hogarth girls in general, is rendered almost fantastically ridiculous by their ages: at the time of his marriage Mary was still only sixteen and Georgina was nine.

Chapter 4 [pp. 135-156]

1. Kitton, *Novels*, 9.
2. Dexter-Ley, *Origins*, 65-6. These facts refute Forster, 90, which states that *Pickwick* appeared "without newspaper notice or puffery."
3. Ibid., 67-8.
4. Ibid., 78.
5. Waugh, *Hundred Years*, 22.
6. Dexter-Ley, 48-9.
7. Ibid., 50.
8. Waugh, *Hundred Years*, 23.
9. *Let.*, I, 69, Seymour, [4/14/36].
10. Ibid., 68-9.
11. Pope-Hennessy, 59, and Straus, 101, say that neither of the publishers was present; Dexter-Ley, 52, that both were. The preface to the Charles Dickens Edition of *Pickwick* in 1868 (*P. P.*, preface, xxiii) says that two persons still living—obviously Catherine and Frederick Dickens—were present at the interview, and that Edward Chapman had "set down in writing . . . his deceased partner's reception" of the Seymour "pretenses." These statements strongly suggest William Hall's presence, since on all other matters connected with the origin of *Pickwick* Chapman's direct knowledge would

be as authoritative as his quotation of his partner.

12. *P. P.*, preface xxiii.

13. I have accepted, here, Ralph
Straus's hypothetical recon-
struction of the scene.

14. Dexter-Ley, 52.

15. Ibid., 53-4.

16. Wright, *Life*, 85, quoting a statement by Henry Burnett.

17. Dexter-Ley, 68.

18. Dexter-Ley, 59; also implicit in
the fact that Thackeray went
to Furnival's Inn to submit his
drawings to Dickens, as told by
Forster, 77, quoting Thackeray's speech at the Royal
Academy Dinner in May, 1858.

19. In Part II of *P. P.*, facsimile in
Waugh, *Hundred Years*, f. 24.

20. *Let.*, I, 78-9, Chapman and Hall,
Leech, [8/?/36].

21. Forster, 77; Thackeray's speech,
Royal Academy Dinner, May,
1858, quoted in Melville, II,
115.

22. Dexter, *Hints*, 11.

23. Forster, 82, n. 91; Dexter-Ley, 60;
Wright, *Life*, 86.

24. Dexter-Ley, 61.

25. Ibid., 64.

26. Waugh, *Hundred Years*, 24, says
"not even the easy good nature
of Edward Chapman would
pass" this plate. Clearly, however, it was the fact of the
number it illustrated having already appeared in print, rather
than the inferiority of the
drawing, that prevented its use.
Leslie Staples, in a letter to me
on 11/8/1947, points out that
it was used in the Victoria
Edition of *Pickwick*, Chapman
and Hall, 1887, I, 51; and
quotes Joseph Grego, *Pictorial
Pickwickiana*, Chapman and
Hall, 1889, I, 109: ". . . the
plate [was] submitted [by
Buss] as an instance of his artistic qualifications as successor

to Seymour"—as a sample, in
short, not a plate offered for
publication.

27. *Let.*, I, 69, Chapman and Hall,
4/27/36.

28. Forster, 82, n. 91, on Buss's payments; cf. Dexter-Ley, 128.

29. Waugh, *Hundred Years*, facsimile
between 24-5.

30. Forster, 82, n. 91.

31. Wright, *Life*, 87; Forster, 82, n.
91, quotes G. S. Layard, who
thinks Dickens insisted on
Browne.

32. Wright, *Life*, 87.

33. Kitton, *"Phiz,"* plates.

34. Dexter-Ley, 129.

35. Ibid., 150.

36. Ibid., 130.

37. Ibid., 140.

38. Ibid., 71.

39. Ibid., 75, 6/12/36.

40. Ibid., 78.

41. Ibid., 79.

42. *Let.*, I, 71-2, Macrone, 5/8/36.

43. Ibid., 70, Hullah, three letters
[1836].

44. Ibid., 76, Hullah, [1836], Macrone, [7/27/36].

45. Ibid., 71, Hullah, [1836].

46. Hansard, 4/21/36.

47. *S. by B., S. U. 3H.*, 499. Wright,
Life, 89-90, suggests that the
name "Timothy Sparks" may
have been intended as an allusion to the pyrotechnical sermons of Timothy Richard
Matthews, a Church of England clergyman who often
preached in Nonconformist
meetinghouses.

48. *S. by B., S. U. 3H.*, 500-3.

49. Ibid., 505.

50. Ibid.

51. Ibid., 506-7.

52. Ibid., 508.

53. Ibid., 512-4.

54. Ibid., 516.

55. Ibid., 517.

56. Ibid., 518.

57. Ibid., 523-5.

58. Ibid., 525.
59. Pope-Hennessy, 60, says the third reading, but Dickens in the pamphlet (511) says the second, and both *Hansard* and the *Mirror of Parliament* bear him out. According to both these, it was voted to defer consideration, as had been done regularly since 1832. For further discussion of the circumstances surrounding the writing of *Sunday Under Three Heads*, see my article "Dickens and the Bluenose Legislator," in the *American Scholar*, Autumn, 1948.
60. Dexter, *Mr. and Mrs.*, 68-9, [5/27/36].
61. Complete report is in *Morning Chronicle*, 6/23/36.
62. Ibid.
63. A verbatim report of the Melbourne - N o r t o n trial fills twenty-six and one-half finely printed columns of the *Morning Chronicle*, 6/23/36. The caustic opening is indubitably by Dickens, with its comment that "if a premium had been offered for the construction of a building in every way inadequate to the purposes for which it was intended," the architect of this Court "would have carried off the prize." He also criticized "the indecent behavior of a large course of barristers of small standing" whose self-importance and "ungentlemanly interruptions" prevented "the progress of business." Though Dickens may have had alternates to relieve him, his share would be of a bulk amply justifying his fatigue the next day.
      The Court of Common Pleas was housed in the old building at Westminster, now destroyed, located where the Cromwell Statue stands, on the lawn west of Westminster Hall.
64. *Let.*, I. 73·4; Macrone, two letters, [7/?/36].
65. Ibid, 73, Macrone, [7/?/36].
66. Ibid.
67. Ibid.
68. Ibid., 74, Macrone, [7/20/36].
69. Ibid., 75, Braham, [7/26/36].
70. Ibid., 79-80, Hullah, [8/29/36].
71. Dexer-Ley, 79.
72. Ley, 120.
73. Dexter-Ley, 83-4.
74. *Let.*, I, 76, Macrone, [7/?/36].
75. Ibid., 78, Chapman and Hall, [8/?/36].
76. Berg MS., Dickens to George Thomson, 7/30/36.
77. *Dick.*, XXVIII, 38.
78. *Let.*, I, 76-7, Macrone, [8/3/36].
79. Ibid., 77-8, Tegg, 8/9,10,11/36.
80. Berg MS., Bentley's "Retrospective Sketch of his Connection with Charles Dickens."
81. *Dick.*, III, 33.
82. Berg MS., Bentley's "Retrospective Sketch."
83. *Let.*, I, 91-2, Hansard, 12/1, 2/36.
84. *Serjeant Bell and His Raree Show*, Tegg, 1839, was not written by Dickens. According to Tegg's son, the engagement was canceled by agreement, Eckel, 208.
85. Berg MS., Dickens letter to Bentley, 8/17/36.
86. *Let.*, I, 79, Fraser, 8/?/36.
87. Ibid., 79-80, Hullah, [8/29/36].
88. Ibid., 79, Chapman and Hall, 8/?/36.
89. Ibid., 79-80, Hullah, 8/29/36.
90. Ibid., 81, Hullah, 9/17/36.
91. Ibid., 82, Beard, [9/23/36].
92. Straus, 90.
93. Kitton, *Minor Writings*, 8; *Dick.*, XXVIII, 38, XXX, 111.
94. *Let.*, I, 87, Easthope, [11/1/36].
95. Ibid., 84, Macrone, [1836].
96. Ibid., 85, Macrone, [10/12/36].
97. Ibid., 84, Macrone, [1836].
98. Ibid., 90, Crewe, [11/?/36].

99. Ibid., 90, Cruikshank, [11/28/36].
100. Ibid., 90, fn.
101. *Let.*, I, 81, Hullah, [9/20/36]. A number of Dickens's biographers have imagined the objection came from the ladies acting in the dramatic production, but this is clearly an error: Cramer's were the publishers of the music, not the producers of the play.
102. *Let.*, I, 92, Editor of the *Examiner*, 12/3/36.
103. Sala, *Things Seen*, I, 50-1.
104. Ibid.
105. Straus, 90.
106. *Let.*, I, 93, Hullah, [12/11/36].
107. *Dick.*, XXX, 17.
108. *P. P.*, preface, xix.
109. Dexter-Ley, 76.
110. *Dick.*, XXXIII, 95.
111. Forster, 91.
112. Mackenzie, 151.
113. Forster, 91.
114. L'Estrange, II, 198.
115. Ibid., 193.
116. Kitton, *Novels*, 14.
117. Straus, 118-20.
118. Kitton, *Novels*, 14.
119. *Let.*, I, 87, Chapman and Hall, 11/1/36.

Chapter 5 [pp. 157-175]

1. *P. P.*, preface, xviii.
2. Ibid., xix.
3. Ibid., xvii.
4. Chesterton, *Criticisms*, 16.
5. Escott, 161.
6. *P. P.*, I, 5.
7. Ibid., II, 7.
8. Wright, *Life*, 87-8, points to Samuel Beazley's farce, *The Boarding House; or, Five Hours in Brighton*, in which a militiaman, Simon Spatterdash, has such speeches as "I am down on you, as the extinguisher said to the rushlight," and "Let everyone take care of themselves, as the jackass said when he was dancing among the chickens." This species of joke was made widely popular by Samuel Vale, a comic actor who played the part of Spatterdash.
9. *P. P.*, II, 9.
10. Ibid., 21.
11. Ibid., LIV, 758.
12. Ibid., VIII, 102.
13. Ibid., 100.
14. Ibid., XXXIV, 475, 482.
15. Ibid., VII, 84.
16. Ibid., XIX, 251.
17. Ibid., VII, 85.
18. Ibid., XXI, 282.
19. Ibid., XXXVI, 512-3.
20. Ibid., V, 60-4.
21. Gosse, 254-5.
22. *Let.*, I, 66, Chapman and Hall, 2/18/36.
23. Wilson, *Wound and Bow*, 10.
24. My discussion in this and the following paragraph parallels that in Wilson, *Wound and Bow*, 10-2.
25. *P. P.*, III, 35-40.
26. Ibid., VI, 74-81.
27. Ibid., XI, 139-47.
28. Ibid., XXI, 282-93.
29. *Let.*, I, 69, Seymour, 4/14/36.
30. *P. P.*, preface, xviii.
31. Possibly Mr. Pickwick's experience with Mr. Nupkins echoes some of John Black's campaigns against the unpaid magistrates.
32. *P. P.*, XXXV, 495-502, XXXVII, 515-28.
33. Ibid., XIII, 157-75.
34. Ibid., XV, 192-207.
35. Ibid., XXVIII, 372-94.
36. Wilson, *Wound and Bow*, 13.
37. *P. P.*, XXXIV, 463-86.
38. Ibid., 467.
39. Ibid., 470.
40. Ibid., 471.
41. Ibid., 472.
42. Ibid., 483.
43. Ibid., 484.
44. Ibid., 474-5.
45. Ibid., 481.

46. Ibid., 476-80.
47. Ibid., 470.
48. Ibid., 485.
49. Ibid., 486.
50. Ibid., XL, 561, XLI, 570, 572, 576, XLIV, 616.
51. Ibid., XLIV, 624-5.
52. Ibid., XLII, 592.
53. Ibid., XLI, 573.
54. Ibid., XLV, 642.
55. Ibid., XLII,594-5.
56. Ibid., XLV, 639.
57. Ibid., preface, xix.
58. Ibid., XLVI, 647.
59. Ibid., XXVII, 364, XXXIII, 456-60.
60. Ibid., XXV, 336-55.
61. Ibid., VII, 88.
62. Ibid., XXXI, 416.
63. Ibid., XXXIX, 553-4.

PART THREE

Chapter 1 [pp. 179-194]

1. Pope-Hennessy, 39.
2. Let., I, 86, Beard, 10/28/36.
3. Berg MS., S. R. Rintoul to Bentley, n.d. [circa 11/27-12/4/36].
4. Berg MS., Contract, 11/4/36.
5. Let., I, 88, Easthope, 11/5/36.
6. Ibid., 11/18/36.
7. Ibid., 99, Collier, 1/6/37.
8. Coll. P., II, 484-5, speech, 5/20/65.
9. Forster, 65.
10. Ibid., Let., I, 726, Forster, [1845].
11. Let., I, 90, Jerrold, [11/?/36].
12. Berg MS., Dickens to Bentley, [12/5/36].
13. Let., I, 84, Macrone, [1836].
14. Ibid., 93, Cruikshank, [12/?/36], 93 fn.
15. Wright, Life, 96, quoting Macrone letter to Strang, 1/2/37.
16. Let., I, 83-4, Macrone, [1836], passim.
17. Ibid., 214, Miton, 5/13/39.
18. Ellis, Ainsworth, I, 305, Ainsworth to Macrone, 11/12/36.

19. Ibid.
20. All these facts are either in or derived from Ainsworth's letter to Macrone, 11/12/36, ibid.
21. Ellis, Ainsworth, I, 305-8.
22. Ibid., I, 306-7, Ainsworth to Macrone, 11/14/36, 11/28/36.
23. Let., I, 91, Hansard, [12/1/36].
24. Ibid., 91-2, 12/2/36.
25. Ibid., 92, Bentley, [12/2/36].
26. Ibid., 214, Mitton, 5/13/39.
27. Berg MS., opinion of Sutton Sharpe on the later, but parallel, case of the Dickens-Bentley dispute, 2/12/40.
28. Harvard, Widener MS., 1/5/37; partially quoted in Let., I, 92 fn.
29. Let., I, 215, Mitton, 5/13/39.
30. Berg, MS., Dickens to Bentley, 2/5/36.
31. Let., I, 93-4, Harley, [12/?/36], 95 fn.
32. Ibid., 94, Harley, [12/?/36], 94 fn.
33. Ibid., [12/?/36].
34. Ibid., Beard, [12/?/36].
35. Ibid., 94-5, Beard, [12/?/36], Mitton, [1836].
36. Ellis, Ainsworth, I, 272.
37. Renton, Forster, passim; Dick., VIII, 119.
38. Forster, 59. It has already been pointed out, however, that Forster was mistaken in recalling the strike as directed against the True Sun.
39. Pearson, 59.
40. See Maclise portrait of Forster as a young man.
41. Espinasse, quoted by Pope-Hennessy, 76.
42. Rosina Bulwer, Chevely, quoted by Jane Carlyle, Letters to Family, 10/31/41.
43. Carlyle, Letters to Mill, Sterling, Browning, 10/31/41.
44. Forster, 84-5.
45. Forster, 85, says the meeting was not until June, when Dickens was in Hampstead, but Berg MS. 3/16/37 shows that they conferred in March.

46. *Let.*, I, 103, Forster, [2/23/37].
47. Ibid., 101-2, Forster, [2/2/37].
48. Ibid., 145-6, diary, 1/6/38.
49. Ibid., 99, Cruikshank, 1/9/37.
50. Ibid., 146, diary, 1/6/38.
51. Barham, II, 16, quoting Barham's letter to Hughes, 3/1/37.
52. Announcement in *Bentley's Miscellany*, June, 1837.
53. *Dick.*, III, 70.
54. Morgan MS., Dickens to J. J. Crackenbottom, n.d.; Madigan catalogue, November, 1928, Dickens to W. B. Archer, n.d.
55. Berg MS., Dickens to Bentley, "Saturday Evening."
56. Ibid., "Tuesday morning," [1/24/37].
57. *O. T.*, II, 12-3.
58. Ibid., I, 3.
59. Ibid., II, 4-5.
60. Ibid., III, 20.
61. *Let.*, I, 102-3, Harley, 2/13/37, Cruikshank, 2/15/37, Beard, 2/22/37, Forster, 2/23/37.
62. Ibid., 100, Hullah, 1/14/37, Culliford, 1/24/37; Berg MS., Dickens to Bentley, 1/24/37.
63. *Let.*, I, 100, Culliford, 1/24/37.
64. Ibid., 101, Hullah, [1837].
65. Ibid., 102, Harley, [2/13/37].
66. *Coll. P.*, II, 153-4.
67. *Let.*, I, 102 fn.
68. Ibid., 103, Beard, [2/22/37].
69. Kitton, *Life*, 41 fn.
70. *Dick.*, XXIII, 213. Not until January 9, 1838, however, did he give notice through Mitton that he was not renewing his lease at Furnival's Inn (*Let.*, I, 153 fn.).
71. Berg MS., Dickens to Bentley, 2/28/37.
72. Christian, 485, 487.
73. Ellis, *Ainsworth*, I, 275-6.
74. *Let.*, I, 102, 106, Cruikshank, 2/15/37, [4/?/37].
75. Ibid., 41, Austin, [1835].
76. Morgan MS., Dickens to Austin, 1/31/37.
77. Rylands MS., John Dickens to Harley, 4/2/37.
78. Kitton, *Novels*, 29.
79. *Let.*, I, 104, Chapman and Hall, 3/31/37.
80. Ibid., 105, Forster, [4/7/37].
81. Berg MS., holograph notation by Bentley, n.d.

Chapter 2 [pp. 195-204]

1. *Let.*, I, 107, Thomson, 5/8/37.
2. Ibid., 119, Johns, 7/12/37.
3. Ibid., 112, unknown correspondent, 6/9/37.
4. Ibid., 133, Mrs. Hogarth, 10/26/37.
5. Ibid., 120, Johns, 7/12/37.
6. Ibid., 109, Beard, 5/17/37.
7. Ibid., 107, Thomson, 5/8/37.
8. Ibid., 108, Chapman, [5/?/37].
9. Ibid., 121, Ainsworth, 7/14/37.
10. *Let.*, I, 359, Mrs. Hogarth, 10/24/41; Berg MS. to Edward Chapman, May '37, only part of which is quoted in *Let.*, I, 108. From the second of these letters, in which Dickens asks Chapman for an advance to help him defray the burial expenses, it must be inferred that he, rather than the Hogarths, paid for the funeral—unless he was reimbursed at a later date. At the moment, however, it was Dickens who had to borrow.
11. *Let.*, I, 108, Ainsworth, 5/17/37.
12. *Let.*, I, 114 fn., points out that Forster, 89, was mistaken in identifying *P. P.*, No. 14, as the delayed issue; it was No. 15. Forster, 85, was also in error in saying that the interruption was for two months. There was an interval of two months between the publication of the numbers, but the writing was delayed by only one month.
13. *Bentley's Miscellany*, June, 1837.
14. Kitton, *Novels*, 13. Cf. Forster, 160 fn., quoting Dickens's own auctorial address to the public, 6/30/37, on resuming publica-

tion of *P. P.*: "By one set of intimate acquaintances, especially
well-informed, he has been killed
outright; by another, driven
mad; by a third, imprisoned for
debt; by a fourth, sent per
steamer to the United States; by
a fifth, rendered incapable of
mental exertion for evermore; by
all, in short, represented as
doing anything but seeking in a
few weeks' retirement the restoration of that cheerfulness and
peace of which a sad bereavement had temporarily deprived
him."

15. *Let.*, I, 108, Beard, 5/17/37.
16. Ibid., 109, Ainsworth, 5/17/37.
17. Forster, 85.
18. *Let.*, I, 113, Beard, 6/16/37.
19. Ibid., 109, Beard, 5/17/37.
20. Ibid.
21. Ibid., 112, unknown correspondent,
    6/9/37.
22. Ibid., 120, Johns, 7/12/37.
23. Elkins MS., Dickens to Mrs. Ho-
    garth, 10/26/37; partly printed
    in *Let.*, I, 133.
24. *Let.*, I, 145, 147, diary, 1/6,
    14/38.
25. Ibid., 158, Catherine, 2/1/38.
26. Ibid., 519, Mrs. Hogarth, 5/8/43.
27. Ibid., 202, Bradbury, 3/3/[39].
28. Ibid., 292-3, Forster, 1/7/41.
29. Ibid., 359, Mrs. Hogarth,
    10/24/41.
30. Ibid., 360, Forster, 10/25/41.
31. Ibid., 10/26/41.
32. Ibid., 441, 4/20/42.
33. Ibid., 624-5, 9/30/44.
34. Ibid., II, 87, 5/7/48.

Chapter 3 [pp. 205-233]

1. Forster, 109, n. 112, quoting
   Ainsworth.
2. Ellis, *Ainsworth*, I, 330; Waugh,
   Hundred Years, 37. There is
   some confusion here, however,
   for Walter Dexter, *Dick.*, XL,
   118, notes the existence of a

receipt from Dickens to Chapman and Hall, 11/18/37, for
£643 for "the balance of the
consideration money for the
license to print and publish, and
for two-thirds of the copyright
of Pickwick Papers." The difference in these figures may represent a mistake by Ainsworth
and Waugh or be covered by
some adustment for advances
made or expenses incurred.
Much less likely, but still not
impossible, if Dickens received
a total of £2,000-£2,500, is that
there were separate payments of
£750 and £643 at this time.

3. *Let.*, I, 87, Chapman and Hall,
   11/1/36.
4. Ibid., 123, 7/27/37.
5. *Let.*, I, 137, Hill, 11/13/37, Macready, 11/15/37, Forster,
   11/16/37; Ellis, *Ainsworth*, I,
   330; Forster, 105, 109-10, n.
   112. Ainsworth mentions the
   presence of Hogarth and John
   Dickens in a letter to James
   Crossley, 11/22/37. The description of Thomas Hill is from
   Hall, *Memories*.
6. Forster, 109, n. 112.
7. Jerdan, IV, 365.
8. Forster, 109, n. 112.
9. Macready, *Diaries*, 11/18/37.
10. *Let.*, I, 116, Ross, [1837].
11. Ibid., 111, Haines, 6/3/37.
12. Ibid., 109, Forster, [6/?/37].
13. Ibid., 109-10, [6/?/37].
14. Ibid., 110, [6/?/37].
15. Berg MS., Bentley holograph no-
    tation, n.d. Included among the
    guests were Barham and his
    son, William Jerdan, and John
    Hughes, author of *The Legend
    of Walter Childe*, which pres-
    ently appeared in the *Miscel-
    lany*. Hughes was the father of
    the more famous Thomas
    Hughes, who was to write *Tom
    Brown's Schooldays*.
16. *Let.*, I, 110-1, Forster, [6/?/37].

17. Forster, 87.
18. *Let.*, I, 111, Forster, [6/?/37].
19. Forster, 87.
20. Ibid.
21. Ibid., 88.
22. Ibid., 87.
23. Forster, 88. *Dick.*, III, 10, gives the date of Chapman and Hall's agreement to purchase the *Sketches* from Macrone as 6/11/37 and the date of Macrone's receipt as 6/24/37. The actual receipt, however, in Harvard, Widener Coll., bears the date 6/17/37.
24. Forster, 88.
25. *Let.*, I, 114, Forster, [6/?/37].
26. Ibid., 124, [7/?/37].
27. Ibid., 126, [1837].
28. Ibid., 109, [6/?/37].
29. Forster, 93.
30. Ibid., 92.
31. *Let.*, I, 135, Forster, [1837].
32. Renton, 58.
33. Ellis, *Ainsworth*, I, 275.
34. *Dick.*, XXXVIII, 182.
35. Chorley, I, 194, diary, 10/31/36.
36. Lytton, *Life*, 1913, 74, letter to Forster, 3/15/46.
37. *Coll. P.*, II, 387, speech, 3/1/51.
38. Hall, *Retrospect*, 259.
39. Macready, *Diaries*, I, 399, 6/17/37.
40. *Let.*, I, 115, Forster, 7/2/37.
41. Ibid., 123, Harley.
42. *Let.*, I, 126, Hullah, Aug., 1837; Macready, *Diaries*, 8/16/37. Dr. Eric George Millar identifies the opera as *The Barbers of Bassova* and tells me it was produced at Covent Garden, 11/11/37.
43. *Let.*, I, 116, Mitton, [1837].
44. Ibid., 122, Beard, 7/21/37.
45. *Forster*, 94, 101, n. 106. Their address on this visit was No. 12 (now No. 31) High Street.
46. Wright, *Life*, 115.
47. R. P., 25, "Our English Watering Place."
48. *Let.*, I, 127, Forster, 9/3/37.

49. Ibid., 128, 9/7/37.
50. The dedicatory letter was dated 9/27/37, but the book was not published until November.
51. *Let.*, I, 128, Forster, 9/7/37.
52. Ibid., 132, Carey and Company, 10/26/37; cf. Kerslake.
53. *Let.*, I, 131, Talfourd, [10/?/37], 133-4, Ainsworth, 10/30/37.
54. *Dick.*, XXXI, 170; *Let.*, I, 133, Ainsworth, 10/30/37; Ellis, *Ainsworth*, I, 308.
55. *Let.*, I, 136, Forster, 11/3/37. Dickens and his wife stayed at the Old Ship.
56. Ibid.
57. Ibid., 140, Laurence, [1837].
58. Waugh, *Hundred Years*, 29.
59. Forster, 105-6. Harvard, Widener MS. Agreement is dated 11/18/37. Forster mistakenly says 11/19, which was a Sunday.
60. Forster, 105.
61. *Let.*, I, 138, Forster, 12/11/37.
62. Ibid., Beard, 12/6/37.
63. Osborne, *Letters*, 29.
64. *Let.*, I, 152, Cruikshank, [1/?/38].
65. Ibid., Mitton, [1838].
66. Ibid.
67. Ibid., 141, Mme. Sala, [1837].
68. Ibid., 147, Diary, 1/14/37.
69. Ibid., 153, Forster, [1/?/38].
70. Ibid., 154, Ainsworth, [1/25/38].
71. Ibid.
72. N. N., preface, xvi.
73. *Dick.*, XI, 260, quotes from a Yorkshire newspaper report of the trials, before the Court of Common Pleas, of Jones vs. Shaw, 10/30/1823, and Ocherby vs. Shaw, 10/31/1823.
74. *Dick.*, XXXV, 10.
75. *Let.*, I, 122, George Beadnell, [7/?/37].
76. *Let.*, I, 157, Catherine Dickens, 2/1/37. Dickens's actual journey is paralleled in the narrative of N. N., V, VI, 49-58 passim.
77. Forster, 127, n. 128. Also *Let.*, I, 157, Catherine Dickens,

2/1/37, which by calling Smithson merely "Mitton's friend" implies that perhaps the two men had not yet become partners.

78. N. N., preface, xvii.
79. Let., I, 185-6, Mrs. Hall, 12/29/38.
80. N. N., preface, xvii.
81. Forster, 128, n. 128, quoting T. P. Cooper, With Dickens in Yorkshire.
82. Let., I, 158, Forster, 2/7/38. Forster, 124, 130, emphatically gives a date as 2/7, but V. and A. MS., dated "Friday morning," means either that Dickens had the day of the week wrong or that it was 2/9/38.
83. Let., I, 159, 2/9/38.
84. Ibid., 162, 3/6/38.
85. Forster, 108.
86. Let., I, 162, Forster, 3/9/38.
87. Forster, 109.
88. Let., I, 165 fn. It was on Isleworth Road, near St. Margaret's Station.
89. Forster, 131; Let., I, 167, Mitton, [1838].
90. Let., I, 165, Beard, [6/12/38].
91. Ibid., 148, Diary, 7/12/38.
92. Ibid., 165, Forster, 6/23/38.
93. Forster, 130; Let., III, 75, B. Jerrold, 11/26/58.
94. Dick., XXXV, 75; Ray, I, 327 fn. This story was about Dando, the oyster-eater.
95. Ellis, Ainsworth, I, 298; Forster, 130. Renton, 61, has further material about Maclise.
96. Let., I, 138, Forster, 12/11/37, 170, Hunt, [7/?/38].
97. Dick., III, 70.
98. Let., I, 171, Giles, [7/?/38].
99. Kitton, Pen and Pencil, Sup. 7, quoting Burnett, but he erroneously says the boy was French.
100. Houtchens, 211-7, quoting Knickerbocker Magazine, October, 1838.
101. Let., I, 172, Forster, [8/7/38].

102. Chesterton, Criticisms, 42.
103. Let., I, 173, Forster, [9/?/38].
104. Ibid., but later in first week of September; see Forster, 111.
105. Forster, 111-2.
106. Let., I, 172, Cruikshank, two letters [1838].
107. Ibid., a third letter to Cruikshank, [8/?/38].
108. Dexter, Mr. and Mrs., 11/5/38; Berg MS., Forster to Bentley, 11/5/38.
109. Berg MS., Forster to Bentley, 11/8/38.
110. Let., I, 176, Cruikshank, [11/9/38]. This letter, and those previously noted, dispose of Cruikshank's story, also dismissed in Forster, 112 fn., that he originated Oliver Twist by drawing a series of plates to which Dickens merely devised a story. Ellis, Ainsworth, I, 130, points out that Cruikshank also claimed to have originated several of Ainsworth's best novels. Cruikshank was not a deliberate liar, but in his later years his memory grew oddly deranged.
111. Berg MS., Forster to Bentley, 11/5/38.
112. Macready, Diaries, 12/5, 11, 12/38.
113. Dick., XXXIII, 95.
114. Let., I, 181, Macready, 12/13/38; Macready, Diaries, 12/13/38.
115. Macready, Diaries, 11/8, 10/38.
116. Forster, 125.
117. Forster, 128, n. 129.
118. Let., I, 178-9, Yates, [11/?/38].
119. Ibid., 179, Yates, [11/?/38];Yates, Recollections, 18; S. J. A. Fitzgerald, 97, 117.
120. Let., I, 148, Diary, 10/30/38.
121. Dexter, Mr. and Mrs., 75, 11/1/38.
122. Let., I, 149-50, Diary, 11/1-7/38.
123. Ellis, Ainsworth, I, 338, 10/31/38, 340, 10/?/38; Let., I, 176, Forster, 11/3/38; Dexter, Mr. and Mrs., 79, 11/5/38.

124. Ellis, *Ainsworth*, 341-3.
125. Hodder, *Shaftesbury*, 120, Dickens to Edward Fitzgerald, 12/29/38.
126. Ellis, *Ainsworth*, 345-6, 348.
127. *Let.*, I, 151, Diary, 12/13,27/38, 191, Diary, 1/29/39.
128. Ellis, *Ainsworth*, I, 349, Ainsworth to Crossley, 1/10/39.
128a. Ibid., 350.
129. Ibid., 342.
130. *Let.*, I, 184, Martin, 12/28/38.
131. *N. N.*, preface, xiv, 175.
132. Hall, *Memories*, quoting Benjamin R. Haydon.
133. Ibid., quoting N. P. Willis.
134. Ley, 157.
135. *Let.*, I, 469, Sumner, 7/31/42.
136. Ibid., 675, Lady Blessington, 5/9/45.
137. Mackay, *Long Day*; Hall, *Memories*.
138. Forster Coll., letters from Kate to Rogers, signed "very affectionately yours."
139. Quoted by Pope-Hennessy, 95-6.
139a. Trevelyan, *Macaulay*, I, 192, Macaulay to Hannah Macaulay, 5/30/31.
140. Lytton, *Life*, 1913, 13.
141. *Let.*, I, 166, Talfourd, 7/9/38. It was the anniversary of the wedding of Austin and Letitia.
142. Quoted by Pope-Hennessy, 103.
143. *Dick.*, XXXVI, 33, Dickens to Lady Holland, 9/?/38.
144. Holland, *Smith*, 547, Smith to Dickens, 6/11/39.
145. *Let.*, I, 216, Mary Berry, [6/3/39], 193, Diary, 7/1/39.
146. Waugh, *Athenaeum Club*, loaned me by courtesy of N. R. Udal, Secretary of the Athenaeum, who also kindly took me through all the members' rooms.

Chapter 4 [pp. 234-253]

1. Berg MS., Dickens to Bentley, [June, 1837].
2. Ibid., Bentley, "Retrospective Sketch of His Connection with Charles Dickens."
3. Ibid., Dickens to Bentley, [3/9/37].
4. Ibid., Dickens-Bentley Agreement, 3/17/37.
5. Ibid., Dickens to Bentley, [3/16/37].
6. *Let.*, I, 118, Forster. Walter Dexter dates this as sometime in July, but it must be June, as it clearly precedes the letter of 7/2/37 in the next reference.
7. Ibid., I, 116, Bentley, 7/2/37.
8. Berg MS., Bentley, "Retrospective Sketch."
9. Ibid., Dickens to Bentley, 7/14/37. Incomplete in *Let.*, I, 120-1.
10. *Let.*, I, 125, Bentley, [8/?/37].
11. Berg MS., Bentley, "Retrospective Sketch."
12. Ibid.
13. *Let.*, I, 117, Beard. July according to Dexter, but probably 8/14/37. There was a meeting at Forster's on 8/15/37, and Dickens's letter to Bentley, 8/18/37, makes it clear that Beard met Gregory on 8/16/37.
14. Berg MS., Dickens to Bentley, 8/18/37.
15. Ibid., Gregory to Bentley, 8/19/37.
16. Ibid., Bentley, "Retrospective Sketch."
17. Ibid.
18. *Let.*, I, 119, Forster. Dexter puts this letter in July, but Cruikshank's letters to Bentley show that it must have been written in September.
19. Berg MS., Cruikshank to Bentley, 9/15/37.
20. Ibid., "Retrospective Sketch."
21. Ibid., Dickens to Bentley, 9/16/37.
22. Ibid., Cruikshank to Bentley, "Saturday Noon," [9/?/37].
23. Ibid., draft letter, Bentley to Dickens, [9/18/37].
24. *Let.*, I, 128, Bentley, 9/19/37.
25. Ibid., Cruikshank, 9/20/37, accord-

ing to Dexter, but probably 9/27/37.

26. Berg MS., Gregory to Bentley, 9/21/37.
27. Ibid., Dickens to Bentley, "Wednesday Morning," [Jan.-April, 1837].
28. Let., I, 196, Forster, 1/21/39.
29. Berg MS., draft memorandum, n.d., [9/22/37].
30. Ibid., Molloy to Bentley, 9/26/37.
31. Ibid., draft agreement, 9/28/37.
32. Let., I, 129, Mitton, [1837].
33. Berg MS., draft agreement, 9/28/37.
34. Let., I, 131, Forster. A revised but unsigned draft agreement in Berg MSS., dated November, has a few trivial changes of detail from the preceding agreement. The only one affecting Barnaby Rudge defers its delivery date to October, 1838.
35. Berg MS., Dickens to Bentley, [10/31/37], another dated "Thursday Morning," [1837], agreement, 11/29/37.
36. Let., I, 163, Forster, [1837].
37. Berg MS., Dickens to Bentley, "Monday Morning," [1837].
38. Ibid., Dickens to Bentley, [1837].
39. Ibid., "Thursday Night," [1837].
40. Ibid.
41. Ibid., "Thursday Morning," [1837-8].
42. Let., I, 159, Bentley, 2/11/38.
43. Ibid., 160, Chapman and Hall, 2/22/38.
44. Ibid., 148, Diary, 7/12/38.
45. Berg MS., agreement, 9/22/38.
46. Let., I, 183-4, Downing, 12/27/38.
47. Berg MS., Forster to Bentley, [11/8/38].
48. Let., I, 196, Forster, 1/21/39.
49. Berg MS., George Mitford to Bentley, 6/5.17/36.
50. Ibid., Forster to Bentley, 6/3/39.
51. Ibid., Barham to Bentley, 9/24/39, 9/4/40.
52. Ibid., correspondence between Bar-

ham and Bentley, 5/11-19/43, Barham to Joseph Hume, [1843].
53. Ibid., Bentley to Dickens, 1/25/39.
54. Ibid., draft in Gregory's hand, marked "Copied 28/1/39."
55. Ibid., holograph note in Bentley's hand, relating to Dickens, n.d.
56. Ibid., Barham to Bentley, outlining Dickens's memorandum, [1/30/39], another, Barham to Bentley, [1839].
57. Ibid., draft agreements, dated 2/15,22,27/39, all virtually identical, another, n.d., dealing with Oliver Twist and Barnaby Rudge, superseding that of 9/22/38.
58. Let., I, 198, Talfourd, 1/31/39.
59. Ibid., 263, Chapman and Hall, 7/2/40. Possibly in February there were not even two chapters, for this letter is six months later still!
60. Kitton, Minor Writings, 66.
61. Berg MS., Dickens to Smithson and Mitton, 12/16/39.
62. Ibid., George Bentley holograph notation on preceding letter.
63. Ibid., copy in Gregory's hand of a letter for Bentley to send to Smithson and Mitton, 12/17/39.
64. Ibid., copy in Gregory's hand of another letter for Bentley to send to Smithson and Mitton, 12/19/39.
65. Ibid., Gregory to Bentley, [1839].
66. Let., I, 237, Beard, 12/17/39.
67. Ibid., 238, Chapman, 12/27/39.
68. Morgan MS., Macready to Dickens, "Saturday," [1839-40].
69. Macready, Diaries, 2/23/40.
70. Morgan MS., Dickens to Macready, "Sunday Morning," [1840].
71. Ibid., Dickens to Macready, [2/24/40].
72. Berg MS., Barham to Bentley, "Monday Night," [1840].
73. Ibid., holograph note by Bentley, n.d.
74. Ibid., legal statement, with opinion of Sutton Sharpe, barrister, 2/12/40.

75. Ibid., Jerdan to Bentley, 6/19/40; cf. Jerdan, IV, 209.
76. *Let.*, I, 263, Chapman and Hall, 7/2/40.
77. Waugh, *Hundred Years*, facsimile f. 44.

Chapter 5 [pp. 254-270]

1. *Let.*, I, 192, Diary, 2/7/39.
2. Strong, 179, quoting letter from Hunt to Duke of Devonshire.
3. Forster, 84.
4. *Let.*, I, 192, Diary, 2/7/39.
5. Ibid.
6. Waugh, *Hundred Years*, 41.
7. Fitzgerald, *Life*, 112, John Dickens to Chapman and Hall, 2/14/37.
8. Waugh, *Hundred Years*, 41; Straus, 110.
9. Waugh, *Hundred Years*, 41.
10. Straus, 110.
11. Waugh, *Hundred Years*, 42.
12. Berg MS., John Dickens to Chapman and Hall, 12/19/37.
13. Straus, 111.
14. *Let.*, I, 201, Forster, [3/1/39].
15. Ibid., 201-2.
16. V. and A. MS., Forster, 3/5/39, inaccurately quoted, *Let.*, I, 203-5; *Let.*, I, 205-6, Mitton, 3/6/39; Dexter, *Mr. and Mrs.*, 81-3, 3/5/39.
17. V. and A. MS., Forster, 3/5/39.
18. *Let.*, I, 205-6, Mitton, 3/6/39.
19. Dexter, *Mr. and Mrs.*, 81-3, 3/5/39.
20. Straus, 151.
21. *Let.*, I, 207, Beard, 3/13/39.
22. V. and A. MS., Dickens to Forster, 7/13/39; Pope-Hennessy, 107.
23. *Let.*, I, 266-7, Forster, 7/31/[40].
24. Ibid., 303,594, Mitton, 3/9/41, 4/17/44.
25. Christian, 484.
26. Forster, 551-2, [5/?/41].
27. *Let.*, I, 207, Forster, [3/?/39].
28. Ibid., 208, Colburn, 3/25/39.
29. Sawyer, *Dickens vs. Barabbas*, Dickens to Ainsworth, 3/26/39, facsimile, frontispiece. This letter is

inaccurate and incomplete in *Let.*, I, 208. It is possible that Bentley's accusations against Forster were partly motivated by irritation over his interference in a dispute between Bentley and Ainsworth: See Ellis, *Ainsworth*, I, 387.
30. Morgan MS., Dickens to Ainsworth, 4/1/39.
31. Berg MS., Barham to Ainsworth, "Garrick 9 o'clock."
32. *Dick.*, XXX, 170; Morgan MS., Smithson and Mitton letter to Foss and Clark, 5/6/39, Clark to Hansard, 5/6/39, Smithson and Mitton to Foss and Clark, 5/15/39; *Let.*, I, 214, Mitton, 5/13/39.
33. Forster, 131.
34. *Let.*, I, 217, Harley, 6/28/39.
35. Forster, 129, n. 131, quoting Thackeray.
36. *Let.*, I, 216, Cruikshank, "Friday Night," and "Monday Morning." See Haight on Dickens's revisions of the ballad, refuting the story that Thackeray was its author. Cf. Ray, I, 380-1, and 381 fn.
37. *Coll. P.*, II, 540, "The Loving Ballad of Lord Bateman."
38. Kitton, *Pen and Pencil*, 137, records that actually the music was taken down, not by Fanny, but by Henry Burnett.
39. *Let.*, I, 216, Cruikshank, [5/?/39].
40. Ibid., 218, Forster, [7/39].
41. Waugh, *Hundred Years*, 45.
42. *Let.*, I, 218-20, Forster, [7/?/39].
43. Ibid., 221-2, Mitton, 7/26/39.
44. Forster, 142.
45. Ibid.
46. *Let.*, I, 222, Mitton, 7/26/39.
47. Macready, *Diaries*, 7/20/39; *Let.*, I, 217, Blanchard, 7/11/39, but this letter is misdated, and should be 7/13/39.
48. *Coll. P.*, I, 123-7, "The Restoration of Shakespeare's 'Lear' to the Stage," *Examiner*, 2/4/38.

49. Macready, *Diaries*, 3/30/39.
50. Clarke, *Recollections*, quoted by Pope-Hennessy, 107.
51. *Let.*, I, 223, Macready, 7/26/39, 223 fn.
52. Macready, *Diaries*, 8/7/39.
53. *Let.*, I, 223, Macready, 7/26/39.
54. Ibid., 193, diary, 9/2, 3/39. The address was No. 40 Albion Street, rented at £21 a month.
55. *Let.*, I, 225, Forster, 9/9/39. The original MSS. letters, in the V. and A., show that Forster has slightly garbled the texts and run together the wording of *two* letters, 9/9/39 and 9/18/37.
56. Ibid., 193, Diary, 9/4/39.
57. Ibid., 225, Forster, 9/9/39.
58. Ibid., 194, Diary, 9/20,21/39; Macready, *Diaries*, 9/22/39.
59. *Let.*, I, 226, Forster, 9/18/39.
60. Ibid., 194, Diary, 9/21,22/39.
61. Ibid., 226-8, letters to Forster, Beard, Cattermole, Hill, Macready, Wilkie.
62. Kitton, *"Phiz."*
63. Macready, *Diaries*, 10/5/39.
64. Forster, 127.
65. Macready, *Diaries*, 10/5/39.
66. Morgan MS., Dickens to Macready, [10/?/39]; Kitton, *Life*, 64.
67. *Let.*, I, 232, Macready, 10/25/39.
68. Dexter, *Mr. and Mrs.*, 198, 10/29/53, establishes the date of birth.
69. *Let.*, I, 234, Macready, 11/14/39.
70. Forster, 640, [1857].
71. *Let.*, I, 213, Forster, [1839].
72. *Coll. P.*, II, 546, "The Loving Ballad of Lord Bateman," n. 10.
73. *Let.*, I, 214, Forster, [1839].
74. Ibid., 134, Ainsworth, 10/30/37.
75. Ibid., 235, Forster, [1839].
76. Ibid., 231, Cruikshank, [10/3/39].
77. Ibid., 233, Forster, [10-11/?/39].
78. Ibid.
79. Ibid.
80. *Let.*, I, 233, Forster, [Oct.-Nov., 1839]; Forster, 133. The New Road is now Marylebone Road.
81. Ibid., 747, Phillips, 4/20/46, gives details about the house.
82. Ibid., 234, J. Hall, 11/14/39.
83. V. and A. MS., Dickens to Forster, [1839]; Pope-Hennessy, 110
84. E.g., *Let.*, I, 235, Snoxell, 11/30/39.
85. Lewes, 246-51.
86. Morgan MS., Dickens to Macready, 3/11/41.
87. Quoted by Crotch, *Secret*, 57.

PART FOUR

Chapter 1 [pp. 273-291]

1. Trevelyan, *British History*, 148-50.
2. Ibid. 147.
3. Ibid., 249-50.
4. Pugh, passim.
5. House, 197-8.
6. *O. T.*, II, 4.
7. Ibid., III, 10.
8. Ibid., 10-1.
9. Ibid., 11; House, 94, quoting *Second Annual Report of the Poor Law Commissioners*, 1836, 56.
10. House, 94.
11. *O. T.*, IV, 28-9.
12. House, 95.
13. *O. T.*, IV, 27.
14. Ibid., III, 18.
15. Gissing, 80.
16. Trollope, I, 11, quoted by House, 43.
17. *O. T.*, preface to 1st cheap edition, xiii-xiv.
18. Ibid., preface to 3rd edition, viii-ix.
19. Ibid., vii.
20. Crotch, *Social Reformer*, 46.
21. *Dick.*, XIII, 213.
22. *O. T.*, preface to 3rd edition, ix.
23. Ibid., x.
23a. Ibid., LI, 399.
24. Ibid., preface, vii.
25. Ibid., xi.
26. Ibid., XLVII, 363.
27. Ibid., XLVIII, 369.
28. Ibid., 371.
29. Ibid., LII, 413.
30. *N. N.*, XXXIV, 430-1, XIV, 169.

31. Ibid., XVI, 206.
32. Ibid., XXIII, 288-300, XXIV, 301-17, XXIX, 375-84, XLI, 536-7, XLII, 546-7.
33. Ibid., IV, 40.
34. Ibid., V, 46, IV, 33.
35. Ibid., XV, 176.
36. Ibid., XXXIV, 432, XXX, 395, XXIII, 291.
37. Ibid., XXIV, 303, LIV, 724.
38. Ibid., preface to 1st edition, xii.
39. Huxley, 54-5.
40. *Fraser's Magazine*, April, 1840, 381-400.
41. Gissing, 98.
42. N. N., VIII, 89.
43. Ibid., 91-2.
44. Young, *Early Victorian England*, II, 3, quoting Horace Mann's *Education in Great Britain*, 1854.
45. N. N., preface to 1st edition, xii.
46. House, 42.
47. Chesterton, *Criticisms*, 47.
48. *Coll. P.*, II, 337, speech, 2/1/42.

Chapter 2 [pp. 292-305]

1. *Let.*, I, 247, Forster, 2/12/40.
2. Ibid., 249, Thompson, [2/?/40]. The Queen's marriage took place 2/10/40; therefore this letter was written shortly after that event.
3. Ibid., 236, Beard, 12/17/39, 235, Hall, [12/?/39].
4. Ibid., 244, Forster, [1/?/40].
5. Ibid., Bradbury and Evans, 1/2/40.
6. Ibid., 247, Landor, [2/11/40].
7. Ibid., 248, Thompson, [2/?/40].
8. Straus, 156-7.
9. Ley, 208.
10. Kitton, *Pen and Pencil*, 142.
11. *Let.*, I, 273; Forster, 9/15/40, 272-3, Forster, 9/9,13/40.
12. Ibid., 306, Hall, 3/16/41.
13. Ibid., 304, Maclise, 3/12/41.
14. Ibid., 326, Fletcher, 6/15/41.
15. Ibid., 315, Coutts, 4/20/41.
16. *Let.*, I, 263, Chapman and Hall, 7/2/40. It is possible, indeed,

that at the first of the year not even the two chapters mentioned in this letter were written. Dickens *had* begun the story, however, the preceding October. See *Let.*, I, 231, Cruikshank, [10/3/39].
17. Morgan MS., Dickens to Macready, [2/24/40].
18. *Let.*, I, 244, Forster, 1/9/40.
19. Ibid., 245, [1/?/40].
20. Forster, *Landor*, 395, April, 1838. Landor's birthday was 1/30, and in later years, whenever Dickens was in England, he and Forster made birthday visits to Bath. Forster's *Landor* says that this first trip was made by rail, but *Mr. and Mrs.*, 89, 3/1/40, and *Let.*, I, 250, Forster, [2/27/40], establish the fact that Forster's memory was at fault and that this time they still took the coach.
21. Linton, 55.
22. Forster, *Landor*, 459.
23. *Let.*, I, 250, Forster, 3/4/40.
24. Ibid., 3/5/40.
25. Forster, *Landor*, 459.
26. Forster, 158; Renton, 61.
27. Maggs MS., unknown correspondent, "Tuesday afternoon," [4/7 or 14/40].
28. Waugh, *Hundred Years*, 48.
29. Forster, 146.
30. *Let.*, I, 254, Forster, [3/?/40].
31. Ibid.
32. Ibid., 259, Forster, [5/?/40].
33. Ibid., Beard, 6/1/40.
34. Ibid., 260, Maclise, 6/2/40.
35. Ibid., 261, Mitton, 6/16/40.
36. Ibid., 262, Forster, 6/17/40.
37. Kitton, *Pen and Pencil*, 142-3, Burnett's reminiscences; Christian, 499-500. Mrs. Christian attributes the episode to a later period (the execution took place 7/6/40), but there is no reason for rejecting her account otherwise.
38. *Let.*, I, 264, Marjoribanks, 7/6/40.
39. Ibid., 266, Maclise, 7/22/40.
40. Ibid., 267, Elliotson, 8/5/40.

41. Ibid., 268, Rogers, 8/13/40.
42. Ibid., 269, Harley, 8/17/40.
43. Berg MS., Dickens to Landor, 7/26/40.
44. Macready, *Diaries*, 8/16/40.
45. *Let.*, I, 269, Macready, 8/17/40.
46. Forster, 147.
47. *Let.*, I, 271-2, Maclise, 9/2/40, 274, Forster, 9/20/40.
48. Ibid., 272, Forster, 9/2/40.
49. Ibid., 274, Chapman and Hall, 10/2/40.
50. Ibid., 275, Forster, 10/4/40.
51. Ibid., 277, Mitton, 11/9/40.
52. Ibid., 277, Forster, [11/?/40].
53. Ibid., 295, Forster, 1/17/41.
54. Ibid., 278, Chapman and Hall, 11/24/40.
55. Ibid., 277, Forster, 11/12/40.
56. Ibid., 283, Cattermole, 12/22/40.
57. Ibid., 292, Forster, 1/7/41.
58. Macready, *Diaries*, 1/22/41.
59. *Dick.*, XV, 35.
60. Pope-Hennessy, 151.
61. *Dick.*, XIV, 96.
62. Kitton, *Novels*, 64.

Chapter 3 [pp. 306-318]

1. *Let.*, I, 297, Forster, 1/29/41.
2. Ibid., 312, Smedley, 4/5/41, Forster, 4/7/41, 296, Ainsworth, 1/25/41.
3. Morgan MS., Dickens to Macready, 3/11/41.
4. *Let.*, I, 307, Forster, 3/18/41.
5. Ibid., 293, 298, 302, Cattermole, 1/14,30/41, 2/26/41.
6. Kitton, *Pen and Pencil*, 178-80.
7. *Let.*, I, 296, Beard, 1/23/41, 298, Mitton, 2/4/41.
8. Ibid., 299, Mitton, 2/8/41.
9. Ibid., 302, Cattermole, 2/26/41.
10. Hunt. MS., Dickens to Mitton, 3/9/41, partly quoted in *Let.*, I, 303.
11. *Victorian Review*, 3/1/84, 439. There is a copy in V. and A. The date of the notice was 3/8/41.
12. *Let.*, I, 308, Scott, 3/22/41.
13. Ibid., 278, Harford, 11/25/40.
14. Ibid., 293, 1/15/41.
15. *Coll. P.*, I, 30-1, Preface to *Evenings of a Working Man*.
16. Morgan MS., Dickens to Macready, 8/21/41.
17. *Coll. P.*, I, 30-31.
18. *Let.*, I, 213, Overs, 5/8/39.
19. Ibid., 229, 9/27/39.
20. Ibid., 248, 251, 254, 256, 2/16/40, 3/7/40, 4/12/40, 4/?/40; a few supplementary sentences to the last of these from a facsimile in a clipping from an unidentified bookseller's catalogue, MS. Division, N. Y. Pub. Lib.
21. *Let.*, I, 285, Overs, 12/30/40.
22. Ibid., 270, Colburn, 8/19/40, 277, Cruikshank, 11/17/40, 310, Colburn, 4/1/41, Forster, 4/1/41, 314, Forster, 4/12/41, 321, Colburn, 5/27/47. The preface to the *Pic-Nic Papers* is dated July, 1841. Dickens collected material for two volumes and Colburn, *without* Dickens's connivance, pirated J. C. Neal's *Charcoal Sketches* from America to bring it up to three. See Eckel, 143-4, and *Let.*, III, 97-8, Yates, 3/29/59.
23. *Let.*, I, 312, Fletcher, 4/18/41.
24. Ibid., 315, Irving, 4/21/41.
25. Ibid., 322, Lady Blessington, 6/2/41.
26. Ibid., 324, Forster, 6/3/41.
27. Forster, 168.
28. *Let.*, I, 349, Forster, 9/12/41.
29. Trevelyan, *British History*, 252; Young, *Early Victorian England*, II, 444; Wilson, *Wound and Bow*, 18.
30. *Let.*, I, 282, Smith, 12/15/40.
31. Ibid., 346, Forster, 8/16/41.
32. Horne, *Spirit of Age*, 65-6, 69.
33. *Let.*, I, 344, Napier, 8/8/41, Forster, 8/16/41.
34. *Coll. P.*, II, 302-3, "The Fine Old English Gentleman"; also in Forster, 191-2.
35. Pope-Hennessy, 121.
36. For Dickens's acquaintance with

these two men, see *Let.*, I, 476, II, 387, Chesterton, 9/11/42, 4/12/52, I, 319, II, 78, Tracey, 5/11/41, 4/8/48.

37. *Let.*, I, 345, Forster, 8/13/41.
38. Dickens did not, however, believe in "physical-force" Chartism, with its willingness to invoke revolutionary violence. See *H. W.*, 10/19/50, "A Poor Man's Tale of a Patent."
39. *Let.*, II, 695, Macready, 10/4/55.
40. Wilson, *Carlyle*, III, 80-1, quoting a letter of Carlyle to his brother, describing the dinner, which took place 2/23/40. Pope-Hennessy, 120, mistakenly says Dickens first saw Carlyle at his lecture on "Great Men" in Willis's rooms; this series was not given until two months later, in May.
41. Wilson, *Carlyle*, III, 104.
42. *Let.*, I, 322, Lovejoy, 5/31/41.
43. *Ibid.*, 325, 6/10/41.

Chapter 4 [pp. 319-337]

1. Chesterton, *Dickens*, 124.
2. *O. C. S.*, VII, 56, VIII, 71.
3. *Ibid.*, 70.
4. *Ibid.*, 71.
5. *Ibid.*, LVIII, 459.
6. *Ibid.*, XXXIX, 313.
7. *Ibid.*, XIX, 153.
8. *Ibid.*, XXVII, 213.
9. Huxley, 54-5.
10. Gissing, 197.
11. Chesterton, *Criticisms*, 53-4.
12. Warner, 43.
13. *O. C. S.*, XLII, 336.
14. *Ibid.*, LXII, 491, XI, 91, XXXIII, 262, LXII, 491.
15. *Ibid.*, V, 41.
16. *Ibid.*, V, 42-3.
17. *Ibid.*, XXXI, 247-8.
18. *Ibid.*, XLV, 361.
19. *Ibid.*, 358.
20. *B. R.*, LXXI, 587-8.
21. *Ibid.*, XIX, 155-6.
22. Mrs. John Wylie Barrow, whose husband was a son of Thomas

Culliford Barrow. Her judgment was communicated to me orally by her son, Mr. Archibald Barrow, of New York.

23. Wright, *Life*, 131.
24. *B. R.*, XXIII, 187.
25. *Ibid.*, LXXVII, 644.
26. *Ibid.*, XXXVIII, 311.
27. *Ibid.*, XLVI, 378.
28. *Ibid.*, XLIX, 402.
29. *Dick.*, VIII, 251.
30. *B. R.*, LV, 456.
31. *Ibid.*, LXVIII, 565-6.
32. *Ibid.*, LXXVII, 645.

Chapter 5 [pp. 338-353]

1. *Let.*, I, 307, Forster, 3/18/41.
2. *Ibid.*, 211, Beard, 4/11/39.
3. Ley, 102.
4. *Let.*, I, 312, Forster, 4/7/41, Fletcher, 4/8/41.
5. *Ibid.*, 327, Forster, 6/23/41.
6. *Ibid.*, 330, 6/30/41.
7. *Ibid.*, 325, 6/15/41.
8. *Ibid.*, 327, 6/23/41.
9. *Ibid.*
10. *Dick.*, XXXIV, 64.
11. *Let.*, I, 329, Cattermole, 6/26/41.
12. *Dick.*, XXVIII, 15.
13. *Let.*, I, 328, Forster, 6/26/41.
14. Forster, 176 fn.
15. *Let.*, I, 328, Forster, 6/26/41; Forster, 176 fn.
16. *Let.*, I, 328, 330, Forster, 6/26/41, 6/30/41.
17. *Coll. P.*, II, 331, speech, 6/25/41.
18. *Let.*, I, 329-30, Forster, 6/30/41.
19. Forster, 177.
20. *Let.*, I, 330-1, Forster, 6/30/41.
21. *Ibid.*, 329, Chapman, 6/26/41.
22. *Ibid.*, 332, Forster, 7/5/41.
23. *Ibid.*, 331, 6/30/41.
24. *Ibid.*, 332-3, 7/5/41.
25. *Ibid.*, 331, 6/30/41.
26. *Ibid.*, 334, 7/9/41.
27. *Ibid.*, 336-8, 7/11/41.
28. *Ibid.*, 285-7, draft letter to Chapman and Hall, [9/?/40].
29. *Ibid.*, 342-3, Chapman and Hall, 7/31/41.

30. Ibid., 342, Chattermole, 7/28/41.
31. Ibid., 344, 8/6/41.
32. Ibid., 341, Beard, 7/25/41.
33. Ibid., 343, 8/2/41; Hunt. MS., Dickens to Mitton, 8/11/41.
34. *Let.*, I, 345, Overs, 8/11/41; Morgan MS., Dickens to Macready, 8/21/41.
35. *Let.*, I, 346, Forster, 8/16/41.
36. Forster, 193-4.
37. Berg MS., Dickens to Mitton, 8/23/41.
38. Forster, 193.
39. Berg MS., Dickens to Mitton, 8/23/41.
40. Morgan MS., Dickens to Macready, 8/21/41.
41. *Let.*, I, 347-8, Macready, 8/24/41.
42. Morgan MS., Dickens to Overs, 8/24/41.
43. Ibid., Dickens to Macready, 8/21/41.
44. Ibid., Dickens to Overs, 8/24/41.
45. Ibid., 10/22/41.
46. *Let.*, I, 358, Overs, 10/14/41.
47. Morgan MS., Dickens to Overs, 10/23/41.
48. Ibid., 11/30/41.
49. *Let.*, I, 349, Mitton, 9/1/41; Christian, 483. Cf. W. B. Maxwell, "Mrs. Christian's Reminiscences of Dickens," *Review of English Studies*, January, 1951, which compares this article with its earlier version in the *Englishwoman's Domestic Magazine*, X, 336-44 (1871), and argues that the two Broadstairs summers referred to must have been in 1841 and 1842, not 1837 and 1839 as Pope-Hennessy, 70-3, 110, dates them. I had come to the same conclusions in this chapter (written in 1948) on the same grounds Maxwell outlines.
50. Christian, 484-7.
51. Ibid., 493.
52. Ibid., 486-7.
53. Ibid., 488.
54. Ibid., 484.
55. Ibid., 481.
56. Ibid., 481-2.
57. Ibid., 484.
58. Ibid., 489.
59. Ibid.
60. Ibid., 484.
61. Ibid., 494-5.
62. Ibid., 490-1.
63. *Let.*, I, 352-3, Chapman, 9/16/41.
64. Ibid., 348, Mitton, 8/30/41, 9/1,3/41.
65. Forster, 194-5.
66. Ibid., 194 fn.
67. *Let.*, I, 352, Hall, 9/14/41.
68. Ibid., Forster, 9/13/41.

PART FIVE

Chapter 1 [pp. 357-377]

1. P. P., XLVI, 650.
2. *Let.*, I, 352, Hall, 9/14/41.
3. Rosenbach MS., Dickens to Andrew Bell, 10/12/41.
4. *Let.*, I, 354, Forster, 9/22/41.
5. Ibid., 546, 11/2/43.
6. Ibid., 353, 9/19/41.
7. Ibid., 354, 9/22/41.
8. Morgan MS., Dickens to Macready, 9/21/41.
9. *Let.*, I, 355, Forster, [9/23/41].
10. Macready, *Diaries*, 9/22,23/41.
11. Hunt. MS., Macready to Dickens, "Thursday," [9/23/41].
12. *Let.*, I, 355, Forster, [9/27/41]; Hunt. MS., Macready to Dickens, 9/28/41; Morgan MS., Dickens to Macready, 9/29/41.
13. Morgan MS., Maclise to Catherine Dickens, [9/20 or 27/41].
14. *Let.*, I, 355, Forster, [9/27/41].
15. Ibid., 355-6, Clark, 9/28/41, 356, Irving, 9/28/41.
16. Forster, 198.
17. *Let.*, I, 357, Beard, 10/12/41.
18. Ibid., 358, Napier, 10/21/41.
19. Forster, 198.
20. *Let.*, I, 358, Mitton, 10/17/41.
21. Ibid., 362, 11/18/41.

22. Macready, *Diaries,* 5/23/40;
Cockburn, I, 272.
23. Clark, *Letters,* 377.
24. Latimer, 338.
25. Oberholtzer, 336, 345.
26. Payne, 7.
27. *Let.,* I, 366, Marjoribanks,
12/11/41.
28. Kitton, *Pen and Pencil,* 36.
29. Forster, 199.
30. *Let.,* I, 365, Alexander, 12/2/41.
31. Ibid., Mrs. Hall, 12/2/41.
32. Ibid., 366, Miss Coutts,
12/14/41.
33. Ibid., 367, Miss Talfourd,
12/16/41.
34. Chorley, I, 187.
35. Pope-Hennessy, 159.
36. Forster, 199.
37. Macready, *Diaries,* 1/1/42.
38. Forster, 199.
39. Ibid., 200, n. 188.
40. A. N., I, 5, 1, 3.
41. *Let.,* I, 372, Mitton, 1/3/42.
42. A. N., I, 3.
43. Ibid., 5.
44. Millar MS., Dickens to Brougham,
9/2/41, 12/17,27/41, 1/3/42.
45. A. N., I, 7; Berg MS., Dickens to
Frederick Dickens, 1/3/42.
46. Forster, 200.
47. A. N., I, 6.
48. Berg MS., Dickens to Frederick
Dickens, 1/30/42.
49. *Let.,* I, 548, Beard, 5/1/42.
50. Ibid., 381, Mitton, 1/31/42.
51. Ibid., 373, Forster, 1/17/42.
52. Ibid., 380, 1/29/41; A. N., II, 14,
16; Berg MS., Dickens to Frederick Dickens, 1/30/42.
53. *Let.,* I, 416, Forster, 3/22/42.
54. Ibid., 374, 1/21/42; Berg MS.,
Dickens to Frederick Dickens,
1/30/42.
55. A. N., II, 19-20.
56. Ibid., 21.
57. *Let.,* I, 374, Forster, 1/21/42.
58. A. N., II, 21.
59. *Let.,* I, 377, Forster, 1/28/42.
60. Payne, 14.
61. Ibid., 9, quoting Worcester *Aegis.*

62. Ibid., 14.
63. *Let.,* I, 373, 377, Forster,
1/17,28/42.
64. Payne, 12-3.
65. *Let.,* I, 379, Forster, 1/28/42.
66. A. N., II, 22.
67. Wilkins, 13, quoting Fields, *Yesterdays.*
68. *Let.,* I, 377, Forster, 1/28/42.
69. Payne, 17, 4.
70. Ibid., 5.
71. Wilkins, 13.
72. A. N., III, 23-4.
73. Payne, 20, 24.
74. Ibid., 27-30, 5, 32.
75. Ibid., 32.
76. Forster Coll., MS. presented by
Joe Field to Dickens and by
Dickens to Forster.
77. Payne, 36, quoting letter from
Charles Parsons to T. W. Hig-
ginson.
78. Winter, 108; cf. *Let.,* I, 419, Maclise, 3/22/42, on similar doings
in New York.
79. Payne, 36.
80. Ibid., 42; Dana MS., Felton to
Cleveland, 1/24/42.
81. Payne, 56, 54.
82. Ibid., 44-7.
83. *Dick.,* VI, 211, quoting Mrs. J. L.
Motley to her husband,
2/5/42.
84. Payne, 40.
85. *Let.,* I, 378-9, Forster, 1/28/42.
86. Putnam, 477-9; Payne, 50.
87. Putnam, 478.
88. *Let.,* I, 378, Forster, 1/28/42.
89. Putnam, 480.
90. *Let.,* I, 381, Mitton, 1/31/42.
91. Ibid., 378, Forster, 1/28/42.
92. Latimer, 338.
93. Payne, 43-4.
94. Ibid., 55, quoting R. H. Dana's
Diary, 1/27/42.
95. Dana MS., R. H. Dana, Jr.,
2/5/42.
96. Ibid., R. H. Dana, Sr., to Mrs.
Arnold, 2/14/42.
97. James, I, 58.
98. Payne, 37.

99. Latimer, 338-9.
100. Dana MS., Felton to Cleveland, 1/24/42.
101. *Let.*, I, 379, Forster, 1/28/42.
102. *Let.*, I, 380, Forster, 1/29/42. It is not clear whether Dickens had the misconception that all New England was one "state" or whether this was merely his way of saying "this state *in* New England."
103. A. N., III, 27-50.
104. Ibid., IV, 61-7.
105. Ibid., 65.
106. Ibid., 66.
107. *Dick.*, VI, 211.
108. A. N., V, 75.
109. *Let.*, I, 379, Forster, 1/29/42.
110. See the Alexander portrait of Dickens and the Thompson portrait of Longfellow, in Dana, frontispiece.
111. Dana, 59-60, quoting Longfellow to his father, 1/30/42; incomplete in Longfellow, 414.
112. Ibid., 60.
113. A. N., III, 55-7.
114. Dana, 61.
115. Payne, 77.
116. Dana, 59, quoting Longfellow to Ward, 1/30/42.
117. *Let.*, I, 378, Forster, 1/28/42.
118. Payne, 93-4.
119. Wilkins, 21-2; Payne, 95.
120. Wilkins, 23.
121. Ibid., 24-9.
122. *Coll. P.*, II, 335-9, speech, 2/1/42.
123. Ibid., 336.
124. Ibid., 337.
125. Ibid., 338.
126. Ibid., 339.
127. Wilkins, 34; Pope-Hennessy, 262.
128. Chesterton, *Dickens*, 142-4.
129. Ibid.
130. Fields, *Yesterdays*, quoted by Payne, 96.
131. Wilkins, 58, 66-7, 77.
132. Ibid., 65-6.
133. Ibid., 86.
134. Ibid., 87.

Chapter 2 [pp. 378-394]

1. *Let.*, I, 379, Forster, 1/29/42; Payne, 110.
2. Payne, 122; Dana, 62-3.
3. Dana, 63.
4. *Let.*, I, 394, Forster, 2/28/42.
5. Payne, 122.
6. Ibid., 131-2.
7. Dana, 64, quoting Felton to Sumner, 2/8/42; also in Payne, 132.
8. A. N., I, 68.
9. Payne, 133. There is a photograph of Governor Davis's house and Dickens's bedroom in Wilkins, f. 90.
10. Dana, 64-5; Payne, 134.
11. *Let.*, I, 407, Sumner, 3/13/42.
12. Prescott, letter to his wife, 6/4-7/42.
13. *Let.*, I, 383-4, Forster, 2/17/42; A. N., V, 69-70. No explanation is ever given for the frequency with which Kate suffered from this swollen face.
14. *Let.*, I, 384, Forster, 2/17/42.
15. Wilkins, 97. This dinner took place 2/7/42.
16. *Let.*, I, 386, Forster, 2/24/42.
17. *Coll. P.*, II, 341-2, speech, 2/?/42.
18. *Let.*, I, 386, Forster, 2/24/42.
19. Ibid., 387.
20. Ibid., 391, Chapman, 2/24/42.
21. Ibid., 386, Forster, 2/24/42.
22. Ibid., 390.
23. Ibid., 386.
24. Ibid., 388.
25. Ibid., 389.
26. Ibid., 388.
27. Putnam, 479.
28. Wilkins, 102, quoting New Haven *Commercial Herald.*
29. *Let.*, I, 385, Forster, 2/17/42.
30. Ibid., 384.
31. A. N., V, 75-6.
32. Minnigerode, 72; A. N., VI, 78-9, 83.
33. Minnigerode, 21, 23.
34. *Let.*, I, 385, Forster, 2/17/42.
35. *Payne*, 56. Payne is mistaken, however, in saying that Colden went

to Boston with the invitation to the ball; Colden was ill and sent the letter by a friend, a Mr. Blake.

36. Williams, *Irving*, II, 117, quoting Maunsell T. Fields, *Memories of Many Men* (1874), 31, accepts Fields's story that Irving disliked Dickens and thought him "outrageously vulgar in dress, manners, and mind." Williams also refers to Pierre Irving's MS. notes of a conversation with Washington Irving, 4/22/51 (in the possession of Gabriel Wells in 1945), and to E. A. Duykinck, MS. Diary, 6/24/59, 12/1/59, as further support. But W. G. Wilkins, *Dick.*, XII, 274, points out that Irving *wept* on parting from Dickens at Washington (*Let.*, I, 409, Forster, 3/17/42) and turned up again at Baltimore for another farewell (*Let.*, I, 411, Irving, 3/21/42, 416, Forster, 3/23/42, 419, William Guy, 3/23/42), which hardly has the appearance of dislike. And Pacey, *Washington Irving and Charles Dickens*, adduces evidence that Fields was an exaggerator, and quotes L. Gaylord Clark's account of Irving's regard for Dickens from *N. Y. Pub. Lib. Bulletin*, XLII, 950. Noting that the conversations with Pierre Irving and Duykinck took place years later, Pacey suggests that after the publication of *American Notes* and *Martin Chuzzlewit*, Irving's patriotic revulsion altered his earlier esteem, and that his memory then magnified and distorted details that had not troubled him in 1842. The combination of these arguments and the letters of the time I think conclusive.

37. Wilkins, 110-4; Minnigerode, 277-80.

38. *Let.*, I, 385, Forster, 2/17/42.

39. Wilkins, 112, quoting N. Y. *Evening Post*, 2/15/42.

40. Minnigerode, 277.

41. Ibid., 281-2.

42. Wilkins, 114, quoting Nichols, *Forty Years in America*; *Let.*, I, 385, Forster, 2/17/42.

43. Minnigerode, 282.

44. Wilkins, 115.

45. *Let.*, I, 385, Forster, 2/17/42.

46. There is a possibility that after dining at the Coldens', they went to the Bowery Theatre, where *The Pickwick Club* and *Nicholas Nickleby* were being performed in Dickens's honor.

47. *Let.*, I, 386, Forster, 2/17/42.

48. Wilkins, 124, 149-50.

49. Forster, 219-20.

50. *Let.*, I, 387, Forster, 2/24/42.

51. Clark, 376.

52. Wilson, *Halleck*, 437. The interrupter was Charles Augustus Davis, "Major Jack Downing."

53. *Coll. P.*, II, 344-5, speech, 2/18/42.

54. Wilkins, 139-47.

55. Ibid., 242-3, quoting N. Y. *Tribune*, 2/14/42; *Dick.*, IV, 206.

56. Wilkins, 244-5, quoting N. Y. *Tribune*, 2/21/42.

57. *Let.*, I, 390-1, Forster, 2/27/42.

58. *Dick.*, XII, 246.

59. Pacey, 332-9.

60. *Let.*, I, 394, Forster, 2/28/42.

61. Wilkins, 116-7.

62. Putnam, 480.

63. *Dick.*, XLIV, 187. The Park repertory, according to Malcolm Morley, included *Nina Sforza*, *London Assurance*, *What Will the World Say*, *Charles O'Malley*, and *The School for Scandal*. From Maurice Inman, Inc., I have a copy of an a.l.s. to Mitchell, 2/16/42, expressing the warm admiration with which Dickens had followed the actor's previous career in London.

64. Dana, 66, quoting Felton to Ward, 2/22/42.

65. A. N., VI, 84.

66. Dana, 67, quoting Dickens to Longfellow, 2/23/42; also in Longfellow, 416.
67. Ibid.
68. A. N., VI, 89-91.
69. *Let.*, I, 398, Forster, 3/6/42.
70. A. N., VI, 85-8.
71. A. N., VI, 80.
72. *Let.*, I, 396-7, Forster, 3/6/42.
73. Ibid., 398.
74. Ibid., 399.
75. Ibid., 394, 2/28/42.

Chapter 3 [pp. 395-410]

1. A. N., VII, 94.
2. *Let.*, I, 390, Forster, 2/27/42, 393,
Maclise, 2/27/42.
3. Berg MS., Dickens to Putnam,
3/2/42.
4. *Let.*, I, 419 fn., Kate's postscript,
Dickens to Maclise, 3/22/42.
5. Ibid., 393-4, Forster, 2/28/42.
6. Ibid., 395, 3/6/42.
7. Ibid.
8. Ibid., 396.
9. A. N., VII, 95.
10. *Let.*, I, 400, Forster, 6/13/42.
11. *Dick.*, XXXVI, 115; Grubb, *Personal and Literary Relations of
Dickens and Poe*, 19-20, 21.
Grubb quotes Dickens's letters to
Poe, 3/16/42, 11/27/42, from
Harrison's *Works of Poe, Letters*, XVII, 107, 109. Dickens
failed to find a British publisher
for Poe, as the second of these
letters shows.
12. Wilkins, 153.
13. Ibid., 159.
14. *Let.*, II, 332; Putnam, 7/24/51.
15. Wilkins, 158.
16. *Let.*, I, 399, Forster, 3/13/42,
Colden, 3/10/42.
17. A. N., VIII, 113; Putnam, 591.
18. Putnam, 591.
19. *Let.*, I, 400, Forster, 3/13/42.
20. A. N., VIII, 117.
21. *Let.*, I, 401, Forster, 3/15/42.
22. Ibid., 402.
23. Ibid., 406, Sumner, 3/13/42; Berg

MS., Dickens to Fonblanque,
3/12/42.
24. Berg MS., Dickens to Albany Fonblanque, 3/12/42. Some of this
material is in A. N., VIII, 118,
120.
25. A. N., VIII, 117-8.
26. Jackson, 49-50.
27. Berg MS., Dickens to Fonblanque,
3/12/42. The interview with
President Tyler was on 3/10/42.
28. Ibid.
29. Ibid.
30. Wilkins, 167.
31. Morgan MS., John Quincy Adams
to Catherine Dickens, 3/16/42.
32. Wilkins, 168-9.
33. *Let.*, I, 401, Forster, 3/15/42.
34. Wilkins, 170.
35. *Let.*, I, 401, Forster, 3/15/42.
36. Ibid., 407, Felton, 3/14/42.
37. Ibid., 400-1, Forster, 3/13/42.
38. Ibid., 409, Forster, 3/17/42.
39. A. N., VIII, 113.
40. Putnam, 592.
41. *Let.*, I, 409, Forster, 3/21/42.
42. A. N., IX, 137.
43. *Let.*, I, 410, Forster, 3/21/42; Putnam, 592-3; Wilkins, 177-92.
Dickens was in Richmond from
the evening of 3/17/42 to the
morning of 3/20. Wilkins gives
a full account of a private supper
in his honor at the Exchange
Hotel on the night of his arrival
there, quoting the speeches, including, 185-7, Dickens's response, which is not among his
speeches in *Coll. P.*, II.
44. *Let.*, I, 410, Forster, 3/21/42.
45. Ibid.
46. Morgan MS., Macready, 3/22/42;
also *Let.*, I, 412-5. The printed
version, however, which is taken
from the text of the Georgina
Hogarth-Mary Dickens edition of
Dickens's Letters, is incomplete
and inaccurate in various details.
47. Ibid.
48. Ibid.
49. Ibid.

50. Berg MS., Dickens to Fonblanque, 3/12/42.
51. *Let.*, I, 415-6, Forster, 3/22/42.
52. A. N., IX, 139.
53. *Let.*, I, 416, Forster, 3/23/42.
54. A. N., IX, 138.
55. *Let.*, III, 616, Lanman, 2/5/68.
56. Berg MS., Dickens to Frederick Dickens, 3/22/42.
57. Putnam, 478.
58. A. N., IX, 140.
59. *Let.*, I, 420, Forster, 3/28/42.
60. Ibid., 421.
61. Ibid., 422.
62. Ibid.
63. Ibid., 422-3.
64. Ibid., 423.
65. Ibid., 425, 4/1/42.
66. Wilkins, 202.
67. A. N., XI, 155-6.
68. *Let.*, I, 425, 421, Forster, 4/2/42, 3/28/42.
69. Ibid., 425-6, Forster, 4/2/42.
70. Ibid., 426, 4/3/42.
71. Ibid., 424, 4/1/42.
72. Ibid., 426, 4/2/42.
73. Ibid., 4/3/42.
74. Ibid., 4/2/42.
75. A. N., XI, 158-60.
76. Berg MS., Dickens to Frederick Dickens, 4/4/42.
77. *Let.*, I, 416, Mitton, 3/22/42.
78. Ibid., 431, Forster, 4/15/42.
79. Ibid., 446, Felton, 4/29/42.
80. Ibid., 432, Forster, 4/15/42.
81. Wilkins, 207-9.
82. A. N., XI, 164; Wilkins, 206, 208.
83. A. N., XII, 166.
84. Ibid., 169.
85. Ibid., 170.
86. Ibid., 171.

Chapter 4 [pp. 411-426]

1. *Let.*, I, 436, Forster, 4/17/42.
2. A. N., XII, 175.
3. *Let.*, I, 436, Forster, 4/17/42.
4. A. N., XIII, 177-81; Snyder, 9, 12, 13, 16.
5. A. N., XIII, 181; Snyder, 15.
6. A. N., XIII, 182.
7. Snyder, 18.
8. *Let.*, I, 435, Forster, 4/16/42.
9. Ibid., 410, 3/21/42.
10. Ibid., 432-3, 4/15/42.
11. Ibid., 433.
12. Ibid.
13. Ibid., 434.
14. A. N., XIV, 186-7.
15. *Let.*, I, 436-7, Forster, 4/20,24/42.
16. Putnam, 596.
17. *Let.*, I, 437, Forster, 4/24/42; A. N., XIV, 192-3.
18. Ibid.
19. Ibid.
20. Ibid.
21. Putnam, 596.
22. *Let.*, I, 438, Forster, 4/24/42.
23. Putnam, 596.
24. *Let.*, I, 438, Forster, 4/24/42.
25. Putnam, 596.
26. *Let.*, I, 438, Forster, 4/24/42.
27. Putnam, 597.
28. *Let.*, I, 438, Forster, 4/24/42.
29. Putnam, 597.
30. A. N., XIV, 195.
31. Berg MS., Dickens to Frederick Dickens, 3/22/42.
32. *Let.*, I, 454, Forster, 5/3/42.
33. Berg MS., Dickens to Frederick Dickens, 3/22/42.
34. *Let.*, I, 429, Mitton, 4/4/42.
35. Ibid., 454, Forster, 5/3/42.
36. Putnam, 478.
37. Ibid., 594.
38. *Let.*, I, 440, Forster, 4/26/42. The newspaper was the Cleveland *Plain Dealer*, and the article, to which Dickens also refers in A. N., 198, was reprinted from the Alexandria (D.C.) *Index*. He evidently did not notice this fact. (Archer W. Shane, *The Plain Dealer: One Hundred Years in Cleveland*, 45. Knopf, 1942.)
39. *Let.*, I, 440, Forster, 4/26/42.
40. A. N., XIV, 199.
41. *Let.*, I, 440, Forster, 4/26/42.
42. Ibid., 450-1, Austin, 5/1/42.
43. Ibid., 452.
44. Wilkins, 232.

45. Ibid., 249-53.
46. Ibid., 253-5.
47. *Let.*, I, 444, Felton, 4/29/42.
48. Ibid., 446, Editor of *Evening Post*, 4/30/42.
49. Wilkins, 249, quoting letter to Seaton, 4/30/42; *Let.*, I, 446 fn.
50. *Let.*, I, 451-2, Austin, 5/1/42.
51. Wilkins, 246-7.
52. Forster, 272.
53. Wilkins, 146.
54. *Let.*, I, 453, Forster, 5/3/42.
55. Ibid., 408, Felton, 3/14/42.
56. Ibid., 413, Macready, 3/22/42.
57. Ibid., 443, Colden, 4/29/42.
58. Ibid., Mrs. Colden, 4/29/42.
59. Ibid., 455, Forster, 5/12/42.
60. Ibid., 448, Beard, 5/1/42.
61. A. N., XV, 201.
62. *Let.*, I, 455, Forster, 5/22/42; A. N., XV, 205.
63. A. N., XV, 211.
64. *Let.*, I, 457, Colden, 5/21/42.
65. A. N., XV, 206-7.
66. *Dick.*, XXXVIII, 85, points out that Dickens was mistaken in believing either that the officers of the garrison belonged to the Coldstream Guards (*Let.*, I, 455, Forster, 5/12/42) or that Lord Mulgrave was conected with that regiment. He was a lieutenant in the Scotch Fusilier guards and the garrison consisted of the 23rd and 85th.
67. *Let.*, I, 442, Colden, 4/29/42.
68. Ibid., 459, Forster, 5/26/42.
69. Ibid., 456, Felton, 5/21/42.
70. *Let.*, I, 456, Felton, 5/21/42. Dickens used a version of *Past Two O'Clock in the Morning* by Mrs. Gore. *Let.*, I, 690, Lemon, 8/6/45.
71. Ibid., 445, Felton, 4/29/42.
72. Transcript given me by Maurice Inman of Dickens's letter to W. B. Mitchell, 2/16/42; *Let.*, I, 447, Mitchell, 4/30/42.
73. *Let.*, I, 452, Austin, 5/1/42.
74. Ibid., 456, Felton, 5/21/42.
75. *Dick.*, XXXVIII, 17-9.

76. *Let.*, I, 458, Forster, 5/26/42.
77. Ibid., 459.
78. Ibid.
79. Forster, f. 276, has a facsimile of the playbill.
80. *Let.*, I, 389, Forster, 2/24/42.
81. Ibid., 457, Colden, 5/21/42.
82. Ibid., 460, Chapman, 6/2/42.
83. A. N., XV, 212-8, XVI, 219.
84. Wilkins, 233, quoting Hone's diary, 6/8/42.
85. *Let.*, I, 417 fn., 461, Mitchell, 6/6/42.
86. Wilkins, 233.
87. *Let.*, I, 459, Forster, 5/26/42.

Chapter 5 [pp. 427-446]

1. *Let.*, I, 464, Mrs. Colden, 7/15/42.
2. Ibid., 471, Felton, 7/31/42.
3. A. N., XVI, 224-6.
4. *Let.*, I, 472, Chapman, 8/3/42; Forster, 287, n. 240.
5. Dent, 255.
6. *Let.*, I, 472, Chapman, 8/3/42; *Dick.*, XXXVI, 253, Dickens to Lady Holland, 7/11/42.
7. *Let.*, I, 471-2, Chapman, 8/3/42.
8. Forster, 228; Broderip, II, 124, quoting Thomas Hood's letter to Mrs. Elliott, 7/11/42, shows that Forster was mistaken in remembering Talfourd as present.
9. *Let.*, I, 462, Beard, 7/11/42.
10. Ibid., 469, Sumner, 7/31/42.
11. *Dick.*, XXXVI, 253, Dickens to Lady Holland, 7/11/42.
12. *Let.*, I, 468, Sumner, 7/31/42.
13. *Dick.*, XXXVI, 253, Dickens to Lady Holland, 7/8/42.
14. Ibid., 7/11/42.
15. *Let.*, I, 463, Smith, 7/14/42.
16. E.g., *Let.*, I, 480, Austin, 9/25/42; others are also detectable by parallels in content and often in wording.
17. *Let.*, I, 463, Smith, 7/14/42, 465, Beard, 7/19/42.
18. Ibid., 464, Forster, 7/18/42.
19. Ibid., 468, Sumner, 7/31/42.
20. Ibid.

21. Ibid., 463, Mrs. Colden, 7/15/42.
22. Charles Dickens, Jr., *Reminiscences*, 8. The comic song quoted is by Thomas Hudson; its complete words are given in *Dick.*, VIII, 278.
23. *Let.*, I, 468, Colden, 7/31/42, 471, Chapman, 8/3/42, 470, Felton, 7/31/42.
24. Ibid., 463, Mrs. Colden, 7/15/42.
25. Ibid., 473, Forster, 8/11/42.
26. Ibid., 472, Chapman, 8/3/42.
27. Ibid., 478, Forster, 9/16/42.
28. Ibid., 473, 8/11/42.
29. Ibid., 480, Austin, 9/25/42.
30. Ibid., 473, Forster, 8/7/42.
31. Ibid., 478, [9/?/42].
32. Ibid., 479, 9/22/42.
33. Ibid., 478, 9/16/42.
34. Ibid., 477, Hone, 9/16/42.
35. Ibid., 474, Felton, 9/1/42.
36. A. N., Dedication, xv; *Let.*, I, 479, Forster, 9/20/42.
37. *Let.*, I, 482, Chapman, 10/15/42.
38. Ibid., 479, Forster, 9/20/42.
39. A. N., Suppressed First Chapter, xx.
40. Ibid., xxi-ii.
41. Forster, 284.
42. *Let.*, I, 479, Forster, 9/23/42.
43. Dana, 69-70, quoting Dickens to Longfellow, 9/28/42; also in Longfellow, I, 438.
44. Dana, 71, quoting Longfellow to Sumner, 10/16/42; also in Longfellow, I, 440.
45. Dana, 72.
46. Ibid.; Macready, *Diaries*, 10/6/42.
47. Dana, 73, quoting Longfellow to Freiligrath, 1/6/43, 79, quoting Longfellow to Forster, 12/15/42.
48. Ibid., 76.
49. Ibid., 73, quoting Longfellow to Freiligrath, 1/6/43.
50. Ibid.
51. Morgan MS., Dickens to Austin, 10/14/42.
52. Forster, 278-9.
53. Ibid., 278.
54. Forster, 279, says October 21st, but Longfellow, I, 440, quotes H. W.

L. letter to Charles Sumner, 10/16/42, giving it as the 22nd.
55. Dana, 76, quoting Longfellow to Forster, 10/19/42.
56. Ibid., 75.
57. *Coll. P.*, I, 13-9, has from this time a review of Lord Londonderry's "Letter to Lord Ashley," which Dickens published in the London *Morning Chronicle*, 10/20/42. Provoked by Lord Londonderry's opposition to the Mines and Collieries Bill, it is a scorching attack sharpened by ironical commendations of its victim's literary "style."
58. Dana, 80-1, quoting Dickens to Longfellow, 12/29/42; also in Longfellow, I, 451.
59. Forster, 288-9.
60. *Let.*, I, 478, Forster, 9/10/42.
61. Ibid., 485, Smith, 10/22/42.
62. Ibid., 497-8, Felton, 12/31/42.
63. Forster, 289.
64. *Let.*, I, 498, Felton, 12/31/42.
65. Forster, 289-90.
66. Christie gives the date of Georgina Hogarth's birth as 1/22/27.
67. *Let.*, I, 519, Mrs. Hogarth, 5/8/43.
68. Ibid., 494, Beard, 12/18/42.
69. Forster, 300, n. 251.
70. Ibid., 290.
71. *Let.*, I, 487, Coutts, 11/12/42.
72. Forster, 290.
73. *Let.*, I, 489, Frith, 11/15/42.
74. Frith, 69.
75. *Let.*, I, 488, Macready, 11/12/42.
76. *Coll. P.*, II, 308, Prologue to *The Patrician's Daughter*.
77. *Let.*, I, 490, Forster, 11/25/42.
78. Longfellow landed on 11/6/42, Longfellow, I, 445.
79. *Let.*, I, 483, Chapman, 10/15/42.
80. Mackenzie, 219; Clark, *Library*, II, 75.
81. Dana, 77.
82. Minnigerode, 283.
83. Dana, 74. Dickens's antislavery material in Chapter XVII, 227-41, was largely borrowed and adapted from Theodore Weld's *Ameri-*

can Slavery as it is, Anti-Slavery Society, 1839. (See Louise H. Johnson, "The Source of the Chapter on Slavery in Dickens's 'American Notes,'" *Am. Lit.* XIV, 427).

84. Dana, 77.
85. Emerson, 312.
86. Minnigerode, 283.
87. *Dick.*, XXXVIII, 10.
88. Forster Coll., newspaper clippings.
89. Trevelyan, *Macaulay*, II, 62, 66-7; Napier, 398, Macaulay to Napier, 7/25/42.
90. *Let.*, I, 494, Mrs. Trollope, 12/16/42.
91. A. N., XVIII, 242.
92. Ibid., 244.
93. Ibid.
94. Ibid., 245.

PART SIX

Chapter 1 [pp. 449-468]

1. *Let.*, I, 503, Hunt, 1/3/43.
2. Ibid., 498, Felton, 12/31/42.
3. Ibid., 506, Stanfield, 2/3/43.
4. *Coll. P.*, I, 142-3, To the *Examiner*, "International Copyright," 7/16/42, 142 fn., observes that it was also published in the *Athenaeum*; same letter in Elkins Coll., addressed to the *United Services Journal.*
5. *Let.*, I, 496, Lea and Blanchard, 12/28/42; Kerslake, 80.
6. *Let.*, I, 504, Napier, 1/21/43.
7. *Coll. P.*, I, 20, To the London *Times*, "International Copyright," 1/16/43.
8. Elkins Coll., rough proof of proposed prospectus of Society of Authors, drafted by Dickens, 5/3/43. The first meeting was 4/8/43; the second was to be 5/13.
9. *Let.*, I, 516, Babbage, 4/27/43.
10. Parrish Coll., resolutions passed 5/17/43, Dickens presiding.
11. Dana, 80, quoting Dickens to

Longfellow, 12/29/42; also in Longfellow, I, 451.
12. N. Y. Pub. Lib., MS. Division, Myers Vol. 2323, Dickens to Clark, 3/2/43.
13. *Let.*, I, 465, Miss Pardoe, 7/19/42.
14. Ibid., 505, Smith, 2/1/43.
15. Ibid., 512, 3/10/43.
16. Ibid., 517-8, Jerrold, 5/3/43.
17. Ibid., 429, Mitton, 4/2/42.
18. Ibid., 493, Pettigrew, 12/7/42.
19. Ibid., Mitton, 12/7/42. There is, indeed, a letter by John Dickens (Morgan MS., John Dickens to 'Miss Coutts and Co.,' 3/24/32), claiming that it had been understood before his son left for America that the Alphington house was to be given up in July, and begging for a loan—which was refused. If its statements are true, there was some intermediate place of residence, but John Dickens in want of money is not a reliable authority.
20. Ibid., 516, Miss Coutts, 4/24/43.
21. Ibid., 507, Mitton, 2/17/43.
22. Ibid., 517, Frederick Dickens, 5/2/43.
23. Ibid., 507, Forster, 2/12/43.
24. Ibid., 513, Beard, 3/21/43, 514, Miss Coutts, 3/21/43.
25. Forster, 294.
26. Ibid.; *Dick.*, XXIII, 30.
27. *Let.*, I, 545, Forster, 11/2/43.
28. Forster, 302.
29. Waugh, *Hundred Years*, 58-9.
30. Forster, 302; M. C., XII, 215.
31. Forster, 302.
32. N. Y. Pub. Lib., MS Division, Dickens to L. Gaylord Clark, 3/2/43.
33. *Let.*, I, 522, Moir, 5/19/43.
34. Ibid., 509, Felton, 3/2/43.
35. Ibid., 517, Forster, 5/3/43; Forster, 295.
36. *Let.*, I, 521, Wilson, 5/13/43.
37. Morgan MS., Dickens to Macready, 5/16/43.

38. Forster, 295, evidently forgot the postponement and gives the date of the dinner as 5/20/43.
39. Let., I, 523, Talfourd, 5/20/43.
40. Ibid., 475, Felton, 9/1/42.
41. Dick., XXXI, 192, quoting Richards, Howe. The dinner was on 5/30/43.
42. Forster Coll., Carlyle to Forster, 12/5/71, often quoted, e.g., Dick., XIX, 45.
43. Let., I, 533, Forster, 8/15/43.
44. Holland, 589, quoting Sydney Smith to Dickens, 7/1/43; Pope-Hennessy, 192-3.
45. Forster, 302.
46. Ibid., 302-3.
47. Calhoun-Heaney, 275.
48. Waugh, Hundred Years, 60-1.
49. Forster, 303.
50. Calhoun-Heaney, 276.
51. Forster, 302-3.
52. Let., I, 526-7, Forster, 6/18/43.
53. Straus, 199.
54. Let., I, 527, Forster, 6/18/43.
55. Forster, 303.
56. Waugh, Hundred Years, 62.
57. Let., I, 529, Mitton, 7/22/43.
58. Morgan MS., Dickens to Felton, 9/1/43; incomplete and inaccurate in Let., I, 534-7.
59. Let., I, 527, Forster, [7/?/43].
60. Ibid., 528, Beard, 7/18/43.
61. Ibid., 529-30, Miss Coutts, 7/26/43.
62. Ibid., 531, Miss Coutts, 7/28/43, 8/7/43.
63. Broderip, 143.
64. Let., I, 532, Miss Coutts, 8/7/43, 533, Gentlemen of the Stock Exchange, 8/28/43.
65. Ibid., 532, Miss Coutts, 8/7/43.
66. Ibid., 534, Forster, [8/?/43].
67. Morgan MS., Dickens to Felton, 9/1/43. See n. 58 above.
68. Ibid.
69. Macready, Diaries, 8/26/43.
70. Forster, 295; Morgan MS., Dickens to Felton, 9/1/43. See n. 58 above.
71. Macready, Diaries, 9/1/43.

72. Morgan MS., Dickens to Macready, 9/1/43; also in Macready, Diaries, where it is mistakenly dated 9/1/49; Let., I, 538, Marryat, 9/6/43, 537-8, Forster, 9/6/43.
73. Morgan MS., Dickens to Macready, 9/1/43.
74. Macready, Diaries, 9/2/43.
75. Let., I, 539, Hood, 9/12/43.
76. Ibid., 538, Marryat, 9/6/43.
77. Ibid., 506, memo to Browne, [1843].
78. Forster, 297.
79. Coll. P., II, 348-51, speech, 10/5/43.
80. Wright, Life, 164-5, gives the founders as John Pound, a shoemaker of Portsmouth, and an unnamed chimney sweep of Windsor.
81. Let., I, 539, Starey, 9/12/43.
82. Barrett MS., Dickens to Miss Coutts, 9/16/43.
83. Let., I, 541, Starey, 9/24/43.
84. Ibid., 542, Forster, 9/24/43.
85. Ibid., 540, Napier, 9/16/43.
86. Ibid., 543, 10/17/43.
87. Ibid., 10/24/43.
88. Forster, 301, n. 260.
89. Wright, Life, 155.
90. Ibid., 159; Forster, 298.
91. Coll. P., II, 353, speech, 10/5/43.
92. Let., I, 546, Forster, 11/2/43.
93. Waugh, Hundred Years, 62.
94. Let., I, 544-5, Forster, 11/1/43.
95. Ibid.
96. Ibid., 545. The name of his Italian teacher is here given as Mariotti.
97. Forster, 307.
98. Let., I, 545-6, Forster, 11/2/43.
99. Ibid., 548, 11/10/43.
100. Forster, 307.
101. Let., I, 549, Forster, 11/19/43.
102. Forster, 308.
103. Let., I, 549, Forster, 11/19/43.
104. Forster, 299.
105. Let., I, 553, Felton, 1/2/44.
106. Calhoun-Heaney, 277; Eckel, 110-5.

107. *Let.*, I, 553, Felton, 1/2/44.
108. Ibid., 556, Macready, 1/3/44.
109. Carlyle, *Letters to Family*, 169-71, Jeannie Welsh, 12/23/43.

Chapter 2 [pp. 469-489]

1. *Let.*, I, 546, Forster, 11/2/43.
2. *M. C.*, XVI, 271. There was actually a General Pogram among the speakers at the Richmond dinner for Dickens on 3/16/42. See Wilkins, 182, 188.
3. *M. C.*, XXII, 375.
4. Ibid., XXXIV, 538. The "Watertoast Association" may have been suggested by the Brandywine Association.
5. Ibid., XVI, 259.
6. Ibid., 267.
7. Ibid., 269-70.
8. Ibid., XVII, 292.
9. Ibid., 290.
10. Ibid., 293.
11. Ibid., XXI, 351.
12. Ibid., XXII, 372.
13. Ibid., XXI, 349.
14. Ibid., XXXIV, 546. For the origin of the Literary Ladies, see Forster, 254, and *Let.*, I, 408, Felton, 3/14/42, and 426, Forster, 4/3/42.
15. *M. C.*, XXXIV, 538.
16. Ibid., XXXIII, 526.
17. Ibid., XVI, 280.
18. The reader will have to be kind enough to accept my assurance that Chesterton wrote this somewhere; but I have not located the source from which I took it down.
19. *Dick.*, XV, 58, quoting from Roosevelt, *Letters to His Children*, ed. Joseph Bucklin Bishop.
20. *M. C.*, XVII, 277.
21. Ibid., XXVII, 445-6.
22. Ibid., XXXVIII, 601-2.
23. Ibid., XLII, 657.
24. Ibid., XLVII, 725.
25. Ibid., XXXVI, 577-8.
26. Ibid., XXXIX, 603-4.
27. Ibid., 605.
28. Ibid., XXXIII, 517.
29. Ibid., 533.
30. Ibid., XIX, 318.
31. Ibid., XXV, 408.
32. Ibid., XLIX, 760.
33. Ibid., 763.
34. Morgan MS., Dickens to Wilkie Collins, 7/13/56, contains one of several statements by Dickens making it clear that the original of Pecksniff was Samuel Carter Hall (1800-89), editor of *The Amulet*, 1827-37, and of the *Art Union Monthly*, 1839-80. Cf. Osborne, *Mr. Pecksniff and His Prototype*.
35. *M. C.*, II, 13.
36. Ibid., 16.
37. Ibid., III, 38.
38. Ibid., XLIII, 672.
39. Ibid., LII, 815-6.
40. Ibid., LIV, 841.
41. Gissing, 123.
42. *C. C.*, III, 57-8.
43. Ibid., 47-8.
44. Ibid., I, 6.
45. Ibid., II, 30.
46. Ibid., III, 44.
47. Ibid., I, 8.
48. Ibid., I, 16.

Chapter 3 [pp. 490-506]

1. *Let.*, I, 553, Felton, 1/2/44.
2. Forster, 314, 316.
3. Ibid.
4. *Let.*, I, Felton, 1/2/44.
5. Morgan MS., Dickens to Mitton, 12/4/43.
6. Waugh, *Hundred Years*, facsimile f. 44.
7. London *Times* Lit. Supp., 1/25/1947, to Charles Smithson, 11/4/43. This letter also indicates that Dickens tried at first to borrow from Smithson in order to finance his trip to Italy.
8. Morgan MS., Dickens to Mitton, 12/4/43.

9. Forster, 101, n. 107.
10. Ibid., 128, n. 130.
11. Ibid., 102, n. 107.
12. Barham, II, diary, 10/17/38.
13. *N. N.*, XVI, XLVIII.
14. Forster, 321; *Let.*, I, 558 fn.
15. *Let.*, I, 559, Mitton, 1/7/44.
16. Application for injunction, quoted by Pope-Hennessy, 200.
17. *Let.*, I, 559, Mitton, 1/7/44.
18. Pope-Hennessy, 200.
19. *Let.*, I, 561, Forster, 1/18/44.
20. Ibid.
21. Ibid., 562, 1/20/44.
22. Ibid.
23. Ibid., 565, Blanchard, 1/29/44.
24. Ibid., 583, Talfourd, 3/19/44.
25. Ibid., 581-2, Mitton, 3/18/44.
26. Ibid., 598, Talfourd, 5/5/44.
27. Forster, 372.
28. *Let.*, I, 780, Forster, 8/?/46.
29. Ibid., 560, Maclise, Stanfield, and Forster, 1/17/44.
30. Rosenbach MS., Dickens to Thompson, 2/15/44.
31. *Let.*, I, 566, Chapman, 2/8/44.
32. Ibid., 567, Forster, 2/10/44.
33. Ibid., Mitton, 2/12/[44].
34. *Let.*, I, 567, Forster, 2/10/44. Possibly Forster dates this letter inaccurately. The letter to Mitton, 2/12/44, immediately following, distinctly says Dickens saw the *Carol* account Saturday night. If this is correct, that to Forster should be "Sunday Morning, 11 February, 1844."
35. Ibid., 568, Mitton, 2/12/[44].
36. Ibid.
37. Ibid.
38. Ibid.
39. Ibid., 598-9, Bradbury and Evans, 5/8/44.
40. Waugh, *Hundred Years*, 65.
41. See *Let.*, I, 567, Forster, 2/10/44. Such a profit would represent 40 per cent of the retail price.
42. Forster, 314.
43. Forster, 314-5 fn., quoting the financial statement.

44. Dexter, *Mr. and Mrs.*, 94-7, 2/26/44.
45. Ibid.
46. *Coll. P.*, II, 354-8, speech, 2/26/44.
47. Dexter, *Mr. and Mrs.*, 97, 2/26/44.
48. *Let.*, I, 572 fn.
49. Ibid., 574, Thompson, 2/28/44.
50. Ibid., 580, 3/11/44.
51. Ibid., 572 fn.
52. Ibid., 576, Weller, 3/1/44.
53. Ibid., 588, Thompson, 3/29/44.
54. Ibid., 572, Miss Weller, 2/27/44.
55. Ibid., 575, Weller, 3/1/44.
56. Ibid., 574, Thompson, 2/28/44.
57. Ibid.
58. Ibid., Fanny Burnett, 3/1/44.
59. Ibid., 573, Thompson, 2/28/44.
60. Ibid., 579, 3/11/44.
61. Ibid.
62. Ibid., 580.
63. Ibid., 3/13/44.
64. Ibid., 3/11/44.
65. Ibid., 3/13/44.
66. Ibid., 3/11/44.
67. Ibid., 3/13/44.
68. Ibid., 586, Fletcher, 3/24/44.
69. Ibid., 578, Mitton, 3/10/44.
70. Ibid., 594, 4/17/44.
71. Ibid., 595, 4/24/44.
72. Ibid., 598-600, Bradbury and Evans, 5/8/44.
73. Forster, 316.
74. Ibid., 325; *Let.*, I, 577, Forster, 3/10/44.
75. *Let.*, I, 578, Mitton, 3/10/44.
76. Ibid., 584, Overs, 3/21/44.
77. Ibid., 600, 5/10/44, 600 fn.
78. Ibid., 608, Forster, 6/28/44. *Evenings of a Working Man* was published by T. C. Newby.
79. Ibid., 576, Forster, 3/5/44.
80. Ibid., 595, 4/23/44.
81. Ibid., 588, Thompson, 3/29/44.
82. Ibid., 589, Mitton, 4/2/44, 590, Alfred Dickens, 4/3/44.
83. Dexter, *Mr. and Mrs.*, 98-9, 4/6/44.
84. *Let.*, I, 592, Miss Weller, 4/8/44.

85. Dexter, *Mr. and Mrs.*, 100, 4/6/44.
86. *Let.*, I, 592, Miss Weller, 4/8/44.
87. Ibid., 593.
88. Ibid., 591.
89. Ibid., 593. This is a curious episode, with strange emotional overtones. One wonders if Dickens does not suspect that he himself was the unknown who had made an impression on Christiana Weller's heart—left "other footprints in the field" —and if, in his letter to her, he may not be assuming a playful manner in order to be able to say at all what he plainly *does* say: "I love you, but I am already married, so I hope you will take my friend Thompson." How seriously Dickens means this the reader will decide for himself, but it does not sound like pure fooling, nor would the circumstances be altogether appropriate for joking.
90. Pope-Hennessy, 210; Forster, 330.
91. *Let.*, I, 602, Fletcher, 5/13/44.
92. Forster, 325; *Let.*, I, 606, Forster. Erroneously dated June, 1844. Should probably be May. The carriage, oddly enough, belonged to Charles Black, whose wife's sister Clarissa was married to George Cattermole.
93. *Let.*, I, 603, Roche, 5/15/44.
94. Dickens to Southwood Smith, 5/28/44, from American Art Association sale catalogue, 4/25-6/1927.
95. *Let.*, I, 604, Forster, 5/28/44.
96. Ibid.
97. Ibid., 604 fn.
98. Forster, 328. See Dickens's speech in *Coll. P.*, II, 364-8, 6/4/44.
99. Forster Coll., Carlyle to Forster, 6/6/44.
100. *Dick.*, XXXVI, 253, Dickens to Lady Holland, 6/30/44.
101. *Let.*, I, 603-4, Landseer, 5/27/44.
102. Ibid., 588, Forster, [3/?/44].
103. Ibid., 581, Thompson, 3/13/44.

Chapter 4 [pp. 507-523]

1. Forster, 329-30.
2. *P. from I.*, "France," 258, 261.
3. Ibid., 261-6.
4. Ibid., "Lyons," 268-9.
5. Ibid., 269-70.
6. Ibid., 270-4.
7. Ibid., 274.
8. Ibid., 273.
9. Ibid., "Avignon," 278-80.
10. Ibid., 280-2.
11. *Let.*, I, 609, Forster, 7/16/44.
12. *P. from I.*, 283.
13. *Let.*, I, 614, Forster, 8/3/44.
14. *P. from I.*, 283.
15. *Let.*, I, 679-80, Forster, 6/2/45.
16. Ibid., 614, 8/3/44.
17. Ibid., 610, Maclise, 7/22/44.
18. Ibid., 611.
19. *P. from I.*, "Genoa," 284.
20. *Let.*, I, 609-10, Forster, 7/16/44.
21. Ibid., 619, [8/?/44].
22. *P. from I.*, "Genoa," 284.
23. *Let.*, I, 613, Maclise, 7/22/44.
24. *P. from I.*, "Genoa," 283.
25. *Let.*, I, 612, Maclise, 7/22/44.
26. Ibid., 613, Forster, 8/3/44.
27. Ibid., 616, 8/10/44.
28. Ibid., 613, 8/3/44.
29. Ibid., 612, Maclise, 7/22/44.
30. Ibid., 610, Forster, 7/16/44.
31. Ibid., 614, Curry, 8/9/44.
32. Pope-Hennessy, 215.
33. *Let.*, I, 623, Forster, 9/16/44.
34. Ibid., 612, Maclise, 7/22/44.
35. Forster, 330.
36. *P. from I.*, "Genoa," 287.
37. Ibid.
38. Ibid., 291-5.
39. Ibid., 300.
40. *Let.*, I, 611, Maclise, 7/22/44.
41. *P. from I.*, 300.
42. *Let.*, I, 611, Maclise, 7/22/44.
43. *P. from I.*, 295.
44. Ibid., 296.
45. *Let.*, I, 616, Forster, 8/10/44.
46. Ibid.; Pope-Hennessy, 215.
47. *Let.*, I, 615, Tagart, 8/9/44.

48. Forster, 333.
49. Ibid., 338.
50. *Let.*, I, 616, Forster, 8/20/44.
51. Ibid.
52. Forster, 340.
53. *Let.*, I, 618, Forster, [8/?/44].
54. Forster, 340-1.
55. Ibid., 341.
56. Hird MS., Stanfield, 8/22/44, inaccurately printed in *Let.*, I, 619-22.
57. Ibid.
58. *P. from I.*, "Genoa," 303.
59. Ibid., 303-4.
60. Ibid., 305.
61. Forster, 342.
62. *Let.*, I, 623, Forster, 9/9/44.
63. Forster, 342-3.
64. *Let.*, I, 623, Forster, 9/14/44.
65. Forster, 344.
66. *Let.*, I, 617, Forster, 8/20/44.
67. Forster, 344.
68. *P. from I.*, "Genoa," 305.
69. *Let.*, I, 626, Forster, 10/6/44.
70. Forster, 345.
71. Ibid., 346.
72. *Let.*, I, 624-5, Forster, 9/30/44.
73. Ibid., 626, 10/6/44.
74. Ibid., 627, 10/8/44.
75. Forster, 346. The quotation is from *Henry IV*, 2, III, 2, 231-2 (Oxford Shakespeare).
76. *Let.*, I, 627, Forster, 10/8/44.
77. Forster, 348.
78. House, 75.
79. *Let.*, I, 627, Forster, [10/?/44].
80. Ibid., 631, [10/?/44—but before 10/11/44].
81. Ibid., [circa 10/11/44].
82. Ibid., 633, 11/5/44.
83. Dexter, *Mr. and Mrs.*, 106-7, 11/8/44.
84. *Let.*, I, 631, Forster. Erroneously dated as October, 1844, but should be 11/2/44, as established by Forster, 353, which says it was eight days after the letter of 10/25/44.
85. Ibid., 632, 11/3/44.
86. Ibid., 633, Mitton, 11/5/44.
87. Ibid., 634.

88. Ibid., 630, Forster, 10/25/44.
89. Ibid., 631. Given as October, but may be early November.
90. Ibid., 631-2.
91. Ibid., 632.
92. Ibid., 11/4/44.
93. Ibid.
94. Ibid., 641, Forster, 11/17/44.
95. *P. from I.*, "Parma," 313.

Chapter 5 [pp. 524-539]

1. Dexter, *Mr. and Mrs.*, 103-5, 11/8/44.
2. Ibid., 105; *P. from I.*, "Parma," 314.
3. *P. from I.*, ibid.
4. Ibid., 315-7.
5. Ibid., 317.
6. Ibid., 319.
7. Ibid., "Bologna," 323-4.
8. Ibid., 325-6.
9. *Let.*, I, 641-2, Forster, 11/17/44.
10. Dexter, *Mr. and Mrs.*, 106-9, 11/8/44.
11. *P. from I.*, "Italian Dream," 328; *Let.*, I, 636, Forster, 11/12/44.
12. *P. from I.*, "Italian Dream," 329.
13. *Let.*, I, 636, Forster, 11/12/44.
14. *P. from I.*, "Italian Dream," 330-1.
15. *Let.*, I, 637, Forster, 11/12/44.
16. Ibid., 639, Jerrold, 11/16/44.
17. Ibid.
18. *P. from I.*, "Verona," 342.
19. *Let.*, I, 639-40, Forster, 11/17/44.
20. Ibid., 640.
21. Ibid., 638, Jerrold, 11/16/44.
22. *P. from I.*, "Verona," 337; *Let.*, I, 642-3, Lady Blessington, 11/20/44.
23. *Let.*, I, 640, Forster, 11/17/44.
24. Ibid., 641.
25. Dexter, *Mr. and Mrs.*, 108, 11/8/44.
26. *P. from I.*, "Verona," 344-6.
27. *Let.*, I, 642, Forster, 11/18/44.
28. Dexter, *Mr. and Mrs.*, 109, 11/23/44.
29. *P. from I.*, "Verona," 347.
30. Dexter, *Mr. and Mrs.*, 110, 11/23/44.

31. *P. from I.*, "Verona," 348.
32. Ibid., 349.
33. Dexter, *Mr. and Mrs.*, 111, 11/23/44.
34. *Let.*, I, 645, Forster, 11/25/44.
35. *P. from I.*, "Verona," 351.
36. Macready, *Diaries*, 11/9/44.
37. *Let.*, I, 647, Macready, 11/28/44.
38. Dexter, *Mr. and Mrs.*, 113-4, 11/28/44.
39. *P. from I.*, "Verona," 351.
40. Forster, 363.
41. Dexter, *Mr. and Mrs.*, 116, 12/2/44.
42. *Let.*, I, 632, Forster, Oct., '44. There is no such comment in the *Westminster Review*; Dickens's remark is either a joke or an error of memory.
43. Dexter, *Mr. and Mrs.*, 116-7, 12/2/44.
44. Ibid.
45. *Let.*, I, 648, Miss Ely, 12/2/44.
46. Forster, 363, is mistaken in giving the date of the reading as 12/2/44; *Mr. and Mrs.*, 117, 12/2/44, says "the reading comes off tomorrow night."
47. *B. H.*, X, 129.
48. *Let.*, I, 633, Forster, 11/4/44.
49. Forster, 363.
50. Forster, 363-4.
51. Barham, *Life*, diary, 12/5/44, gives that evening as the date of the second reading.
52. Dexter, *Mr. and Mrs.*, 117, 12/2/44. It is not clear when Dickens read the story to Macready. Forster, 363, says everyone who heard it at his chambers was dead in 1872 except himself and Carlyle; Macready, however, was still alive. Possibly Dickens read it separately to Macready, 12/1/44: see P.S. to this letter to Catherine. Macready, *Diaries*, 277, shows that he did not leave London until 12/4/44.
53. *Let.*, I, 671, Mitton, 4/14/45.
54. Quoted by Pope-Hennessy, 220, who gives date as 3/12/45.

55. *Let.*, I, 651, Forster, 12/22/44.
56. *Chimes*, I, 103.
57. Ibid., 105.
58. Ibid., II, 115.
59. Ibid., 116.
60. Ibid., 117.
61. Ibid., 117-8.
62. Ibid., I, 107.
63. Ibid., 108.
64. Ibid., III, 144-5.
65. Ibid., 146.
66. Ibid., 149.
67. *Let.*, I, 629, Forster, 10/18/44.
68. *Chimes*, III, 150.
69. Ibid., IV, 169.
70. Ibid.
71. Throughout this paragraph I am indebted to Cazamian, 247-8.
72. Cazamian, 248.
73. *Let.*, I, 648, Miss Coutts, 12/8/44.
74. Ibid.
75. Ibid., 649.
76. Ibid., 666, Forster, 3/30/45.
77. Ibid., 650, 12/17/44.
78. Macready, *Diaries*, 11/9/44.
79. Forster, 364.
80. *Let.*, I, 650, Forster, [12/?/44]; Macready, *Diaries*, 12/11/44. Dickens must have meant by "Madame St. George" Mlle. George (Marguerite Weinser).
81. Forster, 364.
82. *Let.*, I, 650, Forster, [12/?/44].
83. Forster, 364.
84. Pope-Hennessy, 221.
85. Macready, *Diaries*, 12/13/44.
86. *P. from I.*, "Verona," 352.
87. Morgan MS., Dickens to Mrs. Macready, 3/10/45.
88. Forster, 364.
89. Ibid., 365.
90. *P. from I.*, "Verona," 352.
91. Morgan MS., Dickens to Mrs. Macready, 3/10/45.
92. Forster, 365.
93. *P. from I.*, "Verona," 352.
94. Morgan MS., Dickens to Mrs. Macready, 3/10/45.
95. *Let.*, I, 651, Forster, 12/22/44.
96. Ibid., 663, Miss Coutts, 3/18/45.

Chapter 6 [pp. 540-564]

1. Altick, Dickens to Charles Kemble, 9/3/44.
2. Dexter, *Mr. and Mrs.*, 114, 11/28/44.
3. *Let.*, I, 655, Forster, 1/8/45.
4. Ibid., 707, Thompson, 10/17/45.
5. Berg MS., Dickens to De la Rue, 12/26/44.
6. Ibid., 1/15/45.
7. Pope-Hennessy, 217.
8. Berg MS., Dickens to De la Rue, 1/15/45.
9. Forster, 367, says 1/20/45, but see letter above.
10. *P. from I.*, "To Rome," 354.
11. Pope-Hennessy, 222.
12. *P. from I.*, "To Rome," 354.
13. Berg MS., Dickens to De la Rue, 1/27/45.
14. *P. from I.*, "To Rome," 354-5.
15. *Let.*, I, 655-6, Forster, 1/25/45.
16. *P. from I.*, "To Rome," 357-9.
17. Ibid., 360.
18. Berg MS., Dickens to De la Rue, 1/25/45.
19. *P. from I.*, "To Rome," 360.
20. *Let.*, I, 667, Forster, 4/2/45.
21. *P. from I.*, "To Rome," 361.
22. Ibid., 361-2.
23. Forster, 368.
24. *P. from I.*, "To Rome," 362.
25. Berg MS., Dickens to De la Rue, 1/27/45.
26. *Let.*, I, 656, Forster, 1/?/45.
27. *P. from I.*, "To Rome," 363.
28. Forster, 368.
29. *Let.*, I, 656, Forster, 1/?/45.
30. Ibid.
31. Ibid., 657.
32. *P. from I.*, "To Rome," 364.
33. Ibid., 365.
34. Ibid., "Rome," 366.
35. *Let.*, I, 657, Forster, 1/30/45.
36. *P. from I.*, "Rome," 366.
37. Ibid., 367.
38. Ibid., 367-8.
39. Ibid., 368.
40. Ibid., 371-2.
41. Ibid., 373.

42. Ibid., 374.
43. *Let.*, I, 657, Georgina Hogarth, 2/4/45.
44. *P. from I.*, "Rome," 372-3.
45. Ibid., 375-6.
46. Ibid., "Diorama," 411.
47. Ibid., "Rome," 399.
48. Forster, 369.
49. *P. from I.*, "Diorama," 412-3.
50. Berg MS., Dickens to De la Rue, 2/14/45.
51. *Let.*, I, 659, Mitton, 2/17/45.
52. Ibid., 658, Forster, 2/11/45.
53. Ibid.
54. Ibid., 658-9.
55. Ibid., 660, Mitton, 2/17/45.
56. *P. from I.*, "Diorama," 415-6.
57. *Let.*, I, 660, Mitton, 2/22/45.
58. Ibid., 661.
59. Ibid.
60. Ibid., 662.
61. *P. from I.*, "Diorama," 428-30. Forster, 372, notes that at Naples Dickens was also entertained by the English Minister, Mr. (later Sir) Richard Temple, Lord Palmerston's brother.
62. *Let.*, I, 662, Forster, 3/2/45.
63. Ibid., III, 752, Le Fanu, 11/24/69.
64. Ibid., I, 745, Mme. De la Rue, 4/17/46.
65. Ibid., 667, Bodenham, 3/24/45; Pope-Hennessy, 227.
66. *Let.*, I, 666, Forster, 3/?/45.
67. *P. from I.*, "Rome," 401-6.
68. *Let.*, I, 664, Miss Coutts, 3/18/45.
69. Morgan MS., Dickens to Fletcher, 3/26/45.
70. *Let.*, I, 667, Bodenham, 3/24/45; Pope-Hennessy, 227.
71. Ibid., III, 752, Le Fanu, 11/24/69.
72. *P. from I.*, "Diorama," 430-1.
73. Ibid., 432-3.
74. Forster, 371 fn.
75. *Let.*, I, 668, Forster, 4/2/45, 668 fn.
76. Ibid.
77. Forster, 372; Pope-Hennessy, 227.

78. Trollope, I, 110.
79. Dexter, *Mr. and Mrs.*, 227, 12/5/53.
80. *Let.*, I, 669, Black, 4/12/45, 670, Mitton, 4/14/45.
81. Ibid., 678, Beard, 5/20/45.
82. Ibid., 670, Mitton, 4/14/45.
83. Ibid., 678, Beard, 5/20/45.
84. Ibid., 671, Mitton, 4/14/45.
85. Ibid., 671-2.
86. Ibid.
87. Ibid., 676, Mitton, 5/20/45.
88. Ibid., 677.
89. Ibid., 746, Phillips, 4/20/46.
90. Ibid., 670, Forster, 4/13/45.
91. Ibid., 672, 4/27/45.
92. Ibid., 679, 6/1/45.
93. Ibid., 673, Maclise, 5/9/45.
94. Ibid., 674.
95. Ibid., 676, Forster, 5/12/45.
96. Forster, 375.
97. Berg MS., Dickens to De la Rue, 8/19/57.
98. *Let.*, I, 681-2, Forster, 6/7/45.
99. Ibid.
100. Ibid., 679, De la Rue, 5/24/45.
101. Ibid., 676, Curry, 5/13/45.
102. Ibid., 682, Forster, 6/14/45.
103. Ibid., 683.
104. Ibid.
105. *P. from I.*, "Rome," 395.
106. *Let.*, I, 640, Forster, 11/17/44.
107. Ibid., 666, Forster, [3/?/45].
108. *P. from I.*, "Rome," 395.
109. Ibid., 396.
110. *Let.*, I, 639, Forster, 11/17/44.
111. *P. from I.*, "Genoa," 295.
112. Ibid., "Rome," 369.
113. Ibid., "Genoa," 296.
114. Ibid.
115. Ibid., "Rome," 370.
116. Ibid., "Genoa," 296.
117. Ibid., "Diorama," 428.
118. *Let.*, I, 664, Miss Coutts, 3/18/45.
119. *P. from I.*, "Diorama," 434.

Chapter 7 [pp. 565-585]

1. *Let.*, I, 713, Forster, 11/3/45.
2. Trevelyan, *British History*, 266-7.

3. Driver, 452-3, 457.
4. Trevelyan, *British History*, 268.
5. Ibid., 271.
6. Forster, 325.
7. McCarthy-Robinson, 40. So interpreted by McCarthy and Robinson, but so far as the wording of Mahony's letter reveals, it might *possibly* refer merely to a personal correspondence. No other letters between him and Dickens, however, have come to light.
8. *Let.*, I, 684, Forster, [6/?/45].
9. Forster, 379.
10. *Let.*, I, 685, Forster, [7/?/45].
11. Ibid., 691, Beard, 8/6/45.
12. Forster, 364.
13. *Let.*, I, 680, Forster, [6/?/45].
14. Ibid., 686, Stanfield, 7/15/45.
15. Ibid., 699, Cattermole, 8/27/45.
16. *Let.*, I, 687, Forster, 7/22/45. Here, the reader will see, Dickens is parodying Bobadil's manner of speaking.
17. Ibid., 697, Cruikshank, 8/23/45; *Dick.*, XXXV, 231.
18. Forster, 383-4.
19. *Dick.*, XXXVI, 75, quoting Dickens to Mme. De la Rue, 9/27/45.
20. McCarthy-Robinson, 6.
21. *Let.*, I, 688, Napier, 7/28/45.
22. Ibid., 690, Powell, 8/2/45.
23. Ibid., 694, Frederick Dickens, 8/14/45.
24. Ibid., 695, Forster, 8/19/45.
25. Dexter, *Mr. and Mrs.*, 119, [8/24/45].
26. Morgan MS., Dickens to Macready, 9/2/45.
27. Ibid., Dickens to Miss Macready, 9/18/45.
28. Ibid.
29. McCarthy-Robinson, 7.
30. *Let.*, I, 701, Serle, 9/16/45.
31. *Dick.*, XXXVI, 75, quoting letter to Mme. De la Rue, 9/27/45.
32. Carlyle, *Letters to Family*, 253, to Jeannie Welsh, 9/30/45.

33. Carlyle, *Letters and Memorials*, I, 195, 9/23/45.
34. Macready, *Diaries*, 9/20/45.
35. Forster Coll., Bell to Forster, 9/23/45.
36. *Dick.*, XXXVI, 75, quoting Dickens letter to Mme. De la Rue, 9/27/45.
37. *Let.*, I, 703, Macready, 9/18/45.
38. London *Times*, 11/15/45.
39. *Let.*, I, 710, Beard, 10/26/45.
40. Ibid., 711, Stanfield, 10/26/45.
41. London *Times*, 11/15/45.
42. Greville, *Diaries*, I, 566.
43. *Let.*, I, 725, Tagart, 12/22/45.
44. *Dick.*, XXXV, 231.
45. Berg MS., Dickens to Stanfield, 10/4/45.
46. *Let.*, I, 708, Macready, 10/17/45.
47. Ibid., Thompson, 10/17/45.
48. Ibid., 709, Napier, 10/17/45.
49. Ibid., 710, Beard, 10/26/45.
50. Ibid., 709, Talfourd, 10/22/45.
51. Ibid., 710, Beard, 10/26/45.
52. *Let.*, I, 711, Stanfield, 10/28/45. The printed text reads "a chopping boy," but this is probably a misreading for "strapping." In Thackeray's *Catherine*, however, I have come upon the expression "a chopping boy."
53. E. Fitzgerald, *New Letters*, 122.
54. Pope-Hennessy, 240.
55. Markham, 126.
56. Dickens House MS., Dickens to Mitton, 10/20/45.
57. Young, *Early Victorian England*, II, 29; DNB, LIX, 162, "Sir Joshua Walmsley."
58. Bourne, 143.
59. *Let.*, I, 716, Bradbury and Evans, 11/6/45.
60. Ibid., 718, 11/7/45.
61. Ibid., 711, 10/28/45.
62. Ibid., 713, [10-11/?/45].
63. Ibid., 712, Forster, 10/31/45.
64. Ibid., 713, 11/1/45.
65. Forster, 386.
66. *Let.*, I, 713, Forster, 11/3/45.
67. Ibid., Bradbury and Evans, 11/3/45.
68. Ibid., 715, Beard, 11/4/45.
69. Ibid., 716, Bradbury and Evans, 11/6/45.
70. Ibid., 715, Beard, 11/4/45.
71. Ibid., Bradbury and Evans, 11/6/45.
72. Ibid., 718, 11/7/45.
73. Ibid., 716, 11/6/45.
74. Ibid.
75. Ibid., 717.
76. Ibid., 718, 11/7/45.
77. Ibid., 720-2, 11/10/45, Leech, 11/18/45, Bradbury and Evans, 11/19/45, Leech, 11/19/45, Stanfield, 11/21/45.
78. Ibid., 719, Napier, 11/10/45.
79. Markham, 168.
80. Bourne, 143.
81. Lehmann, *Dickens as Editor*, preface, x-xi; Crowe, 71.
82. *Dick.*, XLIV, 104. Possibly this was John Hill Powell.
83. *Let.*, I, 734, Bradbury and Evans, 1/30/46.
84. Ibid., 724, Paxton, 12/1/45.
85. McCarthy-Robinson, 5, 10; Forster, 389, n. 284; Jerrold, *Dramatist*, II, 424.
86. *Let.*, I, 721, Hogarth, 11/19/45.
87. Berg MS., Dickens to Lady Blessington, 1/16/46.
88. Crowe, 70.
89. Ibid. The fact that John Dickens remained on the *Daily News* after the resignation of his son removed any special influence that might have been exerted on his behalf, and the fact that he was still there until the time of his death five years later, are additional signs that he was not lacking in ability or industry.
90. Ibid., 68-9.
91. McCarthy-Robinson, 8.
92. *Let.*, I, 723, Paxton, 12/1/45.
93. McCarthy-Robinson, 1-2.
94. Macready, *Diaries*, 12/27/45.
95. Ibid.
96. N. Y. Pub. Lib., MS Division, T. F. Madigan catalogue, No-

vember, 1928, Dickens to C. Clayton, 1/8/46.

97. S. J. A. Fitzgerald, 196.

97a. McCarthy-Robinson, 7-8.

98. Young, *Early Victorian England*, II, 28.

99. Trevelyan, *British History*, 272.

100. *Let.*, I, 732, Beard, 1/17/46.

101. McCarthy-Robinson, 9-10.

102. Crowe, 70.

103. McCarthy-Robinson, 9.

104. Markham, 171.

105. *Let.*, I, 732, Beard, 1/17/46.

106. Markham, 171.

107. Ibid., 173.

108. *Let.*, I, 732, Fox, 1/21/46.

109. Bourne, 144.

110. *Dick.*, XXXIV, 119-22.

111. McCarthy-Robinson, 1-2.

112. Bourne, 146.

113. E.g., *Let.*, I, 734, Hazlitt, [1846].

114. Bourne, 145. But there is no foundation for A. W. Wood's contention, 73-4, that Dickens was a negligent editor. See Mc-Carthy: "For months and months, he never spared himself....For months and months

he was to be found morning, noon, and night at the offices which had been engaged for the production of the *Daily News*. He went into every detail of the arrangement." See also the various letters in *Let.*, I, 732-4, as examples.

115. *Let.*, I, 734, Bradbury and Evans, 1/30/46; cf. 762, Chapman, 7/13/46.

116. Ibid., 738, Evans, 2/26/46.

117. Ibid., 735, Bradbury and Evans, 1/30/46.

118. Ibid., Forster, 1/30/46.

119. Bourne, 145.

120. *Let.*, I, 738, Evans, 2/26/46.

121. Ibid., 736, Wills, 2/16/46.

122. Ibid., 737, Hill, 2/24/46.

123. Ibid., 744, Mme. De la Rue, 4/17/46.

124. Ibid., 740, Wills, 3/4/46.

125. Ibid., 745, Mme. De la Rue, 4/17/46.

126. Markham, 172.

127. Symons, 191; Bourne, II, 149; Grant, II, 86.

128. Markham, 172.